Principles of
Public Law

Limited

London • Sydney

Principles of Public Law

Andrew Le Sueur, LLB, Barrister

Reader in Laws, University College London

Javan Herberg, LLB, BCL, Barrister

Practising Barrister, Blackstone Chambers

Rosalind English, LLM, MA, Barrister

Cavendish
Publishing
Limited

London • Sydney

Second edition first published 1999 by Cavendish Publishing Limited,
The Glass House, Wharton Street, London, WC1X 9PX, United Kingdom
Telephone: +44 (0) 20 7278 8000   Facsimile: +44 (0) 20 7278 8080
E-mail: info@cavendishpublishing.com
Visit our Home Page on http://www.cavendishpublishing.com

This title was previously published as *Constitutional and Administrative Law* under the Lecture Notes series.

Le Sueur, AP
Principles of public law – 2nd ed – (Principles series)
1 Public Law – Great Britain   2 Great Britain – Constitutional law
I Title   II Herberg, JW   III English, R
342.4'1

ISBN 1 85941 381 1

Printed and bound in Great Britain

PREFACE

This book has been written for law students. Its purpose is to introduce the UK's changing constitutional system and some of the underlying debates about how modern societies should organise themselves.

Part A

In Chapters 1 to 5, we examine what 'principles' motivate people in their attempts to change the way we are governed (or keep it the same). It is the ideals of liberal democracy which today provide the basis for most discussion about what the constitution is or should be. For us, modern liberal democracy has three main features:

(a) respect for people's autonomy from State authorities;

(b) people's participation in collective decision making, primarily by electing representatives at regular multi-party elections; and

(c) the responsibility of the State to provide for people's welfare and security.

We examine when and why these characteristics emerged, what modern day politicians have to say about them and what contribution legal textbook writers have made to our understanding of them.

Part B

In the UK, we have no strong sense of 'the State'. Instead, we have a conglomeration of institutions and officeholders which carry out the tasks of government. Chapters 6 to 8 look at just some of them, focusing on the UK Parliament (and its diminishing importance as the place for robust debate about how we organise ourselves), on the European Union (and its increasing powers and continuing 'democratic deficit') and on administrative bodies such as central government departments, executive agencies and local authorities.

Part C

Part C (Chapters 9 to 18) looks at some of the processes for resolving disputes between State authorities and people, and between State authorities themselves. Since the 1960s, a range grievance redressing institutions, colloquially known as 'ombudsmen', have been established to investigate and make recommendations about instances of maladministration alleged to have caused injustice (Chapter 10). The main focus of this part of the book is, however, on the role of courts. Over the past decade, judicial review of administrative action has assumed a greater significance in the constitutional system – not only as a practical method by which people can seek to challenge the legality of government action, but also as a set of judge developed principles which operate as a constraint on public authorities (Chapters 11 to 17). European Community law also provides a basis for challenge to government (Chapter 18).

Part D

The search for constitutional principle has been clearest in the development of 'human rights'. For several years, British judges have sometimes used the language of 'human rights' in their judgments. With the enactment of the Human Rights Act 1998, the main provisions of which are to brought into force in October 2000, British courts will be required to consider the provisions of the European Convention on Human Rights in making their decisions (Chapter 19). The final chapters of the book (Chapters 20 to 27) provide an explanation and assessment of some of the main human rights: the right to life; liberty of the person; non-retrospectivity of law; respect for privacy; freedom of expression; freedom of assembly and association; equality; and freedom of movement.

This book grew out of a short text in the *Lecture Notes* series by Andrew Le Sueur and Javan Herberg: *Constitutional and Administrative Law* (1995, London: Cavendish Publishing). Although some material from that edition remains, this book is essentially a new one. In the preface to the 1995 book, we acknowledged contributions by Susan Hall to the chapter on ombudsmen and Lucan Herberg to the chapter on the ground of bias in judicial review. Le Sueur and Herberg have been joined for this new edition by Rosalind English, who wrote Chapter 8, revised Chapter 10 (ombudsmen) and wrote Chapters 20 to 27. Le Sueur wrote Chapters 1 to 7 and 17 to 19. Herberg wrote Chapters 11 to 16. The opinions expressed by each author are not necessarily shared by the others.

The law is stated as at May 1999, although it has been possible to incorporate a few later developments at proof stage. The Northern Ireland Act 1998, which provides the framework for devolved government in that part of the UK, has not yet been implemented; at the time of writing, its future remains in doubt.

Andrew Le Sueur
Javan Herberg
Rosalind English
September 1999

CONTENTS

PART A SEARCHING FOR PRINCIPLES

PART B PARLIAMENT AND GOVERNMENT

PART C RESOLVING DISPUTES

Contents

PART D CIVIL LIBERTIES AND HUMAN RIGHTS

TABLE OF CASES

TABLE OF STATUTES

TABLE OF INTERNATIONAL AND EUROPEAN LEGISLATION

PART A

SEARCHING FOR PRINCIPLES

CHAPTER 1

PRINCIPLES IN PUBLIC LAW

1.1 Ask yourself this ...

What do you really want from life? Most people we know hope for similar things. We want to meet someone, fall in love and share a home with them; most people want to have children. We aspire to have a satisfying career, or at least a job that pays well. There is more to life than our family and work, though. We also seek out interesting things to do in our leisure time. For some it is sport; for others it is cultural activities – from going out clubbing to reading novels; many people, though the number is decreasing, spend time practising a religious faith; some people, and the number is growing, enjoy using mood-altering drugs. We also want to feel safe, especially from ill health, the hardships than can come from old age and unemployment, and from crime.

This book is about how we organise ourselves to achieve these aspirations, focusing particularly on the role played by the law.

1.2 How we organise ourselves

The task of organising ourselves takes place in three main realms. First of all, 'ourselves' means each of us, as individuals. In Western societies, it is regarded as important that every person has a considerable degree of personal autonomy. People are encouraged to work out for themselves what makes life worthwhile. Living as a member of a society is not the same as being a recruit in the army; we should not be expected unquestioningly to follow the orders of a superior as to how to live every aspect of our lives.

A second level at which we organise ourselves is through voluntary associations with other people. To live in isolation from others would be just too lonely, too dull for most people to bear. We therefore need to be able to join together with other people, to pursue common purposes. Some voluntary associations (such as family units) are inward looking, established for the well being of their members. Other voluntary associations (for example, many religious organisations and political bodies) are set up in order to influence the behaviour of people outside the association. In the world of work, people set up limited liability companies or partnerships and join professional bodies and trade unions. No one forces anyone to take part in these social activities. Just as it is vital that individuals have personal autonomy, it is also important that voluntary associations have some degree of independence to decide for themselves what they do, whom to have as members and rules which govern how collective decisions are made.

The third level at which we organise ourselves is through the State. This is not a single institution, but a conglomeration of decision making processes, institutions and office holders. In the past, 'the State' was the institutions within a Nation – in our case, the United Kingdom of Great Britain and Northern Ireland (see below, 2.4). These include the UK Parliament, government ministers, local authorities, the National Health Service, the Civil Service and so on. In the age of globalisation and European integration (see below, 2.3, 2.7), however, the idea of the State needs to encompass the multinational organisations such as the European Union, the United Nations and the World Trade Organisation through which Nations co-operate with one another.

State authorities differ from voluntary associations in important ways. We – as individuals and members of voluntary associations – have no choice but to be subject to decisions taken by them. They decide who can be a member of society (by making and enforcing rules on immigration and confining some people to prisons and mental hospitals, for example). State authorities confiscate money from us (tax). They prohibit us from doing things (for example, by making and enforcing criminal laws) and require us to do things (for instance, to educate our children).

Some people are hostile to State authorities, believing that coercion – the threat of punishment which ultimately hovers behind many orders issued by governmental bodies – is not the best way of organising a society. Some also assert that State authorities do not act on behalf of the people under their control, but instead exist to further vested interests (for instance, those of the relatively small number of people who own business enterprises and exploit those who work for them). Views such as these are currently unfashionable, though this has not always been so. On the whole, people today are happy to look at State authorities as desirable agencies through which to organise society. The State provides frameworks for voluntary associations – through the laws on marriage, charities, companies and partnerships, contracts and so on. It is to State authorities which we turn for many of our most basic needs: to protect us from crime and fires, to provide roads, to supply health care free at the point of need, to give our children an education; to dispense a subsistence income in hard times. There is a broad consensus that people cannot be left to fend for themselves in these areas, and that needs such as these cannot be provided entirely through voluntary associations such as business ventures and charities.

1.3   The scope of public law

Public law is concerned with the relationships between 'us', as individuals and members of voluntary associations, and State authorities. It is also about

4

the interrelationships of the various State authorities. Obviously, this is a very broad field.

Practising lawyers often specialise in a particular field of State activity, such as immigration control and land use planning. Their work may also centre on a particular form of legal relationship – for instance, judicial review of government decisions, or the making of bylaws by local authorities. It is only in the past decade that the term 'public law' has become widespread to describe the totality of these fields. Practitioners still often prefer the more specific categories; and, curiously, lawyers working in the areas of criminal law and tax law hardly ever see their work as part of 'public law', despite the fact that these are two of the most direct ways in which State authorities intervene in people's lives.

Academics, too, have, in the past, tended to prefer subdividing the study of law relating to State activity. Like practitioners, academic lawyers began using the term 'public law' extensively only during the 1980s (though it was used intermittently by writers before this and the journal *Public Law* was established in 1956). For university lecturers, it used to be convenient to adopt three smaller subject categories: constitutional law; administrative law; and civil liberties. Constitutional law involves the study of the Parliament and the main institutions of government, especially their legal relationships to one another and to citizens. Administrative law focuses on the legal aspects of day to day administrative activity and on how grievances are redressed. Civil liberties looks at the freedom people have to act, unconstrained by legal regulation; traditionally, this has concentrated on the limits of police powers, but today, it is also concerned with human rights more broadly. One of the main reasons for amalgamating these three categories into the wider one of public law has been the realisation that they share a common foundation. If you want to *understand* and *evaluate* (rather than just state) the laws relating to the constitution, administration or civil liberties, you need to do this by reference to principles.

1.4   What are principles?

This book is about the *principles* of public law. Before going any further, we need to explain what this means. In everyday speech, we criticise a person (often a politician) as 'lacking any principles', or for 'abandoning his principles'; we praise a person for 'sticking to her principles'; we say that some proposal or decision is 'wrong in principle'; and, when faced with a difficult problem, we sometimes tackle it by 'going back to first principles'. We therefore tend to believe that having principles is a good thing; that not having any, or ignoring them, is bad; that they are capable of guiding us; and that they ought not be surrendered and replaced lightly.

This begs questions. First of all, what is a principle? The term is often used in a very broad way to describe some desirable goal or standard of conduct.

For instance, in 1995, the Committee on Standards in Public Life then chaired by Lord Nolan laid down seven 'key principles' for those in public life: selflessness, integrity, objectivity, accountability, openness, honesty and leadership (see *First Report of the Committee on Standards in Public Life*, Vol 1, Cm 2850-I, 1995, London: HMSO) (see below, 6.7). In 1995, the Labour Party adopted a new statement of 'aims and values' which would guide it in government, including, for instance, the desirability of living in a community 'where the rights we enjoy reflect the duties we owe, and where we live together, freely, in a spirit of solidarity, tolerance and respect' (see below, 4.4). All of these are attempts to state maxims which (in the opinion of the authors) should guide the actions of people or how the law should be developed. When the word 'principle' is used in these ways, it is therefore really just a rhetorical device to give greater weight to a *statement of conclusion*.

'Principles' can also be used in a rather different, though connected, sense to mean a reasoned justification for the way we organise ourselves collectively. Principles *explain why* things ought to happen. For example, government ministers regularly attend the House of Commons to make statements and answer questions about their departments' activities (see below, 6.8). To explain why this occurs, one needs to provide a principled justification. Similarly, English law prohibits consensual sado-masochistic sex between adults. Again, to explain why this ought to be so, one needs to provide a reasoned justification – to appeal to some principle.

In our society, there is broad agreement about how people should treat each other and what decision making procedures we should use for making collective decisions. In other words, there is a consensus that good reasons exist for most of our social practices. For example, most judges and politicians accept that there are good reasons for the rules on parliamentary sovereignty which state that Acts of Parliament are the highest form of law in the UK (see below, 5.2). If principles are understood to be arguments of justification, then by definition there is scope for change. Until the 1920s, for instance, women did not have the right to vote in parliamentary elections. Various reasons were put forward to justify this, including that women were generally less intelligent than men and too busy being mothers to participate in public life (see below, 5.1.1). These justifications for the prohibition ceased to be accepted, and the law changed. To summarise: principles are often widely accepted and relatively permanent ways of thinking which justify social practices; they may also be fought over (in Parliament, the courtroom, in the news media, in the street); and they may, therefore, also change.

1.4.1 Principles and reason

In societies based on religious faith, principles may be set out in a holy book, interpreted by priests, and state comprehensively and authoritatively what principles people should follow. The UK is no longer a country run on the basis of faith, so we must look elsewhere for essential foundations for living worthwhile lives – to people's ability to reason, based on facts and moral arguments. The notion that principles are the product of rational, moral reasoning has its root in the Enlightenment – a way of thinking about the world which emerged during the 18th century (see below, 3.7). In Western Europe and the newly colonised America, men and women came to understand that human beings were capable of organising themselves, and discovering scientific truths, in order to make the human society a better place to live. Humans could, in other words, make progress by using their powers of scientific and moral reasoning (rather than relying blindly on superstitious belief and following the edicts of traditional rulers). The central aspiration was that people's freedom could be increased if they understood the natural and human world and applied rationality to the task of living. During the 20th century, two great rival theories, based on rationality and the desire for progress and freedom, came to dominate the world: liberal democracy and Marxism.

The importance of rationality is not accepted by everyone today. Some conservative thinkers believe that, if a society dwells too much on rational problem solving, it looses sight of something equally or even more significant – 'the customary or traditional way of doing things' (see Oakeshott, M, *Rationalism in Politics*, 1962, London: Methuen). During the 1980s, it also became fashionable for some left-wing intellectuals, including legal academics, to deny that there was such a thing as a principled or rational approach to constructing a good society. These postmodernists oppose any theory which purports to provide a universal explanation for how we live or ought to live. They use the label 'grand narratives' for such theories, which include Christianity, liberal democracy and Marxism. For postmodernists, all such grand narratives are inherently authoritarian – they are methods by which a minority of powerful people in a society (church leaders, elected politicians, the Communist Party) seek to control the lives of the rest of us. Rather than enhancing human progress and freedom, grand narratives diminish it. The ideological battles between the world's competing grand narratives has weakened them all, postmodernists argue, so that it is pretence to see any of them as capable of providing principles of universal application; instead, postmodernists urge people to seek out 'difference'. (For an introduction to these ideas, see Sim, S (ed), *Postmodern Thought*, 1998, Cambridge: Icon.)

1.5 Principles and legal rules

If principles are reasoned justifications for doing something, then clearly they are not the same as legal rules, though particular laws may attempt to give effect to principles. It is, therefore, possible to criticise a law (for example, that the monarch of the UK has to be a member of the Church of England, or that the Head of State is a hereditary monarch) as being 'wrong in principle', meaning that no good justification exists for it. In other words, principles provide a way of arguing about what the law should be. In a constitutional system, principles may also be given effect in practices that are not enforceable by the courts (for instance, that government ministers explain and justify their policies to elected representatives in the Parliament). These practices are called constitutional conventions (see below, 2.8.2). The *absence* of a legal rule may also reveal a principle (for example, people in the UK are no longer required by law to attend church on Sundays). To study what principles exert an influence, we therefore need to look at legal rules, the absence of legal rules governing some activities and at well established practices which are not compelled by legislation or courts.

1.6 The characteristics of liberal democracy

The assortment of principles which explain how people in the UK organise themselves can be labelled 'liberal democracy'. Law, lawyers, legislators and judges have important roles in converting these ideals of liberal democracy into a practical system for organising our society. One of the purposes of this book is to explain the function of law in 'constituting' liberal democracy as it exists in the UK. Before we begin doing this, however, we need to say more about modern liberal democracy, by dissecting three of its main elements: (a) autonomy; (b) popular participation; and (c) securing safety and welfare through State authorities. We will see later (below, 1.7) that the version of liberal democracy practised in the UK does not always match up to this model; indeed, it sometimes falls well short. Most debates today between politicians, writers and lawyers are, however, about what liberal democracy means and how it might be improved.

1.6.1 Autonomy

At the heart of liberalism is the idea that it is both possible and desirable to make a distinction between private life and public life. Within the private sphere, individuals have freedom – especially freedom from government officials – to determine for themselves the important things in their lives – such as what they think and read, what opinions they hold and express, with whom they have sex, what, if any, religious beliefs they practise, with whom they associate, and so on. (As we shall see, the '... and so on' is important, because the extent of people's private lives is contentious.) The classic statement of the importance of individual liberty comes from the 19th century philosopher John Stuart Mill in *On Liberty* (1859), 1982 edn, London: Penguin:

> The only purpose for which power can be rightfully exercised over any member of a civilised community, against his will, is to prevent harm to others. His own good, either physical or moral, is not a sufficient warrant. He cannot

rightfully be compelled to do or forbear because it will be better for him to do so, because it will make him happier, because, in the opinions of others, to do so would be wise, or even right. These are good reasons for remonstrating with him, or reasoning with him, or persuading him, or entreating with him, but not for compelling him ... The only part of the conduct of anyone, for which he is amenable to society, is that which concerns others. In the part which merely concerns himself, his independence is, of right, absolute. Over himself, over his own body and mind, the individual is sovereign.

There are two main reasons for saying that personal liberty is of paramount importance. One is that it is wrong for anybody to coerce another *because* a person's freedom to do or be what he or she wants is an essential part of what it means to be a human being. A second reason why a society should value individual liberty – the freedom of each person to experiment with ideas, to debate, to try new ways of living – is that this is more likely to lead to human progress than a society based on rigid and authoritarian ways of life. Liberty encourages people to be independent, critical and imaginative. The truth about things is more likely to emerge if we are allowed to say what we think, and to listen to controversial views of others, than if the government controls what may be published and broadcast or if intolerant social pressures stifle debate and action. (For example, whether humans were created by God in the Garden of Eden or evolved from apes; whether the phenomenon of global warming exists and, if so, what causes it; or whether six million people were killed in Nazi concentration camps between 1941 and 1945.)

Almost all liberals accept that there may, however, be some situations in which individual freedom should be curtailed. The test for determining whether restrictions on liberty are justified is whether a person's unqualified liberty will have adverse affects on, or cause harm to, other people. In other words, freedom may be limited in order to preserve the freedom of others. It is this which forms the boundary between 'private life' (where autonomy should be absolute) and 'public life' (where regulation of conduct by State authorities is permissible). Causing harm is not the same as causing offence or being disgusted. For instance, although attitudes have changed in recent years, many people remain disgusted by the fact that gay men have sex with each other; the fact of a person's revulsion is not a good reason for suppressing homosexuality. Similarly, liberalism takes the view that derogatory speech about a person's race, religion or other status – 'most niggers are muggers', 'faggots deserve to die of AIDS' – is deeply offensive to many people (including the authors of this book), but is not in itself sufficiently harmful to warrant banning the use of such words (though, when combined with threatening actions, it may be).

The *assumption* that liberalism requires to be made is that every adult is equally capable of making decisions for him or herself about what to believe and how to act. It follows from this that people are not in need of paternalistic guidance from State authorities on how to live and what to think. Many people – including most professional politicians – doubt whether this assumption is correct. Their approach to deciding whether people should be left alone often starts by posing the question 'if people were fully informed and wanted to act wisely, what would they do?'. The politician then supplies the answer (because they regard themselves as fully informed and wise) and requires people to act in accordance with what is viewed as 'their best interests'. Liberals view this as dangerous. As Isaiah Berlin puts it:

> All paternalistic governments, however benevolent, cautious, disinterested, and rational, have tended, in the end, to treat the majority of men as minors, or as being too often incurably foolish or irresponsible; or else as maturing so slowly as not to justify their liberation at any clearly foreseeable date ... This is a policy which degrades men, and seems to me to rest on no rational or scientific foundation, but, on the contrary, on a profoundly mistaken view of the deepest of human needs [*Four Essays in Liberty*, 1969, Oxford: OUP, p lxii].

Liberalism in a political system implies tolerance of other people's beliefs, attitudes and decisions. This, in turn, implies pluralism: a society which values personal freedom will inevitably be one in which people choose to live their lives in a variety of ways, some of which will be morally wrong, unhealthy or unsatisfying. People should be allowed to choose their own path through life because, in the end, it is just not possible to reconcile many competing values. In particular, government should not be organised on the basis of religious belief. The liberal stance is that religious faith (or the lack of it) should be in each person's private sphere and that State authorities should not promote one religion above another. But liberalism does not imply relativism (that all ways of living and all opinions are equally valid, true or good). On the contrary, the point of liberalism is to open up possibilities for robust debate in society about what *is* valid, true and good.

For many but not all liberals freedom from coercion extends beyond the moral and social sphere into economic relationships. In the 18th and 19th centuries, notions of 'freedom' were based on property ownership (rather than, as today, on ideas of inalienable human rights): a man who owned property and the means to earn a living had autonomy. From these roots sprang ideas of market liberalism (also called 'neo-liberalism' and *laissez faire*). This stands for the proposition that government and legal regulation should interfere as little as possible in the workplace relationships between employers and their workers. If an employee (an autonomous human subject) agrees to work long hours at low pay, this should be permitted. Market liberals also support a *global* free market – the ability of business to trade across national borders without tariffs and quotas imposed by government in order to protect their own nationals.

1.6.2   Popular participation

Autonomy (see above, 1.6.1) is about 'me' and what 'I' want to do. As such, it provides little basis for explaining why State authorities should exist and according to what principles they ought to operate – other than that they may curtail 'my' freedom if I am harming 'you'. Liberalism tends to begrudge the existence of government, viewing it with hostility or scepticism. It is the combination of ideas of liberalism with the ideal of *democracy* that provides a positive and principled basis for government, which, as we shall see shortly (below, 1.6.3), is capable of making a beneficial contribution to conditions of liberty. Democracy is about what 'we' can and should do together, for each other.

Of course, people disagree about what is the best for society (for example, how crime should be prevented; whether people should be able to smoke cannabis; how to deal with people who want to divorce; whether women should have abortions; how to cope with unemployment). A central feature of democracy is the notion that people ought to have the opportunity to participate in shaping the decisions and actions of State authorities. In particular, the policies pursued by government officials are to which the *majority* of adults *consent*. This does not mean that the majority of people have to be consulted on proposed action and then agree to it – though, in a few places, democracy is very 'direct'. In some cantons of Switzerland, for instance, several thousand people meet together once a year to vote on legislation and set levels of tax and government spending; the majority view is measured by how citizens vote on particular issues. Some theorists urge the need for more such participatory or 'strong' democracy (see Barber, B, *Strong Democracy: Participatory Politics for a New Age,* 1984, Berkeley: California UP). We might, for example, establish neighbourhood assemblies for debating issues and find out what people want by means of information technology (see Walker, C and Akdeniz, Y, 'Virtual democracy' [1998] PL 489).

Some version of *representative* democracy is, however, the norm in liberal democracies. This means that people consent principally by choosing representatives in periodic, multi-party elections to serve for a limited period in government and in the legislature. (On the key role of political parties in constitutions, see Barendt, E, *An Introduction to Constitutional Law*, 1998, Oxford: OUP, Chapter 8.) In representative democracy, consent is, therefore, general; the view of the majority on particular questions of policy is measured by the votes of the elected representatives sitting in a Parliament. Even in representative democracies, however, the direct consent of the people on particular questions may be sought from time to time – for example, by holding referendums. All adults ought to be permitted to give or withhold their democratic consent on an equal basis (see Dworkin, R, 'What is equality? Part 4: political equality' (1987) 22 San Francisco UL Rev 1). In the past, however, many countries have limited voting rights to Caucasians, males or property owners; and some have given additional votes to university graduates and business people.

For democratic consent to be meaningful, it has to be capable of being withdrawn – for instance, by the ability to vote a political party out of government office at a general election. Consent also needs to be qualified – it is important that, between elections, representatives are scrutinised and held to account for their decisions. But once an institution has made a decision or enacted legislation according to fair procedures in which people have been able to participate, it is often thought by many theorists that everyone has an obligation to accept and obey that outcome; people cannot pick and choose which laws to obey (for an introduction to the debate about civil disobedience, see Raz, J, 'The obligation to obey: revision and tradition', in *Ethics in the Public Domain*, 1995, Oxford: Clarendon, Chapter 15).

1.6.3   Securing safety and welfare

A third feature of modern liberal democracy is collective responsibility for our security, safety and welfare through State authorities. People are often afraid. Until very recently, we were most concerned about our country being invaded by foreign enemies and destroyed by weapons of mass destruction. Today, the threat is seen to come from drug traffickers and terrorists fighting for religious causes or rights to national self-determination. We dread being assaulted and our possessions stolen. We fear the consequences of unemployment, accidents, ill health and old age. For most of history, the vast bulk of humans have lived precarious lives. They face starvation, ill health, high rates of infant mortality, illiteracy, ignorance and grinding poverty (while a small proportion of the population avoids or mitigates such catastrophes by the personal accumulation of wealth). To make the private sphere of people's lives meaningful (see above, 1.6.1), and for people's participation in the public sphere to be effective (see above, 1.6.2), a system of social security – a 'Welfare State' – exists in most liberal democracies. Today, it is normal for there to be collective provision of education for children, medical care free at the point of need, accommodation for the homeless and guarantees of a minimum income in times of unemployment and retirement. In practice, collective responsibility for safety and welfare is achieved though institutions of the State such as the armed services, the police, immigration officers, fire brigades, public hospitals, social workers and agencies paying welfare benefits. In short, government institutions are regarded as having a positive contribution to make towards freedom.

During the second half of the 20th century, there has been an immense shift in the nature of government responsibility for safety and welfare. Though important, the task of defence and maintaining law and order now amounts to a relatively small proportion of government expenditure in most liberal democracies. For example, in the UK during 1996–97, only 7% of public spending was on defence and 5% on law and order ((1998) *The Economist*, 28 March, p 36). Today, the main role of governments in liberal democracies is to run the Welfare State. In the UK, for instance, 32% of government spending is on welfare benefits and retirement pensions, 17% on health and social services and 12% on education.

A Welfare State is expensive and is paid for by taxes levied on the incomes of individuals and business enterprises. Collective social security therefore relies upon economic prosperity. Liberal democracies have capitalist economies (though not all capitalist economies are liberal democracies). Business enterprises have freedom to buy and sell commodities and services, employ people, accumulate capital and make profits (see above, 1.6.1). Indeed, government policies and laws encourage this. Most modern liberal democracies, however, recognise that 'freedom' in economic relationships is often a dangerous fiction, enabling employers to exploit their workers, and big businesses to abuse dominant positions in sectors of the market. A major task of government, in order to achieve social security, is, therefore, the regulation of market forces. There is a tendency for some people to think of 'the market' as a natural phenomenon that exists spontaneously in the absence of government regulation; in fact, it is a human institution for producing and distributing goods and services. Markets are dependent on government activity and laws to provide for the enforcement of contracts, the creation of limited liability companies, and the control of monopolies. In most liberal democracies, there is political debate about the extent to which government institutions should regulate market forces (see above, 1.2.3). Government action can take many forms: requiring businesses to pay employees a minimum wage; restricting working hours; imposing standards for health and safety at work; giving people legal protection against unfair dismissal and redundancy; controlling the abuse of monopoly power; supervising the takeovers and mergers of companies. In the UK during the later 19th century (see below, 3.8) and between 1979 and 1997 (see Chapter 4), politicians favoured less rather than more regulation of markets. But, as John Gray explains:

> The *laissez faire* policies ... in 19th century England were based on the theory that market freedoms are natural and political restrains on markets are artificial. The truth is that free markets are creatures of State power, and persist only so long as the State is able to prevent human needs for security and the control of economic risk from finding political expression [*False Dawn: The Delusions of Global Capitalism*, 1998, London: Granta, p 17].

1.6.4 The future of liberal democracy: consensus or crisis?

For its enthusiasts, the spread around the world of systems of government based on liberal democracy and the idea of a Welfare State is one of the great progressive trends of the 20th century. In *The End of History and the Last Man*, 1992, London: Penguin, the American historian Francis Fukuyama argues that 'a remarkable consensus concerning the legitimacy of liberal democracy as a system of government has emerged throughout the world over the past few years, as it conquered rival ideologies like hereditary monarchy, fascism, and most recently communism' (p xi). He points to the fact that whereas, in 1940, 13 countries based their systems on liberal democracy, by 1990, the number was 61. Controversially, Fukuyama goes on to argue that this form of government 'may constitute the end point of mankind's ideological evolution and the final form of human government' (p xi). Although the practical implementation of the principles of liberal democracy is flawed in some countries, his contention is that the ideal of liberal democracy cannot be improved upon as a way of organising any society. The bold claim is that we are now witnessing the development of a universal form of civilisation, for people of all cultures and traditions, replacing the disparate forms of government which once existed around the world.

Unsurprisingly, liberal democracy has many vehement critics. Even among its supporters, few are confident enough to agree with Fukuyama's grand claims. His thesis has been dismissed, often rudely, by other commentators. Sir Stephen Sedley, an English Court of Appeal judge, calls him conceited ('Human rights: a twenty-first century agenda' [1995] PL 368). John Gray, having accused him of 'parochialism', laments that 'it is a telling mark of the condition of the intellectual and political life towards the end of the century that such absurd speculations could ever have seemed credible' (p 121). Many writers – not just postmodernists (see above, 1.4.1) – reject the notion of liberal democracy constituting a set of universal principles; these are, in reality (it is said), just Western values in contrast to, say, 'Asian values', which emphasise 'attachment to the family as an institution, deference to societal interests, thrift, conservatism in social mores, respect for authority' (Mahbubani, K, *Can Asians Think?*, 1998, Singapore: Times Books International). It is commonplace today to talk of liberal democracy being 'in crisis'. What, then, are its alleged failings? Two that are particularly pertinent to constitutions can be highlighted; these ought to be borne in mind when reading the rest of the book.

First, critics point to the practical failure of systems of government based on liberal democracy. In most countries organised according to its principles, there are high levels of unemployment, endemic poverty, poor housing, widespread drug addiction, family breakdown, racism, crime and polluted environments. In the US, social control by government has come to depend on ever higher levels of incarceration – in 1994, one in every 193 adults was in jail. For huge numbers of people, the core features of liberal democracy – personal liberty, voting in elections and welfare benefits – do little to transform their lives. On a global level, there is also no great movement towards liberal democracy. True, its main rival of State communism has (People's Republic of China apart) largely disintegrated with the break up of the Soviet Union and the Eastern Bloc in Europe. But a new rival – government based on the tenets of religious fundamentalism – is emerging. All over the world, there are also armed conflicts in which factions seek ethnic and territorial superiority over others. This includes Europe, where, in the former Yugoslavia, bloody civil war based on ethnic enmity has raged for several years.

Secondly, liberalism misunderstands what it means to be a human who lives in a community. Liberalism is wrong, critics claim, to view society as made up of isolated, adversarial individuals, each shouting 'leave me alone to do what I want!' For a start, it is virtually impossible to draw a boundary between private life and public life: almost everything we do has some adverse impact on other people (see above, 1.6.1). If this cannot be done, then the whole liberal project dissolves away. Feminists point out that the public/private divide has been created with men's – not women's – interests in mind. Some feminists doubt that discussion of 'rights' is helpful to women (see, generally, Millns, S and Whitty, N (eds), *Feminist Perspectives on Public Law*, 1999, London: Cavendish Publishing). More than this, liberalism, its critics say, wrongly prioritises the selfish desires of individuals over their mutual responsibilities and duties to one and other that are part and parcel of living in a community. David Selbourne, for example, describes as 'a hooligan's charter' the liberal assertion that individuals have a moral right to absolute control over themselves and their possessions provided that such a right does not interfere with the right of others to do likewise (*The Principle of Duty*, 1994, London: Sinclair-Stevenson, p 10). Nor can the focus on liberty rights explain the great social movements of Western countries in the 20th century – the demands for new status for women, people in ethnic minorities and homosexuals; these have not been calls for the right to be left alone, but, on the contrary, they have been motivated by a desire to be recognised as having a status of equality within a *community*.

1.7   Constitutions in liberal democracies

In a country organised according to the principles of liberal democracy, a constitution serves to further the broad aims of autonomy, democracy and security. The UK Constitution is not unequivocally committed to liberal democracy; there are many countercurrents. It does, however, share many of the aspirations of liberal democracy; and this political theory is a useful measure against which to test the law and practices of the modern British Constitution. We therefore turn to look at the role of constitutions in liberal democracies.

1.7.1 Autonomy and constitutions

First of all, constitutions in liberal democracies exist to draw the boundary between 'private' and 'public' matters and attempt to ensure that freedom within the private sphere is protected from arbitrary incursions by government. In other words, the constitutional system tries to protect people from the prying eyes and busybody intrusions of State officials. This it does by recognising that people have *legal rights*, which should not be abrogated by public authorities – except, perhaps, if there is some pressing need to do so, and the right is restricted by clear legal rules and established procedures (not mere arbitrariness). Later, we examine the nature of these rights in more detail. For the time being, it is enough for us to note that rights to liberty are often codified in constitutional documents drafted after dramatic reorganisations of societies, such as the French Declaration on the Rights of Man 1789, the American Declaration of Independence 1776 and the Constitution of South Africa 1996 adopted at the end of apartheid. The early statements of rights and freedoms were not conceived as legally enforceable, but as rhetorical statements of political claims. Today, however, in most liberal democracies judges have an important role in adjudicating on whether State authorities – including democratically elected legislatures – have infringed people's basic rights to autonomy. As well as the constitutions of particular countries, several international legal instruments have been made in which governments of many States have committed themselves to upholding principles of individual freedom. These include the United Nations Universal Declaration of Human Rights 1948 and the Council of Europe's European Convention on Fundamental Rights and Freedoms 1950 (see Chapter 19).

Although the UK now lays claim to being a liberal democracy, there is a long tradition of being sceptical or hostile to the practice of codifying the basic rights of individuals in a single legal document (see below, 5.3 and 19.2). It is only as recently as 1998, with the enactment of the Human Rights Act, that such a code became part of national law in this country and capable of adjudication upon by British courts. The absence of a codified set of rights did not, however, mean that no such rights existed: principles of individual freedom, and practical legal rules drawing the boundary between public and private matters, can be found in judge made case law and in particular statutes. Two legal principles underpin the UK's constitutional recognition of individual freedom; they are really two sides of the same coin:

(a) a *principle of negative liberty*: that individuals are permitted to do everything not specifically prohibited by the law (we may smoke cigarettes in the street; reprimand our children by smacking them; read magazines which ridicule government ministers; go to worship in our chosen church or temple);

(b) a *principle of limited government*: all action taken by State authorities must be authorised by a particular legal power recognised by the common law or contained in an Act of Parliament (a police constable is empowered to arrest us if we smoke cannabis only because the Police and Criminal Evidence Act 1984 and the Misuse of Drugs Act 1971 permit him or her to do so; social workers may take children away from neglectful parents only because they are empowered by the Children Act 1989; customs officers may confiscate sexually explicit literature from people, but only within the terms of the Obscene Publications Act 1959).

Most people in the UK consider that they enjoy a considerable degree of liberty to conduct their personal activities and express themselves free from legal regulation. Up to a point, and in contrast with some other societies, this is true. (For an audit of the state of freedom in the UK, look at Klug, F *et al*, *The Three Pillars of Liberty*, 1996, London: Routledge). We may, for instance, listen to the kinds of music we enjoy. If we play it too loudly, however, local council officials have legal powers to confiscate our stereo systems; and if we want to listen to music in the company of others – at a concert or club – we may do so only if the organisers of the event have first obtained a licence from a public authority. Because the UK is not a society in which any religious dietary laws are enforced by those who rule us, people have considerable freedom to consume what they enjoy eating and drinking. But even such an everyday activity as eating is subject to legal regulation. Many laws regulate the production and sale of foods and beverages to ensure they are fit to eat and that retailers (of alcoholic drinks and game birds, for example) are responsible persons to carry on such a trade.

Legal regulation is then, in our society, central to the ways in which we live our everyday lives. There is a broad consensus that most of the laws we have are desirable for a well ordered society. Indeed, political discussion today is often characterised by calls for *greater* legal regulation of human and business activities – for example, tobacco use and advertising, gun ownership and the publication of salacious stories in tabloid newspapers. These constant demands for legislation cause liberals to worry that freedom is, bit by bit, being eroded.

1.7.2 Democracy and the constitution

A second purpose of a constitutional system in a liberal democracy is to provide a settled framework of institutions and processes through which people may participate in government, if only by expressing their consent to be governed. In other words, the constitution creates the practical mechanisms of democratic decision making. This may involve laws relating to elections, referendums, and the tasks of a legislature. Through these mechanisms, people are enabled to *talk about* their rival opinions and diverse, overlapping interests and to mediate conflicts about them – rather than the alternative of resolving disputes between factions by means of physical violence.

In most liberal democracies, the mechanisms are set out in a codified constitutional document. The UK still does not have such a written constitution; instead, the main arrangements for democratic government are contained in statutes – for example, the Representation of the People Act 1983, Parliament Acts 1911 and 1947, the Local Government Act 1972, the European Parliamentary Elections Act 1998 and the Scotland Act 1998. Legal rules contained in Acts of Parliament are, however, only part of the picture. As we shall see (below, 2.2), well established practices – in the UK called 'constitutional conventions' – also guide the operation of democratic governance. It is a constitutional convention, for instance, that the monarch always gives royal assent to bills passed by the UK Parliament; similarly, it is a convention rather than a legal rule that, after a general election, the monarch invites the leader of the largest political party in the UK Parliament to become Prime Minister.

In the UK, one of the great steps forward in the 20th century was the achievement of the universal franchise – the entitlement of all adult men and women to vote in parliamentary elections and so take part in choosing MPs to govern us and legislate for our behaviour. This political project is, however, far from complete. Although reforms are underway, in 1999 the upper chamber of Parliament is still made up of people who inherit their right to be in the legislature from their fathers, people appointed there for life on the recommendation of the Prime Minister and the bishops of one particular church. Nor, in a monarchy, do people have a right to vote for the Head of State in periodic elections. Many people criticise as unfair the 'first past the post' voting system for elections to the House of Commons and advocate a system of proportional representation (see below, 6.4). Another concern is that, in recent decades, the powers of elected local authorities throughout the UK to tax and spend and to pursue policies have been curtailed by successive Acts of Parliament; voter turnout in many local elections is dismal. Moreover, since 1973, when the UK became a member of the European Community, important government decision making and law making powers have been assumed by institutions which are neither elected nor properly accountable to elected representatives (see below, 7.4.2). Later chapters will survey some of the deficiencies in our system, and assess the reforms needed to improve the condition of democracy.

There is, in short, a disillusionment with electoral politics. In June 1999, barely more than one in four of the UK electorate bothered to vote in elections for the European Parliament. According to some opinion polls, almost half the adults under 35 years of age in the UK are 'not very' or 'not at all' interested in politics (but, for a contrasting view, see McCormack, U, *Playing at Politics: First Time Voting in the 1997 General Election*, 1998, London: Politeia). Although they may support pressure groups, particularly those campaigning on the environment and animal welfare, many young people regard elections, Parliament and political parties as irrelevant to their everyday lives and personal aspirations. There are, it has to be said, some good reasons for holding such opinions. The problem for law lecturers is that the study of constitutional law is inextricably bound up with broad political questions: as we have already noted, and will see throughout the book, criteria for evaluating constitutional law are rooted in competing ideas about how we should organise our society in accordance with democratic principles. Twenty years ago, law teachers could confidently assume that many of their undergraduates took an enthusiastic interest in politics, and that most of the rest were well informed bystanders following events and debates by reading a broadsheet newspaper regularly. Times have changed: for many students, politics today is a dismal activity, which is best avoided.

If you are one of those students, reading this or any other law textbook is unlikely radically to alter your perception of the modern political process. What this chapter can do, however, is pose a thought: the fact so many people, including intelligent law students, do not believe that the democratic political process is important *is itself an interesting phenomenon*. Just *why* are so many people, especially young people, disenchanted? One possible answer may be that our particular constitutional arrangements are partly to blame for the problem. Certainly, this has been one widely held view among professional politicians and several pressure groups (such as Charter 88). Both the Conservative Governments of 1979–97 and the Labour Party Government formed after the May 1997 general election have carried out constitutional reform (see Chapter 4). What prompted these changes was the belief that, in various ways, the existing constitutional arrangements ('the Westminster Model') were no longer adequate for our needs at the end of the 20th century.

1.7.3   Safety and security from the constitution

A third function of constitutions in most liberal democracies is to provide a framework of institutions and procedures through which State authorities are expected to achieve security and promote the welfare of citizens. As we have seen, at its most basic, this requires the defence of the country from invasion or attack by other nations. Most constitutions permit governments exceptional powers during war; in time of emergency, the normal procedures of democratic decision making may be suspended or modified, and individual liberties may be curtailed. To an ever-increasing extent, governments of Nation States now recognise that none acting alone is capable of ensuring safety from attack from weapons of mass destruction. States may therefore make collective decisions about security through multinational organisations such as the United Nations, the North Atlantic Treaty Organisation (NATO) and the Western European Union (WEU). In Western Europe, the development of a common defence and foreign policy is now also one of the goals of the European Union (see below, 7.2.2 and 7.7.1). The other rudimentary function of a constitution is to define the powers of police officers and other public authorities to maintain law and order and investigate crime. In a liberal democracy, a constitution seeks to guarantee that the intrusive powers to stop, search, arrest and detain citizens are carried out within the limits set by law in order to carry out the tasks determined by elected representatives (see below, 2.5.7). As with defence, governments of Nation States have come to recognise that each alone is incapable of providing security from internationally organised crime (such as drug trafficking and terrorism). Few national constitutions have yet adapted to these new practices by providing adequate mechanisms for scrutiny and consent-giving.

As we have noted (see above, 1.6.3), in the 20th century, security has come to mean welfare as well as defence and policing. Although the UK has no codified constitution (see below, 2.2), there are numerous statements in laws committing government to furthering the goals of material welfare. The European Union, of which the UK is part, is constitutionally bound to follow policies to promote 'a harmonious, balanced and sustainable development of economic activities, a high level of employment and of social protection ... sustainable and non-inflationary growth ... a high level of protection and improvement of the quality of the environment, the raising of the standard of living and quality of life ...' (Art 2 of the EC Treaty, discussed in Chapter 7). Numerous Acts of Parliament set out more specific responsibilities of government ministers and other public authorities to fulfil certain objectives. Thus, s 1(1) of the National Health Service Act 1977 states:

> It is the Secretary of State's duty to continue the promotion in England and Wales of a comprehensive health service designed to secure improvement –
> (a)   in the physical and mental health of the people in those countries, and
> (b)   in the prevention, diagnosis and treatment of illness, and for that purpose to secure the effective provision of services in accordance with this Act.

Similarly, s 8 of the Education Act 1944 provides:

> It shall be the duty of every local education authority to secure that there shall be available for their area sufficient schools –
> (a)   for providing primary education ... ; and
> (b)   for providing secondary education.

Section 197 of the Housing Act 1996 places on a local authority the duty to provide a homeless person 'with such advice and assistance as the authority consider is reasonably required to enable him to secure such accommodation'. There are many other similar such statutory duties placed on State authorities. It is the function of the constitution to provide procedures for enacting such legislation and ensuring that it is complied with.

1.7.4   Mediating tensions between constitutional goals

The functions of a constitution in a liberal democracy include providing practical arrangements for achieving individual liberty, collective decision making and ensuring collective safety and security. These goals are not always compatible with each other, and so a further task for the constitutional system is to supply a principled basis for resolving such tensions. Two examples of this will suffice at this stage.

Conflicts between liberty and democracy

Although democracy and liberalism coincide in many countries, they are distinct ideas: liberalism is concerned with *restricting the power* of public authorities; democracy is concerned with *placing power* in the hands of people representing the majority of adults in a society. There is room for conflict between these two principles. Consider this: if a majority of the electorate vote for politicians who promise to do X, how can, and why should, the constitutional system prevent X being implemented, even if it would infringe the private sphere of some people? (For X imagine, for instance, prohibiting literature disrespectful of a religion).

The answer so far as traditional British constitutional practices are concerned is 'yes' – Parliament should indeed be able to enact whatever laws it pleases, though it is unlikely to pass legislation which is too draconian (see below, 5.2). More recently, however, thinking on this question has changed. Since 1966, British citizens have been able to petition an international judicial body based in Strasbourg (eastern France) alleging that a public authority has violated the rights and freedoms set out in an international treaty called the European Convention on Human Rights. Article 8 states that 'Everyone has the right to respect for his private and family life, his home and his correspondence' (see Chapter 23). In several judgments, the Court of Human Rights has held that Acts of Parliament have breached the Convention – for example, in *Dudgeon v UK* (1982), statutory provisions making homosexual acts in private illegal in Northern Ireland were declared contrary to Art 8. Until the enactment of the Human Rights Act 1998 (see below, 19.10), the judgments of the court in Strasbourg had no formal affect in national law within the UK, though, in practice, British governments normally tried to change the laws or practices which that court held to be an infringement of human rights. After the Human Rights Act comes into force, however, the Convention will be able to be used by lawyers conducting litigation in the UK and British courts will have the power to make formal declarations that statutes passed by Parliament are incompatible with the Convention. In some other liberal democracies, such as the US, courts have the power to strike down legislation which is incompatible with their constitutions. Is this right? Some commentators and politicians believe that it is wrong for unelected judges to be able to overrule legislation passed by elected politicians; others claim it is an essential requirement in a liberal democracy. We return to this debate in Chapter 19.

Conflicts between liberty and safety and security

Demands that public authorities act on our collective behalf to make us secure and safe from harm (see above, 1.7.3) may also sit uneasily with the competing desire for personal freedom (see above, 1.7.1). Sociologists have identified a preoccupation with avoiding risks in our society. Frank Furedi argues:

> Safety has become the fundamental value of the 1990s. Passions that were once devoted to the struggle to change the world (or keep it the same) are now invested in trying to ensure that we are safe [*Culture of Fear*, 1996, London: Cassell, p 1].

Much recent legislation in the UK is highly paternalistic and seeks to place inflated concerns for public safety above (for instance) the enjoyment people get from participating in an Olympic sport, the consumption of traditional English food and freedom of expression. The Firearms (Amendment) Act 1997 bans the possession of all handguns and owners had to surrender them to the police; implementation of this policy, which including compensation payments to owners, is estimated to cost over £160 million and has stopped people participating in the Olympic sport of pistol shooting. The Beef Bones Regulations 1997 prevent the sale of beef on the bone, meaning that people can no longer enjoy oxtail soup, T-bone steak or a Sunday roast of rib of beef. The reason for the ban was the risk that humans might contract new variant CJD (the human form of BSE) as a result of eating certain cuts of meat, though the predicted risk of this happening was minute. There would have been a one in 20 chance of one person in the whole of the UK contracting the disease from such meat in the next 20 years. Section 1 of the Knives Act 1997 provides:

> (1) A person is guilty of an offence if he markets a knife in a way which –
>
>   (a) indicates, or suggests, that it is suitable for combat; or
>
>   (b) is otherwise likely to stimulate or encourage violent behaviour involving the use of the knife as a weapon.

The assumption here is that people merely seeing an advertisement will be propelled to harm other people. As concerns for public safety increase, the real danger is the one identified by Isaiah Berlin – that paternalistic government degrades human beings (see above, 1.7.1). As we shall see in Part D of the book, such conflicts between liberty and safety are not diminished simply by attempting to set out 'human rights' in a codified document.

PRINCIPLES IN PUBLIC LAW

Public law is concerned with the legal relationships between State authorities and people (as individuals and members of voluntary associations). It is also about the rules that govern the interrelationships between the various State authorities themselves (for example, Parliament and the courts). In the UK at the moment, as in many other countries, there is fairly broad agreement about the basic values which should influence public law – these are the principles of liberal democracy. Three main elements may be identified:

(a) *the idea that it is both possible and desirable to make distinctions between a person's private and public life*. Liberty to speak and act is highly valued and should be constrained by State authorities only when necessary in order to prevent harm to other people. Legal instruments (such as the European Convention on Human Rights) setting out basic rights are now an important method of demarcating the limits of State intrusion into private life. There are also, however, constant calls for greater regulation of human activity to make our society safer;

(b) *the idea that collective decision making should be based on people's consent and participation*. This ideal may be put into practice in different ways, notably by choosing representatives in periodic, multi-party elections to serve for limited periods in government and in the legislature. One of the purposes of a constitutional system and public law is to provide a stable framework of institutions and process through which collective decisions may be made;

(c) *State authorities have responsibility for many aspects of our collective security, safety and welfare*. This includes conducting foreign relations, organising the armed forces and maintaining law and order by the police. In modern times, it also includes the provision of welfare benefits, health care, education and other social benefits paid for by taxation. Detailed legal rules govern all these State activities.

CHAPTER 2

THE NEW CONSTITUTIONAL SETTLEMENT

2.1   Introduction

The previous chapter explained, in a fairly abstract way, the principles of liberal democracy underpinning public law. Before going further, we need to consider in outline the practical constitutional arrangements of the UK. So many changes have been made to the structures of law making and government in the past few years that it is no exaggeration to say that there has been a new constitutional 'settlement'. Many of them have come about as the direct result of a programme of constitutional reform implemented by the Labour Government since the 1997 general election. Other changes stem from broader and deeper transformations that are taking place in the way governments operate – many of them associated with the processes of globalisation and the creation of the 'new world order' (see below, 2.12). Some of the most significant developments include the following:

(a) the continuing evolution of the European Union, most recently with the revisions made by the Treaty of Amsterdam which came into force in May 1999;

(b) new devolved legislative and executive institutions have been established in the three smaller parts of the UK (Scotland, Wales and Northern Ireland) and this will have an impact on the whole of the UK, including England;

(c) the Human Rights Act 1998 incorporates the European Convention on Human Rights into the legal systems of the UK. This will affect not only the constitutional relationship between individuals and the State, but also between the judiciary, legislatures and executive bodies of the UK.

2.2   Allocating decision making powers

One of the main practical functions of a constitution is to define the powers of decision making of the State's office holders and institutions (see above, 1.7). The term 'competences' may be used to describe these powers. A public authority may have competence to carry out a specific kind of constitutional function. Theorists identify a principle called the 'separation of powers', in which three main kinds of constitutional function are distinguished:

(a) the legislative (broadly, making legally binding rules of general application);

(b) the executive (broadly, governmental powers to initiate and implement policy choices); and

(c) the judicial function (broadly, adjudicating on disputes according to legal rules and principles).

Some theorists argue that it is important for each function to be allocated to a separate institution. If they are combined, the fear is that a public authority may have too much power and abuse it. The UK Constitution does not take this view. It has a system of parliamentary, rather than presidential, government which *requires* members of the executive branch (ministers) to be members of the legislative branch (Parliament). Another illustration of the UK's relaxed attitude towards the separation of powers is that the Lord Chancellor is a member of all three branches of government: he is the presiding officer of the upper chamber of Parliament; he sits as a judge in the Appellate Committee of the House of Lords; and he is a member of the Cabinet (see below, 2.4.3). What the UK does attach great importance to, however, is the general independence of the judiciary from the executive (see below, 2.10).

Apart from allocating functional competences, in the ways just described, a constitution needs to allocate competences to deal with particular areas of public policy. We may say that an institution, or set of institutions, has the legal capacity to deal with (say) agriculture or health care – and this may include making legislation about the topic, taking executive action and adjudicating on disputes about it. Many large liberal democracies, such as the US and Germany, allocate policy competences according to a federal system. This means that the constitution recognises two autonomous levels of government, neither subordinate to the other. The UK does not have a federal system, though the trend may be towards something resembling federalism with the creation of devolved legislative and executive institutions in Scotland, Northern Ireland and Wales.

Any description of the allocation of competences now has to be quite technical. A person wanting to know whether public authority has the power to do something needs to understand the content and status of a range of legal instruments, as we shall see. These include the Treaty Establishing the European Communities and the Treaty on European Union (see below, 7.2). Numerous Acts of the UK Parliament deal with the powers, limits on powers, and duties of public authorities. These include the Scotland Act 1998, the Northern Ireland Act 1998, the Government of Wales Act 1998, the Local Government Act 1972, the European Communities Act 1972, the Public Order Act 1986, the Parliament Acts of 1911 and 1947, the Representation of the People Act 1983, the Act of Settlement 1700, the Bill of Rights 1688, Magna Carta 1215 ... the list could go on. Some of these statutes allocate competences, or place restrictions on competence, according to elaborate schemes. Some public authorities also acquire powers, and have restrictions place upon them, by the prerogative (see below, 2.4.3).

Constitutional conventions

In addition, there are constitutional conventions. (The term 'convention' is also used to describe some international treaties, such as the European Convention on Human Rights, but here, the word is used in an entirely different sense.) Some of the features of the constitution described in this chapter – including the existence of a cabinet and the fact that ministers are members of, and make themselves answerable to, the UK Parliament – are not stipulated by statute or the common law. Many institutions exist, and procedures are followed, just because there is widespread agreement that they should. There is academic debate about the nature of conventions and the extent to which their characteristics differ from 'laws' (see below, 5.4). One constitutional authority suggests a practical test for establishing whether a particular convention exists (see Jennings, I (Sir), *The Law and the Constitution*, 1952, London: London UP):

(a) Are there any precedents?

(b) Did the actors in the precedents believe that they were bound by a rule?

(c) Is there a reason for the rule?

In many situations, this test clearly determines that a convention exists. For instance, it is a convention that the monarch does not refuse to give royal assent to a bill passed by Parliament (see below, 2.11). There are many precedents, and the monarch apparently believes that she is bound by this rule – not since Queen Anne attempted to withhold assent in the 18th century has a monarch seriously sought to question its existence. There are also good democratic reasons for the convention. In other cases, the existence of a convention may be less certain. For instance, is it a convention that a minister who has engaged in a discreditable sexual relationship should resign from government?

Lack of a codified constitution

Occasionally, it is suggested that the UK would benefit from a written constitution – that is, a codified legal instrument setting out the principal powers, limits on powers and duties of the main public authorities. The UK remains one of a tiny number of countries without such a document. The flurry of constitutional reform over the past few years has rather diverted attention from the fact that it is often difficult to know what public authorities do and how they relate to each other.

2.3 Allocation of competences between the EC and the UK

Describing the competences of public authorities in the UK is, then, not straightforward – not least because, since 1973, the UK has been a Member State of what is now called the European Union. The most developed part of the European Union is the European Community (see below, 7.2.1); Member States also work together on a common foreign and security policy (see 7.2.2) and there is police and judicial co-operation on criminal matters (see 7.2.3). For simplicity's sake, we focus, for the time being, just on the European Community.

In relation to some fields of government action, the institutions of the European Community have sole competence to develop policy. In relation to other areas of policy, the European Community shares competence to do things with each of the 15 Member States. In yet other categories, Member States remain free to develop policy without any formal co-operation with the European Community. This can be represented in a diagram.

Figure 1

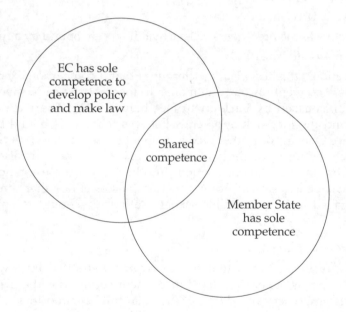

The extent of the European Community's sole or shared competences in policy areas can be seen from Art 3 of the Treaty Establishing the European Communities (see below, 7.2), which states:

> ... the activities of the Community shall include, as provided in this Treaty and in accordance with the timetable set out therein:
>
> (a) the prohibition, as between Member States, of customs duties and quantitative restrictions on the import and export of goods, and of all other measures having equivalent effect;
>
> (b) a common commercial policy;

(c) an internal market characterised by the abolition, as between Member States, of obstacles to the free movement of goods, persons, services and capital;

(d) measures concerning the entry and movement of persons ...;

(e) a common policy in the sphere of agriculture and fisheries;

(f) a common policy in the sphere of transport;

(g) a system ensuring that competition in the internal market is not distorted;

(h) the approximation of the laws of Member States to the extent required for the functioning of the common market;

(i) the promotion of co-ordination between employment policies of the Member States with a view to enhancing their effectiveness by developing a coordinated strategy for employment;

(j) a policy in the social sphere comprising a European Social Fund;

(k) the strengthening of economic and social cohesion;

(l) a policy in the sphere of the environment;

(m) the strengthening of the competitiveness of Community industry;

(n) the promotion of research and technological development;

(o) encouragement for the establishment and development of trans-European networks;

(p) a contribution to the attainment of a high level of health protection;

(q) a contribution to education and training of quality and to the flowering of the cultures of the Member States;

(r) a policy in the sphere of development co-operation;

(s) the association of the overseas countries and territories in order to increase trade and promote jointly economic and social development;

(t) a contribution to the strengthening of consumer protection;

(u) measures in the spheres of energy, civil protection and tourism.

These, then, are the policy competences allocated in whole or in part to the European Community. Chapter 7 examines in more detail how the European Community exercises its functions in relation to these areas of policy. It carries out legislative functions through a network of institutions (the Council, the Commission and the European Parliament), which create directives and regulations. It has an executive function (mainly carried out by the Commission (see below, 7.5.1, and 8.2.5)), but public authorities in the Member States have most of the responsibility for the day to day implementation of Community policy. The European Community also has a judicial function, exercised through the Court of Justice and Court of First Instance in Luxembourg; but national courts and tribunals are responsible for adjudicating on the bulk Community law issues (see Chapter 18). From time to time, disputes arise about whether it is the Community or a Member State which has the competence to do something (see below, 5.2.4). On the other hand, the European Community has, on occasion, mistakenly thought it had competence, when it did not. It is Community law, not national law, which determines where competence lies.

2.4   Allocation of competences within the UK

In relation to some areas of policy, Member States of the European Union retain sole competence to decide what government ought to do (see Figure 1). The Treaty establishing the European Communities does not spell out what these areas are: they are, therefore, any field of policy which does not fall within the competence of the European Community. Policy in relation to families and divorce, constitutional reform, criminal justice and income tax are examples of areas in which each Member State has competence – although, even here, national governments may be constrained to some extent by Community law.

Our focus in this book will be on the arrangements within the United Kingdom of Great Britain and Northern Ireland (as a member of the European Union). The UK, like most other States, has chosen to create smaller units of governance within its territory. The UK is a union of four parts: England, Wales and Scotland (which together form 'Great Britain') and Northern Ireland. Within each part of the UK, government is also organised in still smaller units – local authorities (sometimes called 'counties' and 'boroughs'). Throughout the UK, there are over 600 such units (see below, 2.9.1).

Jersey, Guernsey (Channel Island 'Crown dependencies') and the Isle of Man are not parts of the UK, nor are they members of the European Union. The UK Government is, however, responsible for the defence and external relations of these self-governing islands. The same is true of a number of small dependent overseas territories, which include Gibraltar, the Cayman Islands and the Falkland Islands.

2.4.1   Difficulties in mapping out competences within the UK

For a beginner, understanding the allocation of competences within the UK is made difficult for several reasons. As we have just seen, competences in relation to some fields of government action are shared with the European Community. Careful legal analysis of relevant legislation may be needed in order to work out, for example, whether a particular policy initiative on (say) environmental protection is a matter for the Community, for the UK, for a devolved institution in Scotland, Northern Ireland or Wales, or for a local authority. Another difficulty is that devolution, under the Scotland Act 1998, the Northern Ireland Act 1998 and the Government of Wales Act 1998, has resulted in an asymmetrical arrangement. England, which has 80% of the UK's population and its largest land area, does not have its own Parliament or government separate from that of the UK as a whole: 'England' has no constitutional status. Moreover, there is no common pattern to the schemes for allocating functional and policy competences (see above, 2.2) to the new institutions in Scotland, Wales and Northern Ireland. To explain who has competence to do what, when and how within the UK, we begin with the UK as a whole (and England), and then move on to examine the powers of the devolved institutions.

2.4.2 The UK Parliament

The 659 Members of the UK Parliament (which is also the Parliament for England) are elected to serve for terms of up to five years (the minimum length of a Parliament is not set by law) by a plurality (or 'first past the post') electoral system. The role of Parliament in the constitutional system is considered in more detail in Chapter 6. Here, our concern is to outline its constitutional competence. Much theory and political rhetoric has been spent claiming that the UK Parliament is omnicompetent – that it has power to make and unmake laws on any subject (see below, 5.2). In formal legal terms, this is true; in practical terms, it is misleading.

It is true because, in the absence of a written constitutional code (see above, 2.2), Acts of the UK Parliament are still generally regarded as the highest form of law in the constitutional system. What has happened is that, for the time being, the UK Parliament has delegated law making powers to the institutions of the European Union (see below, 7.6), including the capacity to make rules which override Acts of Parliament. The UK Parliament could, however, at any time reclaim those law making powers. Similarly, in relation to the UK Parliament's relationship with the Scottish Parliament (see below, 2.5.1) and the Northern Ireland Assembly (see below, 2.6.1): the UK has conferred power on those devolved institutions to make legislation, but it could, at any time, take them away. Indeed, the Scotland Act 1998 and the Northern Ireland Act 1998 expressly preserve a residual power for the Parliament of the UK to enact primary legislation for those parts of the UK on any matter, including those envisaged normally to be within the competence of the devolved legislatures (s 28(7) of the Scotland Act; s 5 of the Northern Ireland Act).

This view may, however, be misleading – or at least overly formal. Certainly, it does not capture the day to day constraints that apply to the UK Parliament. Its competence to enact legislation is limited. In summary, the position is that it may enact statutes in relation to the following matters:

(a) any matter relating to England which does not breach a rule of European Community law (see below, 7.9.1);

(b) any matter relating to Wales which does not breach European Community law;

(c) in relation to Scotland, those matters which have been 'reserved' to the UK by Sched 5 of the Scotland Act 1998 (see below, 2.5.1). Again, statutes on these issues may not be enacted in breach of European Community law;

(d) in relation to Northern Ireland, those matters which are 'excepted' or 'reserved' to the UK by Scheds 2 and 3 of the Northern Ireland Act 1998 (see below, 2.6.1).

As a matter of domestic law, the UK Parliament may pass statutes which breach the human rights set out in the European Convention on Human Rights – as it has done on several occasions (see below, 19.6). Following the enactment of the Human Rights Act 1998, however, courts in the UK may grant a declaration that a provision in an Act of Parliament is incompatible with the Convention. This will not affect the legal validity of the enactment.

As a matter of international law, the UK may not enact legislation contrary to the Convention. The European Court of Human Rights in Strasbourg has, in international law, power to make a declaration that a breach has occurred (see below, 19.7). Such a declaration would not affect the validity of the provision at issue so far as UK law is concerned.

2.4.3   Government of the UK

The Government of the UK, which is also the Government of England, is drawn from the UK Parliament. After a general election, the leader of the largest political party becomes the Prime Minister (see below, 2.11) and chooses a number of other MPs and peers (usually about 90) from his or her party to become ministers. It has become practice for the Prime Minister to have an annual cabinet reshuffle in which some ministerial posts are reallocated. Twenty or so senior ministers (mostly styled 'Secretary of State') are the political heads of the main central government departments (such as the Home Office, the Foreign and Commonwealth Office, Department of Trade and Industry and the Department for Education and Employment). The portfolios of some ministers, such as the Foreign Secretary, include responsibilities for the UK as a whole. After devolution in 1999, the responsibility of some ministers in the UK Government (for instance, in the Ministry of Agriculture, Fisheries and Food) is largely confined to government within England.

The interests of Scotland, Wales and Northern Ireland in the Government of the UK are represented, respectively, by the Secretary of State for Scotland, the Secretary of State for Wales and the Secretary of State for Northern Ireland. (These posts are not to be confused with those of leaders of the devolved executives, namely the First Minister of Scotland, the First Secretary of Wales and the First Minister of Northern Ireland.)

Senior ministers of the UK Government join the Prime Minister in the Cabinet, which meets once a week at 10 Downing Street, normally for no more than an hour. What is discussed is a secret, though journalists are normally briefed on some of the issues discussed by the Prime Minister's Press Secretary. There are numerous Cabinet committees of senior and junior (non-Cabinet) ministers, and sometimes senior civil servants, which decide government policy on different issues. It is in these committees that major government policy initiatives are often finalised.

Ministers in the UK Government obtain powers and duties to take action from several different sources. Acts of the UK Parliament may confer powers or impose duties on them (see above, 1.7.4). Such powers often include the capacity to make subordinate legislation (also known as 'delegated' or 'secondary' legislation). Most subordinate legislation is in the form of statutory instruments. These are rules drafted within a minister's department and put before Parliament for approval. In most cases, the scrutiny which Parliament subjects them to is – to say the least – cursory. It is rare for a statutory instrument to be debated (see below, 6.5.2). They are published by Her Majesty's Stationery Office <www.hmso.gov.uk/stat.htm>. Occasionally, the validity of a statutory instrument is challenged by judicial review.

In some situations, ministers may obtain their legal powers, or have duties imposed upon them, by the royal prerogative. In essence, these are powers recognised by the courts as attributes of the Crown. Academic lawyers have disagreed over the exact definition of prerogative powers. For some, they are the legal powers, unique to the Crown, to alter a person's rights, duties or status (Wade, HWR, *Constitutional Fundamentals*, 1989, London: Stevens, p 46). The courts, however, have tended to adopt a broader definition: all the non-statutory powers of the Crown, even if they are not unique to the Crown (for instance, giving money away) and even if they do not alter people's rights. Falling within this definition, for example, would be making ex gratia payments to victims of violent crime under the Criminal Injuries Compensation Scheme (*R v Criminal Injuries Compensation Board ex p Lain* (1967); but note that the scheme has now been made into a statutory one). In the distant past, prerogative powers were exercised personally by the monarch. With the rise of Cabinet government and the coming of democracy (see Chapter 3), decisions about how to exercise most prerogatives came to rest in the hands of ministers. There is no formal, comprehensive list of prerogative powers. They include: entering into treaties with other countries; the disposition of the armed forces; the appointment of judges; and the organisation of the civil service. Ministers cannot create new prerogatives. Nor is there a general prerogative 'to act in the public good' (Vincenzi, C, *Crown Powers, Subjects and Citizens*, 1998, London: Pinter). The Queen still personally exercises some prerogative powers, including the grant of royal assent to bills passed by Parliament and the appointment of the Prime Minister. Mostly, there are well established conventions dictating how such prerogative powers are to be used, and so their exercise is uncontroversial.

When a minister claims to be acting under the legal authority of one of the prerogative powers, the courts may adjudicate on whether that power actually does exist. The courts will not permit the use of a prerogative power where it has been replaced by a statutory power (*AG v de Kaiser's Royal Hotel* (1920), though the fact that an Act of Parliament deals with the same general field as a prerogative will not prevent a minister from using the prerogative (*R v Secretary of State for the Home Department ex p Northumbria Police Authority* (1989); the Home Secretary had prerogative power 'to maintain the peace of the realm' and set up a store of plastic bullets and CS gas for police forces to use). If a prerogative power is held to exist, it must normally be exercised in accordance with the principles of judicial review (*Council of Civil Service Unions v Minister for the Civil Service* (1985)) (see Chapter 11).

2.5 Scotland

The Scotland Act 1998 created the Scottish Parliament, the Scottish Executive and the Scottish Administration.

2.5.1 The competence of the Scottish Parliament

The 129 Members of the Scottish Parliament (MSPs) are elected for fixed terms of four years using the additional member voting system (see below, 6.4.1). In the first election in May 1999, Labour had the most seats, though not an overall majority over all other parties. The Scottish Parliament has limited tax varying powers: MSPs may pass a resolution that the basic rate of income tax for Scottish taxpayers is increased or decreased by not more than 3% of the tax rate set by the UK Parliament. Given this limited power, the Scottish Executive is largely dependent on grants of funds authorised by the UK Parliament.

The limits of the legislative competence of the Scottish Parliament to pass Acts of the Scottish Parliament are set out in s 29 of the Scotland Act 1998:

29 (1) An Act of the Scottish Parliament is not law so far as any provision of the Act is outside the legislative competence of the Parliament.

   (2) A provision is outside that competence so far as any of the following paragraphs apply –

   (a) it would form part of the law of a country or territory other than Scotland, or confer or remove functions exercisable otherwise than in or as regards Scotland,

   (b) it relates to reserved matters,

   (c) it is in breach of the restrictions in Sched 4,

   (d) it is incompatible with any of the Convention rights or with Community law,

   (e) it would remove the Lord Advocate from his position as head of the systems of criminal prosecution and investigation of deaths in Scotland.

The Scottish Parliament is therefore told what it cannot do, rather than what it can do. This is similar to the Northern Ireland Assembly (see below, 2.6.1), but the opposite of the arrangement for the National Assembly of Wales (see below, 2.7). Looking at s 29, we see that the Scottish Parliament cannot enact legislation for anywhere outside Scotland (s 29(2)(a)).

Acts of the Scottish Parliament cannot 'relate to' a 'reserved matter'. These are defined in Sched 5 to the Act. These include some general reservations: the constitution of the UK; registration and funding of political parties; foreign affairs; the Civil Service; defence; and treason. Schedule 5 also sets out a long list of specific reservations, grouped under a number of heads. In some, a description of the nature of the reservation is given; in others, particular Acts of the UK Parliament are set down. The heads, in outline, are:

A – Financial and Economic Matters

B – Home Affairs

C – Trade and Industry

D – Energy

E – Transport

F – Social Security

G – Regulation of the Professions

H – Employment

(There is no letter I; parliamentary drafters avoid it, lest it might be mistaken for the Roman numeral I.)

J – Health and Medicines

K – Media and Culture

L – Miscellaneous.

The contents of these heads vary in their scope. Under J, for instance, there are five subheads reserved to the UK Parliament: abortion; xenotransplantation; embryology, surrogacy and genetics; the licensing of medicines, medical supplies and poisons; and schemes for the distribution of welfare foods.

Section 29(2)(c) denies competence to enact Acts of the Scottish Parliament which are 'in breach of the restrictions in Sched 4'. This Schedule sets out the Acts of the UK Parliament which cannot be modified by the passing of a Scottish Act. These include the Human Rights Act 1998, provisions of the European Communities Act 1972, and most of the provisions of the Scotland Act 1998 itself.

Under s 29(2)(d), enactments of the Scottish Parliament cannot contravene either the Human Rights Act 1998 (see below, 19.10) or any rule of European Community law (see 7.9.1).

Finally, in s 29(2)(e), the Scottish Parliament is prohibited from altering certain of the powers of the Lord Advocate, who is one of the two Law Officers in the Scottish Executive (the other is the Scottish Solicitor General). It is the Lord Advocate who decides whether or not to bring some prosecutions of serious offences, and it was thought desirable to protect his independence in this way.

Section 28(7) states that the arrangement just described 'does not affect the power of the Parliament of the United Kingdom to make laws for Scotland'. This both preserves parliamentary sovereignty (see below, 5.2) and makes it clear that the new devolved settlement does not amount to a federal system. In other words, as a matter of last resort, the UK could legislate for Scotland on a non-reserved matter – or, indeed, repeal the Scotland Act.

2.5.2 The Scottish Administration

As well as the new Scottish Parliament, the Scotland Act creates a new set of government institutions. The Scottish Parliament chooses one of its MSPs to be appointed as First Minister by the Queen (ss 45–46). In practice, that person is likely to be the leader of the largest political party in Parliament. After the first elections to the Parliament in May 1999, Donald Dewar became First Minster. He then selected other MSPs to be appointed ministers by the Queen (s 47). Ten senior ministers, along with the two Law Officers and the First Minister, form a Cabinet. Collectively, the ministers and Law Officers are called 'the Scottish Executive' or 'the Scottish Ministers' (s 44). The other part of the Scottish Administration, in addition to the Scottish Ministers, are the several thousand professional civil servants appointed under s 51.

Scottish Ministers may be conferred with powers by Acts of the Scottish Parliament. Section 53 of the Scotland Act also makes a 'general transfer of functions' to the Scottish Ministers, by which some powers which were formerly exercised by ministers in the UK Government were shifted on a prescribed day. These powers came either from an Act of the UK Parliament or from the royal prerogative (see above, 2.4.3). The Scotland Act sets out a framework for the competences of Scottish Ministers. If a function has been transferred under s 53, then the exercise of that function becomes a matter for the appropriate Scottish Minister. There is, however, also provision for some functions to be 'shared powers' to be exercised jointly by a Scottish Minister and a minister of the UK Government (ss 56–57). Two examples of shared powers are ministerial action on road safety and steps taken under the European Communities Act 1972 to implement obligations under Community law. A Scottish Minister exercises a function 'outside devolved competence' if he or she makes subordinate legislation which is outside the competence of the Scottish Parliament (s 54), and is also prohibited from breaching Community law or the Human Rights Act 1998 (s 57(3)(b)).

If the Secretary of State for Scotland, or any other Secretary of State in the UK Government, has reasonable grounds to believe that action proposed to be taken by a Scottish Minister is incompatible with the UK's international obligations, he or she may direct that the action not be taken. Similarly, the

Secretary of State may require action to be taken, including that a Scottish Minister revoke subordinate legislation which adversely affects a reserved matter (s 58).

2.6 Northern Ireland

Between 1801 and 1922, when the island was partitioned after a civil war (see below, 3.9.2), the whole of the island of Ireland was part of the UK. Six counties in the north east were retained by the UK; the rest of the island became an independent State, which ultimately became the Republic of Ireland. The border between north and south was drawn in such a way that the majority of the population in Northern Ireland wished to be part of the UK; but a large minority of the province's population identify themselves as Irish nationalists, with cultural, religious and political affiliations to the Republic. Between 1922 and 1972, Northern Ireland had its own bicameral Parliament and a government headed by a Prime Minister. Then, the system of devolved parliamentary government broke down amidst mounting civil unrest. The Northern Ireland Parliament was suspended by the UK Government and the province was put under direct rule, with all important governmental powers being exercised by the Secretary of State for Northern Ireland (a member of the UK Government). A turning point came in 1994, when terrorist groups, which had been committing violent crimes to campaign for and against the union with the UK, declared ceasefires. Multi-party talks were set up, and in April 1998, agreement on a new constitutional settlement was reached (the Belfast Agreement). In a referendum the following month, over 70% of people voting in Northern Ireland supported the proposed arrangements; and, in the Republic, over 94% supported the proposed change to the Irish Constitution removing that country's claim to sovereignty over Northern Ireland. The Northern Ireland Act 1998 sets out the legal framework for the new settlement, providing for an assembly, an executive and other institutions.

2.6.1 The Northern Ireland Assembly

Under the Northern Ireland Act 1998, 108 members are elected to the Northern Ireland Assembly for a fixed term of four years by the single transferable vote electoral method. The Assembly is empowered to make 'Acts of the Northern Ireland Assembly' (s 5). The Northern Ireland Act provides a framework for allocating legislative competence to the assembly. A provision of a Northern Ireland Act is outside the Assembly's competence if:

(a) it purports to apply outside the province;

(b) it deals with an 'excepted' or 'reserved' matter;

(c) it is contrary to the Human Rights Act 1998;

(d) it is incompatible with European Community law;

(e) it discriminates against any person or class of person on the ground of religious belief or political opinion; or

(f) it seeks to modify the Human Rights Act 1998, certain provisions of the Northern Ireland Act itself or certain sections of the European Communities Act 1972.

This scheme is different from that for Scotland in several ways. First, the Scotland Act contains no express prohibition on legislating for religious or political discrimination. Secondly, the Scotland Act creates two general categories: matters 'reserved' to the UK Parliament and those that are not (and therefore within the competence of the Scottish Parliament). In the Northern Ireland Act, there are three categories: 'excepted matters', 'reserved matters' and 'transferred matters'.

Excepted matters are defined by Sched 2 and include matters relating to the Crown, international relations, defence, nationality and immigration, the appointment of judges and elections in the province. These are intended always to remain matters for the UK.

Reserved matters are defined in Sched 3; they include navigation, civil aviation, domicile, postal services, disqualification from the assembly, criminal law, public order and prisons, the organisation of the police force, firearms and explosives, civil defence, the courts, many aspects of import and export controls and trade with places outside the UK, and business competition. It is envisaged that these areas of policy will remain within the competence of the UK Parliament until such time as they are transferred to the Assembly.

The third category is 'transferred matters'. These are those areas of policy which are neither 'excepted' nor 'reserved' (s 4(1)). They are not listed in the Act. The Secretary of State for Northern Ireland, the member of the UK Government responsible for the province, will, from time to time, decide what areas of policy in the 'reserved' list should be transferred. Once transferred, they may be 'recalled' into the competence of the UK Parliament.

The Northern Ireland Assembly is required to make standing orders setting up committees of Assembly members 'to advise and assist each Northern Ireland Minister in the formulation of policy' (s 29). These are likely to operate in similar ways to the departmental select committees of the UK Parliament (see below, 6.8).

2.6.2 Northern Ireland executive bodies

After a general election to the assembly, members elect a First Minister and Deputy First Minister (s 16). To ensure that there is a broad consensus on these leaders – in a province which is strongly divided into two communities – special voting arrangements have been devised. Candidates for the posts of First Minister and Deputy have to stand jointly and to win must have the 'support of the majority of the members voting in the election, a majority of the designated Nationalists voting and a majority of the designated Unionists voting' (s 16(3)). Acting jointly, the First Minister and the Deputy appoint ministers to head departments responsible for areas of policy (such as agriculture, health and so on). The First Minster, Deputy and senior ministers form an executive committee or 'Cabinet' (s 20). Northern Ireland ministers are conferred with powers by Acts of the UK Parliament, Acts of the Northern Ireland Assembly and also the prerogative (s 23). The first elections to the Assembly were held in June 1999, but the formation of the executive was delayed owing to disputes over the decommissioning of weapons by paramilitary groups.

2.6.3   The North-South Ministerial Council

The 1998 Belfast Agreement requires several new institutions to be created. One is the North-South Ministerial Council. An agreement was concluded between the UK and Ireland in March 1999 establishing the Council <www.nio.gov.uk>. The body will consist of ministers from the Northern Ireland executive and of the Irish government. The body will be conferred with its powers by an Act of the UK Parliament and similar legislation passed by the Irish Parliament. Its function will be to exchange information, discuss, consult and reach agreement on the adoption of common policies 'in areas where there is a mutual cross-border and all-island benefit'. Such areas include agriculture, teacher qualifications and exchanges, strategic transport planning, environmental protection and inland waterways. Agreements reached by the North-South Ministerial Council will be implemented north of the border by the Northern Ireland executive and Assembly, and in the south by the Irish government and parliament. The work of the North-South Ministerial Council is supported by a secretariat staffed by members of the Northern Ireland Civil Service and the Irish Civil Service. The Belfast Agreement also contained provisions for setting up the British-Irish Council (see below, 2.12).

2.7   Wales

Devolution from the UK Parliament and Government to new institutions in Wales took effect under the Government of Wales Act 1998. Elections for 60 seats in the National Assembly for Wales take place every four years under an 'additional member' electoral system (see below, 6.4.1). The Secretary of State for Wales – the minister in the UK Government responsible for Wales – is entitled to attend and participate in the proceedings of the Assembly, but not to vote (s 76). The official languages of the assembly are English and Welsh; simultaneous translation is provided.

Unlike the Scottish Parliament and the Northern Ireland Assembly, the Welsh Assembly has no power to make primary legislation; Acts applicable to Wales continue to be made by the UK Parliament (see above, 2.4.2). The Welsh Assembly's legislative competence is confined to making subordinate legislation about the areas of policy which have been transferred to it (ss 58, 64–67). What is envisaged is that whereas, in the past, Acts of the UK Parliament conferred rule making powers on to the Secretary of State for Wales (see 2.4.3 and 6.5.2), in future, such rule making powers will be exercised by the Assembly. The Assembly cannot make subordinate legislation which is contrary to European Community law or the Human Rights Act 1998 (s 107).

The Government of Wales Act requires the Welsh Assembly to set up several committees. 'Subject committees' (s 57) participate in making policy and include as a member the relevant Assembly secretary (see below). A subordinate legislation scrutiny committee (s 58) examines legislation proposed by the Assembly. Regional committees (s 61) responsible for different parts of Wales also have to be established.

The Welsh Assembly elects one of its members to the post of First Secretary – the leader of the executive branch of government (s 53). Alun Michael, who was also a Member of the UK Parliament, became the First Secretary in May 1999. The First Secretary appoints a number of Assembly secretaries (in effect, 'ministers') with responsibility for areas of policy such as education and agriculture and the rural economy. Together they form the executive committee (s 56), in effect, a 'Cabinet'.

Functions have been transferred to the Welsh Assembly in accordance with Sched 2 of the Government of Wales Act. These include the fields of: agriculture, fisheries and food; education and training; health and social services; highways; housing; and social services. Future Acts of the UK Parliament may also confer functions on the Assembly. The Welsh Assembly differs from the devolved institutions in Scotland and Northern Ireland because its areas of competence are defined by reference to what is specifically transferred to it (rather than by what competences are retained by the UK). As well as responsibility for these fields of policy, the Government of Wales Act confers other functions on the Assembly – notably, the reform of the Welsh health service (s 27) and reform of other Welsh public bodies (s 28).

2.8 'Intergovernmental relations' within the UK

The process of devolution has created a new area of constitutional law: the framework of rules and understandings governing the relationships between the UK Government (and Parliament) and the new executive bodies (and legislatures) of Scotland, Northern Ireland and Wales. In simple terms, devolution has meant sharing out powers for making law and policy between the UK tier and the new devolved institutions. In reality, this is likely to be a continuing, complex and sometimes contentious process. Several elements have been put into place to stave off disputes about the competence of the devolved institutions, or to deal with disputes when they arise.

2.8.1   Self-scrutiny of Bills before introduction

In Scotland (s 31 of the Scotland Act) and Northern Ireland (s 9 of the Northern Ireland Act) a member of the executive must make a formal statement that that the proposed legislation is within the Scottish Parliament's or Northern Ireland Assembly's competence.

2.8.2   The roles of the Secretaries of State for Scotland, Northern Ireland and Wales

Under the Scotland Act (ss 35, 58), the Northern Ireland Act (ss 15, 26) and the Government of Wales Act (s 108), ministers of the UK Government may intervene to prevent legislation or government action being taken which is outside the competence of the devolved institutions. The minister must have reasonable grounds to believe that a Bill or subordinate legislation contains provisions incompatible with the UK's international obligations, with the interests of defence or national security, or would have an adverse affect on the operation of law as it applies to reserved matters. The minister may issue an order prohibiting the Bill from being submitted to the Queen for royal assent or revoking subordinate legislation.

2.8.3   Concordats

The UK Government has established non-statutory 'concordats' with the devolved executives as a mechanism for regulating intergovernmental relations about some areas on which the devolution legislation does not provide firm rules. These include, for example, how Scotland, Wales and Northern Ireland will participate in deciding the UK's stance within the Council of the European Union (see below, 7.5.3), regulating regional incentives promoting inward investment, and the provision of resources to the devolved legislatures. The concordats do not create legally binding obligations. It is envisaged that they will be signed by senior officials, though on politically sensitive matters they may be signed by UK ministers and their counterparts in the devolved institutions. Critics have argued that important measures such as those envisaged to be dealt with by concordats should be implemented through primary or secondary legislation and subjected to parliamentary scrutiny – rather than 'shadowy and sinister backroom deals' (see Ancram, M, 'Dictatorship of the concordat' (1998) *The Times*, 4 March). Attempts to amend the devolution Acts to require concordats to be placed on a public register, and for them to be subject to approval by the respective Parliaments/Assemblies, were defeated.

2.8.4 Adjudication by the Privy Council and other courts

The Devolution Acts recognise that doubts about the competence of a devolved institution to legislate in a particular manner may arise during the passage of the legislation. Therefore, a Law Officer (the Attorney General of Northern Ireland, the Lord Advocate, or the Attorney General) may refer a question of whether a Bill is within the legislative competence to the Judicial Committee of the Privy Council immediately after its passing. Disputes about 'devolution issues' may also be raised by individuals in ordinary civil and criminal proceedings in any part of the UK (Sched 11 of the Northern Ireland Act; Sched 6 of the Scotland Act; Sched 7 of the Government of Wales Act). Devolution issues include questions about the competence of the Scottish Parliament and Northern Ireland Assembly to pass an Act on a particular issue, competence of any of the devolved legislatures to make secondary legislation, and disputes as to whether an exercise of a function by a member of a devolved executive is compatible with European Community law and the European Convention on Human Rights.

When, in ordinary civil proceedings or a criminal prosecution, a litigant raises a devolution issue before a court or tribunal, that body must give notice of the fact to the relevant Law Officer (the Attorney General of Northern Ireland, the Attorney General of England and Wales or the Lord Advocate). The court of first instance or tribunal may, and sometimes must, refer the case to a higher court. The higher court may, in turn, refer the issue to the Judicial Committee of the Privy Council. Where a devolution issue arises in judicial proceedings in the House of Lords, the issue will be referred to the Judicial Committee unless the House of Lords considers that it would be more appropriate in the circumstances for it to determine the issue. The Appellate Committee of the House of Lords was thought not to be appropriate, as it is, technically, a committee of the UK Parliament and might therefore not appear to be impartial.

The courts are to construe legislation made by a devolved legislature so far as possible as to be within its legislative competence; so, in cases of doubt, where a court is faced with more than one plausible interpretation of an Act and one of these would render the Act *ultra vires*, it will endeavour to avoid the problems that might arise from the latter conclusion being arrived at and steer towards a construction that will keep the Act within the legislative competence of the Assembly.

2.9   Local governance

So far, this chapter has described government at the level of the European Union, the UK and the devolved institutions in Scotland, Northern Ireland and Wales. Beneath all these is a system of local governance. Two institutions are of particular importance: local authorities and police constabularies.

2.9.1   Local authorities

Throughout the UK, there are over 600 elected local authorities, some covering quite small geographical areas. Within the very strict confines set by Acts of Parliament, elected councillors have powers and duties to make decisions on specified issues like town and country planning, ways of collecting and disposing of refuse, schools and social services (such as the provision of home helps for disabled people and the care of neglected children). As in the UK Parliament and devolved institutions, most councillors represent one of the main political parties. During the 1980s and early 1990s, there were tensions between the many local authorities run by Labour Party members and the Conservative central government. This resulted in a great deal of complex legislation (through which central government attempted to control the activities of local authorities), and also numerous judicial review challenges brought by the two tiers of government against each other, questioning the legal validity of the new rules (Loughlin, M, *Legality and Locality*, 1996, Oxford: Clarendon; Cooper, D, 'Institutional illegality and disobedience – local government narratives' (1996) 16 OJLS 255). The first past the post electoral system means that many local authorities have been run by members of the same political party for decades.

Elected councillors work with politically neutral local government officers (the local equivalent of civil servants) to formulate policies and make particular decisions. Policy is made by councillors sitting in committees with responsibility for a particular subject matter, such as leisure facilities and planning. Practical delivery of local authority functions is sometimes done by council employees (such as social workers), but, since the mid-1980s, most service delivery tasks (such as refuse collection) have had to be put out to competitive tender, with the result that they are 'contracted out' to private businesses.

Local government is in a state of malaise. Financial corruption is rife in a few councils. Throughout the UK, the democratic authority of local government has declined as only a relatively small proportion of the electorate bothers to vote in elections. In July 1998, the government published a White Paper aimed at revitalising local authorities (*Modernising Local Government: In Touch with the People*, Cm 4014, 1998). The proposals include directly elected mayors, annual elections for councillors, increased powers to raise local taxation (but only for the most efficient councils), referendums on local issues, and a new independent inspectorate to monitor how councils fulfil their statutory duties.

2.9.2 The police

Police officers possess some of the most direct powers to intervene in people's lives – to stop, search, arrest, detain, to confiscate literature, to prohibit meetings and demonstrations. There are 43 separate police forces (or 'constabularies') in the UK, each under the control of a Chief Constable, or, in the case of the Metropolitan Police, a Commissioner, appointed by the Home Secretary. Every police constable is an independent office holder, not a government or local authority employee (Marshall, G, 'The police: independence and accountability', in Jowell, J and Oliver, D (eds), *The Changing Constitution*, 3rd edn, 1994, Oxford: OUP, Chapter 11). A constable's powers come from the common law, though these are now heavily circumscribed by legislation such as the Police and Criminal Evidence Act 1984 (Chapter 21) and the Public Order Act 1986 (Chapter 25). For each constabulary, there is a police authority – a committee consisting of local councillors, magistrates and people nominated by the Home Secretary – which is responsible for securing 'the maintenance of an adequate and efficient police force' in their area (Police Act 1964). Police authorities cannot intervene in particular cases or give directions to police constables. Complaints against police officers are handled by the Police Complaints Authority.

2.10 The judiciary

In liberal democracies, a high value is placed on compliance with the law. As we have already noted, legal rights are used to demarcate areas of personal autonomy into which public authorities must not step, unless there is some compelling reason for them to do so (see above, 1.7.1). Laws also establish the procedures and institutions through which collective decisions are made (see above, 1.7.2), and laws place duties and confer powers on public authorities to provide for our safety and security (see above, 1.7.3). On top of this, laws provide for orderly interactions between people.

In the UK, there are three distinct legal systems. England and Wales share a common civil and criminal court system, legal profession and almost all Acts of Parliament (see above, 2.4.2) which apply in England also apply in Wales. From the lower courts, appeals lie to the Court of Appeal and the House of Lords. Law in Northern Ireland is similar, but not identical, to that in England and Wales, but it has its own court system and a Court of Appeal of Northern Ireland, from which an appeal lies to the Appellate Committee of the House of Lords in both civil and criminal matters. Scotland's legal system is different.

as happened with the Merchant Shipping Act 1988 (see below, 5.2.4 and 7.9.1). Another significant alteration to the principle of parliamentary sovereignty is the Human Rights Act 1998, under which courts may now make a declaration of incompatibility, formally holding that part of an Act of Parliament without justification infringes a right guaranteed by the European Convention on Human Rights (see Chapter 19).

Two other courts outside the UK also play an important role in the modern constitution. The European Court of Justice in Luxembourg, established under the EC Treaty, is the highest court on matters of Community law (see below, 7.5.5). Most disputes about rights and obligations under Community law are determined by national courts and tribunals, but on difficult points of law they may seek guidance ('make a reference for a preliminary ruling') from the Court of Justice (see 18.2.1). The Court of Justice also has power to deal with some types of legal proceedings directly, but these are mostly brought by the institutions of the Community against Member States (and vice versa). Also of importance is the European Court of Human Rights in Strasbourg, which adjudicates on complaints that public bodies have failed to comply with the European Convention on Human Rights (see 19.6). Since the Human Rights Act 1998, the case law of the Strasbourg Court has become persuasive authority in the UK's legal systems (see below, 19.10).

2.11   Constitutional monarchy

One feature of the UK Constitution remains largely untouched by recent reforms. The Head of State in the UK is a hereditary monarch. It is important to appreciate, however, that the monarch occupies the throne because Acts of Parliament – in particular, the Bill of Rights 1688, the Act of Settlement 1700 and His Majesty's Declaration of Abdication Act 1936 – specify that this be so. The Queen performs ceremonial functions both in public (such as the annual State Opening of Parliament) and in private (for instance, when she formally present seals of office and kisses the hands of MPs chosen by the Prime Minister to be senior government ministers). As we have seen, the Crown exercises a prerogative power to give royal assent to Bills passed by Parliament (see above, 2.4.3). Note the opening words of all statutes of the UK Parliament:

> Be it enacted by the Queen's Most Excellent Majesty, and by and with the advice and consent of the Lords Spiritual and Temporal, and the Commons, in this present Parliament assembled, and by the authority of the same, as follows
> ...

It is now a well established constitutional convention that the monarch always assents to Bills which have been passed by Parliament. Most decisions and actions taken by the Crown under the prerogative are made only on the advice of government ministers (who, in effect, really make the decisions) or a formal body known as the Privy Council (consisting, in this context, of ministers, not the judges who sit in its Judicial Committee). Examples of prerogative powers include the making of international treaties, declarations of war, the appointment of judges and the regulation of the civil service (see above, 2.4.3). There are, conceivably, some circumstances in which the monarch personally might have to take a decision required by the prerogative when advice from ministers will not be available. For instance, the Queen has a duty formally to appoint an MP to the office of Prime Minister. In recent times, there has been no doubt about the person the Queen should invite to take up the post: following a general election, one or other of the main political parties has won a majority of seats in the House of Commons and it is clear who is the leader of that party. If, however, there was to be a 'hung' Parliament (in which no single party could regularly rely upon a majority of MPs to support its legislative programme), the monarch might have to make a difficult choice as to which party leader to approach.

2.12 Globalisation: the world outside the UK

So far, this chapter has described how competences to carry out constitutional functions and responsibilities for fields of policy are allocated to different institutions and office holders at the levels of: the European Community; the UK; devolved legislative and executive bodies in Scotland, Northern Ireland and Wales; and local government. The activities of public authorities in each of these spheres are both facilitated and constrained by laws enforceable in national courts and the European Community's court in Luxembourg. Taken together, these public authorities form the main institutions of our constitutional system. What happens within constitutional systems is becoming increasingly influenced and constrained by transnational institutions and agreements between countries.

The term 'globalisation' is used to describe the momentous and complex changes in the way we live. One strand in the phenomenon is technology: electronic communications and air travel have transformed the ability of people and business enterprises to reach each other. A second strand is the development of a single global market. Goods and services are increasingly traded across national frontiers. The World Trade Organisation (WTO) was established in 1993 to enforce a system of free trade agreed between the majority of the world's countries (see <www.wto.org>; and, for a blistering critique, see Gray, J, *False Dawn: Delusions of Global Capitalism*, 1998, London: Granta). A third thread is the rise and acceptance of the notion of universal human rights and the establishment of international judicial bodies to protect them. The treatment of people by national governments is no longer regarded as a purely domestic matter. Instead, people are viewed as universally having 'rights' by virtue of being human, and these rights cannot be withdrawn by the national laws of any State (see below, 19.1).

Finally, globalisation describes the fact that multinational organisations are more and more determining the collective policies to be followed within Nation States, especially in defence and security matters though bodies such as the United Nations, the North Atlantic Treaty Organisation (NATO) and the Western European Union (WEU). This is a recognition that, in a world where nuclear and biological weapons exist, no single Nation State is any longer capable of fulfilling the most fundamental need of its citizens for physical protection. Policing citizens too, is becoming a matter for international co-operation and collective decision making through bodies such as Interpol: no Nation State in isolation is now capable of dealing with drug smuggling, money laundering, terrorism or international fraud.

In short, it has to be recognised that our constitutional system, and the citizens within it, are not hermetically sealed off from the rest of the world.

2.12.1 Treaties and international organisations

Until recently, many books and courses on public law were able to avoid discussing international treaties – except perhaps to note that, as a matter of national law in the UK, it is the prerogative which enables a minister to make a formal agreement between the UK and another Nation State (see above, 2.4.3). The legal study of treaties and other aspects of international relations has traditionally been hived off to the separate subject of public international law (for an excellent introduction, see Higgins, R, *Problems and Processes: International Law and How We Use it*, 1994, Oxford: Clarendon). To an ever increasing extent, however, treaties are becoming bound up with ways in which governments of Nation States carry out their day to day functions. Legal systems vary as to how they recognise treaties. Broadly, there are two possible arrangements. In monist legal systems, a treaty entered into by a government becomes a source of law in that country. In dualist legal systems (such as the UK), treaties only become a source of national law if and when they are specifically incorporated into the legal system by Act of Parliament. Thus, for example, the Treaty agreed in Ottawa in December 1997 under which many countries undertook to ban the use and trade of anti-personnel landmines was given effect in the UK by the enactment of the Landmines Act 1998. This does not mean that non-incorporated treaties are entirely ignored by British judges. Where a court is called upon to interpret an ambiguous statute (*R v Secretary of State for the Home Department ex p Brind* (1991)) or there is uncertainty as to how a rule of common law should be developed (*Derbyshire County Council v Times Newspapers Ltd* (1993) – see below, 24.4), reference may be made to the UK's treaty obligations. The court will construe the law in a manner that is not incompatible with those obligations. It has also been held that the fact that the government has entered into a treaty obligation may give a person a 'legitimate expectation' that the government will comply with its obligations, even if the treaty has not been incorporated into national law (*R v Secretary of State for the Home Department ex p Ahmed (Mohammed Hussain)* (1998), and see below, 14.2).

International organisations

In terms of the broad constitutional system, treaties exert several significant influences. First, treaties establish multi-national institutions through which the governments of Nation States co-operate with each other. As we have seen, the European Community is an international organisation of profound significance to the way in which the UK is governed (see above, 2.3). The European Community is a new type of international organisation through which its Member States now make policies and laws – particularly in relation to a single market and economic and monetary union – which are directly binding and enforceable in each other's countries (see Chapter 7). Its methods of decision making are unique.

Another international treaty organisation of great importance to the UK is the Council of Europe – a body entirely different from the European Community/European Union (though sometimes journalists and even politicians confuse them!). Whereas the European Community/European Union has 15 Member States, the Council of Europe has 41 members stretching from Iceland to Turkey, to the Russian Federation and France. The Council of Europe was established in 1949 to promote democracy, the rule of law and human rights in Europe in the wake of the Second World War. It is under the auspices of the Council of Europe that the European Convention on Human Rights operates (see below, 19.5). Apart from the Convention, most people are unaware of the Council of Europe's role. One other rights instrument which falls within its remit is the European Social Charter, a statement of 19 economic and social rights. The Council of Europe also issues recommendations and passes resolutions on matters such as administrative justice, 'cyber crime', corruption and the cloning of human beings.

One other regional body which may, in the future, have an important influence on the UK's constitutional system is the British-Irish Council (BIC). This was outlined in the April 1998 Belfast Agreement (see above, 2.6) and established by an agreement between the government of the UK and the government of Ireland signed in March 1999. Members of the BIC will be drawn from the UK and Irish governments, the devolved executive bodies of Northern Ireland, Scotland and Wales and also from Jersey, Guernsey and the Isle of Man. 'England', not being recognised in the UK's new devolved structure, is not represented. The function of the BIC will be to 'exchange information, discuss, consult and use best endeavours to reach agreement' on common policy issues such as transport links, agriculture, the environment, culture, health, education and approaches to European Union matters. Senior representatives of the governments will meet at summit level at least twice and year, with more regular meetings to discuss specific policies (see, further, Bogdanor, V, 'The British-Irish Council and devolution' (1999) 34 Government and Opposition 287).

Individuals and treaties

A second reason why some treaties and treaty organisations have come important for national constitutions is that they deal ever more directly with the rights and responsibilities of individuals. In the past, treaties tended to be concerned with matters, such as regulating trade between Nation States, military alliances and the recognition of diplomats. Since the Second World War, many treaties have established international institutions to monitor and adjudicate on the people's rights (see below, 19.3). Thus, the European Court of Human Rights in Strasbourg adjudicates on complaints made by individuals that their rights have been violated by the countries which are parties to the European Convention on Human Rights (see below, 19.6). Under the auspices of the United Nations, a complex system of committees and officials monitor and report on human rights abuses around the world. And in 1998, countries agreed to establish a permanent International Criminal Court with jurisdiction to try individuals for offences including genocide, crimes against humanity and war crimes. If public law is the study and practice of legal relationships between public authorities and people (see above, 1.3), then we need to recognise that these are now sometimes played out in international forums: policy and law may be made outside the boundaries of national States.

Policy constraints from treaties

Thirdly, treaties constrain the choices that public authorities in the UK may make – including the UK Parliament and government, the devolved executive and legislative institutions in Scotland, Northern Ireland and Wales, and the courts. The incorporation into national law of the European Convention on Human Rights by the Human Rights Act 1998 will require public authorities to avoid infringing Convention rights (see below, 19.10). Although the UK Parliament itself will not be bound, as a matter of national law, by the Convention, clearly the Convention will exert a powerful influence on the content of Acts of Parliament. Outside the field of human rights, many other policy choices are also limited by the treaty obligations of the UK. For instance, the treaty made in Kyoto in December 1997 on climate change commits the UK to pursue policies designed to reduce emissions. If a government of the UK were one day to favour the decriminalisation of cannabis, it may nevertheless feel constrained from doing so by UK treaty obligations, such as those contained in the UN Convention against Illicit Traffic in Narcotic Drugs and Psychotropic Substances 1988.

THE NEW CONSTITUTIONAL SETTLEMENT

Reforms over the past few years amount to a new constitutional settlement for the UK. One of the practical purposes of a constitution is to distribute decision making powers ('competences') to office holders and institutions. Theorists suggest that the principle of separation of powers ought to influence the allocation of competences, but this has not had a great influence on the UK's system of parliamentary government – except for the principle that the judiciary should be independent of the executive.

Sources of constitutional law

In the absence of a codified constitutional document, constitutional laws are found in the form of ordinary laws of the UK. These include the Treaty on European Union and the Treaty Establishing the European Communities, incorporated into national law by the European Communities Act 1972. Numerous other Acts of Parliament deal with matters of constitutional importance and the common law also recognises constitutional principles. Many norms exist as constitutional conventions which are not, as such, enforceable in the courts.

Allocation of competences between the EC and the UK

The first pillar of the European Union, the European Community, has powers to make policy and law in relation to a wide range of areas; policy making in some fields is shared with the Member States. Member States continue to have independence from the EC to make policy on some subjects.

Allocation of competences within the UK

At the level of the UK, Parliament in practice has limited its competence to legislate on some subject areas. This is because it has delegated powers to do so to the Scottish Parliament, the Northern Ireland Assembly and the institutions of the EC. The same is true of the UK Government. Throughout the UK, over 600 local authorities exercise very limited powers to govern. Policing in the UK is also organised mainly on a local level, with 43 separate forces.

Devolved institutions

The Scotland Act 1998, the Northern Ireland Act 1998 and the Government of Wales Act 1998 create legislative and executive bodies for those parts of the UK. The Acts allocate competences to the bodies in different ways. England has no legislative assembly or government separate from that of the UK. Disputes about 'devolution issues' are heard by the Judicial Committee of the Privy Council.

The judiciary

There are three distinct legal systems in the UK: one for Scotland; one for Northern Ireland; and one for England and Wales. It is regarded as important that the judiciary are independent from the executive branch of government. Judges of the higher courts may not be removed from office except by a resolution passed by both Houses of Parliament. Some commentators are sceptical about the notion of independence, arguing that, because of their social background and their status, judges are necessarily conservative. During the early 1990s, however, there was considerable tension between the Conservative government and the higher courts, especially over judicial review cases. Under the Human Rights Act 1998, the courts have new powers to consider the case law of the European Court of Human Rights and to declare Acts of Parliament incompatible with the Convention.

Globalisation

Important government functions are now both facilitated and constrained by treaty obligations and supranational institutions. Treaties do not automatically become part of national law in the UK; only if a treaty is expressly incorporated by an Act of Parliament will it be recognised by courts as capable of creating rights and obligations.

CHAPTER 3

PRINCIPLES FROM HISTORY

3.1 The importance of history

Practising lawyers and judges carry out their work in a brutally anti-historical manner. Although they rely upon precedents, often from earlier centuries, precious little importance is attached to the historical context in which case law was decided and legislation enacted. Consider Lord Donaldson MR's judgment in *R v Secretary of State for the Home Department ex p Muboyayi* (1991), p 78, where he stated, in a case about a Zairian applying for political asylum in the UK, that the 'duty of the courts is to uphold [the] classic statement of the rule of law' in Magna Carta 1215:

> No freeman shall be taken or imprisoned, or be disseised of his freehold or liberties, or free customs, or be outlawed, or exiled, or any other wise destroyed; nor will we not pass upon him, nor condemn him, but by lawful judgment of his peers, or by the law of the land. We will sell to no man, we will not deny or defer to any man either justice or right.

The notions of 'liberty' and who was a 'free man' were profoundly different in the 13th century than they are today (it did not include the majority of adult men, nor any women); yet principles assumed by modern lawyers to be contained in Magna Carta were applied to circumstances of the 1990s.

Understanding how the constitution works is not, however, the same task as practising public law in the courts. For this, history is important for several reasons. First, it reveals how and why constitutional principles emerged – why, for instance, did ideas of democratic government become important in the late 19th century? Secondly, past events and practices *in themselves* have constitutional importance. As we have seen (see above, 2.2), important principles are given effect through constitutional conventions, that is, well established practices which are regarded as mandatory even though they are not enforceable through the courts. And, as we shall see (below, 4.3.3), for conservatives, established constitutional practice is in itself a source of legitimate authority for some features of the modern constitution (for example, hereditary peers sitting in Parliament). Thirdly, the absence, in the UK, of a codified constitution means that there is no single legal text capable of forming the main focus of study. Written constitutions are the product of purposeful design, created by a committee, often after a momentous event such as a declaration of independence, war or revolution. We, though, have no set of such 'founding fathers' or 'framers' of the constitution whose beliefs and attitudes are able to guide us today. In Britain, the principles which permeate the constitutional system have to be gleaned from a much wider range of legal sources, constitutional practices and the day to day operation of public institutions – the roots of which lie in the past. This chapter, therefore, provides a very brief (and therefore incomplete and rudimentary) account of some of the significant features in the historical development of the British Constitution. The main trend is clear. Over the centuries, there has been a shift from the strong personal rule of monarchs and the centrality of the Christian church in the country's constitutional affairs to a system of secular government based on the rule of law, universal suffrage and the formal equality of all adults. There has, in other words, been the development of liberal democracy (see above, Chapter 1).

3.1.1   The need for caution

History is a controversial enterprise. Professional historians disagree not only about facts, but also how to evaluate them, and even about whether such things as 'facts' exist. To take an example: many historians would say that the account of the constitutional events of the 17th century sketched out below (3.6) focuses too much on the rivalries of the ruling elites and pays insufficient attention to the role played by ordinary people – 'the mob' – around the time of the Glorious Revolution in 1688. There is also considerable debate about whether two rival theories of government were a cause or a consequence of the English Civil War. All that this chapter can do, then, is set out a basic chronological narrative.

3.1.2   Principle and pragmatism

In Chapter 1 we suggested that constitutional systems exist to give effect to the underlying political ideals of a society; and that, in the case of the UK, these values are (more or less) those of liberal democracy. The principles of modern liberal democracy did not suddenly spring up one day. Nor are they the product of any defined group of thinkers living at a particular moment in history. They have *emerged* over time, partly from the work of theorists, but also from the changing material conditions of society (such as the rise of the industrial working class during the 19th century). If one theme emerges from the chronology set out in this chapter, it is that change often comes about for pragmatic reasons. Governments respond to pressures (for instance, to extend the franchise) cautiously and in a piecemeal fashion. Grand ideas often carry little weight with the actors in constitutional events. Even the English Civil War – sometimes held up as a battle for parliamentary government over absolute monarchy – is now subject to revision by historians. In *The Causes of the English Civil War*, 1990, Oxford: Clarendon, Conrad Russell argues (p 160) that:

the body of ideas about how the country should be governed were not really
the central element in the cause for which they [the Parliamentarians] fought:
they were, like their medieval predecessors, ad hoc ideas constructed out of
any materials ready to hand, to serve the immediate purpose of clipping the
wings of a king with whom they simply could not cope.

We start in 1066, as this date marks an important break in the continuity of the
form of government.

3.2   The Norman conquest and feudalism

In 1066, William, a Norman duke, invaded England and defeated King
Harold's army in battle. William claimed that he, not Harold, was the lawful
heir of the previous English king and therefore the rightful successor to the
Crown. In the ensuing years, William and his army took over England. A new
feudal system of land tenure was introduced: the monarch owned all land in
the kingdom and granted it in enormous tracts to tenants-in-chief (noblemen)
who, in return, were required to provide certain forms of service to the king –
for example, 'knight service', which obliged the tenant to provide the monarch
with a certain number of armed men. The tenants-in-chief granted parts of the
land they controlled to other tenants, who, in turn, did the same. In time, a
hereditary right to succeed to tenancies became established. In this system of
subinfeudation, there were thus often several intermediate subordinate
tenants between the monarch and the person who actually exercised authority
over an area of the countryside; each tenant swore allegiance and paid
homage to his overlord.

The vast majority of the population, some 70%, did not hold any of these
freehold tenancies, but belonged to the class of serfs who were bound to stay
working for the lord of the manor. In time, however, many serfs were granted
copyhold tenancies, under which they are granted use of fields for cultivation
in return for payments of money or provision of services to the freehold tenant
immediately above them in the chain of land tenure. Unlike freehold tenants,
however, they were not at liberty to move elsewhere. Life was hard: farming
was for subsistence, and famines were frequent.

The Domesday Book, a census of the population and record of tenancies,
was compiled by William to provide an accurate basis for taxation and
military service. The demands of the King were, however, often resisted.
William and his successors were immersed in almost continuous struggle with
their tenants-in-chief. Day to day order was administered through manorial
courts attached to the lands of freehold tenants. There was, from the start, a
close connection between monarchy, church and the freeholders: priests and
bishops often presided in local courts and under the 'benefit of clergy',
churchmen accused of crimes were protected from the worst punishments,
such as castration and blinding. Monarchs claimed the right to conduct the

most important trials personally and, over time, a system of appeals developed from the manorial courts to the king and his justices, who travelled around country on circuit. In this two tier system of justice, tensions were often apparent, with both tiers anxious to preserve or expand their jurisdiction.

3.3   Magna Carta 1215

By the 13th century, towns – which had largely remained outside the feudal system of land tenure – were assuming a greater importance and their leading citizens, 'burghers', asserted considerable influence. In the countryside, the nature of the feudal bonds between the monarch and the cascade of tenants under him was also changing, with money rents rather than service becoming central to relationships. During the reign of King John (born 1167, died 1216), relations between the monarch, his chief tenants and the burghers sank to new depths. In 1215, a group of barons and burghers marched to confront the tyrannous king with numerous demands. Bloody revolt seemed likely and John reluctantly agreed, in a meadow near Windsor, to the Magna Carta ('the great charter of liberties'). In later centuries, this document has assumed an anachronistic significance in practical politics and constitutional discourse – both in the UK and the US – which bears little connection with the pragmatic list of rights extracted by the barons for themselves and other freehold tenants (though not the serfs). Three of the 63 demands are of enduring importance. First, that no man should be convicted without due process of the law (see above, 3.1). Secondly, that the monarch should not levy tax without the consent of the Great Council of the Realm (the meeting of the tenants-in-chief which, in later centuries, transmuted into the House of Lords). Thirdly, the freedom of foreign merchants to travel to Britain and, except in times of war, for all freemen to travel abroad. The feudal system established by the Normans had a profound affect on the way people have conceived the relationship between the ruler and the ruled, as one dependent on mutual obligations and rights.

Later events of the 13th and early 14th centuries shaped the constitution. In time, the monarch adopted a practice of summoning representatives of the shires and boroughs to attend meetings of the Great Council; they represented the interests of the landed gentry in the countryside and merchants in the towns. King Edward III (born 1312, died 1377) conquered Wales and turned his attention to Scotland. Under the leadership of Robert Bruce, the Scots fought a protracted war, culminating victory at in the battle of Bannockburn in 1314 and a peace treaty under which the Scotland remained independent of the English Crown.

3.4 The 15th century: the Wars of the Roses and the loss of France

The 1400s are characterised by intensified violent rivalries within the country's ruling elite and military defeat abroad. English kings still asserted a claim to the Crown of France (as successors to William the Conqueror, duke of Normandy). Henry VI was crowned King of England in 1429 and travelled to Paris to be crowned King of France in 1431, but, by 1450, the English had lost control of Normandy and three years later were expelled from power throughout France (except for the town of Calais, which remained with the English Crown for over 100 years until 1558, and the Channel Islands, which to this day remain a possession of the British Crown).

By the 15th century, a market economy was forming in towns, based on the sale of surplus corn and wool. International trading activity was assuming an ever greater importance. But, at home, growing strains between the monarch and factions within the country's ruling families escalated into ever greater disorder (later romantically dubbed the Wars of the Roses after the white and red roses the two factions adopted as their respective emblems). The Duke of York, his successors and supporters clashed with King Henry VI's army in numerous battles over two decades. Historians disagree over the effect these battles had on ordinary life in the country; what is clear is that many of the noble families were, literally, wiped out by the bloody and complex struggles of the period. These were not clashes of principle, but of grievances between the leading landowners and the monarch, often over the fiscal problems of the Crown and its demands for taxation. In 1485 Henry Tudor won victory at the battle of Bosworth and became King Henry VII.

3.5 The 16th century and the Protestant reformation

During the 16th century, a powerful religious movement spread its influence throughout northern Europe. Encouraged by the ideas of the German theologian Martin Luther (1483–1546) and the French scholar Jean Calvin (1509–66), people of all social classes in several countries began to reject some of the doctrinal teachings and corrupt ecclesiastical organisation of the Roman Catholic church. In Scotland, John Knox (1513–72) converted the official church to the new Protestant version of Christianity. Ireland, like Scotland still independent of the English Crown, remained Catholic.

In England, the reformation movement coincided with the desire of Henry VIII (1491–1547) to divorce his then wife, something the Pope refused to grant. Henry therefore embraced Protestantism and, in December 1533, an Act of Parliament declared him to be the head of the Protestant Church of England. The century and a half that followed is characterised by struggles between the adherents to the Roman Catholic and Protestant branches of the Christian Church.

During Elizabethan times (1533–1603), the feudal system and its manorial courts were giving way to newer forms of land tenure and government. The Tudor 'revolution in government' involved a shift away from the direct personal rule of the monarch and the creation of permanent administrative bodies capable of carrying on the business of the State from one monarch to another. Parliament was meeting more regularly, and represented the interests of landowners and merchants to the Crown. The monarch became dependent on parliamentary approval for levying taxes. At a local level throughout the countryside, prominent landowners were appointed as local Justices of the Peace (JPs) who dispensed summary justice, administered the poor law relieving the destitute, regulated prices and wages, licensed alcohol and had some responsibilities for the upkeep of roads and bridges. They were 'maids of all work'. Statutes conferred wide powers on them and their work was supervised by the Privy Council – prominent churchmen, statesmen and judges called upon to advise the monarch.

3.6 The 17th century: the Civil War, the Restoration and the Glorious Revolution

The 17th century was dominated by three momentous constitutional events: the English Civil War and rule by Oliver Cromwell; the Restoration of the monarchy in 1660; and then the Glorious Revolution of 1688. These were complex events and historians still debate their causes and their significance. The disputes between adherents to three different branches of the Christian Church – Roman Catholics, members of the established Church of England (Anglicans) and dissenting Protestants (non-Catholics who were not Anglicans) lay at the heart of the struggles for power in the 17th century. Also central to the events were notions about the proper relationship between the monarch and the House of Commons.

On Queen Elizabeth's death in 1603, the English Crown passed to James VI of Scotland (born 1566, died 1625), who became James I of England. Thus, a personal union of the Crowns of England and Scotland came about (though it was not until a century later that there was a formal union between the two countries). James survived an assassination attempt on 5 November 1605 when a group of English Catholics, including one Guy Fawkes, were foiled in their plans to blow up the House of Lords during that year's State opening of Parliament.

3.6.1 Conflicts in Parliament and the courts

Both James I and his son Charles I (who reigned from 1625–49) used their prerogative powers extensively to make law and raise taxes without the parliamentary consent – Charles I ruled for 11 years without convening Parliament. James I and Charles I and their courtiers believed monarchal power stemmed from the divine, God-given right of kings to rule rather than any 'contract' between the monarch and his subjects. As Charles I put it: 'The state of the monarchy is the supremest thing on earth; for the kings are not only God's lieutenants on earth, but even by God himself they are called gods.'

Throughout the 17th century, the monarchy was in severe debt. Attempts were made to balance the budget, but during the first half of the century James I and then Charles I lived lives of extravagance and ever-increasing funds were also needed for the defence of the realm. The clashes between the kings and the men of property (represented in the House of Commons) were, for a time, fought out in debates in Parliament and in the courts, where judges were called upon to adjudicate on the legality of the monarchs' demands. The response of the judiciary to disputes about the ambit of royal power was not uniform; but this is not surprising, for some judges were royalists, while the sympathies of others lay with Parliament. One of the early confrontations in the courts was over the attempt by James I to raise revenue from increased customs duties on imports. In 1605 Bates, a merchant, refused to pay the new rate of duty on currants imposed by the King (over and above the 'poundage' tax stipulated by statute) and the matter went to court: *Bates' Case (The Case of Impositions)* (1606). The court found for the King, on the ground that he did indeed have the power to impose duties if the primary purpose of doing so was to regulate foreign trade, rather than merely to raise revenue, as this was an aspect of the Crown's prerogative powers to control foreign affairs. The Commons was unimpressed by the judgment, seeing it both as a threat to subjects' property rights and as damaging to England's competitiveness in international trade. Under pressure from Parliament, James I consented to a compromise: he would abandon some of the new duties, though some remained, and in the future the levying of 'impositions' would only be lawful if done with the consent of Parliament – but he dissolved Parliament before this arrangement could be finalised.

Judges with Parliamentarian sympathies were in a dangerous position, for judges held office only at the King's pleasure: they were his servants and could be removed from the bench if they handed down judgments which displeased the monarch. One such judge was Coke (pronounced 'cook') CJ (1552–1634) who handed down several judgments which sought to curb royal power. He was a Parliamentarian through and through, having been an MP before his appointment. Coke was also a scholar, and he published a series of law reports and *Institutes* (legal commentaries), some volumes of which were banned from publication. In the *Case of Proclamations* (1611), Coke CJ held that the King no longer had the authority to create new offences by proclamation and could only exercise prerogative powers within the limits set by the common law, but James I ignored this judgment and continued to make proclamations. Another decision influenced by Coke was *Prohibitions del Roy*

(1607), where the court (actually a conference of the judges) held that the King had no right to determine cases personally:

> And the judges informed the King, that no king after the Conquest assumed to himself to give any judgment in any cause whatsoever, which concerned the administration of justice within this Realm, but these were solely determined in the Court of Justice ... The King said, he thought the law was founded on reason, and that he and others had reason, as well as the Judges; to which it was answered by me [that is, Coke], that true it was, that God had endowed His Majesty with excellent science and great endowments of nature; but His Majesty was not learned in the law of the realm of England, and causes which concern the life, or inheritance, or goods, or fortunes of his subjects, are not to be decided by natural reason but by the artificial reason and judgment of law ... with which the King was greatly offended, and said, that then he should be under the law, which was treason to affirm, as he said: to which I said, that Bracton saith [the King should not be subject to any man, but to God and the law].

When, six years later in 1617, Coke refused to obey a command of the King not to try a case, he was dismissed by James I and replaced by a royalist judge.

In the years that followed, many judgments finding the use of the prerogative lawful were handed down. Another of the King's schemes to raise revenue – forcing subjects to grant him (by now, Charles I was on the throne) loans – brought questions of the Crown's authority before the courts in 1627. Five knights refused to pay contributions to the loan and were imprisoned. They issued a writ of habeas corpus, alleging their detention was unlawful. The gaoler told the court that the men were held 'by the special command of the King' and Hyde CJ accepted that this amounted to lawful reason: *Darnel's Case (The Five Knights' Case)* (1627). As Christopher Hill has said: 'The judgment was legally sound; but it placed impossibly wide powers in the hands of an unscrupulous government' (*The Century of Revolution*, 1980, London: Van Nostrand Reinhold, p 44). In 1637, yet another of Charles I's attempts to raise revenue without the consent of Parliament was challenged in the court. From feudal times, the monarch had been able to demand ships, or their equivalent in money (Ship Money), from coastal towns in England. Charles now sought to extend this tax to the whole of the country as money was needed to provide protection for English shipping. John Hamden, like Bates and Darnel in previous decades, refused to pay. Again, the court found for the King, though only by a majority: *R v Hampden (The Case of Ship Money)* (1637). Professor Hill, in his classic study, comments: 'Legally the judges had a case; but politics proved stronger than the law'. Many of the rich, upon whom Ship Money was levied, refused to pay, and the Crown's financial difficulties deepened year after year.

3.6.2 The outbreak of the Civil War

Tensions continued to rise between the court of Charles I and the propertied classes represented in the House of Commons – especially over taxation. In 1640, the Commons passed the Triennial Act, which provided for the automatic summoning of Parliament if the King failed to do so (Charles had ruled for 11 years without calling one). The judgment of the court in the *Ship Money* case was declared unlawful. Across the water, there was rebellion in Ireland in which thousands of Englishmen were killed. In England, the King took armed men to the Commons with the intention of arresting the leaders of those who opposed him, but they fled to the City. The King had lost control of London and the Civil War had begun, the first major bloodshed occurring at the battle of Edgehill in October 1642. By the end of 1645, the Parliamentarians controlled most of the country except for Oxford, the south west of England and parts of Wales. Charles I surrendered to the Scots in 1646 and was handed over to the English Parliament the following year. Attempts to agree upon a form of limited monarchy failed, and Charles was executed in Whitehall as a traitor in 1649.

The clashes which shattered 17th century society were not, however, in any straightforward way (as Hill puts it) 'about who should be boss' – the king and his favourites or the elected representatives of the men of property. Contemporaries simply did not think about sovereignty in these terms. The Parliamentarians had 'a stop in the mind': while Royalists had a long tradition of thinking on which to base their ideas of divine right, Parliamentarians, while they could deny sovereign power to the king, were not capable of asserting, on a theoretical basis, a claim that *Parliament* should be sovereign (one reason being that only the king could summon Parliament). Conrad Russell argues:

> the body of ideas about how the country should be governed were not really the central element in the cause for which [the Parliamentarians] fought: they were ... ad hoc ideas ... to serve the immediate purpose of clipping the wings of a king with whom they simply could not cope [*The Causes of the English Civil War*, 1990, Oxford: Clarendon, p 160].

3.6.3 The Commonwealth under Cromwell

For almost 10 years England was without a monarch. During this period of 'the Commonwealth', the country was ruled by the military under Oliver Cromwell. Cromwell was conferred with the title of 'Lord Protector' and, for a while, the House of Lords was abolished. The House of Commons offered the title of king to Cromwell but, after some wavering, he declined it. Although the Parliamentarians (a loose coalition of factions) had won the Civil War, it was no victory for democracy. During the war, some on the Parliamentarians' side had flirted with forms of egalitarianism. By the Self-Denying Ordinance, peers had ceased to be officers in the army and appointments were made by merit rather than social rank. Throughout the period, radical political ideas were debated as never before. One group, the Levellers, advocated giving the vote to all 'free Englishmen', the election of JPs and the abolition of the aristocracy. The sovereignty of Parliament (for there was now no king) could only be justified if that sovereignty derived from the people. Parliament should therefore represent all men (though not the 'unfree' – the destitute, women and servants). The radicalism of another smaller faction, the Diggers, went still further: all land, they said, should be held in common. Cromwell was not for these radical reforms, and he suppressed the Levellers and Diggers and their propaganda. The limited reforms of the franchise during the Commonwealth actually led to fewer rather than more people being entitled to vote for MPs though, as a body, Parliament had more power than before.

Under Cromwell's rule, England was at war with the Dutch (1652–54) and with the Spanish. He needed money, and used familiar tactics: dismissing a judge who, he feared, would declare the collection of a tax unlawful, and manipulating and excluding members from Parliament. Oliver Cromwell died in 1658 and was succeeded by his brother for a few months, but the Commonwealth soon crumbled. Anarchy loomed, and tax payers refused to pay (as they had 20 years before). The propertied classes were afraid. The Parliamentarians were irredeemably split into factions. The men of property, represented in the Commons, summoned Charles II from exile to take the throne.

3.6.4 The Restoration of the monarchy

The country was to be ruled by Stuart kings again (Charles II and then his brother, James II) for almost another 30 years. But there had been 'a change in the minds of men', which made absolutist monarchy an impossibility ever again. 'For nearly 20 years, Committees of Parliament had controlled Army, Navy, Church and foreign trade, more efficiently than the old government had ever done. No longer could these be treated as 'mysteries of state', into which subjects must not pry' (Hill, C, *The Century of Revolution*, 1980, London: Van Nostrand Reinhold, p 193). Religion – or, rather, which particular branch of Christianity was acceptable – remained a defining concern. The Test and Corporation Acts permitted only practising Anglicans to hold office in national and local government and removed the right to worship from Catholics and Unitarian Protestants. Those who opposed toleration did so more on political than doctrinal religious grounds: Protestant dissenters (whose sects had often come to prominence during the Civil War) and especially Roman Catholics (who, it was seen, owed allegiance to a foreign power, the Pope) were regarded as threats to the constitution. After all, the King was supreme governor and 'Defender of the Faith' of the established Church of England. People were prosecuted for being absent from church services.

3.6.5   A Papist king for a Protestant State?

When James II, a convert to Roman Catholicism, succeeded his brother Charles II to the throne in 1685, the stark question was raised: how could Protestant England have a Popish king? For James II, the persecution of Catholics was intolerable. In 1686, he granted a general pardon, and later, by the Declarations of Indulgence, he prohibited prosecutions of Catholic worship (and, in so doing, as Stuarts often had done before, he used prerogative powers to suspend an Act of Parliament). James II's motivation for the policy of tolerance was complex: it was partly to win much-needed political allies among the nonconformist Protestants (who also benefited from the new policy of toleration), but also his cherished hope that England could be converted to Catholicism by persuasion. In fact, there were few converts to Rome. On the contrary, London found itself in the grip of anti-Catholic hysteria and mob violence. Many people in the lower classes feared a Catholic coup (when, in fact, the precise opposite was about to happen!). Catholics were attacked and 'mass-houses' burned down. The King's position was untenable. Within four years of succeeding to the throne, it was clear to James II that his political allies – in particular, the army and navy officers – had deserted him. The country was once again on the verge of anarchy.

3.6.6   The Glorious Revolution

Who was to succeed James II? His eldest daughter, Mary, was married to the (Protestant) William, Prince of Orange. It was therefore for William and Mary that, in 1688, a group of influential Englishmen sent. William sailed from Holland and landed with 15,000 men at Torbay in November. The position in the capital continued to deteriorate, and it became clear to James II that his position was untenable. In December, he left London for exile in France, throwing the Great Seal – the symbol of kingly authority – into the River Thames as William's army marched towards the City. Mobs looted and burnt Catholic churches and the businesses and homes of the Catholics; only the news that William was nearing London helped calm the crowds.

The day after Christmas 1688, an assembly of peers and MPs met and advised Prince William to call a convention of all peers and representatives of the counties and boroughs. The 'Convention Parliament' met in January 1689 and resolved that James, by 'breaking the original contract between king and people, and by the advice of Jesuits and other wicked persons having violated the fundamental laws and having withdrawn himself out of the kingdom, had abdicated the government, and that the throne has thereby become vacant'. The Parliament also passed a resolution 'that it hath been found, by experience, to be inconsistent with the safety and welfare of this Protestant Kingdom to be governed by a Popish Prince'. In fact, there was considerable disagreement among the ruling class as to whether this was an abdication. It was more like a revolution. As FW Maitland (the 19th century legal historian) puts it: 'it was extremely difficult for any lawyer to make out that what had then been done was lawful' (*The Constitutional History of England*, 1908, Cambridge: CUP, p 283).

In February 1689, the two Houses of Parliament formally offered the Crown to William and Mary – subject to clear understandings about the limited powers of the monarchy in the future. The Convention Parliament declared itself to be the Parliament of England and passed the Bill of Rights 1688, firmly limiting the rights of the monarch: William was called upon 'to reign but not to rule'. Like Magna Carta centuries before, the Bill of Rights 1688 has assumed an enduring constitutional importance. Its purpose was not so much to grant liberties to individual subjects, but to give statutory force to the new relationship between Parliament and the Crown. It enacted that the King could not levy taxes or maintain an army without the consent of Parliament; that no legal proceedings could be taken against any MP for any action or speech made in Parliament ('parliamentary privilege'); that only Protestants were permitted to bear arms; that the assumed power of the monarch to dispense with laws was unlawful; and that excessive fines and other 'cruel and unjust punishments' were prohibited. Twelve years later, in the Act of Settlement 1700, Parliament enacted a proposal debated, but rejected, in 1689, that the Crown had no power to remove judges unless requested to do so by resolutions passed by both Houses of Parliament.

Almost immediately, the new king had to cope with a new uprising in Ireland spurred on by James II's arrival there. ('King Billy' going into battle on horseback and the date '1690' remain ideological icons for Ulster Protestantism to this day). William went in person to fight the Battle of the Boyne, a battle as much with the French, whose forces had gone to aid their fellow Catholics, as with the Irish. His victory led, in the years that followed, to Catholics being barred from the Irish Parliament and all public offices, attempts to eliminate Catholic landlords and the general subjugation of the Catholic population who made up the vast majority of the people of Ireland.

It was during the reign of William and Mary that the foundations of the modern English Constitution were laid. A constitutional monarchy had been established. The judges no longer held office 'during the King's pleasure', but on good behaviour, removable only with the consent of both Houses of Parliament. Parliament now asserted clear power to control government finance and the Treasury began to draw up annual budgets for parliamentary approval. The right to criticise royal appointments to government offices was also regularly used. A 'Cabinet' of the Crown's ministers began to meet regularly. But, again, this was no real progress for democracy: as at the beginning of the 17th century, the electorate was no more than 3% of the population – the men who owned substantial land and the merchants of the towns and cities.

The philosopher John Locke (1632–1704), in his *Two Treatises of Civil Government* (1690), provided a rationalisation for the events of the Glorious Revolution. He rejected any form of absolute monarchy, arguing that 'it cannot be supposed that people should give any one or more of their fellow-men an authority over them for any other purpose than their own preservation'. His ideas, including those about the 'natural rights' of men, have had an abiding importance in constitutional thinking (see above, 1.3.1, and below, Chapter 19).

3.7 The 18th century and the Enlightenment

While the 1600s laid the foundations for the relationship between the Crown, government and Parliament, the 18th century established the geographical boundaries of Great Britain. As we have already noted (above, 3.6), since 1603 there had been a 'personal union' of the Crown of England and Scotland when James VI of Scotland succeeded Elizabeth to become King James I of England. Each country, however, continued to have its own Parliament and Privy Council until 1706 when, by the Act of Union, a Parliament of Great Britain was created comprising English, Welsh and Scottish MPs.

3.7.1 Rationality and radicalism

The importance of the 18th century lies not so much in particular constitutional events in Britain, but in changing attitudes of mind. Throughout Europe, intellectuals developed new ways of understanding the world and man's place in it. The movement called 'the Enlightenment' combined belief in the importance of rationality in human affairs with an unprecedented optimism about the ability of mankind to organise government in ways capable of improving social conditions. Most thinkers remained firmly Christian in their beliefs, but there was a growing rejection of religious persecution and a retreat from many of the superstitions (such as witchcraft) which had been widespread in previous centuries.

In Britain, Jeremy Bentham (1748–1832), a philosopher and lawyer, developed the idea of utilitarianism: people inevitably pursue pleasure and avoid pain, he argued, and the judgment of what is socially desirable is 'the greatest happiness of the greatest number'. For Bentham, laws were socially useful tools to bring about this state of affairs, and he was an early advocate of constitutional codes.

A populist radicalism also arose. Newspapers were established all over the country, political pamphlets were sold in their millions and men met, in 'corresponding societies', to talk about new ideas for government. The Wilkite movement was of particular importance. John Wilkes (1727–97) was an MP and founder of the *North Briton* journal, which was outspokenly critical of the government of the day. Intent on suppressing the publication, the government issued a general warrant for the arrest of Wilkes and 48 others. Wilkes was imprisoned and his house searched and ransacked by order of the Secretaries of State. In court, Wilkes and his supporters challenged the legality of the general warrants and won: see *Entick v Carrington* (1765). The judge refused to accept the government's plea of 'State necessity', holding that 'public policy is not an argument in a court of law'. The government had acted without specific lawful authority, and so had unlawfully trespassed on Wilkes's land. The judgment was both a highly publicised political victory for Wilkes and also an enduring precedent in favour of individual liberty. Nonetheless, Wilkes was soon forced to flee to France when the government revealed a sexually obscene poem which their messengers had found among Wilkes's belongings. He later returned, and was re-elected to Parliament several times but, on each occasion, was barred entry to the House of Commons. There was mob violence, and Wilkes again used the courts to publicise his cause – this time, the case was on the reporting of parliamentary debates.

Another radical was Thomas Paine (1737–1819), who rejected the legitimacy of monarchical government altogether. For him 'all hereditary government is in its nature tyranny'. In his writings, including *Common Sense* (a pamphlet written in 1776) and *Rights of Man*, Paine shared the assumption of many Enlightenment thinkers and other radicals that men had universal and inalienable rights – including political equality, free speech and freedom from arbitrary arrest. Paine also advocated a system of social security, financed by taxation, and he welcomed the new rise of manufacturing industry and economic growth as ways of increasing the general welfare of the population.

3.7.2 Revolution in America and France

The government in Britain feared civil strife or even revolution, and many repressive laws were enacted by Parliament curtailing freedom of assembly and free speech. There were good reasons for such fears as, during the last quarter of the century, there was revolt against established forms of government, both in Britain's American colonies and across the Channel in France.

Tensions mounted between Britain and its 13 American colonies. At the beginning of the 18th century, the population of these colonies was only some 200,000 but, by 1770, it had risen to over 2 million. The British Government was levying ever-increasing taxation in America, something deeply resented by the colonists (who had no representation in Parliament). Radicals in England, like Wilkes and Paine, supported the cause of the colonists. In 1776, after 'a war of extraordinary incompetence on both sides', George Washington declared the American colonies independent and, shortly afterwards, drew up the first American Constitution, influenced by the thinking of Paine. It set out in a code:

> ... these truths to be self-evident, that all men are created equal, that they are endowed by the Creator with certain inalienable rights ... That whenever any form of government becomes destructive of these ends it is the rights of the people to alter or abolish it, and to institute new government, laying its foundations on such principles and organising its powers in such form, as to them shall seem most likely to effect their safety and happiness.

Revolution was also brewing closer to home. In the span of a few years, France moved from an absolutist monarchy to constitutional monarchy (1789); to violent, radical revolt and the proclamation of a republic (1792); and then (from November 1799) the personal rule of General Napoleon. In Britain, Paine supported the revolution across the Channel as he had in the American colonies – his influential pamphlet *The Rights of Man* (1791–92), dedicated to George Washington, was a polemical reply to attacks on the French revolution made by Edmund Burke (1729–97). Hundreds of thousands of copies of Paine's pamphlets were in circulation, and the British Government grew increasingly fearful that radical revolution would take place in England. Its response was strong censorship, the suspension of habeas corpus, and to break up the corresponding societies. In 1791, a royal proclamation was issued against 'wicked seditious writing printed, published and industriously dispersed', and Paine was summoned to stand trial. He never did so, however, as he travelled to France to take up his seat in the new National Assembly, to which he had been elected as the representative of Calais.

3.8   The 19th century

3.8.1   The creation of the UK

In 1801, the United Kingdom of Great Britain and Ireland was created by the second Act of Union, and 50 Irish constituencies were given seats in the Westminster Parliament. The new UK was much resented by the majority of the population of Ireland, who were Catholics. Since the 1690s, Catholics living in Ireland had been denied formal equality before the law: they were barred from holding public office, denied the right to own land and access to education. It was not until 1829 that the worst of these legal disabilities were removed. While the rest of the UK was beginning a revolution in manufacturing industry (see below, 3.8.2), Ireland remained a mainly rural economy. Between 1845 and 1849, the potato harvests failed in Ireland, wiping out the staple food. Over a million people starved to death, and millions immigrated to the US, Australia and Canada. The authorities in London provided little assistance during the disaster.

3.8.2   The Industrial Revolution

In parts of England, Wales and Scotland, the economy was transformed within the space of a couple of generations from one based on agriculture to an industrial society. New technologies enabled the mass production of textiles and iron, and railways were built across the countryside, making travel possible like never before. New forms of capitalist enterprise emerged, in which firms employed large numbers of wage labourers in factories. With these changes emerged new social classes: industrial entrepreneurs, different in their outlook from the landowners and merchants who had dominated Parliament and the institutions of government in the previous century; and a rapidly growing urban working class of wage labourers. From the point of view of public law, two themes dominate the development of the constitution during the 1800s: the movement towards parliamentary democracy, and the creation of a government machine capable of coping with the new demands imposed on the State by the new industrial age.

3.8.3   Extending the franchise

As we have seen, neither the Civil War nor the Glorious Revolution of 1688 brought democracy; the struggles between king and Parliament had been about the protection of private property against the arbitrary powers of the Crown. At the beginning of the 19th century, the position was as it had been for many years previously: the House of Commons did not represent 'the people', but the small proportion of men who owned freehold property. Aristocratic landowners, the old merchant classes and the king continued to exercise considerable powers of patronage which influenced, often determined, the outcome to election to the Commons, a task made easier by the fact that elections were not by secret ballot. Society was changing rapidly in the 19th century, but there was no single reform movement campaigning for democracy. For some, the goal was confined to the extension of the franchise to the growing middle class. Radicals – as they had done in the 18th century – demanded more: universal manhood suffrage (literally, for few included women in their proposals). The ruling elite and their representatives in Parliament continued to fear revolution, and the events in France only a decade before were fresh in the mind. The year 1819 was particularly turbulent in England. A crowd of 60,000 met in St Peter's Fields in Manchester to hear radical speakers. It ended with soldiers charging the crowd, killing 11 and wounding many hundreds (dubbed the 'Peterloo massacre' in ironic reference to Wellington's victory over Napoleon at Waterloo in 1815). The government's reaction was to pass the 'Six Acts' which, among other things, banned meetings of over 50 people for the discussion of public grievance, extended newspaper stamp duty to political pamphlets and prohibited the training of men in the use of arms.

But reform, if not immediate radical reform, did occur. The first success was the Representation of the People Act 1832 (the Great Reform Act) which abolished the 'rotten boroughs' and extended the right to vote to men of property who did not own substantial freehold land. In 1867, by the Second Reform Act, many working men in towns were enfranchised and, in 1884, so were male agricultural labourers. Women in the propertied classes were able to vote in local elections from 1869. The coming of parliamentary democracy led to transformations in the dynamic forces of the constitution. Mass political parties became part and parcel of the constitution, and led to the evolution of conventions such as that of collective ministerial responsibility.

3.8.4 The administrative revolution

The agrarian revolution of the 17th century and the Industrial Revolution of the 19th are well known, but the 'revolution in government and administration' produced effects as profound as the better turnip and the steam engine. During the 19th century, ideas and practices of what 'government' should be changed, necessitating new techniques and structures of public administration.

In 1853, two senior civil servants, Sir Stafford Northcote and Sir Charles Trevelyn, conducted a wide ranging review of administration in Whitehall. Their short 20 page report was eventually to transform the British Civil Service. In future, they recommended, young men should be recruited on merit after sitting competitive examinations, rather than on the basis of favouritism and patronage. Uniform conditions of employment should apply in all government departments, the Northcote-Trevelyn report said, rather than the haphazard arrangements and sinecures which still existed. Many people in the establishment viewed these proposals with hostility when they were first published, some even seeing in them 'the seeds of republicanism', because objective examinations (rather than the Crown) were to determine who was appointed to the Civil Service. But public outrage over the lives lost in the Crimean War owing to administrative inefficiencies helped prepare the ground for the adoption of the proposals. In 1870, when Gladstone was Prime Minister, a new Civil Service Order in Council (a piece of primary legislation made under the royal prerogative (see above, 2.4.3) was made, implementing most of the proposals in the Northcote-Trevelyn report. England now had a modern, permanent, 'politically neutral' Civil Service. It was also a bureaucracy that was growing rapidly: it doubled in size between 1853 and 1890.

Throughout the 19th century, government increasingly intervened in commercial activity to ensure basic standards of health and safety by inspecting factories, passenger ships, railways, mines, etc. The government also assumed a role in providing subsistence, basic health care and elementary education to the working classes, and eventually the direct provision of affordable housing. Gas, water, sewerage, street lighting and other utilities were also provided to the public by local authorities. This was the beginning of the modern regulatory, interventionist State: government no longer confined itself to being a 'nightwatchman', responsible only for the defence of the realm and the maintenance of law and order. A variety of new administrative techniques were used. Central government departments sometimes appointed their own inspectors or set up independent bodies of inspectors. Sometimes, specially created 'commissions' or 'boards' were set up (such as the Poor Law Commission in 1834, which later became the Poor Law Board). Above all, local government was a vital part of the new emerging structures of public administration. The justices of the peace (see above, 3.5) were no longer appropriate 'maids of all work', and many of their administrative functions were taken over by elected rate-levying bodies responsible for police, the administration of the poor law and schooling.

As with central government, local bodies underwent a process of reform during the century, both in terms of democratic participation and their administrative effectiveness. During the 19th century, the right to vote in local elections – as for the House of Commons – was progressively widened, first to the middle class (1832), then the working class in towns (1867) and agricultural labourers (1884). Eventually, the morass of different local bodies exercising different responsibilities were amalgamated into general purpose local authorities with paid clerks and treasurers with powers to make bylaws (local regulations). They were subject to financial audit and began to receive financial grants from central government. The work of these authorities was directed by central government departments by means of delegated legislation and ministerial circulars.

3.9   The 20th century

In this brief chronology of constitutional developments, three processes stand out during the 20th century: the creation of the Welfare State; decolonisation; and the reorientation of British trade and political ties towards Europe.

3.9.1   The Welfare State and democracy

We have already noted some early enactments of social legislation intended to improve the lives of working class people. Under the Liberal governments led by Lloyd George and Asquith around the turn of the 19th century, the pace quickened: death duties for the rich were increased; old age pensions for the poor were introduced (Old Age Pensions Act 1908); a national insurance scheme to protect workers against the effects of illness and unemployment was created by the National Insurance Act 1911 (the old poor laws administered locally by justices of the peace had applied only to the absolutely destitute); progressive income tax arrived (and has never gone away) and investment income was taxed differently from earned income. Taxation became a tool for changing society and redistributing income, and was no longer seen merely as a way of raising revenue to pay for the defence of the realm and administration of justice.

The era of 'social security' had arrived; but not without a constitutional struggle. The upper House of Parliament, still representing the interests of the aristocracy as it had done for centuries before, was deeply hostile to the new social democracy. The Lords used their legislative power to block the Bill designed to implement the Liberal Party's 'people's budget' of 1909. There was a crisis. The government responded by calling a general election in January 1910. The Liberals won, and the Lords had little option but to pass the Bill when it was reintroduced in the new Parliament. The government was determined to take away the Lords' powers to block such 'money Bills'. When the Lords refused to pass such a Bill curtailing their powers, a second general election was called. The outcome was another victory for the Liberals and a limited one for democracy; faced with a threat from King George V to create as many Liberal peers as necessary to get the Bill through, the Lords reluctantly gave their approval to the Parliament Act 1911. Henceforth, the hereditary House of Lords had power to delay money Bills for one month only and other Bills for only three sessions of Parliament; thereafter, the elected House of Commons, acting alone, could pass a Bill capable of receiving royal assent. During this period, the Labour Party, representing working class men, gradually grew in strength and, by 1906, there were 29 Labour MPs in the chamber.

3.9.2 Foreign relations

By the outset of the 20th century, the British Empire was the leading world power. It covered almost 25% of the world's land surface (and so 'the sun never set' on the Empire) and held a quarter of the world's population. In 1914, Britain entered into the First World War. On one day alone, 20,000 British soldiers were killed and many more injured at the Somme. The future of Europe also seemed uncertain for reasons other than war with Germany. In 1917, the Bolsheviks seized power in Russia and set about building a society based on Marxist principles. In Western Europe, the armistice was signed in November 1918.

The political agenda in Britain immediately after the First World War was dominated by Ireland: there were ever more forceful demands for home rule or independence. Sinn Fein, a major political party in Ireland, set up an unofficial Parliament in Dublin in 1918 after the general election of that year. This Parliament behaved as if it were an official one; taxes were levied and courts established. At the same time, the IRA began a guerrilla war against the British in Ireland. Over 1,500 people died. Messy, confused negotiations led to the British Parliament agreeing, in 1921, to Prime Minister Lloyd George's negotiated settlement which was to divide Ireland; the six predominantly Protestant counties in the north east were to remain part of the UK and the rest of the island, overwhelmingly Catholic, would officially be recognised as an independent State (which it had, in fact, been for several years already). A large part of the 'UK' had been excised. In 1922, the Irish Free State came into existence, with Dominion status within the British Empire, but these arrangements soon faltered. In 1937, the Republic of Eire was established, with a constitution claiming the counties of Northern Ireland to be an integral part of the Republic.

Changes were also apparent in the nature of the British Empire. From the 1920s onwards, Australia, New Zealand, South Africa and Canada asserted autonomy over their own foreign policies. A Commonwealth of Nations, equal and united by their allegiance to the Crown, was in the process of formation. In 1931, the Statute of Westminster formalised many of the new arrangements: those countries with Dominion status (principally, those listed above) were free to pass legislation in their own national legislatures even if inconsistent with British law, and British law was not to apply to any Dominion without its consent. India – Britain's major trading partner within the Empire – did not have such Dominion status, and there were ever-stronger demands for self-government.

3.9.3   The inter-war economic depression

The Western economies fell into deep depression during the 1920s, and Britain was blighted with mass unemployment. Trade unions called a general strike in 1926, but it lasted for only nine days. A great deal of legislation was enacted during the 1920s which further laid the basis for the modern Welfare State. In 1928, universal suffrage was finally achieved when women were given the vote on an equal footing to men. In Germany, the National Socialists came to power during the 1930s; within Germany, anti-Jewish laws were enacted and, later, a policy of genocide was pursued, resulting in the systematic murder of over 6 million people. Abroad, Nazi Germany embarked on forced expansion of its territories. British fascists began to organise in London, and here the response of the government was to enact the Incitement to Disaffection Act 1934 and the Public Order Act 1936, giving the police new powers and banning provocative assemblies. Britain was set on course for war with Germany, and government spending on armaments brought an end to the mass unemployment. The countries of Western Europe were at war between 1940 and 1945. As in the Great War of 1914–18, the experience of war brought about profound changes in social attitudes.

3.9.4   The 1945 Labour Government

In the first general election after the war, the Labour Party won with a landslide majority and, for six years, embarked on a programme that was to shape Britain for the next three decades. The Welfare State, whose foundations had been laid in earlier years by both Liberal and Conservative governments, was established, notably by the enactment of the National Health Service Act 1946 (granting free medical care to all), the National Insurance Act 1946 (building on early social security legislation to create universal welfare benefits funded by compulsory contribution from employers, workers and the State) and legislation on housing (controlling rents charged by private landlords and encouraging local authorities to build rental accommodation). The Children Act 1948, and other legislation, placed responsibilities on councils to employ a new profession of social workers, with powers to intervene in families' lives.

Apart from these welfare reforms, the Labour government embarked on a programme of nationalisation. The Coal Industry Nationalisation Act 1946, Electricity Act 1947, Transport Act 1947, Gas Act 1947 and the Iron and Steel Act 1949 brought within State ownership and control the 'commanding heights' of the economy. The last of these Acts was delayed by the House of Lords, resulting in the Parliament Act 1949, which reduced the time the upper chamber could delay Bills approved by the Commons to two sessions of Parliament. In 1948, the Representation of the People Act finished the project, begun in the last century, of creating a universal franchise: it took away the right of university graduates and owners of business premises to two votes in parliamentary elections.

During the 1940s, India and Pakistan were given independence (by the Indian Independence Act 1947). In the years which followed, most other colonies also gained self-government, most remaining within the Commonwealth of Nations (though not all retained the Queen as their Head of State).

3.9.5 Building the new Europe

Influenced by American foreign policy, the nations of Western Europe began to rebuild their shattered economies after the Second World War. During the early 1950s, Germany, Italy, France and the three Benelux countries formed free trade agreements, backed up by novel types of institutions. One of these was the European Economic Community, or 'Common Market' as it was called. After some hesitation, the UK became a member in 1973. Another international organisation, the Council of Europe, was established to promote parliamentary democracy and the rule of law in the region. The UK played an influential role in drafting one of its principal legal instruments, the European Convention on Human Rights, and was a signatory to it in 1950. Britain's economic ties to the Commonwealth diminished in the post-war period; its trading links and political future now lay with Europe. The account of how this happened, and the legal implications of it, require separate treatment and are examined further in Chapter 7.

3.10 Conclusions

In the absence of a written constitution, it is the history of events and changing attitudes of mind which reveal what are now regarded as the valuable principles in the modern constitution.

Religious belief has been rejected as the basis for organising constitutional affairs and civil liberties and as the justification for governmental powers. Although the Queen remains the Head of the (Protestant) Church of England, and legislation requires State-funded schools to hold assemblies of a predominantly Christian character (see below, 4.3.1), membership of a non-established church or atheism are no longer general legal disabilities which bar participation in public affairs. Religion has become a private matter. In Northern Ireland, however, religious affiliation continues to be important in the constitution of society (see above, 2.6).

There has been a partial, but not total, rejection of hereditary rights as an organising principle (see below, 4.3.3). True, the Queen remains a hereditary Head of State and, during the 1980s, Mrs Thatcher created several new hereditary peerages (including one for the Macmillan family), but few people now accept that it is legitimate for hereditary peers to sit in Parliament. The Labour government proposes to abolish the rights of hereditary peers to sit in Parliament.

Democratic ideals have assumed importance. The right of all adults to vote for representatives in Parliament and local government came about after a long campaign. The constitution now accords all adults formal equality in the legal system; there is no longer any 'class' of persons (serfs, Roman Catholics, the working class) who are, by reason of law, excluded from participation in the constitutional scheme. But, as in the past, there are also claims today that democracy means more than the right to vote for parliamentary representatives. The notion of 'inalienable rights' against government, which first gained acceptance during the 18th century, is again prominent in discourse about the British Constitution.

The principle of government under law has been established. The monarch, and then government, has been required to act in accordance with laws enacted by Parliament and legal principles established by the courts. Government under law now also includes the principle that the State must comply with international agreements, such as the European Convention on Human Rights.

There have been shifts in the UK's global allegiances. In the past, England lost France, lost the American colonies, and gained and lost an Empire. During the current period, the UK's essential political and economic interests are as part of the European Union.

PRINCIPLES FROM HISTORY

History reveals how and why constitutional principles emerged; past events themselves help establish conventions. Traditional authority is regarded by some people as a legitimate source of power. Without history, it is difficult to understand the UK Constitution. A constant theme that emerges from the historical study of the constitution is that change often comes about for pragmatic reasons.

1066	the Norman Conquest.
1215	Magna Carta.
15th century	English kings continued to assert a claim to the Crown of France. Market economy is emerging.
16th century	Protestant reformation. Some shift away from personal rule by monarch evident; parliaments meeting more frequently.
17th century	conflicts between Parliament and James I and Charles I. Civil War, overthrow of monarchy and establishment of the Commonwealth under Cromwell. Restoration of monarchy. 'Glorious Revolution' 1688 and new constitutional settlement.
18th century	the Enlightenment. Radicals including Bentham, Wilkes and Paine develop new ideas about the constitution. Revolution in America and France.
19th century	the creation of the UK of Great Britain and Ireland 1801. Industrial Revolution. Franchise extended. Administrative revolution.
20th century	the Welfare State emerges, along with the universal franchise. Larger part of Ireland becomes an independent State. Two world wars and economic depression of 1930s cast doubts on Nation States and capitalism. After the Second World War, major industries are nationalised. Nations of Western Europe begin to rebuild their economies, partly through the European Community. The UK's colonies gain independence. The UK joins the European Community in 1973.

CHAPTER 4

POLITICIANS AND THEIR PRINCIPLES

4.1   The importance of political parties

Political parties are important in liberal democracies, even though opinion pollsters tell us that a large proportion of the British public are 'not very' or 'not at all' interested in politics at the moment (see above, 1.7.2). They are voluntary associations of people (see above, 1.2) who compete to occupy positions of power in some State authorities: the House of Commons, ministerial posts and elected members of local authorities.

For more than 50 years, central government in the UK has been led by ministers of one or other of two parties – Labour and the Conservatives. While one has been Her Majesty's Government, the other has formed Her Majesty's Official Opposition in the Commons. The Liberal Democrats have relatively few MPs in the UK Parliament, but they do participate in running a large number of local authorities and, in coalition with Labour, are members of the Scottish Executive (see above, 2.5.2) and Welsh Assembly (see above, 2.7).

One way to understand what principles exist in the modern constitutional system is to dissect what the parties have to say on the subject. This chapter focuses on the Conservatives and Labour and their attitudes to the three core features of liberal democracy – autonomy from government, democracy and security.

4.2   New governments, new constitution

For the Conservatives and Labour alike, modifying important features of the constitutional system has been, and is, a central vehicle for their wider political project to change society. Despite their name, the Conservatives do not want to keep society the same, though they have been wary of using the term 'constitutional reform' to describe the changes they implemented while in government between 1979 and 1997. Indeed, they were often at pains to present themselves as opposed to the reforms being urged by pressure groups such as Charter 88, Liberty and the Campaign for Freedom of Information. In both the 1992 and 1997 general elections, the Conservatives made resistance to devolution to Wales and Scotland a major manifesto commitment. In several areas they did, however, carry through a programme of radical change:

(a) the realignment of relations between central and local government and redefinitions of the functions of local authorities;

(b) changes in the Civil Service, especially the creation of executive agencies;

(c) privatisation of most State owned corporations;

(d) the introduction of market forces within remaining government activities through 'compulsory competitive tendering' and 'market testing';

(e) deregulation of business activities; and

(f) what has been termed 'the Great Codification' of previously internal government custom and practice through the publication of 'Citizen's Charters' and the imposition of financial audits.

Much of the present Labour government's programme of constitutional reform has already been described in Chapter 2 and will be examined in more detail later in the book. The main features include:

(a) devolution of legislative and executive power to new elected institutions in Scotland, Northern Ireland and Wales (see above, 2.5, 2.6, 2.7);

(b) incorporation of the European Convention on Human Rights (ECHR) into the UK's legal systems by the Human Rights Act 1998 (see below, Chapters 5 and 18);

(c) reform of local authorities, including elected mayors and referendums on local issues;

(d) abolition of hereditary peers' right to sit in Parliament (see below, 6.4.3);

(e) consideration of a new proportional representation electoral system for the UK Parliament (see below, 6.4.1); and

(f) a Freedom of Information Act (see below, 24.8).

Both parties have supported the development of the European Union (see below, Chapter 7).

4.3   Do politicians have any principles?

Labour's programme of reform, and the Conservatives' response to it, have been criticised for lacking coherent principles. *The Economist* comments of Labour:

> At some point ... the various constitutional changes have to be meshed together in a framework that works. They also need to be underpinned by some unifying political vision. And so far, alas, there is little evidence either of meshing or of vision [(1998) *The Economist*, 18 April, p 34].

The editor of *The Times* makes a similar point:

> The most compelling criticism of Labour's constitutional agenda is that it is piecemeal and only partly thought through [(1998) *The Times*, 25 February, p 19].

Similar failings are alleged against the Conservative Party. On 25 February 1998, the Conservative leader William Hague delivered a speech at the Centre for Policy Studies, a Conservative think tank, entitled 'Change and tradition: thinking creatively about the constitution'. *The Economist*'s acerbic comment was that 'it exhibited hardly any thinking at all, much less the creative kind' (28 February 1998, p 21). It went on:

> Long sweated over, eloquently phrased, studded through with apt reference to the historic heroes of the Tory constitutional pantheon, a Dicey here, a Disraeli there, Magna Carta everywhere, at the end of the day it fell short of expectations ... When it came to what he would not do, Mr Hague trotted out the clichés. Of change in general: 'It will not be possible to turn the clock back'. Of devolution: 'We cannot unscramble the omelette'. Of human rights legislation: 'Is this another omelette we cannot unscramble?' But while proclaiming the inevitability of change in general, he simultaneously rejected it in almost every particular: the rights legislation, referendums, and the government's proposed reforms of the Lords ... [p 40].

Commentators have also questioned the coherence of the Conservatives' constitutional reforms between 1979 and 1997. In this chapter, we dig beneath these criticisms, trying hard to find out what principles do inform the two main political parties in their approach to the constitution. This is not, of course, to suggest that any such principles are either static or always clearly articulated. Given the fact that all political parties are broad coalitions of people, inevitably the presentation has to be something of a caricature.

4.4 The Conservatives and the constitution

Up until the Second World War, the Conservative Party – or Tories as they are often called – existed to give expression to 'the landed interest' in the country. Even in 1999, almost all hereditary peers in the House of Lords support the Conservatives. An important part of the Conservatives' roots thus lies with traditional ways of life in the countryside and is associated with hierarchical, authoritarian and paternalistic values. There is also another, apparently contradictory, rootstock: members committed to the values of the free market, with its emphasis on individualism and progress through trade. Out of these tensions emerge the policies of the modern Conservative Party.

4.4.1 Conservatives and autonomy

Conservatives are, by inclination, hostile to, or at least sceptical of, most State authorities, seeing them as a threat to freedom. This scepticism extends to State created charters of constitutional rights; Conservatives prefer the concept of negative freedoms (see above, 1.7.1). Lord Cranborne argues that codified constitutions and charters of rights:

> ... are the creation of government. Citizens are thus, by definition, the servants of the State because their freedoms are bestowed upon them by the State. Those freedoms are defined by government and the constitution [*Don't Unbalance our Unwritten Constitution*, 1996, London: Politeia].

The Conservative governments of 1979–97 pledged themselves to 'rolling back the frontiers of the State'. The liberty which Conservatives seek to protect from State intrusion is not, however, necessarily that of 'the individual' of classic liberal theory (see above, 1.6.1). Great importance is attached to voluntary associations, such as the family, churches and charitable bodies (often labelled 'civil society' by Conservatives). For Conservatives, 'The real sign of a civilised society is precisely that voluntary, charitable organisations can meet human needs without coercive taxation and the employment of public officials' (Willetts, D, in Gray, J and Willetts, D (eds), *Is Conservatism Dead?* 1997, London: Profile, p 93). It is these associations, rather than merely atomistic individuals, which need to be protected from government intrusion. The danger posed by an overly intrusive and all-encompassing Welfare State (see above, Chapter 1) is its tendency to destroy voluntary associations and to diminish the incentives of people to organise themselves independently of government. Conservatives do not, however, see strong trade unions as voluntary associations with a beneficial influence on society. Referring to the 1960s and 1970s, David Walker wrote:

> In public law unions are not only consulted by governments on every matter, but assert and dictate their views, arrogantly claim to represent the people of the country and make and unmake governments ... They represent the gravest threat to democracy, liberty and economic progress and prosperity yet known and constantly call for the law to be kept out of industrial relations to enable anarchy to be promoted [*Oxford Companion to Law*, 1980, Oxford: OUP, p 1229].

The Conservative governments of 1979–97 therefore *increased* legal regulation to curb trade union power, outlawing some forms of picketing (see below, Chapter 25) and imposing legislative requirements as to the procedures to be followed by trade unionists in deciding whether or not to strike.

Because (most) voluntary associations are so important to the fabric of society, Conservatives believe that State authorities may sometimes need to intervene in order to support and protect them; paradoxically, government is thus seen both as a potential threat and a potential saviour. Christian Churches are particularly significant and most Conservatives take the view that government should, therefore, further their aims. Thus, the Education Act 1988 requires all publicly funded schools to have a daily act of collective worship 'of a broadly Christian character', though, in practice, this is ignored by many schools, especially those where few pupils and their parents follow the Christian religion. Most Conservatives strongly support the idea that the Church of England remain established (that is, linked to the State), with bishops sitting in the House of Lords. Conservatism, therefore, does not support the classical liberal standpoint that religious faith ought to be a matter within the private, rather than public, sphere (see above, 1.6.1).

The family is another voluntary association in civil society essential for social stability; and here again State authorities are seen to have a positive role in promoting family life and preventing family breakdown. To take just a few examples: during the 1980s, the influence of the gay rights movement was seen by Conservatives as a particular threat to the institution of the family. Section 28 of the Local Government Act 1988, therefore, prohibited local authorities from promoting or teaching the 'acceptability' of homosexuality as 'a pretended family relationship'. The Family Law Act 1996 imposed a 12 month wait for people wanting to divorce, so that they can reflect on whether this is the right course of action; it also requires people intending to divorce to attend compulsory mediation sessions in the hope of saving the marriage. In 1997, Lord Mackay, the Conservative Lord Chancellor, established a 'marriage taskforce initiative' to prevent marriage breakdown, with government funding being given to projects such as telephone helplines and a national telephone counselling service for married couples; marriage preparation programmes; a media campaign to change the culture of marriage; an African Caribbean marriage support helpline; and drop-in marriage and advice centres.

The field in which Conservatives most strongly support personal autonomy, unrestrained by government and law, is the economic sphere. There is a principled virtue in low taxation, as it is at this most rudimentary level – confiscating money from people's pay packets – that government begins to diminish people's liberty. The last Conservative government reduced the highest rate of income taxation to 40%. The Conservatives also attempted to encourage local authorities to set low taxes by replacing 'rates' (a form of property tax) with the Community Charge (or Poll Tax) in which almost everyone in a locality – rich or poor – was expected to pay the same flat rate sum. Electors, it was thought, would vote for the political party (the Conservatives) which promised a low Community Charge. The policy was a catastrophe for the government, with tens of thousands of people refusing to pay the Poll Tax and violent demonstrations in London. The Poll Tax was replaced in 1993 with a new Council Tax, once again based on property values.

For Conservatives, economic freedom extends not only to individuals, but also to business enterprises. An ambitious programme of 'deregulation' was implemented, aimed at cutting out the 'red tape' which hampered commerce, especially small businesses. The Deregulation and Contacting Out Act 1994 gave ministers powers to repeal legislation if, in their opinion, 'the effect of the provision is such as to impose, or authorise or require the imposition of, a burden affecting any person in the carrying on of any trade, business or profession' (s 1(1)). The extent of these powers – enabling ministers, rather than Parliament as a whole, to repeal statutes – was controversial, and many people questioned its constitutional propriety. Opponents also objected that deregulation removed legal standards previously in place for the protection of consumers and employees. In the workplace, the Conservative's deregulation policy was hampered by the adoption by the European Community of a directive which imposed limits on working hours and holiday entitlements (see below, 7.8.1). Where regulation is desirable in a sector of the economy, Conservatives have a preference for *self*-regulation by voluntary associations formed by the trade or profession concerned – though this has created the problem of what powers the courts have to ensure that the self-appointed regulators act fairly (see below, 17.6.2).

4.4.2 Conservatives and democracy

Conservatives recognise the importance of democracy in some spheres, though they also attach importance to traditional practices as a legitimate form of governance (for example, hereditary peers being part of Parliament) and believe that market forces are better then democratic decision making in some fields.

For Conservatives, the main unit of democratic decision making is the Nation State (the UK as a whole) and its representatives in the Westminster Parliament. Conservatives attach great importance to the supremacy of Parliament (its right to make or unmake any law it pleases (see below, Chapter 5)). Many Conservatives therefore oppose the process of European integration, in which the institutions of the European Union are gaining ever more powers to legislate (see below, Chapter 7). They also opposed the Human Rights Act 1998, incorporating the ECHR into UK law, on the ground that this would increase the relative powers of the courts to determine the limits of government policy. Philip Norton, a political scientist appointed as a Conservative peer in 1998, explains that 'disputes as to encroachment on fundamental rights are essentially political disputes and must be resolved politically, not judicially' (*The Constitution in Flux*, 1984, Oxford: Blackwells, p 253).

Because of their commitment to the integrity of the UK, Conservatives also opposed devolution of legislative and executive powers to new institutions in Scotland and Wales in 1998. Nor do they regard local authorities as important democratic institutions. As Martin Loughlin describes, the Conservative governments of 1979–97 introduced a great deal of legislation to regulate the relationship between central and local government, and to curtail the functions of local authorities, in order 'to reduce the political capacity of local government as a tier of government' ('Central-local relations', in Jowell, J and Oliver, D (eds), *The Changing Constitution*, 3rd edn, 1984, Oxford: OUP, p 273). In 1986, Mrs Thatcher's government and its majority in Parliament abolished the Greater London Council (GLC) and six other metropolitan county councils. These had formed a second tier of local government above smaller boroughs in the major urban centres in England. The result in London was that the city came to be governed by 32 quite small borough councils, but there is no elected city-wide authority. After the abolition of the GLC, some functions, such as land use planning and education, were passed down to the borough councils. Other strategic planning responsibilities, such as for fire, transport and waste, were given to new, joint boards (comprising representatives of the relevant borough councils). Many people questioned the lack of democratic control and accountability of these bodies.

Conservatives often viewed local authorities as unnecessary intermediary bodies standing between the users of public services and those who provided them. Legislation introduced by the Conservatives seeking to give parents a greater say in the schooling of their children: the Education Act 1996 created a right to 'express a preference' as to which local authority school their children would attend; the boards of governors of local authority schools were given responsibility for making decisions previously taken by local authorities – for example, on staff appointments and sex education policy; and parents of local authority schools were given the right to vote to 'opt out' of local authority control altogether and in future receive more favourable funding directly from central government (grant maintained schools).

4.4.3 'Established usage' as an alternative to democracy

Conservatives do not believe that democratically elected politicians are the only, or necessarily the best, people to make collective decisions. Tradition is regarded as an important source of legitimacy: an office holder or institution may justify its existence and powers by reason of its 'established usage' – its continuity and practical effectiveness:

> Conservatives contest the theory ... that the application of reason would make the world intelligible to man and that institutions designed by man in accordance with theoretical principles were the only institutions which would have beneficial consequences ... Conservatives reject the notion that it is a simple matter to design a constitution in accordance with abstract principles [Lansley, A and Wilson, R, *Conservatives and the Constitution*, 1997, London: Conservative 2000 Foundation; and see, also, Oakeshott, M, *Rationality in Politics*, 1962, London: Methuen].

Many conservative thinkers argue that the authority or legitimacy of government derives from the long established constitution, not from an abstract, overarching principle such as the need to promote individual freedom, nor from the principle of democracy. From this perspective, it is not self-evident to Conservatives that an institution such as the House of Lords, whose hereditary composition is, for modern thinkers, difficult to justify on a principle basis, ought to be reformed. Indeed, Mrs Thatcher created several new hereditary peerages during her time as Prime Minister. As a second chamber, the House of Lords in fact works, so why reform it? Conservatives, in the end, came to accept the need to extend the franchise for the House of Commons in the last century, but this was for pragmatic reasons – the need to accommodate the system of parliamentary government to changing social conditions – rather than a dogmatic belief that democracy should be an overriding principle spurring on constitutional change. For similar reasons, Conservatives strongly support the continuation of an hereditary monarchy.

4.4.4 Markets as an alternative to democracy

As well as valuing tradition as a source of authority, Conservatives believe that markets are useful mechanisms for making decisions and that they may, in some situations, be better than debate and voting by elected representatives. Many of the Conservative governments' reforms during 1979–97 were implemented to give effect to this belief. Replacing democratic institutions and public officials with market forces is called 'public choice' (for a critical assessment, see Self, P, *Government by the Market? The Politics of Public Choice*, 1993, London: Macmillan). A policy of privatisation became an important part of the Conservative government's programme after 1983. After the Second World War, many industries had been taken into State ownership – including coal mining, steel making, some vehicle manufacture and the telephone system (see above, 3.9.4). To the government, selling its interests in such industries to commercial enterprises and individual investors seemed a solution to several problems. One was that it would help stem government borrowing: when public corporations were turned into companies and the shares sold, this bought revenue into the Treasury; and loss making enterprises ceased to be a drain on public funds. The privatisation policy also fitted into the government's views that 'less government is good government', and that individuals could be empowered by owning property (including shares). By the 1990s, most of the nationalised industries had been sold off, including British Telecom (1984), British Gas (1986), British Airways (1987), British Aerospace (1981), British Airports Authority (1986), British Steel (1989), British Shipbuilders (1983), the regional water and electricity companies (1989) and British Rail (1997). In order to make markets work effectively, it was necessary to stimulate competition, but also to regulate prices and standards; an elaborate system of licensing and supervision by State regulatory bodies was therefore put in place (see below, 8.2.2).

As with the nationalised industries, the Conservative government saw the discipline of market forces and competition as tools which could be used to make local authorities more efficient in the way they provided services to their communities. The Local Government Act 1988 requires councils to advertise, inviting tenders from private businesses to carry out work such as catering in schools and old people's homes, maintenance of leisure facilities and refuse collection. The council's own workforce may also submit a tender, but they will only be allowed to carry out the work if they can show that they will provide better value for money than an outside contractor. Contracts to carry out specified jobs for a period of time (usually a year or more) are then entered into by each council. Compulsory competitive tendering was later extended to the professional services used by the councils themselves – for example, legal advice and conveyancing. The change has, therefore, been profound. One commentator writing in the 1980s even suggested that 'it is quite possible to envisage the local authority of the future as a set of contracts, and a network of internal and external trading' (Walsh, K, in Stewart, J and Stoker, G (eds), *The Future of Local Government*, 1989, London: Macmillan, p 30).

4.4.5   Conservatives and security and welfare

For Conservatives, the maintenance of law and order is one area in which strong powers are needed by State authorities. During the Conservative governments of 1979–97, legislation was introduced giving police and courts new powers over people accused of crimes. They considered that new laws were needed because guilty people were escaping conviction; critics argued that many developments diminished people's civil liberties and prevented fair trials taking place. The Criminal Justice and Public Order Act 1994 removed the so called 'right of silence' from defendants; at trial, judges could, therefore, direct juries to draw adverse inferences from the fact that a suspect said nothing when questioned by the police or decided not to give evidence in court. Critics said that this undermined a person's right to be presumed innocent until proved guilty by the prosecutor (see below, Chapter 21). New legislation was also introduced to strengthen police powers to maintain public order at demonstrations (see below, Chapter 25).

On the Welfare State, modern Conservatives accept that government has responsibility to provide a safety net for people living in poverty due to illness, unemployment and retirement. Because of the importance attached to keeping taxation levels low, benefits ought to be modest, and targeted at those who most need them by means testing.

4.4.6   Accountability and efficiency: the 'great codification'

The Conservative governments of 1979–97 were committed to creating constitutional arrangements to ensure that State authorities used their resources efficiently ('value for money') and that they were responsive to those who used their services. In part, these aims were pursued by the use of market forces, through compulsory competitive tendering and market testing (see above, 4.4.4), and also through a more vigorous system of financial auditing put in place by the National Audit Act 1983. They were also pursued through reform of the Civil Service. As we will see in more detail in Chapter 8, the functions of central government departments were split. A relatively small number of civil servants responsible for giving policy advice to ministers remained within each department, but all operational functions – the day to day practical delivery of services – were hived off to executive agencies linked to the department by a framework document setting out performance targets, but having a considerable degree of independence as to how those were to be met.

As well as identifying efficiency as an important principle, the last Conservative government sought to make State authorities more accountable and responsive to the people who used their services. The Citizen's Charter initiative launched in 1991, headed by a minister, required authorities dealing with the public to set out in a clear form what standard of service could be expected from them, and how people using that service could complain about failings (see Austin, R, 'Administrative law's reaction to the changing concepts of public service', in Leyland, P and Woods, T (eds), *Administrative Law Facing the Future*, 1997, London: Blackstone, Chapter 1). Thus, Customs and Excise put up posters in airport arrivals halls, explaining what their role was and how people would be treated. London Underground and British Rail were required to publish details of how often trains were late, and to provide compensation for users affected by serious delays. At the time, the Citizen's Charter initiative was derided by the Labour Party as banal and inadequate (although, as we shall see, when in government Labour has built on this initiative).

For Conservatives, these developments – compulsory competitive tendering, market testing, new forms of audit and the Citizen's Charter programme – represented a major change in constitutional culture: 'the "great codification" of hitherto internal custom and practice' (Willetts, D, *Blair's Gurus*, 1996, London: Centre for Policy Studies, p 70).

4.5   Labour and the constitution

Labour originated as a political organisation to represent trade unionists in the House of Commons; in 1906, it has 29 MPs. It formed its first (brief) government under Prime Minister Ramsay Macdonald in 1924; it formed a government in 1945, when it set about an ambitious programme of nationalisation and the development of the Welfare State (see above, 3.9.4). During its last long period out of government, from 1979 to 1997, the Labour party reinvented itself. It ceased to be have any commitment to government ownership of industries and infrastructure in the UK and abandoned its hostility or scepticism to the European Community. In 1995, the party symbolically altered clause IV of its constitution which had committed it:

> ... to secure for the workers by hand or by brain the full fruits of their industry and the most equitable distribution thereof that may be possible upon the basis of the common ownership of the means of production, distribution and exchange, and the best obtainable system of popular administration and control of each industry and service.

The new 'aims and values' are as follows:

1.   The Labour Party is a democratic socialist party. It believes that by the strength of our common endeavour we achieve more than we achieve alone, so as to create for each of us the means to realise our true potential

and for all of us a community in which power, wealth and opportunity are in the hands of the many and not the few, where the rights we enjoy reflect the duties we owe, and where we live together, freely, in a spirit of solidarity, tolerance and respect.

2   To these ends we work for:

A dynamic economy, serving the public interest, in which the enterprise of the market and the rigour of competition are joined with the forces of partnership and co-operation to produce the wealth the nation needs and the opportunity for all to work and prosper, with a thriving private sector and high quality public service, where those undertakings essential to the common good are either owned by the public or accountable to them;

A just society, which judges its strength by the condition of the weak as much as the strong, providing security against fear, and justice at work; which nurtures families, promotes equality of opportunity and delivers people from the tyranny of poverty, prejudice and the abuse of power;

An open democracy in which the government is held to account by the people; decisions are taken as far as practicable by the communities they effect; and where fundamental human rights are guaranteed;

A healthy environment, which we protect, enhance and hold in trust for future generations.

3   Labour is committed to the defence and security of the British people, and to co-operating in European institutions, the United Nations, the Commonwealth and other international bodies to secure peace, freedom, democracy, economic security and environmental protection for all.

4   Labour will work in pursuit of these aims with trade unions, co-operative societies and other affiliated organisations, and also with voluntary organisations, consumer groups and other representative bodies.

5   On the basis of these principles, Labour seeks the trust of the people to govern.

For many in the party, this new clause IV left 'only the most attenuated system of public ethics as Labour's core belief' (Rentoul, J, *Tony Blair*, 1997, London: Warner, p 419). Since forming the government in May 1997, Labour has worked on formulating a deeper and more comprehensive understanding of its mission, termed 'the Third Way'. The name adopted for these emerging principles is to distinguish it from market liberalism (which guided the Conservatives between 1979 and 1997) and the old socialism of State ownership (which once was at the core of Labour politics). Radical constitutional reform is a central feature of the Third Way project in the UK. As David Marquand explains:

New Labour ... has embarked on the most far-reaching programme of constitutional reform attempted in this country this century. Ironically, the Thatcherites deserve part of the credit. Old Labour was committed to the doctrines and practices of Westminster absolutism as were the Conservatives.

But in the Thatcher years, when Labour found itself on the receiving end of a ferocious centralism, far exceeding anything it had ever attempted itself, it underwent a death-bed conversion. Slowly at first, but with mounting enthusiasm, as time went on, it embraced most of the constitutional agenda originally put forward by the SDP-Liberal Alliance [the third main party during the 1980s, before the creation of the Liberal Democratic party], and later given a radical twist by Charter 88 ['The Blair paradox' (1998) *Prospect*, May, p 20].

Charter 88 is a pressure group, now with over 75,000 members, set up in 1988 to campaign for constitutional reform. Marquand may overstate its influence on Labour; certainly, there are several other pressure groups which share some of the credit (or blame) for Labour's programme – including Liberty, the Campaign for Freedom of Information, the Labour Campaign for Electoral Reform and the Scottish Constitutional Convention.

4.5.1 Labour and autonomy

The Third Way favours individual rights – but 'on the principle that strong communities must be the basis for individual freedom' (Robin Cook MP, quoted in (1998) *The New Statesman*, 1 May, p 22). Like the Conservatives, Labour is not committed to individualism; but, whereas the Conservatives attach importance to established institutions of civil society – voluntary associations such as the church, the family, charities – Labour uses the far more amorphous term 'community'. Anthony Giddens, director of the LSE and a leading intellectual force behind the development of the Third Way, explains that it is not libertarian:

> Individual freedom depends on collective resources and implies social justice. Government is not ... the enemy of freedom; on the contrary, good government is essential for its development and expansion [(1998) *New Statesman*, 1 May, p 19].

Labour was quick to incorporate the ECHR into British law during its first parliamentary session (see below, 19.10) and (somewhat more slowly) it drew up proposals for a Freedom of Information Act (see below, 24.8). Set alongside these initiatives, however, are laws designed to make 'communities' 'stronger' and 'safer' but which, at the same time, encroach on individual civil liberties and curtail long established constitutional safeguards against abuse of power (see below, 4.4.3). For Labour, rights to personal liberty are far from absolute; they have to be weighed against the desirability of government action aimed at community building. The ECHR is no obstacle to this anti-libertarian aim, as it, too, qualifies rights to personal liberty – including those of freedom of expression, privacy and freedom of association – with caveats that State authorities may curtail them to the extent necessary in a democratic society on the grounds of public safety, the prevention of disorder, the protection of health and morals and the rights of others (see below, 19.5).

In the economic sphere, the Third Way stands against market liberalism and in favour of balancing market forces with appropriate legal regulation. The catch-phrase 'better regulation' replaces the Conservatives' mantra of 'deregulation'. In the workplace, the Labour government has accepted the desirability of the Working Time Directive (long opposed by the Conservatives); and it introduced legislation requiring businesses to pay a minimum wage and to recognise trade unions.

4.5.2 Labour and democracy

The Third Way asserts that liberal democracy is failing 'because it isn't democratic enough ... To regain trust and legitimacy the Third Way advocates a thorough-going package of reforms, which taken together could be said to define a new democratic State' (Giddens, A (1998) *New Statesman*, 1 May, p 20). Unlike the Conservatives, Labour is not committed to the Nation State as the main unit of democratic decision making. As the new clause IV of the Labour Party constitution suggests (see above, 4.4), power is to be reallocated both downwards (to re-invigorated local authorities, cities with directly elected mayors, local referendums and to new assemblies in Wales and Northern Ireland and a Parliament in Scotland) and also upwards (to international bodies, including, especially, the European Union). The concept of 'subsidiarity', developed to explain the relationship between the European Union and its Member States (see below, 7.8.3) is also apt to describe this *whole* process.

The UK Parliament itself is to be 'modernised', with the removal of hereditary peers from the Lords and new procedures in the Commons (see below, Chapter 6). The democratic ideal of the Third Way is not the clash and debate between competing ideas, but the search for consensus and inclusion. Matthew Parris suggests that new Labour's:

> ... instincts are to move our democracy away from ... a bi-polar world of Punch and Judy, throw-the-buggers-out – and towards a political establishment offering more organic change: groupings and regroupings of men and ideas; constantly shifting focuses of power and influence; coalition; compromise; consensus. Under the surface, American politics are more like this. Continental constitutions encourage it too. We are the odd ones out [(1998) *The Times*, 1 May].

The Labour government has included members of another political party (the Liberal Democrats) in a Cabinet committee (see above, 2.4.3) and appointed as a minister someone who was not a member of the Labour Party (Gus Macdonald as Scottish Industry Minister in August 1998). Proportional representation and the creation of competing centres of power in Wales, Scotland, Northern Ireland and in local authorities (especially London) further this aim. With the enactment of the Human Rights Act 1998, British judges are going to have far greater scope for contributing to political debate, in the courtroom, about government policy as expressed in Acts of Parliament (see below, 19.12). One of the first actions by the Labour government was to confer on the Bank of England the power to set interest rates, something that had previously been done by the Chancellor of the Exchequer, answerable to the Commons.

David Marquand argues that the whole *point* of Labour's programme of constitutional reform 'is to dismantle the *ancien règime:* to create institutional and legal checks and balances which will make it impossible for future governments to impose their will on the society and economy in the way that the Thatcher governments did' ('The Blair paradox' (1998) *Prospect*, May, p 20). He adds that 'the process of constitutional change will almost certainly generate a dynamic of its own, carrying the transformation further than its authors intended or expected' (p 21). If this analysis is correct, the reform package will disable the constitution from providing a vehicle for future radical change throughout the UK directed by a government in Westminster. In this way, Labour's view of the constitution as pluralist and co-operative may be entrenched for years to come. This is, perhaps, an exaggeration. In several of its reforms, Labour has been careful to preserve at least the formality of parliamentary sovereignty. In the White Paper, *Rights Brought Home*, Cm 3782, 1997, the government spoke of the importance it attached to this concept and, accordingly, the Human Rights Act 1998 stops short of empowering the courts to strike down statutory provisions incompatible with the ECHR (see below, 5.2.5). The Scotland Act 1998 and the Northern Ireland Act 1998 preserve the right of the UK Parliament to enact legislation for the whole of the UK (see above, 2.4.2).

4.5.3   Labour on security and welfare

Labour recognises that defence and some aspects of policing in the modern world need to be organised on an international, rather than purely national basis (see clause IV). Like the previous Conservative government, Labour has committed itself to strengthening the legal powers of the police and to diminishing the rights of defendants. The Youth Justice and Criminal Evidence Act 1999 restricts the rights of defendants in rape and sexual assault trials to cross-examine complainants. Labour enthusiastically took up and extended the Conservatives' initiative to create the sex offenders' register; the Sex Offenders Act 1997 makes people who have been convicted and *already punished* for a sex offence against a minor subject to requirements that they report their movements to the police for a period of up to 10 years. The Home Office regards the register not as a punishment, but a measure to protect the public. Under the Crime and Disorder Act 1998, people on the register may be made subject to a sex offenders' order. This new form of legal control will work in a similar way to the much wider community safety order (CSO), which gives courts powers to impose injunctions on individuals responsible for 'anti-social behaviour' which causes distress or fear 'in the community'.

The CSOs require named individuals not to carry out, cause or permit to be carried out specified conduct for a minimum of two years. The orders are made according to the civil standard of proof (that, on the balance of probabilities, the anti-social activity alleged to have taken place did take place) rather than the criminal standard (beyond reasonable doubt). Breach of a CSO is a criminal offence punishable by up to five years' imprisonment.

In the economic sphere, the Third Way sees unrestrained free markets as a major source of social instability. It accepts the analysis of commentators such as John Gray (see above, 1.6.3) that communities and families have been undermined the casualisation of labour (short term contracts, low wages). A central role for government is to facilitate education and training for people.

For Labour, rights to benefit from State run services are to be defined so as to 'reflect the duties we owe' (see above, 4.4). Once in power, Labour decided to continue with the Citizen's Charter initiative (see above, 4.4.6) – but with an added twist. Thus, for example, the Department of Health announced in 1997 that the Patients' Charter would be developed to reflect the 'partnership' between patients and the NHS. The new NHS Charter will reflect not only the patients' rights to treatment, but also focus on *their responsibilities* – for example, to treat NHS staff with respect, to turn up on time for appointments and not to make unnecessary night time calls to GPs. Mary Warnock despairs of this trend:

> Of course it is good to set out what the various services hope to provide. But this is very different from issuing a charter of rights. In despair the National Health Service has started to argue that the patients' charter entails duties as well as rights for patients. But this is based on a total confusion. If rights and duties are correlative ... it is in the sense that the right of a patient to treatment entails the duty of the health service to provide it. It is not the case that no one can have a right who does not himself have some duty, though this may be so in the case of contracts ... But the poor health service is now saying that the patients' charter entails the duty on patients not to call out their doctors on frivolous grounds, or not to put their feet on the chairs in the waiting area. This was never part of the charter, which was unconditional [*An Intelligent Person's Guide to Ethics*, 1998, London: Duckworth, pp 70–71].

The Labour government has also emphasised people's responsibilities in relation to receiving jobseeker's allowance by continuing policies begun by the previous Conservative government: entitlement to many welfare benefits is now dependent on a claimant demonstrating, in ever more stringent ways, that they are actively seeking employment, or on requiring attendance at training schemes.

4.5.4 Conservative response to Labour reforms

In his lecture to the Centre for Policy Studies in February 1998 (see above, 4.2), William Hague MP said:

... I believe there is only one practical Conservative response to Labour's constitutional upheaval. We will need to adopt our own programme of constitutional reform. We will have to correct the dangerous imbalances and tensions which Labour's constitutional reforms will unleash. We must seek to construct a set of constitutional relationships which will preserve the key, overarching principles of our existing constitution: limited government, the rule of law, the unity of the kingdom and, above all, democratic accountability.

It has not been difficult to point to problems with Labour's programme. Lord Cranborne criticises the 'crass and ignorant approach' that Labour has adopted to parliamentary reform, dealing with the Commons and Lords separately and having no firm plans as to how to constitute the reformed upper House ((1996) *The Times*, 11 October, p 20). There is, however, little evidence yet that the Conservatives have a coherent vision of their own as to the type of constitutional system they want to see in the 21st century.

4.6 Conclusion

This chapter has revealed several things about the contribution of political parties to the development of constitutional principles. The constitutional system is not a set of neutral and static arrangements and principles which elected politicians inherit and are constrained by. Rather, the constitutional system is something which politicians have the power to reshape in order to further their political projects. Constitutional reform was important to the last Conservative government's term of office (though they did not use the term) and is now central to Labour's programme. Unlike our forebears (see above, Chapter 3) or academics (see below, Chapter 5), politicians competing for governmental power have the real ability to put into practice their beliefs about a good constitutional system. Some commentators suggest that the reforms currently being put in place will disable future governments from using the powers of central government and its majority in the UK Parliament to make far-reaching changes (see above, 4.5.2).

POLITICIANS AND THEIR PRINCIPLES

For politicians in the main UK political parties, modifying important features of the constitutional system has been, and is, a central vehicle for their wider political projects to change society. Journalists and other critics have accused both Labour and the Conservatives of having ill formed and incoherent visions of the constitution. It is, nevertheless, possible to identify principles underpinning the Conservative view of the constitution on the one hand, and on the other, those of Labour and the Liberal Democrats.

Conservatives and the constitution

By inclination, Conservatives are hostile or sceptical of most public authorities, seeing them as a threat to individual freedom. The Conservative governments of 1979–97 pursued policies aimed 'rolling back the frontiers of the State'. Conservative beliefs attach importance to the roles played by traditional voluntary organisations such as Christian churches and the family – sometimes believing that government should intervene to protect them. For Conservatives, the main unit of democratic decision making ought to be the Nation State and the UK Parliament. The transfer of powers to devolved institutions in Scotland and Wales and to the European Union are, on the whole, opposed. Local authorities are thought to be service providers rather than a highly politicised tier of government. Conservatives do not believe that democratically elected representatives are the only, or the best, people to make collective decisions. Tradition is regarded as an important source of legitimacy and so the presence of hereditary peers in the UK Parliament is not objectionable in principle. Markets are also regarded as a useful mechanism for decision making as an alternative to that by elected representatives. Most Conservatives accept the need for a Welfare State, but benefits should be modest and targeted at the most deserving.

Labour and the Liberal Democrats on the constitution

The Labour Party has transformed itself from one with a formal commitment to State ownership of the means of production into a social democratic party committed to 'the Third Way'. On the constitution, it shares many of the views of the Liberal Democrats. Individual autonomy is, up to a point, seen as important – but the existence of individual rights implies also the existence of duties and responsibilities. Labour is not committed to the Nation State as the main unit of collective decision making. Power ought to be reallocated both downwards (to local authorities and devolved institutions for Scotland, Wales and Northern Ireland) and upwards (to the European Union and international organisations, such as NATO). Unrestrained market forces are regarded as a major source of social instability, and so they ought to be regulated by public authorities.

CHAPTER 5

TEXTBOOK WRITERS AND THEIR PRINCIPLES

5.1   Introduction

In the absence of a codified constitutional document in the UK (see above, 1.7.2 and 2.2), generations of law students have been introduced to the constitutional system primarily through the use of textbooks. For better or worse, one long dead textbook writer, Professor Albert Dicey, continues to have a firm foothold in many expositions of the British Constitution by present day writers, and even in the speeches of a few politicians (see above, 4.2). No doubt some modern writers overemphasise the relevance of his thinking to present day conditions. It is something of an exaggeration to say of his best known book, *An Introduction to the Study of the Law of the Constitution* (1st edn, 1885, London: Macmillan), that 'Dicey's word has in some respects become the only written constitution we have' (Jowell, J and Oliver, D (eds), *The Changing Constitution*, 3rd edn, 1994, Oxford: OUP, p v). What is not in doubt, however, is that his analysis still acts as an important point of reference. Questions about this 'Dicey phenomenon' should cross the minds of inquisitive students soon after they begin their studies. Are the views of this one professor of law really so important that, over 100 years after its first publication, his book continues to be on students' reading lists? How can Dicey's work still be relevant to the modern constitution? We need, therefore, to conclude the search for the source of principles by providing a brief critical assessment of what Dicey said about the British Constitution. This book, like many others, will return to Dicey's views, especially in relation to three features of the constitution – parliamentary sovereignty, the rule of law and constitutional conventions. The purpose of the present chapter is to provide an overview of Dicey's thinking on these matters.

5.1.1   A biographical sketch

Albert Venn Dicey was born in 1835 into a middle class, evangelical Christian family; he died, aged 87, in 1922. His life, therefore, spanned a period of great change in government and administration (see above, 3.8–3.9.2). He witnessed the establishment of parliamentary democracy, the Victorian reforms of the Civil Service, the 'administrative revolution' and the formation of an independent Irish State. He was a well known figure during his lifetime and, it is said, twice refused a knighthood. (Had he lived in the 1990s, he would undoubtedly have been a panellist on television and radio programmes such as *Question Time* and *Any Questions*).

Throughout his life, he suffered from a muscular weakness which often made it difficult for him even to write. He failed exams more than once because the examiners could not read his handwriting. His prose style, though, was a model of clarity and succinctness. After graduating from Oxford, he practised at the Bar for several years with no outstanding success. He continued to write articles, regularly had letters published in *The Times* and wrote a book. In 1882, at the age of 47, he was appointed to a chair at his old university and it was as an academic that he exerted a profound influence, though his aspirations were to be an MP or a judge. During his 27 years at Oxford, he wrote two monumental books, both of which are still much used, discussed and criticised: *Introduction to the Study of the Law of the Constitution* (the edition most often used today is the 10th edition, published after Dicey's death with an introduction by Professor ECS Wade in 1959, London: Macmillan) and *Law and Public Opinion in England* (1st edn, 1905, London: Macmillan).

Dicey's political views were those of a market liberal, meaning he had a commitment to individualism and free trade (see above, 1.6.1). Above all, he was against 'State collectivism', believing there was a contradiction between such 'socialism' and democracy. He was concerned by the increasing State regulation of economic activity and the growing provision of services by government. Of all the particular political causes with which Dicey was involved, his strongest pronouncements were about Home Rule and independence for Ireland. He was a passionate, obsessive Unionist and opposed all proposals that any part of Ireland should cease to be part of the UK (see above, 3.9.2). For Dicey, the maintenance of the UK was of fundamental importance, and one of his answers to the growing civil unrest in Ireland was to advocate suspending trial by jury. The Irish Free State came into being shortly after Dicey's death.

Dicey was also outspoken in his opposition to the vote for women, arguing, among other things, that 'nor can it be forgotten not only that women are physically and probably mentally weaker than men, but that they are mentally, as a class, burdened with duties of the utmost national importance, and of an absorbing and exhausting nature, from which men are free' – by which he meant motherhood ('Letters to a friend on votes for women', see McAuslan, P and McEldowney, J (eds), *Law, Legitimacy and the Constitution*, 1985, London: Sweet & Maxwell).

5.1.2 How to read Dicey

Dicey's *Introduction to the Study of the Law of the Constitution* started out as a series of lectures given to undergraduates at the University of Oxford in the 1880s. The book was a runaway success with law students everywhere, not least because of its easy, clear style. They 'were attracted by Dicey's convenient format which encouraged certainty and precision in a subject which was vague and imprecise' (McEldowney, J, 'Dicey in historical perspective – a review essay', in McAuslan, P and McEldowney, J (eds), *Law, Legitimacy and the Constitution*, 1985, London: Sweet & Maxwell, p 41). Dicey's book is arranged around three features of the constitution, as Dicey saw it:

(a) the sovereignty of Parliament;

(b) the rule of law; and

(c) constitutional conventions.

Dicey was not, of course, the first writer to describe and analyse these features of the constitution. In relation to parliamentary sovereignty, for instance, William Blackstone had set down a definition more than a century before when he wrote: 'The power and jurisdiction of parliament, says Sir Edward Coke, is so transcendent and absolute, that it cannot be confined, either for causes or persons, within bounds' (*Commentaries on the Laws of England*, 1765–69). In many respects, Dicey's fame rests on his powers as a popular writer, rather than on being a wholly novel analyst.

It is important to understand not just each of the features of the constitution (set out above) in isolation, but also Dicey's attempt to explain their interrelationships. The last edition of the book to be revised by Dicey himself was in 1908. How should the book be read more than 90 years on? Professor ECS Wade has suggested three possible approaches (see his introduction in *Introduction to the Study of the Law of the Constitution*, 10th edn, 1959, London: Macmillan, p xxviii):

(i) to accept Dicey's principles, and more particularly the sovereignty of Parliament and the rule of law, as portraying only the period of which he wrote;

(ii) to regard these principles critically and in the light of future events to admit that they were only partially true of the 19th century and certainly inapplicable today;

(iii) to accept these principles, supplemented if need be by later developments, and to show how they can be fitted into modern public law.

5.1.3 Dicey's critics

A strange feature of the Dicey phenomenon is that almost everyone disagrees with all, most or some of his analysis. As one commentator has put it, for us to continue to focus on Dicey's work 'is to belabour a horse which is thought to have died so long ago, after assaults so numerous and savage, that humane considerations might dictate another line of investigation' (Arthurs, HW, 'Rethinking administrative law: a slightly Dicey business' (1979) 17 Osgoode Hall LJ 1, p 4). One early, influential riposte to Dicey came from Professor Sir Ivor Jennings, who was professor of law at the London School of Economics, then Cambridge. Jennings was a Fabian socialist who welcomed the increasing government regulation of business and social security provision, and who shared none of Dicey's hostility to the interventionist State. Jennings' own book (*The Law and the Constitution* (1st edn, 1933), 5th edn, 1958, London: London UP) criticised the whole scope of Dicey's analysis, arguing that Dicey failed to deal with the powers of government: Dicey 'seemed to think that the British Constitution was concerned almost entirely with the *rights of individuals*' (p 55). In fact, even when Dicey was writing, central and local government had considerable discretionary legal powers to carry out all sorts of functions, from the compulsory purchase of land to restricting overseas trade. Jennings also makes more specific criticisms of Dicey's analysis of parliamentary sovereignty, the rule of law and the nature of conventions, which we consider below. Jennings' assessment was that Dicey 'honestly tried ... to analyse [the constitution], but, like most, he saw the constitution through his own spectacles, and his own vision was not exact' (p 316).

5.2   Dicey's understanding of parliamentary sovereignty

In Chapter 1 of *An Introduction to the Study of the Law of the Constitution*, Dicey argues that 'the sovereignty of Parliament is (from a legal point of view) the dominant characteristic of our political institutions'. This means that the Queen in Parliament has 'under the English Constitution, the right to make or unmake any law whatever; and, further, that no person or body is recognised by the law of England as having a right to override or set aside the legislation of Parliament'. Dicey distinguished this legal sovereignty from *political* sovereignty, which, he argued, lay with the electors, whose views were represented in Parliament by MPs. Parliament's legal sovereignty was, as a matter of reality, limited externally by the possibility that a large number of subjects might disobey or resist laws. There was also an internal check on sovereign legislative power – 'the moral feelings of the time and society' which MPs, including those in government, shared. Dicey claimed that representative government produced a coincidence between the external and internal limits on sovereign legislative power.

In Chapter 2, Dicey goes on to contrast the powers of Parliament and non-sovereign law making bodies (such as local authorities, railway companies empowered to make bylaws and legislatures in federal systems). He details the characteristics of Parliament. First: 'There is no law which Parliament cannot change ... so called constitutional laws can be changed by the same body and in the same manner as any laws, namely by Parliament acting in its ordinary legislative character.' Secondly, there is no marked or clear distinction between laws which are not fundamental (or constitutional) and laws which are. There is no written constitutional statute or charter. Pausing here, we may note that it was these two features which, for Dicey, made entrenching legislation impossible in the British system.

Thirdly, no judicial body can pronounce void any enactment passed by Parliament on the ground of such enactment being contrary to the constitution or any other ground whatever (except, of course, its being repealed by Parliament). Earlier, Dicey had demonstrated that the courts will not inquire into any alleged irregularities in parliamentary procedure. Nor is the fact that an Act is contrary to international law or morality any basis for the courts declaring it invalid.

In Chapter 3, Dicey then compares the system of parliamentary sovereignty in Britain with systems of federal government, especially those of the US and Switzerland. He argues that a federal State derived its existence from the constitution just as any corporation (such as a railway company!) did from the charter by which it was created. This meant that the constitution of federal countries must necessarily be 'written' and 'rigid'. The distribution of powers was also an essential feature of federalism which led to weak government. Federalism also tended to produce conservatism and 'legalism' (the predominance of the judiciary in the constitution).

5.2.1 Dicey's conception of democracy

Before moving on, we need here to note in a little more detail the way in which Dicey conceived of democracy – something which underlies both his approach to parliamentary sovereignty and the rule of law. Paul Craig, in his challenging book *Public Law and Democracy in the UK and USA* (1990, Oxford: Clarendon), explains that Dicey's approach to the British Constitution was based on 'certain assumptions concerning representative democracy and the way it operated' (p 13). Dicey's vision of democracy was one 'in which the will of the electors was expressed through Parliament, and in which Parliament controlled the government' (p 30). As we have already noted, Dicey thought that MPs reflected the views of the majority of electors; if they did not, this would be 'corrected' at the next general election. It is not at all clear, Craig suggests, how 'Dicey would prevent or forestall the danger of majority oppression' of minorities. If the majority in Parliament enacted legislation which detrimentally affected minority interests, the common law (which, as we shall see shortly, is a key feature of Dicey's conception of the rule of law) could not protect rights, because the principle of parliamentary sovereignty would prevail. In any event, Craig argues, Dicey's image of the British Constitution was flawed even when he wrote, and is certainly no longer sustainable today. Dicey thought that power moved in one direction: from the electors, via Parliament, to the government. But the reality was always more complex; even in Dicey's time 'our constitutional system became one dominated by the top, by the executive and the party hierarchy' (p 42). It needs also to be remembered that Dicey did not regard all adults as fit to participate in the election process: he opposed women's suffrage (see above, 5.1.1).

5.2.2 Jennings attacks Dicey's view of parliamentary sovereignty

Even though Jennings, too, saw Parliament's legislative power as central to the British constitutional system, he was scathing in his criticism of Dicey's version of parliamentary sovereignty. First, he regretted that Dicey used the ambiguous term 'sovereignty' in this context:

> ... this is a word of quasi-theological origin which may easily lead us into difficulties. Sovereignty was a doctrine developed at the close of the Middle Ages to advance the cause of the secular Stage against the claims of the Church ... if sovereignty is supreme power, Parliament is not sovereign [*The Law and the Constitution*, 5th edn, 1958, London: London UP, pp 147–48].

Jennings did not believe that 'legal sovereignty' in the sense described by Dicey was sovereignty at all: it was not supreme power. Rather, for Jennings, 'it is a legal concept, a form of expression which lawyers use to express the relations between Parliament and the courts. It means that the courts will always recognise as law the rules which Parliament makes by legislation' (p 149).

Jennings then goes on to argue (p 150) that Dicey's comparison of sovereign and non-sovereign legislatures is 'entirely beside the point' and ridicules Dicey's suggestion that a local authority in England and the Parliament of Canada share characteristics because they are both non-sovereign. Jennings states that, 'if sovereignty is merely a legal phrase for legal authority to pass any sort of laws, it is not entirely ridiculous to say that a legislature is sovereign in respect of certain subjects, for it may then pass any sort of laws on those subjects, but not on any other subjects' (p 151).

Jennings also attacks Dicey's assertion that a sovereign Parliament was incapable of entrenching legislation. 'Entrenchment' is the process whereby, in some constitutional systems, laws dealing with basic constitutional arrangements and human rights are given a protected status; the legislature may repeal or amend them only by following a special procedure such as a two-thirds vote in favour. Dicey denied that entrenchment was possible in the British system, citing several instances in which Acts with purported entrenchments of their own provisions (as in the Union with Scotland Act 1706) had in fact been repealed or amended by Bills in subsequent Parliaments following the usual parliamentary procedures. For Jennings, the true rule was that 'the courts accept as law that which is made in the proper legal form' (p 152) because 'legal sovereignty' was just the name for the rule that the legislature has, for the time being, power to make laws of any kind in the manner required by the law. Parliament was, therefore, capable of entrenching legislation because the power to change the law *included the power to change the law affecting itself.*

5.2.3 Can the common law provide a basis for declaring Acts of Parliament unconstitutional?

In addition to Jennings' general critique, written in the 1930s, several other characteristics of our modern constitution seem, at first sight, to undermine Dicey's conception of parliamentary sovereignty, perhaps catastrophically. First, some senior judges have, in recent extra-judicial writings, suggested that, in extreme circumstances, a British court would apply common law principles and hold that an Act of Parliament was legally ineffective on the ground that it was inconsistent with a fundamental constitutional principle – something which Dicey vehemently rejected. Lord Woolf has written (*'Droit public* – English style' [1995] PL 57, p 69):

> If Parliament did the unthinkable, then I would say that the courts would also be required to act in a manner which would be without precedent. Some judges might chose to do so by saying that it was an unrebuttable presumption that Parliament could never intend such a result. I myself would consider that there were advantages in making it clear that ultimately there are even limits on the supremacy of Parliament which it is the court's inalienable responsibility to identify and uphold. They are limits of the most modest dimensions which I believe any democrat would accept. They are no more than are necessary to enable the rule of law to be preserved.

The type of oppressive legislation which Lord Woolf has in mind is a statute depriving Jews of their British nationality, or one which prohibits marriages between Christians and non-Christians, or vests the property of all red haired women in the State. At least one other judge, Laws LJ, shares Lord Woolf's opinion ('Law and democracy' [1995] PL 72) and Lord Cooke of Thorndon, while a judge in New Zealand, spoke of the possibility that some common law rights lie so deep that even Parliament cannot override them: see *Fraser v State Services Commission* (1984) and *Taylor v New Zealand Poultry Board* (1984).

Such comments by serving judges, made during the 1990s, reflect both a resurgence of judicial self-confidence about their place in the constitutional order and a re-assertion of 'rights talk' (see below, Chapter 19). For most of the 20th century, judges explained the legitimacy of their power of judicial review of the legality of governmental decisions in terms of the *ultra vires* principle (the notion that the main role for the court is to ensure that ministers, local authorities and other public bodies do not overstep the powers granted to them, or duties imposed upon them, by statutes – see below, 11.3). *Ultra vires* provides no constitutional basis for a court to declare legally invalid an Act of Parliament itself. During the 1980s and 1990s, some innovative judges have come to rely on justifications for judicial review which are based on a conception of democracy in which people have fundamental rights against the State, to be protected, in the last resort, by the courts. These rights include freedom of expression and access to justice. For some judges, such as Woolf and Laws, it has been only a short jump from saying that ministers and other public bodies must not infringe fundamental rights to saying, or hinting, that nor must Parliament itself. These suggestions that the common law may provide a basis for a court refusing to recognise the validity of an Act of Parliament do, however, need to be kept in perspective. They were made outside the courtroom and so carry no formal precedent value; they are clearly intended to apply in only the clearest and most extreme situations; and it is far from certain that other members of the judiciary share such views. Above all, it needs to be borne in mind that the comments of Lord Woolf and Laws LJ were made before the enactment of the Human Rights Act 1998, which now provides a statutory basis upon which the courts may hold a statutory provision incompatible with fundamental rights (see below, Chapter 19). On balance, then, Dicey's assertion that the courts have no *common law* powers to refuse to apply statutes continues to have broad support.

5.2.4 The power of the courts to 'disapply' statutory provisions as incompatible with European Community law

A second challenge to Dicey's understanding of parliamentary sovereignty comes from the UK's membership of the European Union. As we have already noted (see above, 2.3), laws enacted by the institutions of the European Community and the case law of the European Court of Justice are required by Community law to take priority over any other law in each of the Member States (see, further, 7.9.1). On several occasions, courts in the UK have, accordingly, held that provisions contained in an Act of Parliament are legally ineffective. In *R v Secretary of State for Transport ex p Factortame Ltd (No 3)* (1992), provisions in the Merchant Shipping Act 1988 which sought to restrict the right to register fishing vessels in the UK to British owned companies and individuals, were set aside. It was held that this condition of registration was inconsistent with the right of freedom of establishment set out in the EC Treaty. In *R v Secretary of State for Employment ex p Equal Opportunities Commission* (1995), the House of Lords held that provisions in Employment Protection (Consolidation) Act 1978 were indirectly discriminatory against women and were thus contrary to European Community law.

This power vested in the courts to adjudicate on the legal validity of Acts of Parliament seems, at first sight, to be quite contrary to Dicey's version of parliamentary sovereignty. It is, however, possible to attempt a reconciliation in the following way. The power of British courts to 'disapply' provisions of Acts of Parliament as contrary to Community law falls short of a power to 'pronounce void' an enactment 'on the ground of such enactment being contrary to the constitution' (in Dicey's words). This is because the court in this situation is merely faithfully following the will of Parliament as expressed in ss 2 and 3 of the European Communities Act 1972. Although set out in complex language, those sections require judges to give effect to the principle of priority of Community law over national law. If it thought desirable to do so (the argument goes), Parliament could repeal or modify ss 2 and 3 of the 1972 Act (as it can any other Act) and so once again require British judges to recognise the supremacy of Acts of Parliament over all other laws, including those of the European Community. There has, in other words, been a delegation of legislative power by Parliament to the European Community (just as Parliament delegates some rule making powers to ministers and local authorities), which may at any time be revoked and the powers once again be exercised by Parliament itself. This argument, it has to be said, has an air of unreality and sophistry about it. So long as the UK remains a member of the European Union (as surely it will for the foreseeable future), then ss 2 and 3 will remain in place. If some other, later Act of Parliament on a particular subject sought to enact a rule inconsistent with Community law, but expressly stated that the rule was to be treated as valid by British courts 'notwithstanding any incompatibility with Community law' (or some such formula), it is unclear how a British court would deal with the issue. To understand what might happen, we need, however, to delve into several technical matters, and this we will do in Chapter 7. The conclusion there will be that, while the UK remains a member of the European Union, British courts are unlikely to recognise as valid provisions in a future Act of Parliament which expressly enacts laws contrary to Community law (see below, 7.8.1).

5.2.5 The Human Rights Act 1998

As we shall see in more detail later, most of the rights set out in the European Convention on Human Rights (ECHR) were brought into national law by the Human Rights Act 1998 (see below, Chapter 19). Under s 4, the higher courts (in England and Wales this means the High Court, the Court of Appeal and the House of Lords) are empowered to make 'declarations of incompatibility', by which it is formally held that a statutory provision is inconsistent with the ECHR, as interpreted by the British courts. Such a declaration will not invalidate an offending provision in a statute, but merely alert Parliament to the conflict. In its White Paper, *Rights Brought Home*, Cm 3782, 1997, London: HMSO, the Labour government was careful to explain that this constitutional innovation did not undermine the concept of parliamentary sovereignty (para 2.13):

> The Government has reached the conclusion that the courts should not have the power to set aside primary legislation, past or future, on the ground of incompatibility with the Convention. This conclusion arises from the importance which the Government attaches to Parliamentary sovereignty ... To make provision in the Bill for the courts to set aside Acts of Parliament would confer on the judiciary a general power over the decisions of Parliament which under our present constitutional arrangements they do not possess, and would be likely on occasions to draw the judiciary into serious conflict with Parliament. There is no evidence to suggest that they desire this power, nor that the public wish them to have it.

This disappointed many of those people who campaigned for incorporation of the ECHR into national law. These critics argued that the Human Rights Act conferred insufficient power on the courts to insist upon the constitutional invalidity of offending statutory provisions. Under the Human Rights Act, the government is under no legally enforceable duty to introduce legislation rectifying any infringement identified by the court; and nor is Parliament itself under any compulsion to approve legislation which the government does choose to introduce following a declaration of incompatibility.

Another disappointing feature of the Human Rights Act, according to some people, is that it does not 'entrench' itself into the UK legal systems. You will recall that entrenchment means that a piece of legislation is given a protected status, making it capable of being repealed or amended only by a special procedure (such as requiring two thirds of MPs to vote in favour, or for there to be a referendum). For Dicey, parliamentary sovereignty meant that such entrenchment was not possible (see above, 5.2.2). In *Rights Brought Home*, the government appeared to agree with this:

> 2.16   On one view, human rights legislation is so important that it should be given added protection from subsequent amendment or repeal. The Constitution of the United States of America, for example, guarantees rights which can be amended or repealed only by securing qualified majorities in both the House of Representatives and the Senate, and among the States themselves. But an arrangement of this kind could not be reconciled with our own constitutional traditions, which allow any Act of Parliament to be amended or repealed by a subsequent Act of Parliament. We do not believe that it is necessary or would be desirable to attempt to devise such a special arrangement for [the Human Rights Bill].

Although, at first sight, the Human Rights Act seems to be an important constitutional innovation, in formal terms it does not undermine the concept of parliamentary sovereignty popularised by Dicey. What remains to be seen, however, is the extent to which its practical impact may turn out to be a rebalancing of the constitutional relationship between Parliament and the courts. Dicey argued that written constitutions and codified rights legislation in other jurisdictions led to the 'predominance of the judiciary in the constitution'. This may yet turn out to be so in the UK.

5.3   Dicey's view of the rule of law

Let us now move on to consider the second of the main characteristics of the British Constitution discussed by Dicey. In Chapter 4 of *An Introduction to the Study of the Law of the Constitution*, Dicey argues for the importance of the rule of law, which he claimed meant three specific things in Britain.

First, that government officials did not have 'wide, arbitrary or discretionary powers of constraint' (p 188). This meant that no man could be punished or be made 'to suffer in body or goods' except for a distinct breach of law established in the ordinary legal manner before the ordinary courts of the land. He warns sternly 'that wherever there is discretion there is room for arbitrariness [which] must mean insecurity for legal freedom on the part of its subjects'. Dicey's distrust of discretionary powers in the hands of the executive stemmed at least in part from his view that it was only through *Parliament*, which represented the views of the nation, that government ought to be able to affect people's rights. As an adherent to *laissez faire* liberalism, he was also against government regulation in principle (see above, 5.1.1).

A second meaning is that 'every man, whatever be his rank or condition, is subject to the ordinary law of the realm and amenable to the jurisdiction of the ordinary tribunals'. Dicey was not thinking about treating aristocrats and farm labourers equally; rather, he meant that government officials, policemen, ministers, tax collectors, etc, could be sued in tort if they conducted their official duties unlawfully. There was no special body of law administered by tribunals which gave immunity to State officials. (Dicey chose to ignore the common law immunity from being sued which judges enjoyed – and still do. He also ignored the legal position of 'the Crown'; at the time, there were considerable procedural hurdles facing anyone attempting to sue a government department.)

Thirdly, the rule of law meant that 'the constitution is the result of the ordinary law of the land'. The general principles of the constitution to do with civil liberties, such as the right of personal liberty and freedom of assembly, were the result or consequence of judicial decisions in cases where individuals sued government officials. This was to be contrasted with countries which had a supreme written constitution where the rights of individuals resulted from the general principles embodied in that document. In Chapters 5–10, Dicey examined certain areas of substantive rights, including the rights to personal freedom, freedom of discussion and of public meeting.

In Chapter 13, Dicey addresses what many later critics identify as the major weakness in his analysis: the relationship between parliamentary sovereignty and the rule of law. He concedes that there might appear to be tensions – or even a contradiction – between these 'two principles which pervade the whole of the English constitution'. Parliamentary sovereignty means that the legislature can legally do whatever it wants to by enacting a statute; but the rule of law means, in part, that common law principles established by judges protect the civil liberties of subjects. In reality, there was no conflict, Dicey argued, for two reasons. His analysis at this point becomes a little hard to follow. First, he states, 'The sovereignty of Parliament favours the supremacy of the law of the land' (p 406). The will of Parliament can only be expressed through an Act of Parliament which gives great authority to the judges who must interpret the words used in the statute. The principle that Parliament speaks only through an Act of Parliament greatly increases the authority of the judges in the constitution. Also, Parliament, though sovereign, cannot interfere with the day to day administration of justice.

A second main reason why there is no conflict between the two principles is that the 'supremacy of the law necessitates the exercise of Parliamentary sovereignty' (p 411). Dicey argued that the 'rigidity of the law' sometimes prevented government action; in which case the executive needed to obtain from Parliament 'the discretionary authority which is denied to the Crown by the ordinary law of the land'. In other words, statutes do sometimes confer discretionary powers on ministers, local authorities and other public bodies – but these 'powers are never really unlimited, for they are confined to the words of the Act itself, and, what is more, by the interpretation put on the statute by the judges' (p 413). In interpreting statutes, judges 'are disposed to construe statutory exceptions to common law principles in a mode which would not commend itself either to a body of officials, or to the Houses of Parliament, if the Houses were called upon to interpret their own enactments'. His conclusion (p 414), stronger on rhetoric than systematic analysis, is that:

> By every path we come round to the same conclusion, that Parliamentary sovereignty has favoured the rule of law, and that the supremacy of the law of the land both calls forth the exertion of Parliamentary sovereignty, and leads to its being exercised in a spirit of legality.

5.3.1 Jennings' criticisms of Dicey's rule of law

In Appendix II of his book, Jennings considers Dicey's theory of the rule of law. In relation to Dicey's first meaning (the absence of arbitrary and discretionary powers), Jennings explains that what Dicey really meant was that 'wide administrative or executive powers are likely to be abused *and therefore ought not to be conferred'* (*The Law and the Constitution*, 5th edn, 1958, London: London UP, p 307, emphasis added). But the discretionary powers of ministers and local authorities were as much part of the 'regular' law of the land as any others. And while, of course, occasional abuse of power might occur, this was no reason for not conferring discretionary powers on officials. These powers, remember, were used to ensure things like minimum standards of health and safety in workplaces and to clear slum housing. This, Jennings said, was of no interest to Dicey:

> Dicey ... was much more concerned with the constitutional relations between Great Britain and Ireland than with the relations between poverty and disease on the one hand, and the new industrial system on the other. In internal politics, therefore, he was concerned not with the clearing up of the nasty industrial sections of towns, but with the liberty of the subject. In terms of powers, he was concerned with police powers, and not with other administrative powers [pp 310–11].

In relation to Dicey's second definition of the rule of law (equality before the law), Jennings flatly denied that there was any equality between the rights and duties of an official and that of an ordinary person. Dicey surely realised this, but had chosen to ignore the public law position of officials – for example, the duty of local authorities to provide education to children and the powers of the tax inspectors to demand information. Dicey was only writing about the position in tort law – not public law. While it was true that, generally, officials could be sued personally by an aggrieved citizen for a tortious act or omission in the course of their duty, Jennings' withering retort was that 'this is a small point upon which to base a doctrine called by the magnificent name of "rule of law", particularly when it is generally used in a very different sense' (p 312).

Lastly, Jennings questioned Dicey's proposition that the rule of law meant that 'the constitution is *the result* of the ordinary law of the land' rather than a constitutional code. Jennings could not see Dicey's point. 'I do not understand,' wrote Jennings, 'how it is correct to say that the rules are the consequence of the rights of individuals and not their source. The powers of the Crown and of other administrative authorities are limited by the rights of individuals; or the rights of individuals are limited by the powers of the administration. Both statements are correct; and both powers and rights come from the law – from the rules' (p 314).

5.3.2 The rule of law and Parliament

Everyone agrees that an important principle within our constitutional system is that government (that is, all public bodies) carry out their tasks in accordance with the law. The meaning and practical application of this principle, however, continues to be contentious. Most modern writers, as did Jennings, come to the conclusion that Dicey's particular formulation of the concept of the rule of law is an inadequate description both of how the principle actually operates, and also what ought to be regarded as important about it.

As we have seen, Dicey's version of the rule of law did not include the placing of legal restraints on the power of Parliament to pass Acts. The implication of Dicey's approach is that, if it were to be enacted that all blue eyed babies be strangled at birth (to use a classic illustration), the court would be under a duty to recognise the validity of such legislation like any other. Dicey's only answer to people who asked whether a court should recognise even a plainly evil enactment duly passed by Parliament was that such legislation was unlikely to be enacted (see above, 5.2). To a considerable extent, Jennings shared Dicey's confidence in Parliament and so did not disparage him on this ground. More recent critics have not shared this faith. For Ferdinand Mount, 'Dicey's doctrine of the rule of law is inescapably a narrow, shrivelled thing. It applies vigorously enough to the rights of individuals in their dealings with one another and with the State, but it does not really touch the untrammelled quality of parliamentary sovereignty' (*The British Constitution Now*, 1993, London: Mandarin, p 207). As we have already noted, the Human Rights Act 1998 gives courts the power to declare that Parliament itself has failed to respect civil liberties (including, of course, those like personal liberty and freedom of assembly which Dicey regarded as important) set out in the ECHR. The Act stops short of allowing courts to enforce any such finding by refusing to recognise the validity of the offending statutory provision.

5.3.3 The rule of law and governmental discretion

Jennings was clearly right to point out that many statutes confer upon ministers, local authorities and other public bodies discretionary powers necessary for them to carry out their tasks. Later critics have gone further, arguing not only that discretion and the rule of law are not incompatible with one another, but also that discretion, properly exercised, is desirable. The use and occasional abuse of discretionary power is a matter of such importance in administrative law that we need to discuss the issues it raises in more detail (see below, Chapter 8). Here, it suffices to note that no one today agrees with Dicey's position.

5.4 Dicey on constitutional conventions

In Part III of *An Introduction to the Study of the Law of the Constitution*, Dicey examines the last of what, for him, are the three main characteristics of the British Constitution – constitutional conventions (see above, 2.2). He draws a sharp distinction between constitutional 'law' (which is the rules enforced or recognised by the courts) and constitutional conventions which are 'customs, practices, maxims or precepts which are not enforced or recognised by the courts' (p 417). He quickly adds, however, that a lawyer cannot master 'the legal side of the English Constitution' without understanding 'those constitutional understandings which necessarily engross the attention of historians or of statesmen'.

The common characteristic of most conventions was, Dicey argued, that they were rules for determining the mode in which the 'discretionary' (that is, prerogative) powers of the Crown and ministers ought to be exercised. A few conventions also related to the privileges of Parliament. Conventions had one ultimate object: 'Their end is to secure that Parliament, or the Cabinet which is indirectly appointed by Parliament, shall in the long run give effect to the will of that power which in modern England is the true political sovereign of the State – the majority of the electors ...' In other words, conventions secured the sovereignty of the people, he claimed. In the final chapter, Dicey considers what sanctions exist to enforce conventions – he thought that this was 'by far the most perplexing' of questions in constitutional law. Remember that he has just said that conventions are not law (that is, they will not be enforced by the courts). He rejects the idea that it is the force of public opinion which ensures ministers and others follow conventions: this was really just a restatement of the question.

The real reason for obedience was this: 'the fact that the breach of ... conventions will almost immediately bring the offender into conflict with the courts and the law of the land' (p 446). He gives illustrations of how this works. What would happen if a government no longer had the confidence of the majority of MPs, but the Prime Minister defied convention by refusing to request that the Queen dissolve Parliament so that a general election could be held? The government would be unable to steer the annual Appropriation Act through Parliament (this gives legal authorisation for the government to spend money raised by taxation) and this would leave the government without any lawful means of expenditure. Therefore 'the conventions of the constitution are not laws, but in so far as they really possess binding force, derive their sanction from the fact that whoever breaks them must finally breach the law and incur the penalties of a law-breaker' (p 451).

5.4.1 Jennings on conventions

Jennings rejects Dicey's definition of conventions. For Jennings, they are 'rules whose nature does *not* differ fundamentally from that of the positive law of England' (*The Law and the Constitution*, 5th edn, 1958, London: London UP, p 74, emphasis added). There were, he argued, problems with Dicey's sharp distinction between laws and conventions. First, Dicey generally overemphasised the role of the courts: most public law issues never see a court. Public law powers and duties are created by statute and enforced by administrative authorities. Only in the rarest cases do the courts become involved, and even then an Act may restrict or exclude their jurisdiction. For Jennings, a wider definition of 'law' was appropriate which would include rules such as that it is the Prime Minister and not the Cabinet who advises the Queen to dissolve Parliament. As a matter of history, the courts recognised rules (such as parliamentary sovereignty) which were established around the time of the Glorious Revolution, but conventions which developed later (for example, to do with Cabinet government) were, as a matter of formality, treated as not being part of the common law. But there was no distinction of substance or nature between law and convention.

Jennings also sought to show (pp 128–29) that Dicey's argument that a breach of a convention would lead to a breach of law was not necessarily correct.

5.6   Conclusion

What, then, is left of Dicey's work? We noted at the beginning of this chapter that his writings, especially *An Introduction to the Law of the Constitution*, continue to be a source of reference for academic writers, teachers and politicians. To this extent, even though most people disagree with some or all of what he wrote, Dicey's continuing influence is undeniable. Perhaps the most enduring legacy is Dicey's emphasis on parliamentary sovereignty as *the* defining feature of the British Constitution. As Ferdinand Mount puts it:

> The Constitution, we are told, is parliamentary supremacy and nothing but parliamentary supremacy; it admits no considerations of natural law or human rights, just as it admits no powers for subordinate or external law making bodies, except in so far as Parliament has defined and granted such powers [*The British Constitution Now*, 1993, London: Mandarin, pp 32–33].

Thus, even when the new Labour government was 'bringing rights home' in the Human Rights Act 1998, the primacy of Parliament, rather than rights enforced by courts, was insisted upon (see above, 5.2.5).

Dicey's particular version of the rule of law, with its three elements, has endured less well. In fact, almost every part of it is now discredited, and we must look elsewhere for an understanding of the importance of the requirement that State authorities respect the law.

TEXTBOOK WRITERS AND THEIR PRINCIPLES

In the absence of a codified constitution in the UK, textbooks have provided important descriptions of the constitutional system. Dicey's *Introduction to the Study of the Law of the Constitution* has had a unique influence. It deals with the sovereignty of Parliament, the rule of law and constitutional conventions. Dicey did not 'invent' these concepts, but he did write in a way that popularised his own views about them. People reading Dicey's book today have to decide of what relevance it is today. Some commentators dismiss it as being of only historical interest, while others accept Dicey's principled account (though conceding they need to be adapted to fit into the modern world). Dicey's work has long been held up to vehement criticism.

Parliamentary sovereignty

Dicey argued that MPs reflected the views of the majority of electors – and if they ceased to do this, they would not be re-elected. This fact led him to place Parliament's legislative power at the centre of the constitution. Acts of Parliament, Dicey argued, were, and ought to be, the highest form of law. One Parliament could not bind its successors by 'entrenching' legislative provisions. There are several challenges to this view today, though most people continue to accept that parliamentary sovereignty is a characteristic of the constitution. Today, UK courts have power under the Human Rights Act 1998 to declare that an Act of Parliament is incompatible with the European Convention on Human Rights (though this does not affect the validity of the statute in question). A few judges have even suggested that the common law may provide a basis for holding an Act of Parliament unconstitutional. The major challenge to parliamentary sovereignty, however, comes from the UK's membership of the European Union. While membership continues, European Community law is the highest form of law and Acts of Parliament in breach of Community law may be 'disapplied' by UK courts.

Rule of law

Dicey argued that the rule of law was a concept with three meanings:

(a) that public authorities should not have wide and arbitrary powers and they require legal authority for their actions. Today, however, almost everyone accepts that conferring discretion on public authorities, so long as it is properly supervised, is necessary and beneficial;

(b) that the legal system does not confer special immunities on public authorities or set up special tribunals to deal with claims against public authorities. Commentators have pointed out that, even in Dicey's time, there were many specialist courts and tribunals for adjudicating on claims against officials. This continues to be true today;

(c) that the constitution is the result of the ordinary law, not a codified constitutional document.

One problem with Dicey's conception of the rule of law, according to critics, is its weakness: it offers no protection in situations where an Act of Parliament enacts or permits public authorities to carry out oppressive actions.

Constitutional conventions

Dicey defined these as the customs, practices, maxims or precepts which are not enforced or recognised by the courts. He attached special importance to the fact that conventions existed to regulate the use of prerogative powers by ministers. (Today, prerogative powers may be subject to judicial review.) Academic writers have questioned whether there is really a fundamental difference of substance between constitutional conventions and legal rules.

PART B

PARLIAMENT AND GOVERNMENT

CHAPTER 6

THE UK PARLIAMENT

6.1   Parliament: from sovereignty to power-sharing

There once was a time when almost everyone agreed that the UK Parliament was, and ought to be, the pre-eminent institution of the constitutional system. Dicey's explanation of the constitution was filled with Victorian optimism about the role of MPs. These men were able to give legitimacy to the Acts of Parliament by reason of the fact that they were elected representatives expressing the will of the electors; MPs controlled those of their colleagues who went on to form the government for the time being; and MPs would not legislate to infringe people's freedoms because MPs shared the moral feelings of the time and society, which were predisposed to liberty (see above, 5.2). People of very different political outlooks, antithetical to Dicey's, also once looked to Parliament as an institution capable of bringing about potent change in society. For socialists, the universal franchise was a preliminary step to getting representatives of the working class into the House of Commons, from where they could transform life for ordinary people (they thought), by legislating to turn the State into a Welfare State, a State that owned and controlled important industries and redistributed income.

Times have changed. Today, the case for saying that Parliament is, or ought to be, central to the constitutional system is harder to make. Whereas once, campaigns for the right to vote by working class men, and later by women, invigorated the country, now many ordinary people are bored by politics and see the work of Parliament as wholly irrelevant to their aspirations for a better life (see above, 1.7.2). The news media's exposé of sleaze during the 1990s – the sexual, financial and political improprieties of MPs inside and outside government – has added to the malaise (see below, 6.7). Moreover, people who understand how the modern constitution operates know that the UK Parliament's role in ever wider fields of policy and law making has been overtaken by the powers of the institutions of the European Union (see below, Chapter 7). The recent flux of constitutional reform (see above, Chapter 2) can be explained as attempts to inject the whole constitutional system with renewed moral authority, which once attached to Parliament but which has now ebbed away from that institution. Some of the reforms are directed at Parliament itself: the modernisation of procedures; abolishing the powers of hereditary peers in the House of Lords; and the possible replacement of the first past the post electoral system with one of proportional representation. Many other planks in the Labour government's pledge to modernise British politics, however, aim to remove constitutional powers from the UK Parliament, and disperse them elsewhere (see above, 4.4.2). The basic constitutional functions of legislating and calling government to account are to be shared with elected bodies in Cardiff, Edinburgh and Belfast (see above, Chapter 2). (MPs sent to Westminster from these parts of the UK can no longer, it is believed, effectively represent the interests of their constituencies there.) Power sharing also involves giving the courts new powers to prevent Parliament enacting legislation contrary to the European Convention on Human Rights, by making declarations of inconsistency under the Human Rights Act 1998. (MPs are no longer to be trusted to strike the right balance in the public interest between individual rights and the needs of the State to govern.) This lack of confidence in the ability of MPs at Westminster to regulate themselves was evident under the previous Conservative government when faced with various allegations that a small number of MPs, including ministers, had acted improperly. Whereas, in the past, the House of Commons jealously guarded its historic powers to investigate wrongdoing and discipline its members itself, in the 1990s the government turned to outside, independent bodies to do this task – to a committee chaired by Sir Richard Scott (a judge of the Court of Appeal) into the arms to Iraq affair, by establishing a permanent Committee on Standards in Public Life under the chairmanship first of Lord Nolan (a Law Lord), and then Lord Neill QC, and the post of Parliamentary Commissioner for Standards.

6.2   What is the point of Parliament?

During the current period of constitutional flux, it is more important than ever to ask the question what is the constitutional purpose of Parliament? In Chapter 2, we gave some brief pragmatic answers: Parliament provides a body of men and women from whom a government is formed; the remaining MPs act as a watchdog over government and hold its purse strings; and Parliament is a legislature (see above, 2.4.2). In this chapter, we delve deeper into the question. Part of the answer is that, in a system of liberal democracy, people consent to be governed through fair, multi-party elections on the basis of universal suffrage. As early as 1791, Thomas Paine was able to write that the people of England as a whole ought to have three fundamental rights: '(1) To choose our own governors; (2) To chasier them for misconduct; (3) To frame a government for ourselves' (*The Rights of Man*, 1791–92 (1969) London: Pelican, p 62, quoting Dr Price).

In a parliamentary system such as that of the UK, the status of MPs and the functions they carry out are of obvious importance to the practical realisation of this form of governance. To assess the extent to which current parliamentary arrangements are adequate, and whether the various reforms are be an improvement, they need to be measured against a set of criteria. Six principles, which ought to guide the law and practice of Parliament, may be identified:

(a) that MPs are representative;

(b) that MPs are fairly elected to Parliament;

(c) that MPs have power to enact legislation;

(d) that, once elected, MPs are free to speak out on any issue;

(e) that MPs do not act corruptly or otherwise dishonestly;

(f) that MPs are able to call ministers to account for their actions.

In the rest of this chapter, we look at each of these principles in turn.

6.3 That MPs are representative

In our constitutional system, one of the primary mechanisms by which people express their consent to be governed – an essential feature of a liberal democracy – is through their elected representatives in Parliament (see above, 1.6.2 and 1.7.2). As AH Birch explains: 'It is generally agreed that a political system can be properly described as a system of representative government if it is one in which representatives of the people share, to a significant degree, in the making of political decisions' (*Representative and Responsible Government*, 1964, London: Allen & Unwin, p 13). The concept of representation, and its connection to the idea of consent, is a complex one. Elsewhere, Birch states what is at its core:

> Parliamentarians are representatives because they have been appointed by a particular process of election to occupy that role ... Members of Parliament ... are people who have been authorised by the process of election to exercise certain powers. This is their defining characteristic, and they remain legal representatives until they step down, die or are defeated, no matter how they behave in the assembly [*The Concepts and Theories of Modern Democracy*, 1993, London: Routledge, p 74].

This is clearly an important point. You will remember (see above, 5.2) that Dicey argued that the democratic justification for the legislative powers of Parliament was the fact that MPs reflected the wishes – were influenced by – the electorate. What exactly does this mean?

According to one strand of theory, MPs, once elected, are to be regarded as independent, in the sense that they should exercise their judgment on issues debated in Parliament according to their personal views of what is in the nation's best interest. MPs are not merely delegates of their constituents or spokesmen for some particular sectional interest group. Edmund Burke famously propounded such a view in his speech to the electors of Bristol in 1774:

> Parliament is not a *congress* of ambassadors from different hostile interests; which interests each must maintain, as an agent and advocate, against other agents and advocates; but Parliament is a *deliberative* assembly of *one* nation, with *one* interest, that of the whole; where, not local purposes, not local prejudices ought to guide, but the general good, resulting from the general reason of the whole.

For most of the 20th century, such a theory has seemed quaint and of little relevance to political reality. The coming of universal suffrage, mass political parties and working class representation in Parliament made elections appear to be about the clash of two great interests – that of country landowners and capitalists (represented by the Conservative Party) and organised labour (represented by the Labour Party). Research shows that almost all electors cast the vote for a candidate because of the political party to which that candidate belongs, rather than because of the candidate's personal views or attributes. Today, it is uncontentious to say that MPs do not decide how to speak and vote in the Commons merely according to their individual views of what is right, but are strongly influenced by the policy objectives and attitudes of their political party. This has led some writers to go a step further, and propound a theory of representation based on the notion of electoral mandate.

Before a general election, each party publishes a manifesto setting out its policies, often including reference to specific legislation it will introduce if its leaders form the government after the election. The link between the electorate and MPs' powers to enact legislation may, therefore, be explained in terms of the mandate which the majority of the House of Commons derives from a party's electoral victory. Some writers have suggested that notions of a mandate establish constitutional conventions. Jennings wrote:

> It is now recognised that fundamental changes of policy must not be effected unless they have been in issue at a general election. This appears as a limitation upon the Government. But since the Government ... controls Parliament, it is a limitation upon Parliament itself [*The Law and the Constitution*, 5th edn, 1958, London: London UP, p 176].

More specific is the so called Salisbury convention, under which peers do not reject government Bills on their second reading in the House of Lords if the Bill is intended to put into effect a manifesto commitment of the governing party.

There are, however, a number of objections to the notion of a mandate. One is that the current electoral system fails to translate the electoral support gained by each party throughout the country into a proportionate share of seats for the party forming the government in the House of Commons (see below, 6.4). Research has also shown that voters rarely either know about, or, if they do, agree with, many of the policies outlined in the manifesto of the party whose candidate they support. Moreover, legislation and policy may have to be made in response to problems not foreseen, or addressed, in party manifestos. Some writers also object that mandate theories are apt to blur the important distinction between MPs and the government. As Adam Tompkins explains:

> Contrary to Tony Blair's erroneous view, it was not his government, but a new Parliament, which was elected on 1 May [1997]. It is because and only because Parliament allows it and wants it (for the time being) that he and his ministers hold office. That is why they are constitutionally responsible to Parliament. ... It is easy to overlook this. The power of the party machines and the scourge of the whips have successfully managed to blur the formal distinction between Parliament and government [*The Constitution After Scott: Government Unwrapped*, 1998, Oxford: OUP, p 269].

To summarise, it may be said that the constitutional justification for MPs' powers to legislate (including those MPs who go on to form a government) arises simply from the fact that they were elected, or, because the MPs exercising most power – those in government and their supporters – were elected on a the basis of commitments made in a manifesto.

6.4 That MPs are fairly elected

The principle of formal legal equality is central to liberal democracy. In the context of the parliamentary system, this means that all citizens of the UK have one vote (and one vote only) in elections. As we saw in Chapter 3, by 1928, the struggle for the universal franchise was won when first manual workers, then women, were given the legal right to vote. The principle of one person, one vote was not established, however, until the 1940s, when the additional votes of people who occupied business premises and university graduates were abolished. Many people, however, still do not regard the present voting arrangements for the UK Parliament, contained in the Representation of the People Act 1983, as fair. Three main complaints are levelled against the current electoral system: that the first past the post system leads to unfair representation of some political parties in the Commons; that the second chamber of Parliament, the Lords, is wholly unelected; and that the composition of MPs, in terms of their sex and ethnicity, does not reflect that of the general population of the UK.

6.4.1 First past the post elections

MPs are elected to the UK Parliament by a first past the post (or plurality) system, in which voters in each constituency may vote for only one candidate, and the candidate gaining the most votes (which will not necessarily be a majority of votes) is elected. Arguably, such a system fails to give each person a vote of equal value. The plurality system is also used for elections to local authorities (see above, 2.9.1), but elections to other representative institutions are conducted using other schemes. For the Northern Ireland Assembly and for Northern Ireland representatives in the European Parliament, it is a single transferable vote system (see above, 2.6.1). The Scottish Parliament and the National Assembly for Wales are elected using additional member systems (see above, 2.5.1, 2.7). Members of the European Parliament for England, Scotland and Wales are elected under a party list system (see below, 7.5.2). Many campaigners prefer these other systems, claiming they are fairer than the plurality system. Richard Rose puts the problem succinctly, 'The right to vote is not enough; how votes are counted and converted into seats in Parliament is considered equally important' ('Electoral reform: what are the consequences?', in Vibert, F (ed), *Britain's Constitutional Future*, 1991, London: IEA, p 122). The importance arises because the outcome of a general election determines not merely which MP represents a particular constituency in Parliament, but also which political party goes on to form the government.

The first past the post system often results in a disproportion between the number of votes the candidates of a political party receive throughout the UK and the number of parliamentary seats which that party wins. For example, in the 1997 general election, Labour gained a landslide majority with two-thirds of the seats in the Commons, though throughout the UK as a whole, only 44% of people who voted supported Labour candidates. The system can also mean that the party gaining most votes throughout the UK actually loses a general election: in 1951, Labour gained more votes, but fewer seats, than the Conservatives.

In 1997, the government set up an independent commission on the voting system, under the chairmanship of Lord Jenkins of Hillhead, to consider alternatives to the first past the post system. The commission reported in October 1998, recommending what has been described by others as an 'ingenious' 'alternative vote top up' system (*Report of the Independent Commission on the Voting System*, Cm 4090-I, 1998, London: HMSO). Electors would, in effect, each have two votes. The first would be used to choose a constituency MP. However, instead of simply putting one cross next to the candidate of their choice (as at present), electors would rank candidates in order of preference. A candidate getting more than half the first choices would be elected automatically. If no candidate is in this position, then the candidate with the lowest votes would be eliminated, and the other preferences of that candidate's supporters would be reallocated to the remaining candidates. If this did not produce a winner, the process would be repeated until there was a candidate with more than half the preferences. An elector would use his or her second vote to choose a political party (or a particular candidate) from a different list of 'top up candidates'. About 80% of MPs would come from constituency preferences and about 20% from the top up list. The point of choosing 'top up' MPs is that it is a method of correcting the disproportionality in the number of constituency seats political parties win compared with the level of support they have throughout the country. It remains to be seen whether the government will accept the recommendations of the Jenkins commission.

Despite the inconsistencies which sometimes emerge, there is, however, a strong case to be made for retaining the first past the post system. First, most systems of proportional representation would break the tradition that one MP represents one constituency, and this would diminish the authority of MPs to speak out and assist their constituents. Secondly, some forms of proportional representation which use 'party lists' would give too much power to bureaucrats in the headquarters of the main parties to determine who gets on to the lists and so into Parliament. Thirdly, proportional representation is more likely to result in 'hung' Parliaments, in which no single party is able to form a government, and so has to form a coalition, depending on the support of MPs in other parties. Small parties would become disproportionately powerful in the backroom negotiations and deals would inevitably follow. Fourthly, it must be asked whether, given the raft of other far reaching constitutional reforms being put in place – devolution, the Human Rights Act 1988, reform of the Lords, newly empowered local authorities – there is still any pressing need for proportional representation. The argument that used once to be made, that the UK constitution needed proportional representation because there are inadequate checks and balances against an overbearing central government, is far less convincing. The first past the post system has a great virtue: it produces effective and stable single party government which is held to account at the following election for its conduct and the extent to which it has met its manifesto commitments at the previous election.

6.4.2   The unelected upper chamber

A second stark dent in the principle of fair elections is the fact that only one of the two chambers of Parliament is elected. There are 659 elected MPs in the Commons; in the Lords, as at December 1997, there were 1,274 non-elected parliamentarians composed as follows:

Hereditary peers:	750
Hereditary peers of first creation:	9
Life peers:	465
Law Lords:	26
Bishops:	26

Many of the hereditary peers are heads of aristocratic landowning families whose interests have been represented in Parliament for centuries; several have inherited their right to sit and vote in the Lords from a forebear granted a peerage more recently (for instance, Mrs Thatcher recommended to the Queen that former Prime Minister Harold Macmillan be granted an hereditary peerage and his grandson is now a member of the upper house). Since the Life Peerages Act 1957, the Prime Minister has had the power to recommend to the

Queen that a person be made a member of the House of Lords for that person's lifetime.

Although many commentators highlight the effectiveness of much of the work of the Lords, especially in scrutinising legislation, there is long standing and widespread consensus that its composition needs to be altered (see above, 3.9.1). In 1968, the Labour government unsuccessfully attempted reform. The present Labour government plans to start by removing the rights of hereditary peers to sit and vote (*Modernising Parliament: Reforming the House of Lords*, Cm 4183, 1999, London: HMSO). In February 1999, the government set up a royal commission with terms of reference to consider and make recommendations about the role and functions of a second chamber and to suggest methods of composition for the new chamber. The royal commission is expected to report in December 1999. A wholly nominated chamber would not be consistent with the principle of fair elections. If the new chamber is elected, it would have to be according to some method different from that used for the House of Commons. There is, however, a logically prior question: what constitutional function should the upper House serve? If it is mainly to expose legislation and government action to better scrutiny than the Commons is able to carry out, then the answer surely is to improve the effectiveness of the Commons or to give power to some external body, such as the courts, to ensure that legislation passed by the Commons does not infringe basic rights (which is now the case under the Human Rights Act 1998). A bi-cameral Parliament is not essential.

6.4.3   The composition of MPs and peers

A third concern, linked to the principle of fair voting, is that the current composition of the Commons fails to reflect the social make-up of the country as a whole. In former years, the campaigns were for working class people to have a vote and have their representatives sit in Parliament. Social class has ceased to be a defining issue in politics, and instead, the concerns are about imbalances in the ethnicity of MPs and their sex. After the 1997 general election, there were still only 120 women MPs. The Labour Party increased the number of its female prospective parliamentary candidates by requiring some constituency Labour parties to have all-women short lists when selecting their candidate, but this scheme had to be abandoned, as it was held to be contrary to the Sex Discrimination Act 1975. A characteristically radical proposal has come from Tony Benn MP, who suggests that each constituency should return two MPs, one male, one female:

> The point about gender is that while men and women may be black, white, Asian, Christian, Muslim, atheist and sometimes a combination of these, they are either men or women [*Common Sense*, 1993, London: Hutchinson, p 107].

6.5 That Parliament enacts legislation

In a liberal democracy, government regulation ought to take place with the consent of the people and in accordance with the law. Parliament is a central mechanism for achieving this overarching goal, as Dicey's work explained to generations of readers (see above, 6.1, Chapter 5). Before examining the general principle that Parliament enacts legislation, it is necessary to understand how Parliament does this in practical terms.

6.5.1 Primary legislation

Most primary legislation is initiated by government, though there are some opportunities for backbench MPs and peers to introduce draft legislation (see below). Bills (draft Acts of Parliament) may be introduced either into the House of Commons or the Lords, and must pass through a series of stages prescribed by parliamentary Standing Orders:

(a) First Reading. This is a formality at which the title of the Bill is read out and a date set for its Second Reading.

(b) Second Reading. Here, the general policy embodied in the Bill is debated on the floor of the House.

(c) Committee stage. During this part of the legislative process, there is line by line scrutiny of the text of the Bill. In the Commons, this normally takes place in a standing committee of about 40 MPs. They sit in a mini debating chamber, opposing political parties facing each other. They are thus very different in nature from the generally consensual, cross-party select committees (see above, 6.8). The committee stage of some particularly important Bills, especially those dealing with constitutional issues, takes place in the Chamber of the Commons so that all MPs have an opportunity to contribute to the debate. Amendments to the text of the Bill are proposed by opposition MPs and also by the government itself (for example, to deal with matters overlooked during the drafting of the Bill, or to respond to criticisms). Amendments suggested by opposition MPs are only rarely accepted. When a Bill is in the Lords, the Committee stage takes place in the Chamber.

(d) Report stage. This is when the Bill, as amended in committee, returns to the floor of the Chamber. This provides an opportunity for the government to try to change any unacceptable amendments which may have been agreed to in committee.

(e) Third Reading. This is normally a short debate, with only very limited scope for MPs to table further amendments.

Once a Bill has passed through this procedure in one House, it is then introduced into the other. Thus, if the Bill was first considered by the Commons, it will then go to the Lords where it is considered further; and vice versa. Throughout the legislative process, the government is able to exercise a great deal of control over the length of debate. Its supporters in the Commons can normally be relied upon to vote for a guillotine motion which ends debate on a Bill after a certain number of hours.

While in the Lords, each Bill is subject to scrutiny by a select committee to see whether it proposes to enact any undesirable delegated powers – in other words, to give powers to civil servants (acting in the name of a minister or some other body) to make rules with the force of law, usually in the form of statutory instruments. The potential for misuse of delegated rule making powers has, for decades, been of concern to constitutional lawyers, as it is a means by which the executive may legislate with little or no effective parliamentary scrutiny of their proposals (see below, 6.5.2). The increasing use of framework Bills presents problems for Parliament. This is where the Bill seeks to confer broad powers on a minister to make by statutory instrument, at a later date, more detailed rules dealing with the subject matter of the Bill; MPs will often have little idea about the content of that secondary legislation.

In almost all cases, a majority in both Houses of Parliament agree as to the final form of the Bill, and it may then go on to receive the royal assent, which is a formality (see above, 2.11). The Act of Parliament may either state that it comes into force immediately, or on a specified day, or on such day as a minister may determine.

In very rare cases, after scrutiny of a Bill, both Houses of Parliament, the Commons and the Lords, may fail to agree as to its final form. Under the provisions of the Parliament Act 1911 (as amended in 1949), the Commons – which effectively means the government with a majority of MPs – may insist that the Bill go on to receive royal assent after 13 months, even in the absence of consent by the upper house. In recent years, the Parliament Act has only been invoked once (for the War Crimes Act 1991).

In 1992, the Hansard Commission, a pressure group, published a report, *Making the Law*, London: Hansard Society, which contained scathing criticism of the present effectiveness of parliamentary scrutiny of legislation. It called for better consultations between government and particularly parties affected by legislation before Bills are introduced into Parliament. Parliament should, it recommended, play a greater role in the period before a Bill is drafted, for example through cross-party select committees which would take evidence and issue reports on the subject of the proposed legislation. Once Bills are introduced into Parliament, the scrutiny process is far too rushed, the Commission found, and MPs often lack the necessary expertise to understand the likely impact of proposed legislation. Many of these issues are now under consideration by MPs in the select committee on the Modernisation of House of Commons, set up in 1997.

Parliamentary procedure also permits backbench MPs to introduce Bills, though few of these ever complete their passage through both Houses of Parliament. Some important pieces of social legislation, such as the Sexual Offences Act 1967 (decriminalising homosexuality) and the Abortion Act 1967, have been initiated by backbench MPs or peers. When the government is hostile to a particular private members' Bill, it will usually be able to wreck it by its ability to control the legislative timetable, by its supporters tabling numerous amendments at report stage, or by getting a sympathetic MP to filibuster (talking at great length to prevent a Bill making progress). Even if a Private Members' Bill fails to reach the statute book, introducing one may be an effective way of generating publicity for a cause.

6.5.2 Subordinate legislation

As well as enacting Acts of Parliament, peers and MPs are involved in consenting to subordinate (or 'secondary' or 'delegated') legislation drafted by government departments under rule making powers conferred on a minister by an Act of Parliament (see above, 2.4.3). Most secondary legislation is in the form of statutory instruments. One main reason for the use of statutory instruments is to spare Parliament from having to consider in detail highly technical and relatively uncontentious legal regulations. Some statutory instruments, however, deal with matters of considerable practical or constitutional importance. There are, however, a handful of Acts of Parliament which give ministers powers to make statutory instruments which may be of great significance. One such is the Human Rights Act 1998, under which ministers are able to use statutory instruments to amend or repeal primary legislation declared by the court to be inconsistent with the European Convention on Human Rights (see below, 19.10.3). The European Communities Act 1972 also provides ministers with broad powers to make legislation necessary to bring national law into compliance with directives agreed by the Community institutions (see below, 7.6.2).

Statutory instruments are considered by a joint select committee of backbench MPs and peers which has power to draw to the attention of Parliament any statutory instrument which falls foul of one of 11 criteria (such as, that its drafting appears to be defective, or that the minister is seeking to make some unusual or unexpected use of powers conferred by the statute under which the statutory instrument is made). This Joint Committee on Statutory Instruments has no power to question the policy or merits of statutory instruments. It finds only a very small number of the 3,000 or so statutory instruments made each year to be of concern, and on these it reports to both Houses of Parliament. After scrutiny by the committee, an statutory instrument is subject to one of two main types of procedure (which one is specified in the particular enabling Act of Parliament). Most are subject to the negative resolution procedure, under which an statutory instrument becomes law 40 days after being laid before Parliament unless an MP challenges it and calls for a debate. Under the other, affirmative resolution procedure, there is a short debate of no more than 90 minutes. MPs have no power to make amendments to the statutory instrument, only to accept or reject it as a whole. (See, further, Ganz, G, 'Delegated legislation: a necessary evil or a constitutional outrage?', in Leyland, P and Woods, T (eds), *Administrative Law Facing the Future*, 1997, London: Blackstone).

6.6   Once elected, MPs should be able to speak out on any issue

Once MPs are elected to Parliament, it is important that they are able to speak out on any issue without fear that they will be sued or punished by people inside or outside Parliament. This principle was recognised in the Bill of Rights 1688, Art 9 of which provides 'That the freedom of speech, and the debates or proceedings in Parliament ought not to be impeached or questioned in any court or place outside of Parliament'. One effect of this provision is to give MPs absolute immunity from being sued for defamation for statements made during parliamentary business. The Defamation Act 1996 amended the law to allow MPs who are themselves sued for defamation to use proceedings of Parliament – for example, extracts from Hansard – as part of their defence (see, further, Sharland, A and Loveland, I, 'The Defamation Act 1996 and political libels' [1997] PL 113).

Set against this formal protection of MPs' free speech are the pressures which may lead MPs to be less than forthright in challenging government policy in Parliament. Critics argue that the leaders of political parties (especially the party which forms the government) have far too much power over other MPs in their party. When legislation is being considered in the Commons, MPs are instructed by the whips of their party (MPs appointed by the party leader to maintain discipline) exactly which way to vote; failure to follow instructions in an important vote may lead to suspension from a party. Most MPs, however, vote and otherwise support their party because they agree with the policies pursued by the leadership. The suggestion that MPs should be more independent from their party leadership overlooks the fact that most electors vote for a candidate because he or she represents one or other of the main political parties, not because of the candidate's personal views (see above, 6.2).

In principle, the whip system is not meant to operate during select committee investigations – in other words, when MPs are carrying out watchdog functions, rather than acting as legislators, they have independence from their own political party. From time to time, however, it has emerged that whips have sought to influence the course of investigations. When the select committee on employment investigated the banning of trade union membership for GCHQ employees in 1984, allegations were made that some members of the committee were nobbled (see Le Sueur, AP and Sunkin, M, *Public Law*, 1997, London: Longman, p 380). Another instance was revealed in December 1996, when David Willetts MP, the then Paymaster General (a junior ministerial post in the Treasury) was forced to resign from office after it came to light that two years previously, when he was a government whip, he had attempted to influence the chairman of a select committee about how an inquiry should be conducted. It is not only select committees that government seeks to influence: in March 1998, it revealed that Nigel Griffiths MP, a junior minister in the Department of Trade and Industry, drafted a question for another Labour MP to put to him. As well as seeking to control scrutiny by backbenchers of their own party, the government effectively controls the parliamentary timetable with the result, for example, that time is rarely made available for the reports of select committees to be debated in the chamber of the Commons.

6.7 That MPs are not corrupt or dishonest

During the early 1990s, the news media became preoccupied with allegations of sleaze – the sexual, financial or political improprieties of MPs (including ministers). So far as sexual matters are concerned, if nothing illegal has taken place, this ought normally to be an entirely private matter with no bearing on a person's fitness to hold public office (though, for a different view, see Brazier, R, 'It *is* a constitutional issue: fitness for ministerial office in the 1990s' [1994] PL 431).

The more important, if less titillating, area of concern were allegations that MPs or ministers improperly benefited financially from their public office, or had misled Parliament in some way. Two main series of events triggered calls for something to be done. In a constitutional system so heavily influenced by conventions, the study of such episodes is capable of revealing important norms which ought to regulate behaviour.

In the first, a small number of MPs were revealed to have been paid for asking questions of ministers in Parliament on behalf of businesses which paid them to do so (cash for questions), and that, during the legislative process, some MPs had tabled amendments to Bills, on behalf of clients, in the name of other MPs without asking their consent. Partly in response to these events, in 1994, the government established the permanent independent Committee on Standards in Public Life (see above, 6.1). Its first report, in 1995, dealt with MPs, ministers and civil servants. It recommended that a new officer of the House of Commons be established – the Parliamentary Commissioner for Standards; Sir Gordon Downey, a former senior civil servant, was appointed to this post; his successor was Ms Elizabeth Filkin. A code of conduct for MPs was proposed. In the same year a new, cross-party select committee of MPs was also established in the Commons – the Committee on Standards and Privileges. In its first inquiry, one MP, the Conservative Neil Hamilton, came in for particular censure, though he strongly maintained he had not acted with impropriety and claimed that the committee's procedures were unfair.

The second scandal concerned the actions of ministers during the Arms-to-Iraq affair, in which directors of a company called Matrix Churchill Ltd were prosecuted for selling defence-related goods to Iraq in breach of export restrictions contained in delegated legislation. It later emerged that ministers had secretly agreed to alter government policy to permit these exports, while at the same time defending the restrictions in Parliament. At the trial, however, government ministers issued public interest immunity certificates, seeking to prevent the defendants having access to government documents which would have aided their defence. The trial collapsed, and the prosecution was withdrawn in a blaze of publicity. The Prime Minister, John Major, set up a judicial inquiry into the events surrounding the case, chaired by Sir Richard Scott. In 1996, a 1,800 page report was published, finding, among other things, that a minister (William Waldegrave MP) had given answers to Parliament which were neither ... adequate [nor] accurate and answers by other ministers to MPs' questions had deliberately failed to inform Parliament of the current state of government policy on non-lethal arms sales to Iraq (para D4.42). (On arms to Iraq, see, further, Tomkins, A, *The Constitution after Scott*, 1998, Oxford: OUP.)

The practical outcome of these episodes has been significant. New rules governing the conduct of ministers have been published. Parliamentary rules have been amended, but have stopped short of banning MPs from receiving any paid employment from outside bodies. The new rules do prevent MPs being sponsored. In the past, many MPs received funds from organisations (such as trade unions and employers' organisations and pressure groups) which they used to pay for things such as research and secretarial assistance; in return, the MPs were expected to act as spokesmen for their group in the Commons, though such sponsorship always had to be declared when speaking in parliamentary debates. In a further move, amid concern that there was a lack of openness and potential for improper favours being given by government, the Committee on Standards in Public Life conducted an inquiry in 1998 into the funding of political parties. This was partly prompted by the revelation that the Labour Party had received a donation of £1 million from Formula One motor racing, which is heavily dependent on advertising from cigarette companies, and that the government had agreed to exempt this sport from a general ban on tobacco sponsorship (see Fifth Report, *The Funding of Political Parties in the UK*, Cm 4057, 1998, London: HMSO).

Some commentators have questioned the preoccupation with the alleged improprieties of backbench MPs and ministers. For James Heartfield, the debate about sleaze is much more than a symptom of popular disaffection. It is also a self-righting mechanism, employed by the elites to win back the voters' trust in the State. Within the preoccupation with corruption there are two processes intertwined, each pushed forward any the other. 'Sleaze' is about discrediting and delegitimating the old political order – and, at the same time, legitimising and winning authority for a new one ('The corruption of politics and the politics of corruption' (1997) 103 LM 14, p 17).

6.8   That MPs and peers call the government to account

It is one of the basic constitutional functions of MPs and peers that they call ministers to account for their policies and actions. Our consent to be governed is not limited to voting for MPs in elections, but is continued in more specific ways by our elected representatives' actions in the Commons. MPs carry out this task in various ways:

(a) motions on government policy are debated on the floor of the chambers in both Houses. Opposition parties are given some opportunities to choose the subject matters of debate;

(b) written and oral questions are asked of ministers by MPs and peers. The Prime Minister answers oral questions on general government policy once a week for 30 minutes in the Commons. Other ministers take oral questions according to a departmental rota. The answers to written questions are published in *Hansard*;

(c) select committees, which typically comprise 15 backbench MPs or peers, conduct inquiries by taking oral and written evidence from ministers, pressure groups and others. Senior civil servants may also be called to give evidence, but do so on behalf and under directions of their ministers rather than in their own rights. Members are drawn from across the political parties and they sit around a horseshoe-shaped table. Reports containing findings and recommendations are published. In the Commons, select committees scrutinise the work of the main government departments. In the Lords, the select committees on the European Communities and on Science and Technology are especially prominent.

Commentators identify several failings in these arrangements which prevent the principle that ministers should be made accountable to Parliament being given full effect. The first and fundamental problem is said to be the erosion in the constitutional convention of ministerial responsibility. This broad concept includes two main features (see, generally, Woodhouse, D, 'Ministerial responsibility: something old, something new' [1997] PL 262). One is a duty to explain – that ministers give accurate and truthful information to Parliament, refusing to disclose information only when disclosure would not be in the public interest (see the First Report of the Public Service Committee, *Ministerial Accountability and Responsibility* (1996–97) HC 234, Annex 1). The other aspect of ministerial responsibility is that ministers and their departments are expected to take amendatory action in the light of criticisms made in Parliament and, in the final resort, that a minister resign from office and return to being a backbench MP. Very few ministers have resigned in recent years in consequence of criticism made of their department's serious mistakes, and it may, therefore, be doubted whether resignation continues to be a constitutional convention.

Critics suggest that neither the Commons nor the Lords have yet adapted themselves to the new, more diffuse forms of government decision making institutions (see below, 8.2.1) which have been created over the past decade (see Woodhouse, D, *In Pursuit of Good Administration: Ministers, Civil Servants and Judges*, 1997, Oxford: Clarendon). Peter Riddell writes that:

> My worry ... is that Parliament has failed to cope with the growth of alternative centres of power. The formation of Next Steps executive agencies, the creation of regulators for the privatised utilities and the devolution of key decisions over, for example, the setting of interest rates to the Bank of England all have far-reaching implications for accountability. The official line that these bodies are still accountable, via ministers, to Parliament is an unconvincing and inadequate description of the real position [*Parliament under Pressure*, 1998, London: Gollancz, p 32].

Perhaps even more significant than changes to decision making structures within the UK is the fact that more and more governmental decisions are made inside European Union institutions, and the UK Parliament has little or no opportunity to call anyone to account for these (see below, Chapter 7). In short, the traditional focus on ministerial responsibility is outmoded as less and less policy making and practical policy implementation is carried out by ministers themselves or by civil servants in their departments.

6.9 Parliament's diminishing importance

Parliament's status as a forum for great political debates has waned in recent years (see above, 6.1), the result of the decline of adversarial politics. As *The Economist* notes, the chamber 'was suited for great set-piece debates, in eras when politics took place across gaping class and ideological divides. Modern politics and government do not on the whole consist of such issues' ((1998) *The Economist*, 10 January, p 32). The process of European integration (see below, Chapter 7) and Labour's 'Third Way' constitutional reform programme (see above, Chapters 2 and 4) result in political decision making and scrutiny moving to a range of other institutions, including the devolved assemblies and the courts. Parliament's pre-eminence as a legislative body has also waned. Parliament has no choice but to legislate to give effect to directives made by the institutions of the European Community (see below, 7.6.2). Inadequate opportunities for scrutiny of proposed legislation means that the principle of consent to legislation by elected representatives is often illusory. Peter Riddell, the political journalist, captures the prevailing mood when he writes:

I believe that Parliament should be at the centre of our political system but in a stable and creative relationship with other political institutions with their own legitimacy and authority. MPs should not always be whinging about threats to some absolute notion of sovereignty [p 20].

In other words, while the UK Parliament is important, it is not the whole story; and other bodies – not all of them elected – are now to form a new constitutional package.

While some welcome this new diffusion and plurality of State power, others worry. William Hague MP praises the Westminster system that is fast disappearing:

Of all the features of our constitution today, it is this strong democratic accountability which is the most important. Practical political power in our country resides primarily with the national government, not with individual MPs or unelected judges or local or regional parliaments. That power is derived from the national government commanding a working majority in the House of Commons. That working majority is bestowed on political parties by the British people at the ballot box. There is a clear line of accountability. We know who to praise when things go well, and, more importantly, we know who to blame when they do not. And when things do not go well, our voting system allows us to do something about it and kick the Government out ['Change and tradition: thinking creatively about the constitution', lecture at the Centre for Policy Studies, 24 February 1998].

THE UK PARLIAMENT

It is now questionable whether the UK Parliament has a central place in the constitutional system. Developments have transferred practical powers from the UK Parliament to other institutions – the institutions of the European Union, the Scottish Parliament, the Northern Ireland Assembly, the National Assembly for Wales and also, to an extent, to judges. .

Parliaments ought to be an important feature in liberal democracies. In the UK, it provides a body of people from whom a government is formed, and the remaining MPs act as a watchdog over government. Elected assemblies ought also to be the main legislative bodies in a constitution. Six principles should influence the practical arrangements for choosing MPs and guide their practices:

(a) that MPs are representative. There are different constitutional justifications for MPs' rights to legislate. It may be said that their powers arise simply by the fact that they were elected – and that, once elected, MPs ought to exercise their judgment on issues debated in Parliament in according to their own personal views of what is in the nation's best interest. Alternatively, the notion of mandate suggests that MPs representing a political party should be bound by the manifesto promises made to electors at the time of the election;

(b) that MPs are fairly elected to Parliament. Many people believe that the first past the post electoral system is unfair. In 1998, the Jenkins commission on the voting system recommended the adoption of an 'alternative vote top up' scheme. Parliament's upper chamber is unelected, containing people who have inherited their right to sit and vote or people appointed by the Prime Minister. A royal commission is due to report in December 1999 with recommendations for reform of the House of Lords;

(c) that MPs have power to enact legislation. Procedures exist for MPs and peers to debate and vote on Bills before they become Acts of Parliament. In rare cases, Acts of Parliament have been made despite the fact that the House of Lords has not given its consent. Critics question the effectiveness of parliamentary scrutiny of proposed legislation, particularly of subordinate legislation (rules made by ministers);

(d) that, once elected, MPs are free to speak out on any issue. They should be able to criticise and reveal information without fear of being sued or punished. This is recognised by Art 9 of the Bill of Rights 1689. The political parties enforce party discipline and require MPs to vote as instructed. One area where party discipline is less strong is in the work of select committee inquiring into the running of government departments; here MPs often work co-operatively with opponents in other parties;

(e) that MPs do not act corruptly or otherwise dishonestly. During the 1990s, a small number of MPs were revealed to be accepting money from businesses to ask questions of ministers in Parliament and to table amendments to Bills. The scandal led in 1995 to the creation of a permanent Committee on Standards in Public Life and the post of Parliamentary Commissioner for Standards. A second scandal occurred when it became known that ministers had not been open with Parliament about policy on the export of defence-related goods to Iraq, and that several business people had been unfairly prosecuted. An inquiry by Sir Richard Scott led to new rules governing the conduct of ministers and stopped the practice of MPs being 'sponsored' by bodies such as business associations and trade unions;

(f) that MPs are able to call ministers to account for their actions. Procedures exist for MPs and peers to question the actions and policies of the government – through formal written and oral questions, debates and select committee inquiries. Commentators point out that these methods are not always well designed for scrutinising decision making by executive agencies and by the institutions of the European Union.

CHAPTER 7

THE EUROPEAN UNION

7.1   Introduction

Any description of the 'British' constitutional system must include analysis of the law and institutions of the European Union, which today are part and parcel of the way we are governed. There are currently 15 Member States of the European Union: Austria; Belgium; Denmark; Finland; France; Ireland; Italy; Germany; Greece; Luxembourg; The Netherlands; Spain; Sweden; Portugal; and, of course, the UK. Encouraged by the success of the Union, other countries have applied to join. Estonia, Poland, the Czech Republic, Hungary, Slovenia and Cyprus are likely to be the next ones admitted as members, probably in 2003. In deciding which new members to admit, the European Union applies criteria agreed upon in 1993: that the country has 'stable institutions guaranteeing democracy, the rule of law, human rights and the protection of minorities', 'the existence of a functioning market economy' and 'the ability to take on the obligations of membership'.

This chapter considers the major constitutional questions that need to be asked about the European Union. At the outset, we need to ask why European integration is taking place and what it means for the principles of liberal democracy which, we have suggested, underpin the UK's Constitution (see above, 1.6). The European Union is an extraordinary creation. Within living memory, most of its Member States were at war with others, the second time the continent had been wracked by conflict during the 20th century. In the period after 1945, several Member States were governed by anti-democratic military dictatorships (Greece, Spain and Portugal). Several of the countries soon to accede to the European Union were ruled by totalitarian communist regimes (as was the eastern part of Germany). Today, versions of liberal democracy are practised in all Member States. Indeed, this is the main point of the European Union. It is an attempt by Nation States in one part of the world to entrench that form of political organisation – in preference to fascism and communist totalitarianism. The treaty by which Member States created the European Union proclaims that the Union is 'founded on the principles of liberty, democracy, respect for human rights and fundamental freedoms, and the rule of law, principles which are common to the Member States' (Art 6 of the Treaty on European Union). These are the broad principles associated with liberal democracy (see above, 1.6). There is a paradox: the institutions of the European Union themselves suffer from a 'democratic deficit'. We are, however, running ahead of ourselves. Before examining the contribution of the European Union to constitutions based on liberal democracy, we need to understand what it is and what it does.

7.2   The legal base of the European Union

The starting point for an explanation of the European Union are the international treaties that establish it. There are two main treaties: the Treaty on European Union (TEU, or 'the Maastricht Treaty'), dating back to 1992, and the Treaty Establishing the European Communities ('EC Treaty' or sometimes 'the Treaty of Rome') dating back to 1957. Both these treaties were amended by the Treaty of Amsterdam. The revisions came into force on 1 May 1999. The amendments necessitated a renumbering of provisions in the TEU and EC Treaty. In this chapter, we shall, therefore, sometimes consider the EC Treaty and sometimes the TEU. The European Union is often described as 'a temple of three pillars'. More prosaically, this means that policy making in relation to different fields of government activity is carried out using three different processes.

7.2.1   The first pillar: the European Community

This first pillar – which may be referred to as 'the European Community', 'the EC' or simply 'the Community' – is the oldest component of the Union, tracing its roots back to the European Economic Community (EEC) established by six Member States in the 1950s. Although the Community is an integral part of the European Union, its continues to have its own separate treaty, which is linked to the TEU – the EC Treaty. From the outset, the Community contained an overarching political and constitutional aspiration, to establish 'an ever closer union among the peoples' of Europe (see, now, Art 1 of the TEU). Many of the politicians and diplomats who created the original Community in the 1950s envisaged it developing into a European federal constitutional system, similar to that of the US, in which governmental power was allocated by a constitutional document to two tiers of government.

At the heart of the Community are the four basic freedoms – freedom of movement of goods, persons (see below, 27.8), services and capital between the Member States. These are the foundations for the aim of 'establishing a common market and economic and monetary union' (Art 2 of the EC Treaty). As we have seen, the EC Treaty allocates powers to Community institutions to make policy and laws in relation to a wide range of policy areas (see above, 2.3). UK government policy in all these fields is now made in conjunction with other Member States through the elaborate institutional framework and decision making processes laid down by in the EC Treaty. Among the objectives set out in the treaty is 'the principle of an open market economy with free competition' (Art 4(2) of the EC Treaty) and:

> ... a harmonious, balanced and sustainable development of economic activities, a high level of employment and of social protection, equality between men and women, sustainable and non-inflationary growth, a high degree of competitiveness and convergence of economic performance, a high level of

protection and improvement in the quality of the environment, the raising of the standard of living and quality of life, and economic and social cohesion and solidarity among the Member States [Art 2 of the EC Treaty].

Of especial significance is the Community's role in economic and monetary policy (Title VII of the EC Treaty). The Community has been following a policy of progressive convergence of monetary policy in the Member States, and January 1999 was set as the target date for the third and final phase, the adoption of a single currency. At the time of the Maastricht Treaty, the UK negotiated a derogation from this treaty obligation. A protocol to the EC Treaty provides that 'the UK shall not be obliged or committed to move to the third stage of Economic and Monetary Union without a separate decision to do so by its government and Parliament'.

From the outset, the Community has also had a 'social dimension', in which free trade is combined with legal protection for workers, including measures for combating sex discrimination at work, and rights for consumers.

7.2.2 The second pillar: common foreign and security policy

Under the second pillar of the European Union, common foreign and security policy (CFSP), governments of Member States must 'support the Union's external and security policy actively and unreservedly in a spirit of loyalty and mutual solidarity' (Art 11 of the TEU). The treaty envisages the progressive framing of a common defence policy, which, in the future, might lead to a common defence, should the Member States so decide. In the meantime, the Union implements those areas upon which Member States agree by means of the armed forces of Member States under the auspices of other military international organisations, such as the Western European Union (WEU), the North Atlantic Treaty Organisation (NATO) and the United Nations.

7.2.3 The third pillar: criminal matters

Under the European Union's third pillar, the objective of the Union is 'to provide citizens with a high level of safety within an area of freedom, security and justice by developing common action among the Member States in the fields of police and judicial co-operation in criminal matters and by preventing racism and xenophobia' (Art 29 of the TEU). Several forms of criminal activity are highlighted as needing particular action: terrorism; trafficking in persons, illicit drugs and arms; offences against children; corruption and fraud. Member States are also expected to ensure the 'approximation, where necessary, of rules on criminal matters'. We look in more detail later at the decision making procedures of the third pillar (below, 7.7). Member States remain responsible for the internal policing of their own countries.

7.2.4 Sole and shared competences

Policy making and government administration, therefore, now needs to be thought of as falling into three conceptual categories (see above, 2.3 and Figure 1). In one category, the Community has sole competence to decide what should be done. Such areas include agricultural policy and decisions about imports from countries outside the EC. A second category is where there Member States and the Community share competence to make law and policy – for example, in relation to regulating competition between businesses and about imposing value added tax on goods and services. A third category are those areas where each Member State continues to enjoy freedom to make law and policy without having to use the institutions of the European Union (for instance, internal policing and many aspects of family policy and law).

7.3 Is there a European constitution?

So far, we have seen that there are two important treaties. The Treaty on European Union (TEU) sets out the main objectives of the Union and deals with decision making in the second and third pillars. The EC Treaty continues to set out the objectives and institutions of what has become the first pillar of the European Union – the Community. Do these treaties amount to a written constitution? Certainly, the treaties have many characteristics of a written constitution: they lay down institutional structures and processes for making policy, legislating and adjudicating in wide fields of human activity; they confer rights and obligations; and they also lay down broad State objectives. Most of the rights contained in the EC Treaty are essentially economic ones – for instance, the rights of business enterprises, self-employed people and workers to free movement throughout all the Member States, without being discriminated against on the basis of the nationality, in order to create a single market. These rights amount to a constitutional guarantee of free trade. Like some other constitutions, the treaties also lay down broad requirements of governmental policy which have to be pursued.

One reason to suggest that the treaties are not a proper constitution, however, is that constitutions are traditionally understood to express the fundamental legal relationships between people and the State, and between different branches of the State (see above, 2.2). Even though the European Union is assuming more of the attributes commonly associated with States, such as the power to confer citizenship (Art 17 of the EC Treaty), it is not yet a body which amounts to a 'State'; it is still to be regarded primarily as a body created on the plane of public international law (see above, 2.12.1). Another reason why the treaties may stop short of being a constitution is because of what is lacking from its content. Frank Vibert explains:

> The democratic rights and civil liberties of individuals are mentioned only in passing. The Treaty is showing its age: its framers were more concerned with

providing a supranational platform for benevolent bureaucrats than a framework and process for the exercise of political choice by the citizens of Member States [*Europe's Constitutional Future*, 1990, London: IEA, p 88].

For a discussion of the treaty as a constitution, see, further, Harden, I, 'The constitution of the European Union' [1994] PL 609; Seurin, J-L, 'Towards a European constitution? problems of political integration' [1994] PL 625; and Walker, N, 'European constitutionalism and European integration' [1996] PL 266.

7.4 The European Union and principles of liberal democracy

Having considered the scope of the European Union, we can now return to the question of what it has to do with liberal democracy. The causes of the process of integration are debated by historians. Alan Milward argues that there are currently four different, but overlapping ideas (Milward, A, 'The springs of integration', in Gowan, P and Anderson, P (eds), *A Question of Europe*, 1997, London: Verso). For some analysts, integration has occurred as nations pursue their traditional foreign policy objectives: the development of the European Union is, for them, a kind of alliance system, such as existed between European States during the 19th century, but adapted to the modern world. In particular, the European Union has been created to protect Member States from other superpowers, such as the US and the former USSR. Other historians argue that European integration is the result of the modification or rejection of traditional foreign policy objectives by European countries. The rise of the European Union should, from this point of view, be seen as the product of federalist thinkers (like Jean Monnet, the French statesman who was instrumental in initiating discussions about the European Community), who were anti-nationalist, altruistic idealists. Yet other commentators argue that integration is occurring because of the inevitable loss of sovereignty by Nation States because of economic and social developments; with increasing mobility of people and information, frontiers become permeable and new systems of government are created to cope with these facts. Milward's own analysis is that European integration should be seen as having the deliberate goal of preserving the Nation State after its collapse in Europe between 1929 and 1945. As we have noted, the State has continually adapted itself in order to survive – by introducing universal suffrage, by creating rights to welfare benefits and the provision of health care and education (see above, Chapter 3). For Milward, integration buttresses the Nation State in the pursuit of income, welfare, family security and employment. In other words, integration is motivated by the domestic policy choices of governments.

In Chapter 1, we suggested that liberal democracy has three main attributes: the importance it attaches to personal autonomy (see above, 1.6.1); government based on popular participation (see above, 1.6.2); and the role of government institutions in providing safety and welfare for people (see above, 1.6.3). Let us consider what, if any, contribution the European Union makes to each of these characteristics.

7.4.1 Personal autonomy and the European Union

Ideas, policies and laws expressly to do with the personal autonomy of individuals and groups have not, so far, been significant in the growth of the European Union. Two factors help to explain why this is so. First, the earlier periods of development of the European Community (now the first pillar of the European Union) were mainly concerned with industry and commerce. The immediate goal of integration in the 1950s was to place the iron and coal industries, especially those of France and Germany, under the control of a supranational institutional framework in order to prevent them being used again for the purposes of war. The other important aim was to reduce barriers to trade between the Member States.

The second reason explaining why, unlike most national constitutional systems, the European Union has been able to attach little importance expressly to protecting individual autonomy, is the fact that another separate set of European institutions – the Council of Europe and the European Court of Human Rights in Strasbourg (see below, 19.6) – have had this as their main concern. All members of the European Union have also belonged to the Council of Europe (see above, 2.12.1). Some commentators worry about this situation. There have been calls for the European Union itself to become a signatory to the European Convention on Human Rights, to ensure that the institutions of the Union, in their dealings with people, properly respect basic human rights (see below, 19.11). This has not happened, but the European Union now pledges itself to:

> ... respect fundamental human rights, as guaranteed by the European Convention for the Protection of Human Rights and Fundamental Freedoms signed in Rome on 4 November 1950 and as the result from the constitutional traditions common to the Member States, as general principles of Community law [Art 6.2 of the TEU].

Critics point to the very general and vague terms of this provision. The judicial bodies of the European Union (the European Court of Justice and Court of First Instance in Luxembourg (see below, 7.5.5 and Chapter 18)) have no clear competence to deal with human rights abuses by the European Union itself or by Member States implementing European Union policy and law. It has, nevertheless, come to recognise principles of human rights laws in its case law (see below, 19.11).

7.4.2 Popular participation in the European Union

Despite the European Union's professed aim to further a system of governance based on the principles of liberal democracy, critics diagnose deep flaws in its realisation of these objectives. There is, it is said, a 'democratic deficit' (for a general discussion of this concept, see, further, Boyce, B, 'The democratic deficit of the European Community' (1993) Parl Aff 458). Part of the complaint is that decision making and law making within the various Union institutions is insufficiently accountable to elected representatives and that the Union provides inadequate political rights to its citizens. Certainly, the European Union does not replicate the political arrangements common to liberal democracies: there is no mechanism by which citizens can 'vote out' the 'government' of the Union.

The 626 Members of the European Parliament are the only directly elected representatives of the people in the Union system (see below, 7.5.2). This Parliament, it is said, has insufficient power within the law making process and cannot effectively call to account decision makers in other Union bodies – the unelected Commission, Council and European Court of Justice (the role of all of which will be explained shortly). A concomitant of European integration is that the constitutional effectiveness of national parliaments has diminished. For the UK, this means that British ministers, as part of the 15 person Council, now have powers to make legislation which they present as a *fait accompli* to MPs in the UK Parliament, who can do little more than rubber stamp them (see 6.5.2 and 7.6.2).

The European Union's powers also lack legitimacy, critics say, because the people of the UK have not truly consented to the phenomenally speedy and far-reaching growth in the governmental and law making powers of this supranational organisation. Unlike the campaigns for universal suffrage in the past, European integration clearly has not come about as the result of the demands of a mass movement of people; rather, it is was the product of visionary decisions made by a small elite of postwar politicians. The UK government under Conservative Prime Minister Edward Heath acceded to the precursor of the Union (the European Community) in 1973 without any referendum being held. After the Labour Party won the subsequent general election, a referendum was held in 1975, which posed the question 'Do you think that the UK should stay in the European Community ("the Common Market")?' Sixty seven per cent of people who voted answered yes. Nevertheless, since then, the critics argue, the Union has gained considerably greater governmental powers, the full implications of membership have become clearer, yet no further assent has been sought from the people for this project of ever greater European integration.

The counterargument is that the outcome of British general elections since the 1970s has been either a Conservative or Labour Party government committed to continued membership of the Union. The Referendum Party campaigned in the 1997 general election for a referendum on the UK's future in the Union, but received little support. The Prime Minister Tony Blair has also dismissed calls by the leader of the Opposition, saying: 'The idea that this country should have a referendum on the Amsterdam Treaty is one the most absurd propositions that has been advanced in recent times' (HC Deb, Col 933, 9 July 1997). A more general point is that referendums do not form an essential part of the UK's democratic system; there is no legal requirement or constitutional convention that one be held before significant changes are made to the constitution. Parliament has always voted in favour of incorporating the treaties which created the European Union and its forerunner, the European Community, and this, in British law, is all that is needed. It has to be said, however, that debate has sometimes been surprisingly brief. In the House of Commons, the committee stage of the bill incorporating the Amsterdam Treaty into British law was guillotined by the government after only 12 hours.

7.4.3 Security and welfare through the European Union

At their inception, the forerunners of today's European Union were supranational institutional frameworks created by Member States in order to prevent war breaking out once more in western Europe. Member States twice went to war with each other during the first half of the 20th century; they have not done so in the second half. Measured against this, the process of European integration has been a success. As we have noted, under the second pillar, Member States now work closely on issues of common defence (see above, 7.2.2 and below, 7.7.1). But the European Union in about more than just avoiding war; under the auspices of the third pillar (see above, 7.2.3 and below), there is increasingly close co-operation between Member States to combat crime.

Many of the policy areas which fall within the competence of the European Union are directly concerned with improving the ability of governments to provide for people's material welfare. Community law lays down minimum health and safety standards in workplaces and regulates maximum working hours. Laws deal with the safety of food and with environmental issues. Funds are distributed from the richer parts of the European Union to the poorer ones. Sex equality at work is required by Community law. The agricultural and fishery sectors are subject to a great deal of central planning by the European Community. In these and other ways, capitalist enterprises are controlled and the worst consequences of industrial production (or lack of it) are mitigated.

7.5 The institutions

A single set of institutions – notably, for our purposes, the Commission, the Council, the European Parliament and the European Court of Justice – serve the three pillars of the European Union (Art 3 of the TEU). There are, however, very important differences in the ways decisions are taken under each pillar. It is the role of the institutions under the first pillar, the Community, which marks out the European Union as a truly novel form of international organisation. Here, decision making, in those fields identified as matters for the Community by the EC Treaty, does not proceed according to traditional models of international diplomacy, in which ministers or diplomats of Nation States meet at conferences on the basis of formal equality, each having the power to veto proposals put forward when this is desirable in their particular nation's interests. Instead, the 15 Member States have conferred policy and law making powers on the institutions of the European Community, and, in so doing, have dramatically altered the position of national governments, parliaments and court systems. For decision making under the first pillar of the European Union (but not the second and third), there are several innovative features:

(a) the government of a Member State now only rarely retains a power to veto a decision which is favoured by other Member States;

(b) the institutions have independent power under the treaty to enact legislation, in the form of directives and regulations, which are binding on the Member States (even if they have voted against them) and their citizens;

(c) the governments, Parliaments and judicial systems of Member States are now subordinate to the decisions of the European Court of Justice;

(d) Member States no longer enjoy formal equality, as, when votes are taken, ministers from larger Member States have more votes than those from smaller ones (the system of qualified majority voting).

As we will see below, under the second pillar (common foreign and security policy) and the third pillar (criminal matters), decision making retains much more of a traditional, intergovernmental character. Here, the European Parliament and the European Court of Justice do not have the extensive powers which they exercise in Community matters.

7.5.1 The Commission

This consists of '20 members, who shall be chosen on the grounds of their general competence and whose independence is beyond doubt' (Art 213 of the EC Treaty). A practice has arisen that the large European Union Member States each nominate two, and the smaller members each nominate one commissioner; but once appointed, however, the commissioner is forbidden from taking instructions or favouring his or her national government. Nominations are subject to approval by the European Parliament, but the Commission is a relatively undemocratic body in the sense that it is neither elected nor subject to any great degree of accountability by citizens' elected representatives. The justification put forward for this state of affairs is that the Commission needs to be able to act with relative autonomy from political pressure from Member States and from the European Parliament in order to further the overriding goal of European integration.

Recently serving commissioners nominated by the UK are Sir Leon Brittan (once a minister in Mrs Thatcher's Cabinet) and Neil Kinnock (formerly leader of the Labour Party). One of the commissioners becomes the President: currently (1999) the post is occupied by Romano Prodi; his two immediate predecessors were Jacques Santer and Jacques Delors.

The task of the commissioners is to further the general interest of the Community by developing policy and proposing legislation in the fields set down by the treaty. This is done through a series of 'Directorates General' (DGs, which are, in effect, departments) each headed by one of the commissioners and supported by a staff of officials. The Commission regularly meets as a whole, in private, to consider broad issues and to decide important policy. The Commission also has some regulatory functions, particularly in relation to competition and agricultural policy (on this, and the making of 'soft law', see 8.2.5 and 8.3.4). In addition, it provides executive and administrative support for the work of the European Union.

The Commission has frequently been criticised. During the late 1980s, it was seen by governments of some Member States (including the UK) as exercising too much governmental power, leaving too little to the Member States. Since then, a shift has taken place. The EC Treaty was amended to incorporate the principle of subsidiarity, signalling the limits on the powers of the Commission in particular and the Community in general (see below, 7.8.3). The Commission itself recognised the need to reign in some of its ambitions and, in 1995, took as its unofficial motto 'Doing less, better'.

Under the presidency of Jacques Santer, the Commission was subject to mounting opposition. In 1996, the European Parliament refused to approve the Commission's accounts amid accusations of large scale fraud and mismanagement of funds. In January 1999, a senior official in the Commission leaked information to the European Parliament which appeared to show that the Commission was attempting to cover up incompetence and wrongdoing. Under pressure from the European Parliament, the Commission agreed to the setting up of a committee of independent experts to investigate matters. In March 1999, the committee reported its findings of fraud and mismanagement. Several commissioners were found to have indulged in nepotism, recruiting friends and relatives to fill posts in the Community without following proper procedures. All 20 commissioners resigned. Member States, in consultation with the European Parliament, appointed new commissioners, headed by Romano Prodi (a former premier of Italy) as President.

7.5.2　The European Parliament

The European Parliament consists of 'representatives of the peoples of the States brought together in the Community' (Art 189 of the EC Treaty). There are 87 European parliamentary constituencies in the UK, each electing one MEP by a system of proportional representation. Elections are held every five years, most recently in 1998. MEPs group themselves according to political affiliations rather than in national blocks. The EC Treaty expressly recognises that 'political parties at European level are important as a factor for integration within the Union. They contribute to forming a European awareness and to expressing the political will of the citizens of the Union' (Art 191 of the EC Treaty). For these reasons, the European Parliament should be seen as representing political opinion throughout the Union, rather than the interests of the various Member States as such.

7.5.3　The Council

This consists of 'a representative of each Member State at ministerial level, authorised to commit the government of that Member State' (Art 203 of the EC Treaty). The Council makes decisions of policy within the fields laid down by the treaty and adopts, or rejects, legislation proposed by the Commission after it has been considered by the European Parliament.

The Council is more a process than an institution. It has no regular place at which it meets. Which minister attends meetings of the Council depends on the subject matter under discussions, so that, for example, the UK representative when employment issues are considered is the Secretary of State for Education and Employment. More than one meeting of the Council may take place simultaneously. Preparations and preliminary negotiations for Council meetings are done by a permanent committee of senior diplomats from Member States (COREPER). The late Alan Clark MP, a former UK minister, explained the process in his idiosyncratic style:

> it makes not the slightest difference to the conclusions of a meeting what ministers say at it. Everything is decided, horse-traded off by officials at COREPER ... The ministers arrive on the scene at the last minute, hot, tired, ill or drunk (sometimes all of these together), read out their piece and depart [*Alan Clark's Diaries*, quoted in (1998) *The Economist*, 8 August, p 37].

This is probably an exaggeration. When decisions have to be taken by the Council, voting is now usually according to the principle of qualified majority voting in which ministers from larger Member States have more votes than those from smaller ones (for example, a UK minister has 10 votes, whereas Denmark has only three).

7.5.4 The European Council

The European Council is the twice yearly meeting of Heads of State or government of the Member States (for the UK, that is the Prime Minister), the president of the Commission and the foreign ministers of the Member States (Art 4, TEU). Its role is to 'provide the Union with the necessary impetus for its development' and to 'define the general political guidelines thereof'. (Note that the European Council is entirely distinct from the Council of Europe, the international body under which the European Convention on Human Rights has been established (see above, 2.12.1).)

7.5.5 The European Court of Justice and the Court of First Instance

The role of the Court of Justice is to 'ensure that in the interpretation and application of [the EC Treaty] the law is observed' (Art 220 of the EC Treaty). There are 15 judges, one nominated by each Member State. The UK nominee is currently Judge David Edward, a Scottish lawyer; his predecessor was Lord Slynn. Nine Advocates General, who are judicial officers of similar status to the judges, participate in cases by delivering reasoned opinions suggesting the appropriate resolution of each case. The court usually follows the Advocate General's advice, but is not bound to do so. (Francis Jacobs QC has been an Advocate General since 1988.) In 1989, a second court, the Court of First Instance, was created to hear some, generally less important, classes of litigation. The are several different types of proceedings (which will be considered in more detail in Chapter 18):

(a) Under Art 234 of the EC Treaty (formerly Art 177 before the treaty provisions were renumbered by the Amsterdam Treaty in 1998), the Court of Justice may give preliminary rulings on points of EC law when requested to do so by courts and tribunals in the Member States. This important procedure is considered in more detail in Chapter 18.

(b) The Court of Justice is also the final arbiter as to whether the Union institutions have followed the procedures when making legislation and decisions (Art 230 annulment proceedings).

(c) The Commission and Member States may also bring proceedings in the Court of Justice to compel another Member State to fulfil its obligations under European law (Arts 226 and 228).

Through its case law, the court has developed several important principles of law, including proportionality and rights to compensation for breach of EC law.

As we shall see shortly, the court has also developed more fundamental – and controversial – constitutional principles, such as the primacy of Community law and the direct effectiveness of Community law. Indeed, the whole role of the Court of Justice has sparked criticism. Few doubt that the

Court of Justice has been a powerful force in furthering the goal of European integration. Lord Neill (who went on to chair the Committee on Standards in Public Life (see above, 6.1)) wrote, in 1995, that 'a court with a mission is not an orthodox court. It is potentially a dangerous court – the danger being that inherent in uncontrollable judicial power' (*The European Court of Justice: A Case Study in Judicial Activism*, 1995, London: European Policy Forum, p 48). He was critical of the court's approach to interpreting the treaty, saying that its methods 'have liberated the court form the customarily accepted discipline of endeavouring by textual analysis to ascertain the meaning and language of the relevant provision' (p 47). Against this view needs to be set the claim that the creation of a single market would have been impossible without the Court of Justice taking a lead in ensuring the universal application of the common rules of Community law on which it depends.

7.6 How the Community legislates

As we have noted, the novel feature of the Community – the first of the Union's three pillars – is that institutions have power under the treaty to make legislation binding in the legal systems of the Member States. Such legislation is in the form of regulations and directives (defined in Art 249 of the EC Treaty).

7.6.1 Regulations

A regulation has 'general application' and is 'binding in its entirety and directly applicable in all Member States'. In other words, they are a source of law in the UK legal systems without the British Government or Parliament needing to incorporate them into English law. Indeed, it is unlawful for a Member State, through its government or Parliament, to seek to give legal effect to a Community regulation by enacting national legislation: see Case 34/73 *Variola v Amministrazione delle Finanze* (1973). Many regulations are made solely by the Commission under powers delegated to it by the Council.

7.6.2 Directives

A directive is 'binding, as to the result to be achieved, upon each Member State to which it is addressed, but shall leave to the national authorities the choice of form and methods' (Art 249 of the EC Treaty). In other words, this type of Community legislation creates a binding framework for achieving a particular policy, within which Member States are able to fulfil in different ways according to what is most appropriate in their national circumstances. Directives lay down a time limit, often 12 or 18 months, by which all Member States must have achieved the results laid down by the directive. This will often require national legislation, an Act of Parliament or statutory instrument, to be enacted.

The legislative processes by which the Community institutions make directives has, for many years, been notoriously labyrinthine, though the Amsterdam Treaty simplified them a little. The initiative for a proposed directive comes from the Commission and is often the result of protracted consultations with governments of Member States and pressure groups (see Harlow, C, 'A community of interests? making the most of European law' (1992) 55 MLR 331). Once a draft directive has been produced, it has to be considered and approved by the European Parliament and the Council in accordance with one of three main procedures: assent; co-decision (Art 251 of the EC Treaty); or consultation. These differ according to the degree of influence each confers on the European Parliament to make amendments or veto draft legislation and whether voting in the Council is by qualified majority or requires unanimity.

National parliaments are given no formal role during the Community legislative process. In the UK, both the House of Lords and the Commons have, however, established select committees which attempt to exert influence by taking evidence from experts, interested parties and the government and then issuing reports about draft directives (see, further, Denza, E, 'Parliamentary scrutiny of community legislation' [1993] Statute LR 56). In 1980, the UK Parliament passed a resolution which made it clear that British ministers should not vote in favour of a draft directive in Council until any parliamentary committee considering that particular proposal had concluded its deliberations and issued a report, unless there were 'special reasons' for the minister needing to vote. The Protocol on National Parliaments agreed as part of the Amsterdam Treaty has gone a little way to improving opportunities for national parliaments in the legislative process. It requires the Community to provide parliaments with timely information about proposed legislation, and it also formally establishes the Conference of European Affairs Committees (COSAC), at which parliamentarians from the Member States meet to discuss issues. There are continuing calls for national parliaments to be given a greater role in decision making and scrutiny processes in order to fill the democratic deficit.

Once a Directive is adopted by the Community, each Member State has, within the stipulated time, to ensure that its own national law and practices comply with the terms of the directive. Often, this will involve introducing new legislation into the national parliament. In the UK, this can be done by Act of Parliament (for example, the Consumer Protection Act 1987 brought Directive 85/374/EEC into English law). More commonly, directives are brought into domestic law by making a statutory instrument (on which, generally, see above, 6.8.2). The Directive on Unfair Terms in Consumer Contracts 93/13/EEC was transposed into domestic law in this way. Section 2(2) of the European Communities Act 1972 gives ministers a general power to use statutory instruments to implement directives, though Sched 2 prohibits the use of statutory instruments to impose taxation, retrospective legislation, sub-delegated legislation or the creation of new criminal offences. Using statutory instruments has obvious advantages for the government; given the already overcrowded legislative timetable for Bills in Parliament, it would be impossible to use primary legislation to transpose all directives. The downside is that statutory instruments receive little parliamentary scrutiny in comparison to Bills. Greater opportunities to scrutinise would, though, be of little value, as once a directive has been made by the Community, a Member State and its Parliament are required by Community law to give effect to it (see above).

There is no obligation for the Act of Parliament or statutory instrument to use precisely the same wording as the directive. In the past, there was a tendency for British legislative drafters to use a traditional English style, which spells out the policy in great detail and attempts to anticipate as many contingencies as possible. The danger with this is that discrepancies may arise between the Act or statutory instrument and the original directive on which it was based. An alternative approach to drafting, known as the 'copy out' technique, is therefore gaining favour; here the text of the directive is just set out almost word for word. A potential problem with this approach is that directives normally only set out broad principles, and there is a fear that this will give English judges too much discretion to fill in detail when they are called upon to interpret the legislation.

7.7 Institutions and processes in the second and third pillars

In the previous section, we have looked at the institutions and legislative processes within the Community, the first pillar of the European Union. The decision making structures in the second pillar (common foreign and security policy) and the third pillar (police and judicial co-operation on crime) are different. They are often described as 'intergovernmental', to emphasise several features:

(a) they take place outside the procedures applicable to the Community under the first pillar;

(b) in many situations, each Member State retains the right to veto any policy which others favour;

(c) the outcome of the decision making process is not legislation binding in the legal systems of Member States (as are directives and regulations in Community law), but, rather, have a status more like international agreements binding on countries as a matter of public international law.

7.7.1 The second pillar: common foreign and security policy

Overall responsibility for defining 'the principles of and general guidelines for the common foreign and security policy, including for matters with defence implications' lies with the European Council (Art 13 of the TEU), that is, with the twice yearly meeting of the Heads of State or government of the Member States, the president of the Commission assisted by the foreign ministers of the Member States (see above, 7.5.4). The treaty lays down no set procedures for decision making by the European Council.

The Council, that is, the more regular meetings of ministerial representatives of the Member States (see above), recommends common strategies to the European Council 'and shall implement them, in particular by adopting joint actions and common positions'. These measures do not have the direct force of law within the national legal systems of the Member States, unlike directives and regulations made within the Community. The decisions of the Council are generally taken on the basis of unanimity, not qualified majority voting, when they have military or defence implications (Art 23 of the TEU). The European Parliament is, at most, consulted by the Council and concerns are often expressed as to the lack of democratic accountability for the Union's common foreign and security policies. Examples of agreements under the second pillar are a 'Common Position on Albania to support democracy and stability' and a 'Joint Action to help the Palestinian Authority counter terrorist activities in the territories under its control'.

7.7.2 Third pillar

In the third pillar (police and judicial co-operation in criminal matters), co-operation takes place at a number of levels – from that of police forces and customs authorities up to ministerial level. Numerous working groups have been established to take responsibility for discussion of policy on specific issues. Where action is taken at the ministerial level, this is done through the Council. Voting takes place on the basis of unanimity rather than a qualified majority – in other words, each member retains a right of veto. The outcome of discussion may take various forms, including 'common positions', 'framework decisions', 'other decisions' and the adoption of international conventions (Art 34 of the TEU). None of these measures is automatically binding within the legal systems of the UK.

By use of a 'convention', Member States have established Europol, an organisation based in The Hague, through which police forces liase by exchanging information, conducting joint training and having exchange programmes. In March 1998, the Council adopted a 'common action' on indictments for the participation in criminal organisations, with Member States agreeing to make certain activities 'subject to effective, proportionate and dissuasive criminal sanction'. Another field in which there is co-operation is in the enforcement of driving bans imposed in one Member State in all other Member States. Where co-operation takes place in the form of international conventions, the problem is that they have to be ratified in each Member State before coming in to force; they are also often subject to complex 'declarations' and 'reservations' by Member States.

Critics are concerned that this developing field of intergovernmental co-operation is not subject to effective control as it is not supervised by the Commission nor the European Parliament. The role of the European Parliament is limited to being consulted on these measures, and the jurisdiction of the European Court of Justice in relation to these matters is also limited (Art 35 of the TEU). In the UK, concern has been expressed that the decisions of British ministers under the third pillar are liable to sidestep the UK Parliament. In 1997, the House of Lords' select committee on the European Communities reported:

> We believe that Parliament owes a duty to the public to ensure that Ministers are made fully accountable for their actions in Council. The matters falling under the Third Pillar can have serious implications for the rights and freedoms of the individual, and Parliament must ensure that its procedures for monitoring work under the Third Pillar are effective [Sixth Report, Session 1997–98, para 1].

During 1997, Member States took steps towards making third pillar decision making more transparent, with publication of the timetables for discussions of various working groups, progress reports and by allowing the public access (through the internet) of proposals on criminal matters presented to the European Parliament.

7.8 Constitutional relationships between the UK, the Union and citizens

The legal connector between the Union and the UK is the European Communities Act 1972, as amended. Anyone looking there to find an explanation of the principles which regulate this relationship will be sorely disappointed. The 1972 Act is a dismal triumph for impenetrable statutory drafting techniques. Its constitutional novelty lay in the fact that it not only incorporated the text of a treaty into the legal systems of the UK, but also all past and future directives and regulations made by the Community institutions. It also brought into the national legal systems of the UK what is known as the *acquis communautaire* (defined by William Robinson as 'an amorphous phenomenon. It constitutes the body of objectives, substantives rules, policies, laws, rights, obligations, remedies and case law which are fundamental to the development of the Community legal order' in Monar, J *et al* (eds), *Butterworths Expert Guide to the European Union*, 1996, London: Butterworths, p 3).

British law has little to contribute to the discussion of the constitutional relationship between the UK and the Union, other than the overworked concept of parliamentary sovereignty. As we noted, commentators differ in their analysis of the extent to which this has been 'lost', 'pooled' or 'transferred' as a consequences of membership of the Union (see above, Chapters 2 and 5). The notion of sovereignty is, however, only one of a number of principles which regulate constitutional relationships to the Union. As we shall see shortly, although the treaty does not spell this out expressly, the European Court of Justice has held that Community law takes priority over the laws of Member States, including their constitutional law (see below, 7.8.1). This means that the relationship between a Member State and the Union is ultimately a question of Community law.

7.8.1 Loyalty to the project

Membership requires a Member State – which means its government, Parliament, judiciary and its other emanations – to abide by the decisions and legislation made by the Community institutions. Article 10 of the EC Treaty provides:

> Member States shall take all appropriate measures, whether general or particular, to ensure fulfilment of the obligations arising out of this Treaty or resulting from action taken by the institutions of the Community. They shall facilitate the achievement of the Community's tasks.

They shall abstain from any measure which could jeopardise the attainment of the objectives of this Treaty.

This article (formerly Art 5) has been used by the European Court of Justice to justify several of its innovative doctrines. From time to time, governments of Member States are implacably opposed to legislation made by the Community. One recent example was the Conservative government's hostility to the Directive on Certain Aspects of Working Time 93/104/EC, a measure which sought to impose restrictions on working hours, which the British Government at the time saw as contrary to its own desired policy of deregulating working arrangements. After having unsuccessfully challenged the legal validity of the directive in proceedings before the European Court of Justice, the government was obliged to initiate legislation to bring national law into accordance with the directive, and Parliament was under an obligation to pass such legislation.

There is, then, no scope for a Member State to pick and choose which Community legislation it will comply with – so long as it remains a member. Suggestions have been made in the past that if an Act of Parliament were knowingly to enact a provision incompatible with Community law (an unlikely event), then a British court would be bound by the British constitutional principle of parliamentary sovereignty to give effect to the statute rather than the EC legislation: see *obiter dicta* of Lord Denning MR in *Macarthys Ltd v Smith* (1979) and *Blackburn v AG* (1971). This view is unlikely to be followed today. Were the issue to arise, the British court would have to make an Art 234 reference to the European Court of Justice for it to make a preliminary ruling on this point. Article 10 of the EC Treaty (set out above), and the principle of the primacy of Community law even over Member States' constitutions, would seem to indicate only one answer.

7.8.2 Negotiating opt-outs at the treaty revisions

The main scope governments of Member States have for seeking to exempt their country from legal requirements imposed by Community law is to negotiate a formal derogation from the Treaty at one of the periodic intergovernmental conferences set up to revise the treaties (as in Maastricht in 1993 and Amsterdam in 1997). Thus, at the time of the Maastricht agreement, the last Conservative government negotiated an opt-out from the provisions of the Social Chapter of the EC Treaty, which empowered the Community to make legislation affecting working conditions. In the event, the practical implications of this opt-out arrangement was not tested, as the incoming Labour government agreed at Amsterdam that the UK should be bound by the Social Chapter. One important British opt-out which remains relates to Community policy on monetary union and the single currency.

7.8.3 The principle of subsidiarity

Another important feature of the constitutional relationships between Member States and the Union is the principle of subsidiarity, which was set down at the time of the Maastricht Treaty to allay fears in some Member States that the Commission was exercising its powers to take action and initiate Community legislation in too broad a way. Article 5 of the TEU provides:

> The Community shall act within the limits of the powers conferred upon it by this Treaty and of the objectives assigned to it therein.
>
> In areas which do not fall within its exclusive competence, the Community shall take action, in accordance with the principle of subsidiarity, only if and in so far as the objectives of the proposed action cannot be sufficiently achieved by the Member States and can therefore, by reason of the scale or effects of the proposed action, be better achieved by the Community.
>
> Any action by the Community shall not go beyond what is necessary to achieve the objectives of this Treaty.

There has been much academic debate about the meaning and practical implementation of the subsidiarity principle (see, further, O'Keeffe, D and Twomey, P (eds), *Legal Issues of the Maastricht Treaty*, 1994, London: Wiley, especially Chapters 3–5). The Amsterdam Treaty attempts to make it less vague by providing a more detailed framework governing its application. Here we see the start of the process for the principled demarcation of powers between the Union and the Member States, giving some constitutional protection for the rights of the latter.

7.8.4   Closer co-operation

Constitutionally, perhaps the most important innovation in the 1998 Amsterdam Treaty is the enactment of a general concept of 'closer co-operation' (Arts 43–45 of the TEU) under which it will now be possible for a group of Member States to go ahead – in the first or third pillars of the Union – to use the institutional framework of the Union to develop policy initiatives and legislate without all other Member States having to be bound by these outcomes. The aim is to introduce a degree of flexibility into the project of European integration – a so called 'multi-track' Union – without undermining the integrity of the project as a whole. Great uncertainties surround how this new arrangement will operate.

7.9   Community law in national legal systems

The way in which Community law is applied by national courts is a matter of Community law, not national law. In a series of cases in the early 1960s, the Court of Justice asserted the idea that the EC Treaty has created 'a new legal order of international law'. This had two main features. One was that the 'States have limited their sovereign rights' and, accordingly, Community law takes precedence over any inconsistent national law or practice. The second feature of the new legal order is direct effect. This is the idea that 'independently of the legislation of Member States, Community law imposes obligations on individuals' and 'confers upon them rights which become part of their legal heritage'.

7.9.1   Primacy of Community law

The principle that Community law takes precedence over any inconsistent laws in Member States was well established by the Court of Justice before the UK joined the Community in 1973. In Case 26/62 *van Gend en Loos* (1963), the court stated – to the surprise of some of the Member States at the time – that 'the Community constitutes a new legal order of international law for the benefit of which the States have limited their sovereign rights, albeit within limited fields'. Shortly afterwards, the court spelt this out even more fully in Case 6/64 *Costa v ENEL* (1964):

> By creating a Community of unlimited duration, having its own legal institutions, its own personality, its own legal capacity ... and, more particularly, real powers stemming from a limitation of sovereignty or a transfer of powers from the States to the Community, the Member States have limited their sovereign rights, albeit within limited fields, and have thus created a body of law which binds both their nationals and themselves.

> The integration into the laws of each Member State of provisions which derive from the Community, and more generally form the terms and the spirit of the

treaty, make it impossible for the States, as a corollary, to accord precedence to the unilateral and subsequent measure over a legal system accepted by them on the basis of reciprocity. Such a measure cannot therefore be consistent with that legal system. The executive force of Community law cannot vary from one State to another in deference to subsequent domestic laws, without jeopardising the attainment of the objectives of the Treaty.

In 1970, the court held that Community law takes precedence even over the fundamental constitutional law of a Member State: see Case 11/70 *Internationale Handelsgesellschaft* (1970).

By incorporating the treaty into national law by the European Communities Act 1972, the UK constitutional system accepted this principle of primacy, though neither the treaty itself, nor the 1972 Act, actually spell it out clearly and explicitly. It was relatively late on in its membership that UK courts first had to 'disapply' inconsistent national law and give effect to Community law (see above, 5.2.4).

7.9.2 Direct effect of Community law

The basic idea of direct effect is that, in certain circumstances, provisions in Community law – in the EC Treaty itself, and regulations and directives – confer rights on individuals and business corporations which they may enforce in national courts. As we shall see shortly, sometimes the rights are enforceable only against governmental bodies, whereas in other situations, rights under Community law may also be enforced against other individuals and companies.

Direct effect of the treaty

Many provisions in the treaty are not concerned with conferring rights or obligations on anyone, but rather with setting out institutional structures and processes for decision making within the Community. Some articles, however, do deal with the freedom of people to act, and it is these which may be capable of having direct effect in domestic litigation. In Case 26/62 *van Gend en Loos* (1963), the Court of Justice held that an article which 'contains a clear and unconditional prohibition which is not a positive but a negative obligation [and] is not qualified by any reservation on the part of States which would make its implementation conditional upon a positive legislative measure enacted under national law' may be able to benefit the nationals of the Member State. The following treaty provisions, among others, have been held by the European Court to be directly effective: Art 28, which prohibits quantitative restrictions on imports and discriminatory measures having equivalent effect; Art 39, on the free movement workers; Art 43, conferring the right of freedom of establishment for businesses; and Art 141, which states that 'each Member State shall ensure that the principle of equal pay for male and female workers for equal work or work of equal value is applied'.

These rights can be relied on by a person in a British court, both 'vertically' against the Member State and 'horizontally' against another private citizen or business. What bodies count as being an emanation of a Member State has been defined broadly for this purpose by the Court of Justice in Case C-188/89 *Foster v British Gas plc* (1990):

> ... a body, whatever its legal form, which is made responsible, pursuant to a measure adopted by the State, for providing a public service under the control of the State and has for that purpose special powers beyond those which result from the normal rules applicable in relations between individuals.

Direct effect of regulations

As we have seen (above), regulations are defined as being 'directly applicable in all Member States' once made by the Community institutions (Art 249 of the EC Treaty). Like the treaty provisions, however, not all regulations create rights and obligations enforceable in national courts. For a regulation to be relied upon by a litigant in a national legal system as conferring rights or imposing obligations, its provisions must be clear and precise, unconditional and leave no room for the exercise of discretion in its implementation. Like treaty articles, regulations may be directly effective both vertically and horizontally.

Direct effect of directives

It is the application of the concept of direct effect to directives which has caused the most controversy. You may be thinking that, if directives are transposed into English law by Act of Parliament or statutory instrument (see above), then there will be no need for a litigant to seek to rely on the directive itself during the course of litigation in a national court. A variety of practical situations may, however, occur where it is still necessary to look at the directive itself. First, the government may have failed to transpose the directive into national law by the set date and so failed to confer rights set out to be achieved by the directive. Secondly, the UK Act of Parliament or statutory instrument which seeks to incorporate the directive into national law may not properly reflect the provisions of the relevant directive (either because of a mistake in drafting, or because the government took a view of what the directive requires which is not shared by the court). In these circumstances, a litigant may rely on the terms of the directive itself, provided that the rights it confers are unconditional and sufficiently precise: Case 41/74 *Van Duyn v Home Office* (1974).

The European Court of Justice has held that directives (unlike the treaty provisions and regulations considered above) can never have horizontal direct effect, only vertical effect. In other words, an individual cannot directly rely on the provisions of a directive against another individual or private business, only against an institution of the State: see Case 152/84 *Marshall v Southampton and South West AHA (Teaching)* (1986) and *Faccini Dori v Recreb* (1994). One reason for courts limiting the principle in this way is that the wording used in Art 249 of the EC Treaty defines a directive as binding 'upon each Member State to which it is addressed', in contrast to regulations which 'have general application'. Another justification is that a Member State should not be allowed to rely upon its own breach of Community law, in failing to transpose a directive into domestic law, as a ground for denying a person rights. The distinction between horizontal and vertical direct effect can create anomalies. For example, two people – one working for a governmental body, the other for a private businesses – may have exactly the same dispute over (say) sex discrimination, but only the public sector employee will be able to rely upon any relevant directives in taking her employer to court. The private sector employee may, however, be able to apply for judicial review against the government for its failure properly to implement the directive into national law, as in *Equal Opportunities Commission v Secretary of State for Employment* (1995).

7.9.3 Principle of consistent interpretation

The rule that directives can only have direct effect vertically, that is against public bodies, has been slightly undermined by Case C-106/89 *Marleasing SA v La Comercial Internacional de Alimentacion SA* (1992), in which the Court of Justice held that national courts had, so far as possible, to interpret all national legislation so that it conforms with any relevant directives. The practical effect of this is that rights or obligations contained in a directive may, by this sidewind, by enforced by a British court even against a private person or business. The House of Lords have added a gloss to this: the court or tribunal must carry out its task of interpretation 'without distorting the meaning of the domestic legislation' and words of the Act or statutory instrument must actually be capable of supporting an interpretation consistent with the directive: see *Webb v EMO Air Cargo UK Ltd* (1993). In other words, the English courts apply the *Marleasing* principle to choose an interpretation of legislation consistent with a directive where this is one of several plausible interpretations.

7.9.4 Compensation for breach of Community law

Following an important judgment by the European Court of Justice in Joined Cases C-6 and 9/90 *Republic of Italy v Francovich* (1991), citizens and businesses may now claim damages against a Member State which has failed to transpose a directive into its domestic law properly or at all, whether or not it had direct effect. In *Francovich*, the Italian Government should have transposed a directive into its domestic law to set up some sort of scheme (it was up to each Member State to decide precisely what kind) to ensure that employees received any outstanding wages, etc, if their employer became insolvent. Italy failed to do this by the due date. Francovich's employer went bust and he was not paid. The directive was not directly effective against the

Italian Government because the provisions lacked sufficient 'unconditionality' – the government needed to carry out several things before the scheme could be operational. But Francovich sued the Italian Government for their failure to establish a scheme. The Court of Justice held that there was a right to damages for non-transposition of a directive if three conditions were satisfied in a case. These were: the directive had to create individual rights; the content of those rights must be ascertainable from the directive itself; there was a causal link between the government's failure to transpose the directive and the individual's loss. In later cases, the Court of Justice has added the requirement that the breach of Community law must be 'sufficiently serious'. Whether this is so is for the national court hearing the damages action to determine. A failure to implement a directive within the set time limit is, of itself, a sufficiently serious breach warranting compensation: *Dillenkofer v Germany* (1997).

A right to compensation may also exist in relation to other breaches of Community law, including breaches of the EC Treaty (*R v Secretary of State for Transport ex p Factortame Ltd (No 4)* (1997) where the British Government enacted a statute incompatible with the right to freedom of establishment) and the taking of administrative action contrary to Community law (*R v Minister for Agriculture, Fisheries and Food ex p Hedley Lomas (Ireland) Ltd* (1996)).

7.10 Conclusions

Membership of the Union has brought about momentous alterations in basic features of the constitutional system of the UK. The Treaty on European Union and the EC Treaty form an emergent written constitution for western Europe. Until now, the framers of the treaties have placed special importance upon constitutional guarantees for free trade and associated economic rights, some of which are enforceable by individuals and business enterprises in national courts. Through the principles of primacy of EC law, subsidiarity and, now, closer co-operation, the treaty and the European Court of Justice are venturing to set down constitutional principles to govern the developing constitutional relationships between the Union and its Member States. What stands in the way of the treaties being regarded as a proper constitution, however, is the absence of effective civil and political rights for citizens. Though the treaties and the Court of Justice have regard to such rights, especially those contained in the European Convention on Human Rights, the Union continues to suffer from a severe democratic deficit in its systems of decision making and legislation.

THE EUROPEAN UNION

Why European integration is taking place

The European Union is a paradox: it both promotes constitutional systems based on the principles of liberal democracy and undermines them because the institutions of the EU suffer from a democracy deficit. Several explanations have been put forward to explain why integration is taking place in the EU. Some stress that the formation of the EU is an aspect of foreign policy – protecting countries in Europe from other world powers and also preventing war breaking out throughout Europe as it did twice during the 20th century. Other explanations emphasise integration as an aspect of globalisation. Another sees the EU as the method by which States continue to be able to provide welfare benefits and social services to their citizens.

The legal base

The institutions and processes of EU are arranged into a 'temple of three pillars':

(a) the European Community, the longest established part of the EU;

(b) the second pillar in which Member States develop common foreign and security policy;

(c) the third pillar of police and judicial co-operation in criminal matters.

The legal basis for the EU rests on two treaties: the Treaty on European Union and the EC Treaty, both amended by the Treaty of Amsterdam which came into force in May 1999. The treaties set out the institutional and procedural arrangements for decision making. The main institutions are:

(a) the Commission;

(b) the Council;

(c) the European Parliament;

(d) the Court of Justice.

The EC Treaty also includes rights for individuals and businesses – including the 'four freedoms' of free movement of persons, goods, capital and services. It also requires equal pay for equal work between men and women.

The EU institutions, working in the European Community pillar, are empowered to make legislation in the form of directives and regulations. All Community legal rules take priority over inconsistent national laws in the

Member States. The European Court of Justice is the final arbiter on the interpretation of Community law.

In the second and third pillars, Member States have not delegated law making powers to EU institutions. Member States agree upon 'common positions' and 'joint actions'.

Constitutional relationship between the UK and EU

So far as the UK is concerned, it is the European Communities Act 1972 (as amended) which incorporates into the domestic legal systems the TEU and the EC Treaty, directives and regulations and the case law of the Court of Justice. Membership of the EU requires Member States to 'take all appropriate measures' to ensure fulfilment of their obligations, and to 'abstain from any measure which could jeopardise' the objectives of the Community. The only way that a Member State may exempt itself from a particular area of Community law is by negotiating an 'opt-out' from the EC Treaty at one of the intergovernmental conferences held every few years to revise the treaties. Member States who wish to work more closely in a particular field may now do so under the 'closer co-operation' provisions on the TEU; this may result in a 'multi-track' EU. Where competence in an area of policy is shared between Member States and the Community, the principle of subsidiarity limits the scope of Community action.

In national legal systems, Community law has primacy over any inconsistent domestic rule. Some provisions of the EC Treaty are directly effective (vertically and horizontally), meaning they create rights which may be relied upon by people in national courts. Regulations are 'directly applicable', and provisions in them may also be directly effective (vertically and horizontally). Directives may also create directly effective rights – but only vertically and after the time for implementation has passed. National courts and tribunals have an obligation to interpret national legislation so that it conforms to Community law. They may also award damages to people who suffer loss as a result of a breach of Community law by a Member State.

CHAPTER 8

GOVERNMENT AND ADMINISTRATION

8.1   Introduction

One of the purposes of a constitutional system is to provide means by which large scale societies may make collective decisions. The ideal of representative democracy is that important decisions are taken by our elected representatives (see above, 1.6.2). In practice, this is not possible. Parliamentary bodies are too large and fractious to be effective decision making organs. The role of such bodies is, therefore, often confined to scrutinising and passing legislative proposals initiated by a smaller executive committee of their members; and to calling members of that executive committee to account for their actions. As we have seen, the executive committees of the UK Parliament, the Scottish Parliament, the Northern Ireland Assembly and the National Assembly for Wales are known respectively as: the Cabinet (see above, 2.4.3); the Scottish Executive (see above, 2.5.2); the Northern Ireland Executive (see above, 2.6.2); and the Executive Committee of the National Assembly for Wales (see above, 2.7). The role of members of the executive committees ('ministers') is to decide what ought to be done. Ministers do usually set the policy agenda, based on the political manifesto their party issued before a parliamentary election (see above, 6.3).

Generally, ministers do not have the time or expertise to carry out the practical implementation of their policy choices. They do, occasionally, make decisions about the application of law and policy to individual people – for instance, ministers in the UK Government sometimes personally make decisions about whether a particular person should be allowed to enter or forced to leave the country, how long people convicted of serious crimes should serve in prison and whether government should intervene in one business's attempt to take over another enterprise. But most decisions about the implementation of policy and law are left to a staff of unelected, politically neutral officials. Without a large body of staff, government would simply not be able to carry out its functions of securing our safety and security (see above, 1.7).

This chapter examines how executive bodies, and their staffs of public officials, set the framework for implementing policy.

8.1.1   The constitutional status of public officials

The roles carried out by public officials vary greatly. Some are responsible for the very practical delivery of public services, such as issuing driving licences to people who have passed the test, which requires no difficult judgment.

Others are professionally qualified people who have to decide how law and policy are to be applied to particular individuals – for example, a member of the Crown Prosecution Service deciding whether a prosecution should proceed; a social worker deciding whether apparently neglected children should be taken into the care of the local authority; a scientist deciding whether a factory has breached pollution emission standards; an economist calculating whether a business is abusing a monopolistic position.

The legal status of public officials varies according to the level of government at which they are employed. Officials employed by the Government of the UK or the devolved executive institutions in Scotland, Northern Ireland and Wales continue to have their basic status determined largely by rules made under prerogative powers (see above, 2.4.3) rather than an Act of Parliament. Most such officials are in the service of 'Her Majesty's Home Civil Service'; staff of the Foreign and Commonwealth Office serve under different terms and conditions. Public officials with posts in local authorities (see above, 2.9.1) are generally known as 'local government officers' and their status is established by the Local Government Act 1972 and subordinate legislation. Staff of the European Union have their terms of employment determined by EC Regulations.

8.1.2   Political neutrality

An important constitutional principle is that public officials should be 'politically neutral'. In the UK, public officials in more senior posts in the UK Government, the devolved executive institutions, local authorities, and the institutions of the European Union, are banned by law from participating in party political activities or standing for election themselves – in order to maintain the distinction between elected representatives and salaried officials. Clearly, for some individuals, this amounts to a severe curtailment on their rights to freedom of expression (see below, Chapter 24) and association (see below, Chapter 25), but the European Court of Human Rights has held that these are legitimate restrictions (*Ahmed v UK* (1999) discussed below, 25.8). Some commentators and politicians have, however, questioned the whole notion of 'political neutrality', suggesting that senior civil servants, pursing their own agendas, control policy making in departments when ministers ought to be in the driving seat (see, for example, Benn, T, *Arguments for Democracy*, 1982, London: Penguin, Chapter 4).

8.2   Types of administrative bodies

We have seen that the work of government is divided between various departments staffed by civil servants who are accountable to the relevant Secretary of State (see above, 2.4.3). In addition, there are a wide range of institutions which have been established both by government and private interests, which used to be called 'quasi-non-governmental organisations' or quangos, and are now more generally known as 'non-departmental public bodies' or NDPBs. It is difficult to devise any reliable system of categories for them, but they can be divided broadly into three main types: executive, advisory, and regulatory. Local authorities carry out a combination of these functions (see below, 8.2.4).

8.2.1 Executive agencies

Much of the day to day work of central government in the UK (see above, 2.4.3) is carried out by 'executive agencies': the Prison Services Agency, the Benefits Agency, the Highways Agency and the Vehicles Inspectorate, to name but a few. These agencies operate under 'framework agreements', which demarcate the boundaries of responsibility between the chief executive and the parent department (in other words, the responsible minister). Whilst the parent department is responsible for any unlawful decision or act by the agency responding to a ministerial policy, the chief executives of these agencies have considerable leeway in generating their own rules and regulations as to how they run the business of providing public services. The framework documents themselves are not legal instruments, merely means of delegating power down from departments into the agencies. (For a detailed account of the creation of Next Steps Agencies, see Greer, P, 'The Next Steps initiative: an examination of the agency framework document' 68 Public Administration 89; and Freedland, MR, 'Government by contract and public law' [1994] PL 86.) The degree of discretion handed down to the service providers is considerable, since the chief executives of these agencies have to behave like managers of commercial services, producing results. They are thus accountable for those *results* rather than for the *policies* behind the services.

8.2.2 Regulatory bodies

Regulation may be carried out directly, by government, or (as is more frequently the case) it can be delegated to outside agencies. The privatisation of public industries (see above, 4.3.4) has placed the supply of gas, water and telecommunications and other former State-owned corporations in the hands of private shareholders and directors. These industries are no longer subject to direct parliamentary control and accountability. The idea was that the forces of the market would be an efficient substitute, but this does not apply to some, such as the gas industry, where British Gas are effectively operating a monopoly. For this reason, regulatory bodies have been set up by Act of Parliament to monitor their activities; Ofgas, Oftel, Ofrail, Ofsted, and so on, have broad powers to regulate the relevant industries. They are overseen by Directors General, whose duties are set out in the founding statutes. Their existence has been referred to as 'reinvented government' (Harlow, C and Rawlings, R, *Law and Administration*, 2nd edn, 1997, London: Butterworths, p 142), since their role is to act in the public interest, 'traditionally a government prerogative'.

8.2.3   Self-regulatory organisations

Supervision is no longer as hierarchical as it once was; rather, it is splintered across various different types of activities. Julia Black has observed that modern society is divided up into a number of different spheres, notably the spheres of the consumer and the market. One way of ensuring that there is some mediation between them is for the providers of goods and services to set up self-regulating agencies; these are 'mini legal systems' which are allowed to formulate and apply their own rules (see Black, J, 'Constitutionalising self-regulation' (1996) 59 MLR 24). Self-regulation has proved a popular vehicle for supervision and control, and much regulation in this country is conducted by the industry itself, based on an understanding that if self-regulation does not work, government will step in and legislate. Black distinguishes four categories of self-regulating agencies:

(a) *mandated* self-regulation, in which a collective group, an industry or a profession for example, is required by government to formulate and enforce norms in a framework enforced by government. An example of this is the Stock Exchange;

(b) *sanctioned* self-regulation, in which the collective group itself formulates the regulation which is subject to government approval, and, in return, the industry is exempted from other statutory requirements; for example, codes of practice produced by trade associations and approved by the Office of Fair Trading;

(c) *coerced* self-regulation, in which the industry itself formulates and imposes regulation, but in response to threats by the government that, if it does not, government will impose statutory regulation (the Press Complaints Commission is a good example of this);

(d) *voluntary* self-regulation, where there is no active State involvement; for example, sporting bodies, or bodies regulating the professions. Industry itself desires regulation and takes the initiative in the formation and operation of the system.

8.2.4   Advisory bodies

There is, in addition to the above forms of administration, a range of bodies which do not operate under direct government control, but perform a public function, such as the Countryside Commission, the Higher Education Funding Council and the Arts Council. These bodies are usually staffed by respected professional people with expertise in the relevant field; these people are appointed by the minister of the relevant department, not elected. Some of these bodies are created by statute, others by the exercise of the prerogative.

Some bodies are set up to advise the government; others are watchdog organisations established to act in the interests of certain sectors of society, such as the Mental Health Commission, which investigates complaints by patients compulsorily detained under the mental health legislation in this country. They are comparable to the institution of self-regulation, in the sense that many of these commissions and councils have been set up as an alternative to legislation; in the case of the Mental Health Commission, for example, the government opposed campaigns for increased statutory rights for patients, claiming that this would result in 'legalism' and bureaucratic problems for the psychiatric profession. The Commission's decisions, on the other hand, would be non-binding – soft law, in other words. Other types of advisory body include the National Consumer Council, the Medicines Commission and the Independent Television Commission. A sceptical explanation for their existence would be that they make it possible for government to hide behind some unpopular form of regulation by referring the complainant to the relevant NDPB. There are other justifications advanced for the creation of these NDPBs; some activities, it is said, need to be protected from political interference; such institutions avoid the known weaknesses of government departments and there are some areas of public administration which should be remitted to people with the relevant expertise.

8.2.5 Local authorities

Some issues relating to the role of local government have already been considered (see above, 2.9.1). Local authorities have largely become agents of central government, through processes such as rate-capping, compulsory competitive tendering and the transfer of other important responsibilities, such as housing, to the private sector. The real responsibility of local authorities now may be best described as overseeing service provision, purchasing rather than providing services.

The general services for which local authorities are responsible are the allocation of council houses, setting the rents and determining tenancy conditions and granting or refusing permission for the development of land. A range of other local matters are under their control, such as the enforcement of compliance with hygiene and sanitary standards, traffic flow and parking and the provision of care for children and the elderly. They have extensive licensing powers which determine whether certain films, plays or occupations are permitted in their area. A recent addition to local authorities' powers in the area of environmental regulation has come from Europe. Parliament has entrusted the primary task of environmental protection to the Environment Agency and to local authorities, who exercise duties and powers that derive from European Community directives. Under the Environmental Protection Act 1990 and the Water Resources Act 1991, the Agency and local authorities may take enforcement action in the form of criminal proceedings, prohibition, abatement and remedial notices against industries that they deem to be responsible for polluting the area under their control.

In addition to these specific functions, s 235 of the Local Government Act 1972 grants local authorities the power to make bylaws for the 'good rule and government of the whole or any part of the district or borough, and for the prevention and suppression of nuisances therein'. These are subject to confirmation by the Secretary of State and bylaws may be challenged in judicial review proceedings (*Arlidge v Mayor etc of Islington* (1909): a requirement of regular cleansing of lodgings where access was not always available struck down as unreasonable).

8.2.6 Administration in the European Community

Under Art 211 (formerly 155) of the EC Treaty, the Commission (see above, 7.5.1) is given the task of applying the provisions of the treaty and exercising the powers conferred on it by the Council (see above, 7.5.3) to implement delegated legislation. It is, in other words, the main executive body of the Community. The Commission's discretion to formulate policy extends across a wide range of areas, particularly in agriculture, the customs tariff and the setting of technical standards for health, the environment and other matters. Because the Commission is given such a wide discretion under Art 211, the Council requires it to consult a management committee in the formulation of policy. These committees are made up of civil servants representing the particular subject area of the legislation. The committee members scrutinise a draft of the Commission's proposed measures and vote by a qualified majority to adopt or reject the measure. Since these committees have no legal basis in the treaty, the delegation of decision making to them has come under attack (Case C-25/70 *Einfuhr und Vorratsstelle Getreide v Koster* (1970)). The European Court of Justice held, however, that this was not an illegitimate delegation of power. Since that case, a decision was passed (Council Decision 87/373) setting out the structure for this so called 'comitology' procedure. The European Parliament has since challenged the existence of committees, arguing that they diminish Parliament's own power of control over the Commission; however, the Court rejected their application for annulment of Decision 87/373 on the basis that Parliament had no standing (*European Parliament v Council* (1988)).

Apart from ensuring the implementation of Community law, the Commission supplements the role of national bodies in supervising policy implementation in Member States. So while, for example, the Customs and Excise authorities will ensure that the import and export of goods complies with the free movement of goods provisions in the EC Treaty, the Commission supervises the role of the national agencies to ensure the uniform implementation of Community law. The Commission itself may take proceedings in the Court of Justice against defaulting Member States which have not implemented Community directives, or are, in some other way, in breach of Community law, see below, 18.3.2. It also has the power to decide that Member States should abolish State aids (Art 88, formerly 93) and it can take action against individuals under the EC Treaty's competition rules (Arts 81 and 82; formerly 85 and 86). It has the power in all these circumstances to decide upon the level of fines for defaulting States. Although the ultimate decision on enforcement will rest with the European Court of Justice, the Commission's 'policing' powers in these areas give it significant scope for developing policy, allowing it to determine new strategy in relation to State aids and competition.

The Commission's executive role extends to other areas of Community organisation. It manages the Community budget for agricultural support (which accounts for 50% of the Community budget). The decisions it reaches in relation to this fund are overseen by a management committee. It also has some responsibility in relation to other important budgets within the Community, such as the European Social Fund and the European Regional Development Fund. Apart from these functions, the Commission determines and conducts the European Union's external trade relations, managing responsibilities in respect of the various external agreements which the European Union has with many third countries and international organisations.

8.3 Types of decision making

The discussion above demonstrates that a host of public actors, ranging from European Community officials and UK government ministers to a proliferating class of administrative bodies far removed from Westminster, have the power to make *ad hoc* decisions affecting the activities of individuals and the running of international commerce. On the whole, the only visible part of these decisions are those informal 'rules' which they themselves have generated. It will be remembered from the discussion on Dicey that wide discretionary powers exercised by government officials were anathema to Dicey's vision of a constitution based on the rule of law (see above, 5.3):

> ... the rule of law is contrasted with every system of government based on the exercise by persons in authority of wide, arbitrary or discretionary powers [Dicey, A, *Introduction to the Study of the Law of the Constitution*, 10th edn, 1959, London: Macmillan, p 187].

However, it has to be acknowledged that, even in Dicey's time, these 'wide, arbitrary or discretionary powers' were already being invested in officials and boards responsible for implementing early legislative welfare reforms, and over the course of the last century the dictates of the modern Welfare State have brought about a system where discretionary power is routinely granted to ministers and public bodies. This is because there is a very wide gap between the very broad power imposed by welfare legislation and the application of it, and this gap has to be filled by the individual discretion of the decision making body. The existence of this discretion obviously raises issues of accountability and control, which we will look at shortly (see below, 8.4). But before considering these issues in detail, it is worth considering to what extent administrative discretion is delimited by rules.

These rules, known as 'quasi-legislation', or 'soft law', are generated by the European institutions, ministers and public bodies. Thay range from codes of practice, circulars, directions, rules and regulations, to ministerial statements regarding policy changes, and positions taken in official departmental communications (see Ganz, G, *Quasi-legislation: Recent Developments in Secondary Legislation*, 1987, London: Sweet & Maxwell). On a national level, these rules may be promulgated to guide official interpretation of some policy or law; to regulate procedure; to set up voluntary standards of conduct or to impose managerial efficiency standards. Standard-setting rules apply to everybody, from MPs (see above, 6.7) to motorists (the Highway Code is a non-binding set of standards to be observed on roads). The fact that these rules are not legally binding does not mean that they do not have effect; if a newspaper, for example, disregards the provisions of the Press's voluntary code of practice, it may be required by the Press Complaints Commission to publish an apology.

8.3.1   Rules

Most of the rules which restrict this discretion are not legal rules as such, but non-binding general standards. Baldwin has identified eight types of rules (*Rules and Government*, 1996, Oxford: Clarendon):

(a) procedural rules (for example, the PACE codes of practice, governing the interrogation of suspects in police stations);

(b) interpretative guidance as to the policy behind some piece of legislation;

(c) instructions to officials in the department responsible for enforcing the law in its area of remit, such as Home Office Circulars to chief constables, or guidance circulars released by the Home Office to immigration officers exercising their discretion at ports of entry under the Immigration Act 1971;

(d) prescriptive rules made by regulators;

(e) evidential rules, such as the Highway Code, and, to the extent that they provide evidence of prejudicial interrogation of suspects in police stations, the PACE codes of practice;

(f) commendatory rules of good practice, such as the rules issued by the Health and Safety Executive on how to achieve safety standards;

(g) voluntary codes of practice;

(h) rules of practice for legal procedures; for example, the concessions made by the Inland Revenue to taxpayers if certain procedures are followed.

Many non-legislative rules, of course, belong to two or more of these categories. Three main groups may be identified.

Rules attached to legislation

It has been observed that hardly a statute is passed without a provision for a code of practice or guidance (see Cavadino, M, 'Commissions and codes: a case study', in Galligen, DJ (ed), *A Reader on Administrative Law*, 1996, Oxford: OUP, p 216). Such codes are useful to government not only because they offer a useful way to legislate on some difficult regulatory areas without resorting to the full legislative process, but also because codes provide a clue to judges as to the meaning of a statutory provision, thus giving judicial force to the executive's intention behind a particular policy. We have seen already (above, 8.2.2) that much quasi-legislation is developed by regulatory agencies, in their capacity as 'reinvented government'. But where do they get the raw material for the formulation of their regulations? Much of it comes from their founding statutes, which require them to regulate the industries in such a way as to ensure even service distribution, maintain sufficient financial resources, secure economy and efficiency, promote the interests of consumers and ensure competition. Increasingly, guidance for these rules is derived from the institutions of the European Union, which pass laws under the EC Treaty setting minimum standards and requirements for commerce, industry, services and the environment, amongst other things. The role of regulatory bodies in enforcing European law is often overlooked by the concentration on the manner in which Parliament promulgates European Community norms.

Evidential rules

Other codes are developed by public bodies to compel people to act in a certain way, so that even though breach of the code itself is not against the law (codes are non-binding) it is compelling evidence that the law has been broken. The evidentiary value of this kind of non-binding law in legal proceedings is comparable to the standards courts apply, for example, in assessing whether professional conduct has been negligent or not, by taking an accepted (but non-binding) professional standard as their guiding point. Breach of the Highway Code, for example, is not an offence of itself, but it is compelling evidence of civil or criminal liability. Disregard of the Department of Employment's picketing code – which provided that not more than six pickets should be allowed at the entrance to a workplace – provided compelling evidence during the 1984–85 mining dispute that the involvement of more than six pickets might amount to a civil nuisance or the offence of obstruction (DOE, Code of Practice on Picketing, 1980, para 31). This was in spite of the fact that the legislation under which the non-binding code was drafted made picketing lawful without any restrictions as to numbers. In addition, the contents of circulars often take on the status of relevant considerations in the process of determining whether a decision reached by an administrative body is '*Wednesbury* unreasonable'. The significance of circulars in court proceedings was illustrated by the fate of Home Office guidance notes to immigration officers at ports of entry, referring them to Art 8 of the ECHR, which guarantees individuals a right to a family life (often jeopardised by refusal of entry to people wishing to join family members who are lawfully resident in this country). Although this looked good on paper, these circulars backfired when immigration officials were brought to book in the courts for disregarding the reference to the convention. Because this reference was set out in the circular, it was deemed to be a 'relevant consideration' for the purposes of judicial review. Once these were withdrawn, applicants could no longer attack the reasonableness of immigration officials' decisions on convention grounds, because it was not, until recently, part of national law (see *R v Secretary of State for the Home Department ex p Lye* (1994)).

Voluntary codes

We have seen (above, 8.2.3) that self-regulating agencies are set up to ensure compliance with codes of practice. These are, by their nature, not imposed from above, but are developed by an interest group threatened with legislation in order to ward off any more binding form of regulation. Examples of this are the code of practice developed by the press, or the code of standards for advertising monitored by the Advertising Standards Authority.

Codes may be found in the performance standards promulgated under the Citizen's Charter by executive agencies or departments (see above, 8.2.1). The setting of specific standards is at the discretion of the administrative bodies. Executive agencies were themselves created in the interests of speed, economy and efficiency (this being the reason for their replacing the unwieldy powers exercised by civil servants in large departments). These objectives are bound to influence their standard-setting rather more than the less pressing considerations of quality service. The failure by the service provider to meet these performance targets entitles the citizen to some redress, such as a refund or the payment of some compensatory sum, although neither of these is enforceable through a contractual action.

8.3.2 The 'rules' versus 'discretion' debate

Having considered the range of rules that delimit the scope of administrative discretion, it is worth asking at this point whether we should accept that rules are always a necessary and desirable thing. The theory of rules versus discretion has been much expounded in the academic literature (see, in particular, Jowell, J, 'The rule of law today', in Jowell, J and Oliver, D (eds), *The Changing Constitution*, 3rd edn, 1994, Oxford: Clarendon, pp 62–66) . Since this literature emanates from legal experts rather than politicians, rules have been generally held to be desirable. One of Dicey's requirements for a rule of law was that public bodies were not entrusted with arbitrary power, in other words, unlimited discretion (see above, 5.3). But the formulation of rules by public bodies has an instrumental as well as a constitutional purpose. They promote legal certainty and encourage early consultation of and participation by interested parties. The Environment Agency, for example, has the discretion to decide on an *ad hoc* basis whether a particular industry is polluting the atmosphere or the ground water and therefore should be prosecuted. On the other hand, it could adopt a series of upper limits for emissions, specified in advance. These limits, in the form of rules, will enable the industries to take preventative action, which is what environmental regulation is designed to achieve (rather than clogging up the magistrates' courts with a series of criminal prosecutions). The formulation of consistent rules also enables the public body in question to make decisions more quickly and efficiently.

This is, in itself, uncontroversial. But, in many cases, such as the provision of benefits to individual applicants, rigid application of such rules may conflict with an individual's need to have their case determined on its particular merits. The ideal resolution to this conflict would be to allow administrative bodies to develop rules, but to apply those rules only after they have heard individual cases on the merits. Otherwise, the body would be unduly restricting its discretion granted by the power, which itself would be an unlawful act, challengeable by means of judicial review. This requirement that every new case is heard on its merits, and that the administrative body can then apply its policy with impunity, is, however, fraught with difficulties, as the following section on policy as a form of soft law will show.

8.3.3   Policies

As we have seen, it is difficult to draw a dividing line between some types of rule, which limit and guide the discretion of an administrative body, and policy, which often does the same thing. Policy as a form of soft law is different from policy which precedes most forms of legislation; this 'pure' type of policy is settled by departmental or cabinet committee and usually ends in legislative form. It is policy which has no legal basis (in the form of legislation or statutory instrument) that concerns us here. Provided certain statements of policy do not interfere with people's pre-existing rights, there is no need for the full legislative process to be seen through. Ministers may try to influence the direction of legislation by issuing non-binding guidance notes and circulars (a form of soft law) which expresses policy. Ministers' statements in Parliament often enunciate policy changes which are subsequently embedded in guidelines, rather than in legislation. The advantage of this form of 'soft law' is that it does not bind the executive, and subsequent events may necessitate a change in policy which can be effected without the need for new legislation. This is sometimes a source of hardship by those who have relied on some statement of ministerial policy. In the early 1980s, the Hong Kong

Government announced that it would afford all immigrants a personal interview and a chance to put their case before repatriating them to the mainland Chinese. After this policy statement was broadcast on national television, an applicant came forward, but was refused an interview. The Privy Council ruled that the government could not repatriate him without fulfilling their promise, in other words by letting him have an opportunity to present his case (*AG of Hong Kong v Ng Yuen Shiu* (1983)). In this instance, the courts are prepared to intervene to give the non-binding ministerial statement of policy legal effect. This means, sometimes, that the public body concerned cannot switch policies which have given rise to a legitimate expectation that the old policy will be continued without at least giving interested parties an opportunity to make representations (see below, Chapter 14). But as the discussion in that chapter also reveals, the courts are not always willing to come to the assistance of individuals who feel that they have been cheated by changes in government statements of policy.

Policy is not confined to ministerial statements. 'Low level' policy – positions adopted by government departments and executive agencies – may have considerable effects on people and business. A broadcasting authority may be refused a licence by the licensing body, or the Environment Agency might select one polluting industry rather than another for prosecution. An applicant for benefit may lose out in identical circumstances to another person who is successful in his or her claim.

> Low level policy choices of these kinds are nevertheless real policy choices upon which the treatment of people depends. They are policy choices which are often hard to identify, difficult to control, and without proper legal authority; they are the products of the moral and social attitudes of officials, which are in turn to a large degree the results of the social and organisational ethos of a department or agency [Galligan, DJ (ed), *A Reader in Administrative Law*, 1996, Oxford: OUP, p 40].

Sometimes, a minister is empowered by a statute to issue guidance, or directions, to a particular decision making body. Whilst the power itself is governed by statutory controls, the content of the guidance is not. In 1977, Freddie Laker, operator of a cut price air travel service known as Skytrain, challenged guidance issued by the Transport Minister to the Civil Aviation Authority to the effect that only one British airline could be allowed to serve the same route. Lord Denning MR ruled that the policy guidance cut right across the statutory objectives of the Civil Aviation Act 1971, which were designed to ensure that British Airways did not have a monopoly:

> Those provisions disclose so complete a reversal of policy that to my mind the White Paper cannot be regarded as giving 'guidance' at all. In marching terms it does not say 'right incline' or 'left incline'. It says 'right about turn'. That is not guidance, but the reverse of it.

> There is no doubt that the Secretary of State acted with the best of motives in formulating this new policy – and it may well have been the right policy – but I am afraid that he went about it in the wrong way. Seeing that the old policy had been laid down in an Act of Parliament, then, in order to reverse it, he should have introduced an amending Bill and got Parliament to sanction it. He was advised, apparently, that it was not necessary, and that it could be done by 'guidance'. That, I think, was a mistake.

The court therefore granted a declaration that the guidance was *ultra vires* (*Laker Airways Ltd v Department of Trade* (1977)).

The tension between rules and discretion has not been solved by judicial intervention, and it is impossible to say at any point whether a minister has violated the rules of natural justice by too rigidly adhering to a previous policy position and closing his or her mind to the individual merits of an application, or whether he or she has acted illegally by disregarding the policy behind an Act. One of the most important judicial dicta on this problem can be found in an early case involving a challenge by a company against a policy adopted by the Board of Trade (the predecessor to the DTI). Here, the Board was empowered by statute to make grants towards companies' capital expenditure on plant and machinery. No statutory criteria were provided. The Board adopted a policy of not making a grant in respect of machinery costing less than £25, and refused British Oxygen's application on these grounds. On review, the House of Lords upheld the Board's policy:

> The general rule is that anyone who has to exercise a statutory discretion must not 'shut his ears' to an application. There is no great difference between a policy and a rule ... a large authority may have had to deal already with many similar applications and then it will almost certainly have evolved a policy so precise that it could be called a rule. There is no objection to that, provided it is always ready to listen to a new argument [*British Oxygen v Board of Trade* (1971)].

8.3.4   Soft law in the European Community

It is enlightening to note the use made of 'soft law' by the institutions of the European Community, mainly the Commission. Community institutions are authorised by Art 249 of the Treaty to pass various forms of delegated legislation in areas covered by Community competence (see above, 7.6) including regulations and directives. Two other types of delegated legislation, however, are specifically stated by the Treaty to be non-binding: recommendations and opinions. In addition, decisions and agreements adopted by the representatives of Member States meeting in Council (see above, 7.5.3), as well as declarations, resolutions, communiqués and other positions taken by the institutions of the Community, all lack binding force. An example of this was the declaration on human rights adopted by the institutions on 5 April 1977, in which they stated that the exercise of their powers and in the pursuance of the aims of the European Community, they would respect and continue to respect those rights (OJ C103, 27.4.77, p 1). Although this had no force in law, in 1979, the European Court of Justice was invited to consider that declaration in a reference from a German court asking whether a Council regulation prohibiting the planting of new vines could be in breach of the applicant's fundamental right to property under the German Constitution (Case C-44/79 *Hauer v Land Rheinland-Pfalz* (1979)). The Court referred to the declaration, and ruled that human rights such as those protected by the German Constitution formed part of the general principles of European Community law. Although the German wine farmer in question failed on the merits, this case demonstrates that non-binding declarations, amongst others, are capable of having legal effect in the Community. In a later case, Case C-322/88 *Salvatore Grimaldi v Fonds des Maladies Professionelles* (1989), the Court observed that:

> ... such measures in question [recommendations] cannot be regarded as having no legal effect. The national courts are bound to take recommendations into consideration in order to decide disputes submitted to them, in particular where they cast light on the interpretation of national measures adopted in order to implement them.

Whilst it is open to the Community institutions to pass regulations or directives or decisions on any matter within an area of treaty competence, it is often more advantageous to opt for non-binding recommendations or resolutions. This is because, by extending such a piece of quasi-legislation to an area which is not obviously within Community competence, the Community thus acquires exclusive competence in that area for possible future legislative activity. This was confirmed in a decision of the European Court of Justice concerning the European Road Traffic Agreement, a dispute about Community versus Member State competence arising out of a non-binding Council resolution (Case C-122/94 *Commission v Council* (1996)). Here, the Court said that exclusive competence of the Community was established 'each time the Community, with a view to implementing a common policy envisaged by the Treaty, lays down common rules whatever form these may take' (see Klabbers, J, 'Informal instruments before the European Court of Justice' (1994) 31 CML Rev 997, for a more detailed discussion of the use of informal instruments for extending Community competence).

Soft law at a Community level has other uses: because it is non-binding, it is less prone to legal attack. It should be noted that the Member States can always challenge the legality of a Community *legislative* measure through the annulment procedure (see above, 18.3.1). However, the European Court of Justice has no power to scrutinise the legality of a non-binding measure. Baldwin notes:

> Judicial review has limited potential to legitimate secondary and tertiary legislation. This is first, because the Court focuses on the legality rather than the merits or substance of the rules; second, because its interventions are

sporadic and dependent on the actions of other institutions, Member States or individuals (who are subject to restrictions as to locus standi), and, third, because the breadth of legal discretion given to the Community institutions by the Treaty limits their liability to judicial review [*Rules and Government*, 1996, Oxford: Clarendon, p 282].

8.4 Accountability and control

Non-legislative rules, at whatever level they are generated, are, on their face, free of formal controls. Other forms of control need to be invented. The problems of redress that arise out of this system are discussed more fully in Part D of this book, but it is worth noting here that administrative law in this country has not yet caught up with these constitutional developments. As Rodney Austin observes:

> ... for the courts to intervene there must be some legally enforceable basis for or backing to the powers of the authority under review. Where power is conferred and limits are imposed by non legal means, the courts lack the necessary peg upon which to hang the exercise of their powers ['Administrative law's reaction to the changing concepts of public service', in Leyland, P and Woods, T (eds), *Administrative Law Facing the Future*, 1997, London: Blackstone, p 28).

Other forms of control, such as parliamentary accountability, are also lacking in the informal development and application of soft law. We have seen, for example, that the work carried out by executive agencies to implement government legislation is at several removes from the relevant government department (see above, 8.2.1). Therefore, the traditional model of ministerial accountability which applies to government departments, where the minister is answerable to Parliament for the failings of the civil servants working at a departmental level – is not appropriate for executive agencies (see above, 6.8). The division between policy – for which the minister is answerable to Parliament – and operational matters – for which the chief executive of the executive agency is responsible – has led to the practice of MPs writing about their constituents' concerns to the chief executive rather than the minister, and the answers are then published in *Hansard*. However, the division between what is a policy matter, and what is operational, is never very clear, as was demonstrated in the controversy following the mass break out from Parkhurst Prison in January 1995. The Director General (that is, chief executive), of the Prison Services Agency, Derek Lewis, was forced to resign, although he refused to take responsibility for the security lapses and escapes, saying that these were the direct consequence of the then Home Office Minister's policy of allocating resources away from prison staffing levels and security measures. It was also pointed out that constant interventions by the Home Secretary in the day to day running of the prison service rather undermined his argument that he was responsible only for policy formulation (for a fuller account of this episode, see Barker, A, 'Political responsibility for UK prison security: ministers escape again' (1995) Essex Papers in Politics and Government. Despite the problems of the policy/operational divide shown up by the Derek Lewis affair, the division still applies in relation to the functions of executive agencies.

The growth of regulatory agencies also presents problems of control. One of the drawbacks of the system of regulation discussed above, 8.2.2, is known as 'agency capture'. This means that, from the moment they are set up, they come under pressure from the industry they regulate to protect the interests of that industry rather than the interests of the public. Another problem is that the aims of some of the regulatory agencies may come into conflict with others. The Environment Agency, for example, has been set up to monitor and enforce compliance with environmental standards by industry, across the board. The level of effluent in the nation's waterways, for example, is a central concern of the Agency. Ofwat, on the other hand, is dedicated to monitoring competition and ensuring fair prices for consumers of water. Dedicating expenditure to the cleaning up of rivers drives up water prices. The Environment Agency and Ofwat, therefore, often find their aims in conflict.

The available controls over the activities of these regulatory agencies and redress for things that go wrong as a result of their decisions are few and far between. The National Audit Office reviews their efficiency annually, but does not question the merits of their policies. The Ombudsman may look into individual disputes concerning the agencies' activities, but his investigation is subject to severe constraints. Judicial review of their decisions is technically possible. In *R v Director of Passenger Rail Franchising ex p Save Our Railways* (1995), for example, a consumer's group managed to get a declaration that DPRF's decisions specifying minimum passenger service levels for prospective rail franchises were unlawful, since they departed too radically from existing service levels. But, in general, the courts are reluctant to intervene, except where procedural irregularities can be established. There is, significantly, no statutory duty on the Directors General to give reasons for their regulatory decisions, or, indeed, to publish the information on which they have based those decisions. To correct this deficit in accountability and justiciability, proposals have been made to reform the system of regulation in this country by bringing it under the umbrella of parliamentary scrutiny; for example, by establishing a Select Committee on Regulated Industries, and to introduce a common code of practice for all the regulators (see the summary of these proposals in Harlow, C and Rawlings, R, *Law and Administration*, 2nd edn, 1997, London: Butterworths, pp 337–39).

The spread of self-regulation (see above, 8.2.3) has also presented certain control problems, specifically by the courts. Not only is there a question over the justiciability of their decisions, but there are difficulties with the amenability of these quasi-private bodies to judicial review in the first place. Some of these difficulties were dealt with in the leading decision of *R v Panel of Take-overs and Mergers ex p Datafin* (1987) (see below, 17.6.2). The present government has proposed a certain cutting back in self-regulation, particularly in the City, where it is intended to invest the Securities and Investments Board, a regulatory body based on statute, with more powers. This approach has been illustrated, too, in the proposals to set up a statutory agency to monitor food standards (proposed in 1997).

Advisory bodies, like executive agencies, also lack clear control mechanisms. Although ministers exercise some control over NDPBs, they are not accountable in Parliament for their activities, and it has been observed (notably in the First Report of the Committee on Standards in Public Life) that appointment to these bodies was not made on merit, but rather on party political grounds. Since the decisions and advice of these non-departmental bodies often carry considerable weight in the formulation of government policy and the introduction of legislation, there are concerns about the lack of transparency in their operations and their independence from the party in power.

The administrative activities of local authorities are, unlike all the preceding bodies, subject to several forms of effective control. Judicial control on the exercise of discretion by local authorities is a central area of judicial review, and will be explored more fully in Part D of this book. The restrictions imposed by the courts on local authorities' powers to govern, however, pale into insignificance when compared with the intensification of central control through restrictions on capital expenditure through council tax-capping or the withholding of central government grants and sanctions for loans. The system of audit of local government expenditure is also regulated by central government. The Audit Commission, set up under the Local Government Finance Act 1982, has the power to identify and to take legal action to prevent potentially wasteful expenditure by local authorities; whilst any resulting judgment will have the force of 'hard' law, the Commission also generates 'soft law' in the form of guidance issued to local authorities on management in pursuit of economic efficiency, public interest reports on the progress of local authorities, and the development of performance indicators for local government, which serve as the basis for league tables of performance. When the accounts of the local authority are up for audit and it appears to the auditor that an item of expenditure is unlawful, he may apply to the court for a declaration of unlawfulness and an order that the person who authorised that expenditure repay it (Pt III of the Local Government Finance Act 1982). It can be seen, then, that the system of audit and its consequences are as powerful a measure of legal control as judicial review.

Finally, a word must be said about control and accountability of the soft law generated by the European Community institutions, notably the Commission (see above, 7.5.1). In the wake of the mass resignation of the entire Commission in March 1999, following a damning report on corruption inside the Brussels executive, greater emphasis will have to be placed on transparency and justiciability of many of the Commission's decision making powers. Although the allegations in the report of five independent 'wise persons' focused on mismanagement and nepotism, one of the most worrying features of the Commission identified by the report was the loss of control by the authorities over the administration they were supposed to be running. Part of the explanation for this loss of control can be laid at the door of what one critic called 'the nether world of comitology', (see above, 8.2.5). The chief criticism of comitology is that it exacerbates the democratic deficit in Community law making (see above, 7.4.2). The civil servants who sit on these committees are neither elected nor accountable, either to the European Parliament or to Member States, and yet their decisions, particularly on technical standard-setting, have a considerable influence in Community law. Comitology raises similar problems of accountability and transparency to those presented by the role of advisory committees in the formulation of government policy (see above, 8.2.4.

8.5 The advantages and disadvantages of administrative rules

The main focus of this chapter has been on forms of regulation that do not have the force of law. There are arguments against, and arguments in favour of these informal rules. The *disadvantage* of administrative rules is that they are inconsistent. They sometimes have legal effects, although not always. This means that individuals can never be sure whether to base their future conduct on them. And, when things go wrong, recourse to the courts is difficult, because these rules are often couched in non-justiciable language, if indeed they are published at all. Apart from the problems of redress that they present, there are arguments that the presence of administrative rules, or 'soft law', often has the effect of distorting the constitutional balance. It is said that it may influence judges to interpret statutes in accordance with the executive's intentions, not Parliament's. If ministers are aware that the details of any proposed policy are likely to be controversial, they may avoid parliamentary debate by leaving these details to be implemented by non-statutory codes and rules. And, finally, it is often the case that types of soft law, particularly guidance notes and codes, may emerge as a result of disproportionate lobby group pressure, without the balancing effect of parliamentary scrutiny.

In favour of soft law, it is argued that its flexibility is indispensable to modern administration. Statements of policy, performance targets and non-binding codes may be set aside in the interests of justice for individual cases; but the need to draw up these forms of soft law enhances accountability and transparency by informing the public of the way that official discretion is likely to be exercised, so that they can plan their conduct accordingly. Bureaucrats, in other words, are encouraged by these rules to be consistent, without being rigidly inflexible.

As we can see, the range of disadvantages is rather wider than the list of advantages. This may be because there is no constitutional place for informal rule making, and yet it has become one of the most prevalent parts of British and European Community constitutional practice.

GOVERNMENT AND ADMINISTRATION

A range of administrative bodies formulate and implement policy on a day to day level. This administrative activity affects our lives not only in the form of binding laws and regulations, but also by means of 'soft law'; rules, policy decisions, declarations, positions and codes that are not legally binding, but are persuasive and influential on administrative behaviour.

Function of soft law

(a) To guide official interpretation of policy.

(b) To regulate procedure.

(c) To set up voluntary standards of conduct.

(d) To impose managerial efficiency standards.

Types of administrative bodies

Administrative bodies that generate 'soft law' include the following:

Executive agencies

'Next Steps' executive agencies, service providers set up under framework agreements, are led by chief executives who have broad discretion as to the implementation of policy. These agencies have to meet performance targets imposed by the Citizen's Charter, but these are not legally binding.

Regulatory bodies

These monitor the activities of recently privatised industries such as British Rail. They have a broad mandate to regulate these industries by non-legislative means.

Self-regulatory organisations

A network of self-regulating organisations monitor the compliance by businesses and professions with codes of practice. Some of these agencies are judicially reviewable; others are not.

Advisory bodies

These bodies are set up to advise the government or to act in the interests of certain sectors of society. Their decisions are non-binding, but influential.

Local authorities

While the functions of local authorities have been greatly reduced through processes such as rate-capping, compulsory competitive tendering and the transfer of other important responsibilities, such as housing, to the private sector, there are important remaining functions on which local government makes rules and formulates policies: the allocation of council houses, setting the rents and determining tenancy conditions; production of development plans; a range of other local matters, such as the enforcement of compliance with hygiene and sanitary standards, traffic flow and parking and the provision of care for children and the elderly. Local authorities also share with the Environment Agency certain duties and powers for environmental protection that derive from Community directives. In addition to these specific powers, local authorities may, under s 235 of the Local Government Act 1972, make bylaws for the 'good rule and government of the whole or any part of the district or borough and for the prevention and suppression of nuisances therein'.

Types of quasi-legislation

(a) Policy statements by ministers that do not evolve into legislation.

(b) 'Low level' policy adopted by government departments and executive agencies.

(c) Policies or schemes operated by non-statutory bodies, such as the Criminal Injuries Compensation Board.

(d) Ministerial guidance to decision making bodies.

(e) Codes of Practice, such as the PACE rules.

(f) Evidential codes, such as the Highway Code.

(g) Voluntary codes of practice, such as the City code on takeovers and mergers.

Public audit

Central government, local authorities and a range of other administrative bodies are now subject to 'value for money' audits, carried out by the Public Accounts Committee, the National Audit Office and the Audit Commission. One of the functions of this type of audit is to monitor the progress of two of the government's main financial programmes, the Next Steps programme and the Private Finance Initiative.

Soft law in the European Community

The institutions of the European Community act both in a legislative capacity and as administrators. As legislators, the Council and Commission produce non-binding legislation in the form of recommendations and opinions. In addition, decisions, agreements, declarations, resolutions, communiqués and common positions emanate from the Community institutions, which have no legal force, but may have legal effect because, for example, they give rise to the doctrine of legitimate expectation. The European Court of Justice has no jurisdiction to scrutinise the legality of these measures.

As an administrator, the Commission has the power under the EC Treaty to formulate policy and implement subordinate legislation. Such policy, particularly in the areas of agriculture, the customs tariff and technical standards, is subject to scrutiny and veto by management committees. This process is called 'comitology'. In addition to its policy forming role, the Commission also polices the implementation of Community law by Member States and it has the power under the EC Treaty to take infringement actions for breach of Community law, as well as enforcing the abolition of State aids and taking action against individuals who are found to be in breach of Community competition rules.

PART C

RESOLVING DISPUTES

CHAPTER 9

INTRODUCTION TO DISPUTE RESOLUTION

9.1 Why dispute resolution is important

Government based on principles of liberal democracy endeavours to ensure that the people who govern us do so with our consent (see above, 1.1.2). This implies several things: that the constitutional system permits people to choose their rulers in fair and regular elections; that between elections, rulers and officials working for them allow people to participate in collective decision making; and that laws and executive actions are open to challenge once they have been made. It is with the last of these things that we are now concerned.

Chapters 9–18 examine some of the ways in which disputes between people and government, and between different governmental institutions, are resolved. The election of office holders does not give them or their employees *carte blanche*. One of the responsibilities of government is, therefore, to provide adequate opportunities for citizens to challenge the good sense and lawfulness of its decisions, and seek reparation for harms wrongfully inflicted on them; only if these exist will government be 'limited'.

The existence of institutions and procedures for redressing grievances is also important for government itself. The fact that an apparently independent third party (a judge, tribunal, ombudsman) can be called upon to correct mistakes and remedy abuses of power helps to *legitimate* government action by reassuring citizens. Some commentators identify a ploy here: by providing 'a symbolic appearance of legality', dispute resolution procedures can deflect attention from the harsh or unfair substance of government policy on, say, immigration control or entitlement to welfare benefits (see Prosser, T, 'Poverty, ideology and legality: supplementary benefit appeal tribunals and their predecessors' (1977) 4 BJLS 39). Dispute resolution procedures may also assist government by providing information about what is, and is not, acceptable conduct. For instance, the grounds of judicial review (see below, 11.2) provide not only a basis for challenging public authorities in the High Court, but also principled guidance on how power ought to be exercised in a democracy. There is some evidence to suggest that UK government departments attempt to learn lessons from judgments for their future work and, to this extent, the case law improves the quality of public administration (see Richardson, G and Sunkin, M, 'Judicial review: questions of impact' [1996] PL 79). The various ombudsmen also publish reports of their investigations into cases of alleged maladministration and may make recommendations for improving decision making within public authorities (see below, Chapter 10). Finally, government bodies themselves may need to use dispute resolution mechanisms. In the modern constitution, litigation has become an important way for determining conflicts about the allocation of governmental power between different institutions. During the 1980s, for instance, local authorities used numerous judicial review challenges to question new limits placed on their powers to tax and spend imposed by central government. Litigation is also useful for central government: on several occasions, the UK has brought actions in the European Court of Justice to challenge the legality of Community legislation (see below, 18.3.1).

For people and for public authorities, the provision of appropriate dispute resolution mechanisms is therefore an important function of the constitution.

9.2 Types of dispute

Public law disputes take many forms, ranging from relatively trivial grievances that civil servants have been rude or incompetent, to conflicts about the existence or application of important constitutional principles and the validity of legislation. To make sense of these disputes, it is helpful to begin by highlighting some of the conceptual distinctions which exist, although, in practice, these differences may be blurred.

9.2.1 Disputes about the existence of legal power

These are complaints that a decision maker lacks legal authority. There is, in other words, a dispute about legal power or duty. The Latin word *vires* is often used (pronounced 'vie-rees', meaning power). Commonly, the public body in question has done something which a citizen claims it had no capacity to do (for example, the Foreign Secretary pays a grant to the government of Malaysia to construct a uneconomic hydro-electric station); or it has failed to do something which the law required it to do (for instance, a local authority declines to pay for a home help for a disabled person). To work out whether or not a legal power or duty exists, the court has to examine all relevant legislation and sometimes (in the case of government ministers) the extent of the prerogative.

Within the UK, government institutions and officials normally stand in a different position to that of ordinary citizens. Whereas we may do anything that is not expressly prohibited by the law, government may do only that which it is authorised to do by law (see above, 1.7.1). Central and local government, and other public bodies must, in other words, be able to point to a positive law before the take coercive action against us. The institutions of the European Community – the Commission, Council, Parliament and the Court of Justice – likewise have only those legal powers which are conferred on them by the EC Treaty and legislation made under the treaty. If they act beyond those powers, they act unlawfully. On several occasions, the UK has gone to the Court of Justice to argue that the Council has acted beyond its powers (see below, 18.3.1), for instance, by adopting the controversial Working Time Directive in 1996, or that the Commission has overstepped its legal authority (for example, by making an EC Regulation banning the export of beef from Britain in 1996).

The creation of devolved legislative and executive bodies in Scotland, Northern Ireland and Wales has brought with it the inevitability of disputes about their powers. As we have seen, the 1998 Acts provide for 'devolution issues' to be determined by the Judicial Committee of the Privy Council (see above, 2.8.4).

At an abstract level, disputes about the existence and extent of legal power involve 'the rule of law'. We have already examined how AV Dicey and his critics have conceived this principle (see above, 5.3) and, in the chapters which follow, we see how this precept is put into practice.

9.2.2 Disputes about the manner in which decisions are made

Disputes also arise about the *way* in which a public body has set about reaching its determination. There is, in other words, disagreement over the decision making procedures which have been used. The issue here may, for instance, be whether a local authority ought to have heard representations from parents before closing a school, or whether it was unfair for a public authority to revoke a person's licence to carry on a trade without first giving her a chance to answer the allegations made against her. Some such complaints involve an allegation that the public authority has breached the law by not following correct procedures, so making the decision flawed, and may be the subject of an application for judicial review to set it aside (see below, Chapters 13 and 14). Other grievances are merely that a public body was unhelpful or inefficient in making its decisions. These disputes do not necessarily involve an allegation that government officials have breached the law. Officials who are rude, incompetent, or misleading may not have acted unlawfully, even though they cause offence and inconvenience. Such complaints may, however, amount to 'maladministration' and be investigated by an ombudsman (see below, Chapter 10); or be the subject of an internal inquiry (see below, 9.3.1).

9.2.3 Disputes about the motives of public officials

Citizens and business enterprises may sometimes question the motive for a public official's decision. At its most extreme, this involves an allegation of corruption. In many constitutional systems, corruption is endemic and bribes are needed to obtain what is due from public authorities. When the Committee on Standards in Public Life (see above, 1.7 and 6.7), then chaired by Lord Nolan, published its First Report (Cm 2850-I) in May 1995, it concluded that there was no evidence of systematic corruption in British public life. It does, however, occasionally occur – especially in some local authorities and police forces. The corruption of public office holders is primarily regulated by the criminal law. In March 1998, the Law Commission called for reform of the common law offence of bribery and the Prevention of Corruption Acts of 1889–1916, recommending the ending of the distinction between public and private sector corruption, not least because it is unclear how the present law applies to privatised utilities and the many tasks that are now contracted out by government (*Legislating the Criminal Code: Corruption*, Law Com No 248). As part of the international effort to suppress corruption, in 1998, the UK ratified the international Convention on Combating Bribery of Foreign Public Officials in International Business Transactions, and Parliament passed the International Bribery and Corruption Act 1998, making it an offence for people in the UK to bribe officials in other countries to gain contracts.

In England and Wales, the tort of misfeasance in public office makes it possible to sue a public authority or official who causes harm by taking action or omitting to do something which the person knows is unlawful, or where the motivation is malice towards the injured claimant (see *Three Rivers DC v Bank of England (No 2)* (1996)). There have been very few successful claims in this tort, in part, perhaps, because of the difficulties claimants have in obtaining evidence sufficient to satisfy the court that an improper motive was present.

'Bias' – in the sense of a public official having a financial or other personal stake in the decision he makes – is a ground for seeking judicial review (see below, 13.7).

9.2.4 Disputes about wrong conclusions

In many conflicts between citizens and government, it is common ground that the public official had the legal authority to make a determination (see above, 9.1.1) and did so using the correct procedures (see above, 9.1.2). What is at stake is whether the official exercised his or her judgment in the right or wisest way. Sometimes the decision making task for the public authority is to apply set criteria to a person's circumstances, but, even in these circumstances, some public authorities are notoriously incapable of reaching correct conclusions. In 1997, for example, the National Audit Office (see above, 8.4) refused to accept the Child Support Agency's accounts after finding errors in 85% of its determinations; one in six of these errors exceeded £1,000. In other contexts, the decision making task is more subtle and complex; and disputes are, for example, over whether an immigration officer is correct in thinking that a person who claims asylum from persecution is, in fact, merely seeking entry to the UK for economic reasons, or whether a disabled person is sufficiently incapacitated to be entitled to a welfare benefit. Here disputes are about facts, or inferences drawn from facts, and qualitative assessments of people's conduct, circumstances and motives are required. These cannot be settled just by burrowing away in a law library or testing rival legal submissions.

The courts are very reluctant to interfere with a public authority's conclusion merely on the basis that inappropriate inferences were drawn from facts or that an official weighed up competing factors in a particular way. In judicial review, the High Court will set aside a public body's conclusion only if it is 'so outrageous in its defiance of logic or accepted moral standards that no sensible person who applied his mind to the question to be decided could have arrived at it' (Lord Diplock in *Council of Civil Service Unions v Minister for the Civil Service* (1985), discussed below, Chapter 15). The European Court of Human Rights, in deciding whether there has been a violation of the ECHR, is also aware that there may sometimes be a range of permissible conclusions open to a signatory State. They are permitted by the Strasbourg Court to have a 'margin of appreciation' in deciding, for example, whether, in relation to Art 10, a restriction on freedom of expression is 'necessary in a democratic society' (see below, 19.5).

Acts of Parliament have established tribunals to hear appeals from government decisions in areas such as immigration control, welfare benefits and taxation. Typically, the function of tribunals is to look at the original decision and satisfy itself that the official reached the correct conclusions, in effect giving a person a second chance to put his or her case – before, say, being deported or excluded from receiving a social security payment (see below, 9.3.2).

9.3 Types of dispute resolution

Because this is a book written by lawyers for law students, we focus on the role of law, lawyers and litigation in dispute resolution. Over the past few years, something curious has been happening (see below, 9.4). On the one hand, there is a trend towards 'alternative dispute resolution'. This means that, rather than leaving disputes to be resolved by litigation in court, other mechanisms are established. These include the informal settlements of grievances through internal complaints procedures, the use of ombudsmen to investigate complaints of maladministration, and adjudication by tribunals. On the other hand, courts are being called upon to adjudicate on new and important issues; an ever wider range of decisions are becoming 'justiciable' (that is, subject to litigation), including whether Acts of Parliament are consistent with European Community law and the European Convention on Human Rights (see below, 9.4).

9.3.1 Internal complaints procedures

The tendency today is to believe that going to court should be a last resort; litigation is seen as expensive, long winded and, more often than not, unnecessary. Successive governments have, therefore, encouraged the proliferation of alternative methods of dealing with disputes. Under the Citizen's Charter initiative (see above, 4.3.6 and 4.4.3), public authorities have been exhorted to establish their own internal procedures for dealing with complaints. These range from recording complaints via telephone 'hotlines' to more elaborate reviews by the public body itself of what allegedly went wrong. The shift to informal dispute resolution has, in large part, been motivated by the desire to reduce public spending (tribunal hearings and litigation in court are expensive). However, in so far as the aim of internal complaints procedures is to provide cheap and quick resolution of disputes, they are good things. There is, however, also a darker side. The Council on Tribunals (see below, 9.3.3) several years ago identified 'a trend to compromise and downgrade [external] appeal procedures in a way which may endanger the proper application of the principles of openness, fairness and impartiality which should underpin tribunal systems in general' (*Annual Report 1989–90*, HC 64, p 1). Informal grievance handling takes place behind closed doors; and if public authorities are not called to account in public, the wider public interest that justice is not only done, but seen to be done is compromised (see Mulcahy, L and Allsop, J, 'A Woolf in sheep's clothing? Shifts towards informal resolution of complaints in the NHS', in Leyland, P and Woods, T (eds), *Administrative Law Facing the Future*, 1997, London: Blackstone).

9.3.2 Ombudsmen

One form of alternative dispute resolution which avoids the potential pitfalls of internal systems are the so called ombudsmen. In Chapter 10, we see how the Parliamentary Commissioner of Administration, the Local Commission for Administration and other ombudsmen investigate cases in which complainants allege they have suffered injustice because of the 'maladministration' of a public body.

9.3.3 Tribunals

Under many Acts of Parliament, tribunals have been set up to hear appeals against the determinations of public bodies. Tribunals dwarf the ombudsmen and judicial review in terms of the number of complaints they deal with each year. They operate in different contexts, often resolving disputes of great importance to individuals – such as applications by to remain in the UK by asylum seekers, and the entitlement to welfare benefits of people living on the edge of subsistence.

Typically, tribunals consist of three people, one of whom is legally qualified. The term tribunal may also be used to encompass single adjudicators, such as the Social Security and Child Support Commissioners and the Special Adjudicators in immigration and asylum cases. The grounds on which a person may appeal to a tribunal are set out in legislation. Generally, the task of a tribunal is to consider whether public officials have understood the law and any relevant administrative guidance, whether their assessment of the facts of a case are correct, and whether they have applied it correctly to the facts of the particular case. Unlike the High Court on an application for judicial review (see below, 9.3.4), the decisions of tribunals do not act as binding precedents in later cases, though the determinations of some tribunals are published in series of reports.

In the 1950s, the government of the day asked a committee chaired by Lord Franks to investigate and make recommendations on the future of tribunal adjudication (*Report of the Committee on Administrative Tribunals and Enquiries*, Cmnd 218, 1957, London: HMSO). It concluded that tribunals were better for resolving some disputes than courts. People with specialist knowledge could be appointed to sit on them; for instance, doctors on tribunals hearing complaints against refusal of welfare benefit for disablement. Tribunal hearings could also be conducted with less formality than litigation in court, and so be speedier and less costly. The Franks Committee was, however, quite clear that tribunals should be viewed as independent adjudicative bodies, not part of the internal complaints mechanisms of government departments and other public bodies. The Franks Committee urged that three principles – 'openness, fairness and impartiality' – should inform the design and practices of appellate tribunals. This meant that, so far as appropriate, tribunals should use procedures similar to those of courts: the chair of a tribunal should be a barrister or solicitor; hearings should be in public; appellants should have the right to be legally represented; tribunals should give formal reasons for their adjudications; and there should be an appeal from the findings of tribunals to the High Court.

The many tribunals which exist today are regulated by the Tribunals and Inquiries Act 1992 (formerly the 1952 and 1971 Acts), which imposes on them a legal duty to give reasons (s 10) and allows appeals on points of law to the High Court or Court of Appeal from their decisions (s 11). It may also be possible to seek judicial review of a tribunal decision. The Tribunals and Inquiries Act also creates the Council on Tribunals, an advisory body which carries out research and gives guidance on good practice both to government and tribunals (see Bradley, AW, 'The Council on Tribunals: time for a broader role?' [1990] PL 6).

Major concerns with the current operation of the tribunal system persist. Legal aid is not available to pay for legal representation, and so almost all complainants have to act as their own advocates. It is also often difficult for people to obtain affordable and competent legal advice about their rights before going to a tribunal; highly complex legislation governs decision making in fields such as welfare benefits and immigration control. Tribunal hearings can, therefore, be very uneven contests. Anxieties have also arisen about the impartiality of tribunals (see Council on Tribunals, *Tribunals: their Organisation and Independence*, Cm 3744, 1997, London: HMSO).

9.3.4 Courts

Although ombudsmen and tribunals deal with far more grievances against public authorities than do the courts, what happens in the courtroom is of great constitutional importance. Court proceedings against governmental bodies and office holders take many forms: tort actions; applications for judicial review on the grounds of illegality, procedural impropriety and irrationality; claims in European Community law; and petitions to the European Court of Human Rights in Strasbourg. Litigation procedures, remedies and legal arguments differ somewhat in the three legal systems of the UK (see above, 2.10); our focus will be on those of England and Wales, rather than Scotland and Northern Ireland.

In tort actions, citizens and businesses may sue government institutions, their employees, police officers and even ministers for negligence, trespass, assault, false imprisonment and other tortious wrongs committed in the course of official work. The primary role of tort law is to provide compensation. Public authorities and office holders are generally liable in tort on the same basis as businesses and individual citizens, but the courts have made many adaptations to how normal principles apply in this context. A public authority will not, for instance, owe a duty of care in negligence for 'policy' decisions which cause harm unless that policy decision is so unreasonable that no reasonable authority could have made it (see *X (Minors) v Bedfordshire CC* (1995) and Cane, P, 'Suing public authorities in tort' (1996) 113 LQR 13). On the grounds of public policy, the courts have also created immunity from tort actions for police investigations (*Hill v Chief Constable of West Yorkshire* (1989)) – though the European Court of Human Rights has recently held that such an immunity breaches Art 6 of the ECHR (see below, 20.3).

The common law does, however, recognise that the special powers of public authorities may justify the imposition of liability where none would normally attach to private bodies. Thus, the torts of misfeasance in public office (see above, 9.2.3) and malicious prosecution only lie against public authorities. Exemplary damages (over and above that which is needed to compensate a claimant) are also more readily available against public authorities for the 'oppressive, arbitrary or unconstitutional action by the servants of the government' (*Rookes v Barnard* (1964)), though the Court of Appeal has recently laid down the guideline that the maximum penalty for bad conduct by police officers of superintendent rank and above should be £50,000 (*Thompson v Commissioner of Police for the Metropolis* (1997)) and the Law Commission has recommended reforms (*Aggravated, Exemplary and Restitutionary Damages*, Law Com No 247)).

Judicial review is another type of proceeding in which public authorities are challenged (see below, Chapter 11). The purpose here is not to obtain compensation, but to set aside a legally flawed decision. Until the 1950s, this area of law lacked conceptual coherence and was regarded as a disparate collection of legal rules and archaic procedures. Since then, the courts and academic lawyers have developed a principled approach to the legal control of governmental powers and the court procedures have been modernised. In Chapters 12–15, we examine the main grounds for seeking judicial review, which for convenience are categorised under the headings of illegality, procedural impropriety and irrationality. Chapter 17 considers the procedure for making an application for judicial review in the High Court and the remedies which are available.

Since the accession to the European Community in 1973 (see above, Chapter 7, below, Chapter 18), citizens and businesses have been able bring legal proceedings to enforce Community law rights in the UK. There is no separate court in the UK dealing specially with Community law; on the contrary, every national court and tribunal is obliged to apply relevant Community law and, where there is a conflict with national law, to give priority to Community law (see above, 7.9.1). Sometimes, litigation in the UK is suspended while the court or tribunal seeks guidance from the Court of Justice (see above, 7.5.5) on a question of Community law (see below, 18.2.1). The Luxembourg Court also has jurisdiction to determine legal actions itself, but such direct adjudication is mostly confined to proceedings brought by Member States and other Community institutions; individuals and businesses have relatively little scope for commencing such litigation (see below, 18.3).

Since 1966, citizens in the UK have been able to bring legal proceedings against the UK in the 'other' European court – the European Court of Human Rights based in Strasbourg in eastern France (see below, 19.7). The rulings of this international tribunal on violations of the European Convention on Human Rights are not binding in the national legal systems of the UK, though the government usually complies with its findings. The Human Rights Act 1998 brings about significant changes to the status of the Convention in British law. From now on, all British courts and tribunals are required to interpret Acts of Parliament and statutory instruments 'in a way which is compatible with Convention rights' (see below, 19.10) and violation of the Convention has become a new ground for seeking judicial review of public authorities. In Chapters 19–27, we look at the rights protected by the Convention in more detail.

9.4   Conclusions

Like much else in the British constitutional system at the moment, ideas and practices about redressing grievances against public authorities are in a state of flux.

Although litigation in courts is regarded as slow and expensive, and ill suited to resolving many of the day to day disputes between citizens and public authorities, more people than ever before are using legal proceedings. The annual number of applications for judicial review has risen from 544 in 1981 to over 4,000 in 1998; there are also record numbers of tort actions against public bodies, especially local authorities and the police. Courts and tribunals in the UK, the European Court of Justice and the European Court of Human Rights have all faced persistent backlogs in the case loads, and procedural reforms have had to be introduced to help cope with the demand. Why has there been such an increase in litigation against public authorities? One possible explanation is that, even though legal advice is expensive and fewer people than ever qualify for legal aid, citizens now have a growing knowledge of their legal rights and are more likely to be aware of their capacity to challenge government action. On this view, the rise in litigation is no bad thing: it demonstrates a robust citizenry willing and able to stand up for its rights. A different interpretation is that public authorities are more often making unlawful decisions. Another possible analysis is that the growth in litigation has occurred because there are simply more opportunities for it. Since the early 1980s, the courts have developed new grounds on which judicial review may be sought; these include more rigorous requirements of procedural fairness in administrative decision making (see below, Chapter 13) and the principle of legitimate expectations (see below, Chapter 14). European Community law and the ECHR have both also provided new bases for challenges.

A second feature of recent developments in the UK is the belief that 'alternative dispute resolution' is preferable to courtroom litigation (see above, 9.3.1). In part, this development has occurred as a way of helping courts cope with increasing case loads. As we have already noted, while alternatives to courts may be speedier and less costly, these mechanisms for redressing grievances have disadvantages. What is sometimes now lost sight of is the great equalising virtue of courts, backed by the provision of legal aid: both the aggrieved citizen and the powerful public authority are represented by counsel; both have to make out their case according to settled criteria, and the trial takes place in public.

A third area of rapid innovation in the UK is in the reach of the courts' jurisdictions. New issues are becoming 'justiciable', meaning that they are amenable to adjudication. Since 1985, the ways in which ministers exercise prerogative powers are, in principle, subject to judicial review and are no longer a matter solely for Parliament to oversee (*Council of Civil Service Unions v Minister for the Civil Service* (1985), discussed below, Chapter 15). Most significantly, there have been important changes in functions of the courts in relation to legislation passed by Parliament: courts may now 'disapply' statutes inconsistent with Community law (see above, 7.8.1) and may, under the Human Rights Act 1998, make a 'declaration of incompatibility' in relation to any statutory provision which violates the European Convention on Human Rights. As we shall see in the ensuing chapters, while some commentators welcome these as progressive developments in the protection of citizens from abuse of power by government, others worry that litigation is beginning to replace debate among elected representatives as the method by which we make the important decisions about how society is organised.

INTRODUCTION TO DISPUTE RESOLUTION

Why dispute resolution is important

In a liberal democracy, it is important that legislation and executive action are open to challenge. The election of office holders does not give them, or their employees, carte blanche. One of the responsibilities of government is therefore to provide people with adequate opportunities to question the good sense and lawfulness of public decisions.

Types of dispute

- Disputes about the existence of legal power – people may argue on an application for judicial review that a public authority lacks '*vires*' (power) to take action. The UK government has, from time to time, challenged measures adopted by the European Community on the ground that they are unlawful.

- Disputes about the manner in which public bodies reach decisions. Allegations of procedural impropriety may be a ground for judicial review and complaints to ombudsmen.

- Disputes about the motives of public officials. Corruption in public authorities is not rife in the UK, but it does occur and may be the subject of criminal prosecutions. Allegations of malice may also be the basis for an action in the tort of misfeasance of public office.

- Disputes about wrong conclusions. Even if a public authority does have legal power and makes a decision free from procedural irregularity and improper motives, there may still be dissatisfaction with it.

Types of dispute resolution

- Internal complaints procedures, encouraged by the Citizen's Charter programme.

- Ombudsmen investigate cases of injustice resulting from 'maladministration'.

- Tribunals have been established by many Acts of Parliament.

- Courts: legal proceedings against public authorities take many forms, including tort actions and applications for judicial review. In some circumstances, people may be able to begin proceedings in the European Court of Justice or the European Court of Human Rights.

CHAPTER 10

COMMISSIONERS FOR ADMINISTRATION ('OMBUDSMEN')

We saw in Chapter 9 that, despite policies aimed at steering people away from the courts, the public appetite for litigation has not abated, particularly as a means of calling public authorities to account for their actions. Nevertheless, there are many types of public activity which cause dissatisfaction, and these may not always be subject to legal challenge either before the courts or in the many tribunals that are available, because there has been no technical breach of the law. This is where the ombudsmen come in. The term 'ombudsman' is a borrowing from Swedish administrative law. The first ombudsman in this country was the Parliamentary Commissioner for Administration (PCA), a post established in 1967. Since then, the role of the ombudsman has spread to other sectors of public life: there is an ombudsman for the National Health Service and an ombudsman for local government. While their areas of remit may differ, they all have in common the important role of making public authorities accountable to individuals for administrative failure. This administrative failure is known in ombudsman terms as 'maladministration', and people's complaints must concern themselves with the way decisions are reached, and the manner of their implementation, rather than the quality of the decisions themselves. Any findings or recommendations made by an ombudsman at the end of the investigative process are not legally binding on the public authority complained against. The ombudsmen have no sanctions, but rely, instead, on co-operation.

Maladministration is not a cause of action or ground of judicial review recognised by the courts. Therefore, the ombudsmen provide a form of redress where the complainant cannot take legal action. Nevertheless, in many cases there may be an overlap between the ombudsmen's jurisdiction and those of the courts; the complainant may be able to point, for example, to a breach of natural justice, which is actionable in judicial review proceedings, in addition to a case of maladministration. The current reforms to the civil justice system include a number of mechanisms for discouraging people from pursuing their disputes through the courts; judges will be obliged, for instance, to ask litigants whether they have tried alternative dispute resolution before proceeding to formal litigation. In disputes with public authorities, where there may be an overlap between the ombudsman's jurisdiction and judicial review procedures, it is suggested that the aggrieved individual ought to allow the ombudsman to investigate the complaint first, before going to court. This may not prevent the complainant from returning to court; indeed, an adverse finding by the ombudsman may trigger successful judicial review proceedings. This happened in *Congreve v Home Office* (1976). The PCA here upheld the complaint of maladministration by the Home Office in failing to renew television licenses at the old rate, and this finding led to successful judicial review proceedings where the court found that the minister had acted illegally in revoking the licences of people who had sought to avoid the new, increased licence fee by renewing their previous licence ahead of time.

It can be seen from this brief introduction that recourse to the ombudsman may have some advantages where the complainant has no recognisable legal cause of action. It is not, however, possible to evaluate the efficacy of this institution without some evidence as to the level of co-operation the ombudsmen secure from the public authority into which they conduct their investigation, because, without this co-operation, there is no redress for the complainant. This can be gleaned to a certain extent from the annual reports put out by the ombudsmen themselves. There are also a number of 'no-go' areas, with obvious implications for the redress of grievances. The PCA may not, for example, investigate any action taken for the purposes of the investigation of crime, or action in relation to passports, nor any action taken in matters relating to contractual or other commercial transactions by central government. The list of excluded activities is given below, 10.4 (and is to be found in s 5(3) and Sched 3 of the Parliamentary Commissioner Act 1967). But first, it is worth looking at the roles of the four main public service sector ombudsmen.

10.1   Who are the ombudsmen?

The first main public sector ombudsman to be set up was the PCA. He investigates cases of injustice caused by maladministration in central government departments and some other institutions. The current office holder is Michael Buckley, a former civil servant. The PCA is based in London and is staffed by civil servants on secondment from government departments; this is sometimes said to be a weakness, since the ombudsman's office should be seen to be neutral and independent. This PCA enjoys similar status and tenure of office to that of a High Court judge, which means that he is formally appointed by the Queen and holds office during 'good behaviour', and, more importantly, can only be removed by the Queen following addresses by both Houses of Parliament. Mr Buckley also holds the post of Health Service Ombudsman, established in 1973 to look at allegations of maladministration in the National Health Service.

The Local Commission for Administration (LCA) was set up in 1974 to deal with complaints of maladministration against local authorities in England and Wales. England is split into three areas, with a commissioner for each. The current local ombudsmen are Mr Osmotherly, Mrs Thomas and Mr White. They deal with complaints concerning maladministration by local authorities, mainly in the fields of social services, planning and housing. We will look in more detail at some of their casework below.

In addition to the above, it is worth mentioning another public sector ombudsman with special responsibilities. The Prisons Ombudsman Office (formally known as the Independent Complaints Adjudicator) was instituted in 1994 on the recommendation of the Woolf Report into the serious riots at Strangeways Prison. This was part of a package of reforms introduced in 1992, in which Prison Boards of Visitors ceased to hear disciplinary charges against prisoners; prison governors are now entirely responsible for this. If a prisoner believes that a disciplinary finding is wrong, or that proper procedures were not followed, he can now appeal to the Prisons Ombudsman (see Morgan, R, 'Prisons accountability revisited' [1993] PL 314).

There is also an ombudsman for the European Community to deal with complaints concerning instances of maladministration in the activities of the Community institutions or bodies (with the exception of the Court of First Instance and the Court of Justice acting in their judicial role). The current holder of the post is Jacob Soederman, formerly Parliamentary Ombudsman in Finland. Although the ombudsman played no direct role in the mass resignation of the Commission in February 1999 in response to a damning report on corruption, his investigations into transparency, or lack of it, in Commission recruitment procedures, and public access to Commission documents, will have an important impact on the newly constituted Commission.

In addition, a plethora of private sector ombudsmen have been created to investigate complaints in service industries such as banking, insurance and estate agencies. Most of these ombudsmen have been established and financed by the industries themselves, and have no special statutory powers. They form part of the system for self-regulation (see above, 8.2.3). Other private sector ombudsmen have been set up by statute, such as the Building Societies Ombudsman and the Legal Services Ombudsman, established under the Courts and Legal Services Act 1990. This ombudsman oversees how the professional bodies deal with complaints against solicitors, barristers and licensed conveyancers. He is, however, precluded from investigating allegations relating to matters for which there is immunity from actions in tort, such as advocacy in court. The fact that some private sector ombudsmen are set up by statute, and others are just voluntary, creates an untidy picture – especially when it comes to the way in which complaints against the ombudsmen may be made. If an ombudsman has statutory powers, then a person dissatisfied with a decision not to investigate a case of maladministration (for example) can apply for judicial review of that ombudsman (for example, *R v Parliamentary Commissioner for Administration ex p Balchin* (1997)). But, if the ombudsman is merely 'voluntary', and has no statutory powers, then judicial review is probably not possible (for example, *R v Insurance Ombudsman Bureau ex p Aegon Life Insurance Ltd* (1994)).

Ombudsmen for both the public and private sectors have begun to work closely together, and meet regularly under the auspices of the UK and Ireland Ombudsmen Association formed in 1993, the aims of which include improvement of public awareness of the functions performed by ombudsmen.

10.2   Injustice as a consequence of maladministration

What all these very different ombudsmen have in common is the power to deal with 'maladministration'. None of the statutes establishing the various ombudsmen actually define what is meant by 'maladministration'. A useful, but not comprehensive, guide was provided by Richard Crossman, a minister at the time the PCA was first established. It is now known as the 'Crossman Catalogue': 'bias, neglect, inattention, delay, incompetence, ineptitude, perversity, turpitude, arbitrariness, and so on'. 'And so on' may prove useful to the Commissioners, giving some discretion and flexibility regarding that which can be investigated.

Since the Crossman Catalogue, the annual PCA reports have revealed additions to these categories, including unwillingness to treat a complainant as a person with rights, neglecting to inform, failure to monitor faulty procedures, and the failure to mitigate the effects of rigid adherence to the letter of the law where this produces manifest inequity. It is not enough, however, to complain simply that there has been 'maladministration'; the complainant must establish that he has been caused some 'injustice' thereby; there must be some causal link, in other words, between the public authority's behaviour and the loss caused to the complainant (*R v Local Commissioner for Administration ex p Eastleigh BC* (1988)).

The best way to understand what maladministration means is to look at some reports of ombudsman investigations, and then consider the statistical evidence of the rate of success of these complaints. The following sections focus on the work of the PCA, the Health Service ombudsman and the local ombudsmen respectively.

Here are some recent PCA investigations (summarised in its report of 1997–98):

(a) the PCA upheld a taxpayer's complaint that the Inland Revenue had delayed resolving his tax affairs after he left the UK, with the result that he continued to pay tax unnecessarily. The Revenue did refund this overpayment, but only after the investigation by the PCA did they deal with the complainant's claim for lost interest and costs, making him an ex gratia payment of £1,500;

(b) an increasing number of complaints reaching the office of the PCA concern the activities of the controversial Child Support Agency set up by the government in 1993 to trace absent parents (usually fathers) and make them contribute towards their children's upkeep. When the CSA failed for three years to secure regular payment of child support maintenance by an absent parent (one of the agency's key functions), the ombudsman upheld a complaint that the delay had caused financial loss, distress and inconvenience to the mother. The CSA awarded her *ex gratia* payments of £2,384.26;

(c) a complainant on income support had declared to the benefits office that she was working part time. A fraud officer interviewed her about her employment, but took no account of her declaration of earnings, even though that information was available to him. The ombudsman upheld her complaint declaring that she had been caused distress by being wrongly suspected of dishonestly claiming income support, and that there were serious failures in the handling of her complaint.

So financial compensation does not always follow an adverse finding by the PCA. Over the 15 month period covered by the 1997–98 report, the ombudsman's recommendations of compensation resulted in payments ranging from £30 (to a member of the public who had experienced difficulty in booking a driving test using a credit card) to £50,044.30 (compensation paid by Customs and Excise for losses, costs and inconvenience to a member of the public who, for a period, had been denied a certificate of VAT paid on a boat he wished to import into France). The availability of other remedies, such as a recommendation by the ombudsman to the erring public authority to apologise to the complainant, fits in with the ombudsman's remit, which is to 'emphasise the value placed on the admission of mistakes and the attempt to make right any harm done' (Select Committee on the PCA, *First Report for Session 1994–95 on Maladministration and Redress*, HC 112).

These reports may make for anodyne reading, but they perform the important function of attracting publicity to the ombudsman's findings. The contents of these reports are privileged from defamation.

Some examples of the Health Service Ombudsman's investigations, summarised in his annual report of 1996–97, are as follows:

(a) Staff at University College Hospital failed to inform the complainants of their father's deterioration and death. There followed a delay in giving the family an opportunity to see the body and general lack of tact in dealing with the complaint. The complaint was upheld, and the NHS Trust concerned was criticised for lack of instructions to staff on informing patients about the condition of patients near to death. The ombudsman's office also criticised the trust for a 'disgraceful lack of sensitivity to a bereaved relative'.

(b) An individual submitted a formal complaint through the internal complaints procedure about the clinical mismanagement of his late father's cardiac condition. The Newham Healthcare NHS Trust failed to make a substantive reply to the letter for five months, and when it did, the response was addressed to the deceased patient and not to the complainant. The ombudsman upheld the complaint that the matter had been dealt with inadequately, and he also recommended that individuals should be informed about avenues of appeal from the internal complaints procedure, either to independent review or to the ombudsman himself.

(c) A man suffering from acute appendicitis was kept waiting for about eight hours on a trolley in the Accident and Emergency Department of Hillingdon Hospital before being attended to. He complained that he had received inadequate care, and also alleged that insensitive personal remarks had been made within his hearing. Both complaints were upheld, and the ombudsman recommended that better procedures were put in place to ensure that staff contact the on-call surgical team; the fact that the complainant's arrival in hospital had coincided with the national changeover day for junior doctors, when they change appointments, was no excuse. The hospital also apologised for the alleged insensitive remarks, although they had not been substantiated.

The local ombudsmen conduct investigations into claims of injustice form maladministration by a local authority, local police authority or water authority. Many complaints are about housing and planning. As can be seen from the cases below, recommendations for compensation, when they are made, tend to be modest:

(a) Mr and Mrs H contended that a local council had failed to deal properly with their complaints about dust caused by quarry workings close to their home. They said that they had suffered consequent nuisance from limestone dust settling on their property. The local ombudsman upheld the complaint that the local council had failed to ensure compliance with the conditions for authorisation of the quarry works and the council's delay in responding to the property owners' complaints amounted to maladministration. She recommended that the council pay the complainants £250 to reflect the frustration and distress they had experienced in seeking a response from the council to their complaints. The council accepted this recommendation.

(b) Mrs J, who owned a guest house close to the city centre, complained on behalf of seven resident guest house owners on her street that the council had failed to carry out proper consultations about the introduction of residents' parking in the area. As a result, the complainants said that they had to pay for parking that was formerly free, that the amount of overall parking space had been reduced, and that they had suffered subsequent loss of trade because of insufficient parking space for their guests. The local ombudsman held that the lack of proper consultation had amounted to maladministration by the local council and he recommended that the council should give Mrs J and the six others on whose behalf she had taken the complaint six months' free parking time each and that Mrs J should be awarded £150 for her 'time and trouble' in pursuing these complaints. The council accepted these recommendations.

(c) A complainant informed the local ombudsman that her local council had failed to ensure the protection of a group of mature trees, when approving a planning application for a development close to her home. The local ombudsman found that the council had not considered the probable effect of the development on the trees (which were subject to a preservation order). As a result of the ombudsman's report, the council undertook to fund a replanting scheme to replace the trees that had been lost and to carry out remedial works on remaining damaged trees and to compensate residents for costs incurred in removing dead trees (a total expenditure of £4,000).

10.3 The statistics

The reports indicate not only the nature of some of the individual cases investigated, but are illustrative of the general pattern of the types of complaints brought and the rate of investigation:

1997–98	Complaints	Percentage investigated in full
PCA	1,528	20%
HSC	2,660	4%
LCA	14,969	3%

The number of complaints received by the Health Service Ombudsman has increased most dramatically of all the public sector ombudsmen. In 1989–90, he only received 794 complaints; the current figures represent a 24% increase on the previous year. This is partly because this ombudsman's jurisdiction has recently been extended to cover complaints about the exercise of clinical judgment by health service professionals and complaints about family practitioners, and the very small percentage of investigations undertaken is partially explained by the fact that clinical investigations take much longer, because of the need for the involvement of expert assessors. In contrast to the office of the Health Service Ombudsman, the PCA and the local ombudsmen receive relatively few complaints when one considers the width of their respective jurisdictions. The number of complaints submitted to the PCA has barely increased since 1993, when 1,244 letters were received, 24% of which were investigated. Bear in mind the vast number of decisions taken by public servants on behalf of a population of almost 60 million, and then the tiny number of complaints can be put in perspective. Later, we shall consider the causes of this, and whether it is a problem.

It is also worth noting how few complaints receive a full investigation by all the public sector ombudsmen. As we shall see, this is, in part, because many complaints made fall outside the scope of the ombudsmen's jurisdiction, and so are filtered out at a preliminary stage. Also, the ombudsmen often manage to resolve complaints by informal contact with the public authority without any need for a full formal investigation. The Health Service Ombudsman, for example, sends the majority of the complaints he receives back to the internal complaints procedure set up under the NHS, which is the more appropriate body for dealing with many of the matters raised.

A potentially important area of the current PCA's jurisdiction concerns complaints under the Code of Practice on Access to Government Information, a non-statutory code in operation since 1994. This imposes a non-binding obligation on public authorities to provide certain types of information, and the responsibility for seeing that the government acts in accordance with this Code of Practice is placed on the PCA. The basis for his jurisdiction here is based on the twin criteria of maladministration and injustice; the failure by the public authority in question to provide the information in accordance with the code is deemed to constitute an injustice. However, since the code was put in place, relatively few complaints have been received under this head; only 27 complaints came into the office in 1997–98. When the Freedom of Information Act passes into force, this subject will pass out of the PCA's jurisdiction, since the Act will give legal backing to the right to certain categories of information and a special Commissioner for Information will be appointed to adjudicate on disputes. The current PCA has expressed his concern that 'the creation of yet another public sector complaints authority will make an already complex and fragmented system still harder for complainants to use and understand' (1997–98 Report, para 1.15).

10.4   Limits on the ombudsmen's powers

Not every incident of 'maladministration' by a public authority can be taken to the ombudsmen for investigation. The ombudsmen are able to investigate only those public bodies specifically referred to in the ombudsmen's respective statutes. Some of these limitations are relatively uncontroversial; others less so. The following are all excluded from the PCA's jurisdiction:

(a) complaints relating to matters affecting the UK's relationship with other countries or international organisations;

(b) criminal investigations and national security;

(c) the commencement or conduct of civil or criminal proceedings;

(d) any exercise of the prerogative of mercy by the Home Secretary;

(e) matters relating to contractual or commercial transactions of government departments;

(f) grievances concerning the pay, discipline, pensions, appointments and other personnel matters in the armed forces and Civil Service;

(g) the grant of honours, awards and privileges within the gift of the Crown.

An area of real concern has been the exclusion from the jurisdiction of both the PCA and the Health Service Ombudsman and the local ombudsmen of matters relating to commercial or contractual transactions. Since the 1980s, many public services have been 'contracted out'. These services include the care of the elderly and chronically sick, refuse collection, and catering and cleaning in public institutions. Recent legislation has gone some way to meet these criticisms. The Health Service Ombudsman can now investigate complaints relating to services provided through the internal market created by the NHS and Community Care Act 1990 (s 7(2) of the Health Service Commissioner Act 1993). The Deregulation and Contracting Out Act 1994 extends the PCA and local ombudsmen's jurisdiction to contracted out functions of central and local government.

It should be mentioned here that not all these activities are amenable to judicial review by the courts either. We will see from Chapters 11–16 that some of these are expressions of the prerogative power of the Crown, such as the making of international treaties and the grant of honours. Other areas, such as the employment conditions of civil servants, may be excluded from the purview of judicial review by statute. However, the power of the courts to scrutinise these activities in judicial review proceedings is not so clearly curtailed as it is in the case of the ombudsman, as we will see in looking at the range of public activities which could properly be described as contractual or commercial which have been successfully challenged in judicial review proceedings.

In addition, complaints are subject to a time limit; they have to be made within 12 months from the day the aggrieved person first had notice of the problem. This would appear to be more generous than the time limit imposed for the institution of judicial review proceedings – within three months from the date of the offending administrative act – but, again, the courts do have the discretion to extend the time for application for permission in cases where there is a 'good reason' so to do (see below, 17.3). The PCA does not enjoy this discretion. This is one of the limits on the jurisdiction of the PCA which he himself believes should be removed. He has expressed regret, for example, that he is not able to investigate personnel matters in the public service.

10.5 The ombudsman process

In this section, we trace the steps that have to be followed when complaining to either the PCA, Health Service Ombudsman or the local ombudsmen, highlighting the most controversial features. The first point to make is that the process can take a long time: all the ombudsmen have backlogs of cases waiting to be dealt with. In its 1997–98 report, the PCA noted that the average throughput time for investigations completed was over 87 weeks; in his judgment, he says in his report, 'these figures were unacceptable' (see above,

1.4). Equally, the Select Committee on Public Administration commented in 1997 that the average time taken for Health Service Ombudsman investigations – nine months – is 'too long', particularly since many complaints are months old by the time they reach his office.

10.5.1 The PCA

If a person is aggrieved by the maladministration of a central government body, he cannot complain to the PCA directly: only complaints referred to the PCA office by an MP will be considered. The MP need not be the complainant's own constituency MP. This so called 'MP filter' is regarded by most commentators (but not all) as a major weakness in the institution of the PCA. The bar on direct access to the PCA needs to be set in a historical context. Parliament became the supreme law making body following the English Civil War and the constitutional settlement of the 17th century (see Chapter 3). Three centuries later, Parliament is still seen, or at least sees itself, as the forum for the redress of grievances. This is the reason – apart from administrative convenience – for the MP filter. The ombudsman system is, therefore, firmly attached to Parliament, rather than the people: the PCA is perceived to be a creature of Parliament rather than a citizen's champion, as he is in other democracies.

The MP filter has two main functions. First, to give the MP a chance to deal with the complaint himself or herself – for example, by writing a letter to the relevant government department. Sometimes, this is all that is needed to resolve a problem. Secondly, it is suggested that MPs play a useful role in weeding out unmeritorious complaints, or complaints about matters which fall outside the PCA's jurisdiction. In reality, this does not happen, as many MPs seem not to understand what types of complaints the PCA is able to investigate; a large proportion of complaints referred to the PCA by MPs have to be rejected by the Commissioner's office, on the ground that they fall outside his jurisdiction as set down by the 1967 Act.

Drewry and Harlow carried out research into how MPs were using the PCA in the mid 1980s (see '"The cutting edge"? The PCA and MPs' (1990) 53 MLR 745). They found that every year, about 70% of MPs refer between one and six complaints to the PCA. Interestingly, over 26% of MPs had received a request from a person living in another MP's constituency to pass a complaint on to the PCA. There was considerable uncertainty as to what an MP should do in such circumstances. Drewry and Harlow conclude that the office of the PCA 'is held in low esteem' both by MPs and the public.

Whether or not such low esteem is justified, it has been pointed out in a study of the constituency case work of MPs that the MPs sometimes have to monitor ombudsmen investigations themselves to ensure that investigations are conducted thoroughly and effectively (see Rawlings, R, 'The MP's complaints service' (1990) 53 MLR 22 and 149.) The PCA in fact receives more complaints directly (which he has to reject) than he receives from MPs. The PCA was so concerned about this that, in 1978, he introduced machinery whereby, with permission of the complainant, he would pass on the complaint to an MP, who in turn could pass it back to the PCA to investigate.

The debate over direct access to the PCA continues. In 1977, a report by JUSTICE, *Our Fettered Ombudsman*, recommended direct access, as did the JUSTICE/All Souls Review in 1988. The PCA himself would also like to see direct access. In his report, he again complains about the obstacle of the MP filter:

> That hurdle is not required before an approach is made to me as Health Service Commissioner. It applies to almost no other national ombudsman throughout the world. I remain of the view that the filter serves to deprive members of the public of possible redress.

However, not everyone accepts the need for the removal of the MP filter. Carol Harlow has argued against this, and has challenged the assumptions that underlie the calls for direct access ('Ombudsman in search of a role' (1978) 41 MLR 446; Harlow, C and Rawlings, R, *Law and Administration*, 2nd edn, 1998, London: Butterworths, Chapter 7). She is not keen to see a huge increase in the number of cases investigated by the PCA which would be likely to occur if the MP filter were to be removed. On the other hand, it has been argued that the relatively low numbers of complaints made to the ombudsmen is a fundamental flaw in the institution, and without an expansion of their case load, which could be achieved by removing the MP filter and expediting the investigations undertaken, they cannot properly perform their task of correcting maladministration in the public sector.

10.5.2 Access to other ombudsmen

In contrast to the PCA, the Health Service Ombudsman and the local ombudsmen allow complainants direct access. In the early years of the local ombudsmen, there was a requirement that complaints had to be referred by a councillor, but this was removed by the Local Government Act 1988, since when the public have been able to approach the local ombudsmen directly. This led to a dramatic rise of 44% in the number of complaints received; now over 83% of complaints are made directly, rather than via a local councillor. This strongly suggests that the removal of the MP filter for the PCA would result in a considerable increase in work for that office.

10.5.3 The ombudsman filter

Once a complaint has been received by one of the ombudsman's offices, the first task is to determine whether it falls within that ombudsman's jurisdiction and whether it shows a *prima facie* case of maladministration. As we will see, a very large proportion of cases are rejected at this stage, because the subject matter falls outside the jurisdiction of the relevant ombudsman or the complaint is not about 'maladministration'.

The ombudsman's office also has to consider whether the aggrieved person should be taking legal proceedings. As was mentioned in the introduction to this chapter, there may be an overlap between ombudsman redress and a judicial review matter. It has to be said that, in many of the complaints listed above, 10.2, 'maladministration' simply involves incompetence, failures in communication and insensitivity on the part of public authorities and their employees. In such cases, there would be no grounds for the complainant to apply for judicial review; there has been no illegality, irrationality or procedural impropriety. But, at other times, the complaint of 'maladministration' may also give grounds for some sort of legal challenge. Careless administration – for example, losing documents – could possibly give the basis for suing for negligence. A public authority's inordinate delay in complying with a statutory duty might give grounds for judicial review. This can cause problems. All the main ombudsmen are precluded from investigating complaints of injustice caused by maladministration if the complainant has a legal remedy available. For example, the Parliamentary Commissioner Act 1967 provides:

> 5(2) Except as hereinafter provided, the Commissioner shall not conduct an investigation under this Act in respect of any of the following matters, that is to say–
>
> (a) any action in respect of which the person aggrieved has or had a right of appeal, reference or review to or before a tribunal constituted by or under any enactment or by virtue of Her majesty's prerogative:
>
> (b) any action in respect of which the person aggrieved has or had a remedy by way of proceedings in any court of law:
>
> Provided that the Commissioner may conduct an investigation notwithstanding that the person aggrieved has or had such a right or remedy if satisfied that in the particular circumstances it is not reasonable to expect him to have resort or have resorted to it.

The ombudsmen have tended to interpret this restriction on their powers to investigate cases with a good degree of flexibility. Sir Cecil Clothier, a former PCA, said that 'where process of law seems too cumbersome, slow and expensive for the objective gained, I exercise my discretion to investigate the complaint myself' ((1980–81) HC 148).

10.5.4 The investigation

If the complaint does pass the initial screening, then it is fully investigated. The ombudsman's method is inquisitorial rather than adversarial. This will normally involve a person from an ombudsman's office interviewing the aggrieved person to hear his or her account of the events alleged to constitute 'maladministration'. The civil servant, or local government officer in the public authority, will also be interviewed, and will be given a chance to answer the allegations made. Sometimes, the matter will end there, with an informal resolution; one of the advantages of this form of dispute resolution is that the ombudsman may put some pressure on the public authority at this pre-investigation stage to provide a suitable remedy to the complainant. Such informal inquiries avoid the time consuming process of putting a complaint formally to the department and receiving their comments, then starting a full investigation. Many complaints are resolved at this stage when the ombudsman finds that, though there may have been mistakes, they have not caused 'injustice' to the complainant.

If a formal investigation does proceed, the ombudsman has extensive statutory powers to compel witnesses to give evidence under oath and disclose documents. The ombudsman is not hindered by a number of common law and statutory rules which restrict the production of certain documents in court proceedings, such as the withholding of documents on grounds of public interest immunity or under the Official Secrets Acts (although cabinet documents can only be seen if certified by the Prime Minister or the Cabinet Secretary). An investigation cannot be stopped by a minister; indeed, any obstruction of the ombudsman's investigation may be referred to the High Court for punishment for contempt.

10.5.5 The report

If the investigation has failed to produce an informal negotiated settlement of the complainant's grievances, then staff in the ombudsman's office produce a written report. A copy is sent to the aggrieved person, the public authority which has been investigated, and the MP or any councillor who referred the complaint.

10.5.6 The response to the report

The public authority has an opportunity to respond to the report. In practice, the details of the report often meet with indifference. A recent survey revealed that over 50% of MP respondents said that they 'hardly ever' or 'never' read PCA reports, and 11% found these reports 'not at all useful' (Select Committee on the PCA, *First Report Session 1993–94*, HC 33, para 25). However, this indifference has appeared to have relatively little impact on redress. Central government departments almost invariably assent to the PCA's findings and, where this has been recommended, they pay compensation to the victim of the injustice caused by maladministration.

There are, however, very real problems with non-compliance with local ombudsmen reports by some local authorities. Following the Local

Government and Housing Act 1989, local councils which refuse to take satisfactory action following adverse reports from the local ombudsman are required to publish a statement in a local newspaper at their own expense. This can cost more than the sum that the local ombudsman had recommended as compensation! Only four such statements were issued in 1996–97, as opposed to 11 in the previous year. The 1989 Act also created monitoring officers to follow up cases where redress has been refused. These reforms have resulted in some improvement, but non-compliance remains a problem for the local ombudsmen. In the Citizen's Charter of 1991 (discussed in some detail in the previous chapter), the government stated:

> ... if difficulties continue we will take the further step of introducing legislation to make the Local ombudsman's recommendations legally enforceable, as those of the Northern Ireland Commissioner already are.

10.5.7 The ombudsman reacts

In fact, none of the ombudsmen are keen on the idea of court enforcement proceedings, because they fear that the threat of the courts could harm the co-operative relationships they usually enjoy with public bodies. This view was supported by the JUSTICE/All Souls Review only with regard to the PCA: with regard to the local ombudsmen, where real problems of non-compliance exist, it was recommended that the disappointed complainant should be able to apply to the county court for relief.

The final stage in the 'ombudsman process' is for the ombudsman to react to the public authority's response: as we have just noted, none of the ombudsmen has any powers to enforce their findings, whether it be that the public authority give an apology, revoke a decision or pay compensation. The ombudsmen rely on persuasion and publicity to encourage compliance.

That the PCA is a servant of Parliament is emphasised by the fact that he makes quarterly and annual reports to Parliament. Sometimes special detailed reports are made on investigations of particular importance, such as the one into the Barlow Clowes affair (discussed below, 10.6), or into the matter of 'planning blight' cast over properties in the vicinity of the proposed Channel Tunnel link, due to the confused signals coming from government as to where the link was going to be placed (*Channel Tunnel Rail Link* (1994–94) HC 819). The PCA's close association with Parliament is further enhanced by the existence of a Select Committee on the PCA for Administration (consisting of backbench MPs), which scrutinises the work of the ombudsman, liaises with the office, and produces its own reports on the PCA and the Health Service Ombudsman. The Health Service Ombudsman submits reports to the Secretary of State for Health, who must then lay the report before Parliament.

10.6   The Barlow Clowes affair

Having sketched out what typically happens during the course of an ombudsman investigation, we can now go on to look in more detail at one particular investigation – that of the Barlow Clowes affair.

10.6.1 The background

Barlow Clowes was set up in 1973 by Elizabeth Barlow and Peter Clowes; it was a brokerage business selling relatively secure gilts-based investments. Put very simply, the company acted as middleman, investing customers' money on their behalf, in the hope of gaining a profit. Any profit would go to the investor who supplied the money, and the company would claim a fee for its efforts. Following government deregulation of the money markets, Barlow Clowes prospered and expanded in the 1980s. An important part of government policy was to open the markets to small investors; rather as the Conservatives had worked to extend home ownership, so they encouraged ordinary people to take their chances in the City of London. Barlow Clowes specialised in services for such people; all its advertising in the popular press was aimed at small, inexperienced investors. Many investors dealt directly with Barlow Clowes, but many also used financial intermediaries with whom Barlow Clowes' portfolios were a popular product for their small investors. The intermediaries often made no effort to spread the risk of individual investments, putting all of an individual's life savings into Barlow Clowes. The typical profile of a Barlow Clowes investor was of a Conservative voter of modest means and advancing age, who wished to invest so as to gain financial security in old age.

The investors 'knew' their savings would be safe. All of Barlow Clowes' brochures and letterheads were stamped with the words 'licensed by the DTI' (Department of Trade and Industry). This department had a system of inspection of financial institutions, and if the company passed muster, it was given a licence and required, by the DTI, to publicise this in its literature and on letterheads.

In June 1988, Barlow Clowes went into liquidation following a demand by the Securities and Investment Board (a regulatory body) that they be wound up. Barlow Clowes owed a total of £190 million in high risk ventures. Instead of investing money in safer government securities, it had invested £100 million in high risk ventures. Large funds had been removed from Britain and taken offshore to Jersey, where financial controls are weaker. Mr Clowes had been able to lead a luxurious lifestyle, which included the purchase of property and yachts. As early as December 1984, the Jersey funds were £3.65 million less than obligations. The DTI had failed to notice the existence of the Jersey partnership and the department's procedures were inadequate to reveal this capital shortfall. This happened despite warnings from the accountants,

Touche Ross. Despite having licensed Barlow Clowes for 13 years, the DTI had no useful mechanism for monitoring its licensee.

Unfortunately for the investors, they could not institute proceedings in the courts, since English tort law does not recognise a duty of care owed to people in their position by the DTI (see a similar matter currently going through the courts in *Three Rivers DC v Bank of England* (1999)). In consequence, many of them complained of maladministration to the PCA, saying that the DTI had failed properly to investigate the group when granting licences to the investment companies and that these failures led to their losses. Following nearly 200 requests from MPs, the PCA began what was to be the 'most complex, wide-ranging and onerous investigation' he had undertaken.

10.6.2 The report of the PCA

The report of Barlow Clowes by the PCA found five areas of maladministration by the DTI, including licensing errors and failure to monitor the company. The DTI was also responsible for an unnecessary delay in acting that resulted in further losses. The PCA strongly recommended compensation be paid by the DTI.

10.6.3 The government's response

The initial government response to the report in 1988 was defensive, reminding the PCA that all investments involved risks. It refused to accept the report unreservedly (see *Observations by the Government of the PCA* (1989–90) HC 99. The Secretary of State for Trade and Industry (Lord Young) refused to compensate investors. The PCA was not the only source of pressure on the government. The media condemned the whole affair, calling it a 'scandal on a grand scale'. *The Times* wrote of 'amateurish arrangements' and the *Financial Times* of 'tunnel vision' at the DTI. A highly effective pressure group, the Barlow Clowes Investors' Group, campaigned with the media, putting considerable political pressure on the government. By the end of 1989, Nicholas Ridley, the new Secretary of State for Trade and Industry, agreed that compensation should be paid. Ridley made a statement to the House of Commons on 19 December 1989. He said that 'in the exceptional circumstances of this case and out of respect for the office of PCA' he would make substantial ex gratia payments amounting to over £150 million.

Why the change of heart by the government? There was more than one reason. The media and the investors' group had embarrassed the government. Also, the Select Committee on the PCA voiced strong concern regarding the government's reaction to the scandal. The final factor in the government's change of heart was the publication of the PCA's thorough and condemnatory report. Although no one took political responsibility for the fiasco, this episode marked an important triumph for the office of the PCA. Without his investigation and report, it is unlikely that such a level of compensation for the investors would have been achieved.

10.6.4 General lessons

The PCA did not win this victory on his own. A powerful political pressure by the investors' group, the media, MPs and the Select Committee all played a vital role. Indeed, it could be said that the Barlow Clowes affair highlights some of the weak areas in the ombudsman system:

(a) the PCA's report need not be accepted by the government, although the Barlow Clowes affair shows that the government will often not dare ignore a report entirely;

(b) one of the criticisms made by the government of the report was that the ombudsman had mistakenly questioned the merits of decisions by the DTI, rather than mere maladministration. There is no easy dividing line between policy and operation in public services, and too strict an interpretation of the ombudsman's remit could unduly restrict his decision;

(c) an important point is that the jurisdiction of the PCA is limited to the investigation of governmental bodies, with the consequence that the other personnel involved in the scandal, such as the Stock Exchange, FIMBRA, and the intermediaries, accountants and solicitors (all of whom were involved and probably at fault) could not be investigated. Whilst it would not be appropriate to the role of the PCA to investigate non-governmental bodies, this limitation meant that the report was not able to include adequate recommendations to protect investors in the future.

10.7 The future for ombudsmen

In many ways 'ombudsmen' are a growth area, with many private sector industries, such as banking and insurance, deciding to set up investigative complaints mechanisms for their customers. The public sector ombudsmen, by contrast, are looking less successful. As we have noted, the PCA is held in low esteem by many MPs and has a very low public profile. Things are little better for the local ombudsmen, whose reports are often flouted by local authorities. All the ombudsmen have backlogs of cases waiting to be investigated, a product of inadequate resources. Some cynics argue that the ombudsmen were never really intended to work effectively, merely to give the illusion that grievances could be redressed. But if there is to be reform, what should it try to achieve?

10.7.1 Fire fighting and fire watching

One fundamental choice that may have to be made is between the ombudsman as 'fire fighter' and 'fire watcher' (to use Harlow's terminology). The former clears up the mess and tackles problems as they occur (responding to individual grievances), the latter looks to the future and attempts to prevent problems. Harlow has argued that the PCA is not equipped to deal with numerous small complaints; we have a Rolls-Royce service which is put to best effect by giving a quality service, rather than dealing in quantity. Harlow therefore opposes direct access to the PCA. She chooses to emphasise the effect that the ombudsman can have on improving administration: 'a complaint is primarily a mechanism which draws attention to more general deficiencies'. To boost his powers, Harlow suggests that the PCA should be able to investigate and intervene on his own initiative. In a report in 1978, the Select Committee on the PCA recommended that the PCA should have the jurisdiction to carry out a systematic investigation of a particular area of the administration, if a tally of individual complaints pointed to a general problem. This was firmly rejected by the government on the grounds that it was not necessary and would distract the PCA from investigating individual complaints (Cmnd 7449, 1979).

For Harlow, the desirable output of the PCA's office should be a limited number of high quality reports which result from investigations initiated by himself or MPs. These reports would have a beneficial effect upon the administration, which could learn from past mistakes, and thereby improve future performance. The bulk of citizens' complaints should be tackled by MPs, or at a local level, or by specialist agencies, such as tribunals. The problem with the latter is that many complaints involving maladministration could not be handled unless the matter there also involved a legal right; in this sense, tribunals are constrained by the same limitations as courts. The PCA is all too aware of the need for this type of 'fire watching', but does not regard this to be mutually exclusive with his role of handling grievances. Of some of his reports, he writes: 'These should be read by public servants. They should learn from others' similar errors.' He believes that there should be a publication of guidance for public servants, as there already is by the local ombudsmen. The PCA is concerned not just to redress individual grievances, but also to benefit all in similar positions. The plethora of complaints generated by the Child Support Agency, for instance, led to a practice by the PCA of limiting his investigations to those cases where a new problem not previously investigated appeared to have occurred.. The PCA commented in his 1997–98 report that 'It continues to be a cause for concern that, all too often, the CSA's performance shows the same, often easily avoided, basic errors as have featured in successive Ombudsmen's reports since CSA's inception' (Chapter 3, para 3.3).

The local ombudsmen were enabled by s 23 of the Local Government and Housing Act 1989 to produce a Code of Guidance called 'Devising a complaints procedure for authorities'. Since this has been produced, many more complaints are dealt with internally by local government. The local ombudsmen now view a failure by a local authority to establish a proper internal complaints procedure as, in itself, amounting to maladministration. But the local ombudsman has no enforcement powers.

Another possible reform is to raise the public profile of the ombudsmen. Some commentators argue that the PCA is too much an 'invisible ombudsman'. Since 1997, modest efforts have been made to publicise the role of the PCA – publicity leaflets have been issued, the ombudsman himself has held meetings with voluntary organisations in the advice-giving sector, and a website has been put up giving basic information about the ombudsman's role (<http://www.ombudsman.org.uk>). However, this level of publicity compares poorly with ombudsmen in other countries such as Austria. Here the ombudsman (the *Volksanwaltschaft*) goes out on circuit, a sort of assize, and he advertises his intention of sitting in a particular location. He advertises on television, where he explains and reports on cases recently resolved. His office has a well publicised direct telephone line for the public, and the complainant pays only 1 schilling for the call, regardless of the real cost. The Irish ombudsman also travels around his country and the Commonwealth ombudsman of Australia advertised himself on milk bottle tops by arrangement with the suppliers! In *When Citizens Complain*, 1993, Milton Keynes: Open UP, N Douglas Lewis and Patrick Birkinshaw argue that there is an urgent need for a different culture in the PCA: they believe that he is too much an adjunct to Parliament, too much of an insider. They call for the PCA to have greater visibility and accessibility.

10.7.2 Ombudsmen and internal complaints procedures

The Citizen's Charter initiative laid the stress on the establishment of internal complaints procedures to allow individuals to complain about the inadequacies in public service. Concerns have also been expressed that such informal internal complaints procedures deprive the wider public of an opportunity to see that justice is done in open proceedings (see above, 9.3.1). In any event, when these internal complaints procedures fail, the Charter recognised that 'there must be an external route for taking things further'. A new grievance redressing mechanism was to be created. The White Paper had proposed 'lay adjudicators', who would be volunteers, use common sense and deal with 'small problems'. By the end of 1994, not a single lay adjudicator had been appointed. The Office of Public Service and Science, which has overall responsibility for the Citizen's Charter, says that there are no plans for any in the future, though there is still a possibility that some may be appointed. It was felt that lay adjudicators would prove to be just another tier with which the complainant had to deal. Instead, the public information leaflets on various public services produced under the auspices of the Citizen's Charter often refer complainants to the relevant ombudsman if the complaint has not been addressed. Overall, the Citizen's Charter programme looks set to rely heavily upon the ombudsman system. Indeed, it is the policy of the Office of Public Service to attract complaints.

The PCA himself recognises his partnership with the Citizen's Charter programme. The predecessor of the present PCA stated, in 1993, that that he communicated with the Office of Public Service and uses the 'Charter targets' (performance levels to which the various public services set and aspire to achieve) to help him, taking account of failures to meet targets.

A good example of the relationship between an internal complaints structure and ombudsman jurisdiction is to be found within the NHS. In 1996, a new unified procedure was introduced into the NHS for dealing with all complaints, whether they concerned hospital services, family practitioners, or clinical complaints about hospital doctors. A 'convenor', who is generally a director of the relevant health authority, determines which complaints should go to a special panel, which then adjudicates upon it and provides a solution. Since this procedure takes much less time than a full investigation undertaken by the ombudsman, it has significant advantages. However, the Health Service Ombudsman reported, in 1996–97, that a large number of complaints that come his way were ones which should have been dealt with by the internal complaints system, but which had remained unresolved. Many cases were referred back to the NHS trusts, thus giving the complainant a frustrating sense of buck-passing and delaying the resolution of the complaint even further.

It seems that the Citizen's Charter is affecting the role of the ombudsmen in various ways. If, in the future, the Charter results in growing numbers of 'small problems' being referred to ombudsmen, then the limitations on the ombudsman's role – whether caused by jurisdictional limits, the MP filter or lack of publicity – may become less significant.

COMMISSIONERS FOR ADMINISTRATION ('OMBUDSMEN')

The ombudsman system is a method of redress of individual grievances which does not necessitate using the courts. The work of the ombudsmen can be used to improve the administration of services to the public.

The public sector ombudsmen are:

(a) the PCA (PCA Act 1967);

(b) the Health Service Ombudsman (NHS Reorganisation Act 1973; HSC Act 1993);

(c) the Local Government Ombudsmen (Local Government Act 1988);

(d) the Prisons Ombudsman (Woolf Report 1992, set up 1994).

In addition to these, there is the European Parliament Ombudsman, who investigates complaints relating to maladministration by the Community institutions, and there are also ombudsmen for handling complaints in various service industries, some of whom are part of statutory regulatory framework.

The PCA and local ombudsmen investigate injustice as a result of maladministration, and do not review the merits of a decision. All ombudsmen have public access, except for the PCA, for which there is an MP filter.

The public sector ombudsmen, and especially the PCA, have a low public profile and a poor reputation amongst some MPs. The ombudsmen receive very few complaints as a proportion of the population.

The ombudsman system should be reviewed in the political and social context of the UK. The Citizen's Charter has affected the work of the ombudsmen.

CHAPTER 11

INTRODUCTION TO JUDICIAL REVIEW

11.1 Judicial review in the UK

The purposes of a legal system in a liberal democracy include setting limits on the powers of public authorities, providing a framework of rules and procedures for making collective decisions, and imposing legal responsibilities on public authorities to secure people's safety and welfare (see above, 1.7). Judicial review is one field of legal activity concerned with all of these purposes. A central objective of judicial review is to give judges power to ensure that public authorities act within the limits of the powers conferred on them directly or indirectly by the UK Parliament, and to ensure that public authorities fulfil their statutory duties. Judicial review is also used to ensure that, when ministers in the UK government exercise prerogative powers (see above, 2.4.3) they do so in accordance with the law. In recent years, judicial review has also been used as a way of making non-statutory self-regulatory bodies, such as the Press Complaints Commission, act according to recognised legal principles.

This chapter introduces two things. First, it outlines the grounds of judicial review – the practical legal arguments used by lawyers to challenge or defend the actions and omissions of public authorities (they will be examined in more detail in Chapters 12–16). The chapter then goes on to ask and to consider possible answers to an important question: what is the constitutional basis of the courts' power to engage in judicial review?

As we saw in Chapter 2, there are three separate legal systems in the UK (see above, 2.10). In England and Wales, it is the High Court which has responsibility for determining the 4,000 or so judicial review applications made each year. Some applications go on appeal to the Court of Appeal and House of Lords. In Northern Ireland, the procedures and grounds of judicial review are similar to those in England and Wales; the High Court of Northern Ireland determines applications in the province. In Scotland, the procedure for making a petition for judicial review and the grounds of judicial review are different (see Himsworth, CMG, 'Judicial review in Scotland', in Hadfield, B, *Judicial Review: a Thematic Approach*, 1995, Dublin: Gill and Macmillan). The focus of this and the following chapters is on England and Wales.

The new constitutional settlement has opened up the need for a court to adjudicate on 'devolution issues' – questions about the legislative competences of the assemblies in Wales and Northern Ireland and the Scottish Parliament, the matters reserved to the UK Parliament, and the powers and duties of the executive bodies in Wales, Northern Ireland and Scotland. So now, in addition to judicial review in the constituent parts of the UK, a new field of judicial review has been created by the Government of Wales Act 1998, the Scotland Act 1998 and the Northern Ireland Act 1998. Devolution issues are determined by the Judicial Committee of the Privy Council (see above, 2.8.4). It is not yet clear what methods of judicial reasoning the Privy Council will use in such cases, or to what extent new principles ought or need to be developed (see Craig, P and Walters, M, 'The courts, devolution and judicial review' [1999] PL 274).

11.2 The grounds of review

The grounds of judicial review are the arguments which a lawyer can put forward as to why a court should hold a public authority's decision to be unlawful. They can be categorised in various ways. If you look at the contents pages of the standard textbooks on judicial review and administrative law, you will notice a startling lack of uniformity; the same material is divided up in quite different ways, with different chapter headings and subheadings. To some extent, the differences are merely terminological and organisational. In one sense, it does not matter whether the court's power to review a decision for reasonableness comes under a chapter labelled 'Abuse of discretion', or labelled 'Unreasonableness', or labelled 'Irrationality'. On the other hand, the differences of terminology should not be ignored altogether. For one thing, it is necessary to be aware that someone else (a judge, or an academic) may be using a word in a different sense from that which you expect. This is even the case with regard to quite central concepts such as 'illegality' (considered further below), where differences in meaning can cause spectacular misunderstandings.

Further, changes in vocabulary can be a sign of more substantive shifts in the nature of the ground of review in question. For example, the gradual shift of vocabulary from 'natural justice' to 'fairness' (a process still not complete) has coincided with a relaxation of many of the previous rigidities of the doctrine, and a recognition that it could apply to areas previously considered out of bounds to procedural intervention. This is so even though, today, the terms 'natural justice' and 'fairness' are frequently used entirely interchangeably. Similarly, the move away from the phrase 'Wednesbury unreasonableness' and the adoption of the term 'irrationality' (still not universally accepted) may highlight a change in the nature of that ground of review; we examine this in more detail in Chapter 15.

For now, it is useful to set out the terminology which we have adopted in this book. We have followed the well known division of the grounds of review enunciated by Lord Diplock in the GCHQ case (R v Minister for the Civil Service ex p Council of Civil Service Unions (1985)). Lord Diplock divided the grounds of review under three heads:

Judicial review has I think developed to a stage today when without reiterating any analysis of the steps by which the development has come about, one can conveniently classify under three heads the grounds upon which administrative action is subject to control by judicial review. The first ground I would call 'illegality', the second 'irrationality' and the third 'procedural impropriety'. That is not to say that further development on a case by case basis may not in course of time add further grounds. I have in mind particularly the possible adoption in the future of the principle of 'proportionality' which is recognised in the administrative law of several of our fellow members of the European Economic Community; but to dispose of the instant case the three already well-established heads that I have mentioned will suffice.

To get an overview of what follows in the next chapters, it is worth briefly considering each of these heads of review in turn.

11.2.1 Illegality

In the *GCHQ* case, Lord Diplock gave a very brief definition of 'illegality':

> By illegality as a ground for judicial review I mean that the decision-maker must understand correctly the law that regulates his decision-making and must give effect to it.

Lord Diplock's meaning is best illustrated by a simple example. If a decision maker is given the power to decide between options (a), (b) and (c), then he would be acting outside his powers if he were to choose a different option (d); he would be acting outside the 'four corners' of his jurisdiction. Under the heading of illegality may also be classified the requirements that a decision maker must not 'fetter' his discretion (by committing himself as to how he will exercise it in advance of the decision), nor unlawfully delegate his discretion (by giving the power of decision to another person). We will look at all these different aspects of illegality in the next chapter.

11.2.2 Procedural impropriety

By 'procedural impropriety', Lord Diplock sought to include those heads of review which lay down procedural standards to which public decision makers must, in certain circumstances, adhere. These include the duty to give a fair hearing to a person affected by a decision, and the duty not to be affected by bias (all of which are considered in Chapter 13). It also includes, as we shall see, the obligation not to disappoint a legitimate expectation (dealt with in Chapter 14) – although to the extent that a legitimate expectation may be protected 'substantively', it may be seen as moving beyond 'procedural' protection.

11.2.3 Irrationality

In the *GCHQ* case, Lord Diplock explained this term as follows:

> By 'irrationality' I mean what can by now be succinctly referred to as 'Wednesbury unreasonableness' (*Associated Provincial Picture Houses v Wednesbury Corporation*). It applies to a decision which is so outrageous in its defiance of logic or of accepted moral standards that no sensible person who had applied his mind to the question to be decided could have arrived at it. Whether a decision falls within this category is a question that judges by their training and experience should be well equipped to answer, or else there would be something badly wrong with our judicial system.

Whether or not this is an adequate, or indeed an accurate, definition of this ground of review will be considered in Chapter 15. For now, it is merely worth noting that under this head comes what may be characterised (in spite of judicial protestations to the contrary) as review of the *merits* of the decision (however limited a scrutiny of the merits that may turn out to be). An important issue here is the extent to which the decision under challenge should be judged against the yardstick of 'substantive' principles of judicial review. Advocates of such an approach argue that these substantive principles include the doctrine of proportionality, referred to by Lord Diplock in the passage above as a possible fourth ground of review, as well as other principles, such as the legal certainty and consistency.

11.2.4 Other heads of judicial review

We should re-emphasise that these categories are not set in stone. They are mere 'chapter headings' for the grounds of judicial review (*per* Lord Donaldson MR in *R v Secretary of State for the Home Department ex p Brind* (1990)). Furthermore, the grounds are themselves divided into subcategories, which are often more convenient to use as tools in the day to day task of establishing whether the decision of a public body is unlawful. For example, a subcategory such as the rule against the 'fettering of discretion', which we have located under 'illegality', could justifiably be placed under 'procedural impropriety' – or, conceivably, under 'irrationality'. However it is identified, the content of the rule is the same, and as a matter of day to day practicality it will be applied in the same way however it is regarded. For an alternative approach to the classification of the grounds of review, it is worth referring to the position in Australia, where the grounds have been codified by ss 3–7 of the (Australian) Administrative Decisions (Judicial Review) Act 1977 (as amended) (which are set out at Appendix 8 in JUSTICE/All Souls, *Review of Administrative Law in the United Kingdom*, 1988, Oxford: OUP). Rather than attempting to classify the different grounds of review under 'chapter headings' like illegality or irrationality, the statute sets out, in s 5(1), a long list of grounds (nine basic ones) upon which an applicant may rely.

To complete Lord Diplock's classification, three other possible heads of review should be borne in mind.

Breach of European Community law

An applicant for judicial review may also argue that a public authority has breached a rule of European Community law. As we have already seen, important provisions of European Community law are set out in provisions of the EC Treaty and may be relied upon directly in courts in the UK (see above, 7.9.2). Rules contained in directives and EC regulations may also be directly effective. Thus, breach of such a directly effective provision may be seen simply as a facet of the head of review of 'illegality'. In addition, however, the European Court of Justice has, in its case law, developed 'general principles', which are applicable both to Community institutions and to national bodies in making decisions affecting community rights. These general principles include proportionality; legitimate expectation and legal certainty; equality; respect for human rights; the right to be heard; and the requirement to state reasons.

Human Rights Act 1998

The Human Rights Act creates a broad ground of judicial review. Section 6 provides that 'It is unlawful for a public authority to act in a way which is incompatible with one or more of the Convention rights'. The scope of this new provision is considered below, 19.10.4. Arguably, breach of s 6 of the Act can be seen merely as an aspect of 'illegality'. However, the courts will have to consider the body of case law which has been developed by the European Court of Human Rights since the 1950s. It is also likely that the court will develop distinctive principles for dealing with human rights issues. Breach of s 6, therefore, needs to be recognised as a head of review in its own right.

Devolution issues

As we have already noted, devolution issues are dealt with by the Judicial Committee of the Privy Council and the approach that the court is likely to take is not yet known (see above, 2.8.4 and 11.1). The main task of the court will be to interpret the devolution Acts, and so the issues may be seen as just an element of 'illegality'. The Privy Council may, however, develop distinct principles for dealing with devolution issues; if this happens, a separate head of review may emerge.

11.3 The constitutional basis of the court's power to intervene

From where do the courts derive their power to review the decisions and actions of public authorities, such as ministers and local councils? Such a question may, at first glance, seem unnecessary, but in public law this apparently theoretical question often arises in the most practical contexts; it is of central importance to an understanding of the present day scope and limitations of judicial review. The question also has a constitutional significance in public law, because the courts are deploying a specialised body of law to control and confine the exercise of power by or deriving from democratically elected bodies.

11.3.1 The traditional analysis: *ultra vires*

The traditional explanation of the court's power to intervene can be stated briefly, if crudely. The twin doctrines of the sovereignty of Parliament and the rule of law (see above, 5.2 and 5.3) require that a public authority entrusted with statutory powers can only exercise those powers which have been conferred, either expressly or impliedly, by Parliament. Statutory bodies (sometimes called 'creatures of statute'), such as local authorities, cannot create their own powers. The courts, in judicially reviewing an action of such a public body, are merely adjudicating upon the exact limits of a particular allocation of power; they are checking whether the public body has been given the power to act as it did.

Ultimately, the court's power to perform this 'checking' role is not, itself, conferred by any statute. How could it be, since how would the law which purported to confer the 'checking' role on the courts itself be checked? (The court's role has, however, been recognised in statutes, for instance in s 31 of the Supreme Court Act 1981, which regulates the procedure on an application for judicial review: see below, 17.5.) The court's power simply rests upon the fact that society generally accepts that the courts possess this role because the courts have always had it, or because we continually consent to their having it, or because judges have the power to enforce it, or for one of a number of different reasons which a legal philosopher could provide. The court's power to intervene is often referred to as the court's 'inherent jurisdiction'.

11.3.2 System of review versus system of appeals

However, the important feature of judicial review, so the traditional theory goes, is that the court's power is *limited* to this 'checking' role. A court, in judicially reviewing a decision of a public body, does not have a right to re-take the challenged decision, or to hear an appeal from the decision. Its role is simply to ensure that the public authority has not acted outside its powers or, to use the ubiquitous Latin terminology, to check that the authority has not acted *ultra vires*.

There is, therefore, a fundamental distinction between a system of judicial review and a system of *appeals*. On an appeal, the court can concern itself (at least to some extent) with the merits of the decision under challenge. In judicial review, the court is concerned merely to check the *legality* of the decision which the public body has made – whether the decision is *ultra vires* or *intra vires*. If the court finds that the public body has exceeded its powers, then it has the power to quash the decision, or to require the public body to act in accordance with a duty placed on it by the law, but the court does not ordinarily have the power to re-take the decision itself, or to exercise the discretion in the way which it, the court, thinks would be best. The reason that it does not have this power is simple: Parliament has conferred the discretion upon the public body in question, not upon the court. The court merely has the role of supervising the exercise of power by the public body. For this reason, the court's power to intervene by way of judicial review is sometimes described as the court's *supervisory jurisdiction* (derived from the idea that the court is supervising the exercise of public power). This is distinct from the *appellate jurisdiction* that the courts exercise in other areas.

11.3.3 The concept of jurisdiction

Another concept frequently used in this context is that of *jurisdiction*. In essence, jurisdiction simply means power; the limits of the jurisdiction of a public body are the limits of its power. A public body which acts *ultra vires* may also be described as acting 'outside its jurisdiction'. When it does so, it commits what is known as a *'jurisdictional error'* – that is, an error which takes it outside its jurisdiction. Thus the *ultra vires* doctrine and the concept of jurisdiction are closely linked; according to the *ultra vires* doctrine, a court can only intervene by way of judicial review if a jurisdictional error is established. How far this theory is actually consistent with practice will be examined below.

11.3.4 Summary of the *ultra vires* doctrine

A useful recent summary of the traditional theory of the court's power of review – demonstrating its continuing influence today – is contained in the judgment of Lord Browne-Wilkinson in the decision of the House of Lords in *R v Hull University Visitor ex p Page* (1993):

> Over the last 40 years the courts have developed general principles of judicial review. The fundamental principle is that the courts will intervene to ensure that the powers of public decision making bodies are exercised lawfully. In all cases, save possibly one, this intervention ... is based on the proposition that such powers have been conferred on the decision maker on the underlying assumption that the powers are to be exercised only within the jurisdiction conferred, in accordance with fair procedures and, in a *Wednesbury* sense ... reasonably. If the decision maker exercises his powers outside the jurisdiction conferred, in a manner which is procedurally irregular or is *Wednesbury* unreasonable, he is acting *ultra vires* his powers and therefore unlawfully.

This passage is particularly useful because it shows how the traditional theory seeks to explain each of the different 'grounds' of judicial review, considered above.

11.4 Problems with the traditional analysis

Having sketched out the traditional theoretical explanation for the court's power to exercise powers of judicial review, it is necessary to look at some of the elements of that explanation rather more closely. Commentators have increasingly suggested that the *ultra vires* doctrine does not provide a neat explanation for the whole of judicial review. There are a number of problems which that theory has to overcome.

11.4.1 *Ultra vires* is artificial in some situations

Lord Browne-Wilkinson, in the passage from *ex p Page*, quoted above, 11.3.4, explained that the traditional theory is based on the 'underlying assumption' that powers given to a public body were only intended to be exercised in accordance with fair procedures, etc. But is this realistic? For example, in relation to natural justice, it may be unconvincing to claim that Parliament intended that the public authority exercising a particular power should give a fair hearing before it takes the decision. Parliament may not have thought (in so far as Parliament can collectively be said to 'think') about the question of a prior hearing; it may even have assumed that no prior hearing would be required. A similar criticism can be levelled at the justification of judicial review for irrationality. In each case, the objection goes, it is entirely artificial to claim that the court is merely 'supervising' the exercise of power by the public body; or that the court is merely ensuring that the body only exercises the power in accordance with the wishes of Parliament. When the court reviews a decision for breach of the principles of natural justice, it does not do so (the objection runs) because it has looked at the legislation and decided that Parliament impliedly included the principles of natural justice in the legislation. Instead, the court simply asserts that the principles of natural justice are important, and that the decision maker has failed to live up to them. This last sentence is the seed of the alternative theory, to which we shall return shortly.

11.4.2 Existence of 'error of law on the face of the record'

Lord Browne-Wilkinson stated (in the quotation from his speech in *ex p Page*, above, 11.3.4) that intervention by way of judicial review can be explained by the traditional theory 'in all cases, save possibly one'. The exception to which he was referring is review for 'error of law on the face of the record'. Some commentators dismiss this ground of review as being anomalous and obsolete

– but it is a major headache for supporters of the *ultra vires* doctrine. Put simply, a decision may be reviewed under this head if the court detects an error of law which appears 'on the face of' (that is, 'obvious on') the record of the decision of the tribunal or other public body. If such an error exists, then the court can review the decision even if the error is not one which is *ultra vires* the decision maker (that is, *even if* it is not an error which takes the decision maker outside its jurisdiction). For practical purposes, as we shall see, the existence and ambit of error of law on the face of the record is not important today, but the significance from our perspective is that:

(a) error of law on the face of the record, even if now obsolete, is long established, arising out of a traditional jurisdiction asserted over inferior tribunals and courts (see, for example, *R v Northumberland Compensation Appeal Tribunal ex p Shaw* (1952)); and

(b) it is entirely inconsistent with the *ultra vires* doctrine, and with traditional theory of judicial review, because a decision may be struck down under this head even if the decision maker (or inferior court) has not acted outside its jurisdiction.

11.4.3 The court's ability to review the exercise of prerogative powers

Thus far, we have been considering judicial review of statutory powers and duties – that is, those which are conferred (directly or indirectly) on public authorities by Acts of Parliament. But, as we saw in Chapter 2, some government powers are derived from the prerogative rather than Acts of Parliament. The courts are prepared to review the exercise of prerogative powers: *R v Criminal Injuries Compensation Board ex p Lain* (1967), reaffirmed in *R v Minister for the Civil Service ex p Council of Civil Service Unions* (1985)). This is not easily explainable in terms of the *ultra vires* doctrine. How, for example, can the doctrine justify the ability of the courts to hold that an exercise of the prerogative is *Wednesbury* unreasonable? Where the power to make the decision originated in an Act of Parliament, the doctrine would hold that there is a presumption that Parliament did not intend the decision maker to exercise it unreasonably. However, this explanation is not available in the case of the prerogative, because no one 'confers' the power on the person exercising the prerogative (certainly not Parliament). That person (whether the sovereign, or a minister) cannot be 'presumed' not to want to allow himself or herself to exercise the power unreasonably. Thus, the critics argue, the traditional theory fails to explain the fact that the prerogative is judicially reviewable.

11.4.4 The court's discretion to refuse a remedy

Finally, the *ultra vires* doctrine is hard to reconcile with the court's undoubted discretion to decline to grant a remedy to an applicant for judicial review, even once a ground of review has been established (see below, 17.4). If one applies the *ultra vires* doctrine strictly, then where the court finds that a public authority had no power to act as it did, it should logically find that the purported decision was a *nullity* (that is, was void and of no effect), because it is as if a decision had never been made. Where a decision is held to be *ultra vires*, it should automatically follow that the court holds it to be void. But, if that were the case, how is it that the court has a discretion not to grant a remedy? Once it has found that a ground of review has been made out, then there is no valid 'decision' for the court to decide not to overturn. It would, therefore, appear that the traditional theory is not consistent with the existence of the discretion to refuse to grant a remedy.

11.5   A new theory of judicial review?

An alternative theory has emerged from the objections set out above. It starts from the premise that the court has now become more confident of its constitutional role, which is to uphold the rule of law. The court no longer needs to resort to the fiction of 'jurisdictional error' to strike down a defective decision; it does not need to pretend that Parliament did not 'intend' to allow the decision maker to act as it did. Instead, the courts have the power to strike down errors of law (whether due to failure to give a fair hearing, irrationality, or whatever) simply because they have asserted the power do so, and because that abrogation of power is generally accepted in our society. This view has been well expressed by Dawn Oliver, when she suggests that 'judicial review has moved on from the *ultra vires* rule to a concern for the protection of individuals, and for the control of power ...' ('Is the *ultra vires* rule the basis of judicial review?' [1987] PL 543). She concludes:

> Notwithstanding the supremacy of Parliament, the courts impose standards of lawful conduct upon public authorities as a matter of common law, and it is arguable that the power to impose such standards is a constitutional fundamental ... In place of the *ultra vires* rule a doctrine is emerging that, in the public sphere, the courts in exercising a supervisory jurisdiction are concerned both with the vires of public authorities in the strict or narrow sense ... and with abuse of power. If abuse of power is established, the courts may properly intervene [p 567].

So, on this view, the court's power to intervene (in cases of 'abuse of power', at least) is justified not by reference to the presumed intention of Parliament, but by the court's own self-asserted constitutional right to interfere when it detects abuse of power. Judicial review has, it is said, outgrown the need to rely upon fictions like the *ultra vires* doctrine. This is particularly so given the artificiality of the *ultra vires* doctrine in explaining the power of the courts to disapply primary legislation where it is not in conformity with directly effective EC legislation (see above, 5.2.4 and 7.9.1) or the impending power to interpret legislation against its natural meaning to ensure conformity with the

Human Rights Act 1998 (see below, 19.10.1). It also has difficulty in explaining the increasing readiness of the courts to strike down delegated legislation or rules which infringe what the courts regard as a 'common law constitutional right', such as the right of access to the court (see *R v Lord Chancellor ex p Witham* (1997)), unless expressly authorised by primary legislation.

We will see some of the practical implications of this debate in the next few chapters. It is important to remember, however, that the *ultra vires* doctrine is certainly not dead and buried. Indeed, it remains the conventional explanation for at least most of judicial review (as illustrated by Lord Browne-Wilkinson's recent endorsement of the doctrine in *ex p Page*; see, also, for a recent re-assertion of the conventional view, Forsyth, CF, 'Of fig leaves and fairy tales: the *ultra vires* doctrine, the sovereignty of Parliament and judicial review' (1996) 55 CLJ 122); its advocates would question whether the alternative view has any legitimate constitutional basis (relying simply upon self-asserted judicial power). But it would appear that adherents of the 'newer view' have increased in number, and include senior members of the judiciary; see, for example, Lord Woolf, '*Droit public* – English style' [1995] PL 57, p 66; Sir John Laws, in Supperstone, M and Goudie, J (eds), *Judicial Review*, 2nd edn, 1997, London: Butterworths; and Craig, P, '*Ultra vires* and the foundations of judicial review' (1998) 57 CLJ 63.

INTRODUCTION TO JUDICIAL REVIEW

The grounds of review

The grounds of review are the bases on which the court can hold that a public authority's decision is unlawful. They may be divided up in a number of different ways; the most convenient is to follow the approach of Lord Diplock in the *GCHQ* case (*R v Minister for the Civil Service ex p Council of Civil Service Unions* (1985)), where he separated the grounds under three headings.

Illegality

In essence, this is the principle that 'a decision maker must understand correctly the law that regulates his decision making and must give effect to it'. Under this head may also be included the requirements that a decision maker shall not *fetter his discretion* (by deciding how to exercise it in advance of the decision), nor unlawfully *delegate his discretion* (by giving the power of decision to another person).

Procedural impropriety

This covers those heads of review which specify procedural standards to which public decision makers must adhere. These include:

(a) the duty to give a fair hearing to a person affected by a decision;

(b) the duty not to be affected by bias (both examined in Chapter 13); and

(c) the obligation not to disappoint a legitimate expectation (Chapter 14).

Irrationality

This includes what is sometimes known as *Wednesbury* unreasonableness. To a limited extent, this ground ventures into principles of 'substantive' review – that is, into the merits of the decision.

In addition, there are arguably the following heads of review:

(a) breach of EC law;

(b) breach of s 6 of the Human Rights Act;

(c) devolution issues.

The constitutional basis of judicial review

The court's power to review public law decisions is traditionally explained by the *ultra vires* doctrine. This states that a body exercising statutory powers cannot act outside the powers conferred upon it, either expressly or impliedly, by statute. If the body acts outside its powers, then it goes beyond its *jurisdiction*, and its decision may be reviewed for *jurisdictional error*. The court's power to intervene in this way is not conferred by statute; it is part of the court's *inherent jurisdiction*. The power is (in principle) confined to 'checking' the limits of the decision maker's power; it is not an appeal against the decision. Thus, judicial review is a *supervisory jurisdiction*, not an appellate jurisdiction.

Objections to the traditional analysis

There are a number of objections to the traditional explanation of the basis of judicial review. It is said that:

(a) *the theory is artificial* in its reliance on 'presumed' parliamentary intention;

(b) it fails to explain the power of the court to review for *error of law on the face of the record*;

(c) it fails to explain *judicial review of prerogative powers*;

(d) it is inconsistent with the *court's discretion to refuse to grant a remedy*.

New theory of judicial review

As a result of these objections, it has been suggested that judicial review does not need to rely upon the 'fiction' of the *ultra vires* doctrine. Instead, the courts may intervene simply because they detect an abuse of power; because of a self-asserted constitutional right to control errors of law, and procedural and substantive abuses of power. However, the *ultra vires* doctrine is still influential (see, for example, Lord Browne-Wilkinson in *R v Hull University Visitor ex p Page* (1993)). The practical implications of the debate will appear in the next few chapters.

CHAPTER 12

GROUNDS OF JUDICIAL REVIEW I: ILLEGALITY

12.1   Introduction

As we saw in the last chapter, the basic idea behind the ground of review called 'illegality' is very simple: a public authority must act within the 'four corners' of its powers or jurisdiction. It is the ground of review which most closely reflects the preoccupations of the traditional *ultra vires* view of judicial review, with its concentration upon ensuring that the exercise of power is confined within the limits prescribed by the empowering legislation or rules. Let us take a fictitious scenario, which we can follow throughout the chapter:

(a) Parliament decides to pass legislation to control local markets. It enacts a statute called the 'Market Stallholders (Control) Act 1998'. This Act provides that it is unlawful for anyone to trade from a market stall without a licence. The Act sets up a authority called the 'Market Traders Licensing Board' (MTLB) to issue licences;

(b) s 2 provides 'the MTLB shall have the power to issue or renew market stall licences to applicants as it sees fit';

(c) s 3 provides 'in considering whether or not to issue a licence to an applicant, the MTLB shall consider whether the applicant is a fit and proper person to hold a licence';

(d) s 4 provides 'the MTLB shall have power to prevent anyone from trading from a market stall without a licence, and can confiscate equipment used in market trading by any such person'.

12.2   Acting 'outside the four corners'

In this (fictitious) example, it is easy to imagine a straightforward case of illegality. The MTLB warns Marks & Spencer that it cannot continue trading without a licence, and threatens to confiscate its cash tills (pursuant to s 4 of the Act) if it opens its stores on the following day. Marks & Spencer could challenge this decision on the ground that the MTLB is acting outside its powers; that it is acting illegally. Parliament has not given the MTLB the power to regulate shops, but only to regulate market stalls. The MTLB is threatening to act *ultra vires* (or, in other words, outside its jurisdiction). ✔

In practice, illegality is by far the most common ground of judicial review. The day to day work of a lawyer specialising in public law does not concern abstruse questions as to the meaning of the concept of legitimate expectation, or as to the existence of the doctrine of proportionality, but involves examining and arguing over whether individual Acts of Parliament, statutory instruments and other sources of power (including EC sources) do, or do not, confer power on a decision maker to act as it did. This work is, first and foremost, an exercise of interpretation, not of knowledge of law or of precedent. Every statutory situation is different, and it is not usually very helpful to know what has happened in different situations. This fact is important to bear in mind in answering judicial review problem questions. One cannot prepare oneself by 'learning' cases in which illegality has been used as a ground of review. Rather, it is important to understand the 'logic' behind the idea of illegality: the different types of reasons that a court may give in concluding that a decision maker has acted outside its powers. Then, one can apply that reasoning to any problem situation with which one may be confronted. In other words, one must absorb the thinking processes which courts and lawyers typically follow.

12.3 'Incidental' powers

This is not to suggest that questions of illegality are necessarily straightforward or mechanical to resolve. It may be a finely balanced question as to whether a function or power conferred by statute upon a public authority carries with it other 'incidental' powers, which are not spelt out in the statute, but which may be necessary or helpful for the discharge of the primary function or power. On the other hand, a power which, on its face, appears to be extremely wide may, when construed in its context, be much more narrowly confined. Thus, for example, s 111 of the Local Government Act 1972, which confers upon local authorities the broad power to 'do any thing (whether or not involving the expenditure ... of money ...) which is calculated to facilitate, or is conducive or incidental to, the discharge of any of their functions', has been held, in a series of recent cases, to be impliedly limited by statutory controls on the borrowing and expenditure of local authorities, so that an authority could not rely upon s 111 to conduct interest rate 'swaps' (*Hazell v Hammersmith and Fulham LBC* (1992)) or to establish a limited company and guarantee its loans in order to facilitate a swimming pool and associated timeshare development in its area (*Credit Suisse v Allerdale BC* (1997)).

The next few sections (12.4–12.7) identify some of the 'thinking processes' which the courts follow in considering questions of illegality. Although each is often referred to as a separate subground of review (for example, a court will grant judicial review because the decision maker has been 'influenced by an irrelevant consideration'), you should be able to see how each is merely a 'working through' of the basic idea of illegality – that an authority is not allowed to exceed the powers which it has been given.

12.4 Relevant and irrelevant considerations

A decision maker acts illegally if it 'fails to take into account a relevant consideration' – that is, it does not consider something which it ought to consider. Let us go back to our example.

The MTLB grants a licence to trade to Albert, who has just been released from prison after serving time for running protection rackets and intimidation. The MTLB decides, in considering whether to grant Albert a licence, to ignore the question of whether he is fit and proper, because it feels that 'he has already been punished enough'.

This decision could be challenged for failure to take into account a relevant consideration. Section 3 of the Act requires that the MTLB shall, in considering whether or not to issue a licence, take into account whether it thinks the applicant is a fit and proper person to hold a licence. The MTLB has failed (indeed, refused) to do so; to ask whether he is a fit and proper person in the light of his convictions.

In this example, the relevant consideration which the MTLB ignored was actually spelt out in the statute ('shall consider' whether the applicant is fit and proper): it was 'an express consideration'. But the decision maker may also have to take into account relevant considerations which are not actually spelt out in the statute, but which are merely implied by the statutory context. For example: the MTLB's decision to grant Albert a licence is quashed, for the reason given above. It has to decide his application again (because he still wants a licence). This time, it does consider whether he is fit and proper, but, in doing so, it excludes the evidence of his past convictions, again on the basis that 'he has been punished enough for that'. It concludes that he is fit and proper.

This time, the MTLB has followed the letter of the statute: it has considered whether he is fit and proper. But the decision could still be challenged for failure to take into account a relevant consideration – namely, Albert's past convictions. This consideration is not 'express': the legislation does not actually state that the MTLB is required to take into account past convictions. But there is surely a very strong argument for saying that, in considering whether someone is fit and proper, it must be relevant to consider any recent convictions for serious offences. To ignore such an issue is to ignore an (implied) relevant consideration. Once again, the courts would be likely to quash the MTLB's decision to grant Albert a licence.

There are no clear rules for deciding whether a statute impliedly requires a decision maker to take a particular consideration into account. In every case, it is a matter of interpretation for the court, looking at the words of the statute, the context, and making certain assumptions or educated guesses about the intention of Parliament. Thus, for example, in *R v Gloucestershire CC ex p Barry* (1997), the House of Lords differed from the Court of Appeal in holding that a local authority was entitled to take into account, in assessing the degree of need of the applicant and the necessity to make arrangements to meet it under the Chronically Sick and Disabled Persons Act 1970, the cost of making the arrangements and the availability of resources to the council.

As the obverse of the above, a decision maker also acts illegally if he or she takes into account an irrelevant consideration. Once again, irrelevant considerations may be either express in the statute, or implied. An example of an implied irrelevant consideration may be as follows: the MTLB refuses a licence to Belinda on the basis that she has red hair. The MTLB has quite obviously taken into account an irrelevant consideration, even though it is not expressly stated in the Act that 'the MTLB shall not consider the colour of an applicant's hair'. The decision will also be unreasonable (see Chapter 15). A recent example of a court quashing a decision because an irrelevant consideration was taken into account is *R v Home Secretary ex p Venables* (1997). The House of Lords held that the Secretary of State, in fixing the tariff period of detention to be served by the defendants in the James Bulger murder case, could not take into account public petitions or public opinion as expressed in the media; these were irrelevant considerations to what was a function comparable to that of a sentencing judge.

Note that not every consideration will be either irrelevant (in the sense that the decision maker may not have regard to it) or relevant (in the sense that the decision maker must have regard to it). There is also a category of considerations to which the decision maker may have regard if, in his or her judgment and discretion, he or she thinks it right to do so. Within this third category, as Simon Brown LJ explained in *R v Somerset CC ex p Fewings* (1995), the decision maker enjoys a 'margin of appreciation within which ... he may decide just what considerations should play a part in his reasoning process' (pp 1049–50). In that case, the Court of Appeal held that the council was entitled, in resolving to ban stag hunting from land owned and held for amenity purposes by the council, to the 'cruelty argument'; Simon Brown LJ characterised that argument as either an argument to which the council was obliged to have regard (as a relevant consideration), or at least an argument to which it was entitled to have regard within the third category referred to above (thus differing from the judge at first instance, Laws J, who had held that it was an irrelevant consideration). In fact, the majority of the Court of Appeal overturned the council's decision, because the council had failed to take into account the objects and purposes of the statutory power under which it was acting: see below, 12.5.

In practice, it may not be easy to discover whether or not a consideration has been taken into account by the decision maker – unless the decision maker reveals that it has been influenced by that factor by giving reasons for its decision. It may be particularly difficult if the decision maker does not have a duty to give reasons (as to which, see below, 13.6.5), especially since discovery is rarely ordered in judicial review proceedings (certainly nothing in the nature of a 'fishing expedition' will be ordered).

12.5 Improper purpose

A decision maker ought only to use a power given to it by Parliament for the purpose or purposes for which it was given the power. The decision maker acts *ultra vires* if it uses the power for a different purpose. The classic case in which this principle was set out is *Padfield v Minister of Agriculture, Fisheries and Food* (1968). The minister had a discretion conferred by the Agricultural Marketing Act 1958 to refer complaints about the operation of the milk marketing scheme to a commission. The minister refused to refer a complaint from milk producers to the commission because he feared that, if the complaint was upheld, it would undermine the whole milk marketing scheme. The House of Lords held that this decision was unlawful, because he was exercising his discretion not to refer for a wrong purpose: to protect the existing scheme. The statute conferred the power to refer on the minister just so that such challenges could be made. As Lord Reid (p 1034) put it:

> The minister's discretion ... must be inferred from a construction of the Act read as a whole, and for the reasons I have given I would infer that the discretion ... has been used by the Minister in a manner which is not in accord with the intention of the statute which conferred it.

A more recent example is *R v Inner London Education Authority ex p Brunyate* (1989). Under the Education Act 1944, local education authorities were given powers to appoint school governors, and had an (apparently) unfettered power to remove them from office. The ILEA decided to remove certain governors because it disagreed with the policies which they were pursuing. The House of Lords held that, construing the statute as a whole, the governors were given an independent function. Therefore, the ILEA was acting with an improper purpose in attempting to remove them for a reason which would undermine that independent function. Once again, working out whether a decision maker is acting with an improper purpose is a matter of fact in each case, looking at the statutory context. We can look at one more illustration, using our example.

The MTLB resolves that in considering licence applications, it will favour 'active followers of an organised religion' in order 'to promote the growth of spiritual awareness in the country'.

This decision could be challenged on the ground that the MTLB has adopted an improper purpose (promoting spiritual awareness) in exercising its discretion to issue licences. Looking at the statute as a whole, it is clear that this was not one of the purposes for which Parliament conferred the power on the MTLB, rather (from the extract of the statute which we have seen), it would appear that the primary purpose was to ensure that market stalls are run by honest ('fit and proper') persons.

Do not be too worried about the precise distinctions between categories such as 'irrelevant considerations' and 'improper purpose' – they tend to run into each other. For example, in the last example above, one could say that the MTLB has acted illegally because it has taken an irrelevant consideration into account (promoting spiritual awareness) rather than saying that it has adopted an improper purpose. It doesn't matter how you describe it; what is important is to identify that the decision maker has acted outside its powers by exercising its discretion wrongly. A good recent example of a case which can be categorised under either heading is *R v Somerset CC ex p Fewings* (1995) (council's ban on stag hunting on council land unlawful; discussed above, 12.4).

12.6   Fettering of discretion

If Parliament gives a discretion to a particular public decision maker, then that authority must actually exercise the discretion. 'Discretion' means, essentially, making a choice between two or more options. So the courts insist that the decision maker actually makes that choice in each case: that is, applies its mind to the different possible decisions which it could make, and chooses between them. The courts will not allow a decision maker to prejudge cases, or to bind or 'fetter' its discretion by adopting a rigid policy so that the outcome of individual cases is decided in advance. This is known as the rule against the fettering of discretion. It is best illustrated by our example.

The MTLB, in a state of shock after twice having its decisions quashed in relation to Albert, goes to the other extreme. It decides to adopt a policy which provides that 'any applicant with any criminal convictions (other than driving convictions) cannot be considered fit and proper, and so must be refused a market stall licence'. Albert applies for a licence for a third time, and this time he is refused, because of the policy. He challenges the decision.

The decision is unlawful. The MTLB has adopted a rigid policy which binds it as to how it decides future applications. Even if that policy was completely reasonable (in this case you may think it is not), it is still unlawful, because it fetters the MTLB's discretion to decide each individual case according to its merits. Albert would succeed in an application for judicial review.

A more complex recent example of a decision relying upon the rule against fettering of discretion is *R v Secretary of State for the Home Department ex p Fire Brigades Union* (1995). This case concerned the Criminal Injuries Compensation Scheme, which was originally set up by way of prerogative power in 1964, but was put on a statutory basis by the Criminal Justice Act 1988 which, however, provided that its provisions (in this regard) would come into force 'on such day as the Secretary of State may ... appoint'. The Secretary of State did not appoint a date, but rather, in 1993, indicated that he would, instead, bring in a new non-statutory 'tariff' scheme. The applicants, who regarded the 'tariff' scheme as less favourable than the statutory scheme under the 1988 Act, challenged the decision of the Secretary of State on the basis that, by introducing the 'tariff' scheme, he was thereby unlawfully fettering his discretion in relation to the statutory scheme. The House of Lords held, by a bare majority, that the statutory power to appoint a date for the coming into force of the 1988 Act imposed a continuing obligation or discretion upon the Secretary of State to consider whether to bring it into force, and that he could not, therefore, bind himself not to exercise that discretion by introducing the inconsistent tariff scheme.

In practice, many, if not most, public bodies develop policies which they adopt to help them take decisions; large scale decision making would be impossible without them. Indeed, there are obvious advantages to having clear policies in organisations: it promotes consistency between different decision makers, it speeds up decision making, and it enables senior people in the organisation to communicate to the actual people making the decisions the factors which they ought to consider.

The rule against the fettering of discretion does not prevent decision makers adopting such policies. It simply insists that policies shall not be applied rigidly, so as to remove any ability to depart from the policy in an appropriate case. A good example of this distinction can be seen in *British Oxygen v Board of Trade* (1971). In this case, the Board of Trade had a discretion to make investment grants for certain purchases. It refused to pay British Oxygen an investment grant for the purchase of a large number of metal cylinders which cost less than £25 each, because it had a policy of not awarding grants for the purchase of items which individually cost less than £25. British Oxygen challenged this policy as a fetter on the Board's discretion to make grants. The House of Lords decided that the policy did not fetter the Board's discretion. The judgments reaffirmed that public bodies are allowed to develop policies to deal with a large number of applications, as long as they are prepared to 'listen to someone with something new to say', and to waive the policy in appropriate cases. In other words, one can have a policy, but it must not be 'set in stone'. There was evidence that the Board of Trade did not apply its policy rigidly, and so the House of Lords rejected British Oxygen's case.

An example of a case going the other way is *Stringer v Minister of Housing and Local Government* (1970). A local authority made a written agreement with Manchester University, by which it undertook to discourage development near the site of a large telescope operated by the university – the university was worried that, if houses were built nearby, the telescope's operations would be disrupted. Later, a builder's application for planning permission to build houses near the telescope was turned down by the local authority, on the ground (partly) that the development would interfere with the telescope. The builder challenged this decision by way of judicial review, and the court agreed that (a) the agreement between the authority and the university was invalid, because it fettered the authority's statutory discretion to consider applications for planning permission on their merits in each case; and (b) therefore, the particular refusal of planning permission in this case was void also (although an appeal against that refusal to the minister, in which he had confirmed the local authority's decision, was valid for other reasons).

Note that the courts will not necessarily automatically accept the claim by a decision maker that it has 'kept its mind open' in applying its policy; after all, it is a very easy claim to make. In *R v Secretary of State for Transport ex p Sheriff and Sons* (1986), the Department of Transport had circulated a departmental handbook, in which it was stated that a certain grant would be refused in specified circumstances. This was challenged as an unlawful fetter of discretion. The Secretary of State argued that his department did not really rely on the handbook – that he had kept his mind open. The court rejected this, holding that the handbook was 'so much a part of the Department's thinking' that his discretion was clearly fettered.

12.7 Delegation of discretion

If an Act of Parliament confers a discretion on a particular public authority, the courts normally require that the discretion be exercised by that same authority. The decision maker is not normally allowed to delegate that discretion to someone else, because that would be contrary to the intention of Parliament as expressed in the words of the statute. If Parliament had wanted that other person to exercise the discretion, it would have conferred the power on them in the first place. To revert to our example: after the Albert debacle, the MTLB resolves that 'decisions as to the fitness and propriety of all applicants for licences shall be taken by the local police force of the relevant area'. The MTLB refuses Albert's (fourth) application for a licence, because the local police state that, as far as they are concerned, he is entirely unfit.

This decision is invalid, because it is flawed by an unlawful delegation of discretion. Parliament conferred the discretion to decide whether the applicant is fit and proper on the MTLB, not on the police.

Note that the courts will examine who *actually* exercises the discretion, and will not be satisfied merely because the authority on whom the discretion is conferred exercises it in name. A decision maker may not *'act under dictation'*, by simply adopting someone else's decision as its own. On the other hand, a decision maker is usually allowed to take someone else's view into account. It is a question of judgment in each case which side of the line the decision maker has fallen. Thus: the MTLB adjusts its policy, and resolves that the MTLB will itself decide whether the applicant is fit and proper; but that in each case it will seek the view of the local police on that question. It rejects Albert's application once again, after hearing the police's view.

It is impossible to tell from these facts whether the MTLB has acted lawfully or not. If it has taken the police's view into account and decided independently whether or not it agrees with it, then the decision is likely to be valid. If, however, it has effectively simply deferred to the police's view, then it has unlawfully acted under dictation. Which of the two is the case might be apparent from the MTLB's records of its decision making process – otherwise, Albert may have an uphill task in trying to show that the decision is flawed.

A good example of the distinction in practice is the case of *Lavender v Minister of Housing and Local Government* (1970). Here, the Minister of Housing and Local Government refused Lavender's application for planning permission to develop land for use as a quarry, after hearing objections from the Minister of Agriculture. The decision was challenged on the ground that the minister had acted under dictation – he had effectively abdicated his decision to the Minister of Agriculture. The House of Lords held that the minister was entitled to listen and to pay close attention to the views of the Minister of Agriculture – but that he could not in effect turn the decision over to the Minister of Agriculture because, under the statute, the decision was his alone. On the facts, the House of Lords held that the minister had wrongly delegated his discretion to the Minister of Agriculture, because he had adopted a policy stating that he would not grant this class of planning applications 'unless the Minister of Agriculture is not opposed'.

Remember that some statutes expressly allow the decision maker to delegate the decision to someone else. Obviously, in that case, the decision maker is allowed to delegate, and the rule against delegation has no effect (save, of course, that the decision maker can only delegate to those to whom the statute permits). Further, the courts may sometimes be prepared to *infer* that a statute permits delegation – that is, the statute contains an implied right to delegate. However, since there is a presumption against delegation, the courts will only find that this is the case if the implication is clear.

The Carltona *principle*

In one exceptional situation, the general presumption against the delegation of discretion is reversed. Where a discretion is conferred upon a minister, the courts presume, in the absence of evidence to the contrary, that the minister is allowed to delegate the discretion to officials in his department – even though the statute does not expressly say so.

The *Carltona* principle takes its name from the well known case of *Carltona v Commissioner of Works* (1943). An official in the Ministry of Works wrote a letter to Carltona Limited, requisitioning the building which it occupied. Carltona challenged the decision to requisition on the basis that, while the letter was written (and the decision taken) by an official, the statute only conferred the power to requisition on the minister. But the Court of Appeal held that there was a presumption that the minister was allowed to delegate the decision to officials in his department. In part, this decision was simply a recognition of the fact that it would be physically impossible for the minister personally to discharge all the decisions given to him by statute. But the court also pointed out that, because of the doctrine of ministerial responsibility, the minister was responsible to Parliament for what happened in his department (for the decisions taken, for whether he was delegating to people who were too junior, and so on), and therefore there was an additional safeguard in cases of this sort which would not be present in a normal case of unauthorised delegation. The officials in the minister's department are sometimes called his 'alter ego': that is, they are effectively treated as being part of the minister, so that (in one sense) no delegation takes place at all.

The *Carltona* principle is still alive and well today; it is sometimes suggested that it is a dangerous principle which allows excessive delegation (particularly as the doctrine of ministerial responsibility may not be as effective as it used to be, or was assumed to be). In *R v Secretary of State for the Home Department ex p Oladehinde* (1990), for example, the question was whether the Secretary of State had the power to delegate to immigration inspectors the power to deport aliens. Oladehinde argued that Parliament could never have contemplated that such an extreme delegation would occur; he contended that the statute contemplated that decisions might be taken by Home Office officials (as well as by the Secretary of State), but not by immigration inspectors. However, the House of Lords held that, since immigration inspectors are civil servants, they therefore came under the Carltona principle. The principle applied because there was nothing in the statute to exclude it (either expressly or impliedly). The delegation was therefore lawful.

The *Carltona* principle even applies to the 'Next Steps' executive agencies of government, even though in such cases decision making has been devolved out of the traditional departmental structure into the separate agencies (see Freedland, MR [1996] PL 19). Thus, in *R v Secretary of State for Social Security ex p Sherwin* (1996), the Divisional Court held that, since the Benefits Agency was part of the Department of Social Security, and Agency staff belonged to the civil service, the *Carltona* principle applied.

12.8 Errors of law and fact

At this stage, we must step back again, and refocus on 'illegality' as a ground of review in more general terms. Up until now, in the example which we have been following through the chapter, the errors which the MTLB has been making have, on the whole, been errors of law. For example, in refusing to consider Albert's criminal record, or taking account of Belinda's red hair, the MTLB has not been making errors of fact, but has been misinterpreting the extent of its powers: making errors of law. But an authority may sometimes be judicially reviewed for making factual errors, as well as legal errors. For example: the MTLB confiscates Cassandra's stall because it discovers that she is trading without a licence. In fact, Cassandra claims that she does have a licence, but that her registration number has accidentally been omitted from the MTLB's record of licensees.

Cassandra would have grounds to seek review of the MTLB's decision to confiscate her stall because of error of fact: in mistakenly believing that she was unlicensed. However, the courts are, on the whole, reluctant to become involved in reviewing alleged errors of fact. For one thing, the courts may know much less than the decision maker about the factual issues in question (especially in 'specialist' areas) – if the court intervenes, who is to say that, in fact, the decision maker did not get the fact right, and the court wrong? Secondly, the courts' powers to assist them to get to the true facts are very limited. Courts on judicial review applications rarely hear live witnesses, and very rarely order cross-examination (although they have the power to do so), and they are also reluctant to order a party to produce documents or give discovery. Once again, therefore, the original decision maker may be better placed to discover the true facts than the court. Finally, the courts are very nervous about the sheer number of cases which might result if they were to entertain applications for judicial review every time it was alleged that a decision maker had gone wrong on the facts. They are concerned that to do so might effectively turn a system of 'review' into a system of appeals. To take a practical example: the MTLB considers whether to renew David's licence after allegations that he has been selling alcoholic drinks from his stall without the necessary separate drinks licence. After hearing evidence from Oliver that he bought alcoholic drinks from David's stall and hearing David deny it, the MTLB find the allegations proved, and refuse to renew David's licence on the basis that he is not fit and proper.

Could David obtain review of the decision of the MTLB on the basis that it committed an error of fact in concluding that he had sold alcoholic drinks to Oliver? If so, how would the court decide whether the MTLB had or had not made such a mistake? In fact, David probably could not obtain judicial review for such an alleged error.

Compare these difficulties with the courts' attitude to errors of law. When an error of law is alleged, the court can, at least, be confident that it has the necessary expertise to decide the question, and it has a procedure specially designed to help it do so (for example, disclosure of legal arguments very early, in the form 86A). Furthermore, the court has the permission stage to help it filter out cases where the alleged error of law is simply not arguable (by contrast, is very difficult to weed out bad factual arguments at the permission stage). For all these reasons, the courts are far more reluctant in judicial review applications to interfere with findings of fact than with findings of law.

The result of the above is that the courts have to make two sets of distinctions. First, the courts have to distinguish errors of law (which, subject to 12.9 below, are always reviewable), from errors of fact (which may or may not be reviewable). Secondly, the courts have to distinguish reviewable errors of fact ('jurisdictional errors of fact') from non-reviewable errors of fact ('non-jurisdictional errors'). Both of these distinctions are of extreme complexity, and in a typical constitutional and administrative law course you will not be expected to know a vast amount about the area. Nevertheless, it is important to understand the problems which make the area so difficult.

12.8.1 Errors of law versus errors of fact

A good illustration of the difficulties which the distinction between errors of law and errors of fact can cause can be seen by going back to our first example: the MTLB's threat to stop Marks & Spencer trading for not having a licence. There, the question at issue was whether the words 'market stall' in the statute include a shop, or a department store. The answer is pretty obviously not – but, for present purposes, the important point is, is the question of the interpretation of 'market stall' a question of fact or law? On the one hand, it seems to be a question as to what ordinary people understand by the term; one might ask: Is the stall outside? Is it temporary? etc. On the other hand, the court has to interpret the wording of the statute: it has to ask what meaning Parliament intended to attribute to the words 'market stall' in the legislation. Is this not a question of law?

Judges have introduced the concept of 'mixed questions of law and fact' to deal with cases in this grey area. Thus one question (Does a Marks & Spencer store come within the definition of a market stall?) may include questions of fact (What are the characteristics of a Marks & Spencer store?) and questions of law (What did Parliament intend by the phrase 'market stall'?). But you should not assume that any question as to the meaning of a word in a statute is necessarily a question of law, even in part; in *Brutus v Cozens* (1973) it was suggested that, when a word in a statute is intended to bear its 'ordinary' everyday meaning, then its interpretation in any particular case is a question of fact, not law.

12.8.2 Reviewable and non-reviewable errors of fact

When are the courts prepared to review decisions for alleged errors of fact? Once again, there are no easy answers. A cynic would say that the reason that this issue (and the previous issue, about the distinction between fact and law) is so confused is because the courts are result-driven: they form a view as to whether or not they want to intervene, and then seek to formulate a reason to justify that conclusion. The result is inconsistent and confused decisions. However, trying to simplify a confused area, one can say:

(a) normally, the courts will not review a decision simply because an applicant alleges that the decision maker has made a mistake of fact. Questions of fact are for decision makers, not for the reviewing court. Thus David (above) cannot obtain review of the MTLB's decision just because he says it made a mistake in finding that he sold alcoholic drinks;

(b) however, where the decision maker's entire power to decide (or 'jurisdiction') depends upon it making a finding of fact, then that finding of fact is reviewable (sometimes called a *'precedent fact'*). A decision maker cannot increase its power by mistakenly thinking that it has a power to decide something which it does not. As Lord Wilberforce put it, in *Zamir v Home Secretary* (1980), in some cases:

> ... the exercise of power, or jurisdiction, depends on the precedent establishment of an objective fact. In such a case, it is for the court to decide whether that precedent requirement has been satisfied.

To go back to our example: the MTLB's power to take any action against Marks & Spencer depends upon it making a finding of fact that Marks & Spencer's stores are 'market stalls'. If the correct answer is that the stores are not market stalls, then the MTLB has no power to act against Marks & Spencer. The MTLB cannot, by mistakenly finding that a Marks & Spencer store is a market stall, give itself extra powers. So the courts will intervene to strike down such an error, because the fact in question is a 'jurisdictional fact' – a fact on which the authority's jurisdiction depends.

Another example of a jurisdictional error of fact is the case of *White and Collins v Minister of Health* (1939). A local authority had power (by statute) to acquire land compulsorily – but not if the land in question was part of a park. A landowner objected that a particular order was invalid because the local authority had mistakenly failed to realise that the land in question was part of a park. The Court of Appeal held that it could review the decision on that basis;

(c) the court will also entertain a challenge for error of fact (even if not a jurisdictional fact) where it is alleged that there is no evidence to support the finding of fact at all (it is occasionally suggested that the test is, or should be, no substantial evidence: *Secretary of State for Education and Science v Metropolitan Borough of Tameside* (1977)). This is sometimes seen as part of review for unreasonableness/irrationality (how can one reasonably reach a finding of fact where there is no evidence to support it?). It is, for obvious reasons, not at all easy to establish.

12.9   Are all errors of law reviewable?

We have seen that the courts will only review some errors of fact. We have noted that the courts are, for various reasons, much more reluctant to review errors of fact than errors of law. The question then arises – are there any errors of *law* which the courts will not review? In the past, this was yet another highly complex area. There were cases suggesting that something called a 'non-jurisdictional error of law' did exist – that is, an error of *law* that the courts would not review – a point of law which the decision maker had the final authority to determine, whether rightly or wrongly. Unfortunately, there were almost no cases actually identifying what such errors of law were, and no one was able to produce a satisfactory definition so that one could identify them in the abstract.

The position has today been reached where, in all but a few exceptional circumstances, one can assume that all errors of law are jurisdictional errors. That means that whenever a public decision maker makes an error of law, the court automatically has power to judicially review the decision, without having to worry about whether or not the error 'goes to jurisdiction'. This has great advantages for dealing with a problem question raising a possible error of law. One still has to analyse it to work out whether there is, in fact, an error of law, but, once one is satisfied that there is, one can go straight on to consider whether or not the courts are likely to grant a remedy. In other words, one can usually entirely ignore the whole debate about jurisdictional versus non-jurisdictional errors. And if you look at recently reported cases, you will see, in 99% of them, the courts doing exactly that: ignoring the jurisdictional/non-jurisdictional debate. It is simply assumed that, if there is an error of law, it is reviewable by the courts on judicial review.

The one main exception to this happy assumption is where you are dealing with an 'ouster clause': a statutory provision which seeks to oust the power of the court to review the decision. We deal with this difficult topic in Chapter 16, and also consider there whether the distinction still has some life where one is trying to review not an administrative decision maker or tribunal, but an inferior court. There are also a few anomalous situations where the jurisdictional/non-jurisdictional distinction is still relevant, which you may come across – the most prominent being in relation to the powers of university visitors, where the House of Lords recently reaffirmed the distinction (*R v Hull University Visitor ex p Page* (1993)). The case can be explained as resting on the historically exclusive jurisdiction of university visitors.

12.10 A practical approach to errors of law

To conclude what is a fairly complex area, the good news is that, in an ordinary case, most of the problems are ignorable or bypassable. Most errors are errors of law. If you are dealing with an error of law, then you can assume that, once the error is established, the decision is reviewable. To work out whether there is an error of law or not, you need to have in mind the logical tests which we have labelled relevant/irrelevant considerations; improper purpose, fettering and delegation of discretion.

Errors of fact are rarer. Although the dividing line between errors of law and fact is hard to define, in most cases the distinction is, in practical terms, relatively clear (as with the 'David' example, above). Once you spot an error of fact, you need to think carefully about whether it is a fundamental or 'jurisdictional' fact – that is, one on which the authority's entire power depends. If so, it is reviewable. If not, it is probably not reviewable, unless there is 'no evidence' to support the finding of fact.

GROUNDS OF JUDICIAL REVIEW I: ILLEGALITY

Illegality rests on the fundamental principle that a public authority can only act within its powers or 'jurisdiction.' The courts have developed a number of 'reasoning processes' by which they may conclude that a decision maker has acted outside its powers. These may be summarised as follows:

(a) *acting outside the 'four corners' of the statute* (where the decision maker simply does something which it has no power to do);

(b) *failing to take into account a relevant consideration*. The relevant consideration may be either actually set out in the statute ('express'), or merely implied;

(c) *taking into account an irrelevant consideration*, which again may be either express or implied;

(d) *adopting an improper purpose* (for example, *Padfield v Minister of Agriculture* (1968));

(e) *fettering of discretion*. Whilst it is legitimate for decision makers to adopt policies to help them take decisions (as in *British Oxygen v Board of Trade* (1971)), it is unlawful for anyone exercising a discretion to apply a policy rigidly: *Stringer v Minister of Housing and Local Government* (1970);

(f) *delegation of discretion*. A decision maker must itself exercise a discretion conferred on it unless authorised to delegate that discretion to another. It must exercise that discretion in substance as well as in form; in other words, it must not act under dictation from another authority (*Lavender v MHLG* (1970)). However, under the Carltona principle, a discretion conferred upon a government minister may be exercised by a departmental official, even if the statute does not so provide: *Carltona v Commissioner of Works* (1943); *R v Secretary of State for the Home Department ex p Oladehinde* (1990).

Public decision makers may be reviewed for errors of law as well as errors of fact. Whereas errors of law are always reviewable (for present purposes), errors of fact are not. It is therefore necessary to distinguish *errors of law from errors of fact*. In this complicated area, a good rule of thumb is that the interpretation of a word in a statute is a question of law (unless, possibly, the word is intended to bear its ordinary everyday meaning: *Brutus v Cozens* (1973)).

Most errors of fact are not reviewable. Summarising a difficult area, one can say that an error of fact is only reviewable if:

(a) the issue of fact is 'fundamental' to the decision maker's power to decide (a *'precedent fact'*); see: *Zamir v Home Secretary* (1980); and *White and Collins v Minister of Health* (1939); or

(b) there is no evidence to support the finding of fact at all.

By contrast, given the recent developments in the law, it is safe to assume that all errors of law are reviewable (because all such errors are 'jurisdictional'). There is a possible exception to this convenient rule in the context of ouster clauses, which we examine in Chapter 16.

CHAPTER 13

GROUNDS OF JUDICIAL REVIEW II: FAIR HEARINGS AND THE RULE AGAINST BIAS

13.1 Introduction

The courts may review a public authority's decision on the ground of 'procedural impropriety' if the decision maker has failed to meet required standards of fair procedure. It is difficult to define precisely what is meant by the word 'procedure' in this context, but, in essence, it concerns *the way in which the decision is reached* rather than the *actual decision* itself (in contrast, the grounds of review known as illegality and irrationality both look, in different ways, at the actual decision). Over the years, the courts have built up detailed rules setting out what is required of decision makers in different circumstances – in other words, what procedures they have to follow in order to ensure that their decisions comply with the requirements of 'fairness'.

Different types of decisions, and different decision makers, have to conform to different standards of procedural propriety. At one extreme, almost all decision makers are required not to be biased when taking decisions. On the other hand, only some decision makers are required to offer a person likely to be affected an oral hearing before taking a decision. The crucial skill which one therefore has to develop is to be able to recognise what the courts are likely to require by way of procedural fairness in any given situation. This is not an easy task, because there are few fixed rules to act as a guide. Over the past few years, the courts have increasingly emphasised that what is required of a decision maker is simply what is 'fair in the circumstances' – and they have emphasised that 'fairness' is a flexible concept. This means that, in order to predict what the courts might require in any particular situation with which one is faced, one has to be aware:

(a) of what the courts have done in similar situations in the past; and

(b) of the general principles which the courts follow in applying the 'fairness' concept,

so that one can be alert to differences between this case and past cases, and thus have an idea as to how the courts might react to the particular situation.

13.2 Terminology: a brief history

It is easy to be confused by the different terminology used in this area. As is so often the case in judicial review, the language is far less important than the actual concepts. But some awareness of differences in terminology is necessary, because the labels are of more than merely historical interest. A wide variety of terms is still used today.

Traditionally, the requirements of procedural fairness have been known collectively as 'the rules of natural justice'. This phrase reflects the courts' original explanation of the source of the doctrine: that it was not invented by judges, but reflected 'natural' or even God-given laws of fairness. (In one 18th century case, Fortescue J even traced the doctrine back to Old Testament roots!) The rules of natural justice were traditionally categorised under two headings, each known by a Latin tag:

(a) the principle *audi alteram partem* (meaning 'hear the other side'), encompassed the group of rules that required a decision maker to offer a hearing, either written or oral, to an affected individual before a decision was taken;

(b) the principle *nemo judex in causa sua* (or 'no man a judge in his own cause') covered the rules which ensured that a decision maker was not biased, and should not appear to be biased, in coming to a decision.

These rules were slowly developed by the courts, relying heavily on analogies with court procedures. In other words, the courts looked at the procedural protections which a person would be entitled to in court (such as a right to an oral hearing, a right to call witnesses, a right to be represented by a lawyer, a right to cross-examination, and so on) and applied similar rights to persons affected by decisions of public bodies who were entitled to natural justice.

In the 1970s, this rather rigid approach was softened, as the courts began to state that the rules of natural justice were not necessarily uniform in different situations; that what was required in each case was simply whatever 'fairness' demanded. There was then a long debate in the late 1970s and early 1980s about whether there was any difference between 'natural justice' and 'fairness'. The answer today is, probably not. The best evidence of this is the number of judges who simply talk about 'the requirements of natural justice or fairness' without even attempting to distinguish them. One can still use the language of 'natural justice', as long as one remembers that it is a much more flexible concept than it was 20 years ago.

In the *GCHQ* case (1984), Lord Diplock proposed that, rather than the terms 'natural justice' or 'procedural fairness', we should use the term 'procedural propriety'. He explained that:

> I have described the third head as 'procedural impropriety' rather than failure to observe the basic rules of natural justice or failure to act with procedural fairness towards the person who will be affected by the decision. This is because susceptibility to judicial review under this head covers also failure by an administrative tribunal to observe procedural rules that are expressly laid down in the legislative instrument by which its jurisdiction is conferred, even where such failure does not involve any failure of natural justice [p 411].

We have adopted Lord Diplock's categorisation here. Under the heading of 'procedural impropriety', therefore, there are three broad areas to be examined. These are:

(a) *the right to a fair hearing*. A fair hearing may be required *either* by statute, *or* by the common law (the latter being what is known as the rules of natural justice or fairness). This is dealt with in the first part of this chapter;

(b) *the rule against bias* (dealt with in 13.7 and following);

(c) *the doctrine of legitimate expectation* (dealt with in Chapter 14). This is the idea that decision makers ought, where possible, to fulfil expectations which they have, by their actions, aroused in affected individuals.

13.3 A framework for thinking about the right to a fair hearing

There are a huge number of cases dealing with the right to a hearing: this is the most litigated area of procedural impropriety. Most of the cases deal with different aspects of the same basic question: in the circumstances of the individual case, has the applicant any entitlement to procedural protection before the decision is taken, and, if so, what protection can he or she demand? We have broken this question down into three separate elements:

(a) *When* is a fair hearing *prima facie* required (see below, 13.4)?

(b) Is there any reason why the *prima facie* entitlement to a hearing should be *limited* or *defeated* (see below, 13.5)?

(c) If a some sort of hearing is required, *what* procedural protection can the applicant actually demand (see below, 13.6)?

13.4 When is a fair hearing required?

This is certainly the most difficult of the three issues. Let us go back to the example which we followed in the last chapter.

· Alice applies to the MTLB for a market stallholder's licence. She has never had a licence before. She fills in the short application form, and sends it to the MTLB. Some time later, she gets a letter from the MTLB turning down her application on the ground that the MTLB believes that she is not a fit and proper person. The MTLB states that its decision is final, and that it will not listen to further representations.

Alice wants to know if she can challenge this decision, because the MTLB has not given her an opportunity to make representations. She says she would have liked to make oral representations, or, failing that, to put representations in writing. She would also like to know the grounds on which the MTLB has found that she is not fit and proper. Has she got a good ground of challenge on the basis that the MTLB has failed to give her a fair hearing?

13.4.1 'Judicial/administrative' and 'rights/privileges'

In answering this question, the first golden rule to remember is, don't trust any cases decided before the mid-1960s! Until that time, the courts used to insist that, to be entitled to a fair hearing, it would have to be shown that the decision maker was a 'judicial body' (that is, it had the characteristics of a court or tribunal) rather than an 'administrative body'. It would also have to be shown that the decision in respect of which the hearing was sought was one which concerned legally enforceable rights, rather than merely 'privileges' or 'expectations'.

In Alice's case, although she may be able to show that the MTLB was a 'judicial body' (depending on the MTLB's precise character), she would not be able to show that the decision concerned any legally enforceable 'right'. She has no right to a licence – only a hope of a getting one. So, under the old law, Alice would have had no right to a hearing.

13.4.2 Rigid distinctions swept away

These distinctions have now been swept away. In many ways, the law is now closer to what it was in the mid to late 19th century, before these rigid distinctions arose (so that the old case of *Cooper v Wandsworth Board of Works* (1863) is still (in broad principle) good law). The case that really confirmed the death of these old distinctions between judicial/administrative bodies and rights/privileges was the landmark decision of *Ridge v Baldwin* (1964). Ridge was the chief constable of Brighton, until he was dismissed from his post without a hearing by the local authority (which had the power to dismiss him 'at any time' if, in its opinion, he was 'negligent in the discharge of his duty, or otherwise unfit for the same'). His dismissal followed a corruption trial at which he was acquitted, but where the judge had made various criticisms of him. Ridge challenged his dismissal on the ground that he should have been given an opportunity to make representations to the local authority, defending himself against the allegations made against him. The local authority argued (following the old case law) that, since Ridge had no 'legal right' to his position, he had no entitlement to a hearing before dismissal.

The House of Lords found that Ridge should have been given a hearing before being dismissed. Lord Reid held that whenever a decision by a public authority resulted in a person being deprived of his employment, or resulted in his reputation being significantly diminished, that person ought to be given a chance to make representations before the decision was taken. It was irrelevant whether the person had a 'right' to his position or whether it was merely a 'privilege'. In a case a few years later (*Re HK (An Infant)* (1967)), it was confirmed that the effect of *Ridge v Baldwin* was also to sweep away the judicial/administrative distinction: in other words, Ridge would have been entitled to a hearing even if the local authority were not acting 'judicially' (this was not clear from the judgments in *Ridge* itself). In *Re HK*, the court for the first time talked of the requirement 'to act fairly'. *Ridge* and *Re HK* together are so important because they opened up for debate the question of whether a hearing was required in any particular situation, irrespective of its formal categorisation. They did not, of course, provide a complete answer to that question, beyond suggesting that a hearing would be required when livelihood or reputation was significantly put at risk by a decision (as in *Ridge v Baldwin*), or where a fundamental right, such as the right to enter the county by immigration was at issue (as in *Re HK*).

Those decisions do not, however, assist us in our example. Alice's existing livelihood has not been put at risk, because we know that she has never traded in the past. It could be argued that a finding that she is not fit and proper does significantly affect her reputation, but if no one else knew of the MTLB's decision, this is doubtful.

To decide, therefore, whether Alice is entitled to a hearing, it is necessary to look for authorities dealing with situations which are more similar. This is the same process which has to be gone through each time one is confronted with a novel situation in which it is not immediately clear whether the requirements of procedural propriety apply.

13.4.3 Fair hearings and licensing decisions

Licensing is an important function of government and self-regulatory organisations. In many areas – whether practising a profession or trade, broadcasting or sport – people are required to obtain a licence before engaging in the activity. A useful case in this area is *McInnes v Onslow-Fane* (1978) (although since the case was decided before Ord 53 was introduced, it does not address the difficult issue of whether such licensing authority is amenable to judicial review: see below, Chapter 17). McInnes sought a boxing manager's licence from the British Boxing Board of Control. He had held a licence in the past, but not for several years before this application. The Board refused to grant him a licence without giving him an oral hearing, and without disclosing to him the basis of their decision. McInnes challenged this decision, claiming that the Board had acted in breach of natural justice and unfairly. In his judgment, Sir Robert Megarry VC divided up licence cases into three categories:

(a) the first category consisted of *'revocation cases'*: where someone holding an existing licence has it revoked for some reason. In that type of case, he held, the person should normally be offered a fair hearing before being deprived of the licence;

(b) at the opposite end of the spectrum were *'application cases'* – where a person who doesn't hold an existing licence applies for one. Here, he held, there would not normally be any obligation on the decision maker to offer a hearing;

(c) thirdly, the judge identified a category which he called *'expectation cases'* but which, for reasons which we will deal with later, it is better to call 'renewal cases', where someone has held a licence which has expired by passage of time, and he or she applies for it to be renewed. The judge did not have to decide on this last category, but suggested that it was 'closer to the revocation cases' – that is, closer to the situation where a hearing would be required.

On the facts, the judge found that McInnes came within the 'application' category, because he did not hold an existing licence, and therefore he was not entitled to a hearing or to know the case against him.

Although *McInnes* is as good a starting point as any in the context of licensing cases, it is not the last word on the subject. It is a little misleading in suggesting that classes of case can be divided up in the abstract, when in fact, as judges have subsequently emphasised, all depends on what is 'fair' in the particular circumstances. Since the *McInnes* decision, it has become clearer that 'renewal cases' are indeed closer to 'revocation cases' – that is, that unless there is a very good reason to the contrary, a person applying to continue a licence which has expired is entitled to a hearing before he or she is refused (see, for example, *R v Assistant Metropolitan Police Commissioner ex p Howell* (1986)). It has also become clearer that even in 'application cases', where the applicant has never held a licence before, there may be a limited right to a fair hearing. After all, a person can be as badly affected by being rejected in a 'first time' application as when losing an existing permit; she may be prevented from following a trade or vocation which she had set her heart on. In *R v Huntingdon DC ex p Cowan* (1984), an applicant was refused an entertainments licence (after a first time application) without being told of various objections which the council had received, and without being given a hearing. The court held that the applicant should, as a minimum, have been informed of the nature of the objections made, and have been given a chance reply in writing. Similar reasoning will apply outside the narrow 'licensing' context. In *R v Secretary of State for the Home Department ex p Fayed* (1997), the Court of Appeal held that applicants for British citizenship were entitled to an opportunity to make representations (and entitled to be informed of matters on which the application might be rejected), on the basis that the refusal of the application would lead to adverse inferences being drawn about the applicants' characters.

On this basis, we might advise Alice as follows: since Alice has not previously held a licence, she falls into the category known as 'application cases' which Megarry VC in *McInnes* suggested would not normally attract an entitlement to a hearing. However, the *Huntingdon* case suggests that, even in this situation, a hearing may sometimes be required. Since the MTLB has turned Alice down on a very serious ground – that she is not fit and proper – without giving her any opportunity to comment and, moreover, on an issue which is personal to her, and upon which she might well be expected to have something relevant to say, it is likely that a court would find that the MTLB has acted unfairly here. (However, she is probably not entitled to an oral hearing, but only to be told of the objections against her and to have the opportunity of submitting written representations: see *ex p Cowan* (above, and below, 13.6.2).

This is how you might deal with one particular situation; you should try to build up a picture from your lectures and textbooks as to what the courts have done in other factual contexts. What is most important is to try to develop an 'instinct' as to how the courts are likely to react. This is partly a matter of common sense. For example, it is fairly obvious why Megarry VC drew a distinction between application cases and revocation cases in *McInnes*. In a revocation case, an applicant may be losing his or her livelihood (or at least an important right) by being deprived of a licence. A first time applicant, on the other hand, has no existing rights to lose. Further, the class of people in the 'revocation' situation is limited (only those people who already have licences can be deprived of a licence), so the number of people to whom the authority might have to give a hearing is restricted. By contrast, the class of 'first time applicants' is potentially entirely unlimited. What would happen if the courts held that every applicant for a licence had to be given an oral hearing, and then one million people applied? It is important to realise that judges are influenced by practical considerations of this sort.

13.4.4 Summary of entitlement

It is possible to suggest some general principles which the courts employ in assessing entitlement to procedural fairness today (assuming that there is no statutory requirement of a hearing) – always remembering that they are not rules, and that the answer is dependent upon what is fair in each individual case:

(a) as a very general rule, the courts tend to require that a fair hearing be given whenever an applicant's rights or interests are adversely affected in any significant way by a decision, unless there is good reason not to require a hearing;

(b) this general rule does not apply in the 'legislative' context – for example, where an individual may be significantly affected by a proposed statutory instrument. Here, the courts incline against any right to a hearing (*Bates v Lord Hailsham* (1972)), although the position is not so rigid as it once was;

(c) otherwise, if an applicant is deprived of a private law 'right', then a hearing is almost certainly required before the decision is taken;

(d) if an individual is, by reason of the decision, to be deprived of his or her livelihood, or a significant part of it, then a fair hearing is very probably necessary before the decision is taken;

(e) if an individual's reputation will be seriously affected by the decision, or if the individual's interests will otherwise be seriously affected, then a fair hearing is very probably necessary;

(f) more generally, where a decision is made on the basis of considerations which are personal to an applicant, a fair hearing is more likely to be necessary.

13.5 Restrictions on entitlement to a hearing

Even in a case where, by following the above analysis, one might expect an applicant to be entitled to a fair hearing, there are a number of reasons why that entitlement may be excluded. Below, we list some of the more common reasons why this may happen. This list should not be regarded as set of rigid rules; it is simply a collection of some of the reasons that the courts have given for holding that applicants have no entitlement to a fair hearing, even though they might fall into a class which would normally be entitled. In addition, it is important to remember that the court in judicial review cases always has a discretion not to grant a remedy, even where a ground of review, such as failure to grant a fair hearing, is made out. Some of the restrictions on entitlement listed below are sometimes used by the courts in this different way – as reasons why a remedy should not be granted. For present purposes, however, the distinction is not particularly important.

13.5.1 Express statutory exclusion

A statute may expressly exclude the right to a hearing in particular circumstances. Where this happens, the courts must give effect to the statute because, like the rest of the common law, the rules of natural justice are subservient to the will of Parliament. Express statutory exclusion therefore presents no difficulties.

13.5.2 Implied statutory exclusion

In theory, implied exclusion is no different from express exclusion. If the way in which a statute is worded implies that Parliament must have intended that the right to a fair hearing be excluded (even though the statute does not actually say so), then the courts must give effect to that implied intention, and exclude any right to a hearing. However, in practice, the courts are reluctant to interpret a statute in this way, because the right to a fair hearing is regarded as of fundamental importance. The courts are more likely to be persuaded that Parliament intended to exclude natural justice if the legislation provides for some procedural protection (for example, the right to make written representations); the court may then presume that the words of the Act impliedly intended to exclude greater protection (for example, the right to an oral hearing): see, for example, *Abdi v Secretary of State for the Home Department* (1996) (specific provision in Asylum Rules for disclosure of certain documents impliedly excluded any duty to disclose other documents). But, even where specific rules exist, the courts may supplement the statutory procedures with natural justice, provided that such supplementation is not inconsistent with the scheme of the rules. In *Re Hamilton; Re Forrest* (1981), the court was faced with a decision of magistrates to commit Hamilton to prison, without giving him a hearing (and in his absence), for failing to pay sums due under a court order. The magistrates thought that they did not have to give him a hearing as Hamilton was already in prison for other offences, and the relevant legislation only required a hearing 'unless ... the offender is serving a term of imprisonment'. However, the House of Lords found that the legislation only exempted the magistrates from giving prisoners an oral hearing, and held that natural justice required that Hamilton be given an opportunity to make written representations.

13.5.3 Where a hearing, or disclosure of information, would be prejudicial to the public interest

This is an argument which may lead the court to refuse to grant a remedy whatever ground of judicial review is established; that is, illegality or irrationality as well as breach of natural justice. The best example is the *GCHQ* case (1985), where the House of Lords held that the trade unions would have been entitled to consultation, but that, on the facts, this entitlement was defeated by an argument relying on national security: that if the government had consulted the trade unions before instituting the ban on trade unions, this would have risked precipitating the very disruption to essential services protecting national security that the ban was intended to avoid.

Where the government seeks to rely upon national security, there is a difficult question as to the extent to which it has to be established by evidence. Traditionally (as in *GCHQ*), the courts have been willing to accept the assertion of government (provided that there is some evidence to support it); the courts have not ventured into the issue of whether the national security considerations are sufficiently compelling to justify overriding the applicant's procedural rights. However, particularly under the influence of the case law of the European Court of Human Rights, the courts have begun to adopt a slightly more interventionist stance; see *Chahal v UK* (1997), where the European Court unanimously held that the failure of the English courts to carry out or supervise effectively a balancing test (weighing national security considerations) was a breach of Art 5(4) of the Convention (see below, 21.4.1).

13.5.4 In an emergency

This is self-explanatory; if a public authority has to act very urgently, then it may be exempted from offering a hearing beforehand. A good example is *R v Secretary of State for Transport ex p Pegasus Holidays (London) Ltd* (1988), where the court held that the Secretary of State's decision to suspend the licences of Romanian pilots without first giving them a hearing was justified in circumstances in which he feared an immediate threat to air safety (the pilots had failed a Civil Aviation Authority test). Note that there will normally still be a duty on the decision maker to offer the individual a fair hearing as soon as possible after the decision – as and when time permits.

13.5.5 Where it is administratively impracticable to require a hearing

As we have already seen, administrative impossibility may be a reason for the courts finding that there is simply no *prima facie* entitlement to a fair hearing (remember the example of the one million licence applications, above, 13.4.3). But it may also, in rare cases, be a reason for the courts refusing to grant a remedy even where there is a *prima facie* right to a hearing. So, in *R v Secretary of State for Social Services ex p Association of Metropolitan Authorities* (1986), even though the Secretary of State had failed in his statutory duty to consult before making certain regulations, the court would not quash the regulations (although it did grant a declaration) because, by the time of the court's decision, the regulations had been in force for some while, and it would have caused great confusion to revoke them at that stage. The judge also took into account the fact that the regulations were a form of delegated legislation, which the court is always more reluctant to overturn.

It is only in very exceptional circumstances that the court will refuse to quash a decision on this ground. Usually, the maxim 'justice and convenience are not on speaking terms' applies. It may be inconvenient for a decision to be quashed, but this is not a good reason for allowing an *ultra vires* decision to stand.

13.5.6 Where the unfair decision has been 'cured' by a fair appeal

What if an individual is wrongly denied a fair hearing, but there is then an internal appeal to an superior authority, which hears the case properly? Does the fair appeal 'cure' the unfair hearing? This is a difficult issue. On the one hand, it might be said that, if a person is entitled to a hearing and to an appeal, then he or she is entitled to expect each to be fair, not merely the appeal. On the other hand, the individual has at least received one fair hearing (the appeal), and natural justice would not, of itself, normally require that there be more than one hearing.

The general rule is that both the hearing and the appeal must be fair. The reason for this is that a fair appeal may be no substitute for a fair hearing: it is often easier to convince someone of your case first time round, rather than persuading someone to change a decision on appeal; the burden of proof may be different on appeal; the appeal may not re-open issues of fact, etc.

However, where the appeal is a 'full' one (that is, it is effectively a re-hearing of the original hearing), then the appeal may 'cure' the unfair hearing so that the individual cannot challenge the result. In *Lloyd v McMahon* (1987) (see, also, the Privy Council decision in *Calvin v Carr* (1980)), the House of Lords were faced with a situation where a district auditor had surcharged local authority councillors for deliberately failing to set a rate, after a 'hearing' which the councillors alleged was in breach of natural justice (because he had only offered them an opportunity to make written representations rather than an oral hearing). The councillors had made use of a statutory appeal to the High Court, which had rejected their appeal (after hearing oral submissions). The House of Lords held that, in fact, the district auditor had not acted unfairly in not offering an oral hearing, but further held that even if that failure was unfair, it was 'cured' by the statutory appeal to the High Court, because the appeal was a full re-hearing of the matter, rather than simply an appeal; there was 'no question of the court being confined to a review of the evidence which was available to the auditor' (Lord Keith).

13.5.7 Where the decision is only preliminary to a subsequent decision before which a hearing will be given

Although there are a number of confusing cases on this issue, the same basic considerations arise here as in the preceding section. The test is essentially the same as before: has any real unfairness been caused by the fact that the applicant has not been granted a fair hearing at the preliminary stage?

13.5.8 Where the error made 'no difference' to the result, or where a hearing would be futile

On various occasions, courts have suggested that an applicant is not entitled to a fair hearing if the court thinks that the procedural error made 'no difference' to the decision reached, or where, because of the bad conduct of the applicant or for some other reason, the court thinks that it would be 'futile' to grant a remedy because the decision maker would inevitably come to the same decision a second time. Both these lines of reasoning have in common the fact that the court is looking beyond the defect in procedure, and is taking into account the actual merits of the case. This is normally regarded as the cardinal sin of judicial review – the court is not meant to second guess the decision maker, by finding what would have been the result if the decision maker had acted properly. The courts, therefore, normally refuse to accept this type of argument. To take an example: Alice (in the example above, 13.4.3) takes your advice and seeks judicial review of the decision to refuse her application without a hearing. The MTLB admits that it should have given her an opportunity to make written representations, but puts evidence before the court to show that Alice is a notorious thief and confidence trickster, and therefore would be a completely unsuitable person to hold a licence. The MTLB argues that the court should not quash its decision, because the error (the failure to entertain written representations) did not affect the result since, given her bad character, she could say nothing in her representations which could lead the MTLB to grant her a licence. Making us take the decision again, say the MTLB, would be futile.

The answer to this is that it is not for the court to judge whether or not the MTLB would necessarily come to the same decision. The role of the court is to quash the decision, if a ground of review is made out, and to remit the case back to the MTLB for it to re-take the decision with an open mind. It might be different, however, if Alice admitted the evidence put before the court. In that case, the court might be tempted to hold that, on the basis of such evidence, the MTLB would inevitably have come to the same decision.

There is always a great temptation for the court to find against an unmeritorious applicant by holding that the decision would inevitably have been the same, so that the error made no difference. For example, in *Glynn v Keele University* (1971), the court refused to overturn a disciplinary decision in respect of a university student, even though the court found that the hearing was defective. This was because the offence (nude sunbathing!) merited a severe penalty 'even today', and all that was lost was a chance to plead in mitigation. In *Cinnamond v British Airports Authority* (1980), the Court of Appeal upheld an order excluding six minicab drivers from Heathrow airport, even though BAA had wrongly failed to give the drivers a hearing, because (as Lord Denning put it), the past records of the six were so bad (convictions, unpaid fines, flouting of BAA's regulations) that they could not expect to be consulted over the decision, and there was, therefore, no breach of natural justice. And, more recently, the courts have been prepared to find that cases fall within a 'narrow margin of cases' where it is 'near to certainty' that the flaw made no difference to the result (see, for example, *R v Camden LBC ex p Paddock* (1995); *R v Islington LBC ex p Degnan* (1998)). However, these are unusual cases. More representative of the law is the well known *dictum* of Megarry J in *John v Rees* (1970):

> As everybody who has anything to do with the law well knows, the path of the law is strewn with examples of open and shut cases which, somehow, were not; of unanswerable charges which, in the event, were completely answered; of fixed and unalterable determinations that, by discussion, suffered a change. Nor are those with any knowledge of human nature ... likely to underestimate the feelings of resentment of those who find that a decision against them has

been made without their being afforded any opportunity to influence the course of events [p 402].

13.6 Content of the fair hearing

So far in this chapter, we have spoken in general terms of 'fair hearings'. We need now to consider what precisely is meant by the phrase. Assuming that an entitlement to a fair hearing does exist, what procedural rights can the applicant actually expect? The answer depends, as always, upon what fairness requires in the individual circumstances of the case. Once again, the best way to get a 'feel' for what is required in different circumstances is to look at what the courts have done in past cases, and to put that together with the principles on which the courts tend to act. What follows is a 'menu' of different procedural protections, starting from the most basic and widespread, and progressing to rights which are certainly not required in every case.

13.6.1 Disclosure to the applicant of the case to be met

Whenever an individual has any right at all to be consulted or heard before a decision is taken, he or she will almost inevitably also have a right to disclosure of the case to be met (assuming that there is a 'case' against the applicant), or the basis upon which the decision maker proposes to act. The courts have recognised that it will often be meaningless to give someone a right to make representations if they do not know the case against them, because they will not know to what issues to direct their representations. As Lord Denning MR put it, 'If the right to be heard is to be a real right which is worth anything ... [an applicant] must know what evidence has been given and what statements have been made affecting him' (*Kanda v Government of Malaya* (1962)).

An example of a case where the decision maker failed to make proper disclosure is *Chief Constable of North Wales v Evans* (1982). Here, a probationer police constable was required to resign by the chief constable following various allegations as to his 'unsuitable' lifestyle, of which he was not informed at the time at which he was effectively dismissed. Most of the allegations turned out to be untrue or very misleading. The House of Lords held that the chief constable had acted in breach of his duty of fairness in not putting to Evans the adverse factors on which he relied.

This duty of disclosure may be an ongoing one. Where a decision maker discovers evidence, or forms views, in the course of his investigation adverse to the applicant upon which he proposes to rely in making his decision, there may be a duty to put such concerns to the individual: see, for example, *R v Secretary of State for the Home Department ex p Fayed* (1997).

There are, however, limits on the right to disclosure. Public decision makers are not normally obliged to disclose every relevant document to an affected individual, as if they were giving disclosure in civil litigation. The test is normally whether the individual had sufficient information and material as to the case against him so that he was able to make informed submissions. Further, in some situations, the material which the applicant wants to see may be confidential or sensitive. In such cases, the applicant may have to make do with rather less than full disclosure. In *R v Gaming Board ex p Benaim and Khaida* (1970), the applicants re-applied for gaming licences. The Board gave them a hearing and indicated the matters which were troubling the Board, but refused their application without indicating the source or precise content of the information upon which the Board relied. The Court of Appeal held that, in the circumstances, it was enough that the applicants were given a general nature of the case against them, sufficient to prepare their representations. The Board did not need to 'quote chapter and verse' against them, nor did it have to disclose information which would put an informer to the Board in peril of discovery, or which would otherwise be contrary to the public interest.

13.6.2 Written representations versus oral hearings

Ordinarily, where a hearing is required, then it will be an oral hearing. But, in some circumstances, the courts have held that the requirements of fairness are satisfied by an opportunity to submit written representations. For example, in *R v Huntingdon District Council ex p Cowan* (1984) (discussed above in relation to licence applications, 13.4.3), it was held that, in considering an application for an entertainments licence, a local authority was not under a duty to give the applicant an oral hearing; it was sufficient to inform him of objections made and to give him an opportunity to reply. Part of the reason for this, as noted above, is the sheer impracticality of insisting on oral hearings in circumstances where there is an entirely open ended category of applicants.

In general, the requirement that a hearing should be oral is only likely to be relaxed where there is no good reason for anything more than written representations. If, therefore, the decision may turn on the applicant's credibility, or on contested evidence of witnesses, then an oral hearing will have to be given. Similarly, where the applicant faces disciplinary charges, or any other decision which will have a serious impact on his or her reputation, the courts are likely to require the decision maker to allow the applicant to address it in person.

13.6.3 Statutory consultation

Many statutes provide that the minister, or other public authority, shall undertake 'consultations' before arriving at a decision, or before delegated legislation is enacted. In general, the courts have interpreted this as requiring no more than allowing affected parties to submit written representations (see, for example, *R v Secretary of State for Health ex p United States Tobacco International Inc* (1991)). The courts will try to ensure, however, that such consultation is more than a mere formality. Thus, in *R v Secretary of State for Social Services ex p Association of Metropolitan Authorities* (1986), Webster J stressed that 'the essence of consultation is the communication of a genuine invitation to give advice and a genuine consideration of that advice'.

13.6.4 The right to call witnesses

Fairness may require that the decision maker allow the persons affected to call witnesses to give evidence to support their case. This tends to be required in more 'formal' proceedings, such as in disciplinary hearings. The courts have held that tribunals and other decision makers have a *discretion* as to whether or not to allow witnesses to be called; however, this discretion must be exercised reasonably, and in good faith. In this context, the courts will be prepared to intervene to strike down a decision not to allow witnesses to be called not only if they think that the decision is *Wednesbury* unreasonable or irrational (see Chapter 15), but on the much narrower ground that they believe that the decision was unfair. Thus, in *R v Board of Visitors of Hull Prison ex p St Germain (No 2)* (1979), the court struck down as contrary to natural justice the decision of a prison board of visitors at a disciplinary hearing (following a prison riot) not to allow a prisoner to call witnesses because of the administrative inconvenience involved in calling the witnesses – who were fellow prisoners, then at different prisons. The court also (not surprisingly) rejected the argument that the witnesses were unnecessary because the tribunal believed that there was ample evidence against the prisoner.

In other circumstances, the courts may be more respectful of the tribunal's decision not to allow witnesses to be called. In *R v Panel on Take-overs and Mergers ex p Guinness plc* (1989), the Court of Appeal stated that it felt the 'greatest anxiety' about the panel's decision not to grant an adjournment to allow witnesses for Guinness to attend. However, the court found it impossible to say that that decision had been wrong, bearing in mind that the panel did not exercise a disciplinary function, and was an 'inquisitorial' rather than 'adversarial' body. The court also, in that case, took into account the 'overwhelming' evidence in favour of the panel's view.

13.6.5 The right to legal representation and to cross-examination of witnesses

Essentially, the same principles apply here as to the entitlement to call witnesses. The entitlement to legal representation or cross-examination is a feature only of the more 'judicialised' forms of decision making. Even then, the tribunal or other decision maker has a discretion as to whether or not to allow an applicant to be legally represented. However, the courts may intervene to strike down a decision not to allow representation if the decision is unfair. Unfairness will almost certainly exist if the tribunal allows one side to be legally represented and not the other. It may also exist, particularly in formal disciplinary proceedings, if the questions at issue are complex and the applicant is not genuinely capable of representing him or herself. Thus, in *R v Home Secretary ex p Tarrant* (1984), the court quashed a disciplinary decision of a prison board of visitors for unfairness caused by a failure to allow legal representation. The court set out a number of factors which together required that representation be allowed: the seriousness of the charge and penalty which the prisoner faced; the likelihood that points of law would arise; the prisoner's capacity to present his own case, and the need for fairness between prisoners, and between prisoners and prison officers. The House of Lords approved the decision in *Tarrant* in *R v Board of Visitors of HM Prisons, The Maze, ex p Hone* (1988) – but remember that each case must be considered on its merits; there are other prisoners' discipline cases where the opposite conclusion has been reached, where the charges were straightforward (legally and factually), and where the prisoner was articulate (*R v Board of Visitors of Parkhurst Prison ex p Norney* (1989)). The entitlement to legal representation must also be considered in the context of the more general right of access to a lawyer, a right protected under the European Convention: see Art 6(1) and (3), and *Murray v UK* (1996); see below, 21.2.1.

The question of entitlement to cross-examine witnesses produced by the other side normally (although not always) arises where the parties are legally represented. As a general rule, it can be said that if a witness is allowed to testify orally, then the other side should be allowed to confront the witness by cross-examination. But, once again, this is a matter of discretion for the tribunal or adjudicator, and if the tribunal feels that cross-examination will serve no useful purpose, then the court may be slow to disturb that decision. The most important case on this question is *Bushell v Secretary of State for the Environment* (1981), where the House of Lords refused to overturn the decision of an inspector at a public inquiry in relation to a proposed motorway not to allow cross-examination as to the basis of the Department's predictions of future traffic flow. Although the decision can be read as suggesting that cross-examination should not be allowed into 'policy'-type issues, in reality, the crucial point was that the House of Lords (and the inspector) did not regard the issue of future traffic flow as a relevant question for the inquiry to decide; hence, it was reasonable not to allow cross-examination on the point (there is, however, an unanswered question as to why, if this was right, the Secretary of State was allowed to adduce evidence as to traffic flow forecasts at all).

13.6.6 The right to reasons for the decision

The issue of whether or not a person affected by a decision has a right to be provided with reasons explaining or justifying that decision is an important and fast growing one in public law and it is worth considering the subject in some detail. Before looking at the current position in English law, it is worth asking whether an entitlement to be given reasons for a decision of a public authority is really so important, and if so, why. It is clear that eminent contemporary public law writers do regard an entitlement to reasons as important. As Lord Woolf has said (41st Hamlyn Lectures, *Protection of the Public – A New Challenge*, 1990, London: Sweet & Maxwell):

> I regard the giving of satisfactory reasons for a decision as being the hallmark of good administration and if I were to be asked to identify the most beneficial improvement which could be made to English administrative law I would unhesitatingly reply that it would be the introduction of a general requirement that reasons should normally be available, at least on request, for all administrative actions.

Professor Wade has stated that the lack of a general duty to give reasons is an 'outstanding deficiency of administrative law'; and that 'a right to reasons is an indispensable part of a sound system of judicial review' (Wade, HWR and Forsyth, CF, *Administrative Law*, 1994, Oxford: Clarendon, pp 544, 542). And the JUSTICE/All Souls Committee Report, *Administrative Justice, Some Necessary Reforms*, 1988, Oxford: OUP, devoted an entire chapter to the duty to give reasons, and concluded by endorsing the 1971 Justice Committee report *Administration Under Law* that 'no single factor has inhibited the development of English administrative law as seriously as the absence of any general obligation upon public authorities to give reasons for their decisions'.

As we shall see, the extent of the duty to give reasons has greatly expanded since the passages quoted above were written, but it is still worth asking why these writers think the duty to give reasons is so important. Note, particularly, that reasons are not only valuable for the individual or individuals who will be affected by the decision; many writers believe that it is also in the interests of the decision maker itself to give reasons. To summarise greatly, one can categorise the advantages of the duty to give reasons as follows.

From the affected individual's point of view:

(a) to satisfy his expectation of just and fair treatment by the decision maker, both in his particular case and as a decision making authority in general;

(b) to enable him to decide whether the decision is open to challenge (by way of appeal, further representations, or judicial review).

From the decision maker's point of view:

(a) to improve the quality of decision making (if someone knows that they have to justify their decision, that fact alone may make them take the decision more responsibly, may improve the articulation of their thought processes, etc; reasons may, therefore, be a check on arbitrariness);

(b) to help 'legitimation' of decision making process: whether the decision maker is generally regarded as a fair and reasonable authority;

(c) to *protect* the administration from hopeless appeals or other challenges (the idea is that if an individual has a decision explained to him, he may be more inclined to accept it and therefore not challenge it).

Finally, courts and other reviewing or appellate bodies may need reasons in order to assess whether or not the original decision was lawful or correct.

Obviously, some of these arguments in favour of a right to reasons are stronger than others; you may think some of them carry little weight or are even insignificant. And, when considering how important it is for English law to include a duty to give reasons, it should be borne in mind that there are also significant disadvantages. The most obvious is the extra administrative burden on public bodies; the sheer time and effort involved in justifying every decision to every affected individual. You will notice that Lord Woolf, quoted above, suggests that reasons should be available 'at least on request'; this suggests one way in which the burden might be cut down – but it still leaves decision makers whose decisions affect a large number of persons potentially exposed to a great administrative burden. Also, some might argue that a duty to give reasons would *increase* the number of challenges against public bodies, since people will want to challenge reasons which they believe are wrong. That might be no bad thing, if the reasons really are wrong, but it might also expose decision makers to large numbers of unmeritorious challenges.

One caution should be noted at this point: it is very important to distinguish the right to reasons for a decision from the right to be informed of the case against the applicant before the decision – of proper disclosure in advance. The latter is, as we have seen above, 13.6.1, a basic requirement of natural justice, and is quite different from the duty to give reasons, because it relates to the provision of information before the decision is taken, rather than after the event. In a nutshell, disclosure is important so that one knows what representations one should make, while reasons are important so that one knows how and why the decision was made. Reasons are, nevertheless, typically viewed as a facet of the right to a fair hearing (even though provided after the decision), in part because the obligation to provide reasons after the event may well have an effect upon the way in which the decision itself is taken.

Ultimately, different people will have different views about the relative strengths of the arguments for and against reasons. Of course, the debate is not simply black and white: either for or against reasons. English law is increasingly attempting to identify those situations where it would be valuable for reasons to be given, and to distinguish those from others where the decision maker does not have to justify the decision. In considering the case law, it is worth keeping in the back of one's mind the general arguments for and against reasons, and 'measuring' the decisions in the cases against one's views of the strengths of different arguments.

No general duty to give reasons?

The traditional position in English law has always been that there is no general rule of law (or, in particular, rule of natural justice) that reasons should be given for public law decisions (although there have always been a considerable number of situations in which there is a statutory obligation upon the decision maker to provide reasons). This view was reaffirmed in the important House of Lords case of *R v Secretary of State for the Home Department ex p Doody* (1993), and, more recently, by the Lord Chief Justice in *R v Ministry of Defence ex p Murray* (1998). But the case law has been developing at such a speed in this area, and new cases imposing a duty to give reasons have multiplied at such a rate, that it is becoming increasingly difficult to place much weight on the 'general rule'; the rule itself is becoming the exception. If fairness requires it in any particular situation, the courts now insist that decision makers provide reasons for decisions.

Judges have not developed the law in any 'organised' way; they have not laid down a series of clear propositions which set out in the abstract those categories of case in which reasons are required. Instead, they have developed (and are developing) the law on an incremental, case by case basis. Although this development has been to a large extent judge-led, it has been reinforced by (and has, perhaps, itself influenced) the recent Woolf reforms to civil law procedure, which have placed increasing stress upon early disclosure by parties to litigation. You may wish to compare, as examples of judicial creativity, the emergence of a duty to give reasons with the doctrine of legitimate expectation, examined in the next chapter.

Recent cases in which the courts have held that a right to reasons exists include: *R v Civil Service Appeal Board ex p Cunningham* (1992), where the Court of Appeal held that fairness required that a prison officer be given reasons for an (unexpectedly low) award of damages for unfair dismissal by the Civil Service Appeal Board (the Board, unlike the Industrial Tribunals on which it was modelled, was not required by statute or regulation to give reasons); *Doody* (above) (Home Secretary must give reasons for the 'tariff' period to be served by certain life sentence prisoners); *R v Harrow Crown Court ex p Dave* (1994) (Crown Court should give reasons for all its decisions, except possibly some interlocutory and procedural decisions); *R v Lambeth London BC ex p Walters* (1993) (local authority should give reasons for its decision on an individual's application for local authority housing – the judge went so far as to suggest that there is now usually a general duty to give reasons). See, also, *ex p Murray* (above; reasons at court martial); *R v Mayor of the City of London ex p Matson* (1996) (reasons for decision not to confirm appointment of Alderman after election); *R v Islington ex p Rixon* (reasons for decision as to community care entitlement).

There are still cases, however, where reasons are not required to be given. In *R v Higher Education Funding Council ex p Institute of Dental Surgery* (1994), the court held that the HEFC was not required to give reasons for its decision to assess the Institute at a relatively low level in its comparative assessment of the research of all higher education establishments. Although the fact that the decision was one of academic judgment, arrived at by a panel of experts, did not of itself mean that reasons could not be required, the court found that given the 'combination of openness in the run-up [to the decision]', and 'the prescriptively oracular character of the critical decision', the HEFC's decision was 'inapt' for the giving of reasons. Even here, however, the court rejected that argument that the duty to give reasons could any longer be seen as an 'exceptional' one.

In general, one can summarise the present position by saying that, while each case depends on what is 'fair' in the circumstances, the following factors may dispose a court in favour of requiring reasons:

(a) the decision affects individuals' fundamental rights (such as liberty);

(b) the decision maker in question must make a 'formal' decision – that is, after a judicialised hearing;

(c) the decision is one for which the person affected needs reasons in order to know whether to appeal or seek judicial review;

(d) it would not be administratively impracticable for the decision maker to give reasons for each decision.

The third reason above is, of course, potentially very wide, and will, in practice, open up a vast range of decision making processes to a requirement of reasons, subject only to the fourth consideration.

Where reasons are required, they may usually be brief; the courts do not readily entertain challenges to the adequacy of reasons. And even where a decision maker fails to give reasons for a decision where it is obliged to do so, the court will not necessarily quash the decision. If it has remedied the error by providing proper reasons in an affidavit sworn in judicial review proceedings (or otherwise later notified the individual of the reasons for the decision), then the court may well, in its discretion, decide not to overturn the decision.

Reasons to the court?

So far, we have examined the circumstances in which the common law requires a public authority to give the person affected reasons for its decision. A different situation exists where an application for judicial review is made on any of the grounds of review; does the public authority then have to give reasons for its decision to the court? While the court may not compel the decision maker to justify the decision, it may well be more willing to strike down a decision if no reasons are given for it, even though fairness/natural justice does not require that reasons be given. This is really based on common sense: a decision which the decision maker does not justify may well be more vulnerable. In *Padfield v Minister of Agriculture* (1968), the House of Lords went so far as to suggest that if an applicant could establish a *prima facie* case of unlawfulness, then, in the absence of reasons, the court could infer unlawfulness. Another example of this line of reasoning is *Cunningham* (above), where Sir John Donaldson MR was prepared to infer, in circumstances where the Civil Service Appeal Board had not attempted to justify to the court an apparently unusually low award of compensation to a prison officer, that the decision was irrational. Of course, this line of cases is not really an example of 'procedural impropriety' at all; it is merely an example of the court effectively shifting the evidential burden onto the respondent. However, it is worth taking into account in this context, because it provides another route by which decision makers may ultimately be forced to give reasons for their decisions; if not immediately, to the individual, then later, to the court.

13.7   The rule against bias – introduction

A decision may be challenged on grounds of procedural impropriety if it can be established that there was 'bias' on the part of the decision maker. Bias can take many forms. At one extreme, there are blatant cases which break the rule that nobody may be a judge in his or her own cause (*nemo judex in causa sua*) – where, for example, the decision maker knowingly has a financial interest in the outcome of the case. At the other end of the spectrum are cases where people may disagree as to whether 'bias' exists, and if so, whether it matters; where, for example, a decision maker has strong views about the subject matter of the case before him.

In considering what constitutes bias, it is necessary to look not only at public law cases, but also at criminal cases, because here too, the same considerations of 'natural justice' and the need to maintain public confidence in decision making processes apply. The modern leading case on bias is in fact a criminal one, *R v Gough* (1993), and in his judgment, Lord Goff confirmed that it was:

> ... possible, and desirable, that the same test should be applicable in all cases of apparent bias, whether concerned with justices or members of other inferior tribunals, or with jurors, or with arbitrators.

13.8 Bias and the appearance of bias

What a court is usually looking for when it reviews a decision for bias is whether the appearance of bias is sufficient to justify intervention, rather than whether there was in fact any bias (although, if it is shown that there was in fact bias, this will also justify intervention). This distinction might appear inconsistent with the notion that the rule against bias is a facet of 'natural justice', which is normally concerned with what the decision maker actually did; it might be argued that the fact that there is an appearance of bias does not mean that a biased decision is inevitable or even likely, because it is perfectly possible for a decision maker with an interest in the outcome of a case to decide purely on the merits of the case. There are, however, sound reasons of policy why the law should ordinarily take apparent bias as a sufficient reason for intervention:

(a) it is often extremely difficult to determine the actual state of mind of an individual who is alleged to be biased;

(b) bias can operate even though the individual concerned is unaware of its effect;

(c) even where no bias has, in fact, occurred, it is important that public confidence in the integrity of a decision making process is maintained, such that, in the often-quoted words of Lord Hewart CJ in *R v Sussex Justices ex p McCarthy* (1924), 'justice should not only be done, but should manifestly and undoubtedly be seen to be done';

(d) if a court was obliged to investigate the actual state of mind of a decision maker, the confidentiality of the decision making process might be prejudiced (*R v Gough*, *per* Lord Woolf, p 672, although you may question how serious this would be in many cases).

Accordingly, a decision may be quashed merely if there is found to be a sufficient degree of possibility of bias, even if there is no suggestion that actual bias occurred. It is rare, therefore, for actual bias to be shown to exist, but if it is proved, relief will, of course, be granted too.

On the other hand, if the court can be satisfied on the facts that there was no possibility of actual bias, then the court may be willing to reject allegations of 'apparent bias'. In a recent case in which relatives of some of the victims of a collision involving *The Marchioness* passenger launch on the River Thames sought to have the coroner at the inquest removed on the ground of apparent bias, the Court of Appeal appeared to set limits on the extent to which courts should consider allegations of apparent bias. It was suggested that, where it has to consider allegations of unconscious bias, the court is not strictly concerned with the appearance of bias, but rather with establishing the possibility that there was actual bias. The term 'apparent bias' was even considered by one of the judges (Sir Thomas Bingham MR) to be an unhelpful term, because:

... if despite the appearance of bias the court is able to ... satisfy itself that there was no danger of the alleged bias having in fact caused injustice, the impugned decision will be allowed to stand [*R v Inner West London Coroner ex p Dallaglio* (1994)].

The position today, in summary, is therefore that:

(a) actual bias will almost inevitably provide good grounds for challenging a decision;

(b) apparent bias, if sufficiently serious, will also provide grounds for challenge; unless

(c) it can be proved that, despite the appearance of bias, there was, in fact, no actual bias; in that case, the decision will be allowed to stand (on the authority of *Dallaglio*).

13.9 The test for the appearance of bias

Where it can be shown that a decision was actually affected by bias, then, as we have seen, the court will intervene. In cases where the appearance of bias is alleged, however, the court must determine whether the appearance of partiality is sufficiently serious to justify intervention. Two different tests have traditionally been employed to assess this, and although the confusion this caused has seemingly been resolved by a recent decision of the House of Lords, it is worth considering both approaches briefly, because they are revealing about the kind of apparent bias that the law has set out to prevent.

The first test was whether the facts, as assessed by the court, gave rise to a '*real likelihood*' of bias. This approach was often applied in cases where the possibility that actual bias had occurred seemed remote. Under the second test, the court considered whether a reasonable person would have a 'reasonable suspicion' of bias. This test inevitably begged the question of how much knowledge of the facts the hypothetical reasonable person had. In practice, courts tended to choose whichever terminology best suited the particular case.

In *R v Gough* (1993), the House of Lords decisively came down in favour of the first of the two competing approaches, but preferred the phrase '*real danger*' to 'real likelihood' of bias, so as 'to ensure that the court is thinking in terms of possibility rather than probability of bias'. The requirement for the court to postulate the view of a 'reasonable person' was expressly discarded in favour of the opinion of the court, which 'personifies the reasonable man'. Lord Woolf emphasised the universal nature of this 'real danger' test, stating that it could 'ensure that the purity of justice is maintained across the range of situations where bias may exist'; the recent case of *R v Secretary of State for the Environment ex p Kirkstall Valley Campaign* (1996) has confirmed that the *Gough* test applies to decision makers, whether judicial or administrative. The decision of the Court of Appeal in *R v Inner West London Coroner ex p Dallaglio*

(1994) (the *Marchioness* case) is consistent with *Gough*, although it adds the explanation that 'real danger' can be interpreted as 'not without substance' and as involving 'more than a minimal risk, less than a probability'. On the other hand, decisions in other jurisdictions have declined to follow *Gough* (see, for example, the decision of the High Court of Australia in *Webb v The Queen*, preferring the test of whether the events gave rise to a 'reasonable apprehension on the part of a fairminded and informed member of the public that the judge was not impartial'), and the House of Lords in *R v Bow Street Magistrate ex p Pinochet* (1999), discussed below, hinted that *Gough* may need to be reconsidered in the future (see, for example, *per* Lord Browne-Wilkinson).

13.10 Direct pecuniary interest

Cases where a person acting in a judicial capacity has a financial interest in the outcome of proceedings (where the judge is literally *judex in causa sua*: judge in his own cause) are sometimes regarded as being in a special category. These circumstances are treated as being conclusive of apparent bias and therefore as justifying intervention, regardless of the extent of the interest (unless negligible) and regardless of whether the interest has actually had an effect on the decision in question (see, for example, *Dimes v Proprietors of Grand Junction Canal* (1852). In such situations, there is no need to apply the usual test of whether there was a 'real danger' of bias; instead, the nature of the interest is such that public confidence in the administration of justice requires that the person be disqualified from acting as decision maker in the matter, and that the decision should not stand.

The House of Lords has recently held that this special category of 'automatic' disqualification for apparent bias is not restricted to cases of financial interest. In *R v Bow Street Magistrate ex p Pinochet (No 2)* (1999), the House of Lords had to consider whether Lord Hoffmann's connection with Amnesty International (AI) (he was the unpaid director and chairman of a charity which was wholly owned and controlled by AI, and which carried on that part of AI's work which was charitable) meant that he should have been automatically disqualified from sitting in the House of Lords hearing the appeal of Senator Pinochet on his application to quash extradition warrants issued against him – an appeal on which AI appeared as a party, having been given leave to intervene. The House of Lords, on the second hearing, held that there was no need to consider whether there was a likelihood or suspicion of bias; the judge's interest, although not financial or proprietary, was such that it fell within the category such that he was 'automatically' disqualified as being a judge in his own cause. As Lord Browne-Wilkinson noted, the case was highly unusual, in that AI was party to a criminal cause, although neither the prosecutor nor accused. AI's interest in the litigation was not financial, but was to secure the principle that there is no immunity for ex-Heads of State in relation to crimes against humanity. In such circumstances, Lord Hoffmann's interest as a director of the AI charity was equivalent to a pecuniary interest in an ordinary civil case.

It is arguable that it is not necessary to place cases such as these in a special category of 'conclusive' apparent bias. It may simply be that, in such a case, the 'real danger' test is almost inevitably made out on the facts. Indeed, in rare cases it might still be that even a direct financial interest would not be sufficient to establish bias; for example, where it is demonstrably clear that a decision maker was not aware at the date of his decision that he possessed the financial interest. On the other hand, Lord Goff in *Gough* and the House of Lords in *ex p Pinochet* restated the traditional view that, where direct pecuniary (or equivalent) interest of a person in a judicial capacity can be shown, it is unnecessary to inquire whether there was any real likelihood of bias.

13.11 Different manifestations of bias

One common cause of objectionable bias is where a decision maker has previously been involved with the case in some other capacity. In one such example, an individual who had already supported a measure in his capacity as a member of the local authority was disqualified from adjudicating on it as a magistrate (*R v Gaisford* (1892)). In another case, a conviction for dangerous driving was invalidated, because the clerk to the justices was also a solicitor in the firm which was acting against the defendant in a civil action (*R v Sussex Justices ex p McCarthy* (1924)). In another example, a decision of a local council to grant planning permission was quashed because one of the councillors was the estate agent of the owner of the property to whom permission was granted (*R v Hendon RDC ex p Chorley* (1933)).

An individual will not necessarily be barred from adjudicating if he is a member of an organisation which is one of the parties in an action, provided he has himself been inactive in the matter. Thus, a magistrate was allowed to hear a prosecution brought by the Council of the Law Society even though he was himself a solicitor (*R v Burton ex p Young* (1897)).

'Bias by predetermination' may occur where it can be shown that a person acting in a judicial capacity has committed himself to one outcome before hearing part or all of a case. For example, bias was established where a magistrate was found to have prepared a statement of the defendant's sentence halfway through a trial (*R v Romsey Justices ex p Green* (1992)). However, the mere fact that an adjudicator is known to have strong personal beliefs or ideas on a relevant matter need not mean that he will be disqualified. In such cases, it is a question of degree as to what extent the decision maker is to be credited with the ability to act impartially despite his or her views, and thus, for example, a licensing magistrate's ruling was allowed to stand although he was a teetotaller (*R v Nailsworth Licensing Justices ex p Bird* (1953)).

The rule against bias is often enforced very strictly, going well beyond the original principle that what is to be avoided is for a person to decide in their own cause. Sometimes, mere contact between the adjudicator and one of the parties can amount to bias. For example, a disciplinary committee was overruled because it had consulted privately with the chief fire officer who had reported a fireman for lack of discipline (*R v Leicestershire Fire Authority ex p Thompson* (1978)).

13.12 Ministerial bias

It is common for a government department to initiate a particular proposal and for the relevant minister also to be given the power to confirm that proposal after hearing objections to it. A ministerial decision of this kind cannot be objected to on the grounds that the minister was biased simply because the decision was made in accordance with government policy, since the whole purpose of Parliament giving the deciding power to a political body is so that the power may be exercised politically.

In *Franklin v Minister of Town and Country Planning* (1948), it was alleged that the minister's political support for the establishment of a new town had prevented him from an impartial consideration of objections made at a public inquiry, and, therefore, he should be disqualified from ruling on whether or not the proposal should be adopted. However, it was held that, provided that the minister fulfilled his statutory duty of considering the objections, his decision could not be impugned on the ground of bias.

On the other hand, the suggestion in *Franklin* and other early cases that the rule against bias did not apply (or fully apply) to 'administrative cases' has been firmly rejected; as with the right to a fair hearing, the distinction between 'judicial' and 'administrative' functions is no longer part of the test for bias (see above, 13.4.1 and 13.4.2). Thus, the requirement that a decision maker should not be biased applies to all decision makers – unless exceptional circumstances exist.

13.13 Exceptions: where bias will not invalidate a decision

In three types of case, bias has been held not to constitute a vitiating factor:

(a) a party may waive its right to object to a biased adjudicator. This rule can operate harshly; if a party fails to object as soon as the fact of the alleged bias is known, it may be held to have waived its right to do so;

(b) the rule against bias will also cease to take effect in cases of necessity, such as where no replacement is available for an adjudicator who is allegedly biased. One situation in which this can arise is where the case concerns one or more members of the judiciary – for example, where a Canadian court had to determine the tax status of judges' salaries (*The Judges v AG for Saskatchewan* (1937)). More commonly, if a statute allows only one particular minister or other official to decide on a particular issue, the courts will not allow that decision to be frustrated by disqualifying the individual for bias. However, even in a case where all the available qualified adjudicators could appear to be biased, a decision would probably be quashed if actual bias was proved;

(c) in some cases, Parliament has deliberately acted to prevent the operation of the rule against bias by granting specific exemptions. Statutory dispensation can be effective to exclude the rule, but clear words of enactment must be used, and any ambiguity is likely to be interpreted narrowly, so as to minimise the circumstances in which the decision maker is exempted from disqualification. By statute, for example, a liquor licensing justice is permitted to hear an appeal from a refused application, even if he was also a member of the licensing committee which decided on the original application (see *R v Bristol Crown Court ex p Cooper* (1990)).

GROUNDS OF JUDICIAL REVIEW II: FAIR HEARINGS AND THE RULE AGAINST BIAS

By articulating standards of procedural propriety, the courts control *the way in which* decision makers arrive at their decisions. This is achieved by a number of different techniques, which we have categorised under three headings:

(a) the right to a fair hearing;

(b) the rule against bias;

(c) the doctrine of legitimate expectation.

The *entitlement to a fair hearing* depends, in essence, upon what fairness requires in any given set of circumstances. This can be broken down into three elements.

When is a fair hearing prima facie *required?*

In essence, whenever an applicant's rights or interests are adversely affected in any significant way by a decision, unless there is a good reason not to require a hearing.

Is there any reason why the prima facie *entitlement to a hearing should be limited?*

Some possible reasons are:

(a) express statutory exclusion;

(b) implied statutory exclusion;

(c) where a hearing, or disclosure of information, would be prejudicial to the public interest;

(d) in an emergency;

(e) where it is administratively impracticable to require a hearing;

(f) where the unfair decision has been 'cured' by a fair appeal;

(g) where the decision is only preliminary to a subsequent decision before which a hearing will be given;

(h) where the error made 'no difference' to the result, or where a hearing would be futile.

If some sort of hearing is required, what procedural protection can the applicant actually demand?

A 'menu' of possible procedural rights includes:

(a) disclosure to the applicant of the case to be met;

(b) written or oral representations, or consultation;

(c) the right to call witnesses;

(d) the right to legal representation and to cross examination of witnesses;

(e) the right to reasons for the decision.

What is appropriate in any given case is, once again, a matter of asking what 'fairness' requires. Broadly, the above list is in descending order of importance: while (a) and (b) are fundamental to almost any case in which a fair hearing is required (and within (b), the representations will more usually be required to be oral rather than written), (c) and (d) are more likely to be required only in 'formal' proceedings, such as disciplinary hearings or other hearings of an adversarial nature. Traditionally, (e) has been seen (where it has been recognised at all) as only available in 'exceptional' circumstances, but its rapid development may mean that it must be promoted up the list – we may be seeing the development of a general duty on public bodies to give reasons for decisions.

The rule against bias

A decision may be quashed for bias if it can be shown either:

(a) that the decision maker in fact had an interest in the decision which he reached, either financially or otherwise ('actual bias'); or

(b) even if there is no proof of actual bias, that the facts, as assessed by the court, disclose a 'real danger' of bias (*R v Gough* (1993)) – by which the court means a danger which is more than a minimal risk, if less than a probability (*Dallaglio* (1994)).

This latter test for bias – what has been known as 'apparent bias' – is important, principally because (in Lord Hewart's words) 'justice should not only be done, but should manifestly and undoubtedly be seen to be done'.

However, if it can be established that, on the facts, there was no actual bias, then the decision will be allowed to stand even if the facts would otherwise disclose apparent bias (*Dallaglio*). On the other hand, if a person acting in a judicial capacity has a financial interest (or *pace ex p Pinochet* (1999), an equivalent non-pecuniary interest) in the outcome of the case, then this may be treated as conclusive of apparent bias.

Bias may be held not to invalidate a decision if it can be shown:

(a) that a party (with knowledge of the facts) has waived its right to object to a biased adjudicator;

(b) that the situation is one of 'necessity'; in other words, there is no realistic alternative to an adjudicator who appears biased;

(c) that the rule against bias has been excluded, either expressly or (very unusually) impliedly, by legislation (for example, *R v Bristol Crown Court ex p Cooper* (1990)).

CHAPTER 14

GROUNDS OF JUDICIAL REVIEW III: LEGITIMATE EXPECTATION

14.1 Introduction

The doctrine of legitimate expectation is a recent development, even by fast moving public law standards. The term was first mentioned in an English case in 1969 (in *Schmidt v Secretary of State for Home Affairs*; it was an emergent doctrine in Continental legal systems and European Community law before then), but it was not until the early to mid 1980s that the doctrine had settled into anything like a clear body of law. It is fair to say that that 'settling down' process has now occurred, and the legitimate expectation is now a familiar and frequently invoked ground of challenge on applications for judicial review. However, real uncertainties, particularly relating to the ambit of the substantive legitimate expectation, still remain.

The basis of the doctrine is rather like the principle underlying estoppel in private law: that, if possible, the law ought to require people to keep to their promises or representations, even where the promise does not constitute a contract. More specifically, where a public authority has represented to an individual that it will or will not do something, then (even though the authority has not formally bound itself to follow that representation), it ought not to be permitted to depart from the representation, at least unless it first gives the individual a hearing.

14.2 The doctrine

The most useful definition of the legitimate expectation is contained in the *GCHQ* case (*Council of Civil Service Unions v Minister for the Civil Service* (1985)). It is worth quoting from two of the judgments. First, Lord Diplock stated that, for a legitimate expectation to arise, the decision:

> ... must affect [the individual] ... by depriving him of some benefit or advantage which either (i) he had in the past been permitted by the decision maker to enjoy and which he can legitimately expect to be permitted to continue to do until there has been communicated to him some rational grounds for withdrawing it on which he has been given an opportunity to comment; or (ii) he has received assurance from the decision maker will not be withdrawn without giving him first an opportunity of advancing reasons for contending that they should not be withdrawn [pp 408–09].

Lord Fraser put it rather more simply:

> Legitimate ... expectation may arise either from an express promise given on behalf of a public authority or from the existence of a regular practice which the claimant can reasonably expect to continue [p 401].

Drawing on these two passages, we can summarise the basic doctrine of legitimate expectation in a number of propositions:

(a) *a legitimate expectation always arises from the conduct of the decision maker*. It is always something which the decision maker does or says which gives rise to the expectation;

(b) the expectation may arise in one of two ways. First, it may arise *from an express promise given by the decision maker* that, for example, a benefit will be continued, or not withdrawn;

(c) secondly, it may arise *from conduct on the part of the decision maker*, such as a regular past practice or pattern of settled conduct by the decision maker, which the individual can reasonably or legitimately expect will continue;

(d) the legitimate expectation appears (at least from the quotation from Lord Diplock, above) to be only an expectation of having an *opportunity to make representations* before the benefit is withdrawn (that is, before the expectation is disappointed). Thus, on this view, it is only a 'procedural' concept, because all that one can obtain if one establishes a legitimate expectation is an opportunity to put one's case at a hearing. We will consider later whether there is more to the doctrine: whether (and when) one can claim a legitimate expectation of a *'substantive benefit'*, and not just of a hearing.

We can illustrate the doctrine by reference to our example from Chapter 12.

The MTLB issues a policy statement, which it sends to all applicants, in which it states that 'if we decide to grant you a licence, then the licence will run for at least a year, and will be renewable thereafter'. The empowering Act is silent on the question of the term of licences. Paul applies for a licence, and the MTLB grants him one for six months only.

Paul has a legitimate expectation (based on the express promise contained in the MTLB's policy statement) that, if he is granted a licence, it will have a term of at least a year. The MTLB cannot withdraw this 'benefit' without first giving Paul an opportunity to make representations on why the MTLB ought not to depart from its stated policy. Since it has not given him such an opportunity, Paul would have a good case for applying to quash the decision on judicial review. (We reserve for now the question of whether Paul could claim not simply an opportunity to make representations, but rather the substantive benefit: a year-long licence.)

Let us look at some examples of legitimate expectation in practice. First, examples of the 'express promise' type of case. In *AG of Hong Kong v Ng Yuen*

Shiu (1983), a senior immigration officer made an announcement of government policy that, in future, before illegal immigrants were repatriated, they would be interviewed, and further, that each case would be treated 'on its merits'. The Privy Council held that this announcement gave the applicant, who was an illegal immigrant, a legitimate expectation that he would be able, before the decision to repatriate him was taken, to state his case as to why he should not be repatriated.

In *R v Liverpool Corporation ex p Liverpool Taxi Operators' Association* (1972), Liverpool Corporation was responsible for issuing taxi licences in the Liverpool area. It promised the LTOA that it would be consulted before a decision was taken to grant new taxi licences (the LTOA was worried that to increase the total number of licences would have an adverse impact on its members). When the corporation went ahead and increased the number of licences without giving the LTOA a hearing, the Court of Appeal quashed the decision, effectively on the basis that the corporation could not depart from its promise (in fact, the reasoning in the case is not entirely clear – but note the early date of this case relative to the age of the doctrine).

The best example of the 'past practice' limb of the doctrine is the *GCHQ* case itself (1985). The government had, for many years, consulted the Civil Service unions which represented employees at GCHQ, Cheltenham, about proposed changes to employees' terms and conditions of employment. Although there had never been any formal agreement as to this consultation, this was 'the way things were done'. The government decided to change the employees' conditions by removing their right to trade union membership, and purported to do so without consulting the unions first. The unions challenged the government's action, and the House of Lords held that the unions did indeed have a legitimate expectation, based on the past practice of consultation, that they would be consulted before any major alteration to employees' conditions, such as the removal of the right to trade union membership. However, on the facts, it was held that this entitlement to consultation was defeated by national security considerations.

Identifying a past practice which gives rise to a legitimate expectation is not always easy. It is important to resist the temptation to conclude that a legitimate expectation exists merely because something has occurred more than once in the past. In *GCHQ*, it was not merely the fact that the unions had been consulted in the past that gave rise to the expectation, but rather the practice, combined with the general recognition of all involved that that was the 'way things were done'. In contrast, in *R v Secretary of State for the Environment ex p Kent* (1988), a past practice did not give rise to a legitimate expectation. There, a person who was affected by someone else's planning application was not notified of either the council hearing of the application, nor of the subsequent appeal to the Secretary of State. The council had, in the past, notified people of hearings and appeals relating to applications affecting them. The court held, however, that there was no legitimate expectation of such notification; the mere fact that the council had notified people in the past was not sufficient.

These examples demonstrate some further characteristics of legitimate expectations which we can summarise:

(a) *The express assurance or the conduct which gives rise to the expectation does not need to be personally directed at the individual applicant.* It is enough that the expectation is directed at a group of people of whom the applicant is one. Thus, for example, in *Shiu*, the applicant was one of a group (alleged illegal immigrants) at whom the circular was directed. In each case, the question is: was it reasonable, or legitimate, for the individual applicant to rely on the representation?

(b) In the ordinary case, *it is not necessary for the individual applicant to demonstrate that he has relied upon the representation or assurance to his detriment before he can rely upon a legitimate expectation.* In *Shiu*, for example, there was no evidence that the applicant had done, or had not done, anything in reliance upon the announcement of government policy; similarly in the other cases. This is an important difference between the doctrine of legitimate expectation and the private law concept of estoppel, where detrimental reliance is ordinarily required. Indeed, it is not even clear that it is necessary, in order to establish a legitimate expectation, to show that the applicant was aware of the relevant representation or assurance. In the Australian case of *Minister of Ethnic Affairs v Teoh* (1995), the High Court of Australia held that the applicant did not have to show that he was aware of the international treaty upon which the expectation was founded, nor that he personally entertained the expectation: it was enough that the expectation was reasonable.

Teoh illustrates one other facet of the doctrine; namely, its potential power and width of application. Legitimate expectations are not confined to specific promises or representations in defined policy contexts. Rather, they may have potential effects for a great many recipients across a wide range of individual circumstances. In *Teoh*, for example, the court held that the ratification of a treaty by the Australian Government created a legitimate expectation that executive government and its agencies would act in accordance with the treaty provisions, even though the treaty had not been incorporated into national law. An individual was therefore entitled to be consulted before the government treated him in a way which was not in accordance with the treaty (compare Lester (Lord), 'Government compliance with international human rights law: a new year's legitimate expectation' [1996] PL 187).

14.3 Distinguishing legitimate expectations from the right to a fair hearing

We have now looked at two different ways by which a person may become entitled to a hearing before a decision adverse to him or her is taken. First, an entitlement may arise by virtue of the rules of natural justice/fairness (examined in Chapter 13). Secondly, the person may be entitled to a hearing by virtue of a legitimate expectation which they hold. Both these routes to a fair hearing depend, in the final analysis, upon the concept of 'fairness'. The doctrine of legitimate expectation is often described as being a facet of the public decision maker's general duty of fairness: 'the doctrine is rooted in the ideal of fairness' (*per* Laws J in *R v Secretary of State for Transport ex p Richmond-upon-Thames LBC* (1994)). It is for this reason that we have included it as a ground of review under the head of 'procedural impropriety'.

However, it is very important to distinguish between these two different routes to a fair hearing, because within the general concept of fairness, they are based on quite different arguments. A hearing flowing from the rules of natural justice arises because the right or interest which the applicant seeks to claim or protect is considered so important that it merits protection (in the form of a hearing) before it is taken away or not granted (for example, in *Ridge v Baldwin*, the applicant was entitled to a hearing because of the effect of the decision on his livelihood and reputation). What is crucial is that the hearing is granted because of *the importance of the interest affected*. By contrast, the doctrine of legitimate expectation does not generate an entitlement to a hearing because of the importance of the interest, but simply because of the *way in which the decision maker has acted – because he has encouraged the expectation*.

The best way to appreciate this distinction is to look at a case which involves both natural justice and a legitimate expectation. In *R v Great Yarmouth BC ex p Botton Brothers* (1987), the applicants were amusement arcade owners. They claimed that they should have been permitted to make representations to the council before it granted planning permission for a new amusement arcade – they feared that the new arcade would reduce their own custom. The Divisional Court held, first, that the applicants did not have a legitimate expectation to a hearing. The council had never made an express promise of a hearing, and there was no past practice in the *GCHQ* sense of the term. Thus, there was nothing upon which a legitimate expectation could be founded. However, the court went on to find that the council was in breach of its duty to give the arcade owners an opportunity to make representations. It reasoned that, because they would be substantially prejudiced by the new arcade, which would have a potentially serious effect on their livelihoods, they were entitled, in the unusual circumstances of the case, to a fair hearing before the decision was taken. The entitlement to a hearing thus arose from the rules of natural justice, not from the doctrine of legitimate expectation.

14.4 Substantive protection of legitimate expectations?

We must now return to the question which we postponed when considering the example of Paul and the MTLB (above, 14.2): can an individual ever rely upon a legitimate expectation to claim not simply an opportunity to make representations, but rather to claim the substantive 'thing' that was promised? In some cases, this question simply does not arise, because the individual was never promised more than a hearing. For example, in *AG of Hong Kong v Ng Yuen Shiu* (1983) (above), the promise was simply that illegal immigrants would be interviewed before they were repatriated; in the *GCHQ* case, the past practice upon which the unions relied was that there had always been consultation before changes were made to employees' conditions of employment. In such cases, the substance of the legitimate expectation was only ever of a hearing or of consultation, and so, if successful, the individual is obviously only entitled to a hearing.

Sometimes, however, the assurance or promise upon which the alleged legitimate expectation is based is not of a hearing, but of a 'substantive benefit'. For example, in *R v Secretary of State for the Home Department ex p Khan* (1984), the Home Secretary had issued a circular specifying the criteria upon which he would exercise his discretion to allow parents to bring a foreign child to the UK for adoption. The circular specified four conditions which intending adoptive parents would have to satisfy. The Khans fulfilled all the four conditions, but were still refused permission to bring a child to the UK for adoption, the Home Secretary turning them down for a reason which was not contained in the circular. The Court of Appeal held that the circular gave the Khans a legitimate expectation that entry decisions for such children would be made in accordance with the circular; that is, that the Home Secretary would not refuse entry for a reason not contained in the circular.

But the court was then faced with the question of what remedy it could grant. If the doctrine of legitimate expectation is merely procedural, then it would follow that the Khans would only be entitled to a *hearing* before the Home Secretary disappointed their expectation; that is, they would get a chance to persuade him not to refuse their application for a reason not contained in the circular (but he could go on to do just that if he was not persuaded by them). The Khans argued, however, that they were entitled to a *substantive* remedy; in other words, to an order from the court restraining the Home Secretary from refusing their application for a reason not contained in the circular. This would be, in effect, to force the Home Secretary to apply the circular.

You might think that there is a major difficulty with the Khan's argument. If the Home Secretary was forced by the court to apply his own circular, without even the power to depart from it if he considered the case to be exceptional, would he not thereby have unlawfully fettered his own discretion (see above, 12.6)? The Home Secretary might appear to be in an impossible position; accused of fettering his discretion if he automatically followed his policy; accused of breaching a legitimate expectation if he did not! This might make it impossible for any public decision maker to adopt a policy.

The Court of Appeal in *Khan* adopted a middle course. It held, by a majority, that the Home Secretary ought not to have disappointed the Khan's legitimate expectation as he did, and quashed the decision refusing entry. In an important passage, Parker LJ stated:

> ... the Secretary of State, if he undertakes to allow in persons if certain conditions are satisfied, should not in my view be entitled to resile from that undertaking *without affording interested persons a hearing, and then only if the overriding public interest demands it* ... The Secretary of State is, of course, at liberty to change the policy but, in my view, vis à vis the [holder of an existing legitimate expectation], the new policy can only be implemented after such a recipient has been given a full and serious consideration whether there is some overriding public interest which justifies a departure from the procedures stated in the letter.

The decision in *Khan* therefore did two things:

(a) it allowed a measure of substantive protection to substantive legitimate expectations: it held that a decision maker cannot depart from an assurance previously given (whether contained in a policy or elsewhere) unless he can point to overriding public interest reasons for doing so;

(b) it sought to avoid conflict with the rule against the fettering of discretion by ensuring that a decision maker *can*, in exceptional cases, depart from the legitimate expectation.

The decision in *Khan* (which itself was not unanimous) has been followed by a number of cases which have continued to grapple with the boundaries, and indeed the concept, of the substantive legitimate expectation. The number of decisions which have unambiguously endorsed the doctrine are still – more than 15 years after Khan – remarkably few.

In *R v Home Secretary ex p Ruddock* (1987), various officers of the Campaign for Nuclear Disarmament discovered that their telephones had been tapped by the security services. They contended that the interceptions were ordered by the Home Secretary in breach of their legitimate expectation that interceptions would only be ordered when certain criteria published in a government circular were met. The Divisional Court held:

(a) that the doctrine of legitimate expectation was *not* restricted to cases where the expectation was merely of a hearing, or of consultation;

(b) that the applicants did have a legitimate expectation that the Home Secretary would only authorise interceptions where the criteria set out in the published circular had been met; but

(c) that, on the facts, there was no evidence that the Home Secretary had deliberately flouted the criteria.

This is a case where obviously there could be no 'procedural' protection of the legitimate expectation: one could not imagine a court ordering the Home Secretary to consult with the applicants before he authorised the tapping of their telephones. The case did not, however, raise the more difficult question of whether the Home Secretary was entitled to change his policy as embodied in the circular.

In *R v Inland Revenue Comrs ex p Preston* (1985), the Revenue had agreed with the applicant that it would not press certain tax demands against him if he abandoned certain claims for tax relief. Later, when it was too late for applicant to claim the reliefs, the Revenue changed its mind and sought to reinstate the claims against him. Preston challenged the claims as an 'abuse of power'. The House of Lords held that, in principle, it would be an unfairness amounting to an abuse of power for the Revenue not to honour its undertaking – but that, on the facts, the applicant had not been entirely open with the Revenue at the time that the earlier agreement was made, and therefore the Revenue was justified in going back on its word.

It should be noted that the term 'legitimate expectation' was not used at all in their Lordships' judgments; the ground of review which succeeded was described as 'abuse of power'. Nevertheless, commentators have pointed out that, in essence, Preston was arguing that he had a legitimate expectation (based on an express promise: the Revenue's agreement) that he would not be pursued for the tax claims (a substantive expectation), and the House of Lords in effect found that such a claim was in principle valid, but that, on the facts, his expectation was not 'legitimate' because of his non-disclosure. Thus, in principle, *ex p Preston* would appear to support the concept of a substantive legitimate expectation, even though the term was not mentioned in the case. Indeed, the decision was followed in *R v Inland Revenue Comrs ex p MFK Underwriting Agencies Ltd* (1990), where the Divisional Court did use the language of 'legitimate expectations'.

On the other hand, the House of Lords has more recently upheld and followed *ex p Preston* without mentioning the doctrine of legitimate expectation, and analysing the position solely in terms of 'abuse of power' (*Matrix-Securities Ltd v Inland Revenue Comrs* (1994)). And the Court of Appeal in *R v Inland Revenue Comrs ex p Unilever* (1996) preferred, in finding that a settled past practice by the IRC of allowing Unilever to file tax claims late precluded the IRC from refusing a claim simply on the basis that it was filed late, to rest its decision upon grounds of *Wednesbury* unreasonableness rather than a straightforward legitimate expectation.

A number of recent decisions have considered whether the doctrine of substantive expectation is available in the context of changes of government policy. In *R v Ministry of Agriculture, Fisheries and Foods ex p Hamble Fisheries*

(Offshore) Ltd (1994), fishermen who had purchased two small boats under the expectation that they could (under government policy) transfer the boats' fishing licences to one larger vessel claimed a substantive legitimate expectation when that policy was changed to prevent them doing so. Sedley J rejected the claim, on the basis that the fishermen could not have a legitimate expectation that the minister would not change his policy. The judge suggested, however, that where a respondent claims to be entitled to change or depart from a policy which is relied upon by an applicant as giving rise to a substantive legitimate expectation, the court should perform a balancing exercise to determine whether or not it was 'legitimate' for the applicant to rely upon the policy in the particular circumstances.

This approach was, however, overruled by the Court of Appeal in *R v Secretary of State for the Home Department ex p Hargreaves* (1997). In this case, prisoners sought to rely upon a written 'compact' signed by a representative of the prison governor as founding a substantive expectation that they would become entitled to home leave after having served only a third of their sentences. The Home Secretary had, after the date of the compact, altered the policy so that home leave was only available after half the sentence had been served. The Court of Appeal rejected the application, holding (*inter alia*) that the approach of Sedley J in *ex p Hamble* was 'heresy'. Where a substantive, rather than a procedural expectation is claimed, it is for the decision maker, not the court, to judge whether or not that expectation should be protected or whether the public interest necessitates the overriding of the interest, subject only to the court's control on grounds of perversity or irrationality (upholding another first instance decision in *R v Secretary of State for Transport ex p Richmond-upon-Thames LBC* (1994)).

However, the position has changed once again, following the very recent decision of the Court of Appeal in *R v North and East Devon Health Authority ex p Coughlan* (1999). Here, the Court of Appeal disapproved of the criticisms of *ex p Hamble* expressed by the Court in *ex p Hargreaves* (pointing out that they wcre *obiter*), and embarked upon an extensive and important review of the development of the substantive legitimate expectation. In particular, the Court relied upon *Preston* and the 'abuse of power' cases to hold that, where an individual holds a 'substantive' legitimate expectation (at least if it is personally directed at the individual), it is for the court to decide whether it would be an abuse of power for the respondent to disappoint the expectation or whether the respondent has demonstrated sufficient reasons of overriding public interest. The court's decision is not limited to ensuring that the respondent has acted reasonably in the *Wednesbury* sense; rather, the court has to weigh the matter as a substantive question of fairness.

Ex p Hargreaves and *ex p Richmond* clearly appeared to signal a more restrictive approach to the substantive legitimate expectation (for a commentary, see Forsyth, C [1997] PL 375), whereas *ex p Coughlan* suggests precisely the opposite. However, it should be borne in mind that *ex p Hargreaves* was a case concerned with whether the minister was entitled to *change* his policy, so as to affect those already in prison and, furthermore, to change his policy generally, rather than disappointing the individual expectations of the applicants. As such, it does not appear that the decision in *Hargreaves* is inconsistent with *Coughlan*, although the reasoning plainly is. To seek to sum up what is still an unsettled area:

(a) where a public authority has created a legitimate expectation of a substantive benefit, by express promise or past practice, then in principle it appears that (subject to what follows), that expectation may be 'substantively protected' (*ex p Khan*; *ex p Ruddock*; *Preston*) – that is, the public authority can be compelled to fulfil that expectation;

(b) no individual can legitimately expect the discharge of public duties to stand still, or that policies will not change (*Hamble*). Where a public authority decides to change its policy, an individual will not normally have a legitimate expectation to be dealt with under the old policy, subject only to the requirement that the change of policy be rational and not perverse (*Hargreaves*). The position may be different, however, if the individual has been given a particular promise of continued treatment under the old policy (*ex p Coughlan*);

(c) where a public decision maker has adopted a policy, then a person affected by that policy has a substantive legitimate expectation that, while the policy remains in existence, he or she will be treated in accordance with its terms, and this expectation can be substantively enforced (*ex p Ruddock*). Similarly, a promise that an existing state of affairs will continue may generate a substantive expectations (*Coughlan*). A respondent may, however, be permitted to disappoint such an expectation where it can demonstrate that there is an 'overriding public interest' that it be allowed to depart from the policy. Whether the existence of an 'overriding public interest' is ultimately a question for the decision maker (subject to rationality: *Hargreaves*) or for the court (*Khan/Hamble*) is not entirely clear, although *Coughlan*, as the most recent decision at Court of Appeal level, certainly suggests the latter;

(d) in any event, where a decision maker claims to be entitled to depart from an existing policy on grounds of 'overriding public interest', it may well be that fairness requires that the affected individual should be consulted before the policy is changed (*ex p Richmond* (1994), p 596b–c; *Khan*). This point was not specifically addressed in *Hargreaves*;

(e) the existence of the entire doctrine of substantive expectation still, however, awaits endorsement by the House of Lords. In the taxation cases which have reached the Lords, there has been no inclination to adopt the language of the substantive expectation.

GROUNDS OF JUDICIAL REVIEW III: LEGITIMATE EXPECTATION

A legitimate expectation always arises from the conduct of the decision maker, and is, thus, quite distinct from the fair hearing considered in Chapter 13, which is based upon an individual's protectable rights or interests (see above, 13.3). The legitimate expectation arises (*per* Lord Fraser in *GCHQ*) either from:

(a) an *express promise* given by the decision maker; or from

(b) the *existence of a regular past practice which the claimant can reasonably expect to continue* (this does not mean any past practice, but one which is sufficiently well established).

If such a legitimate expectation exists, then general principles of fairness will ordinarily mean that a decision maker cannot disappoint the expectation, at least without offering the applicant a hearing ('a *procedural expectation*'), and sometimes even then ('*substantive protection*').

The legitimate expectation does not depend for its enforcement upon the applicant proving:

(a) that the express assurance or conduct which gave rise to the expectation was 'personally directed' at him or her (that is, a general policy is sufficient);

(b) that he or she has relied upon the representation to his or her detriment.

If a person has a legitimate expectation of a *substantive benefit* (that is, if the public authority promises the person not simply 'a hearing', but rather that he or she will receive a benefit), then the court may offer substantive protection of the legitimate expectation by restraining the public authority from acting otherwise than in accordance with that expectation. However:

(a) a public authority is ordinarily entitled to change its policy; normally an individual cannot have a legitimate expectation that he or she will be unaffected by such a change of policy (*ex p Hamble* (1994); *ex p Hargreaves* (1997)), subject only to the authority establishing the rationality of the change and subject to any particular promise to the applicant (*ex p Coughlan* (1999)). There may be a right to be consulted over such a change: *ex p Richmond* (1994), p 596b–c; not addressed in *ex p Hargreaves*;

(b) a substantive expectation that an existing policy will be applied in an individual case may be protected unless the public authority can demonstrate that there is an 'overriding public interest' that it be allowed to depart from the policy, and that it has consulted (*Khan* (1984)). It may be that the judgment of public interest is, ultimately, for the decision maker subject to establishing rationality (*Hargreaves*), but the better view appears to be that it is a matter for the court to determine on grounds of fairness (*Coughlan*);

(c) this is a new development, and is still potentially vulnerable to a reconsideration of the law by the House of Lords.

CHAPTER 15

GROUNDS OF JUDICIAL REVIEW IV: IRRATIONALITY

15.1 Introduction

In this chapter, we examine the principles governing the ground of review which Lord Diplock, in the *GCHQ* case (*R v Minister for the Civil Service ex p Council of Civil Service Unions* (1985)), called 'irrationality'. In the broadest of terms, we can characterise this head as involving review of the *substance of the decision (or rule) challenged*; in other words, review (however limited) of the merits of the decision or rule. Judges have, in the past, been very reluctant to concede that this ground of review does involve a judgment of the merits of the decision; indeed, to a cynic's eye, the courts appear sometimes to have almost deliberately declined to clarify the basis upon which they do or do not intervene. As we shall see, one important task in this chapter is to distinguish what judges say from what they actually do.

It is helpful to highlight at the outset two fundamental issues which run throughout the chapter. The first concerns the *level of scrutiny* which the courts exercise when reviewing for irrationality: that is, *what degree of irrationality or unreasonableness must be shown before the court will quash a decision?* As we shall see, it is not enough that a judge thinks that he or she would have come to a different conclusion if he or she rather than the decision maker had been responsible for the decision. Something 'more extreme' is required before the court will be prepared to intervene. But how extreme? Is there any way of defining it, or, at least, is there any agreed formulation against which one can measure the rationality or reasonableness of the decision? And is the standard always the same, or is scrutiny more 'intense' in some circumstances (for example, where fundamental human rights are at stake) than in others?

The second issue is even more basic: *what is it that an applicant must show is irrational or unreasonable in order to establish a basis for judicial review?* Usually, the answer is simply 'the decision' or 'the result' itself: the court may decide that the conclusion which the decision maker reached (or the rule which the authority has enacted) is so unreasonable or irrational that it may be quashed. But there is another possible route by which an applicant may establish irrationality. If the process by which the decision maker has arrived at the decision is irrational (for example, tossing a coin), then the court may quash the decision even if the decision itself is one which, if it had been reached by a normal process of decision making, would not inherently be irrational or unreasonable.

It is worth considering a little further the difference between these two types of irrationality at this early stage.

(a) a classic example of a decision which is, of itself, 'inherently' irrational or unreasonable was suggested by Warrington LJ in *Short v Poole Corporation* (1926) (quoted by Lord Greene MR in his landmark judgment in *Associated Provincial Picture Houses Ltd v Wednesbury Corporation* (1948)), namely, a decision to dismiss a red haired teacher on the ground that she has red hair. But while Warrington LJ's example is relatively straightforward, it does give rise to some difficult questions. In particular, what are the principles upon which the courts act in holding certain decisions or rules to be 'irrational' or 'unreasonable'? At times, the courts simply appear to operate on an 'instinctive' basis: they 'know' when a decision is so perverse that they can strike it down for irrationality. We must try to identify principles upon which the judges act (even if they are not articulated), and we will therefore need to look at principles such as proportionality and certainty;

(b) irrationality of the *'process'* by which a decision was reached may be established in a number of ways. We have already encountered some of them in earlier chapters. For example, the process by which a decision is reached may be held to be irrational if a decision maker has taken into account a consideration which is so irrelevant that no reasonable decision maker could have considered it (compare above, 12.4 on irrelevant considerations). In Chapter 12, we focused on considerations which the courts found were irrelevant because they were contrary to the express or implied meaning of the legislation; the court may, on the other hand, conclude simply that the consideration taken into account is so unreasonable that no reasonable decision maker could have entertained it. Again, a decision which is reached in *bad faith* is sometimes described as being irrational; this may overlap with review for bias, considered above, 13.7. The dividing line between a challenge for irrationality and a challenge on other grounds may not, therefore, be as clear cut as first appears.

15.2   Judicial review of the 'merits'?

In Chapter 11, we contrasted judicial review, which is a supervisory jurisdiction ensuring the *legality* of public law decisions, with an appellate jurisdiction in which the court may be concerned with the *merits* of the decision under challenge (above, 11.3.1–11.3.3). It is frequently suggested that judicial review for irrationality infringes this distinction (or, more forceful critics would say, completely undermines it), because review for irrationality does involve a scrutiny of the merits of the decision.

As we noted earlier, defenders of the *'ultra vires'* theory do have an answer to this criticism. Review for irrationality, they would admit, may involve some scrutiny of the merits of the decision (although not, perhaps, in cases of irrationality challenges to the decision making *process*). It is, in fact, only a 'light' degree of scrutiny, because, as we shall see, the court will not intervene simply because it would have come to a different decision; it will only intervene if the decision is irrational. But even this 'light' level of scrutiny is explicable by the *ultra vires* theory, they would say: the court intervenes because there is a *presumption* that Parliament cannot have intended, in conferring the decision making power or rule making power upon the public body challenged, to have allowed that power to be exercised in an irrational or unreasonable way. Hence, if the judge comes to the conclusion that the decision or rule is irrational or unreasonable, then it is outside the powers conferred on the decision maker by Parliament and can be quashed. The power to review for irrationality is, therefore, explicable in the terms of the ultra vires theory; it is part of a system of review.

We noted, in Chapter 11, that this explanation can be criticised for its artificiality (above, 11.4.1). However, it should be noted that judges do take the 'traditional' explanation seriously. In cases with a high profile, particularly with a political dimension, judges frequently emphasise that their view of the merits of the decision under challenge is quite irrelevant to the case before them; that they are simply charged with assessing the legality of the decision. But this will only remain true, at a practical level, for so long as review for irrationality remains a 'light touch' scrutiny. If the court intervened every time it found a decision 'a little unreasonable', or every time the court would have come to a different decision from the decision maker, the judicial disclaimer would soon ring obviously hollow. The courts therefore have a strong interest in limiting the intrusiveness of review for irrationality; of restricting it to an 'extreme case' remedy. This, in general terms, is what happens. In practice, it is rare for review on the ground of irrationality to succeed. And it is extremely rare for an applicant to succeed purely on the ground of irrationality; where irrationality succeeds, it is normally in conjunction with another ground of review. Whilst irrationality is an important ground of review, its modest practical significance should be borne in mind.

15.3 *Wednesbury* unreasonableness

The traditional starting place for a consideration of this ground of review is the judgment of Lord Greene MR in *Associated Provincial Picture Houses Ltd v Wednesbury Corporation* (1948). The case involved a challenge by APPH to a condition imposed by Wednesbury Corporation upon a cinema licence, that no children under 15 should be admitted to Sunday performances. The corporation had a wide power to impose conditions upon licenses 'as the authority think fit'. APPH challenged the condition upon several grounds, one of which being that it was unreasonable. In his judgment, Lord Greene MR considered the nature of a challenge for unreasonableness:

It is true to say that if a decision on a competent matter is *so unreasonable that no reasonable authority could ever have come to it*, then the courts can interfere. That, I think, is quite right, but to prove a case of that kind would require something overwhelming ... It may be possible to say that although the local authority have kept within the four corners of the matters which they ought to consider, *they have nevertheless come to a conclusion so unreasonable that no reasonable authority could ever have come to it*. In such a case ... I think the court can interfere (emphasis added).

This formulation describes what has come to be known as '*Wednesbury* unreasonableness', after the name of the case. It was, for many years, adopted as (and, some would argue, still is) the best characterisation of this ground of review. It is not enough, to succeed on this ground, to convince a judge that the decision is unreasonable; instead, it must be shown that the decision is *so unreasonable that no reasonable decision maker could ever have come to it*. Of course, as a definition of unreasonableness it is tautologous, because it defines unreasonableness in terms of itself. But it does, in practice, indicate that 'unreasonable' means 'extremely unreasonable', or, as Lord Greene said, 'overwhelming'. What it does not do is to give any indication of any principled basis of assessing whether a decision is so unreasonable that this high hurdle of '*Wednesbury* unreasonableness' has been met.

Two further points should be made about the *Wednesbury* case. First, Lord Greene, in his judgment, also considered in general terms the different grounds of judicial review, setting out a list of different heads of challenge. This list is sometimes referred to as 'the *Wednesbury* catalogue', and the grounds of review are sometimes still referred to collectively as 'the *Wednesbury* principles'. It is important to distinguish these general references from the concept of *Wednesbury* unreasonableness, with which we are dealing here.

Secondly, it is worth bearing in mind the actual decision in the *Wednesbury* case. The court decided that the condition imposed by the corporation could not be said to be unreasonable in the sense set out by Lord Greene MR, and it therefore refused to overturn the condition. Whether the result of the case would be the same if the facts were repeated today is a different question; this is a useful reminder that caution is required in citing older cases as authority in this area. Standards of reasonableness, and even standards of 'overwhelming' unreasonableness, may change from generation to generation. Perhaps the best illustration of this is the even earlier decision of *Roberts v Hopwood* (1925), which involved a challenge to the decision of Poplar Borough Council to pay its employees, both male and female, an equal wage, and to set that wage at a rate above the 'market' rate of pay. The House of Lords held that the decision was not reasonable; there was 'no rational proportion between the rates of wages ... and the rates at which they would be reasonably remunerated'. Lord Atkinson made his view of the merits clear, criticising the council for 'allow[ing] themselves to be guided in preference by some eccentric principles of socialistic philanthropy, or by a feminist ambition to secure the equality of the sexes in the matter of wages in the world of labour'. You may well consider that the decision is of dubious authority today; indeed, compare *Pickwell v Camden LBC* (1983), where Ormrod LJ was of the view that an allegedly overgenerous wage settlement with striking employees by Camden was 'a matter for the electorate at the next election', and not a ground for review of the decision.

15.4   Irrationality

As we have noted (above, 11.4), in the *GCHQ* case, Lord Diplock preferred the term 'irrationality' to '*Wednesbury* unreasonableness'. He stated that irrationality

> applies to a decision which is so outrageous in its defiance of logic or of accepted moral standards that no sensible person who had applied his mind to the question to be decided could have arrived at it. Whether a decision falls within this category is a question that judges by their training and experience would be well equipped to answer, or else there would be something badly wrong with our judicial system ... 'Irrationality' can now stand upon its own feet as an accepted ground on which a decision may be attacked by judicial review [pp 410–11].

An important element of this definition is Lord Diplock's recognition that the test involves an assessment of both the *logic* which led to the decision, and the *moral standards* which it embodies. Some judges have, however, been less than welcoming to the adoption of the word 'irrationality' itself. In *R v Devon CC ex p G* (1988), Lord Donaldson MR expressed a preference for the old term '*Wednesbury* unreasonable':

> I eschew the synonym of 'irrational', because, although it is attractive as being shorter than '*Wednesbury* unreasonable' and has the imprimatur of Lord Diplock in [the *GCHQ* case], it is widely misunderstood by politicians, both local and national, and even more by their constituents, as casting doubt on the mental capacity of the decision maker, a matter which in practice is seldom, if ever, in issue.

Lord Donaldson's point is that the term 'irrational' surely implies a lack, or absence, of rational justification for the decision under attack. This may be a good description of some unreasonable decisions – for example, it will cover the decision maker who consults an astrologer, or spins a coin (examples given by Diplock LJ, as he then was, in *R v Deputy Industrial Injuries Commissioner ex p Moore* (1965)). But there are other decisions which might be described as unreasonable, even though the decision maker has acted in a deliberate and 'coldly rational' manner. For example, in *Backhouse v Lambeth LBC* (1972), the council attempted to avoid a requirement that it increase rents generally in its area by loading the whole of the required increase onto a single property (on which the rent was increased from £7 to £18,000 per week), while leaving all the other properties with unchanged rents. While such a decision may be held to be unreasonable, it is perhaps not accurate to describe it as irrational.

Thus, the term 'irrational', while frequently used by judges, has by no means been universally adopted. The phrase '*Wednesbury* unreasonableness' is still in use, and has been joined by other formulations; it has been suggested that a decision is reviewable if, for example, it can be said that 'the public body, either consciously or unconsciously, are acting perversely' (*per* Lord Brightman in *R v Hillingdon LBC ex p Puhlhofer* (1986)), or (even) if the decision provokes the reaction, 'My goodness, that is certainly wrong!' (*per* May LJ in *Neale v Hereford and Worcester CC* (1986)).

15.5 Substantive principles of review?

There have been a number of attempts to formulate 'substantive principles' which underlie and explain review for irrationality; see, for example, Jowell, J and Lester (Lord), 'Beyond *Wednesbury*: substantive principles of administrative law' [1987] PL 368, and Peiris, GL, '*Wednesbury* unreasonableness: the expanding canvas' [1987] CLJ 53. Jowell and Lester have emphasised the advantages of developing such principles:

> The recognition and application of substantive principles would satisfy the need in a fast developing area of law for clarity and coherence. Far from encouraging judges to meddle with the merits of official decisions, it would we believe promote consideration of the proper role of the courts in the growing common law of public administration. It would also enable the courts to strengthen the protection of fundamental human rights against the misuse of official discretion without usurping legislative or executive powers [pp 368–69].

Until recently, however, the courts have been reluctant to take up this invitation, perhaps because 'clarity and coherence' of reasoning, while desirable in principle, may, in fact, expose judges more readily to the charge that they are intervening in the merits of decisions. It is, therefore, sometimes necessary to read between the lines of the decisions, rather than looking for clear statements of principle. Recently, however, one may detect a greater judicial readiness to accept and articulate the reasoning behind the concept of irrationality. This has gone hand in hand with a growing debate as to the appropriate intensity of review, as forecast in the last sentence of the passage quoted above; there has been increasing judicial recognition that heightened scrutiny is appropriate in cases engaging fundamental rights.

15.5.1 Decisions affecting fundamental human rights

Is a rule or decision more susceptible to review for irrationality if it impinges upon important rights of the individual affected? In such circumstances, is the decision subject to 'heightened scrutiny'? As a matter of common sense, it is surely right that in deciding whether a decision or rule is unreasonable, it is inevitable that one of the factors which must be taken into account is the effect which that decision or rule is likely to have. We will explore this further when considering the concept of proportionality (below, 15.6), but, if this is right, then it follows that a decision having a serious impact upon fundamental human rights may be more susceptible to challenge for irrationality/unreasonableness simply because such an important decision requires greater justification.

There are a number of older decisions which provide some support for this line of reasoning. The old case of *Kruse v Johnson* (1898) involved a challenge to a bylaw which sought to prohibit singing 'in any public place or highway within 50 yards of any dwelling house' (a measure clearly impinging upon what would now be described as freedom of speech or expression). Lord Russell CJ held that the courts had the power to strike down even a bylaw for unreasonableness 'if, for instance, they were found to be partial and unequal in their operation between different classes; if they were manifestly unjust; [or] ... if they involved such oppressive or gratuitous interference with the rights of those subject to them ...' – although, on the facts, the court found that the bylaw was not unreasonable. In *R v Secretary of State for Transport ex p de Rothschild* (1989), there was a challenge to the Secretary of State's decision to approve a recommendation of a planning inspector in favour of the compulsory purchase of the applicant's property. Slade LJ appeared to accept that increased judicial scrutiny was appropriate where property rights were affected:

> ... in cases where a compulsory purchase order is under challenge, the draconian nature of the order will itself render it more vulnerable to successful challenge on *Wednesbury* ... grounds unless sufficient reasons are adduced affirmatively to justify it on its merits ... Given the obvious importance and value to land owners of their property rights, the abrogation of those rights would, in the absence of what he perceived to be a sufficient justification on the merits, be a course which surely no reasonable Secretary of State would take [pp 938–39].

And, in the House of Lords decision in *Bugdaycay v Secretary of State for the Home Department* (1987), Lord Bridge stated that the courts are entitled, within limits:

> ... to subject an administrative decision to the more rigorous examination, to ensure that it is in no way flawed, according to the gravity of the issue which the decision determines. The most fundamental of all human rights is the

individual's right to life and when an administrative decision under challenge is said to be one which may put the applicant's life at risk, the basis of the decision must surely call for the most anxious scrutiny.

(Lord Templeman delivered a similar opinion on this point.)

The matter was further considered by the House of Lords in *R v Secretary of State for the Home Department ex p Brind* (1991). This case concerned a directive by the Secretary of State requiring the British Broadcasting Corporation and Independent Broadcasting Authority not to broadcast any matter which included words spoken by persons representing certain organisations proscribed under the Prevention of Terrorism (Temporary Provisions) Act 1984 (such as the IRA and Sinn Fein). The directive was challenged by journalists who argued (*inter alia*) that it involved a significant infringement of the right of freedom of expression, and that it was *Wednesbury* unreasonable and disproportionate. One question which arose was as to the 'intensity' of scrutiny appropriate in a case where fundamental human rights were at issue. It is not at all easy to derive a clear *ratio* from the five speeches of their Lordships. On the one hand, Lord Ackner appeared to deny that the fact that a decision impinged upon fundamental human rights would alter the degree of scrutiny appropriate on a challenge for unreasonableness; he denied that Slade LJ in the *Rothschild* case was in any sense 'increasing the severity of the Wednesbury test' (p 757), although Lord Ackner did accept that 'in a field which concerns a fundamental human right – namely, that of free speech – close scrutiny must be given to the reasons provided as justification for interference with that right'. On the other hand, Lord Bridge (with whom Lord Roskill agreed) appeared to take a more interventionist line:

> I do not accept that ... the courts are powerless to prevent the exercise by the executive of administrative discretions, even when conferred, as in the instant case, in terms which are on their face unlimited, in a way which infringes fundamental human rights ... We are ... perfectly entitled to start from the premise that any restriction of the right to freedom of expression requires to be justified and that nothing less than an important competing public interest will be sufficient to justify it ... We are entitled [to ask] whether a reasonable Secretary of State, on the material before him, could reasonably make [that decision] [pp 748–49].

Lord Templeman, the 'swing' member of the House of Lords on this issue, did not come to a clear conclusion on the question, but did appear to have regard to the fact that human rights were affected by the decision; he stated that 'the courts cannot escape from asking themselves whether a reasonable Secretary of State ... could reasonably conclude that the interference with freedom of expression which he determined to impose was justifiable' (p 751). On the facts, none of the members of the House of Lords thought that the broadcasting ban was a significant infringement of freedom of speech or expression, because there was nothing to prevent the words of the 'banned' person being spoken by an actor (see, also, below, 24.3.6).

Post-*Brind*, the Court of Appeal in *R v Ministry of Defence ex p Smith* (1996) has accepted that the majority judgments in *Brind* are authority for the proposition that 'the more substantial the interference with human rights, the more the court will require by way of justification before it is satisfied that the decision is reasonable in the sense [that it is within the range of responses open to a reasonable decision maker]' (*per* Sir Thomas Bingham MR). On the facts of the case, the court held (with some reluctance) that the ministry's policy that homosexuality was incompatible with service in the armed forces, whilst plainly affecting the human rights of the applicants (discharged servicemen and women) and thus calling for close scrutiny, could not be stigmatised as irrational.

Ex p Smith appears to mark an increasing recognition by the courts that they are entitled to impose a lower threshold of unreasonableness (that is, heightened scrutiny) in cases involving fundamental rights. As Laws J has put it (writing extra-judicially) 'the greater the intrusion proposed by a body possessing public powers over the citizen into an area where his fundamental rights are at stake, the greater must be the justification which the public authority must demonstrate' 'Is the High Court the guardian of fundamental constitutional rights?' [1993] PL 59); see, also, the interventionist approach of Simon Brown LJ in *R v Coventry Airport ex p Phoenix Aviation* (1995). On the other hand, there have been warnings (not least from Lord Irvine: see 'Judges and decision makers: the theory and practice of *Wednesbury* review' [1996] PL 59) that to impose stricter scrutiny is 'to stray far beyond the limits laid down in *Brind*, and to lead the judges into dangerous territory' (p 65). Lord Irvine suggests that the *Brind* judgment, properly understood, holds that the *Wednesbury* threshold is not lowered in fundamental rights cases, and asserts that this limitation should be respected (see, also, *R v Secretary of State for the Environment ex p NALGO* (1993), *per* Neill LJ).

Whatever the outcome of this debate (and it looks increasingly as if the courts are prepared to engage in stricter scrutiny), the courts have, in any event, devised (and been handed) other tools to ensure strict scrutiny of decisions affecting fundamental rights. The most obvious are the powers conferred by the Human Rights Act 1998, considered in Chapter 19. But, in an important parallel development, the courts have, in two recent cases, held that where a statutory power does not clearly authorise the infringement of a fundamental right (whether a treaty right or, simply, an implied domestic 'constitutional right'), the courts will infer that the statutory intent was not to infringe that right. Accordingly, a delegated rule or decision infringing the right will be *ultra vires* the statutory power (*R v Secretary of State for the Home Department ex p Leech (No 2)* (1994); *R v Lord Chancellor ex p Witham* (1997)). This reasoning is perhaps more accurately characterised as falling under the ground of illegality rather than irrationality, but it is worth noting here because its impact is similar to that flowing from the 'heightened scrutiny' cases. Thus, in *ex p Witham*, the Divisional Court held that increased court fees deprived citizens of their constitutional right of access to the courts, and (not being authorised by the Supreme Court Act 1981 to such a level) were *ultra vires* and unlawful.

15.5.2 Decisions subject to reduced scrutiny?

At the other extreme, there appear to be types of decision which the courts are reluctant to scrutinise even on the *Wednesbury* test. In general terms, the courts are particularly chary of involvement in decisions involving questions of resource distribution, and matters of 'high policy'. Normally, the courts will simply dismiss irrationality challenges to such decisions with the minimum of analysis, but, on occasions, the courts have gone further and held that the *Wednesbury* test should not even be applied. In *R v Secretary of State for the Environment ex p Nottinghamshire CC* (1986), the House of Lords had to consider a challenge to a decision of the Secretary of State to reduce the grant paid by central government to Nottinghamshire (because of overspending by the council). The decision to reduce the grant had been approved (as the legislation required) by an affirmative resolution of the House of Commons, and was not only highly 'party political', but was part of a very complex settlement of grants with local authorities throughout the country. Nottinghamshire's submission that the Secretary of State's decision was unreasonable was not even entertained by the House of Lords; Lord Scarman (with whom the rest of the House agreed) held that, where a decision concerned matters of public expenditure, and where it had been approved by resolution of House of Commons, then it was constitutionally improper for the court to entertain a challenge on *Wednesbury* grounds. Instead, a challenge could only succeed if 'the consequences of the [decision] were so absurd that he must have taken leave of his senses'. It is almost inconceivable that a decision which the House of Commons had approved by resolution could fail to pass such a test (see, also, the later decision of the House of Lords in *Hammersmith and Fulham LBC v Secretary of State for the Environment* (1991), approving *Nottinghamshire*).

It does appear, however, that the *Nottinghamshire* principle is only of application in the limited situation where the challenged decision has been approved by resolution of the House of Commons. The courts have recently rejected the submission that there should be reduced scrutiny merely because there is a high policy content (or resource allocation content) to a decision: *R v Ministry of Defence ex p Smith* (1996); cf Irvine (Lord), 'Judges and decision makers: the theory and practice of *Wednesbury* review' [1996] PL 59, pp 65–67.

15.5.3 Other substantive principles of review

Commentators have drawn on European legal principles to put forward other substantive principles of review which, it is suggested, underlie review for *Wednesbury* unreasonableness or irrationality. A principle of equality has been proposed. Jowell and Lester, in the article cited above, suggest that both the principle of legal certainty and the principle of consistency are nascent in our administrative law. The latter principle underlies the concept of the substantive legitimate expectation, which we have already considered in Chapter 14 (see above, 14.4 and, for example, *R v Inland Revenue Comrs ex p Preston* (1985)). It is also beginning to be invoked as a free-standing principle; see, for example, *R v Secretary of State ex p Urmaza* (1996), *per* Sedley J (and can itself be seen (along with legal certainty) as a fundamental human right: see Chapter 22). An example of the former principle, Jowell and Lester suggest, can be seen in the decision of the House of Lords in *Wheeler v Leicester CC* (1985), which concerned a resolution of the council to ban Leicester Rugby Football Club from continuing to use a council-owned ground (pursuant to a statutory power to grant permissions for the use of its sports grounds), because three members of the club had participated in a tour of South Africa. The House of Lords quashed the resolution, at least in part on the basis that it was *Wednesbury* unreasonable; as Lord Templeman put it, 'the club having committed no wrong, the council could not use their statutory powers in the management of their property or any other statutory powers in order to punish the club'. Jowell and Lester suggest that the decision 'could be justified more convincingly than [it was] by spelling out more clearly the notion that legal certainty requires no punishment without the breach of established law' (p 377). This case should be considered in the context of subsequent cases such as *R v Lewisham LBC ex p Shell UK Ltd* (1988) (where Lewisham's decision not to contract with Shell as part of a South African sanctions campaign was held to be unlawful), and *R v Somerset CC ex p Fewings* (1995) (where Somerset's ban on stag hunting on council land was held to be unlawful – although, in this case, the court preferred to base the decision on the ground that Somerset had adopted an improper purpose, rather than on irrationality).

The place of a 'principle of equality' in English law has also recently been considered in some depth, by Laws J in *R v MAFF ex p First City Trading Ltd* (1997). He concluded that the European principle (requiring a substantive justification of unequal treatment) was not a part of domestic law, or the *Wednesbury* test, but did note that 'if a public decision maker were to treat apparently identical cases differently there would no doubt be a *prima facie Wednesbury* case against him, since on the face of it such an approach bears the hallmark of irrationality.' However, he accepted that where an explanation of the unequal treatment was offered, the court would only be entitled to reject it, in the usual way, on grounds of perversity.

15.6 The doctrine of proportionality

As we have noted, Jowell and Lester draw on the jurisprudence of European Community law and the European Convention of Human Rights to suggest substantive principles underlying review for irrationality (see above, 15.5). It is important to remember, however, that the European Convention was not, until the Human Rights Act 1998, part of UK law, save by virtue of treaty obligation (see above, 2.12.1), and European Community law is applicable only in so far as a Community law right is in issue (see below, 18.1). This raises the awkward question (likely to be increasingly awkward post-Human Rights Act) of the extent to which the courts are obliged to use different legal principles according to whether a case falls under 'European' principles. Nowhere is this question starker than in relation to the doctrine of proportionality.

The doctrine of proportionality requires that the means employed by the decision maker to achieve a legitimate aim must be no more than is reasonably necessary – no more than is *proportionate* – to achieve that aim. It is sometimes described as requiring that 'one must not use a sledgehammer to crack a nut', or as requiring that the means adopted are the 'least intrusive' to another's rights sufficient to achieve the aim. The European principle allows a 'margin of appreciation' for the decision maker, but would clearly require judicial intervention in circumstances where the decision would not, on domestic principles, be held to be *Wednesbury* unreasonable or irrational (see, generally, Jowell, J and Lester (Lord), 'Proportionality: neither novel nor dangerous', in Jowell, J and Oliver, D (eds), *New Directions in Judicial Review*, 1988, London: Sweet & Maxwell).

The status of proportionality as a ground of review in UK law (which Lord Diplock, in the *GCHQ* case, had contemplated as a possible future development) was considered by the House of Lords in *R v Secretary of State for the Home Department ex p Brind* (1991) (see above, 15.5.1). The journalists submitted that the directive banning the broadcasting of the voices of members of proscribed organisations was unlawful because it was disproportionate to the legitimate aims of the Secretary of State. Whilst all the members of the House of Lords rejected the argument based on proportionality (not least because they considered that, on the facts, the interference with freedom of speech and expression was minimal), there was a wide variation of approach between their Lordships. Any attempt to summarise the different speeches is difficult, given the ambiguities which exist, but the following propositions can be put forward:

(a) all the members of the House of Lords agreed that reference to the law of the European Convention on Human Rights was only permissible if there was an ambiguity in the relevant domestic legislation (*Garland v British Rail Engineering* (1983)), and agreed that no ambiguity existed where (as in *Brind*) the legislation simply conferred a wide discretion upon the Secretary of State (this must, of course, now be read in the light of the Human Rights Act);

(b) hence, the applicants could not refer to the ECHR. The issue was simply whether proportionality existed in domestic law. Their Lordships were unanimous that proportionality, as a separate doctrine, could not, on the facts of *Brind*, be invoked;

(c) Lords Ackner and Lowry were of the view that proportionality was simply not part of domestic law: 'there appears to me to be at present no basis upon which the proportionality doctrine applied by the European Court can be followed by the courts of this country' (*per* Lord Ackner, p 763);

(d) on the other hand, Lords Bridge and Roskill expressly left open the possibility of the future adoption of the principle in an appropriate case. What sort of case might be appropriate was not indicated;

(e) Lord Templeman expressed no views either way as to the possible future development of the doctrine;

(f) however, all the members of the House of Lords appeared to accept that the test of proportionality, as outlined above, had a role within the confines of *Wednesbury* unreasonableness; that it might be useful as a way of helping to decide whether a decision is irrational or *Wednesbury* unreasonable. Thus, even Lord Ackner asked whether the Secretary of State had, in issuing the directive, 'used a sledgehammer to crack a nut' (the classic description of 'proportionality' reasoning); he commented: 'Of course, that is a picturesque way of describing the *Wednesbury* 'irrational' test. The Secretary of State has in my judgment used no sledgehammer' (p 759).

The use of proportionality in the limited sense envisaged by Lord Ackner and the other members of the House of Lords was clearly assumed to be very different from the more interventionist test applicable under European law. But as UK courts have increasingly used proportionality in this more 'limited' sense – as assisting in '*Wednesbury* scrutiny' – it may increasingly be asked whether the latitude accorded to a decision maker under *Wednesbury* is so different from the margin of appreciation allowed in European law. The 'convergence' of the two principles is, ironically, assisted by the fact that *Wednesbury* scrutiny now appears to require 'heightened scrutiny' in cases affecting fundamental rights (see above, 15.5.1). This development is itself clearly prompted by the philosophy of proportionality: that the more intrusive a decision on the rights of others, the more is called for in terms of justification.

To the extent that proportionality is not fully developed within UK law, domestic judges face the prospect of having to employ the doctrine in cases where a European Community right is in issue or where recourse can be had to the European Convention (see, for example, *Stoke-on-Trent CC v B & Q plc* (1991); *R v Intervention Board ex p ED and F Man (Sugar) Limited* (1986)), but of having to foreswear the principle in other cases, save as an 'aid to construction' in applying the test of *Wednesbury* unreasonableness or irrationality. The divergence will become increasingly marked after the entry into force of the Human Rights Act 1998, which requires courts determining convention rights to take into account Strasbourg jurisprudence (by s 2) (see below, 19.10).

Whilst there is no juridical basis for arguing that merely because the doctrine of proportionality has been imported into cases involving European Community or convention rights, it should, or will, thereby be translated into the common law, it is nevertheless reasonable to suggest that that importation may provide a stimulus for further development of the doctrine in the common law. It would appear that the majority of the House of Lords in *Brind* did leave the door at least a little ajar to further judicial development of the doctrine, and it would also appear that the courts are beginning to push at that door, by way of cases involving both proportionality and 'heightened scrutiny'.

GROUNDS OF JUDICIAL REVIEW IV: IRRATIONALITY

The ground of review known as irrationality involves (to a limited degree) review of the 'substance' or 'merits' of the decision or rule challenged. In the traditional formulation (as set out in the judgment of Lord Greene MR in *Associated Provincial Picture Houses Ltd v Wednesbury Corporation* (1948)), the applicant must show that *the decision is so unreasonable that no reasonable decision maker could ever have come to it* ('*Wednesbury* unreasonableness').

Lord Diplock reformulated the test in the *GCHQ* case, preferring the term '*irrationality*', and describing it as applying to 'a decision which is so outrageous in its defiance of logic or of accepted moral standards that no sensible person who had applied his mind to the question to be decided could have arrived at it'.

Both the terms 'irrationality' and '*Wednesbury* unreasonableness' are still in use – along with 'perversity' (*ex p Puhlhofer* (1986)), and other terminological variations. In practice, it matters little which phrase is used; what is more significant is the 'level of scrutiny' which the courts require.

A decision may be flawed for irrationality *either* because the decision itself (the 'end result') is irrational or unreasonable (for example, the dismissal of the red haired teacher), *or* because the process by which the decision is reached is irrational (tossing a coin or consulting an astrologer). Standards of irrationality may change between generations!

Lord Greene's definition of 'unreasonableness' was (intentionally) tautologous. Academics and judges have attempted to clarify the principles on which the courts act by developing '*substantive principles*' of review, such as the following:

Decisions impinging upon fundamental human rights may be susceptible to 'heightened' scrutiny for irrationality

See *Bugdaycay v Secretary of State for the Home Department* (1987); *R v Secretary of State for the Home Department ex p Brind* (1991) – where the court was divided on the issue; *R v Ministry of Defence ex p Smith* (1996); Jowell, J and Lester (Lord), 'Beyond *Wednesbury*: substantive principles of administrative law' [1987] PL 368. But see also warnings to the contrary: Irvine (Lord), 'Judges and decision makers: the theory and practice of *Wednesbury* review' [1996] PL 59.

Compare decisions construing legislation as not authorising action interfering with fundamental rights: *R v Secretary of State for the Home Department ex p Leech (No 2)* (1994); *R v Lord Chancellor ex p Witham* (1997).

The principle of legal certainty

The law must be accessible and foreseeable; no one should be punished except for breach of an established law); see *Wheeler v Leicester CC* (1985).

The principle of consistency

Compare the doctrine of substantive legitimate expectation, above, 14.4.

The doctrine of proportionality

The means employed by the decision maker to achieve his legitimate aim must be no more than is reasonably necessary – no more than is proportionate – to achieve that aim). The status of the doctrine is uncertain in domestic law after the decision of the House of Lords in *R v Secretary of State for the Home Department ex p Brind* (1991):

(a) it is clear that the European doctrine has not been incorporated into domestic law (although the better view is that the majority of the House of Lords left open the possibility that this could happen by judicial intervention in a future suitable case); but

(b) it would appear that the doctrine is of relevance in assessing whether a decision is *Wednesbury* unreasonable or irrational; if a decision maker uses an excessively large sledgehammer, then the decision may be unreasonable/irrational.

The doctrine must be applied by the domestic courts with full rigour when dealing with a European Community or Convention law right); see *Stoke-on-Trent CC v B & Q plc* (1991); Human Rights Act 1998, s 2. It may well be that the further development of the doctrine in the common law will be stimulated by its use in a European context.

CHAPTER 16

RESTRICTIONS ON REVIEW: OUSTER CLAUSES

16.1 Introduction

Government may want to protect public decision makers from judicial review of their decisions for a number of reasons. In some cases, there may be a pressing need for 'finality in administration'; for example, where a large public project, such as the construction of a motorway, is at risk of being held up by uncertainty during the period in which a person could ordinarily apply for judicial review. In such a case, even the requirement that an application for permission to apply for judicial review be made 'promptly and in any event within three months' (see below, 17.3.1) may be considered too long to leave such a project 'in the air'. Another reason that government may be 'anti-' judicial review may be simply that it believes that the public authority would be better off without the interference of the courts in its decision making process. Bearing in mind that the government is the most frequent respondent to judicial review applications, we might expect this latter train of reasoning not to be uncommon!

One way in which the opportunities to challenge a decision by way of judicial review may be reduced is by providing the applicant with an alternative remedy. Where, for example, there is an appeal from a decision to a tribunal or other 'appellate' body, then, in the ordinary course of events, a person wishing to challenge the decision must avail himself or herself of that statutory appeal rather than seeking judicial review (see below, 17.2). Alternatively, it may be possible to 'divert' people from making a formal challenge to the decision at all, by providing alternative means of redress, such as the ombudsmen (see Chapter 10).

A more radical way of limiting the scope of judicial review is by means of a statutory provision which seeks either to limit or to exclude entirely the right to challenge the decision in the courts. It is these types of provision, often called 'ouster clauses', with which we are concerned in this chapter. The history of the court's attitude towards ouster clauses is a complex one, and even today the law on the subject is far from straightforward. On the one hand, the courts, in dealing with such clauses, are faced with what is often a fairly obvious intention of Parliament – to exclude or limit their power to intervene. On the other hand, the courts are often hostile to ouster clauses on the basis that they present a challenge to the rule of law, because they displace the court's proper constitutional role of scrutinising and regulating the actions of public bodies. It is feared that, if the courts are precluded from adjudicating on the legality of the actions of government departments or other public bodies, there may be no effective check on their actions. It may also constitute a breach of the right of access to a court, which is constitutionally protected both under Art 6 of the ECHR (see Chapter 21) and under the common law (see *R v Lord Chancellor ex p Witham* (1997)). There is, therefore, a general presumption that such clauses have as narrow an ambit as possible. Indeed, the court's restrictive interpretation of some ouster clauses has limited their effect almost to nothing, notwithstanding the clear intention of the parliamentary drafter to the contrary.

The difficulty has been that, in their attempts to avoid the apparent legislative intention of such clauses (that is, that the court's jurisdiction is to be limited or excluded), the courts have developed principles of statutory construction which, if consistently applied, would have *too great* an effect, because they would logically lead the courts to bypass most, or all, ouster clauses entirely. The courts have shied away from such a radical result, which would so obviously flout the intentions of Parliament. There has thus been an uneasy attempt to walk a fine line between the theory and the practice; the result has been apparent, and real, conflicts between different authorities, and distinctions of almost excruciating complexity. Students often have great difficulty with this topic; indeed, some courses avoid the subject altogether. There is some sense in doing so, because, in practice, cases on ouster clauses are comparatively rare; no more than a very few every year, if that. On the other hand, for those who do have to deal with the topic, some path through the minefield is required.

In what follows, we seek to give an overview of the subject, although it not possible in the space available to discuss the full intricacies of even the major decisions. We have divided ouster clauses into two types.

16.2   Two types of ouster clause

Although ouster clauses come in a number of different formulations, there is a broad distinction between two types of clause, which the courts treat in very different ways. On the one hand, there are clauses which do not try to exclude the court's jurisdiction completely, but only seek to *time limit* it by providing for a specified period of time (almost always six weeks) within which any challenge to the decision must be brought; after that time, any challenge is excluded (and there is no discretion to extend time, unlike the time limit for applying for judicial review under Ord 53, considered below, 17.3). On the other hand, there are the so called *total ouster clauses*, which seek to exclude the court's powers entirely, by providing that 'the decision shall not be challenged in any court of law', or some similar formulation.

The history of the two types of ouster clause is very different. Whilst total ousters, often known as 'no *certiorari* clauses', have a statutory pedigree going back centuries, six week ousters are a more recent invention. The first such clause was enacted in s 11 of the Housing Act 1930, and dealt with slum clearance orders; indeed, many early six week ouster clauses were enacted in the context of public works schemes, and were framed to combat difficulties which had arisen following a series of cases in which successful applications for certiorari had been made to quash orders of local authorities, when the schemes concerned had been brought almost into operation, and after considerable expense had been incurred. Since that time, six week ouster clauses have been enacted in a wide variety of statutory contexts; some modern examples of their use being:

(a) s 14 of the Petroleum Act 1987;

(b) s 49 of the Airports Act 1986;

(c) s 18 of the Telecommunications Act 1984;

(d) ss 287, 288 of the Town and Country Planning Act 1990;

(e) s 55 of the Ancient Monuments and Archaeological Areas Act 1979;

(f) Sched 2 to the Highways Act 1980.

We will have to look in some detail at how the courts respond to the two different types of ouster clause, and examine how they distinguish between them. It is worth summarising straight away, however, the end result of the discussion:

(a) the courts will almost invariably give effect to a six week ouster clause. If such a clause provides that a decision may not be challenged in any way after a six week period, then the courts will not entertain a challenge after that period – even, apparently, if the applicant claims that the reason that he or she did not bring a challenge within six weeks was due to bad faith on the part of the decision maker (see *R v Secretary of State for the Environment ex p Ostler* (1976), discussed below);

(b) by contrast, the courts are very unwilling to give effect to a total ouster clause – although there are occasions where the courts have accepted that judicial review is barred by such a clause.

16.3 General principles: the court's attitude to ouster clauses

The court's 'respectful' attitude to ouster clauses is best illustrated by a classic decision of the House of Lords which concerned a six week ouster clause. In *Smith v East Elloe RDC* (1956), Mrs Smith wished to challenge a compulsory purchase order made by the council in respect of her property. She had various grounds of challenge, including an allegation that the order had been procured in bad faith by the clerk of the council. Unfortunately, she did not bring her challenge until almost six years after the order was made; indeed, until after a house on her land had been demolished and new houses had been built. She was therefore met with the argument that her claim could not succeed, because the Acquisition of Land (Authorisation Procedure) Act 1946 (Part IV of Sched 1) provided that:

> 15(1)   If any person aggrieved by a compulsory purchase order desires to question the validity thereof ... on the ground that the authorisation of a compulsory purchase thereby granted is not empowered to be granted under this Act, ... he may, within six weeks from the date on which notice of the confirmation or making of the order ... is first published ... make an application to the High Court ...

> 16   Subject to the [above], a compulsory purchase order ... shall not ... be questioned in any legal proceedings whatsoever.

The House of Lords unanimously held that this six week ouster clause precluded *any* challenge after the six week period had expired – even a challenge on a ground such as bad faith. As Viscount Simonds put it,

> I think that anyone bred in the tradition of the law is likely to regard with little sympathy legislative provisions for ousting the jurisdiction of the court ... But it is our plain duty to give the words of an Act their proper meaning and, for my part, I find it quite impossible to qualify the words of paragraph [16] .... What is abundantly clear is that words are used which are wide enough to cover any kind of challenge which any aggrieved person may think fit to make. I cannot think of any wider words.

It is important to note that the House of Lords did not suggest in *East Elloe* that their decision was dependent upon the fact that para 15 of the Schedule allowed a challenge within a six week period. If you read Lord Simonds' words quoted above, it appears that he would have come to the same conclusion if the legislation had simply contained a *total* ouster clause, framed as in para 16.

However, the decision in *East Elloe* was called into question by another decision of the House of Lords, in the landmark case of *Anisminic v Foreign Compensation Commission* (1969). This case involved a 'total' ouster clause: the Foreign Compensation Act 1950 provided that determinations of the FCC 'shall not be called into question in any court of law.' Anisminic wished to challenge a determination of the FCC on the ground that the FCC had misconstrued the legal effect of the statutory framework under which it operated, and had therefore reached a decision which was a nullity. Could Anisminic avoid the ouster clause? Or did the reasoning of *East Elloe* apply, so that the statutory words were wide enough to exclude 'any kind of challenge'?

The House of Lords held, by a majority, that the ouster clause did not prevent Anisminic from challenging the decision of the FCC. The leading speech of Lord Reid is well worth reading in full, but its essential reasoning can be summarised in a series of propositions. He held:

(a) Anisminic's challenge involved a claim that the FCC had, by misconstruing the statutory framework, acted beyond its powers (that is, 'outside its jurisdiction');

(b) if Anisminic was right, the FCC's decision was therefore a 'nullity' – the determination had no legal effect;

(c) although the ouster clause provided that determinations of the FCC 'shall not be called into question in any court of law', this could have no effect because *the FCC had never made a determination* – it had simply made a purported determination, which was a nullity. Thus, Lord Reid did not *ignore* that statutory wording; rather, he found a way round it, by holding that *there never was a valid determination in respect of which the court's powers could be ousted*. The court was not 'calling into question' a determination; instead, it was pointing out that a determination had never been made.

The reasoning in (c) is clearly the crucial step which enabled the House of Lords to avoid the total ouster clause without simply defying the words of Parliament. But the case left at least two important questions unanswered: which grounds of judicial review, if established, mean that the public authority has acted 'outside its jurisdiction' in the sense of (a) above? All errors? Only misconstructions of law? And what was the status of *East Elloe* after *Anisminic*? The House of Lords, in the latter case, did not overrule *East Elloe*; instead, it purported to distinguish it. But surely the reasoning of Lord Reid at (c) above applies with equal force to the *East Elloe* ouster contained in para 16 of the Schedule of the Acquisition of Land Act: it could be said that the compulsory purchase order was a nullity, and that the court could, therefore, quash the purported purchase order even within the six week period without infringing the ouster's prohibition on 'questioning' any determination. Was *East Elloe*, therefore, impliedly overruled by *Anisminic*?

It is easier to examine these two questions in reverse order.

16.4   Six week ouster clauses

The answer to the second question is quite clear: *East Elloe* has survived *Anisminic,* and the former decision remains good law in respect of six week ouster clauses. The Court of Appeal was given the opportunity to choose between (or to attempt to reconcile) the two decisions in *R v Secretary of State for the Environment ex p Ostler* (1976). In that case, Mr Ostler asked the courts to quash an order authorising the construction of a new road, and associated compulsory purchase orders, on the basis that they were vitiated by a breach of natural justice and by bad faith on the part of the Secretary of State or his Department. As in *East Elloe*, the legislation in question contained a six week ouster clause providing that, after the six week period, the scheme 'shall ... not be questioned in any legal proceedings whatsoever'. And, like Mrs Smith, Mr Ostler had failed to challenge the scheme within six weeks. However, he submitted that at least part of the reason why he had not brought his challenge earlier was that he had been unaware of a secret agreement between the Department and a particular firm. In other words, he blamed the Secretary of State for the fact that he had not brought his challenge within the statutory time limit. The Court of Appeal rejected the argument that *East Elloe* was inconsistent with *Anisminic*. Lord Denning MR (with whom Shaw LJ agreed) advanced a number of distinctions between the two cases, not all of which are totally convincing (indeed, Lord Denning himself later 'recanted' in his book, *The Discipline of Law* (1979)). Perhaps his most important distinction was that whereas Anisminic concerned a total ouster clause, in *East Elloe* (and in *Ostler*):

> ... the statutory provision has given the court jurisdiction to inquire into complaints so long as the applicant comes within six weeks. *The provision is more in the nature of a limitation period than of a complete ouster.*

In other words, Lord Denning was suggesting that a six week ouster is more in the nature of the three month time limit for judicial review applications: simply a stipulation as to the time for bringing a claim, rather than an 'ouster' of the court's jurisdiction. But it may be objected that, while this provides a practical reason for distinguishing the two types of ouster (and, indeed, a potential justification of the constitutional legitimacy of six week ousters), it does not provide a *principled* answer to the question posed above: why is it that Lord Reid's reasoning does not apply to ouster clauses where a six week 'grace period' is allowed? There is no simple answer to this objection. In one sense, Lord Reid's reasoning is just too strong: its logic impels the conclusion that all ouster clauses providing that decisions 'shall not be questioned' or 'are conclusive' are of no effect (as long as the decision in question is a nullity) – whether or not an applicant is afforded a six week period within which to bring a challenge.

Nevertheless, *East Elloe* and *Ostler* have been followed in a number of more recent cases. Thus, in *R v Secretary of State for the Environment ex p Kent* (1988), the applicant was frustrated by a six week ouster clause, even though the reason that he had not challenged the decision in question (a grant of planning permission) within six weeks was that the local council had mistakenly failed to notify him of the application for planning permission! (See also *R v Cornwall CC ex p Huntingdon* (1992)).

The absence of principle in the case law can be illustrated by asking a simple question: what would happen if legislation included a 'one week' ouster clause? Or a 'one day' ouster clause? Presumably, at some point, the courts would conclude that such a provision was no longer 'more in the nature of a limitation period than of a complete ouster', to quote Lord Denning's words – and when that dividing line had been crossed, the court would treat the provision according to the principles governing total ouster clauses (see below, 16.5). But, at present, the basis upon which such a dividing line could be drawn is not clear.

16.5   Total ouster clauses

In relation to total ouster clauses, the reasoning of Lord Reid in *Anisminic* remained undisturbed by *Ostler* and the other six week ouster clauses cases. We therefore need to return to the first of the two questions which we asked at the end of 16.3. Which grounds of judicial review will, if established, lead the court to conclude that the decision in question is a 'nullity', such that Lord Reid's reasoning that 'there never was a decision' can operate? This is the same question that we touched on, in a different context, above, 12.9, where it was asked whether all errors of law are now 'jurisdictional'.

Lord Reid himself did not, in *Anisminic*, provide a formal answer to the question. But he made it clear that his answer would have been a wide one, from the range of examples which he gave:

> There are many cases where, although the tribunal had jurisdiction to enter into the inquiry, it has done or failed to do something in the course of the inquiry which is of such a nature that its decision is a nullity. It may have given its decision in bad faith. It may have made a decision which it had no power to make. It may have failed in the course of the inquiry to comply with the requirements of natural justice. It may in perfect good faith have misconstrued the provision giving it power to act so that it failed to deal with the question remitted to it and decided some question which was not remitted to it. It may have refused to take into account something which it was required to take into account. Or it may have based its decision on some matter which, under the provisions setting it up, it had no right to take into account. I do not intend this list to be exhaustive ...

Lord Reid may not have meant the list to be exhaustive, but, in fact, with the exception of irrationality, it is difficult to think of any head of review which does not fall within Lord Reid's catalogue. He himself clearly did not think that all errors which a authority might make would lead to the decision being a nullity, because he continued the above passage as follows:

> But if [an authority] decides a question remitted to it for decision without committing any of these errors it is as much entitled to decide that question wrongly as it is to decide it rightly.

The difficulty, post-*Anisminic*, has been to identify any errors which fall within this latter category; that is, errors which do not take the authority outside its powers (which are not 'jurisdictional errors'). Without going through the subsequent case law in enormous detail, the following different (and contradictory) views of the law can be suggested.

View 1: All errors of law are jurisdictional; any public law decision which is judicially reviewable takes the decision maker outside its powers

You may remember that we suggested that this is the everyday working assumption of the courts in cases where an ouster clause is not involved (above, 12.9). It was also the view taken by Lord Denning MR in *Pearlman v Governors of Harrow School* (1978). There, the question was whether a challenge to the decision of a county court judge that a central heating system was not a 'structural alteration' for the purposes of the Housing Act 1974 was barred by a provision that 'any determination [of the judge] shall be final and conclusive'. Lord Denning (in the minority of the Court of Appeal on this point) held that the distinction between jurisdictional and non-jurisdictional errors of law was so fine that it could now be 'discarded'; all errors of law were jurisdictional, and, since the judge had (he thought) made an error of law, the Court of Appeal could avoid the ouster clause and quash the decision by holding that there never was a valid 'determination' for the ouster clause to protect.

View 2: There is still, for all public decision makers, a distinction between 'jurisdictional' and 'non-jurisdictional' errors of law

This was the view of the other two members of the Court of Appeal in Pearlman, Lane and Eveleigh LJJ. Unfortunately, the two judges then disagreed as to whether the particular decision before them was or was not jurisdictional! Eveleigh LJ held that the error did take the county court judge outside his powers, and the decision could therefore be quashed (thereby agreeing with Lord Denning in the result), while Lane LJ, dissenting, held that the decision was one on which Parliament had given the judge the power to decide wrongly as well as rightly – and that his decision, therefore, could not be questioned. Lane LJ's view has been supported by the Privy Council in *South East Asia Fire Bricks v Non-metallic Mineral Products Manufacturing Employees Union* (1981), and by the High Court of Australia.

View 3: The compromise position of Lord Diplock in Re Racal Communications Ltd *(1981)*

In the decision of the House of Lords in *Re Racal*, Lord Diplock (with whom Lord Keith agreed), set out a position midway between Lord Denning's and Lane LJ's views in *Pearlman*. He held:

(a) that as regards *administrative tribunals and authorities*, the effect of *Anisminic* is effectively (as Lord Denning said) that any error of law takes such a authority outside its powers; there is no longer any distinction between jurisdictional and non-jurisdictional errors of law;

(b) however, as regards *inferior courts of law* (such as county courts), there was 'no similar presumption'; Parliament may have given an inferior court the power to decide questions of law wrongly. The 'subtle distinctions' between jurisdictional and non-jurisdictional errors of law thus survive in this context. Since *Pearlman* concerned the decision of a county court judge, Lane LJ's dissenting judgment was, on the facts, correct.

The practical reasoning behind Lord Diplock's distinction between administrative bodies and inferior courts is that Parliament is more likely to have intended to leave the ultimate power to adjudicate upon questions of law to a court than to an administrative authority which may not be legally qualified. This has been translated by Lord Diplock into a 'presumption' about the intention of Parliament.

Many students find the above distinctions not only of great complexity theoretically, but confusing practically, because the present state of the law is so uncertain. However, strictly in point of authority, it can now be said that neither view 1 (Lord Denning's view in *Pearlman*) nor view 2 (Lane LJ's approach) have been followed by later decisions. Instead, Lord Diplock's view in *Re Racal* now represents the law. Even though only Lord Keith of the House of Lords explicitly agreed with him in that case (and even though Slade LJ did not accept Lord Diplock's view in the later case of *R v Registrar of Companies ex p Central Bank of India* (1986)), Lord Diplock's view appears to have been approved (*obiter*) by the House of Lords in *R v Hull University Visitor ex p Page* (1992), and followed in *R v Visitors to the Inns of Court ex p Calder* (1993).

One is still left with no clear answer to the question of *how* one identifies those errors of law which an inferior court has the power to decide rightly or wrongly. Lord Diplock, in *Re Racal*, suggested that, where the question at issue is 'an interrelated question of law, fact and degree' (for example, does the installation of central heating count as a 'structural alteration'?), the courts should be slow to hold that Parliament did not intend a county court judge to have the power ultimately to decide the question. Nevertheless, it is difficult not to have some sympathy with the view of Lord Denning in *Pearlman* that, in reality, the tail is wagging the dog:

> So fine is the distinction [between errors within and without jurisdiction] that in truth the High Court has a choice before it whether to interfere with an inferior court on a point of law. If it chooses to interfere, it can formulate its decision in the words: 'The court below had no jurisdiction to decide this point wrongly as it did.' If it chooses not to interfere, it can say: 'The court had jurisdiction to decide it wrongly, and did so.' Softly be it stated, but that is the reason for the difference between the decision of the Court of Appeal in *Anisminic* and the House of Lords.

16.6 'Super-ouster clauses'?

In this chapter, we have not, for reasons of simplicity, distinguished between different types of total ouster clause. On the whole, this is justifiable, because Lord Reid's basic *Anisminic* reasoning applies to all such clauses, however worded. Thus, the courts have found that review for jurisdictional error is not excluded notwithstanding a provision that:

(a) the decision 'shall not be questioned' (*Anisminic* itself);

(b) the decision is 'final and conclusive': *R v Medical Appeal Tribunal ex p Gilmore* (1957);

(c) the decision 'shall not be removed by certiorari': *per* Lord Denning, *obiter*, in *Gilmore*.

However, it should not be assumed that this will necessarily always be the case. It is at least possible that a super-ouster clause could be framed so as to defeat Lord Reid's reasoning, thereby excluding judicial review entirely. For example, consider a clause providing that:

> ... any decision or *purported decision* made or *purported to be made* under the authority of [the statutory power] shall not be called into question in any proceedings whatsoever.

It could not be argued that, because the decision was a nullity, there was no *purported* (as opposed to actual) decision; thus it might be that a court would hold that such an ouster was effective to exclude judicial review. The question is largely theoretical, because no ouster clause in such terms has been enacted. However, you might want to consider the effect of s 4 of the Local Government Act 1987, which provides that:

> Anything done by the Secretary of State before the passing of this Act for the purposes of the relevant provisions ... shall be deemed to have been done in compliance with those provisions.

Whilst there is no reported case dealing with s 4, it may be that the courts would still seek to resist the 'deeming' effect of the provision by holding that anything done by the Secretary of State which was in fact *not* for the purposes of the relevant provisions is not, by reason of the provision, to be the subject of the 'deeming' clause. In that way, the court would preserve, at least in a limited measure, the ability to scrutinise by way of judicial review decisions taken under the relevant provisions. In addition, it is important to have in mind the right of access to a court guaranteed by Art 6 of the ECHR, enforceable in English law by virtue of the Human Rights Act. If the underlying right at issue is one which is protected by Art 6 (as to which, see Chapter 21), then a super-ouster clause may violate the convention, and would not be a legitimate device to protect the decision from review.

RESTRICTIONS ON REVIEW: OUSTER CLAUSES

An ouster clause is a legislative provision which purports to limit or exclude the power of the courts to review a decision.

The courts interpret ouster clauses as restrictively as possible; there is a presumption that Parliament did not intend to prevent the courts from exercising their constitutional role of scrutinising exercise of power by public bodies, and of quashing decisions flawed by errors of law. In addition, an ouster clause in interfering with the right of access to the court may violate Art 6 of the European Convention.

There is a clear distinction between the court's attitude to two types of ouster clauses:

(a) *six week ouster clauses* (providing that a decision may not be challenged in any way after a six week period); and

(b) *total ouster clauses* (which purport to exclude the jurisdiction of the court completely by providing, for example, that a decision 'shall not be questioned' in any court of law).

The courts will almost invariably respect a *six week ouster clause*. An applicant may not challenge a decision after the six week period, even if it is alleged that the delay is the responsibility of the respondent: *Smith v East Elloe RDC* (1956); *R v Secretary of State for the Environment ex p Ostler* (1976); *R v Secretary of State for the Environment ex p Kent* (1988).

There is a far greater reluctance to accept that the court's jurisdiction has been excluded by a *total ouster clause*. In *Anisminic v Foreign Compensation Commission* (1969), the House of Lords held that, if the error of law allegedly committed by the decision maker takes the authority outside its powers (that is, if it is a 'jurisdictional error'), then the court's ability to intervene is not excluded by a 'shall not be questioned' clause, because the court, in reviewing the decision, is not 'calling into question' the decision, but, rather, finding that a valid decision was never made.

Anisminic left open the question of which errors of law are 'jurisdictional errors' such that the court can avoid the effect of a total ouster clause and intervene. This generated great confusion in the subsequent case law. The position now appears to be that enunciated by Lord Diplock in *Re Racal Communications Ltd* (1981):

(a) as regards *administrative tribunals and authorities*, all errors of law are jurisdictional errors, so that the court, if it finds that the decision maker has made an error of law, can always evade the ouster clause and intervene to quash the decision (approving, in this context, the view of Lord Denning MR in *Pearlman v Governors of Harrow School* (1978));

(b) as regards *inferior courts of law*, it may be that, in particular circumstances, Parliament did intend to give an inferior court the power to decide questions of law wrongly as well as rightly – that is, in this context, an error of law may be 'non-jurisdictional' (approving, in this context, the dissenting opinion of Lane LJ in *Pearlman*).

This distinction was approved by the House of Lords in *R v Hull University Visitor ex p Page* (1992). It is not, however, very clear how one identifies which errors of law are non-jurisdictional, beyond the point that 'interrelated question of law, fact and degree' are more likely, in so far as they are treated as questions of law, to be non-jurisdictional. As Lord Denning has suggested, in practice, the tail appears to wag the dog; if the court wishes to intervene, then it will label the error of law as going to jurisdiction.

CHAPTER 17

JUDICIAL REVIEW
PROCEDURES AND REMEDIES

17.1 Access to justice

Each year about 4,000 people in England and Wales are so aggrieved by decisions taken by public authorities that they begin applications for judicial review in the High Court. The previous four chapters have examined the grounds on which such applications may be made, that is to say the legal arguments which may be put forward by applicants to show that a decision is legally flawed. This chapter looks at the procedures litigants must use in order to make an application for judicial review – in other words, the practical steps they, or their lawyers, must take to get a complaint of unlawfulness heard by a High Court judge. It also describes the remedies which successful applicants may obtain, the formal orders which a judge may make.

Court procedures and remedies are not just nitty-gritty considerations for practising lawyers. Questions of when and how litigants are allowed take grievances to court, and what a judge may do to rectify a problem, raise important issues of constitutional principle. If fair, effective and affordable procedures and remedies do not exist, the rule of law cannot be put into action. This is recognised by Art 6 of the European Convention on Human Rights which declares that:

> In the determination of his civil rights and obligations or of any criminal charge against him, everyone is entitled to a fair and public hearing within a reasonable time by an independent and impartial tribunal established by law. Judgment shall be pronounced publicly but the press may be excluded from all or part of the trial in the interests of morals, public order or national security in a democratic society, where the interests of juveniles or the protection of the private life of the parties so require, or to the extent strictly necessary in the opinion of the court in the special circumstances where publicity would prejudice the interests of justice.

(Chapter 21 examines in more detail the rights to fair trials in criminal cases.)

Access to the courts for people to challenge the legal validity of government action is of obvious importance (though they also need the means to settle disputes against their fellow private citizens and business enterprises). An important aspect of the rule of law is that, generally, public authorities, unlike ordinary citizens, only have those powers which have been specifically conferred on them by some positive law. If people are unable to question whether a particular power exists – and, if it does, whether it has been exercised reasonably and fairly – then government institutions and officials will effectively be able to decide for themselves what powers they have at their disposal. Commentators have often praised English judges for their vigilance in ensuring that government does not hamper the right of people to take their grievances to court. It is certainly possible to find judgments in which the courts emphasise the importance of this principle. In *R v Secretary of State for the Home Department ex p Leech (No 2)* (1994), Steyn LJ asserted that there was a 'constitutional right' of access to the courts and the Court of Appeal quashed a statutory instrument which permitted prison governors to read and stop letters between inmates and their legal advisors. Recently, in *R v Lord Chancellor ex p Witham* (1998), a statutory instrument removing exemptions from court fees previously given to people on very low incomes was held to be unlawful. Only if an Act of Parliament expressly 'permits the executive to turn people away from the court door' (as Laws J put it) will the courts allow this to be done.

In European Community law, too, the importance of 'effective remedies' is recognised (see below, 18.2).

Governments too, both Conservative and Labour, have acknowledged the importance of access to justice. For government, though, facilitating access for aggrieved people to independent courts and tribunals is often balanced against:

(a) the desire to keep the cost of the justice system in check;

(b) the need for legal certainty – public authorities should be able to make speedy and effective administrative decisions unhindered by legal challenge.

For many years, there has been concern that the procedures and remedies in litigation challenging government decisions failed to strike the right balance between the competing goals of access to justice, cost and the need for efficiency in government decision making. The Law Commission of England and Wales has twice investigated the matter. Recommendations in its 1976 Report led to the creation of the modern judicial review procedure set out in RSC Ord 53 (see below, 17.3). Ten years later, an influential pressure group published a scathing report: JUSTICE/All Souls, *Administrative Justice – Some Necessary Reforms* (1988). In 1994, the Law Commission again considered the procedures for making judicial review applications (*Administrative Law: Judicial Review and Statutory Appeals*, Law Com No 226) and made a series of recommendations, but shortly afterwards, Lord Woolf was requested by the then Lord Chancellor (Lord Mackay) to carry out a far-reaching review of the whole civil justice system. Lord Woolf's report, *Access to Justice – Final Report* (1996) urged the need for radical reform. The Civil Procedure Act 1997 (CPA) gives effect to many of his recommendations. It confers powers on a committee to make new rules governing the practice and procedure for civil litigation. The rule making powers of the committee are required to 'be exercised with a view to securing that the civil justice system is accessible, fair and efficient' (s 1(3) of the CPA). The new Civil Procedure Rules came into force in April 1999. At this date, the rules committee had not completed the task of revising the procedures by which applications for judicial reviews are made. For the time being, the previous rules on judicial review were therefore re-enacted with only minor amendments to terminology (CPR Sched 1, Ord 53).

Against this background of constant reform and importance attached to the constitutional principle of access to justice, this chapter examines the operation of the main procedure for challenging the legal validity of government decisions in court in England and Wales – applications for judicial review. Different litigation procedures apply in Scotland (see Wolffe, WJ, 'The scope of judicial review in Scotland' [1992] PL 625; Mullen, T, Pick, K and Prosser, T, 'Trends in judicial review in Scotland' [1995] PL 52) and in Northern Ireland (see Hadfield, B and Weaver, E, 'Trends in judicial review in Northern Ireland' [1994] PL 12). It should also be remembered that special procedures exist for questioning decisions taken under some Acts of Parliament, especially in the field of town planning (see above, 16.4).

17.2 Exhausting alternative remedies

Before starting an application for judicial review, a would-be applicant is expected to have exhausted other adequate alternative remedies. In a long series of cases, the High Court has said that it will normally exercise its discretion to turn away judicial review applications where the applicant has failed to pursue another remedy. Thus, if a person has available an appeal to a tribunal set up by statute, that should first be used (*R v Secretary of State for the Home Department ex p Swati* (1986), and the discussion of tribunals in Chapter 9). It should be noted that legal aid is not available for tribunal hearings. The possibility of making a complaint of maladministration to an ombudsman may also be viewed as an adequate alternative remedy (*R v Lambeth LBC ex p Crookes* (1997)), even though the jurisdiction of the ombudsmen is to investigate maladministration, not unlawfulness (see below, Chapter 10).

17.3 Using the Ord 53 procedure

To begin an application for judicial review, applicants, or more often their barristers, fill in a form. This needs to set out the facts of the applicant's case and the legal submissions which are being relied upon, supported by the citation of relevant authorities. Written evidence, verifying that the facts are true, must also be submitted to the court.

Order 53 r 4 requires all this to be done 'promptly and in any event within three months' of the date when the grounds of the application for judicial review arise. This is not long, especially if an applicant has to realise that his or her problem is a legal one, find a solicitor who recognises that judicial review is appropriate, and possibly apply for legal aid to fund the litigation. An application may be refused because the applicant failed to make it promptly, even within the three month period (*R v Swale Borough Council ex p Royal Society for the Protection of Birds* (1990)). The court does, however, have discretion to extend the time limit if there is a good reason to do so (*R v Dairy Produce Quota Tribunal for England and Wales ex p Caswell* (1990). In general civil proceedings – for example, tort and contract claims – limitation periods are three years or more. The rationale for the short time period in judicial review is the need to protect public authorities from the uncertainty which tardy challenges may create.

17.3.1 Obtaining the permission of the court

In general civil proceedings, once a claimant submits pleadings to the court and pays a fee, these can be served on the defendant, and litigation begins. Not so in judicial review. Section 31(3) of the Supreme Court Act 1981 stipulates that every application must first be vetted by a judge before it may be served on the respondent public authority. This used to be known as obtaining 'leave', but the new terminology is obtaining 'permission'. Only if the judge is satisfied that the applicant has a proper case will permission be given for the case to proceed any further. The procedure dates back to the 1930s, and today performs two main functions: it protects public authorities from the time and expense of having to respond to unmeritorious judicial review claims; and it also helps the High Court cope with the ever-growing case load (Le Sueur, AP and Sunkin, M, 'Applications for judicial review: the requirement of leave' [1992] PL 102). Typically, up to 50% of applications for permission are refused each year, which means that many judicial reviews are disposed of without the need for a full hearing.

Order 53 r 3(3) gives the applicant a choice as to how to apply for permission. It can be done entirely 'on paper', when the judge looks only at the applicant's form and written evidence. If permission is refused, a very short statement of reasons – often no more than a sentence or two – is given by the judge and sent on to the applicant's lawyers. Alternatively, an oral application for permission may be made in open court when counsel for the applicant will be allowed up to 20 minutes to address the judge and persuade him to grant permission. Two important characteristics of the permission stage are that the judge normally hears only the applicant's account of events and the law (not the public authority's) and the process is usually very summary, that is, decisions are made on a quick perusal of the documents or after hearing brief submissions from counsel. An applicant who is refused permission by the High Court may renew the application to the Court of Appeal.

There is no comprehensive official statement of the criteria which the judge should apply when considering whether to grant or refuse permission. One common reason given for refusing permission is that the applicant's case is 'unarguable'. Another is that the applicant has failed to seek an alternative remedy (see above, 17.2). Research has demonstrated that there is an astonishingly wide variation in the proportion of cases granted permission by different judges: some judges refuse 75%, whereas others refuse less than 25% (see Bridges, L, Mészáros, G and Sunkin, M, *Judicial Review in Perspective*, 2nd edn, 1995, London: Cavendish Publishing, Chapter 7). Clearly, this a cause for concern.

In the past, there have been calls for the abolition of the permission stage, on the ground that it was an unwarranted obstacle to access to justice. Now, however, the new Civil Procedure Rules encourage judges to take on a role of 'case management' in general civil proceedings. The permission requirement in judicial review therefore seems less anomalous. It also needs to be remembered that many other grievance procedures have mechanisms to 'filter out' some complaints at an early stage – including the ombudsmen (Chapter 10) and the European Court of Human Rights (see below, 18.3.1).

17.3.2 The interlocutory period

Assuming permission is granted, the respondent public authority has 56 days to submit a formal written reply to the applicant's form, disputing any facts and answering the applicant's legal submissions. It currently takes about 10 months from the grant of permission to an application receiving a full hearing in the High Court.

The time between starting litigation and a trial is called the interlocutory period. During this period, an applicant may fear that if the public authority's impugned decision is allowed to stand, then irreparable damage may be suffered. An applicant may, therefore, request that the court make an interim order suspending the operation of the decision which is being challenged – for example, to prevent the publication of an allegedly legally flawed and commercially damaging report (*R v Advertising Standards Authority ex p Direct Line Financial Services Ltd* (1998).

During the interlocutory period, it is quite usual for the applicant and the public authority to attempt to reach an out of court settlement. If an agreement is reached, then the applicant withdraws the case. In general civil proceedings, such settlements are generally regarded as a good thing. It has, however, been argued that, in judicial review cases, out of court settlements may not be so desirable (Sunkin, M, 'Withdrawing: a problem for judicial review?', in Leyland, P and Woods, T (eds), *Administrative Law Facing the Future*, 1997, London: Blackstone). One concern is that applicants may be pressurised to accept unfair settlements by powerful respondent public authorities. Another is that judicial review is an important way of holding government to account publicly for its actions. Because cases often affect third parties and the wider public interest, decisions to discontinue a legal challenge perhaps ought not be left entirely to the parties to the application.

17.3.3 The full hearing

The full hearing of an application for judicial review is in open court before a single judge, or sometimes a Divisional Court consisting of two or three judges. Counsel for the applicant makes submissions (based on the grounds set out on the application form) and counsel for the respondent public authority then responds. It is highly unusual for any witnesses to be called to give oral evidence or to be cross-examined. Because the outcome of public law litigation can be of concern to people other than just the applicant and the respondent public authority, other interested parties may be allowed to put in evidence and be represented at the hearing. For example, in a judicial review against a hospital's detention of a mentally retarded man, the Secretary of State for Health, the Mental Health Commission and the Registered Nursing Homes Association were granted leave to intervene (*R v Bournewood Community and Mental Health NHS Trust ex p L (Secretary of State for Health intervening)* (1998) and also Schiemann, K (Sir), 'Interventions in public interest cases' [1996] PL 240).

17.4 Remedies

After judgment is given, the court has at its disposal several different types of formal order which may be granted if the applicant is successful:

(a) an order of certiorari, to quash the public authority's decision;

(b) an order of mandamus, or a mandatory injunction, requiring the public authority to carry out its duties;

(c) an order of prohibition, or a prohibitory injunction, restraining the public authority from continuing to act unlawfully;

(d) a declaration, stating what the law is.

Even if the applicant wins all the legal arguments at the hearing, there is no guarantee that the decision will be set aside or the public authority's actions declared unlawful. All remedies on an application for judicial review are discretionary and may be withheld by the court for a number of reasons: for example, the remedy would serve no useful purpose, or the applicant delayed making the application and to grant relief would be detrimental to good administration or would prejudice the rights of third parties (s 31(6) of the Supreme Court Act 1981). Even if a remedy is granted, the applicant's victory may sometimes be a pyrrhic one. If a public authority's decision is set aside on the ground that it was made using improper procedures (see Chapter 13), the court will remit the matter back to the authority to redetermine and the authority may well reach the same decision, though this time being careful to use the proper procedures.

The fact that a decision is quashed because it was procedurally improper, irrational or illegal of itself gives no basis for claiming damages (see de Smith, SA, Woolf (Lord) and Jowell, J, *Judicial Review of Administrative Action*, 1995, Supplement, London: Sweet & Maxwell, Chapter 19). Order 53 allows an applicant to include a claim for damages on an application for judicial review, but damages will only be awarded if the applicant is able to prove that an actionable tort has been committed by the public authority: for example, negligence, trespass, false imprisonment or misfeasance in public office. Successfully arguing on a judicial review that a government authority has breached one or more of its statutory duties is not sufficient to show that the tort of breach of statutory duty has been committed (*O'Rourke v Camden LBC* (1998)).

An unsuccessful applicant who does not qualify for legal aid will usually be ordered to pay the legal costs of the respondent public authority, which will normally amount to several thousand pounds. Except for rich people and businesses, this risk is a major disincentive to applying for judicial review.

17.5 Who may apply for judicial review?

Over the past 15 years, in a series of important cases, the courts have had to determine whether particular applicants have had the necessary 'standing' to make an application for judicial review (Himsworth, C, 'No standing still on standing', in Leyland, P and Woods, T (eds), *Administrative Law Facing the Future*, 1997, London: Blackstone). This is because s 31(3) of the Supreme Court Act 1981, which creates the judicial review procedure, stipulates that:

> No application for judicial review shall be made unless the leave [now 'permission'] of the High Court has been obtained in accordance with the rules of court; and the court *shall not grant leave to make such an application unless it considers that the applicant has a sufficient interest in the matter to which the application relates* [emphasis added].

In fact, since the House of Lords' decision in *R v Inland Revenue Comrs ex p National Federation of Small Businesses and the Self-employed Ltd* (1982), any dispute as to whether or not an applicant has standing is normally not dealt with at the permission stage, but is postponed until the full hearing if the applicant is thought in other respects to have good grounds for obtaining judicial review. This is because it is a mixed question of fact and law, and normally cannot be determined during the permission procedure when the court looks only briefly at the applicant's side of the case.

Judges have been divided over how strictly the 'sufficient interest' requirement should be interpreted. Those who favour a high threshold often do so because they see the standing requirement as a way of reducing the judicial review case load; but as few applications are refused permission on the basis of lack of standing, it is arguable that a high standing threshold merely increases the work load of the courts, as it creates another issue to be resolved at the full hearing. Another reason for wanting a strict standing rule is to deter the tactical use of judicial review by individuals and pressure groups contesting controversial government policy. Even if an application fails, campaigners may believe that judicial review generates publicity for their cause and is a useful delaying tactic.

The main counterargument is that a legal system is discredited and the rule of law weakened if an allegedly unlawful decision is immune from challenge in the courts just because there is no one with a 'sufficient interest' in the matter (as in the *Rose Theatre* case, considered below, 17.5.2). Situations may also arise where an individual does have standing, because his interests are directly affected, but he is reluctant to risk the cost and stress of pursuing legal proceedings. Surely, it may be argued, pressure groups (such as Age Concern and the Child Poverty Action Group) should be allowed to bring an application for judicial review on behalf of people whose interests they represent (for a general discussion, see Cane, P, 'Standing up for the public' [1995] PL 276).

17.5.1 Strict approaches

Clearly, the 'sufficient interest' formula used in s 31(3) of the Supreme Court Act gives a considerable degree of discretion to the judges. In *National Federation*, a well respected and influential group lobbying for the interests of small businesses sought judicial review to challenge the Inland Revenue's 'amnesty' to casual print workers in the newspaper industry who, for many years, had used false names (such as Mickey Mouse) to avoid paying income tax. As a quid pro quo for the newspaper owners and workers regularising the position, the Inland Revenue agreed not to demand back taxes from the employees. The National Federation thought that this was unfair (as their members were always being hounded by the tax authorities) and unlawful. The majority of the House of Lords held that the National Federation did not have sufficient interest to seek judicial review of the tax affairs of other citizens. Lord Diplock dissented on the point, stating:

> It would in my view be a grave lacuna in our system of public law if a pressure group, like the Federation, or even a single public-spirited taxpayer were prevented by outdated technical rules of locus standi from bringing the matter to the attention of the court to vindicate the rule of law and get the unlawful conduct stopped.

In the years which followed *National Federation*, some judges in the High Court used the majority's approach to justify a high threshold. In *R v Secretary of State for the Environment ex p Rose Theatre Trust Company Ltd* (1990), a company formed to act as a pressure group campaigning to have the archaeological site 'listed' and protected by the government as an ancient monument was held not to have standing to challenge the minister's refusal. Applying *dicta* from the majority speeches in the *National Federation* case, Schiemann J said that a group of people, none of whom had standing individually, could not confer standing on themselves by forming a company. He believed that there were good reasons for having standing rules: they reduced uncertainty and chaos and discouraged overcautious decision making by public authorities. He conceded that his decision meant that nobody had sufficient interest to challenge decisions under the Ancient Monuments Act 1979, but this was an inevitable consequence of the statutory requirement that applicants have sufficient interest. The decision was much criticised, and Schiemann J took the unusual step of defending his decision by writing an academic article (*'Locus standi'* [1990] PL 342).

17.5.2 Whittling away the threshold

The stance taken in *Rose Theatre* turned out to be a high water mark and, in later cases, High Court judges have approached the 'sufficient interest' test far more generously – so much so, in fact, that Lord Diplock's dissenting speech in National Federation now reflects the current position. In *R v Secretary of State for the Environment ex p Greenpeace Ltd (No 2)* (1994), the environmental pressure group was held to have standing to challenge a licence allowing the testing of a new nuclear reprocessing plant. Several factors were regarded as justifying this result. Greenpeace had over 400,000 supporters in the UK and, of these, 2,500 were in the region where the plant was situated. Also, if standing were denied to Greenpeace, there might be an application by an individual employee at the nuclear plant or a local resident. If that happened, such an applicant would not be able to command the scientific expertise which was at the general disposal of Greenpeace. Consequently, a less well informed challenge might be mounted which would stretch unnecessarily the resources of the court and which would not afford the court the assistance it required in order to do justice between the parties. The decision of Schiemann J in *Rose Theatre* was distinguished on the basis that the pressure group in that case had been formed for the exclusive purpose of saving the archaeological remains and no individual member of the group could show any personal interest in the outcome.

The next step in the liberalisation of the standing requirement was *R v Secretary of State for Foreign and Commonwealth Affairs ex p World Development Movement Ltd* (1995), in which a pressure group sought judicial review of a decision by the Foreign Secretary to make a substantial grant to the government of Malaysia towards the construction of a hydro-electric project on the Pergau Dam under the Overseas Development and Co-operation Act 1980. In deciding whether the WDM had a sufficient interest in the Foreign

Secretary's decision, the Divisional Court could not simply apply *Greenpeace (No 2)*: whereas a number of Greenpeace members would themselves have had standing to challenge the licence granted to the nuclear plant because they lived near the plant, no supporter of WDM was any more affected by the Foreign Secretary's grant to the government of Malaysia than any other taxpayer or citizen living in Britain. This fact did not, however, prevent the court from holding that WDM had the standing necessary to bring a judicial review challenge. Among the factors to which the court attached importance were: the strength of the applicant's legal arguments (here, WDM went on to win the case); the importance of vindicating the rule of law (a phrase used by Lord Diplock in his dissenting speech in *National Federation*); the importance of the issue raised (here, the legal question had far-reaching implications for government overseas aid policy); the likely absence of any other challengers; the nature of the breach of duty against which relief was sought (here, the argument was that the minister had misunderstood the constraints on his statutory powers); and the prominent role of WDM in giving advice, guidance and assistance in the field of overseas aid policy (in other words, the applicants were well established and well respected, not least because it had consultative status with several United Nations organisations).

The emerging broad and flexible approach was reinforced by Sedley J in *R v Somerset CC ex p Dixon* (1997), where he held that the applicant – who was a local resident, a parish councillor and a member of several environmental campaigning groups – had sufficient interest to seek judicial review of a council's decision to grant planning permission for the extension of a limestone quarry. Sedley J held that there was no authority for the proposition that a court was compelled to refuse leave where the 'interest' of the applicant was shared with the generality of the public (and, if *dicta* in *Rose Theatre* suggested otherwise, they should not be followed). While he accepted that, in the majority of cases, such a greater interest might be necessary to establish that an applicant was more than just a busybody, Sedley J said that 'there will be, in public life, a certain number of cases of abuse of power in which any individual, simply as a citizen, has a sufficient interest to bring the matter before the court'.

The process of liberalising standing ends (for the time being) with a twist in the tail – in another judicial review challenge made by Greenpeace. In *R v Secretary of State for Trade and Industry ex p Greenpeace* (1998), the pressure group sought to argue that the minister had acted unlawfully in granting licences for offshore petroleum drilling because this would harm a special type of coral, protected under an EC directive. It was accepted by all parties that Greenpeace did, indeed, have a sufficient interest to make the application. Laws J commented that litigation of this kind, in which applicants bring challenges in the public interest and have no rights of their own, 'is an accepted and greatly valued dimension of the judicial review jurisdiction'. In such public interest litigation, however, applicants have to act 'as a friend to the court'. This means, for example, that the rules about delay in making judicial review applications (see above, 17.3) would be applied with particular strictness against such applicants – and, in the circumstances of the present case, Greenpeace could and should have applied for leave much earlier. Laws J also made it clear that an applicant's motives for bringing a case (here, Greenpeace's opposition to drilling for oil) formed no part of the public interest equation. The only public interest asserted by Greenpeace was the upholding of the rule of law.

As we shall see in Chapter 19, the problem of defining an appropriate standing test is not confined to s 31(3) of the Supreme Court Act 1981. Standing requirements are also contained in the Human Rights Act 1998 (see below, 19.10.5) and in Art 230 of the EC Treaty, under which legal proceedings may be taken before the European Court of Justice to annul legislation and actions by Community institutions (see below, 18.2.5).

17.6 Which decisions may be challenged by judicial review?

Judicial review developed as a constitutional mechanism for controlling the misuse of statutory powers by magistrates and local government and, later, by ministers (see de Smith, SA, Woolf (Lord) and Jowell, J, *Judicial Review of Administrative Action*, 1995, London: Sweet & Maxwell, Chapter 14). The body of case law which now exists setting out the grounds upon which judicial review may be sought – illegality, procedural impropriety and irrationality – regulates the powers of a much broader range of institutions and office holders. In everyday language, these decision making authorities are often referred to collectively as public authorities. As the High Court has extended its supervisory jurisdiction to cover new types of public authority, it has become important to provide a principled justification to explain against whom applicants may bring judicial review challenges. Why, for instance, have to courts held that the Jockey Club (the non-statutory authority regulating the multimillion pound British racing industry) is not subject to judicial review, whereas the Press Complaints Commission (the non-statutory self-regulatory authority for newspaper publishers) is amenable to challenge in this way? Compare *R v Jockey Club ex p Aga Khan* (1993) and *R v Press Complaints Commission ex p Stewart-Brady* (1997).

17.6.1 Source of power test

Until the 1980s, the courts applied a rather mechanistic test and asked, in effect, only if the particular decision challenged was made under statutory powers. After the House of Lords' decision in *Council of Civil Service Unions v Minister for the Civil Service* (1985) (the *GCHQ* case), decisions which based their legal authority on prerogative powers (see above, 2.4.3) ceased, for that reason alone, to be immune from judicial review. Thus, the Home Secretary's refusal to recommend the exercise of the prerogative of mercy was held to be reviewable (*R v Secretary of State for the Home Department ex p Bentley* (1994)). The issue, in other words, was: what was the source of the decision maker's power? If it was conferred by statute or the prerogative, then, in principle, the decision was amenable to judicial review challenge. If the power was contractual (for example, the relationship between a member and a private club), then judicial review was not available.

17.6.2 Functions test

The courts then abandoned the test based solely on the source of power and devised a more sophisticated approach which rested on the nature of the 'function' being performed by the decision maker, or the nature of the decision's consequences. The leading case is *R v Panel on Take-overs and Mergers ex p Datafin plc* (1987). The panel is a non-statutory authority staffed by people on secondment from merchant banks, law firms and accountants. Its operations are financed by a levy on equity deals in the City and its role is to ensure 'fair play' during takeovers and mergers of companies in accordance with a code. The panel was not set up by, and receives no funds from, government – though its functions complement those of statutory authorities, such as the Monopolies and Mergers Commission and the Securities and Investment Board. Datafin plc was involved in a takeover bid. The panel made certain decisions which the company believed to be unlawful; in particular, it refused to investigate a complaint that the code had been breached by a rival. How could Datafin challenge this decision? It applied for permission to apply for judicial review; the judge applied the 'source test' (see above, 17.6.1) and held that the panel was not amenable to judicial review because it was not exercising statutory powers. The leave application was renewed to the Court of Appeal, which held that the panel was subject to judicial review because the source of a decision maker's power was not always conclusive of the issue. What powers did the panel have? This question caused the Court of Appeal to scratch its collective judicial head. The panel clearly had no statutory or prerogative powers. Nor was it in a contractual relationship with those it sought to regulate. Its power derived merely from their consent. Lloyd LJ devised a test:

> The source of the power will often, perhaps usually, be decisive. If the source of the power is a statute, or subordinate legislation, then clearly the body will be subject to judicial review. If, on the other end of the scale, the source of power is contractual ... then clearly [the body] is not subject to judicial review ... But between these two extremes there is an area in which it is helpful to look not just at the source of the power but at the nature of the power. If the body in question is exercising public law functions, or if the exercise of its functions have public law consequences, then that may be sufficient to bring the body

within the reach of judicial review. It may be said that to refer to 'public law' in this context is to beg the question. But I do not think that it does.

In other words, to work out whether a decision can be challenged in Ord 53 proceedings, it may be necessary to ask three questions:

(a) What was the source of the decision maker's power (the old test which, in most cases, will still provide the conclusive answer)?

(b) What functions was the decision maker carrying out?

(c) What were the consequences of the decision?

When *Datafin* was decided, some commentators predicted that there would be virtually no limit to the reach of judicial review, but this has not been the case. *Datafin* has, however, spawned a morass of case law. There have been several judicial attempts to refine the rather fluid language used by Lloyd LJ (see de Smith, SA, Woolf (Lord) and Jowell, J, *Judicial Review of Administrative Action*, 1995, Supplement, London: Sweet & Maxwell, para 3-027). A number of criteria have emerged; the following two are the most important ones:

(a) the 'but for' test – whether, but for the existence of the non-statutory body, the government itself would almost inevitably have intervened to regulate the activity in question? In *R v Football Association Ltd ex p Football League Ltd* (1993), one of the reasons why the FA was not reviewable was because, had it not existed, a television company, rather than the government, would most likely have stepped in to run professional soccer;

(b) whether the government had 'underpinned' the activities of the body with legislation or had in some other way woven into a statutory framework. On this basis, most of the self-regulatory organisations in the financial services industry (such as IMRO and the PIA) have been held to be amenable to judicial review because the voluntary regulatory regime is tied into statutory regulation under the Financial Services Act 1987.

Applications for judicial review by people who are members of, or have contracts with, non-statutory regulatory authorities have been refused because (among other reasons) such applicants have an alternative remedy, namely, to sue in contract: *R v Jockey Club ex p Aga Khan* (1993) and see, also, *Andreou v Institute of Chartered Accountants in England and Wales* (1998).

The attempt to distinguish between public powers (which are challengeable by judicial review) and private powers (which are not) has introduced slippery concepts into English law. Whether this dichotomy between public and private is plausible or helpful in this context is open to doubt (Oliver, D, 'Common values in public and private law and the public/private divide' [1997] PL 630). The policy justifications for confining the court's power of judicial review are rarely spelt out by the courts. As with the standing requirement (see above, 17.5), one factor is that this is seen as a way of rationing judicial review to prevent the High Court becoming overburdened. Another is that it would be unfair to expect small organisations (such as amateur sports clubs) to have to comply with the decision making standards established by the grounds of judicial review – principles developed over the years to control abuse of power by government institutions.

As we shall see in Chapters 18 and 19, the problem of demarcating public from private persons is not confined to applications for judicial review. First, in European Community law, such a distinction has been made for the purpose of deciding against which authorities directives may have vertical direct effect. The test formulated is based on the notion of 'emanation of the State'(Case C-188/89 *Foster v British Gas plc* (1991) (see above, 7.9.2); and *National Union of Teachers v Governing Body of St Mary's Church of England (Aided) Junior School* (1997)). Secondly, the Human Rights Act 1998 defines 'public authority' to determine whether a body may be subject to claims in UK courts that it has acted unlawfully by violating one or more of the rights protected by of the European Convention on Human Rights (see below, 19.10.4).

17.7   Do litigants have to use Ord 53?

The previous section examined the proposition that an applicant may only use judicial review to challenge the legality of a public law decision. But what if a person wants to argue that a public authority's decision is unlawful in some other sort of legal proceedings? You might, for instance, be prosecuted for breaching a bylaw – can you, as a defence in a criminal court, seek to argue that the bylaw is invalid? Or, you may want to claim that a local authority has failed to pay a grant to which you are entitled under a statute – can you, in these circumstances, bring proceedings in the county court? Issues such as these are sometimes referred to as questions of 'procedural exclusivity'. Generally, the courts prefer public law issues to be dealt with by way of judicial review in the High Court, rather than by other courts using other procedures. Arguably, the pursuit aim has sometimes led to the principle of access to justice being harmed; certainly, it has led to a great deal of wasteful litigation over which court and procedure is the most appropriate for the resolution of a particular grievance.

The problem of procedural exclusivity began in 1982, when the House of Lords held that it was 'an abuse of the process of the court' for a person to seek a declaration using the general civil procedure rather than the application for judicial review procedure in Ord 53 (*O'Reilly v Mackman* (1983)). Following a riot at Hull prison, a number of prisoners were subjected to punishment ordered by a disciplinary tribunal; some of them argued they had not been given proper opportunity to present their side of the events. The claimant's lawyers commenced litigation in the High Court by writ (one of the methods of starting general civil proceedings before the Civil Procedure Rules 1999), claiming a declaration. The reason given by the House of Lords for striking out the claimant's case before it got to trial was that the Ord 53 application for judicial review procedure provided public authorities with certain procedural protections: the requirement that permission be obtained; the fact that the application form requires all legal and factual submissions to be revealed from the very outset; the absence of oral evidence, so keeping hearings shorter; and the requirement that applications be made promptly and, in any event, within three months. Lord Diplock said that the whole purpose of these protections would be defeated if a person could use general civil procedures to obtain a declaration to challenge public law decisions. Professor HWR Wade criticised *O'Reilly* as a serious setback for administrative law:

> It has caused many cases, which on their merits might have succeeded, to fail merely because of the choice of the wrong form of action. It is a step back towards the time of the old forms of action which were so deservedly buried in 1852. It has produced great uncertainty, which seems likely to continue, as to the boundary between public and private law since these terms have no clear and settled meaning ... the House of Lords has expounded the new law as designed for the protection of public authorities rather than of the citizen [Wade, HWR and Forsyth, CF, *Administrative Law*, 7th edn, 1994, Oxford: Clarendon, p 682].

In the years following *O'Reilly v Mackman*, a number of exceptions have emerged.

First, public law issues may be raised as a *defence* in general civil proceedings. In *Wandsworth LBC v Winder* (1985), the council passed a resolution raising the rents of council houses. Mr Winder, a tenant, refused to pay the new sum, and possession proceedings were commenced against him in the county court. He argued that the council's resolution was unlawful. The council tried to strike out his defence on the basis that he could not raise such a public law issue other than by Ord 53. The House of Lords disagreed, holding that public law issues could be raised by way of a defence in general civil proceedings. It was not an abuse of process, because the tenant was merely trying to defend himself.

Where a defendant in a criminal prosecution attempts to defend himself on the basis of the invalidity of a public law measure (for instance, where he is prosecuted for breaching rules set down in a statutory instrument), the House of Lords has held that there is a strong presumption that he should be allowed to do so: *Boddington v British Transport Police* (1998) (a defendant charged with unlawfully smoking on a train could defend himself in the magistrates' court by arguing that the bylaw creating the offence was invalid). It has also held, however, that the statute under which the prosecution is bought may, by implication, bar such a defence – and so require the defendant to bring a separate application for judicial review to challenge to validity of the statutory instrument: *R v Wicks* (1998) (a defendant charged in the Crown Court with failing to comply with an enforcement notice issued under the Town and

Country Planning Act 1990 could not argue that, in deciding to serve the enforcement notice, the local authority took into account irrelevant considerations and acted in bad faith).

The second main exception to the principle of procedural exclusivity is that, if a person has some sort of private law claim against a public authority, as well as public law rights, then the court may permit a private law claim to be pursued. This new degree of flexibility emerged from *Roy v Kensington and Chelsea and Westminster Family Practitioner Committee* (1992). The plaintiff, a general practitioner, claimed he was entitled to a full basic practice allowance in accordance with a statutory instrument, but the family practitioner committee refused to pay, alleging that he had been out of the country for periods of time and had been employing a locum. The doctor's lawyers began general civil proceedings (rather than an application for judicial review), seeking a declaration and payment of the sums he claimed due to him. Lawyers for the committee, relying on *O'Reilly*, sought to strike out parts of his claim, arguing that he should first challenge the committee's decision by judicial review and only if he won could he commence an action for payment of the sums due. The House of Lords held that there was no abuse of process. Lord Lowry said that there were two ways of looking at *O'Reilly*:

(a) the 'narrow approach': the exclusivity rule applies to all proceedings in which public law decisions are challenged, subject to some exceptions when private law rights are involved;

(b) the 'broad approach': *O'Reilly* applies only when private law proceedings are not at stake. (The prisoners in *O'Reilly* had no private rights.)

His Lordship preferred the broad approach, but said that he did not need to choose. There were many indications in favour of a liberal approach. One was that the Law Commission's 1976 report (see above, 17.1) on which the Ord 53 procedure was based had not recommended a strict rule of procedural exclusivity – in fact, quite the opposite. Another was that the litigation in *Wandsworth v Winder* had included private law rights. Lord Lowry's conclusion was that 'unless the procedure adopted by the moving party is ill suited to dispose of the question at issue, there is much to be said in favour of the proposition that a court having jurisdiction ought to let a case be heard rather than entertain a debate concerning the form of the proceedings'.

The pragmatic approach advocated in *Roy* has been followed in several later cases. In *Mercury Communications Ltd v Director General of Telecommunications* (1996), the House of Lords allowed a dispute about licensing of telecommunications operators to be dealt with in the Commercial Court because the procedures in that court were equally, if not more appropriate, for resolving the challenge. In *British Steel plc v Customs and Excise Comrs* (1997), the Court of Appeal held (overturning Laws J) that it was permissible for the claimant to bring private law proceedings for restitution of duty on oil demanded by Customs if they could show that the demand was unlawful. In *Trustees of the Dennis Rye Pension Fund v Sheffield CC* (1998), the Court of Appeal held that the claim for payment of an improvement grant under the Housing Act 1989, which the claimants said the council owed them, could proceed by general civil proceedings which was a suitable procedure for dealing with disputed facts and collecting debts. See, also, *Andreou v Institute of Chartered Accountants in England and Wales* (1998).

The Law Commission noted three fundamental criticisms of the procedural exclusivity rule (Consultation Paper No 126, July 1993). First, it automatically gives protection to public authorities without taking account of the real administrative inconvenience that might, or *might not*, be caused if a litigant could sidestep the Ord 53 procedure. Secondly, no sharp distinction can be drawn between public and private rights. Thirdly, public authorities are not given similar procedural protections when they are sued in contract or tort – so why do they need them in respect of judicial review? In its 1994 Report (Law Com No 226), the Law Commission concluded that:

> ... the present position whereby a litigant is required to proceed by way of Order 53 only when (a) the challenge is on public law and no other grounds, that is, where the challenge is solely to the validity or legality of a public authority's acts or omissions and (b) the litigant does not seek either to enforce or defend a completely constituted private law right is satisfactory.

In other words, the report supported the broad approach outlined by Lord Lowry in *Roy*. In *R v Secretary of State for Employment ex p Equal Opportunities Commission* (1995), where the House of Lords declared that statutory provisions treating part time workers less favourably than full timers were contrary to European Community law, Lord Lowry added this as a footnote to his speech:

> I feel bound, however, to add (as can perhaps be inferred from my speech in *Roy*) that I have never been entirely happy with the wide procedural restriction for which *O'Reilly v Mackman* is an authority, and I hope that the case will one day be the subject of your Lordships' further consideration.

Clearly, the principle of procedural exclusivity requires rationalisation (see Emery, C, 'Public law or private law? – The limits of procedural reform' [1995] PL 450). Although *Roy* introduced a welcome element of flexibility into the courts' approach to procedural exclusivity, it has not stemmed the flow of wasteful litigation about which court and which procedure should be used to determine issues. As we have noted, one of the main reasons for its existence is the desire to channel public law disputes through the Ord 53 procedure because this offers respondent public authorities greater protections than do general civil proceedings. Another reason for the procedural exclusivity rule has been to ensure that important issues of public law are determined by High Court judges, rather than in the county court, in the Crown Court or by magistrates. Two other features of modern public law litigation are, however, undermining the goal. First, European Community law requires every court and tribunal in the UK to set aside national laws which are inconsistent with the EC Treaty, directive, regulations or the case law of the European Court of Justice (see above, 7.9). Even a bench of lay magistrates hearing a criminal prosecution may refer questions about the validity of an Act of Parliament to the Luxembourg Court for a preliminary ruling and, having received guidance, disapply that legislative provision if needs be (see below, 18.2.1). Secondly, the Human Rights Act 1998 now requires every court and tribunal to consider the ECHR and the case law of the European Court of Human Rights in Strasbourg when interpreting and applying national legislation (see below, Chapter 19).

JUDICIAL REVIEW PROCEDURES AND REMEDIES

Access to justice is a constitutional right recognised by the common law, in statute, in Art 6 of the ECHR and in the European Community law principle of effective remedies. Access to justice is of constitutional importance to enable people to challenge the legal validity of actions by public authorities.

Different procedures exist for judicial review in the three legal systems of the UK. In England and Wales, the steps which must be taken in judicial review litigation are now contained in Sched 1, Ord 53 of the Civil Procedure Rules 1999. All judicial review cases are dealt with in the Queen's Bench Division of the High Court in London. For many years there have been demands for reform to the procedure – including calls by the Law Commission.

In outline, the following steps must be complied with:

(a) applicants should exhaust any alternative remedies before commencing a judicial review challenge;

(b) an application must be commenced 'promptly and in any event within three months' from the date when then the applicant first had grounds to seek judicial review;

(c) unlike general civil proceedings, the decision to commence litigation is not that of the applicant alone. Only if a judge is satisfied that there is an arguable case and grants 'permission' may the applicant serve proceedings on the respondent public authority;

(d) the full hearing of the application for judicial review is either before a single High Court judge or a Divisional Court of two or three;

(e) the court has several remedies which it may grant to a successful applicant, including: certiorari (an order quashing a public authority's decision); prohibition, or an injunction preventing unlawful action being continued; mandamus, or a mandatory injunction. The grant of these remedies is discretionary. Damages may also be awarded, but only if the applicant has a cause of action in tort arising from the same facts as the application for judicial review.

Three aspects of the judicial review procedure have been problematic:

(a) who has standing to apply for judicial review? Applicants are required by s 31 of the Supreme Court Act 1981 to have 'a sufficient interest in the matter to which the application relates'. In some cases, the courts have interpreted this strictly and turned people away who were not directly affected by the decision they sought to challenge. Today, however, the courts take a far more liberal approach; it is unlikely that a person with an otherwise good case will be refused permission to apply for judicial review because they lack standing;

(b) which public authorities are amenable to judicial review? In the past, the courts applied a 'source based' test, asking whether the public authority's powers emanated from an Act of Parliament or the prerogative. Now, the courts may also apply a 'function' test, asking whether the public authority is performing a public function. This has resulted in self-regulatory organisations (such as the Panel on Take-overs and Mergers) being subject to review;

(c) is it necessary to use the judicial review procedure? In *O'Reilly v Mackman*, the House of Lords established the rule of procedural exclusivity. If an applicant has grounds to apply for judicial review, the procedural rules contained in RSC Ord 53 must be followed, and it is not permissible for an applicant to use general civil proceedings. This is because Ord 53 contains a number of procedural safeguards for public authorities. In subsequent cases, procedural exclusivity has been applied less stringently.

CHAPTER 18

EUROPEAN COMMUNITY LITIGATION

18.1 Introduction

In the modern UK constitution, the choices of public authorities are enabled and constrained by Community law in a wide range of policy areas (see above, 2.3 and Chapter 7). The importance of Community law has increased, is increasing and is unlikely to diminish. The UK Parliament (see above, 2.4.2 and Chapter 6), the devolved assemblies (see above, Chapter 2), government ministers and local authorities must work within the boundaries set by Community law. Any public official ought always to ask: 'Is what I propose to do, and the manner in which I intend to do it, compatible with Community law?' Judges and members of tribunals must also ask a similar question. Answers to these questions cannot, of course, be found simply by looking at national law, because national law itself may be incompatible with Community law. Where there is conflict, precedence must be given to the rules of Community law (see above, 7.9.1).

For individuals and businesses, Community law is now an essential aspect of their relationship to public authorities. The source of law under which a public authority in the UK claims to be acting may be the EC Treaty, a regulation or a directive (see above, 7.6). It is of constitutional importance that such claims be open to challenge in the courts. For individuals and businesses, there are few possibilities for bringing a direct action before the Court of Justice. Instead, the focus is on national courts and tribunals – which my, as we shall see, request a preliminary ruling from the Court of Justice on the correct interpretation of the Community law.

18.2 European Community law in national legal systems

The Court of Justice has observed that the European Community:

> ... is a Community based on the rule of law, inasmuch as neither its Member States nor its institutions can avoid a review of the question whether the measures adopted by them are in conformity with the basic constitutional charter, the Treaty [Case 294/83 *Les Verts-Parti Ecologiste v European Parliament* (1986), para 23].

Most litigation involving Community law rights and obligations is dealt with by *national* courts and tribunals (Maher, I, 'National courts as European Community court' (1994) 14 LS 226). Having established the four basic building blocks in the relationship between national and Community law – primacy, direct effect, consistent interpretation and Member State liability –

the Court of Justice has been content to leave the design of litigation procedures and scope of remedies as a matter for each national legal system. Member States have not been required to create separate procedures or new forms of remedies for the enforcement of Community law (though inadequate procedures and remedies may be held to be in breach of Community law). Certainly, there is has been no need for any Member State to create special courts for Community law issues. On the contrary, the task of enforcing Community law is dispersed throughout national legal processes, from the lowest tribunal to the highest court. Each and every judge and tribunal member is under the same duty as all other office holders, to:

> ... take all appropriate measures, whether general or particular, to ensure the fulfilment of the obligations arising out of this Treaty or resulting from action taken by the institutions of the Community. They shall facilitate the achievement of the Community's tasks. They shall abstain from any measure which could jeopardise the attainment of the objectives of the Treaty [Art 10 of the EC Treaty, discussed above, 7.8.1].

More specifically, national litigation systems must provide an 'effective remedy' for protecting Community law rights. If a national procedural rule or remedy fails to achieve this, it must be set aside by the national court whose task is hampered by it. Thus, in *R v Secretary of State for Transport ex p Factortame Ltd (No 2)* (1991), the House of Lords had to disapply the rule of English law that no interim relief suspending the operation of an Act of Parliament could be granted. European Community directives may include requirements on the the need for effective remedies. For instance, Art 6 of the Equal Treatment Directive 76/207 requires Member States to take the necessary measures to enable all persons who consider themselves wronged by discrimination to pursue their claims by judicial process. In the UK, the Sex Discrimination Act 1975 limited the compensation which an industrial tribunal could award a person who had been unfairly dismissed to £11,000. One industrial tribunal hearing such a claim correctly 'disapplied' the statutory limit, which had not been increased in line with inflation, believing that an *a priori* limit on damages could not be an effective remedy for breaches of the Directive (Case C-271/91 *Marshall v Southampton and South West Hampshire AHA (No 2)* (1994)). The government subsequently amended the Sex Discrimination Act to remove the cap on damages.

18.2.1 Preliminary references under Art 234

The work of national courts and tribunals is assisted and directed by the Court of Justice. Any national court or tribunal in the UK – from an industrial tribunal, a bench of lay magistrates, the High Court, up to the House of Lords – may seek guidance from the Court of Justice on how to decide a particular point of Community law. The preliminary reference procedure is governed by Art 234 of the EC Treaty (formerly Art 177 before the renumbering of the

Treaty provisions after the Amsterdam Treaty revision) and a *Practice Direction* issued by the Court of Justice (see [1997] All ER (EC) 1). It is through the preliminary ruling mechanism that many of the basic principles of Community law, including those of primacy and direct effect (see above, 7.9), have been established. Article 234 states (emphasis added):

> The Court of Justice shall have jurisdiction to give preliminary rulings concerning:
>
> (a) the interpretation of this Treaty
>
> (b) the validity and interpretation of acts of the institutions of the Community
> [...]
>
> (c) the interpretation of the statutes of bodies established by an act of the Council, where those statutes so provide.
>
> Where such a question is raised before *any* court or tribunal of a Member State, that court or tribunal *may*, if it considers that a decision on the question is necessary to enable it to give judgement, request the Court of Justice to give a ruling thereon.
>
> Where any such question is raised in a case pending before a court or tribunal of a Member State, against whose decisions *there is no judicial remedy* under national law, that court or tribunal *shall* bring the matter before the Court of Justice.

The national court or tribunal formulates the issues of Community law before it as abstract questions and it must also define the factual and legislative context in which they arise. The question has to be 'necessary' for the resolution of the case before the national court or tribunal. The Court of Justice will not accept references made merely to get an authoritative ruling on a point of hypothetical issue of Community law: Case C-104/79 *Foglia v Novello (No 1)* (1980) and Case C-244/80 *Foglia v Novello (No 2)* (1981). Nor will it hear matters which are entirely internal to a Member State; in other words, cases which involve no inter-State element to which Community law can attach: Case C-346/93 *Kleinwort Benson Ltd v City of Glasgow DC* (1996).

Some months after a reference has been made to the Court of Justice, the parties to the litigation – and often the government of the Member State concerned – may attend the court to make oral submissions. One of the Advocates General (see above, 7.5.5) then writes an opinion setting out his reasoned view as to how the Court of Justice ought to answer the questions posed. Some time later, the Luxembourg Court delivers its judgment, 90% of the time adopting the view favoured by the Advocate General. The whole process of seeking and receiving a preliminary ruling takes many months, sometimes several years. On an Art 234 reference, the function of the Court of Justice is to interpret and rule upon issues of Community law only, not to decide on the facts. Having received guidance from the Court of Justice, the national court or tribunal then resumes its determination of the litigation and applies the ruling of the Court of Justice to the particular facts of the dispute.

Article 234 states that any national court 'may refer' a question which is necessary. Every national court and tribunal, therefore, has a discretion whether to make an Art 234 reference; this discretion is not fettered in any way by that court's position in the judicial hierarchy or any ruling of a superior court on the point (Case C-166/73 *Rheinmühlen v Einfuhr-und Vorratsstelle für Getreide und Futtermittel* (1974). Article 234 also provides that, in certain circumstances, a court 'shall' make a reference. If a point of Community law arises in a hearing before a court of last instance (one from which there is no appeal), that court is under an obligation to refer the Community law question to the Court of Justice. This obligation has, however, become so hedged about with exceptions that it is no more certain now that litigants in a court of last instance will get their Community point referred to Luxembourg than it would have been if they had requested that this happen in a lower court. In Case C-283/81 *CILFIT Srl v Minister of Health* (1982), the Court of Justice held that courts and tribunals and courts of last instance had no need to seek a preliminary reference if:

(a) the question of EC law is irrelevant;

(b) the provision has already been interpreted by the Court of Justice; or

(c) the correct application is so obvious as to leave no scope for reasonable doubt.

The last two criteria, (b) and (c), are referred to as the *acte clair* doctrine, and they are strictly construed to prevent national courts evading their obligation to refer matters to Luxembourg because they think they know the answer. In particular, a decision not to refer on the basis of (c) will only be justified if the question has been assessed in the light of the specific characteristics of Community law, the particular difficulties to which this gives rise, and the risk of divergences in judicial decisions within the Community. There was, for example, no preliminary reference before or after the House of Lords declared in *R v Secretary of State for Employment ex p Equal Opportunities Commission* (1995) that provisions of an Act of Parliament were contrary to Community law. The condition set out in (b) acknowledges the emerging concept of precedent in Community law. This was not the original purpose of the Court of Justice, which was designed to exist in a horizontal relationship with national courts, issuing guidance on Community law, but not creating a body of case law which would be binding on them. The doctrine of precedent can only emerge from a hierarchical system of courts, with the Court of Justice at the top, laying down the most authoritative interpretation of Community law.

18.2.2 Challenging Community law in national courts

Most applications for judicial review, and other litigation in the UK raising issues of Community law, seek to challenge the *implementation* of Community law by the Member State – for example, whether an Act of Parliament or statutory instrument conforms to Community law, whether a licence was withdrawn or planning permission granted, and so on. In some cases, however, an applicant may want to argue in a judicial review that a decision of a governmental body in the UK is unlawful because the *Community* directive or regulation it was seeking to follow is itself invalid. One such case is *R v Secretary of State for Health ex p Imperial Tobacco Ltd* (1999), in which cigarette manufacturers applied for judicial review seeking an order preventing the UK Government taking steps to implement into national law a directive restricting cigarette advertising which, the applicants argued, was unlawful. A national court has no power to declare a Community instrument unlawful (Case C-314/85 *Firma Foto-Frost v Hauptzollamt Lübeck-Ost* (1988)). This would be inconsistent with the principle of the primacy of Community law (see above, 7.9.1), and it would also threaten the uniform application of Community law throughout all Member States. If this situation arises, the national court is therefore required to make an Art 234 preliminary reference to the Court of Justice, which will make an binding determination on the issue.

18.3   Direct proceedings before the Court of Justice

As we have just noted, it is national courts and tribunals, occasionally assisted by the Art 234 reference procedure, which shoulder the main burden of enforcing and applying Community law in the Member States. In some circumstances, however, the Court of Justice and the Court of First Instance (see above, 7.5.5) have jurisdiction to deal with legal actions made directly to them when it is alleged that a Community institution (rather than a Member State) has acted unlawfully. There are three main procedures for direct actions:

(a) actions for annulment under Art 230 (formerly Art 173);

(b) proceedings by the Commission to enforce compliance with Community law under Art 226 (formerly Art 169); and

(c) claims for compensation against Community institutions under Art 288 (formerly Art 215(1)).

We now look at each of these in turn. It is the Court of First Instance, not the Court of Justice, which usually has jurisdiction to hear direct actions brought by individuals and businesses against Community institutions.

18.3.1 Annulment actions

Just as the system of judicial review at a national level is necessary to ensure that government bodies remain within the boundaries of their powers, it is equally important to ensure that the institutions of the European Community itself, particularly the Council and the Commission, do not stray beyond the limits of their powers under the treaties in reaching decisions or making directives and regulations. Actions of the Community may be annulled by the Court of Justice under Art 230 if the Community institution:

(a) lacks competence (does not have the legal authority to carry out the act);

(b) infringes an essential procedural requirement (for example, failure to consult the European Parliament before passing an Act under the co-decision procedure, or failure to give sufficient reasons for the measure under Art 253 (formerly Art 190));

(c) has infringed a rule of law derived not only from the treaty, but from the general principles of law approved by the Court of Justice, such as equality, legal certainty or proportionality; or

(d) has adopted a measure with the main purpose of achieving an end other than that stated in the preamble (abuse of power).

Annulment proceedings may be brought by one Community institution against another: for example, the European Parliament sought to annul a regulation made by the Council of Ministers on transport of waste: Case C-187/93 *European Parliament v Council* (1995). Member States may also bring annulment actions – for example, the UK unsuccessfully argued that a Commission had acted unlawfully in making regulations banning the export of live cattle and beef products (Case C-108/96 *UK v Commission* (1998)) and against the Council of Ministers for adopting the Working Time Directive (Case C-84/98 *UK v Council* (1996)).

It is very difficult indeed for individuals and companies to apply for annulment. In no circumstances are such applicants permitted to challenge the validity of a directive (only Member States and Community institutions may do so). Individuals and companies may, however, institute annulment proceedings 'against a decision addressed to that person'. In this context, a 'decision' means a formal legal instrument – distinct from EC regulations or directives – addressed to a particular named person or Member State (see Art 249 of the EC Treaty). Such decisions are often issued by the Commission in carrying out its administrative functions (see above, 8.2.5), especially in the fields of competition and common agricultural policy. Unlike EC regulations (see above, 7.6.1), decisions are not intended to be legislative in character; they are binding only on the person (which may be a Member State) to whom they are addressed.

Individual applicants may also bring annulment proceedings 'against a decision which, although in the form of a regulation or a decision addressed to another person, is of direct and individual concern to the former'. This means that if the Commission or the Council has laid down a rule in an EC regulation (rather than a decision) which has a 'direct and individual' impact on an identifiable person, that person may take annulment proceedings against the regulation if there are grounds for arguing that it is unlawful. The Court of Justice thus looks at the substance of the measure, and if it decides that it has

been passed to control the activities of one or more identifiable con
such as a particular producer of sparkling wine (Case C-309/89 *Cor*
Council (1994)), that company may have standing to seek an annulment.

Annulment proceedings must generally be begun within two months of
the publication of the measure which is challenged. This is a very short time
period, even in comparison to that for applications for judicial review in the
High Court (see above, 17.3).

18.3.2 Enforcement proceedings by the Commission

One of the functions of the Commission (see above, 7.5.1), 'in order to ensure
the proper functioning and development of the common market' is to 'ensure
that the provisions of [the] Treaty and the measures taken by the institutions
pursuant to it are applied' (Art 211 of the EC Treaty). Article 226 gives teeth to
this:

> If the Commission considers that a Member State has failed to fulfil an
> obligation under this Treaty, it shall deliver a reasoned opinion on the matter
> after giving the State concerned the opportunity to submit its observations.

> If the State concerned does not comply with the opinion within the period laid
> down by the Commission, the latter may bring the matter before the Court of
> Justice.

A Member State may also bring enforcement proceedings against another
Member State (Art 227). The court has power to direct that the Member State
in default of its obligations take action and, if this is not done within the time
limit stipulated by the court, then the court 'may impose a lump sum or
penalty payment on it' (Art 228).

18.3.3 Tortious claims against the Community

As we have noted, Member States may be liable to pay damages for loss
suffered by people as a result of their breach of Community law (see above,
7.9.4). The institutions of the Community itself may also be liable. Article 288
of the EC Treaty (formerly Art 215(2)) provides that:

> In the case of non-contractual liability, the Community shall, in accordance
> with the general principles common to the laws of the Member States, make
> good any damage caused by its institutions or by its servants in the
> performance of their duties.

There are no *locus standi* conditions; anyone can sue the Community
institutions provided they establish one of the following: negligent acts by
servants of the Community; operational failures in administration; adoption
of illegal acts having legal effect. As in English law, there is a high threshold
for liability for legislative acts. The rationale for this is that the exercise of

legislative functions should not be hindered by the prospect of damages actions. While it is proper that unlawful legislative measures should be annulled in judicial review proceedings, the imposition of damages should be limited to cases where there has been bad faith or improper motive or, in the words of the Court of Justice, there has been a 'sufficiently serious' breach of a 'superior rule of law' for the protection of the individual. Advocate General Tesauro observed, in Case C-46/93 *Brasserie du Pêcheur SA v Germany* (1996), that, by 1995, only eight actions for damages against Community institutions had been successful.

EUROPEAN COMMUNITY LITIGATION

National courts and tribunals hear most cases in which a litigant argues that a rule of Community law has been breached, or a duty under Community law has not been fulfilled. Rules of Community law may bind individuals, businesses and (the focus of this chapter) public authorities. To ensure consistency in the application of Community law throughout the Member States, the Court of Justice has created four general rules:

(a) any rule of Community law has primacy over inconsistent rules of national law;

(b) in certain circumstances, provisions in the EC Treaty, directives and regulations may have 'direct effect' and be relied upon as creating rights enforceable in national courts;

(c) national legislation is to be interpreted in a manner consistent with Community law;

(d) Member States who breach rules of Community law may be liable to pay damages to people who suffer loss as a result.

The Court of Justice operates in two main ways:

(a) at the request of national courts and tribunals, it issues guidance on the correct interpretation of Community law. The procedure for referring a question to the Court of Justice for a 'preliminary ruling' is established by Art 234 of the EC Treaty. In some situations, it is mandatory for a national court or tribunal to seek a preliminary ruling. One such circumstance is where a litigant seeks to argue that a Community measure (such as a directive or regulation) itself breaches Community law;

(b) the Court of Justice also has jurisdiction to hear some types of case directly:

- actions for the annulment of decisions and legislation of the Community. Proceedings are brought by Member States against the Community, and by institutions of the Community against each other. Stringent rules of standing have prevented individuals and businesses using annulment actions, except in rare cases;

- enforcement actions, mostly brought by the Commission, to compel Member States to comply with their obligations under Community law. The Court of Justice has power to impose financial penalties;

- actions for compensation against Community institutions. Very few are successful.

PART D

CIVIL LIBERTIES AND HUMAN RIGHTS

CHAPTER 19

CIVIL LIBERTIES AND HUMAN RIGHTS

19.1 Introduction

People use the word 'rights' in different senses, and so we need to clarify what they mean.

'Rights' may refer to legally enforceable entitlements or freedoms. Thus, when lawyers talk about the 'right to vote', they may be referring to legal rights contained in the Representation of the People Act 1985 and perhaps also to the international treaty obligations which place a duty on governments to organise elections. For instance, the countries which have ratified the First Protocol to the European Convention on Human Rights (ECHR) 'undertake to hold free elections at reasonable intervals by secret ballot, under conditions which will ensure the free expression of the people in the choice of the legislature' (Art 3).

'Rights' may also be used to mean something else. Campaigners for voluntary euthanasia in the UK, for example, say that people have the right to die with dignity and with the assistance of their doctor. They are not suggesting that there is currently such a legal right; rather, they use the word 'right' as a rhetorical device to add weight to their moral argument in favour of mercy killing. Many philosophers prefer to avoid using the language of rights in such contexts. Mary Warnock, for instance, asks:

> Why should we not prefer simply to talk about the ways in which it would be right or wrong, good or bad, to treat our fellow humans? This would be to adopt the language of morality itself, with no quasi-legal implications [*An Intelligent Person's Guide to Ethics*, 1998, London: Duckworth, p 63].

People sometimes slip backwards and forwards between the two senses of 'rights'. Indeed, the distinction (or lack of one) between moral reasoning and legal reasoning is a deeply contentious one which divides thinkers. The practical difficulty arises because many constitutional documents confer broadly expressed rights on people (or lay down wide duties on State authorities which create corresponding rights). When originally drafted, some such documents were often no more than rhetorical claims that people be treated in a certain way. As Lord Hoffmann observes in *Matadeen v Pointu* (1999), in a discussion on the right to equality in the French Declaration of the Rights of Man and the Citizen of 1789 ('All men are born and remain free and equal in their rights'):

> ... the notion that [the National Convention's] decrees should be subject to review by a court of independent judges would have been greeted with incredulity.

Today, however, in most liberal democracies, courts have powers to adjudicate on whether State authorities (including democratically elected legislatures) have infringed rights codified in their written constitutions.

19.2   Civil liberties

In the UK, until recently, the ability of people to go about their lives without interference from State authorities tended to be spoken about as their 'civil liberties', rather than as 'human' or 'constitutional' rights. The legal systems of the UK had no codified statement of such liberties. The reasons for this lie in history. In England, power had shifted in important ways from autocratic monarchy in 1688 to Parliament, albeit one which was elected on a narrow franchise (see above, 3.6.6). Although some 18th century British radicals, notably Thomas Paine (1737–1819), demanded a written constitutional code of 'rights' for Britain, such an innovation was, for most people, inextricably tied up with the experiences of Britain's enemies – the freedoms proclaimed in the French and American Revolutions became associated with foreign powers that threatened Britain (see above, 3.7.2). Later, in 1838, one of the earliest socialist movements, the Chartists, campaigned for a 'People's Charter', focusing on the political emancipation of workers and male suffrage on the basis of equality (see above, 3.8.3). These radical demands all met with defeat. As in other countries, these early demands for 'rights' were intended as statements of political claims, not documents containing *legal* obligations upon which courts would adjudicate.

By the time Dicey wrote his *Introduction to the Study of the Constitution* ((1st edn, 1885), 10th edn, 1959, London: Macmillan), the whole notion of a formal document recording people's basic rights seemed an alien and unnecessary exercise (see above, 5.3). For over a century, the lack of a charter of rights in the British Constitution was considered not a 'failure' at all, but one of its great strengths. What people in the UK had to protect them from arbitrary intrusions by government were residual liberties and elected MPs and peers who respected the need for personal liberty and who would not enact legislation which unduly infringed it. British judges had an important role to play in ensuring liberty was protected, Dicey argued, even though they had no power to strike down Acts of Parliament as 'unconstitutional' on the basis of infringing a provision in a charter of rights. The judges had two main tools (see above, 1.7.1): the principle of negative liberty (people were permitted to do everything not specifically prohibited by law); and the requirement that action by State authorities must normally be authorised by a particular legal power recognised as valid by the common law or contained in statutes. Before the incorporation of the ECHR into domestic law by the Human Rights Act 1998 (discussed below), Laws J felt able to assert confidently that:

The contents of the European Convention on Human Rights, as a series of propositions, largely represent legal norms and values which are either already inherent in our law, or, in so far as they are not, may be integrated into it by the judges ['Is the High Court the guardian of fundamental constitutional rights?' [1993] PL 59].

Many people could not share Laws J's confidence. For one thing, Parliament was able, at any time, to overturn the effect of a court's judgment seeking to protect a liberty right; and, on several occasions, Parliament has been found by the European Court of Human Rights to have violated rights contained in the European Convention on Human Rights (see below, 19.6). Some critics also saw the common law as 'a catalogue of unprincipled decisions' revealing an 'ethical aimlessness' (Lester, A, 'English judges as law makers' [1993] PL 267).

19.3 Human rights

Today, the term 'human rights' is often used to describe people's residual liberties from interference by State authorities. In the wake of the atrocities of the Second World War, the UK, like other countries around the world, came to recognise that rights against State interference and coercion were no longer a question solely for national law. Since the late 1940s, many international treaties have been established under which governments of Signatory States agree with one another to respect the basic freedoms of their citizens. (On the status of international treaties in the UK legal system, see above, 2.12.1.) Under the auspices of the United Nations, the Universal Declaration of Human Rights was established in 1948. Several regional treaties were subsequently created, including the ECHR, which came into force in 1953. These treaties were novel forms of international law. First, the countries which are parties to them agree with one another to respect the rights of *people* within their jurisdiction; hitherto, international law had been regarded as only regulating the relations between States. Secondly, these treaties established tribunals and procedures for monitoring and enforcing the parties' compliance with their treaty obligations.

The term 'human rights' is not limited to the freedoms people have from unjustified coercion by State authorities. Several international treaties seek to protect political rights to participate in collective decision making, such as the First Protocol to the ECHR (see above, 19.1). 'Human rights' also extends to some economic and social entitlements. For instance, the International Covenant on Economic, Social and Cultural Rights (UNTS No 14531, Vol 993 (1996), p 3) , the text of which was finalised in 1966 under the auspices of the United Nations, seeks to protect rights such as 'the enjoyment of just and favourable conditions of work' including 'reasonable limitation of working hours and periodic holidays with pay' (Art 7), 'paid leave or leave with adequate social security benefits' for mothers (Art 10.2), and 'the right of everyone to the enjoyment of the highest attainable standard of physical and mental health (Art 12.1). Until recently, the status of these as legal rights, rather than just political claims or aspirations, was controversial.

19.4 What is the source of human rights and are they universal?

There are many jurisprudential debates about the nature of rights and how they are expressed in law (for an introduction to some of these, see Raz, J, 'Legal rights' (1984) 4 OJLS 1). Here we can highlight two particular controversies: what is the source of human rights; and are they universally applicable to all times and places? For many legal theorists, human rights exist because they are 'natural' or 'inalienable' attributes to being a human being. Rosalyn Higgins states that:

> Human rights are rights held simply by virtue of being a human person. They are part and parcel of the integrity and dignity of the human being. They are thus rights that cannot be given or withdrawn at will by any domestic legal system [*Problems and Processes: International Law and How We Use It*, 1994, Oxford: OUP, p 96].

In the past, there have been great philosophical debates over whether such 'natural' rights existed, but with the drafting of international legal charters to human rights after the Second World War, these controversies have become less pressing for lawyers and politicians, as they are now able to see those instruments themselves as the source of human rights. But although this has allowed awkward theoretical questions to be put to one side, the problem is that many of the rights instruments drafted during the 1940s and 1950s have (according to some) become outdated. Sir Stephen Sedley, writing of the ECHR, argues that it 'is a full generation out of date. The Convention, devised in 1950, took a limited view of human rights, based on the 19th century paradigm of the individual whose enemy is the State; I don't believe that is a workable premise' ((1994) *The Times*, 10 October). What this criticism has in mind is that the ECHR itself fails to provide for economic rights and rights to health care, housing, education and so on (so called 'red rights' or 'second generation rights') or any comprehensive rights to environmental protection ('green rights').

Another debate around the nature of human rights is, therefore, whether they are universal and timeless, or contingent on culture and temporary. This is often part of a more general debate about the nature of liberal democracy and Fukuyama's claim that we are witnessing the rise of a global civilisation and 'the end of history' (see above, 1.6.4). Some legal scholars are anxious to stress the universal aspects of human rights. Higgins, for instance, writes:

> I believe, profoundly in the universality of the human spirit. Individuals, everywhere, want the same essential things: to have sufficient food and shelter;

to be able to speak freely; to practise their own religion or abstain from religious belief; to feel that their person is not threatened by the State; to know that they will not be tortured, or detained without charge, and that if charged, they will have a fair trial. I believe that there is nothing in these aspirations that is dependent on culture, or religion, or stage of development. They are as keenly felt by the African tribesman as by the European city-dweller, by the inhabitant of a Latin American shanty-town as by the resident of a Manhattan apartment [p 97].

Others are less certain. Sedley warns that 'ideas which pretend to universality are historical delusions' ('Human rights: a twenty-first century agenda' [1995] PL 386, p 387). He explains:

That free speech or family life is today a fundamental individual right is by no means self-evident in a good number of the contemporary world's States, where history and conditions have made it apparent that they are primarily the State's business; and its is entirely conceivable that the States of Western Europe may during the coming century recast their thinking about family life and the right of the incurably or expensively ill to life itself as social and economic pressures bear down on ethics and theology. Who then will be right: our grandchildren or us?

The rights set out in international treaties seeking to protect liberty rights are important to the UK's system of liberal democracy for two main reasons. One is that, as Higgins suggests, rights to liberty go to the core of what it means to be a human being. Without them, a person is little more than an automaton – a member of an army rather than a citizen belonging to a community. In other words, such rights provide a basis from which to argue that there are areas of personal freedom which should not be violated by State authorities (including Parliament and the judiciary). A second reason is that many liberties are the pre-conditions for meaningful democracy (see above, 1.1.2). Parliamentary elections and the process of legislation are valuable ways of making collective decisions for a society only if people's basic freedoms are respected. Suppose, for example, a government calls an election, but bans other political parties, suppresses dissenting opinion, confiscates critical literature, puts its opponents in jail without fair trial, kills them or imposes internal exile. Even if the governing party wins a majority of votes, its election and its subsequent actions would lack legitimacy.

19.5 The European Convention on Human Rights

For people living in the UK today, one international human rights treaty has special importance – the European Convention on Human Rights and Fundamental Freedoms (ECHR). This treaty was created under the auspices of the Council of Europe (see above, 2.12.1), a key objective of which was to secure democracy in Europe after the Second World War. A supra-national judicial tribunal exists to adjudicate on alleged violations of the rights set out in the ECHR and enforce them against signatory States, currently 41 in number (see below, 19.6). And, since the enactment of the Human Rights Act 1998, people have also been able to argue in British courts that a 'public authority' has violated the ECHR (see below, 19.10), though many other international treaties have not (yet) been incorporated into national law, including the International Covenant on Civil and Political Rights (see above, 19.3).

Among the rights set out in the ECHR are: the right to life (Art 2); prohibition of torture, inhumane and degrading treatment (Art 3); prohibition of slavery and forced labour (Art 4); rights to liberty and security of the person (Art 5); right to a fair trial to determine civil obligations and criminal charges (Art 6); no punishment without law (Art 7); right to respect for a person's private and family life, his home and his correspondence (Art 8); freedom of thought, conscience and religion (Art 9); freedom of expression (Art 10); freedom of assembly and association, including the right to form and join trade unions (Art 11); and the right to marry (Art 12). There are a number of Protocols to the ECHR, not all of which the parties have yet agreed to be bound by. The First Protocol provides that 'every natural and legal person is entitled to the peaceful enjoyment of his possessions' (Art 1), that 'no person shall be denied the right to education' (Art 2) and that the parties to the Protocol 'undertake to hold free elections at reasonable intervals by secret ballot, under conditions which will ensure the free expression of the opinion of the people in the choice of the legislature' (Art 3).

Some rights, such as the protection against slavery (Art 4), the prohibition on torture and inhuman treatment (Art 3) and the prohibition on retrospective criminal legislation (Art 7) are unqualified; there are no permissible limitations. Many of the other rights are, however, qualified. Article 5 (right to liberty and security), for example, sets out specific situations where limitations by the State may be permissible. In others, Arts 8, 9, 10 and 11, competing interests which may countervail over the right in question are set out. These include:

(a) the interests of national security or public safety;

(b) the prevention of disorder or crime;

(c) the protection of health or morals; and

(d) the protection of the rights of others.

Articles 8(2) and 11(2) also include the protection of the freedoms of others, and Art 8(2) allows invasions of privacy which are in the interests of 'the economic well-being of the country'. These qualifications must be 'prescribed by law', in pursuit of a 'legitimate aim' and 'necessary in a democratic society'. The ECHR is, therefore, not a charter of libertarian values which upholds individual liberty against the State in all situations.

The Court of Human Rights conducts a strict inquiry into the legality of these qualifications. For a measure 'necessary in a democratic society' to be accepted as valid by the court, a three part test has to be satisfied. First, is the measure rationally connected to the end it purports to serve – in other words, is it at all effective in actually achieving this aim? Did the measure respond to a pressing social need? Secondly, were the effects of the measure in proportion to its aim? Thirdly, even though it fulfils these first requirements, is the measure, on balance, proportionate to the impact on the rights of the individual? In assessing whether the measure is proportionate to the aim, the Court of Human Rights takes into account the 'margin of appreciation' of the signatory State concerned, which means the area of discretion left to signatory States to determine the best solutions to their own national problems.

Since the Court of Human Rights is a supranational body determining liability under an international treaty, it is incumbent on the judges to recognise that governments of the signatory States are in a better position than they are to decide both on the presence of a particular risk and the measures necessary to combat it. The scope of this 'margin of appreciation' varies, depending upon the circumstances and subject matter of the case before a court. We will see from the chapters to follow that the court is reluctant to interfere with national measures which are justified, for example, by reference to public morality (*Handyside v UK* (1979), see below, 24.6). However, in the context of free speech rights (Art 10), the margin of appreciation will be a narrow one; the Court will scrutinise very closely any measure adopted which has the effect of quelling vibrant journalism and free debate in a democracy (*Sunday Times v UK* (1979)).

Article 14 states that:

The enjoyment of the rights and freedoms set forth in this Convention shall be secured without discrimination on any ground such as sex, race, colour, language, religion, political or other opinion, national or social origin, association with a national minority, property, birth or other status.

This does not create a free standing right to equal treatment, but is parasitic on other rights. In other words, it is only if a person is able to show that there has been differential treatment in relation to one of the other rights contained in the ECHR that an infringement of Art 14 may be alleged.

19.5.1 Derogations and reservations

Under Art 15 of the ECHR, parties may 'derogate' from complying with some of the articles of the Convention in certain defined circumstances, including the existence of a 'public emergency'. By lodging a formal document with the Council of Europe, a State may remain a party to the ECHR while declaring that it will not comply with a particular provision in it. Thus, in 1988, the UK entered a derogation in relation to Art 5 (rights to liberty and security of the person) after the Court of Human Rights had held, in *Brogan v UK* (1989), that police powers in the Prevention of Terrorism (Temporary Provisions) Act 1984, allowing suspects to be detained for seven days without charge, were contrary to the ECHR. No derogations are permitted in relation to Arts 3, 4 and 7.

A party may also enter a 'reservation' at the time it signs a Protocol to the ECHR. Thus, in relation to the right to education protected by Art 2 of the First Protocol, the UK agreed to the second sentence ('In the exercise of any functions which it assumes in relation to education and teaching, the State shall respect the right of parents to ensure such education and teaching in conformity with their own religious and philosophical convictions') only 'in so far as it is compatible with the provision of efficient instruction and training, and the avoidance of unreasonable public expenditure'.

19.6   The European Court of Human Rights

The ECHR is more than merely a codified text of rights and freedoms. It also establishes a judicial system for adjudicating upon complaints by individuals, companies and groups that they were victims of violations of the Convention by their own country. The UK agreed that, from 1966, people within its jurisdiction could have this right of individual petition (for a fascinating historical account, see Lester, A, 'UK acceptable of the Strasbourg jurisdiction: what really went on in Whitehall in 1965' [1998] PL 237).

At the time when the UK ratified the ECHR in the 1950s, the government was confident that British laws and government practices were 'consistent with our existing law in all but a small number of comparatively trivial cases' (Memorandum to Cabinet by Foreign Office Minister of State, Kenneth Younger, 25 July 1950). In the years which followed, many complaints against the UK have been made. Notable cases include: *Golder v UK* (1975) and *Silver v UK* (1983) (delegated legislation and internal rules under which prisoner refused access to a solicitor was contrary to Art 6 and Art 8); *Republic of Ireland v UK* (1978) (police in Northern Ireland held to have violated Art 3); *Sunday Times v UK* (1979) (common law contempt rules violated Art 10); *X v UK* (1981) (Mental Health Act 1959 violated Art 5); *Brogan v UK* (1988) (Prevention of Terrorism Act 1984 violated Art 5); and *McCann v UK* (1995) (rules of military engagement under which IRA members on bombing mission in Gibraltar were shot contrary to Art 2).

This dismal record dented the belief that the UK enjoyed a 'culture of liberty' and led to a long campaign for the ECHR to be incorporated directly into the UK's legal systems so that British courts would be empowered to adjudicate on Convention rights. But in comparison to the overall incidence of litigation in the UK courts, the number of people going to Strasbourg is relatively small. Between 1959 and 1995, the Court of Human Rights made 60 judgments in relation to the UK, and in 35 of them found that there had been at least one violation of the ECHR. Many other petitions were rejected at the initial stage as inadmissible (including, for example, that of the GCHQ trade unionists, whose application for judicial review, based on the ground of procedural impropriety, had been refused by the House of Lords in *Council of Civil Service Unions v Minister for the Civil Service* [1985] AC 374). During 1994, 236 applications against the UK were formally received in Strasbourg; 141 were held to be inadmissible; 16 were declared admissible; and there was one friendly settlement (see below). Up to 1998, the UK was third only to Italy and Turkey in the number of complaints made against it, though this crude statistic says little about the relative human rights record of the signatory States.

19.7 Procedures and remedies in the European Court of Human Rights

'Going to Strasbourg' is not an appeal from a national court, as the proceedings are entirely separate from those in each signatory State. As we shall see shortly, however, a person who intends to complain to the Court of Human Rights is required first to have tried to obtain justice in his own State. Until recently, there were two bodies responsible for dealing with grievances: the European Commission of Human Rights and the European Court of Human Rights. Both these institutions sat on a part time basis. The Commission was responsible for deciding whether a complaint was admissible and, if it was, attempting to reach a 'friendly settlement' between the State and the complainant. If no such settlement was achieved, the case was then adjudicated upon by the Court of Human Rights. The Commission filtered out approximately 97% of the 2,000 to 3,000 petitions received each year. This two tier system of decision making contributed to delays in dealing with cases: on average, it took five years from lodging a petition to the date of judgment.

On 1 November 1998, important procedural changes made by the Eleventh Protocol to the ECHR came into force. An entirely new court (though having the same name as its predecessor) replaces the two bodies. There is one judge from each of the ECHR's signatory States, currently 41 in number, and the new Court of Human Rights sits in permanent session. The judges are elected for terms of six years, and may be reappointed, by the Parliamentary Assembly of the Council of Europe. (Be clear! This institution is not part of the European Union, see above, 2.12.1.) The short term of office and the compulsory retirement of judges at 70 years of age have both been criticised: arguably, these arrangements compromise judicial independence and deprive the court of experienced candidates: see Mowbray, A, 'A new European Court of Human Rights' [1994] PL 540). The UK judge is Sir Nicolas Braza QC, who previously served on the European Commission of Human Rights.

Under the new procedures, a committee of three judges first considers the admissibility of each individual petition registered with the Court of Human Rights. The committee may, by unanimous vote, reject the application as inadmissible. If the committee is not unanimous, the question of admissibility will be determined by a Chamber of the Court. The criteria for admissibility, set out in Art 35, are:

(a) the applicant has exhausted all domestic remedies;

(b) the application is made within six months of having done (a);

(c) the applicant is not anonymous;

(d) the application raises a matter which is not substantially the same as one already ruled upon by the Court of Human Rights;

(e) the application is incompatible with the provisions of the Convention; and

(f) that the procedure is not being used as an 'abuse of right' or on the grounds of a 'manifestly ill-founded claim'.

If an application is held admissible, the parties are encouraged to reach a friendly settlement. If this cannot be achieved, the case then proceeds for hearing. The parties submit written evidence, and there is also power to send delegates to the signatory State to investigate the matters complained about. A chamber of seven judges hears oral submissions from the parties. The court gives judgment. Unlike the European Court of Justice (see above, 7.5.5), the Court of Human Rights' judgments need not be unanimous, and dissenting decisions may be delivered. In Chapters 20–27, we look in more detail at how the court approaches its task of adjudicating on violations of the Convention.

Remedies

Using less than crystal clear language, Art 41 (formerly Art 50) of the ECHR states:

> If the Court finds that a decision or measure taken by [... a signatory State ...] is completely or partially in conflict with the obligations arising from the present Convention, and if the internal law of the said Party allows only partial reparation to be made for the consequences of this decision or measure, the decision of the Court shall, if necessary, afford just satisfaction to the injured party.

(See, further, Mowbray, AR, 'The European Court of Human Rights' approach to just satisfaction' [1997] PL 647.) In many cases, the Court has regarded the fact of a finding that a Convention right has been violated is sufficient remedy. Compensation may also be awarded for pecuniary damage (financial loss consequent on a breach of a Convention right that can be quantified). It may also be awarded for non-pecuniary loss: for example, where an applicant has been held for an unreasonable period in detention in breach of Art 5, or has suffered distress or anxiety as a result of the violation of any of the protected rights. It is not easy to predict the level of damages that will be awarded for a breach of a Convention right from the relevant Strasbourg case law; awards for non-pecuniary damage tend to vary widely. Damages for distress and anxiety experienced by applicants as a result of the violation of a particular right have ranged from £1,000 per applicant in one case (*Papamichalopoulos and Others v Greece* (1995)) to £12,000 in another (*Hokkanen v Finland* (1994)).

The legal costs of taking a case to Strasbourg are recoverable if the applicant is successful. The applicant may also have incurred considerable costs at the domestic level, particularly if he or she has lost on the merits in a series of hearings, with consequent costs orders made against him or her. The Court of Human Rights does allow the recovery of domestic costs under Art 41, provided that they were incurred to prevent or remedy breaches of ECHR rights.

Where there is 'a serious question on interpretation or application of the Convention ... or a serious issue of general importance' (Art 43 of the ECHR), a party to an application may request that, within three months of the Chamber's judgment being delivered, the case be referred to a Grand Chamber of 17 judges. This is a re-hearing rather than an appeal, since a number of judges who have sat on the first panel will hear the case a second time. A case may also be referred to the Grand Chamber without first being determined by a chamber.

19.8 Who may be an applicant in Strasbourg?

Complaints under the ECHR may only be brought by 'a person, non-governmental organisation or a group of individuals claiming to be the victim of a violation of a Convention right' (Art 34, formerly Art 25 before the Eleventh Protocol came into force). Legal entities such as companies, and bodies such as trade unions are, therefore, also able to benefit from some of the 'human' rights contained in the Convention, though obviously some rights, such as to marriage, are inapplicable. This reflects the fact that autonomy from the State is important for voluntary associations (see above, 1.2) as well as for individuals, though some critics express unease that business enterprises may be able to claim rights such as freedom of expression (for an analysis, see Penner, R, 'The Canadian experience with the Charter of Rights: are there lessons for the UK?' [1996] PL 104).

The applicant must have been in some way adversely affected by the act complained of, even if the detriment is threatened rather than actual. In *Dudgeon v UK* (1982), an application was made by a gay man who had been questioned under laws in Northern Ireland which made homosexual activity a criminal offence. The fact that no prosecutions had been pursued under these laws in recent years did not detract from his status as victim, since there was always a possibility that the law would be enforced. Although actions by non-governmental organisations are permitted, this is on the premise that they have suffered the detriment. There is no scope for 'public interest' challenges in ECHR law (compare the position in judicial review in England and Wales (see above, 17.5.2).

The jurisdiction of the Court of Human Rights is not limited to individual complaints. One signatory State may apply to the court for a judgment on an alleged violation of the ECHR by another State. In 1971, Ireland brought an application against the UK which resulted in the Court of Human Rights holding that methods of interrogating suspects in Northern Ireland between 1971 and 1975 amounted to inhuman and degrading treatment contrary to Art 3 (*Ireland v UK* (1971)). In practice, however, between 1956 and 1995, only 12 inter-State applications were lodged.

19.9   Who is subject to challenge in Strasbourg?

The Court of Human Rights enforces the ECHR only against 'the High Contracting Parties' – the States which have ratified the Convention (Art 1). Complaints may allege that any State authority has violated the ECHR, including parliaments in enacting legislation (for instance, *Brogan v UK* challenging the Prevention of Terrorism Act 1984) and courts in deciding cases (for example, *Tolstoy v UK*, challenging a £1.5 m libel award by a High Court jury).

A State may sometimes be held responsible for actions of citizens or businesses. For example, the UK was held answerable for the action of a teacher in a private school who had 'slippered' the child of parents opposed to corporal punishment. The First Protocol to the ECHR states that 'In the exercise of any functions which it assumes in relation to education and teaching, the State shall respect the right of parents to ensure such education and teaching in conformity with their own religious and philosophical convictions'. The Court of Human Rights held that 'the State cannot absolve itself from responsibility [to secure an ECHR right] by delegating its obligations to private bodies or individuals' (*Costello-Roberts v UK* (1995)) and, since Acts of Parliament made it mandatory for parents to educate their children, and authorised private schools to provide education, the UK was implicated in such a school's breach (see below, 23.2.10).

The concept of *Drittwirkung der Grundrechte* (German for 'third party effect of fundamental rights') – or 'horizontal effect' – is beginning to be developed. In essence, this is the idea that one of the responsibilities of a State is to ensure that one citizen (or company) does not violate the human rights of another. Thus, if there is a 'right to privacy', this might apply not only to the prying eyes of police surveillance and intrusions of social workers, but may also mean that government should prevent newspaper journalists snooping on people (for instance, by enacting privacy legislation).

19.10 The Human Rights Act 1998

A central feature of the Labour government's constitutional reform programme after the 1997 general election was to 'bring rights home' by incorporating the ECHR into the legal systems of the UK. The UK's dualist approach to international law means that unless specifically transposed into national law by an Act of Parliament, litigants in national courts cannot generally rely upon rights contained in treaties (see above, 2.12.1). There was, therefore, little scope for people in Britain to use the ECHR in their own courts, except perhaps to persuade a judge to interpret an ambiguous statutory provision so that it was in accordance with the Convention. After the enactment of the Human Rights Act 1998, the position has altered significantly. As a last resort, people will still be able to petition the Court of Human Rights, but now they will also be able to advance arguments in British courts about the rights contained in the ECHR.

19.10.1 The duty of interpretation

Section 3 of the Human Rights Act 1998 places the following duty on all courts and tribunals in all types of legal proceedings:

> So far as it is possible to do so, primary legislation and subordinate legislation must be read and given effect in a way which is compatible with the Convention rights.

It is not entirely clear what this means (see Marshall, G, 'Interpreting interpretation in the Human Rights Bill' [1998] PL 167) and it remains to be seen how British judges carry out this new function. UK courts and tribunals must 'take into account' the judgments of the Court of Human Rights and the opinions of the former European Commission on Human Rights (s 2(1) of the Human Rights Act 1998). This means that Strasbourg case law will be influential, although not binding, on the national courts' interpretation of the scope of the rights and limitations set out in the ECHR.

19.10.2 Declarations of incompatibility

If the High Court finds that it is impossible to 'read and give effect' to an Act of Parliament or statutory instrument so that it is compatible with the ECHR, it may make a formal 'declaration of incompatibility' (s 4). Such a declaration has only limited effect as it '(a) does not affect the validity, continuing operation or enforcement of the provision in respect of which it is given; and (b) is not binding on the parties to the proceedings in which it is made'. The limited nature of the remedy is explained by the statement in the White Paper *Rights Brought Home: The Human Rights Bill*, Cm 3782, 1997 (para 2.13):

> The Government has reached the conclusion that courts should not have the power to set aside primary legislation, past or future, on the ground of incompatibility with the Convention. This conclusion arises from the importance with the Government attaches to Parliamentary sovereignty.

The only legal consequence of a declaration of incompatibility is that it may prompt a government minister to use the 'power to take remedial action' in Parliament contained in s 10.

19.10.3 Remedial orders in Parliament

Section 10 empowers a government minister to introduce a statutory instrument to amend or repeal the provision which a British court has declared to be incompatible with the ECHR. This is known as a 'remedial order'. A minister may also use the power to make a remedial order if it appears to him that a finding of the Court of Human Rights suggests that UK legislation is incompatible with the Convention. Section 10 is therefore a 'Henry VIII' clause, enabling primary legislation to be altered by subordinate legislation – something which is potentially of concern, given the limited opportunities for Parliament to scrutinise such legislation (see above, 6.5.2). There is a 'fast track' procedure of 40 days during which both Houses of Parliament debate and pass resolutions affirming the changes proposed by the draft remedial order (s 12). Section 10 grants the minister a power, rather than imposing a duty, to amend incompatible legislation; if a minister decides not to introduce a remedial order into Parliament, he cannot be challenged in the courts for this decision: s 6(6).

Legislation does not normally have retrospective effect. Section 11, however, hints that ministers making remedial orders may deal with the specific circumstances which led a litigant to seek a declaration of incompatibility. The remedial order may 'be made so as to have effect from a date earlier than that on which it is made' and may 'make different provision for different cases': s 11(1)(a) and (c).

19.10.4 Using the ECHR as a ground of judicial review or appeal

Section 6 of the Human Rights Act 1998 states that: 'It is unlawful for a public authority to act in a way which is incompatible with one or more of the Convention rights'. In effect, this creates a new ground of judicial review in addition to illegality, irrationality and procedural impropriety (see above, 11.2). Section 6 also creates a defence to such a challenge. A public authority will not be held to have acted unlawfully if, as a result of one or more provisions in an Act of Parliament or a statutory instrument, 'the authority could not have acted differently'. In other words, a public authority may argue that it was merely following national legislation. In the chapters which follow, we examine some of the rights contained in the Convention and how they may now be used as the basis for judicial review challenges. For the time being, however, the focus is on the modifications to the judicial review procedure which occur when a ECHR point is raised.

As we saw, the courts have struggled to devise a workable common law test for determining which decisions of what bodies are amenable to judicial review (see above, 17.5). Broadly, there has been a shift from focusing only on the source of the decision maker's power to looking also at the functions the decision making body is performing (*R v Panel on Take-overs and Mergers ex p Datafin plc* (1987)). Obviously, the Human Rights Act 1998 needs to demarcate in some way which bodies and office holders' actions may be challenged as violating the ECHR. It could have adopted the approach used in the legislation creating ombudsmen (see above, Chapter 10) and merely listed in a schedule to the Act which public authorities fall within its ambit. The Human Rights Act 1998 does not do this, however; instead, it uses a broad and flexible, but also potentially uncertain, definition of 'public authority'. Applicants are allowed to use incompatibility with the Convention as a ground of review only against 'public authorities'. According to s 6(3), this includes:

(a) a court,

(b) a tribunal which exercises functions in relation to legal proceedings, and

(c) any person certain of whose functions are functions of a public nature, but does not include either House of Parliament or a person exercising functions in connection with proceedings in Parliament.

It is also provided that 'In relation to a particular act, a person is not a public authority by virtue only of sub-section (3)(c) if the nature of the act is private' (s 6(5)). Each of these elements of the definition needs to be considered more closely.

Challenging court and tribunal decisions

Clearly, s 6(3)(a) and (b) includes the types of courts and tribunals which are already amenable to judicial review on the common law grounds of illegality, procedural impropriety and irrationality: for example, magistrates' courts, the Immigration Appeals Tribunal and the Criminal Injuries Compensation Board. The broad term 'court' in s 6 goes further than this, however. It includes the 'superior courts' – in England and Wales, the Crown Court, the High Court, the Court of Appeal and the Appellate Committee of the House of Lords – which have not been subject to judicial review. (This is because judicial review developed historically as a method for supervising decision making of 'inferior' courts, and for the obvious practical reason that the High Court could not review itself or the courts above it in the hierarchy.) The duty of the superior courts to act only in ways compatible with the ECHR cannot, therefore, be enforced by means of a judicial review challenge. Instead, their duty will be enforced by making violation of the ECHR (for instance failing to develop the common law in accordance with Convention rights) a ground of appeal from their judgments.

Challenging self-regulatory and similar bodies

The definition of 'public authority' in s 6 states that

(3) (c) any person certain of whose functions are functions of a public nature

...

(5) in relation to a particular act, a person is not a public authority by virtue of subsection 3(c) if the nature of the act is private.

This mirrors the common law test propounded in *ex p Datafin*, to define when decisions of non-statutory bodies are subject to judicial review (see above, 17.6.2). Thus, organisations such as the Advertising Standards Authority will have to be wary of infringing Art 10 of the ECHR (freedom of expression), and the Press Complaints Commission, the self-regulatory body of the newspaper industry, will have to ensure that, in its determinations, it does not violate Art 8 (respect for privacy).

By adopting this 'public function' test, the Human Rights Act 1998 may go far further than the Court of Human Rights can in applying Convention rights. In Strasbourg, the ECHR is enforceable only against the signatory States and their agents – though, as we have seen, this may include private institutions (see above, 19.9).

Challenging legislation

Section 6(3) of the Human Rights Act 1998 excludes from its definition of public authorities 'either House of Parliament'. This means that a person cannot directly apply for judicial review of a provision in an Act of Parliament on the ground that it violates one or more Convention rights. This restriction is anomalous for two reasons. First, it *is* possible to challenge directly the validity of an Act of Parliament on the ground that it is incompatible with *European Community* law and for the High Court to grant a declaration to this effect (see *R v Secretary of State for Employment ex p Equal Opportunities Commission* (1995), above, 7.9.2). There seems little good reason to prohibit the court from carrying out the same task in relation to the ECHR. Secondly, under s 3, the court is empowered to make a declaration of incompatibility when it tries, but fails, to 'read and give effect' to an Act in a way which respects Convention rights. In practical terms, the exclusion of Parliament from the definition of 'public authority' therefore means that:

(a) an application for judicial review form (see above, 17.3) cannot boldly name a statutory provision as the 'judgment, order or other proceedings in respect of which relief is sought'; however

(b) if the applicant is complaining about a public authority's decision or action and an issue of interpretation arises, then, in the course of the application, the court may grant a declaration that an Act of Parliament is incompatible with the ECHR.

There are two possible justifications for omitting Parliament from s 6. One is that the restriction is necessary in order to preserve parliamentary sovereignty; but as the court can make declarations of incompatibility in other circumstances, this carries little weight (see above, 5.2.5 and 19.10.2). A better justification is that a court ought to have a factual context, not just statutory words in a vacuum, in which to examine whether words in an Act are incompatible with the Convention. If people were allowed to challenge statutory provisions under s 6, the court might have to ask itself hypothetical questions to establish whether the words of enactment breached the ECHR.

The Human Rights Act contains no prohibition on a person directly seeking judicial review of a provision contained in a statutory instrument (see above, 6.5.2) on the ground of incompatibility with an ECHR right. In other words, a statutory instrument can be named as the 'judgment, order or other proceedings in respect of which relief is sought' on an application for judicial review form (see above, 7.3). Even though statutory instruments may be debated and affirmed by resolution of one or both Houses of Parliament, they are regarded as 'made' by the office holder or body (normally a minister) stipulated in the enabling Act of Parliament (see above, 6.5.2). They are not 'proceedings in Parliament'. The Human Rights Act 1998 does, however, prevent the court quashing a statutory instrument if it is in accordance with the enabling Act of Parliament and that Act 'cannot be read or given effect in a way which is compatible with Convention rights' (s 6(2)(b)); all an applicant will obtain in these circumstances is a declaration of incompatibility under s 4(4).

Challenging proceedings in Parliament

Section 6 of the Human Rights Act excludes from its definition of 'public authority' any 'person exercising functions in connection with proceedings in Parliament'. This reflects the law on parliamentary privilege and Art 9 of the Bill of Rights 1698, which provides that 'the freedom of speech, and the debates or proceedings in Parliament ought not to be impeached or questioned in any court or place outside Parliament' (see above, 6.6). Thus, for example. a Member of Parliament being investigated for alleged improper conduct by the Parliamentary Commissioner for Standards (see above, 6.7) will not be able to seek judicial review on, say, the ground that there has been a breach of Art 6 of the ECHR (fair trials). While this exclusion from the Human Rights Act 1998 may protect violations from challenge in the UK courts, parliamentary proceedings have no immunity under the ECHR itself and the Court of Human Rights is able to consider complaints in respect of them (*Demicoli v Malta* (1992)).

19.10.5 Standing to apply for judicial review on ECHR grounds

The requirement for applicants to have 'sufficient interest in the matter to which the application relates' (s 31(3)of the Supreme Court Act 1981) has been considerably relaxed in recent years to allow pressure groups, such as the World Development Movement and Greenpeace, to apply for judicial review in the public interest, even though their own rights have not been affected any more than those of any other person (see above, 17.5.2). In s 7(3), the Human Rights Act modifies the standing requirement for applicants wishing to use the Convention as a ground of judicial review:

> If the proceedings are brought on an application for judicial review, the applicant is to be taken to have a sufficient interest in relation to the unlawful act only if he is, or would be, a victim of that act.

The test, by introducing a requirement of victimhood, is thus stricter than for applications which do not raise ECHR arguments. The unconvincing justification for this is that the status of victim is a requirement for individuals who, having exhausted their remedies in national courts, wish to take a case to the Court of Human Rights (see Art 34 of the ECHR, discussed above, 19.8). The incorporation by the Human Rights Act of the victim test into national law has the unfortunate consequence that, in judicial review applications brought in the public interest – 'an accepted and greatly valued dimension of the judicial review jurisdiction' (see above, 17.5.2) – the public authority challenged will be able to oppose the application on the basis that the applicant is not a 'victim' and so cannot raise a violation of the ECHR as a ground in the judicial review application – even if the applicant has sufficient interest to argue illegality, irrationality or procedural impropriety.

19.10.6 Damages for violation of the ECHR

Generally, when a public body is held to have acted unlawfully by making a decision which is illegal, irrational or procedurally improper, this in itself gives an applicant for judicial review no basis for claiming damages (see above, 17.4). The applicant has to establish that an actionable tort has been committed in order to obtain damages. Section 8 of the Human Rights Act provides:

(1) In relation to any act (or proposed act) of a public authority which the court finds is (or would be) unlawful, it may grant such relief or remedy, or make such order, within its jurisdiction, as it considers just and appropriate.

(2) But damages may be awarded by a court which has power to award damages, or order the payment of compensation, in civil proceedings.

The court is prohibited from awarding damages unless it 'is satisfied that the award is necessary to afford just satisfaction to the person in whose favour it is made' (s 8(3)) and the court 'must take into account the principles applied by the European Court of Human Rights in relation to the award of compensation under Art 41 of the Convention' (s 8(4)). Section 8 ends by stating that 'unlawful' means unlawful under s 6(1)'.

Section 8(1) thus begins by creating generous empowering provisions, which are then whittled away in each ensuing sub-section. As we have seen, the Court of Human Rights' approach to Art 41 compensation is both cautious and inconsistent (see above, 19.7). If a public authority is following national legislation which a court declares to be incompatible with the ECHR under s 3, the litigant will not be entitled to damages, because the public authority will not have been acting 'unlawfully' within the meaning of s 6. Damages will, therefore, not be available to buttress the remedy of the declaration of incompatibility (see above, 19.10.2).

19.11 Human rights and European Community law

As we have noted, the European Union and European Community law is a legal system quite distinct from that of the Council of Europe and the ECHR (see above, 2.12.1). There are, however, important interconnections between them. First, all Member States of the European Union are parties to the ECHR.

Secondly, the European Court of Justice in Luxembourg regards the rights protected by the ECHR as forming part of the 'general principles' of Community case law. The manner in which the court has done this has come in for scathing criticism by some academics. It has been argued that the ECJ prefers to interpret Convention rights in a way that best suits the purposes of the Community institutions, the rationale for Community legislation being very different from the guiding principles of the Court of Human Rights. Sceptics of this jurisprudence point out that by 'grabbing the moral high ground' of ECHR principles, the Community institutions are seeking to do no more than promote commercial interests over real human rights priorities maintained by individual Member States. So far, no individual application for judicial review of Community law on ECHR principles has succeeded. (For an introduction to this debate, see Coppel, J and O'Neill, O, 'The ECJ: taking rights seriously?' (1992) 29 CML Rev 699; and, for a contrasting view, Weiler, J and Lockhart, N, 'Taking rights seriously: the ECJ and its fundamental rights jurisprudence' (1995) 32 CML Rev 51).

One interconnection between the two European systems which is missing is that the European Union itself is not a party to the ECHR. (To be accurate, it would be the European Community which would become a party, as it has legal personality, whereas the European Union does not). This means that a person or business claiming that an institution of the European Union (for instance, the Commission) has breached human rights cannot take a case to the Court of Human Rights. There are several reasons why the European Union has not become a party to the ECHR. In Opinion 2/94 *Re Accession of the Community to the European Human Rights Convention* (1996), the Court of Justice held the EC Treaty contained no express or implied powers enabling the Community to become a party to the ECHR. In any event, some Member States take the view that, because the European Community is not a 'State', it ought not, itself, to participate in treaty organisations such as that of the ECHR. It is also far from certain that parties to the ECHR which are not Member States of the European Union would welcome it joining.

The question therefore arises whether one or more Member States of the European Union, which are parties to the ECHR, may be liable before the Court of Human Rights for a violation of the ECHR following a decision reached by the European Union's institutions. The Court of Human Rights has recently answered this in the affirmative. In *Matthews v UK* (1999), a resident of Gibraltar complained that people living there had no vote in elections for the European Parliament (see above, 7.5.2) contrary to Protocol No 1 of the ECHR, Art 3 (set out above, 19.1). Gibraltar is not part of the UK, but people living there are British nationals (see above, 2.4). The provisions of the EC Treaty apply there, though Gibraltar is excluded from the operation of some of its provisions, notably on free movement of goods. In 1976, the Member States of the European Community concluded a treaty agreement between themselves on direct elections to the European Parliament; the Council subsequently made a Decision under EC Treaty, Art 249 setting out in more detail the voting arrangements; Gibraltar was not included in the franchise. The Court of Human Rights accepted that the European Community as such could not be challenged because it was not a contracting party to the ECHR; but it held that the UK, by its actions in participating in making the Council Decision, was responsible for the violation of the ECHR.

19.12 A triumph for judges over elected representatives?

The emergence of broadly expressed legal rights to liberties in international law, European Community law and national laws causes some people concern. Rights such as those we are about to examine in Chapters 20–27 are really 'political' conflicts, it is said, which are not appropriately resolved by litigation processes and the formal legal reasoning used by lawyers and judges. JAG Griffith is one such trenchant critic. He describes Art 10 of the ECHR protecting freedom of expression as sounding 'like a statement of political conflict pretending to be a resolution of it' and he warns us that 'law is not and cannot be a substitute for politics' ('The political constitution' (1979) 42 MLR 1, p 19). Litigation about violation of the Convention, he argues, has for lawyers just become a 'happy and fruitful exercise of interpreting woolly principles and even woollier exceptions'. Keith Ewing and Conor Gearty, looking at US Supreme Court decisions dealing with homosexual rights and abortion, write:

> The difficulty is that on closer inspection these cases do not look very much like a strictly legal search for principle. When their outer layers are peeled away and they are stripped of their grandiloquent language, they resemble far more closely the dressing up of the judges' policy preferences in legal clothes. It is difficult for advocates of sophisticated philosophical theories about judicial law-making to realise that most tough decisions emerge from the personality of the judge – with all the prejudice, chance happenings and experiences which

come with it' [*Democracy or a Bill of Rights*, 1994, London: Society of Labour Lawyers].

The same is true, some suggest, of decisions of the Court of Human Rights and, after the enactment of the Human Rights Act 1998, of human rights litigation in the UK. The accusation, in short, is that it is wrong for us to have diverted debate about important issues from the political to the judicial arena.

One trend in UK constitutional law is clear: judges in London, Luxembourg and Strasbourg now have more power than ever before to adjudicate on whether legislation passed by elected representatives the UK Parliament matches up to the requirements set by the ECHR and Community law. It is only in relation to Community law that judges have the power actually to set aside an offending legislative provision; but the capacity of British judges to make declarations of incompatibility under the Human Rights Act 1998 and the capacity of the Court of Human Rights to make findings enforceable in international law in reality falls only a little short of this.

Of all the 'sophisticated philosophical theories' which seek to justify the courts' powers to question the enactments of elected legislatures, one of the most persuasive is provided by Ronald Dworkin. Dworkin accepts that democracy based on the wishes of the majority (or their representatives) is a desirable way of organising society. But he argues that certain conditions have to be met before majoritarian decision making has any moral advantage over types of government. What are these preconditions to majority rule? Perhaps the most controversial is what he calls 'moral independence'; for Dworkin, a genuine political community must be a community of independent moral agents: 'It must not dictate what its citizens think about matters of political or moral or ethical judgment, but must, on the contrary, provide circumstances that encourage them to arrive at beliefs on those matters through their own reflective and finally individual conviction' (*Freedom's Law*, 1997, Oxford: OUP, p 26). Some institution other than the representative legislature whose legislation is challenged has to judge whether the preconditions to democracy exist. In most liberal democracies, this function has been assigned to a court, though it could, perhaps, also be carried out by a body of non-lawyers hearing arguments about alleged infringements of constitutional rights.

CIVIL LIBERTIES AND HUMAN RIGHTS

The term 'rights' is used both:

(a) to refer to existing legally enforceable entitlements or freedoms; and

(b) as a rhetorical device to lend weight to an assertion about how to treat other people morally.

The tradition in the UK has been to attach importance to 'civil liberties'. Personal autonomy is the freedom to do anything not expressly prohibited by law and many people have considered that the common law adequately protects these liberties. Until recently, codified statements of people's rights were eschewed by domestic law.

After the Second World War, international treaty organisations were established to protect human rights. The concept of human rights is not limited to protecting people from the improper incursions by the State into personal freedom; it extends to include civil, political, social and economic rights. Many commentators regard human rights as being held universally by all people, everywhere in the world, by reason of the fact that they are human beings. Therefore, such rights in international law 'cannot be given or withdrawn at will by any domestic legal system'.

The European Convention on Human Rights, in force since 1953, is a particularly developed regional system for protecting human rights. There are now 41 parties to it. Although some rights set out in the ECHR (for instance, the prohibition of torture) are held by people without qualification, other rights (such as privacy and freedom of expression) may be lawfully curtailed by government in the interests of national security or public safety, the prevention of disorder or crime, the protection of health or morals and the protection of the rights of others. The ECHR is, therefore, not a libertarian charter.

The European Court of Human Rights in Strasbourg is the judicial body to which individuals may bring a complaint after all domestic remedies have been exhausted. To bring a complaint, a person must be a 'victim' of a violation of the ECHR. Companies and other organisations are entitled to protection in respect of some of the rights in the ECHR. The violation must have been committed by a public authority (which may be a parliament, government or courts), or by a body (such as a private school) which is acting under powers delegated by the State. A State may also be required to ensure that one individual or private body does not violate the human rights of another (*Drittwirkung der Grundrechte*).

In the UK, the Human Rights Act 1998 enacts a scheme for incorporating the ECHR into national law. Courts and tribunals hearing any type of case have an interpretative obligation to ensure that Acts of Parliament and subordinate legislation are, so far as possible, 'read and given effect in a way which is compatible with the Convention rights' (s 3). Higher courts in the UK may make a 'declaration of incompatibility' when it is not possible to interpret a statutory provision in this way. The Human Rights Act 1998 also makes it unlawful for a public authority to act in a way which is incompatible with Convention rights' (s 6). This will, in effect, form a ground of judicial review – but only applicants who are 'victims' of the violation will be permitted to apply for judicial review. Courts may award damages for unlawful action.

The European Community is not a party to the ECHR, though the Court of Justice seeks to uphold human rights as part of the 'general principles' of Community law. The European Court of Human Rights may find Member States of the European Community responsible for violations of the ECHR by Community legislation in which the Member State participated in making.

Not all commentators welcome the emergence of broadly expressed human rights in international law, Community law and national law. Critics fear that law will become a substitute for politics.

CHAPTER 20

RIGHT TO LIFE

20.1 Introduction

The right to life operates in relation to two aspects of State power. The first is the ability of public authorities to kill people, through capital punishment or the mobilisation of its police and armed forces to quell civil unrest. The second is the role of public authorities in regulating individuals' decisions over their own life and death, by way of terminating pregnancy, assisted suicide, or the killing of other citizens. In addition to these direct controls, the State, as the largest supplier of medical services, has an indirect role in making decisions about the rationing of health care, which may lead to people's death.

The right to life as it is formulated and interpreted in rights instruments is not absolute. Article 2 of the European Convention on Human Rights (ECHR), for example, allows for a number of situations in which deprivation of life will not violate the Convention:

1   Everyone's right to life shall be protected by law. No one shall be deprived of his life intentionally save in the execution of a sentence of a court following his conviction of a crime for which this penalty is provided by law.

2   Deprivation of life shall not be regarded as inflicted in contravention of this Article when it results from the use of force which is no more than absolutely necessary:

   (a) in defence of any person from unlawful violence

   (b) in order to effect a lawful arrest or to prevent the escape of a person lawfully detained

   (c) in action lawfully taken for the purpose of quelling a riot or insurrection.

The Sixth Protocol to the ECHR, which the UK ratified in 1999, abolishes the use of the death penalty in peacetime. Under the Protocol, individuals are granted a right not to be condemned to such a penalty or executed. The use of the death penalty in time of war or imminent threat of war is permitted. Until 1998, the UK retained the death penalty for treason and piracy with violence, and, for this reason, it did not sign the Protocol at the time, since it obliges States to abolish the death penalty as it exists in law, even though in practice it is never carried out. These remaining capital offences were abolished by the Crime and Disorder Act 1998.

On a personal level, the right to life is said to oblige States to recognise and uphold autonomy of choice. This right, the argument goes, protects an individual's ability to make personal decisions about life and life's values for him or herself. In this chapter, we examine the role of the State in preventing assisted suicide and euthanasia and the exercise of choice as part of the right to life (see below, 20.6). The inclusion of this freedom of choice in the right to life is not universally accepted, and it is a feature of the rather open ended nature of this right that it can be deployed by opposing sides of an argument; the right to independent choice by a terminally ill patient as part of his or her quality of life is often set against the argument that the right to life is so absolute that the State cannot be called upon to condone its termination. Sedley LJ has observed recently that:

> It is one of history's ironies that, having now put the judicial taking of life behind us, the law's ability to sanction the taking, or more urgently the non-prolongation, of life by others is likely to come dramatically to the fore ... in matters of life and death the law has a fraught journey ahead which is going to jolt our notions of justice.

The law is thus inextricably involved at each end of the spectrum of the right to life, however unrelated the issues may appear: whether they involve the use of lethal force by special security forces, or the administration of morphine to a terminally ill patient.

20.2   State killing

The right to life, as set out in the ECHR, is limited in a number of situations (see above, 20.1). Despite these limitations, it is arguable that the threshold requirements for the legitimate exercise of State power, in the context of the right to life, should be high. For example, the police should not be permitted to justify a shoot to kill policy under any of the exceptions to the right to life. After a death occurs at the hands of the police or armed forces, the State should provide full judicial investigation into the circumstances of death to ascertain whether the killing was justified or not. Neither of these requirements is actually specified in the article. It is a matter of interpretation for the court determining the scope of the right in any particular instance. In the UK, the issue of State killing by the police and armed forces arises most often in Northern Ireland, where the Criminal Law (Northern Ireland) Act 1967 permits the use of lethal force to prevent crime or to effect the arrest of offenders or suspected offenders or of 'persons unlawfully at large'. The force used must be 'reasonable in the circumstances'. Judges in the UK are, on the whole, reluctant to rule that the use of force in combating terrorism is unreasonable, although in *McCann and Others v UK* (1996), the question was raised as to whether the criterion of 'reasonability' in English law matches up to Art 2(2) of the ECHR which stipulates that lethal force can only be justified on the basis of 'necessity'.

McCann was the first case to reach the Strasbourg Court on the question of Art 2. The Court ruled, by a slim majority, that the killing of three unarmed members of the IRA in Gibraltar by undercover British soldiers who apparently believed they were on a bombing mission did not come within any of the permissible exceptions to Art 2. On the facts, the Court found that the soldiers' 'honest belief' that the shooting was necessary to prevent the people detonating bombs was sufficient to exonerate them from liability, as State actors, for breach of Art 2. This aspect of the judgment suggests that the Strasbourg approach to the issue of justification for lethal force is not far from the British one. However, the Court did find a violation of Art 2 by the UK, because there had been other ways in which the arrest operation could have been planned without risk to the suspects' lives. Under the relevant prevention of terrorism legislation, such action could be justified if it were 'reasonable'; under the Convention it could only be justified if it was 'necessary'. The European Court of Human Rights did not rule that the legislative standard itself was in terms a breach of Art 2; the Court is generally reluctant to examine, in abstract, the compatibility of the wording of particular laws with the terms of the Convention. The view of the majority of the judges was that, in relation to the standard of reasonableness in national legislation, 'the difference between the two standards is not sufficiently great that a violation of Art 2(1) could be found on this ground alone'. The finding that the action against the suspected terrorists could have been planned differently and therefore violated Art 2 has important implications for the organisation of police operations, since it will be incumbent on police authorities to explain in legal proceedings after the event why they did not take a less risky course of action.

The European Court of Human Rights does not always find a violation where an alternative course of action could have been possible; if the planning of the operation survives ECHR scrutiny, the Court is slow to condemn operational failure. In *Andronicou v Cyprus* (1998), the Cypriot police and security forces attempted a rescue operation on a besieged house where A was holding C at gunpoint. During the operation, both A and C were shot dead. The victims' families claimed that Art 2 had been breached. The court held that the use of force by the police for the 'defence of any person from unlawful violence' under Art 2(2) could be justified by the policemen's honest belief that it was necessary to kill A in order to rescue C, even if this honest belief later turned out to be wrong. This case, therefore, suggests that the approach of the Court in future claims under Art 2 is to find that the 'absolutely necessary' test under Art 2 will be satisfied by the honest belief of the agents of the State.

20.3 Duty to prevent death

The State should observe the right to life by criminalising killing by private individuals. The case law under Art 2 of the ECHR indicates, however, that this obligation extends only so far as a duty on the State to provide police and security forces to enforce the criminal law against killing. The Strasbourg authorities have so far refrained from ruling on the appropriateness and efficiency of signatory States' anti-crime measures.

It is not clear either from the ECHR or from the common law to what extent the duty to prevent death applies beyond the scope of deliberate killing. There is no duty to rescue in English law, so there is no obligation on a passer-by on right to life principles to extract a victim from the wreckage of a car or a drowning child from a lake. This contrasts with the position in French law, under which it is a criminal offence, even for a stranger, to fail to come to the assistance of victims of an accident. This made it possible for the authorities to press charges against the paparazzi who pursued the Princess of Wales' car to the site of the fatal crash in August 1997, although the prosecutions were subsequently dropped because no causal link could be established between the paparazzi's activities and the fatal accident. The immunity from a duty to rescue also extends in English law to official rescuers. In a case involving the deaths of four children on a canoeing party, the company which had organised the expedition settled the claims by the victims' families for their allegedly negligent handling of the outing. The company then sought an indemnity from the Coastguard service for failing to answer emergency calls promptly and failing to come to the assistance of the troubled expedition. The court held that the Coastguard service had no private duty of care to the families (*OLL v Secretary of State for Transport* (1997)).

In general, the European Commission and Court of Human Rights have taken a similar view of the obligations arising out of Art 2:

> Whether risk derives from disease, environmental factors or from the intentional activities of those acting outside the law, there will be a range of policy decisions, relating, *inter alia*, to the use of State resources, which it will be for Contracting States to assess on the basis of their aims and priorities [*Osman v UK* (1999)].

Neither national courts nor the European Court of Human Rights wish to impose liability on the State under the right to life where such liability would have resource implications. For example, the Commission has ruled that Art 2 does not extend to an obligation on States to provide indefinite bodyguard services in order to protect one of their citizens from threatened attack: *X v Ireland* (1973).

On the other hand, the police, and other public bodies, are sometimes liable for the deaths of people who are in their care, even though they have not caused the deaths. In *Kirkham v Chief Constable of Manchester* (1989), the Court of Appeal held the police liable for the suicide of a man in their custody whom they knew to be suffering from clinical depression. The police may also be held liable for the suicides of prisoners of sound mind. However, recently, the House of Lords has ruled on this issue, saying that where a prisoner of sound mind commits suicide by taking advantage of a breach of duty by the authorities (in this case, the prisoner hanged himself from a cell hatch which had been negligently left open) the police, though liable, would not have to pay full damages. The award would be reduced to take account of the prisoner's responsibility in causing the loss by his own intentional act (*Reeves v Commissioner of Police for the Metropolis* (1999)).

Until recently, the police have enjoyed an immunity from liability for any step they take, or may fail to take, in the course of the investigation into behaviour which may result in one individual killing another. When the family of one of the Yorkshire Ripper victims attempted to sue the police in negligence for failing to identify and detain the murderer, the House of Lords took the view that the police owed no general duty of care to identify and capture an unknown criminal, even though there might be a foreseeable risk to a class of potential victims – in that particular case, young women (*Hill v Chief Constable of West Yorkshire* (1989)). The House of Lords considered that any finding of such a duty would paralyse police activity, because the police would have to justify every step they took in the investigation of a crime with the result that manpower and resources would be diverted from the investigation and prevention of crime to the defending of procedures in court cases.

This immunity from suit in English law has come up for consideration in the European Court of Human Rights under Arts 2 and 6 (the right to a fair trial). In *Osman v UK* (1999), the Court considered an argument that the failure of the police and social services to prevent the murder of a schoolboy's father by one of the teachers after they had been warned about the teacher's suspicious activities was a violation of the victim's right to life under Art 2 of the ECHR. The applicants also argued, inter alia, that the immunity of the police under the rule in *Hill* was a breach of their right of access to court under Art 6. The Court rejected the claim under Art 2. On the facts of the case, they concluded that the police had not erred in concluding that the deceased had been at risk. However, the Art 6 argument was successful. The Court took the view that blanket immunity of the police from negligence actions by victims' families violated the applicants' right under Art 6 to air the substance of their claim before a court of law. Although it concerned Art 6 rather than Art 2, the decision in *Osman* has certain implications for the enforcement of criminal legislation in national law. If agents of the State know that they may have to justify in future litigation each step they have taken to prevent a murder, or each opportunity missed, in the course of an investigation, it may have the effect of making them more alert to the sort of early warnings of impending catastrophe they received in *Osman's* case.

20.4 Asylum, deportation and extradition

Appeals to the right to life are often made in judicial proceedings challenging the State's decision in refusing entry or enforcing departure of aliens. In *Bugdaycay v Secretary of State for the Home Department* (1987), the applicant challenged the Home Office's decision to disallow his asylum application on the basis that he faced a real risk of death if he returned to his home country. The court, upholding his application on *Wednesbury* grounds (see above, 15.5.1), stated that, in cases where 'the most fundamental of all human rights' were at stake, in other words the individual's right to life, judges must apply the 'most anxious scrutiny' to the lawfulness and reasonableness of the administrative decision in question. The failure, in other words, of the immigration authorities to take on board the risk to the applicant's life amounts to a failure to take account of a legally relevant consideration, one of the preconditions for *Wednesbury* unreasonableness.

Strasbourg case law in this area often involves a consideration of the prohibition under Art 3 of inhuman and degrading treatment. Article 3 is pleaded together with Art 2, where the threat to the applicant's life is covered by one of the permitted exceptions to Art 2. This Article, it will be remembered, permits the death penalty in countries which have not yet ratified the Sixth Protocol. In *Soering v UK* (1989), the Court was therefore unable, on the basis of Art 2, to prevent the UK from extraditing S to the US where he faced the death penalty. However, his argument under Art 3 succeeded, since the 'death row phenomenon' in the view of the Court amounted to 'inhuman and degrading treatment'. It did not matter that the UK itself was not responsible for the conditions suffered by prisoners awaiting the imposition of the death penalty in the US. The liability of the State was engaged by the fact that it was prepared to expose him to that risk.

20.5 The right to medical treatment

[handwritten: Positive obligation under Art.3]

Appeals to the right to life have been couched not only in negative terms, urging the State not to take action that would lead to the violation of that right, but in positive terms as well, requiring the State to take positive action to ensure the preservation of the right. Although doctors are private parties and medical negligence actions against doctors are governed by private law principles, the State, as the main supplier of medical services, is implicated in many decisions taken by doctors with wider application. In *R v Cambridge Health Authority ex p B* (1995), the health authority was advised by medical experts that the applicant, a child suffering from a rare form of leukaemia, had only a very slim chance of surviving a bone marrow operation. Relying on this opinion and on the fact that they had finite resources, the authority decided to withhold funding for the operation, although they acknowledged that the applicant would probably die if she did not have the transplant. The High

Court ruled that the health authority had acted illegally: 'where the question was whether the life of a girl aged 10 might be saved by however slim a chance the responsible authority had to do more than toll the bell of tight resources'. In Laws J's view, once the infringement of the right had been established, the health authority had to prove that there was a substantial public interest justification in refusing medical treatment. This conclusion was overturned on appeal. The Court of Appeal ruled that it was for the authority concerned to allocate its budget in the way it thought best. One bone marrow transplant operation may mean 20 fewer hip replacement operations; it was not for the courts to conduct this difficult balancing exercise. We can conclude from this decision that, whilst a State may be under a positive obligation to legislate in order to prevent individuals from killing each other, this positive duty will not be extended to the provision of medical treatment, since this involves the allocation of scarce resources. Whilst this seems harsh on the individual patient, it has to be acknowledged that the exclusion of a certain number of patients from treatment due to the scarcity of resources should not be a justiciable issue, since there are no 'right' or 'wrong' decisions that the authorities can make in these circumstances, except on clinical medical grounds, which judges on the whole are not qualified to consider.

The European Commission and Court of Human Rights take a similar view of the State's obligations to prevent risks arising from disease. Although the Commission has said in the past that Art 2 'enjoins the State not only to refrain from taking life intentionally but, further, to take appropriate steps to prolong life' (*X v UK* (1978), and in *LCB v UK* (1998)), the European Court of Human Rights suggested that Art 2 might impose an obligation on the authorities to provide individuals with information about life threatening environmental conditions. The hint that such a duty was within the scope of the State's obligations to safeguard the lives of those within its jurisdiction has been tempered by later *dicta* in *Osman*. Here, the Court observed that:

> ... such an obligation must be interpreted in a way which does not impose an impossible or disproportionate burden on the authorities. Accordingly, not every claimed risk to life can entail for the authorities a Convention requirement to take operational measures to prevent that risk from materialising.

20.6 The right to refuse medical treatment

Medical intervention usually involves the invasion of bodily integrity, which amounts to a trespass in civil law and a battery in criminal law in the absence of the patient's consent. A mentally competent adult can effectively refuse treatment, even if this leads to his or her death (*Re T (An Adult) (Consent to Medical Treatment)* (1993)). A Jehovah's Witness patient, for example, is perfectly entitled to refuse a blood transfusion (*Re T* (1992)). To get round the problems this creates for doctors treating patients who are not in a position to give that consent, the law has had to come up with a variety of somewhat artificial solutions. In emergency situations, the patient is deemed to have given (implied) consent for life saving treatment.

Much more difficult questions arise in non-emergency situations, again involving patients who cannot, for one reason or another, give consent, where doctors should only take action when it is necessary (*Re F* (1990)).This question arose in the case of *Airedale Trust v Bland* (1993), where the parents of a victim of the Hillsborough football stadium disaster had asked the hospital to withhold all treatment to enable their son to end his life with dignity and with the least possible suffering. The doctors, concerned that such an action would expose them to a charge of murder, sought a declaration from the court on the lawfulness of the proposed action. The House of Lords said that the test of what is in the best interests of a patient must be determined not by the court itself, but by reference to a reasonable and competent body of medical opinion (the so called *Bolam* test).

It might be asked why, if the State is under no positive obligations to ensure life – for example, to rescue – it should provide limitless funds to hospitals to keep patients alive who are in reality enduring what Lord Hoffmann described in the *Bland* case as a 'living death'. The answer is partly practical; allowing doctors to respond to pressure from unscrupulous relatives to hasten their patients' death and hence the distribution of their estate would place an unbearable burden of responsibility on doctors.

With the advance of medical science, it is increasingly difficult to determine when 'death' actually occurs; this definitional difficulty makes it much harder to determine when it is legitimate to withdraw life support from a comatose patient.

One way around this problem is to enable individuals to make their wishes known in advance by means of a 'living will'. This sets out the intentions of a patient which should be observed by the family and medical profession when the person concerned is no longer in a position to give rational consent. The present government is considering proposals to give the concept of living wills statutory force, so that any doubts about the voluntariness of the wishes expressed by the patient about future medical care can be matched against specific statutory requirements.

It is still unlawful for a doctor to administer drugs which would positively shorten life – the only way to avoid prosecution is via the doctrine of 'double effect'. This means that, in a reasonable body of professional opinion, the quantity and combination of drugs administered were indeed necessary and indispensable to prevent suffering, even though they carried with them the risk of shortening life, and that the patient consented. Otherwise, 'assisted suicide' – a doctor's compliance with a competent terminal patient's wishes to die – is still a crime.

Whatever position one takes in the euthanasia debate, there are important democratic arguments to be acknowledged. If we accept that the core value of democratic rights is the right to choose according to one's own convictions and not those of society in general, the argument in favour of controlled euthanasia acquires some moral weight. The difficulty of regulating 'assisted suicides', so that doctors do not risk being pressured by relatives or the exigencies of hospital administration from hastening death in the wrong situation, is not an excuse for the failure to the State to recognise the fundamental right of a patient to choose when to die:

> Of course the law must protect people who think it would be appalling to be killed, even if they had only painful months or minutes to live anyway. But the law must also protect those with the opposite conviction: that it would be appalling not to be offered an easier, calmer death with the help of doctors they trust. Making someone die in a way others approve, but he believes contradicts his own dignity, is a serious, unjustified, unnecessary form of tyranny [Dworkin, R, *Freedom's Law*, 1997, Oxford: OUP, p 146].

Dworkin's view is that the State has to balance its duty to protect individuals from irrational decisions to hasten their own death against the citizen's right to choose to die without being subjected to the religious or ethical convictions of society as a whole. The right to life – which includes the right to choose to die – is an important democratic right, since it contains within it not only the individual's right to choose freely his or her next course of action, according to his or her own moral perceptions, but the person's fundamental right to privacy.

In a case concerning the constitutionality of laws prohibiting assisted suicide in the US, a group of philosophers, including Dworkin, submitted an *amicus curiae* brief to assist the Supreme Court in its deliberations. They commented:

> Most of us see death – whatever we think will follow it – as the final act of life's drama, and we want that last act to reflect our own convictions, those we have tried to live by, not the convictions of others forced on us in our most vulnerable moment.

The respondents in this case – three terminally ill patients and four physicians – argued that a mentally competent person had a constitutional right to control the circumstances of his or her imminent death. The Supreme Court rejected their application, holding that:

> The value to others of a person's life is far too precious to allow the individual to claim a constitutional entitlement to complete autonomy in making a decision to end that life [*Washington v Glucksberg* (1997)].

In this country, suicide was a criminal offence until 40 years ago. While the felony was still being punished, families of suicides would be left destitute as the State forfeited all the property of the offender. The harshness of the law was finally alleviated when the Suicide Act 1961 abolished the common law offence. But the fear of voluntary death still runs deep in society, as the Supreme Court decision above demonstrates, and it may be many years before the terminally ill who are suffering from severe pain can claim a right to autonomy to choose the manner of their death.

20.7   Pre-birth medical intervention

Abortion

Foetuses have limited protection in English law. Abortion is legal before 24 weeks of gestation when carried out by a medical practitioner, provided that any of the circumstances listed in the Abortion Act of 1967 are present, such as risk of injury to the physical or mental life of the mother. However, foetuses themselves do not have rights in English law until they are born alive (*C v S* (1988)); so a father cannot apply for an injunction on behalf of a foetus to prevent an abortion (*Paton v British Agency Service* (1979)), and a foetus cannot be placed under the wardship jurisdiction (*Re F (In Utero)* (1988)).

The father in the *Paton* case took his complaint to Commission of Human Rights, saying that the proposed abortion would violate the foetus's right to life under Art 2 (*Paton v UK* (1980)). The Commission ruled that Art 2 did not grant an absolute right of life to a foetus. The lack of consensus on when life begins (gamete? blastocyst? embryo? 10 day old foetus? 20 week foetus?) has made it difficult for the Strasbourg institutions – or any other international rights body for that matter – to arrive at any definitive position as to the right to life of unborn children under Art 2. Abortion issues that are brought before the court by the pregnant mother are usually linked with the mother's right to privacy under Art 8. It is clearly easier for such a claimant to satisfy the 'victim' requirement for admissibility purposes than a foetus, which has no legal status. Nevertheless, in *Bruggeman and Scheuten* (1978), the Commission indicated that the protection of 'others', which constituted one of the permissible infringements to the right to privacy, included 'the life growing in the womb'. Pregnancy was held to compromise a woman's right to privacy, since her life was bound up with that of the developing foetus.

Provision of information about the availability of abortion services may not be suppressed under anti-abortion laws: *Open Door Counselling v Ireland* (1992). This case, which arose as a result of a provision in the Irish Constitution criminalising abortion. However, in arriving at their decision that there had been a breach of Art 10, the Court in this case did consider that the right to life under Art 2 may sometimes restrict the availability of abortion. We will see from the discussion of Art 10 that it can be limited in the interests of the rights of 'others' (see below, 24.6). The respondent State argued that the foetus was an 'other' whose interests the law should protect; but the Court did not address this argument, since it was peripheral to the central issue of freedom of expression. Instead, it based its decision on the finding that the prohibition of abortion information was a disproportionate measure to achieve the protection of morals. Since the laws of different countries on abortion differ considerably from each other, the Court allows a very wide margin of discretion in this area.

So we can see that, by simply ruling that the foetus is not a constitutional person and therefore not a rights holder, we have not circumvented the problems presented by the abortion debate. We have to recognise that the State does prohibit abortion at a certain stage of viability. If the foetus is not a rights holder, why should the woman's right to privacy be infringed at all, at whatever stage of pregnancy? This is a difficult question, to which there are no easy answers. One possible answer is that the State interferes with our rights to protect all sorts of things and creatures who have no 'rights' recognisable under orthodox constitutional theories – so, for example, our freedom to hunt and eat is curtailed in respect of endangered species, and laws have been passed protecting certain types of landscapes and habitats from development. In the same way, the development of the foetus towards infancy in the late stages of pregnancy engages the State's interests, due to the medical risks inherent in late termination of pregnancy and lack of scientific consensus as to the level of sentience of the developed foetus. This, it is generally accepted, justifies the interference with the pregnant woman's freedom of choice, although at no stage is it established that the foetus has a right independent of that of its mother.

Birth

Similar issues arise where a mother's freedom of choice as to the method of delivery conflicts with the medical profession's opinion as to her safety and the risk to the life of the unborn child. In *Re MB (Caesarean Section)* (1997), the Court of Appeal ruled that a mentally competent patient had an absolute right to refuse consent to medical treatment (in this case, a Caesarean section) for any reason, irrational or rational, even though this might lead to the death of the child or herself; but, in the case of the mentally incompetent, a declaration should be sought from the court in order for the correct decision to be made. In this case, the court deemed the woman to have been rendered temporarily incompetent by her fear of the anaesthetic injection necessary to the performance of the operation. On the other hand, the court specifically rejected the argument that it should take into account the interests of the foetus and balance them against the mother's interests. That case appears to suggest that incompetence may be quite easy to establish; however, that aspect of the ruling in *MB* has to be reconsidered in the light of the judgment by the Court of Appeal in *R v Collins ex p S* (1998). Here, the court confirmed that the rights to autonomy of a mentally competent woman outweighed the interests of the unborn child, as well as her own interests in her self-preservation. The applicant was suffering from pre-eclampsia, a condition which involved serious risks to her life and that of the foetus during the natural birth process. Despite medical advice to this effect, she refused treatment and advice to proceed with a Caesarean delivery. The hospital authorities applied for a declaration from the High Court to dispense with her consent, whereupon a Caesarean section was carried out. In ruling the action of the authorities to be unlawful, the Court of Appeal observed that:

> When human life is at stake the pressure to provide an affirmative answer authorising unwanted medical intervention is very powerful. Nevertheless the autonomy of each individual requires continuing protection even, perhaps particularly, when the motive for interfering with it is readily understandable. If it has not already done so medical science will no doubt one day advance to the state when every minor procedure undergone by an adult would save the life of his or her child, or perhaps the life of a child of a complete stranger. The refusal would rightly be described as unreasonable, the benefit to another human life would be beyond value, and the motives of the doctors admirable. If however the adult were compelled to agree, or rendered helpless to resist, the principle of autonomy would be extinguished.

The current position in national law, then, is clear: that the rights of a mentally competent adult override those of the foetus, even if the process of giving birth threatens the life of the adult as well as the unborn child.

Pre-birth diagnosis

Health authorities are frequently sued for the costs of caring for severely handicapped children who are born as a result of the failure of the medical staff to detect congenital abnormalities which would have given the mother the opportunity to terminate the pregnancy. These claims, somewhat bizarrely labelled 'wrongful life' claims, can be brought in the name of the children themselves in some jurisdictions such as the US. Such actions are really disguised claims for insurance from the State to ease the burden of the parents responsible for looking after a child. In this country such claims for wrongful life, taken by the child itself, are ruled out by legislation, although it is possible for the parents to take legal action. It is also possible for a perfectly healthy child to be the subject of litigation for negligent failure to diagnose early pregnancy where the mother would have proceeded with an abortion, or if the child has been born as a result of a negligent sterilisation operation (*Thake v Maurice* (1988)).

20.8   Assessment

Although the right to life is recognised both in the common law and the legislation of the UK, we have seen that case law of the European Court of Human Rights has cast some doubt on the adequacy of domestic measures for protecting it.

The immunity of the police from liability in respect of failure to investigate and take measures that may prevent a murder, where the potential victims and the suspect are well known, is arguably a shortcoming in the State's duty to prevent private killing; the relationship of proximity between the police and the potential victims in some cases should give rise to a duty of care. The European Court of Human Rights has held an immunity to be contrary to Art 6 of the ECHR (see above, 20.3).

As we have seen from the foregoing pages, the approach by the European Court of Human Rights to right to life claims is somewhat cautious. It is Art 2 more than any of the other articles in the Convention which makes it aware of its position as a supranational body whose decisions should not interfere excessively with the laws and policies of Signatory States. An adverse judgment under Art 2 is a significant statement about the Member State's human rights record, one that, as we have seen, the Court has only arrived at once against the UK.

In the light of this, the right to life has been given relatively restricted scope under the ECHR. It is suggested that national judges should have more leeway in extending the article to cover a greater range of activities that threaten life in the UK. The Indian Constitution, for example, has been relied upon by individuals claiming that severe pollution by industrial plants have threatened their right to life; these claims have been upheld by the Indian Supreme Court. Article 2 could become a valuable tool for environmental regulation in this country. That this is not a wholly unlikely development has been illustrated in a recent judgment by the European Court of Human Rights in *Guerra v Italy* (1998). This case involved claims that the applicants' right to life, the right to freedom of information and the right to privacy and family life had been violated by the failure of the State to provide important information about hazardous pollution emanating from a factory 1 km away from the applicants' village. Although the Court upheld their claim on the right to family life alone, two of the judges considered the claim to fall within the scope of Art 2 as well, 'where substantial grounds can be shown for believing that the persons concerned face a real risk of being subjected to circumstances which endanger their health and physical integrity, and thereby put at serious risk their right to life'. It has to be acknowledged, however, that even if the scope of the protection offered by Art 2 were to be extended in accordance with these dissenting judgments, the link between the failure to supply information and the risk to the applicant's life would have to be more direct than is evident from the *Guerra* case. It has been stressed in the foregoing sections that Art 2 does not impose positive obligations on States, apart from obliging them to pass criminal legislation prohibiting murder; however, it is suggested that it would not be too radical an extension of the Court's current jurisprudence to propose that the right to life under Art 2 covers the provision of a safe environment.

RIGHT TO LIFE

Negative obligations: the prevention of State killing

The right to life prohibits State killing and also engages the State's liability in its capacity of regulator of individuals' decisions over life and death.

Article 2 of the ECHR protects the right to life, subject to certain exceptions; capital punishment is permitted and agents of the State can use lethal force to quell riots, prevent arrests or prevent violence. The Sixth Protocol to the ECHR, shortly to be ratified by the UK, requires the abolition of the death penalty in all Member States.

In *McCann v UK* (1996), the first case to reach the European Court of Human Rights on the question of Art 2, the court ruled that the killing of three unarmed members of the IRA in Gibraltar by undercover British soldiers who apparently believed they were on a bombing mission could not be justified by any of the permissible exceptions to Art 2 because there had been other ways in which the arrest operation could have been conducted without risk to the suspects' lives.

Positive obligations

The right to life is generally recognised as a negative right only. This means that it prevents violations by States of the protected interest rather than requiring the State to take positive measures, apart from passing legislation criminalising private killing. The common law position is the same; the police enjoy immunity from negligence suits in respect of the steps they take to prevent murder, and there is no common law duty to rescue where no relationship of care exists. Neither national courts nor the European Court of Human Rights are prepared to impose liability under right to life principles where this would involve non-justiciable questions of policy and resource allocations. This is particularly true in the case of medical treatment: *R v Cambridge Health Authority ex p B* (1995).

Asylum and deportation decisions

The State may be liable under Art 2 (right to life) or Art 3 (prevention of inhumane treatment) of the ECHR if it allows an asylum seeker or a deportee to return to a country where he or she faces persecution or possible death, even if that risk does not arise out of direct action by the authorities in the receiving State. A State is prevented, for example, by Art 3 from deporting a person suffering from a life threatening disease to a country where there is inadequate health care.

The right to die

The right to life has provided no easy answer to the euthanasia debate. In the UK, 'assisted suicide' is still a crime. Neither Art 2 of the ECHR or any other formulation of the right to life has been extended to permit the medical profession or private individuals to take positive measures to assist someone to die, whatever the circumstances. In extreme cases, where the patient is in a coma, the court will consider whether a reasonable body of professional medical opinion would agree whether cessation of medical treatment is in the patient's best interests. On the other hand, the law recognises the absolute right of individuals to refuse consent to medical treatment, even where such refusal would lead to the death of that individual or to the death of a foetus.

Pre-birth intervention

Foetuses do not enjoy rights under national or international law, so abortion is not a breach of the right to life, although termination of pregnancy is prohibited at a certain stage of the development of the foetus. The parents of a severely handicapped child may take legal action against the medical profession for failing to diagnose deformities before birth which would have given the mother the opportunity to terminate the pregnancy, although actions for 'wrongful life' in these circumstances, taken by the child itself, are prohibited by legislation in the UK.

CHAPTER 21

LIBERTY OF THE PERSON

21.1 Introduction

The most basic of all freedoms is personal liberty from detention. This is recognised in Art 5 of the European Convention on Human Rights (ECHR) which states that 'everyone has the right to liberty and security of the person'. The term 'security' means simply that detention by a public authority must not be arbitrary; individuals should be secure from the unexplained and unlawful actions of the State: *Bozano v France* (1987). There are, however, circumstances in which it may be desirable for public officials – police constables, prison officers, judges, social workers, hospital managers, immigration officers and others – to deprive someone of this liberty. This is so, for example, where people are suspected or convicted of committing crimes; when people become so mentally ill that they are at risk of harming themselves or others; and also when people from overseas arrive in Britain who are suspected of being dangerous or of seeking to gain illegal entry into the country. Article 5(1) provides an exhaustive list of reasons for depriving a person of liberty, which the European Court of Human Rights has interpreted strictly. Arrests, detentions and imprisonments are constitutionally legitimate only if they are carried out in accordance with the law and if the law is fair. This, of course, begs many questions. To be constitutional, a person's detention must be both in accordance with the UK's national laws and also the ECHR: see *Loukanov v Bulgaria* (1996).

This chapter focuses mainly on the criminal justice system – the work of the police, criminal courts and the prison service – as it is within this sphere of government responsibility that people are most likely to lose their liberty. A significant proportion of people in this country will, at some time during their lifetime, be questioned by the police, charged with a criminal offence, stand trial and then be convicted. Many more are questioned and released without trial. Others stand trial and are acquitted. The constitutional system attempts to strike a balance between two competing demands. On the one hand, it facilitates the control of criminal activity by conferring powers on the police, courts and prison service; on the other, it emphasises the rights of suspects to be treated fairly. Whether the system hits the right balance is a deeply contentious question that can only be answered by examining the legal powers which public authorities have to detain people and the legal limitations placed upon those powers.

Central to those limitations is the concept of 'due process', a term which is shorthand for a package of safeguards for people detained by public authorities. In the UK, due process is recognised and protected by statute, common law and the ECHR (especially Arts 5 and 6), which will be considered in the following pages). This country has not ratified Protocol 7 to the ECHR, parts of which are relevant to this issue. Article 1 of Protocol 7 prohibits the expulsion of aliens from the territory of a State except in pursuance of a decision reached in accordance with the law. This Article also includes the right of an alien facing expulsion to have his case reviewed and an opportunity to submit reasons against his expulsion. Article 2 obliges signatory States to provide a mechanism of review of an individual's conviction for a criminal offence, and Art 3 guarantees compensation for miscarriages of justice. European Community law has, as yet, relatively little to say on the right to liberty of the person, though this is likely to change in the future with the development of the 'third pillar' of the European Union on police and judicial co-operation on criminal matters (see above, 7.2.3 and 7.7.2).

In the following sections we look, first, at the powers of and constraints on police during the process of investigating crimes; secondly, at the constitutional requirements for fair trials of criminal cases; and thirdly, at the rights of people sentenced to imprisonment after conviction.

21.2 Police powers during criminal investigations

Before a police officer in England and Wales reaches the point of formally charging a person with a criminal offence and sends a case to the prosecuting authorities (generally, the Crown Prosecution Service) who decide whether the person should be sent for trial, sufficient evidence has to be gathered. The law permits police officers to obtain that necessary evidence in several different ways: a suspect may be stopped and searched, formally arrested and questioned. (On police powers to enter and search premises, see below, 23.2.2.) The constitutional precondition for taking such actions is that the officer has 'reasonable suspicion'. Article 5(1)(c) of the ECHR allows:

> ... the lawful arrest or detention of a person effected for the purpose of bringing him before the competent legal authority on reasonable suspicion of having committed an offence or when it is reasonably considered necessary to prevent his committing an offence or fleeing after having done so.

This does not permit arrest solely for the purpose of gathering evidence; there must be a reasonable suspicion of an offence having been committed. The production of evidence is, in other words, an incidental consequence of the arrest, not one of the conditions for it.

English law also reflects this imperative of reasonable suspicion before taking action. It is set out in the Police and Criminal Evidence Act 1984 (PACE). When this legislation was enacted, it sparked off great controversy: critics claimed that it overemphasised the importance of securing convictions at the expense of suspects' rights. The police may only stop and search people on the basis of the officer's reasonable suspicion of an offence or the presence of stolen goods, drugs, unlawful weapons, tools to be used in a burglary, etc. PACE lays down detailed steps to be followed (ss 2 and 3 and Code of Practice A) before a police officer may lawfully conduct a search, such as the provision of his or her name and police station and the object of the search, as well as the requirement to make a record of the search to be provided to the subject. Under s 24 of PACE, police officers have a discretion to arrest people on 'reasonable suspicion' that an arrestable offence has been committed.

In English law, the test of reasonable suspicion is twofold: it requires the arresting officer to have formed a genuine suspicion in his or her own mind; but also that a reasonable person would have also reached the same conclusion based upon the information available – see the House of Lords' decision in *O'Hara v Chief Constable of the Royal Ulster Constabulary* (1997). Merely acting on the instructions of a senior officer cannot, in itself, give an arresting officer 'reasonable suspicion' to satisfy the first limb of the test; there has to be some further basis, such as the officer's own observations or a report from an informer.

The European Court of Human Rights has also had to consider the meaning of the 'reasonable suspicion' requirement in Art 5. As we have noted, Art 5(1)(c) only permits the arrest of a person when there is a 'reasonable suspicion' that he or she has committed an offence. The 'reasonable suspicion' standard is, therefore, a cornerstone requirement of Art 5(1)(c). The clearest interpretation of this standard is provided by the ruling in *Fox, Campbell and Hartley v UK* (1990), where it was held that the signatory States had to satisfy the Court that there existed sufficient evidence to establish the objective 'reasonableness' of the suspicion. The arresting constable's 'honestly held suspicion' was not sufficient, as it had been held to be by the English courts. In *Loukanov v Bulgaria* (1997), the Court ruled that the level of reasonable suspicion required by Art 5 had not been satisfied when the applicant, a minister in the previous government, was arrested and detained, allegedly for misappropriation of funds. The Commission found that the grounds of the accusations referred solely to the applicant's transfer of money in aid to the Third World, which was not an offence. Therefore, the facts invoked against the applicant at the time of his arrest and during his continued detention could not, in the eyes of an objective observer, be construed as amounting to the criminal offence of misappropriation of funds and, therefore, there was no reasonable suspicion of his having committed an offence to justify his detention. The level of objectivity required by the European Court of Human Rights depends, to a certain extent, on the length and circumstances of the detention imposed. In *Murray v UK* (1995), the Court was satisfied that evidence from the national court proceedings that the applicant had been involved in terrorist activities, coupled with evidence about these activities from Murray's family members, constituted reasonable suspicion justifying four hours' detention, the brevity of which was clearly influential on the Court's findings. It appears, therefore, that the Court will not require external evidence as a basis for 'reasonable suspicion' in all cases, and, therefore, the standard laid down by the House of Lords in *O'Hara* (above), is probably consistent with the Convention.

There are three main sanctions for police officers who carry out searches or make summary arrests without having the sine qua non of reasonable suspicion. One is that they may eventually find themselves being sued for damages in tort by the suspect for wrongful arrest and unlawful imprisonment. Secondly, police officers ought to be aware that, if an unlawful search or questioning produces evidence which the prosecuting authorities seek to rely upon at the defendant's trial, the court may exclude such evidence (see below, 21.2.3). Thirdly, police officers may be subject to internal disciplinary proceedings by their police force.

21.2.1 Arrests

Arrest in England and Wales may either be under warrant or without a warrant. A magistrate may issue a warrant to arrest a person where the suspected offence is one which carries the sentence of imprisonment, or where the person's address is unknown so it is impossible to serve a summons requiring attendance at the magistrates' court. The police can arrest people without a warrant for a number of 'arrestable offences' set out in s 24 of PACE. They can also arrest for non-arrestable (generally, less serious) offences where the offence is in the process of being committed or where it would be impracticable to serve a summons on that person, either because their identity or address is unavailable or because they might harm themselves or someone else or cause damage to property (s 25 of PACE).

PACE also authorises 'citizens' arrests', provided the offence in question is an 'arrestable offence', listed in the Act and it has actually been committed, or is about to be committed. Members of the public are therefore at risk of being liable for wrongful arrest if their suspicions are not grounded in fact: *Walters v WH Smith and Son Ltd* (1914).

21.2.2 Police interrogation

The PACE rules require an arrested person to be taken straight to a police station, since it is only when he or she gets there that the process of monitoring the conduct of the investigation can begin. The rules on the treatment of suspects detained after arrest, but before charge, are laid out in PACE and its codes of practice (for a detailed analysis, see Zander, M, *The Police and Criminal Evidence Act 1984*, 3rd edn, 1995, London: Sweet & Maxwell). At the police station, a designated 'custody officer' has the statutory responsibility for supervising the investigative process by checking that all the requirements of PACE are fulfilled. His or her first task is to determine whether in fact it is necessary to detain the suspect at all, or whether there is enough evidence to charge then and there and release the suspect on bail. In principle, if there is not enough evidence to charge, the suspect should be allowed to go free immediately, since there is nothing to justify their continued detention. However, PACE permits the custody officer to authorise continued detention if there are reasonable grounds for believing that pre-charge detention is 'necessary to secure or preserve evidence relating to the offence' in order to obtain such evidence from the suspect (s 37).

Provided they observe certain procedural requirements, the police may enter and search the arrested person's property for material relating to the offence and seizure and retention of items in the property (ss 18, 19 and 32). Separate provisions under PACE set up safeguards for detainees being searched in police stations (s 54); controls on the taking of fingerprints (s 61) and the conduct of intimate searches (s 55). Intimate samples such as urine, blood or pubic hair may only be taken with appropriate consent (s 65). While in detention, the suspect has the right to inform a person of their arrest (s 62).

A person detained by the police generally has a right of access to a solicitor (s 58) and for that lawyer to be present during questioning. There are exceptions, however, particularly in the context of anti-terrorism legislation. This right may be delayed on several grounds listed in PACE and in the relevant provisions of the Prevention of Terrorism (Temporary Provisions) Act 1989. In cases of a serious arrestable offence, the superintendent may delay access to a solicitor if there are reasonable grounds for believing that the exercise of such a right will lead to interference with evidence related to the offence, or physical injury to other people; or if it is likely that contacting a solicitor might alert accomplices or hinder the recovery of property obtained as a result of the offence for which the suspect has been arrested, s 58(8). Where a person has been detained for a terrorist offence, access to legal advice may also be delayed if there are reasonable grounds to believe that the exercise of such a right will interfere with the gathering of information about the commission and preparation of acts of terrorism, or will alert someone preparing to commit a terrorist act, which would make it more difficult for preventative action to be taken.

These exceptions have been held by the European Court of Human Rights, in certain situations, to be a violation of Art 6(3)(c) of the ECHR (set out below, 21.3) which guarantees the right of a person charged with a criminal offence to legal representation. This right applies to pre-trial questioning, as well as the conduct of the trial itself: in *Murray v UK* (1996), the applicant was denied access to a lawyer for the first 48 hours of his detention and after that period his solicitor had not been permitted to be present during interviews with the police. The court ruled that, in view of the fact that remaining silent had serious consequences at the trial (see below, 21.3.4), the pressure on the accused to speak to the police was sufficiently great to warrant the presence of a lawyer. Therefore, Art 6(3)(c) had been violated.

If the police flout the safeguards contained in PACE, they run the risk that a trial judge will rule that confession and other evidence be excluded at trial. Section 76 requires the courts to exclude confessions obtained as a result of oppression, or in consequence of anything said or done which might render that confession unreliable. Judges have a common law discretion to exclude unreliable confessions: *R v Miller* (1986). Section 78 gives the judge a general discretion to exclude evidence, including confessions, which was unfairly obtained. The problem for suspects is that they have to wait until trial to find out whether the breach of PACE safeguards will lead to the exclusion of prosecution evidence; in some cases it does, in other cases it does not. In general, courts do not regard it as their duty to penalise the police by excluding evidence unlawfully obtained (see Sanders, A and Bridges, L, 'Access to legal advice and police malpractice' [1990] Crim LR 494). This position is unlikely to be changed by the Human Rights Act 1998 and the incorporation of the ECHR, Art 6(1) of which does not lay down specific rules as to the admissibility of evidence. In practice, unlawfully obtained evidence has not been found to have automatically rendered the trial unfair: *Schenk v Switzerland* (1988).

The difficult balance between efficient investigation of crime and the rights of suspects has been analysed by Ashworth ('Should the police be allowed to use deceptive practices?' (1998) 114 LQR 109), who identifies a hierarchy of police 'tricks', which may or may not amount to breaches of PACE and its Codes, but do constitute deception of one sort or another. In Ashworth's view, tape recording and electronic surveillance are lowest on the scale of objectionability. Slightly more dubious, but still justifiable in some criminal investigations, is the use of informers or agents, or 'sting' operations. The activities that should not go unsanctioned, however, are the tricks which impact upon suspects' rights, such as the failure to inform them of their right to a solicitor.

In the past, suspects have been able to refuse to answer questions in the police station, and could also refuse to give evidence on their own behalf at trial, without any adverse inference being drawn from their silence. The position was changed by the Criminal Justice and Public Order Act 1994, ss 34, 36 and 37 of which stipulate that if the defendant wishes to rely during his trial on any fact or piece of material evidence which he had failed to mention or account for to the police whilst being questioned before charge, it is open to the trial court to draw adverse inferences from his silence. Before commencing questioning, the police caution suspects in the following manner:

> You do not have to say anything. But it may harm your defence if you do not mention when questioned something which you later rely on in court. Anything you do say may be given in evidence [Code C, para 10.4].

21.2.3 Duration of detention

Clearly, once the custody officer makes the decision to detain without charge, there must be some limit on how long this period of detention lasts. An initial period of 24 hours is prescribed by PACE, renewable for up to a period of 36 hours (ss 41 and 42). Detention may only be extended in these circumstances if it is necessary for the purposes of obtaining evidence and if the offence forms one of the 'serious arrestable offences' listed under s 116 of the Act. After the first 36 hours have elapsed, the investigating officers may only extend the detention under a magistrates' court warrant, which gives the suspect an opportunity to oppose the application in court. Magistrates' warrants may extend the total time spent in detention before charge up to a period of 96 hours.

Different, and more controversial, time limits apply to people arrested under the Prevention of Terrorism (Temporary Provisions) Act 1984 (PTA). This Act permits detention without charge for 48 hours. When this period elapses, the Home Secretary can authorise another five days, making the total period of detention for terrorist offences a full week. These powers of detention have brought UK law into conflict with the ECHR. Article 5(3) provides: 'Everyone arrested or detained ... shall be brought promptly before a judge or other officer authorised by law to exercise judicial power and shall be entitled to trial within a reasonable time or to release pending trial. Release may be conditioned by guarantees to appear for trial.' In 1988, the European Court of Human Rights held that detention under the PTA for seven days breached this requirement: *Brogan v UK* (1988). This judgment turned not on the legality of the detention itself, but on the length of time a suspect could continue to be held before having access to a judge to assess the justification for this prolonged detention. The government's response was not to amend the PTA to bring it into line with the Convention, but to serve a derogation notice under Art 15 in respect of its obligations of 'promptness' in this Article. This means that, for the duration of the derogation notice, it is not obliged to observe this particular requirement and no one can allege a violation of it before the European Court of Human Rights (see above, 19.5.1). A challenge to the terms of the derogation itself failed: *Brannigan v UK* (1994).

The ECHR does not require that the accused should be released on bail the minute he or she is charged with an offence. Article 5(3) permits detention on remand if there are 'relevant and sufficient grounds': *Wemhoff v Germany* (1979). There are four grounds which the European Court of Human Rights accepts as justification for continued detention. If, from the severity of the proposed sentence, and the detainee's own circumstances, it is likely that he or she will escape, continued detention will not breach Art 5(3). Equally, if it appears likely that the accused person will interfere with the course of justice, by destroying documents, or colluding with other possible suspects and interfering with witnesses, continued detention will be justified. The public interest in the prevention of crime is another ground for justification; this will be relevant if there are good reasons to believe that the accused will reoffend on release. The difficulty of this argument is that the accused is presumed to be innocent until proved guilty by a court of law; this seems inconsistent with allowing the authorities to continue detention on the basis that the accused might repeat the offence of which he or she has not yet been proved guilty – see the dissenting opinions in *Matznetter v Austria* (1979). The final ground for continuing detention is the preservation of public order; this argument will only succeed if there is objective justification for the prospect of a risk to public order posed by the accused's release: *Letellier v France* (1991). In any event, this detention cannot extend beyond a reasonable time; the arrangements for trial must be reasonably expeditious, although the ECHR does not set any maximum length of pre-trial detention.

21.2.4 Ill treatment during interrogation

It was mentioned earlier (see above, 21.2.2) that, if confessions are obtained from suspects in circumstances which are 'oppressive', the judge has a discretion to exclude the evidence in the subsequent criminal proceedings (s 76(2)(a) of PACE). The burden is on the prosecution to prove beyond reasonable doubt that the police did not behave oppressively. Such oppressive behaviour was found to have taken place when suspects were subjected to 13 hours of hostile questioning in the *Cardiff Three* case (1993). The Convention prohibits 'torture, inhuman or degrading treatment' under Art 3, and many complaints under this provision are made in relation to police or prison officer brutality. A number of Turkish cases have come within the scope of Art 3, where suspects have been subject to Palestinian hanging, beating on the feet and rape (*Yagis v Turkey, Aydin v Turkey* (1998)). In less extreme cases, the European Court of Human Rights has said that, in respect of a person deprived of liberty, any recourse to physical force which has not been made strictly necessary by his or her own conduct diminishes human dignity and is in principle an infringement of the right in Art 3 (*Ireland v UK* (1978); *Ribitsch v Austria* (1995)).

21.3 The conduct of criminal trials

After a person has been formally charged with an offence in England and Wales, the decision whether to proceed with a prosecution is made by the Crown Prosecution Service which assesses the strength of the evidence gathered by the police, and also whether a trial is in the public interest. It is important that criminal trials are conducted fairly; many detailed rules of evidence and criminal procedure, which fall outside the scope of this chapter, attempt to ensure that this is so. There are also some basic constitutional principles which need to be adhered to. They are set out in Art 6 of the ECHR (the first paragraph of which also applies to civil proceedings).

6(1) In the determination of his civil rights and obligations or of any criminal charge against him, everyone is entitled to a fair and public hearing within a reasonable time by an independent and impartial tribunal established by law. Judgment shall be pronounced publicly but the press and public may be excluded in the interest of morals, public order or national security in a democratic society, where the interests of juveniles or the protection of the private life of the parties so require, to the extent strictly necessary in the opinion of the court in special circumstances where publicity would prejudice the interests of justice.

(2) Everyone charged with a criminal offence shall be presumed innocent until proved guilty according to law.

(3) Everyone charged with a criminal offence has the following minimum rights:

(a) to be informed promptly, in a language which he understands and in detail, of the nature and cause of the accusation against him;

(b) to have adequate time and facilities for the preparation of his defence;

(c) to defend himself in person or through legal assistance of his own choosing or, if he has not sufficient means to pay for legal assistance, to be given it free when the interests of justice so require;

(d) to examine or have examined witnesses against him and to obtain the attendance and examination of witnesses on his behalf under the same conditions as witnesses against him;

(e) to have the free assistance of an interpreter if he cannot understand or speak the language used in court.

21.3.1 Criminal and civil trials distinguished

It should be noted that Art 6 places greater safeguards on a defendant's rights in criminal trials than in civil proceedings, although many of the guarantees set out in Art 6(2)–(3) have now been implied into the general concept of 'fairness' in Art 6(1) for civil proceedings. Article 6(2) and (3)(a)–(e) contain rights specific to individuals subject to a 'criminal charge'. The application of these rights depends on there being a 'criminal charge' in the first place; the European Court of Human Rights will not accept the State's definition of a case as 'civil' or 'administrative' if, in substance, it amounts to a criminal charge: *Engel and Others v The Netherlands* (1979). The characterisation of a charge as criminal rather than civil depends upon the imposition of a penalty. The more severe the sanction, the more likely it will be that the European Court of Human Rights will classify a matter as 'criminal'. Thus, the imposition of prison sentences on people who, during the 1980s, refused to pay the Community Charge (a controversial local tax, dubbed the 'poll tax') was held to be a 'criminal charge' even though, under English law, defaulting on payment was a civil matter and the applicant ought to have been provided with free legal assistance: *Benham v UK* (1996).

21.3.2 Trial by jury

In England, the right to trial by jury is often regarded as of constitutional importance. Magna Carta 1215 (see above, 3.3) provided that 'No freeman shall be taken or imprisoned ... except by lawful judgment of his peers or the law of the land'. The ability to have serious criminal charges determined by a random selection of ordinary fellow citizens is an important safeguard against government. While some questions before a court turn on complex issues of law, appropriate only for a qualified judge to decide on the basis of the arguments and evidence before him, criminal trials usually involve questions of fact – whose story is most credible – and issues relating to public notions of morality, such as whether an item is 'degrading' in the eyes of the public for the purposes of censorship legislation (see below, 24.6). There is much to be said for a group of lay people deciding both types of question on the basis of common sense; legal learning adds little, if anything, to these issues. The judge directs a jury on the law, leaving the issues of fact for the jury to decide. But sometimes, a judge's direction is designed to lead the jury towards a conviction; on a few occasions the jury has demonstrated its independence by refusing to convict. A famous example of this was the trial of a civil servant in 1985 for breach of the Official Secrets Act 1911. Clive Ponting had supplied classified information to an MP on the sinking of the Argentine ship Belgrano during the Falklands War. In the subsequent criminal trial, the jury returned an acquittal, despite the judge's direction to the effect that they had no choice but to find Ponting guilty of the offence charged (*R v Ponting* (1985)). This – and other – celebrated instances of the jury's independence, however, have not ensured the survival of the right to trial by jury for the indefinite future. In early 1998, the government adopted proposals that had been made by the Runciman Commission on Criminal Justice five years previously that this right should be abolished for certain types of crime, such as burglary, if the magistrates recommend summary trial in a magistrates' court. There are also moves afoot to abolish lay juries in complex fraud trials, possibly substituting for them a panel of experts.

As far as the ECHR is concerned, there is no express right within Art 6 to trial by jury (most of the signatory States to the Convention do not use juries anyway). Indeed, when the so called Birmingham Six argued that new evidence of terrorist offences should not have been considered by the Court of Appeal, submitting that they could not receive a fair trial unless the evidence was heard in its entirety by a jury, the Commission found no reason why new evidence could not be fairly and properly assessed by an appellate body of professional judges (*Application No 14739/89*).

21.3.4 Self-incrimination and the right to silence

Article 6(2) of the ECHR lays down the basic constitutional principle that everyone charged with a criminal offence shall be presumed innocent until proved guilty according to law. This does not, however, bar adverse inferences being drawn at trial from an accused's decision to remain silent during police interrogation (*Murray v UK* (1996)) and the new form of police caution (see above, 21.2.3). What Art 6 does prohibit, however, is the use of compelled evidence in criminal trials. This is the so called 'privilege against self-incrimination', which has been implied into the general concept of fairness in Art 6(1), the principle being that the State should bear the general burden of establishing the guilt of the accused, and the accused is entitled not to be required to furnish any involuntary assistance by way of a confession. The privilege against self-incrimination does not apply at hearings conducted by regulatory bodies: *R v Morissey and Staines* (1997). Under the Companies Act 1985 and some other legislation, special investigators have been given powers to compel evidence, documentary or oral, in their proceedings. Difficulties have arisen in the UK when people investigated in this way have subsequently been prosecuted. In *Saunders v UK* (1996), Ernest Saunders claimed a violation of his right to a fair trial under Art 6. He had been compelled to give evidence to Department of Trade and Industry inspectors during an investigation into the take-over battle between Guinness plc and the Argyll Group for Distillers, and that evidence had been used against him in subsequent criminal proceedings. The European Court of Human Rights upheld his claim. In *Funke v France* (1993), Funke claimed that his conviction for failing to produce bank statements relevant to investigations into suspected customs offences was a violation of Art 6. The Court held that, by attempting to compel him to produce incriminating evidence, the State had infringed his right to silence. In *Saunders*, what the Court objected to was not the procedure used by financial regulatory authorities to compel evidence from a witness in their investigations – the Court acknowledged the very special difficulties of proof in these fraud investigations and such procedures are not themselves covered by Art 6 – but the subsequent criminal proceedings are, and if the compelled evidence is used as part of the prosecution's case in a criminal trial, there will be a violation of the defendant's fair trial rights under Art 6. In *Funke*, on the other hand, the Court found that the level of coercion exercised by the customs in that particular case was not justified by the economic interests of the State, and such primitive measures brought the applicant within the protective ambit of Art 6.

21.3.5 Right to cross-examination

A defendant has a right to cross-examine witnesses under Art 6(3)(d) of the ECHR. Although this right is not absolute, it may be that the Youth Justice and Criminal Evidence Act 1999 falls short of ECHR requirements here. Section 34 of this Act prohibits defendants in rape cases who represent themselves cross-examining their alleged victims about the offence itself or any other offence, of whatever nature, with which that person is charged in the proceedings. This amendment to the law was introduced as a consequence of a controversial case where a rape defendant spent six days questioning his victim, dressed in the clothes which he had been wearing when he assaulted her. This restriction of a defendant's rights of cross-examination in person has yet to be tested for its compatibility with Art 6. However, the European Court of Human Rights' case law suggests that such a challenge will not meet with success, not least because the legislation does not abolish the right to cross-examine altogether. In *Baegen v The Netherlands* (1995), the Commission found no violation where an accused was able to confront the alleged victim of sexual abuse during police investigations, but did not have the opportunity to question her during the criminal proceedings. It was significant, in the Commission's view, that the accused in this case had had the opportunity to challenge the reliability of her evidence on file, a challenge which had failed in the event. In this and another case, *Doorson v The Netherlands* (1996), the Court case law tends to recognise that States should take into account the interests of 'witnesses in general, and those of victims called upon to testify in particular'. Therefore, the rights of the defence should be balanced against those of the individuals called upon to testify, particularly if the life, liberty or security of the person is at stake. In a later case, the Court has upheld a complaint under Art 6(3)(d), where the evidence against the applicants was given by anonymous police officers to a judge in chambers. The court considered that the interrogation of the anonymous officers by the judge was not a proper substitute for allowing the defence to question the witnesses and form their own judgment as to their reliability (*Van Mechelen and Others v The Netherlands* (1997)). It is probable, in the light of the above, that courts will be less ready to find a breach of Art 6(3)(d) where the interests of the witness, who may be vulnerable in some way, can be balanced against that of the accused.

21.3.6 Imprisonment after conviction

Once a defendant has been convicted of an offence, he or she may be sent to prison. Under Art 5(1)(a) of the ECHR, imprisonment will only be authorised if it follows conviction by a competent court and with a procedure prescribed by law. The requirement that a conviction must be 'lawful' not only refers to the national laws of the signatory States, but applies to the obligations set out in Art 6, in particular, those relating to the specific protections of defendants in criminal trials, discussed above. That means that, if the trial leading to a conviction did not satisfy all the requirements laid down in the Article, the conviction will not be lawful and the imprisonment will be outside the permitted categories of Art 5.

In England and Wales, the length of a prison sentence is, in most cases, determined by the sentencing judge within the limits imposed by the statute relevant to the offence. However, for the mandatory life sentence for murder and discretionary life sentence for other serious offences, the sentencing power is, in effect, divided between the judiciary and the executive. The judiciary recommends a minimum period of detention the convicted person must serve before his or her sentence comes up for review by the parole board; their release thereafter is down to the discretion of the Home Secretary. The judicial recommendation for the minimum period served for the first 'penal' part of the sentence for 'lifers' has been followed in the past by successive Home Secretaries when they have come to operate their release decision. However, in recent years, public demand for retribution in murder trials has led to minimal 'tariff' periods being extended by the executive in a way that departed, not only from judicial guidelines (*R v Secretary of State for the Home Department ex p Doody* (1994)), but from minimum periods proposed by previous executive statements (*R v Secretary of State for the Home Department ex p Pierson* (1997)). In both cases, the period imposed by the Home Secretary was overturned in judicial review. In *Doody*, it was held that, where the Home Secretary was carrying out a quasi-judicial role, he should give reasons for his decision, to allow the prisoner some inkling as to when he or she would be considered eligible for release. In *Pierson*, it was held, for the same reason, that the Home Secretary had no more power than a judge to increase a sentence retrospectively (see below, 22.3).

Once the prisoner starts serving a sentence, the rights available to free citizens should, in theory, continue to be available to him or her, subject to limitations that are indispensable to prison management. At its most basic, the common law protects prisoners from unnecessarily oppressive treatment during their detention. If the physical conditions under which prisoners are kept are intolerable, or if they are subject to extreme psychological discomfort, such as denial of sleep, they may apply for judicial review (*R v Deputy Governor of Parkhurst Prison ex p Hague* (1991)), although there will be no opportunity to challenge the merits of their sentence of imprisonment, only the conditions under which they are being held. One prisoner, awaiting extradition to the US, took the bold step of alleging that the conditions in which he was being held were in breach of the prohibition of 'cruel and unusual punishment' in the Bill of Rights 1689. He was successful. The court ruled that a punishment was 'cruel' within the meaning of the Bill of Rights, if it did not serve any penal objective which could not be achieved otherwise (*Williams v Home Office (No 2)* (1982)).

Apart from these basic rights of challenge to length of sentence and prison conditions, most of the conditions governing prisoners' other civil rights are contained in the Prison Rules passed under the Prisons Act 1952. An important restriction imposed by these regulations concerned prisoners' rights of correspondence. There was a time when the prison governor was entitled to censor all letters passing from prisoners to the outside world. When a prisoner challenged such an interception of his letter to a solicitor seeking advice about a proposed legal action, the European Court of Human Rights declared that such a restriction was a breach not only of his right to freedom of expression under Art 10 of the ECHR, but also an interference with his right of access to a court under Art 6 (*Golder v UK* (1975)). This case furnished an important precedent for future expansion of prisoners' rights in the UK. When a prison governor refused to forward to the High Court a prisoner's application for judicial review, the High Court ruled that his actions amounted to contempt of court, observing that 'Under English law, a convicted prisoner, in spite of his imprisonment, retains all civil rights which are not taken away expressly or by necessary implication'. Even before incorporation of the Convention with its due process safeguards, the Court of Appeal had no hesitation in declaring that the rules empowering the prison governor to intercept prisoners' letters of 'inordinate length' were *ultra vires* the Prison Act, on the basis that Parliament could never have intended to impose such an impediment on prisoners' rights to confidentiality and to legal advice (*R v Secretary of State for the Home Department ex p Leech* (1994)). A more recent development in the area of prisoners' rights was the recent decision in *R v Secretary of State for the Home Department ex p Simms and Another* (1999), where the House of Lords ruled that prison rules which banned oral interviews between prisoners and journalists concerning potential complaints about miscarriage of justice undermined a prisoner's fundamental right to free speech.

A high percentage of complaints lodged with the European Court of Human Rights come from prisoners, since they are particularly vulnerable to rights violations by the State. The relevant provisions – apart from Art 5 – are Arts 3, 6, and 10. The case law of the European Court of Human Rights has been reluctant, on the whole, to uphold allegations of degrading and inhuman treatment under Art 3, since they take the view that the minor unpleasantnesses of prison life do not fulfil the requirement of severity in that Article (*Ensslin and Others v Germany* (1976). Enforced medical treatment has not been held to breach Art 3 (*Herczegfalvy v Austria* (1992): therapeutic necessity for force feeding rendered measures proportionate). Exceptionally, the Commission or the European Court of Human Rights have found the UK in breach of the right to family life under Art 8 where prisoners have been deprived of visits from members of their families (*McCarter v UK* (1991): IRA prisoners transferred to mainland Britain away from their families in Northern Ireland).

People may lay claim to the fair trial provisions of Art 6 even after they have been convicted to a term of imprisonment. This right is particularly important in relation to disciplinary proceedings which used to take place before a 'Board of Visitors' – a panel of magistrates and other local citizens who determine sanctions for a range of offences which may lead to the loss of remission – the part of the sentence which may not need to be served, depending on the prisoner's record. The European Court of Human Rights ruled that, even within the prison walls, the basic requirements of criminal justice should be met, so that a prisoner who lost a substantial period of his remission when he was denied legal representation before the Board of Visitors was held to have suffered a violation of his Art 6 rights (*Campbell and Fell v UK* (1985). As a result of this ruling, and a number of reforms which were introduced into the prison system in 1993, all serious disciplinary offences by prisoners are now prosecuted by the Crown Prosecution Office through the ordinary criminal courts, where the normal safeguards for defendants apply.

21.4 Detention outside the criminal justice system

So far in this chapter we have examined the powers of public authorities to detain people for the purpose of controlling criminal activity, and the constitutional safeguards which exist to prevent abuse of those far-reaching powers. Powers to deprive people of their physical liberty also exist in other contexts, notably in relation to control of immigration into the UK and for the treatment of the mentally ill.

21.4.1 The detention of immigrants

Under the Immigration Act 1971 and the Immigration (Places of Detention) Direction 1996, people entering the UK may be held in custody pending a decision to remove them from the country. Persons may be detained at examination areas at ports, prisons, immigration detention centres and police cells. Only nationals and EC citizens have the right to enter the country without restriction (see below, Chapter 27). Since aliens have no such rights, either under immigration legislation, the common law or indeed the Human Rights Act 1998, this form of detention is not considered to be an invasion of a freedom recognised by law. However, the courts have set up a requirement of reasonableness on the length of time deportees may be held in detention, so that the period must not extend beyond that which is necessary to allow the process of deportation to take its course. In practice, this criterion is not very strictly imposed, so that, in a case involving the detention and proposed deportation of a Sikh separatist on grounds of national security, neither the domestic courts nor the European Court of Human Rights considered that the time he had spent in custody – five years – was unreasonable, given the complexity of his case (*R v Secretary of State for the Home Department ex p Chahal* (1996); *Chahal v UK* (1997)). However, the European Court of Human Rights did rule that he had been deprived of his right under Art 5(4) to take proceedings to have the lawfulness of his detention determined speedily by a court.

Article 5(1)(f) permits the lawful arrest or detention of a person to prevent his effecting an unauthorised entry into the country or of a person against whom action is being taken with a view to deportation or extradition.

The deprivation of liberty must, as always, be in accordance with the laws of the country concerned; so a person cannot be subject to a removal order if there are no conditions justifying the imposition of such an order under the municipal laws, and instead, the order is a disguised form of extradition (*Bozano v France* (1986)). If an applicant for asylum or entry is restrained to the airport holding zone and permitted only to leave on board a plane to a destination country, he may still be said to be 'deprived of his liberty' even though, in theory, he is at liberty to leave the country. In *Amuur v France* (1996), the Court found that the mere fact that asylum seekers – Somali nationals in this case – can leave the country does not exclude the deprivation of liberty, since this freedom to depart is only a theoretical freedom if no other country is prepared to take them in.

As with all forms of detention, the right to review by an independent legal authority under Art 5(4) applies; so, in *Zamir v UK* (1983), the Commission held that an illegal immigrant who had been detained pending removal from the country was entitled not only to a court hearing, but also to free legal representation, since the proceedings would have a decisive impact on his future.

21.4.2 The detention of the mentally ill

The powers of mental institutions to detain people of unsound mind are governed by the provisions of the Mental Health Act 1983. As with all statutes providing for detention, there is a tension between two conflicting ambitions. The first is to protect society from the risks posed by the mentally ill, the second is to safeguard the liberty of the subject. The conditions prescribed by the Act for lawful detention are strict, and the courts scrutinise very closely the justifications advanced for detention on the basis of mental disorder. In a case involving the legality of the admission and detention of a patient under the Act, the High Court observed:

> There is no canon of construction which presumes that Parliament intended that people should, against their will, be subject to treatment which others, however professionally competent, perceive to be in their best interests. Parliament is presumed not to enact legislation which interferes with the liberty of the subject without making it clear that this was its intention. It goes without saying that, unless clear statutory authority to the contrary exists, no

one is to be detained in hospital or to undergo medical treatment or even to submit himself to medical examination without his consent. That is as true for a mentally disordered patient as that of anyone else [*R v Gardner ex p L* (1986)].

Given that the autonomy of the patient is paramount, even after he or she is admitted to an institution, the Mental Health Act provides for limited periods of detention for a patient's condition to be assessed (ss 2 and 4); admission and detention of patients for treatment on confirmation by two doctors that the grounds of mental impairment exist (s 3), and the continued compulsory detention of patients already receiving treatment (s 5). The social worker who applies for the patient to be admitted to hospital is responsible for observing certain statutory formalities, such as consulting the patient's nearest relative. Otherwise, the detention will be unlawful, and the patient may be able to apply for habeas corpus (see below, 21.5). Hospital managers have a continuing duty to consider whether the patient is fit for discharge, and under Part 5 of the Act the justification for continued detention may be considered by a panel of experts on a Mental Health Review Tribunal. In deciding whether they are obliged to release a patient, the tribunal has to decide whether he or she is suffering from a mental disorder which makes it appropriate for detention to be continued – the fact that the condition may be untreatable anyway does not lead inevitably to release. This means that patients can be detained simply because they pose a risk to the general population. This type of 'protective detention', not being based on any actual or threatened threat to society, is particularly in need of due process safeguards, particularly in view of the government's plans to extend this type of detention to many more cases of mental disorder (see below, 21.4.3).

Mental detainees may be searched at random without their consent, despite the fact that the Mental Health Act 1983 contains no express power for searching patients. This does not amount to a battery and tort of trespass because the courts have held that the Act, which authorises detention for treatment, implies that the authorities should have a power to control the detainees, and this includes the power of search without cause, even in the face of medical objection (*R v Broadmoor Special Hospital Authority ex p S* (1998)). Even where the statute does not imply any additional powers of detention or treatment, the common law doctrine of necessity supplements the Mental Health Act. In *R v Bournewood Community and Mental Health NHS Trust ex p L* (1998), the House of Lords ruled that a patient who was unable to express consent had been lawfully detained in a hospital even though the authorities had not invoked the compulsory powers of detention under s 3 of the Act. He was not a 'compulsory' patient for the purposes of the statute because he had co-operated on entry to the hospital; and his subsequent detention and treatment were justified by the common law doctrine of necessity. The court was influenced by the fact that the psychiatrist who admitted him said that L's behaviour of persistent self-injury persuaded him that, if L had not co-operated, he would have invoked the compulsory powers of detention under the Act. This decision was reached before Art 5 of the ECHR became part of national law. This Article sets out an exhaustive list of conditions where loss of liberty is allowed, suggesting that any form of detention outside these categories would be in breach of the ECHR. The arrest conditions under Art 5(1) include 'the lawful detention of persons for the prevention of the spread of infectious diseases, of persons of unsound mind ... or vagrants' (5(1)(e)). The action of the authorities in Re L would only survive scrutiny under Art 5 if the common law doctrine of necessity were found to satisfy the requirement of 'lawfulness' under this section. According to Strasbourg case law, the notion of necessity implies that the interference corresponds to a 'pressing social need', and, in particular, is proportionate to the legitimate aim pursued. Strasbourg authorities generally accept the legitimacy of the respondent States' action if there was no alternative; it is likely, therefore, that the action taken in Re L would be justified under Art 5.

The obligation on the State to allow judicial review of detention under Art 5(4) has led to a number of decisions against measures in the UK relating to the detention of psychiatric patients. As we have seen from the discussion of national mental health laws above, the system has acknowledged that psychiatric conditions change over time and patients are entitled to periodic review by Mental Health Tribunals. However, until quite recently, the decisions reached by these tribunals used to be subject to the overriding opinion of the Secretary of State, who could order the continued detention of a patient, despite the fact that he or she had been cleared by the tribunal. This was ruled by the European Court of Human Rights to breach the patient's right under Art 5(4) to have recourse to review of their detention by a court of law (X v UK (1982)), and the law now gives these tribunals (considered to be courts of law for these purposes) the final say in the matter. More recently, in Johnson v UK (1997), the Court held that the detention of a mental patient had been unlawfully extended, breaching his rights under Art 5. The Mental Health Review Tribunal had recommended that he be released, but subject to the condition that he spend a period in a special hostel for rehabilitation. However, none of the hostels in the area would agree to take him because of his history of violent attacks on women. He was released on trial leave, but was returned to the hospital after assaulting another patient. All the experts agreed that he was no longer suffering from mental illness; it was just that, when he was allowed access to alcohol, he was liable to 'explode' and create a threat to the public. The Court found that the validity of continued detention under Art 5 depended upon the persistence of the mental disorder; since this did not apply in this case, his Art 5 rights had been breached.

21.4.3 Proposals for preventive detention

In July 1999, the government published a consultation on proposed legislation to 'safeguard the public from people with dangerous personality disorders', an assortment of measures applying to people re-entering the community after detention in prison or hospital under the Mental Health Act. The proposal which has created greatest concern is the plan to give the courts powers to impose indefinite detention on a person with a severe personality disorder who presented a serious risk to the public; such an order could be attached to any sentence imposed for a crime (no matter how trivial) and could be given to a person who had not committed an offence, but was believed to be a public risk. An inevitable difficulty in implementing this policy will be to find a reliable criterion of 'dangerousness' on which mental health professionals might agree, in order to submit consistent assessments to the courts.

These measures are to circumvent the provisions in the Mental Health Act that allow the continued detention of mentally ill people only on the certification of a doctor that their condition is treatable. If the government's proposals reach the statute book before the coming into force of the Human Rights Act 1998, they will inevitably be challenged under Arts 5 and 6 of the ECHR when these become part of national law. Recently, the European Court of Human Rights had the opportunity to consider the compatibility with the Convention of preventive detention of persons of unsound mind in *Eriksen v Norway* (1997). Norwegian law permits preventive detention 'if punishable acts are committed by a person with an underdeveloped or permanently impaired mental capacity, and there is a danger if the offender, because of his condition, will repeat such acts'. The applicant, who had committed a series of offences, argued that his continued detention was not justified by any of the circumstances set out in Art 5(1)(a)–(e), and, in any event, an expert psychiatric report had advised against his continued detention. The Respondent State said that the applicant's detention on special security grounds came within Art 5(1)(a), (c) and (e). The Court upheld the Respondent State's case, observing that the applicant's impaired mental state and his propensity for violence justified the detention. This decision suggests that, provided the applicant has, at some point, committed a criminal offence, challenges to the Convention compatibility of further preventive detention may not meet with success. However, where, as is envisaged, the 'dangerous' person is not before the court for any offence, detention may not be justified under Art 5 unless it satisfies the specific requirements of Art 5(1)(e).

21.5 Habeas corpus

This is an ancient prerogative remedy for unlawful detention which survives today largely in the context of immigration matters, and, to a certain extent, in relation to detention in mental institutions. As we shall see, the Home Secretary may detain someone pending deportation if his departure from the country is 'conducive to the public good' (see below, 27.5). If the detainee wishes to contest the lawfulness of his detention in these circumstances, it is possible for him to apply for a writ of habeas corpus. This will only secure his release if the court, on examining the circumstances of the detention, concludes that the decision to detain goes beyond the discretion conferred by the relevant statute. This remedy, although somewhat limited in its scope, has the advantage over other judicial review remedies in that it is not discretionary.

The remedy of habeas corpus has, on several occasions, been held to fail to measure up to the requirements of the ECHR. In *X v UK* (1981), the European Court of Human Rights considered that an inmate in a hospital for the criminally insane had been unlawfully deprived of his right under Art 5 to have the legality of his continued detention scrutinised by a court. This was because his detention was at the discretion of the Home Secretary, and review under habeas corpus did not allow the court to examine whether the patient's disorder still persisted, or whether the Home Secretary was entitled to think that continued detention was necessary in the interests of public safety.

21.6 Assessment

Before coming to power, the Labour Party promised to be 'tough on crime, and tough on the causes of crime', and one of the ways in which it is carrying out these manifesto pledges is by widening the reach of criminal law to cover a range of activities that, until recently, have not amounted to criminal offences at all. We have seen from the foregoing sections how important it is that due process safeguards are observed in the prosecution of crime, since the accused risks losing his or her liberty if convicted. In the Crime and Disorder Act 1998, there is a new offence of 'anti-social behaviour', which blurs the distinction between civil and criminal remedies. An order may be applied for by the police or by the district council, and on a (civil) burden of proof of balance of probabilities, the court may grant the order if it is satisfied that the person in question was acting 'in a manner that caused or was likely to cause harassment, alarm or distress to two or more persons not of the same household as himself'. The order, if granted, would list a range of activities that are prohibited or restricted for a minimum of two years; if the terms of the order are breached, that individual risks being held criminally liable, with a possible sentence of up to five years' imprisonment. In essence, what is happening here is that the civil law is being used as a proxy for the imposition of criminal offences (see above, 4.4.3). 'Anti-social behaviour' could cover anything from failing to control noisy children to the waving of banners presenting dissident views. The Prevention of Harassment Act 1997 creates a similar liability in respect of undefined behaviour which gives rise to civil liability, but is ultimately punishable in the criminal courts.

The Crime and Disorder Act 1998 has also introduced a raft of provisions to tackle youth crime by giving local authorities the power to impose local child curfews on children below the age of criminal responsibility. It will also be possible for courts to issue 'child safety orders' to require children under the age of 10 who are at risk of being involved in crime, to be at home by a certain time, or to avoid a certain area. Parents of children between the ages of 10 and 17 who have offended, or of younger children who are subject to a child safety order, may be required to attend training sessions and comply with other requirements regarding the care of their child. Breach of a parenting order will be punishable by a fine of up to £1,000. These proposals may be objected to on the grounds that they permit certain types of detention on the broad basis of risk, rather than actual behaviour.

Much of the current debate about due process in English criminal law arises out of concerns about these 'cross-breed orders'; cross-breed because they allow civil courts to identify behaviour on a civil burden of proof which may later lead to criminal penalties being imposed, thus depriving the defendant of the safeguards of the criminal law. The main objection to this merger of criminal and civil law is that it undermines legal certainty. It is the function of criminal legislation to define in very specific terms the nature of an offence, and it is only if these specific terms are fulfilled that imprisonment may be justified. 'Harassment' and 'anti-social behaviour' are the subject of civil orders, obtainable on civil standards of proof, and thus their scope remains vague and far reaching, covering a vast range of eccentric, but otherwise innocent, activities. As we have seen, the strict safeguards for defendants in criminal proceedings guaranteed by Art 6 of the ECHR apply, irrespective of whether the matter before the court is classed as 'civil' or 'criminal' (see above, 21.3.1). In view of the fact that the proposed measures for 'anti-social behaviour' and harassment carry with them criminal penalties, it is likely that any legal proceedings taken as a consequence will be tested for compatibility with all the guarantees in Art 6, not just those applying to civil cases.

A similar blurring of categories is achieved by the proposals to legislate for preventative detention of people with 'severe personality disorders', discussed above, 21.4.3; if these proposals are implemented, it will put psychiatrists and other health care workers in the position of crime prevention officers for people who do not have a certifiable mental illness, without the safeguards and guidelines of PACE. The power to deprive someone of their liberty before they commit an offence is one that is properly hedged out with carefully worked out standards of honest belief and requirements for justification (see above, 21.2). The need for such safeguards cannot be avoided by shuffling off the responsibility to the psychiatric profession; as one expert declared, on seeing the Consultation Paper:

The position of most psychiatrists is that we would be opposed to a form of preventive detention in which the notion of psychiatric treatment is used as an excuse to deprive people of their liberty.

LIBERTY OF THE PERSON

The most basic of all freedoms is personal liberty from detention. This is recognised in Art 5 of the ECHR, which states that 'everyone has the right to liberty and security of the person'. The State only has the authority to control and detain people whose activities threaten public order if the detention is 'lawful'; in other words, it must comply with the provisions of certain statutes and the basic requirements of due process. Due process is recognised in Arts 5 and 6 of the ECHR; Art 5 requires that detainees are allowed periodic access to an independent tribunal to examine the legality of the detention and Art 6 guarantees basic minimum rights to ensure that persons charged with a criminal offence are fairly tried, such as the right to legal aid and the right to cross-examine witnesses. Protocol 4 of the Convention provides additional guarantees, such as a mechanism of review of an individual's conviction of a criminal offence, and compensation for miscarriages of justice.

Police powers

Reasonable suspicion

Most of the powers of the police to stop, search and detain people on suspicion of having committed an offence are contained in the Police and Criminal Evidence Act 1984 (PACE). Both PACE and Art 5 of the Convention provide that detention is only lawful if the police have a 'reasonable suspicion' of an offence.

Procedures for detention and interrogation

Once a suspect is under arrest, PACE lays down a number of specific procedures that have to be followed by the police, such as the recording of all interrogations and the provision of reasons for continued detention by the custody officer. One of the most important safeguards is the requirement that the detainee may consult a solicitor, which may only be delayed if there is a likelihood that communication with a legal adviser will alert accomplices or interfere with evidence, or, in the case of terrorist offences, if the investigation and prevention of further acts of terrorism are impeded by the suspect contacting his legal adviser. Article 6 of the Convention entitles suspects to legal advice both during pre-trial questioning and during the trial itself, so any restriction of access to a suspect's legal adviser may fall foul of this Article.

Disregard of any of the safeguards laid down in PACE may lead the judge to exclude the evidence or confessions obtained by the police as unfair or oppressive.

The suspect's refusal to answer questions during interview may be mentioned to the jury at trial if the accused wishes to rely for his defence on any evidence that he failed to mention to the police whilst being questioned.

Length and review of detention

The police may only continue detention after the first 24 hours by application for a magistrates' court warrant, and the entire period of detention may only extend to 96 hours. Article 5(3) provides that 'Everyone arrested or detained ... shall be brought promptly before a judge': this provision was held to be breached by anti-terrorism legislation which permits the holding of terrorist suspects without judicial scrutiny for up to seven days. The UK has, therefore, derogated from the requirement of 'promptness' under the Convention for the purposes of investigation of terrorist offences.

After charge, the suspect must be let out on bail pending trial unless there are good reasons to detain him or her in custody. The State only has the authority to imprison convicted people by virtue of specific legislation; however, once a competent court has convicted an accused, he or she has no grounds to challenge the imprisonment itself apart from on limited judicial review grounds.

Criminal trials

Article 6 guarantees criminal suspects a right to be presumed innocent until proved guilty; the right to be informed of the nature of the offence; adequate time to prepare a defence; a right to free legal representation; the right to examine witnesses and the right to an interpreter. The Convention does not guarantee a right to trial by jury and in the UK such a right – laid down in the Magna Carta – is to be removed for certain types of crime such as burglary. There are also proposals to replace juries in complex fraud trials with panels of experts.

The right to be presumed innocent under Art 6 has been held to be violated when evidence that had been compelled during regulatory investigations from the applicant were used against him in subsequent criminal proceedings: *Saunders v UK* (1996).

The rights of prisoners

In certain types of life sentence, prisoners have been held by the courts to be entitled to be given reasons for the length of their sentences, and the right not to have their sentences retrospectively increased. Other minimum rights are guaranteed to prisoners, such as the right to freedom of expression, which limits the restrictions prison governors may impose on prisoners' correspondence, and the right of access to justice: prisoners are entitled to uncensored communication with their legal advisers. The minimum guarantees for a fair trial under Art 6 apply to decisions by the Board of Visitors relating to sanctions for a range of offences which lead to loss of remission. Prisoners are now entitled to a range of due process rights in these proceedings, such as the right to be legally represented.

Detention of immigrants

Article 5 permits the detention of aliens for the purposes of extradition or deportation, or to prevent a person effecting an unauthorised entry into the country. There is no specific statutory restriction on the amount of time a non-national may be detained pending removal from the country. However, the courts have imposed a requirement of reasonableness, so that the period must not extend beyond that which is necessary to allow the process of deportation to take its course. This 'reasonableness' criterion is sufficiently flexible to extend to a period of five years in a complex case. As with all forms of detention, Art 5 requires that any illegal immigrant who is being detained has the right to review by an independent authority.

Mental patients

Article 5 permits the detention of persons of unsound mind, subject to the requirement under Art 5(4) that the detention is periodically reviewed by an independent authority. Mental health legislation in this country authorises admission and detention of mentally ill patients subject to a range of safeguards. Hospital authorities are under a continuing duty to consider whether a patient is fit for discharge and an independent panel of experts on Mental Health Tribunals will assess from time to time the necessity for the patient's continued detention. The powers of detention under the Mental Health Act are supplemented by the common law doctrine of necessity: *Re L* (1998).

Habeas corpus

If a detainee wishes to contest the lawfulness of his or her detention, it is possible to apply for a writ of habeas corpus. This will only secure the release of the applicant if the court, on examining the circumstances of the detention, concludes that the decision to detain goes beyond the discretion conferred by the relevant statute.

New proposals

A number of measures to combat crime introduced by the present government have raised concerns that people accused of certain crimes will be deprived of the due process safeguards normally available in criminal prosecutions. The offence of anti-social behaviour, for example, may be established on a civil burden of proof, but the breach of an order imposed to prohibit such behaviour will lead to a sentence of up to five years' imprisonment. Similar issues arise in respect of the new offence of harassment and the jurisdiction of the courts to issue 'child safety orders' imposing obligations on parents to restrict the activities of their children.

CHAPTER 22

RETROSPECTIVITY

22.1 Introduction

Lon Fuller lists eight principles of what he terms the 'principles of legality', or the requirements for the rule of law. These are the requirements of generality, promulgation, non-retroactivity, clarity, non-contradiction, possibility of compliance, constancy through time and congruence between official action and declared rule (*The Morality of Law*, 1969, Yale: Yale UP). 'Non-retroactivity' – or non-retrospectivity, as it will be referred to in this chapter – is an important requirement of the rule of law since individuals cannot be expected to abide by the laws of a democratic society unless they are in a position to know what those laws are. Above all, the rule of law demands non-retroactivity in the criminal sphere; in other words, laws should not be passed to criminalise past activities which were innocent at the time they were carried out. The principle of non-retrospectivity is closely linked with that other pillar of the rule of law, legal certainty. The certainty principle condemns the enactment of excessively vague laws that delegate to administrators the power to deal arbitrarily with the citizen, particularly in criminal law. In Nazi Germany, for example, people could be prosecuted for 'acts deserving of punishment according to the healthy instincts of race' and, in the Soviet Union, criminal charges could be brought under the Soviet Criminal Code which prohibited all 'socially dangerous acts'. In a sense, the rule against retrospectivity is a sub-set of the requirement of legal certainty, since you cannot know what your liability under the law is until that law has been properly formulated.

But why have these rules in place at all? Fuller's thesis is that law, to be good law, has to work. Laws passed now to control past conduct are an absurdity and therefore unworkable. They offend against another rule of law criterion: possibility of compliance. Joseph Raz stated that an important aspect of the rule of law is that laws properly passed by Parliament must be capable of guiding one's conduct so that one can plan one's life. Laws should, therefore, be prospective,, rather than retrospective and they should be relatively stable. These views have also been espoused on the political right by FA von Hayek:

> Nothing distinguishes more clearly conditions in a free country from those in a country under arbitrary government than the observance in the former of the great principles known as the rule of law. Stripped of all technicalities this means that government in all its actions is bound by rules fixed and announced *beforehand* – rules which make it possible to foresee with clear certainty how the authority will use its coercive power in given circumstances,

and to plan one's individual affairs on the basis of this knowledge [quoted in Harris, JW, *Legal Philosophies*, 2nd edn, 1997, London: Butterworths, Chapter 11].

The repugnancy of retroactive laws to a democracy has been clearly demonstrated in the difficult business of prosecuting 'crimes' committed by agents for the State in countries of the former Communist bloc. In East Germany, for example, under the Honecker Government, the shooting of fugitives by border guards was not an offence, since these actions were authorised by a special 'border law'. After reunification, German courts, including the Constitutional Court, held border guards criminally liable on a complex construction of 'natural' and West German law. The issue has also arisen in relation to war crimes. Germany has attempted to get round the problem of prosecuting Nazi war criminals by declaring that their acts had been illegal in pre-Nazi law and by stating that the 'laws' of the Nazi regime that legitimised their action were invalid. The Nuremberg Trials which took place in post-war Germany from 1945–46, where representatives of the victorious Allied powers prosecuted Nazi leaders for war crimes, were themselves criticised for violating the principles of *nulla poena sine lege* – no punishment without breach of the law. The American jurist Judith Shklar argues that, in these trials, the pretence of legalism was a mere sham, since there were no pre-existing rules (Shklar, JN, *Legalism, Law, Morals and Political Trials*, 1974, Harvard: Harvard UP). The application of international rules of war to the defendants did partly answer the criticism of retrospectivity – since those rules were prevailing at the time of commission – and theoretically, at least, prosecutions of agents of the Allied powers were still possible in Allied national courts.

The European Convention on Human Rights (ECHR), as we will see, allows for the retrospective application of criminal liability where justified by international law, and also allows for the retrospective reach of criminal liability to acts which were 'criminal according to the general principles of law recognised by civilised nations' (Art 7(2)). Apart from this exception, the prohibition on criminal retrospectivity is non-derogable. Although there is no prohibition in the ECHR on retrospectivity outside the criminal sphere, the requirement of legal certainty underlies its provisions – meaning, in effect, that all law, particularly measures which impinge upon basic freedoms, be certain and predictable. Legal certainty is also one of the general principles of European Community law developed through the case law of the European Court of Justice. Although it is not specified anywhere in the EC Treaty, it is applied in relation to regulations and directives (see above, 7.6) by the European Court of Justice and by national courts to domestic laws enacted to implement Community law.

The UK prides itself on respecting the principles of the rule of law, non-retrospectivity being one of its components. In the following sections, we will consider to what extent the rule against retrospectivity is in fact respected in this country.

22.2   Retrospective civil measures

Common law

Every day, judges settle disputes by reaching decisions on novel issues which retrospectively determine the rights and obligations of the parties before them. In theory, this offends against principles of non-retroactivity and certainty discussed above. However, the argument here – advanced by Fuller, amongst others – is that rule of law problems do not arise here so much because in private adjudication the function of settling disputes prevails over the function of governing conduct. While Acts of Parliament set out in certain terms what we should or should not do, most rules of the common law apply only at the point of contact with a court: judge made precedents do not, on the whole, govern our behaviour. An individual publishing a libellous article about another individual runs the risk of being sued for defamation. If the judge or jury decide against the publisher, that risk is realised. But the court has not changed the law retrospectively to make him liable when he would not otherwise have been.

There are, of course, landmark decisions making whole sections of the public liable for common law wrongs where no liability had existed before, and there are decisions removing previously existing liability. An example of this may be found in the development of the case law concerning the liability of local authorities for economic loss in building defects. In *Anns v Merton LBC* (1978), the House of Lords ruled that local authorities could be held answerable in negligence for their administration of building regulations even though there had been no clear precedent for imposing a duty of care in previous similar circumstances. The result of *Anns* was that, for the next 13 years, building inspectors imposed unnecessarily strict requirements on the sinking of foundations for buildings, in order to avoid liability, thereby increasing the financial burden on members of the community. Then, in 1991, the House of Lords overruled *Anns*, in *Murphy v Brentwood BC* (1991). By distinguishing the two cases (inadequate foundations in *Anns* were held to constitute damage to property, whereas inadequate foundations in *Murphy* were held to give rise to economic loss only), the Lords radically altered the scope of tortious liability, with retrospective effect in the sense that all acts or omissions committed before the decision, but not yet adjudicated upon, were covered. On the whole, however, the effect of these decisions is prospective. The unfairness, so far as it exists, is on the losing party to the litigation.

Statute law

Statute law presents more intractable difficulties to the rule against retrospectivity. Parliament is supreme. In areas not involving Community law, Parliament can pass any law it pleases, including Acts which may have retrospective operation. Nevertheless, successive governments have been persuaded of the importance of observing the requirements of the rule of law and retrospective legislation rarely survives its passage through Parliament. One notable occasion in 1965 involved the government introducing a Bill to reverse the decision of the House of Lords in *Burmah Oil v Lord Advocate* (1965). Here, it was decided that a large industrial company was entitled to compensation for damage done by virtue of the prerogative powers of the Crown to its oil installations during the Second World War. Whilst this was a perfectly justifiable decision to reach on the facts, it became a focus for controversy since most people who had been deprived of their property under the statutory powers of the Crown were denied compensation under a 'battle damage' exception. In response to public pressure, Parliament passed the War Damage Act 1965, overruling the precedent set in *Burmah Oil* and effectively disentitling the successful applicant in that case from its award. It is an interesting indication of the approach of the Upper House to issues touching on the rule of law that the Bill nearly met its end in the Lords (see the acrimonious debate recorded in *Hansard* HL Deb Vol 266).

Although the ECHR does not contain a specific prohibition on retrospectivity outside the scope of criminal measures, the European Court of Human Rights has, on a number of occasions, considered claims that retrospective measures by the State have interfered with the applicants' property rights or fair trial rights. In *Stran Greek Refineries Andreadis v Greece* (1995), the applicants complained that national legislation which cancelled an arbitration award made in their favour was a breach of their rights to a fair trial under Art 6(1). The arbitration proceedings related to the termination of a contract entered into with the Greek State while it was under a dictatorship; the same contract was terminated after the restoration of democracy. The State appealed against the arbitration award but, when the courts successively upheld it, the government passed legislation declaring the arbitration award void and unenforceable and invalidating any relevant court proceedings continuing at the time of the enactment of the new law. The European Court of Human Rights held that there had, indeed, been a violation of Art 6(1), stipulating that:

> The principle of the rule of law and the notion of fair trial enshrined in Art 6 preclude any interference by the legislature and the administration of justice designed to influence the judicial determination of the dispute.

The Court is not always prepared to strike down the retrospective extinguishing of claims, either on fair trial or right to property grounds. One area in which both national courts and the European Court of Human Rights are prepared to tolerate retrospectivity is tax legislation. Taxation involves a complicated game of cat and mouse between the Inland Revenue and companies whose teams of accountants and lawyers dedicate their careers to finding loopholes through which their clients may legally avoid revenue obligations. In 1990, the Woolwich Building Society successfully challenged the legality of tax regulations, obtaining a declaration from the House of Lords that the 1986 Regulations were *ultra vires* the enabling Finance Act 1970 (*R v Inland Revenue Comrs ex p Woolwich Equitable Building Society* (1990)). They then obtained restitution of approximately £100 million. The Government was faced with the prospect of paying similar sums to other building societies bringing actions on the same ground, so, admitting it had no defence to these actions, it introduced retrospective legislation in 1991 to stifle such claims. The Woolwich itself was excluded from the scope of the retrospection. The other building societies took their cases to the European Court of Human Rights, alleging breach of their right to property under Art 1 of Protocol 1 of the ECHR, and breach of their right of access to court under Art 6 (*National & Provincial Building Society and Others v UK* (1998)).

The Court doubted that the restitutionary legal claims at issue amounted to 'possessions' within the meaning of the First Protocol, but, assuming that they did, it ruled that the interference with property was justified, having regard to signatory States' wide discretion in the tax field and to the public interest considerations at stake. As to the claim under Art 6, the court acknowledged:

> ... the dangers inherent in the use of retrospective legislation which has the effect of influencing the judicial determination of a dispute to which the State is a party, including where the effect is to make pending litigation unwinnable. Respect for the rule of law and the notion of a fair trial require that any reasons adduced to justify such measures be treated with the greatest possible degree of circumspection.

However, the Court took the view that the tax sector was an area where recourse to retrospective legislation was widespread and, therefore, the applicants must have appreciated the likelihood of the government placing the 1986 Regulations on a secure legal footing. Accordingly, the Court found that the applicant societies could not justifiably complain that they were denied a right of access to a court for a judicial determination on their rights.

This judgment was handed down shortly before the enactment of the Human Rights Act 1998. The position taken by the European Court of Human Rights on retrospectivity in the field of tax law in this case will signal to the Government that, in the field of tax legislation, at least, measures with retrospective effect are likely to survive any challenge under the incorporated Convention; provided, of course, that the tax authorities are able to establish that there is a genuine public interest behind these measures.

Community law

It was pointed out above that changes in common law and statute may interfere with vested interests. Established rights and liabilities may also be disturbed by developments in Community law. Here, issues of retrospectivity arise because national courts are obliged to interpret national law in conformity with Community law, even when the national law was passed before the relevant Directive was published (see above, 7.9.3). In other words, Community law creates retrospective rights and obligations which appear to infringe the principles of legal certainty and non-retroactivity. The European Court of Justice dealt with this anomaly in Case C-106/89 *Marleasing SA v La Comercial Internacionale de Alimientacion SA* (1990), saying that, if the effect of pro-Community interpretation is to create retrospective civil penalties, such as rendering contracts null and void, the interpretative obligation would not apply. In *Marleasing* itself, the Court of Justice held that no penalties were at stake, either civil or criminal. The applicant was seeking to rely on provisions of Spanish law to obtain a declaration that the contracts which set up the defendant company were null and void. However, these particular contracts were not void under the relevant (non-implemented) Community Directive. The Court of Justice ruled that national law should be construed in accordance with the directive, thereby leaving the applicant without the remedy it obviously understood would be available when it entered the contract with the respondent company.

The Court of Justice has drawn a certain amount of criticism for this disregard of the significance of legal certainty and non-retroactivity in national law, particularly where the temporal effects of its rulings are concerned. The difficulty is that, once the Court of Justice has ruled on a particular fundamental right, such as the requirement under Art 141 that men and women are entitled to equal pay for equal work, an innumerable number of parties wake up to the fact that they may have a similar claims, with the result that businesses are faced with an indeterminate number of claims against them stretching back over many years, even decades. The Court of Justice did predict this problem in its first ruling on this particular issue, Case C-43/75 *Defrenne v Sabena* (1979), where they ruled that, in the light of the 'important considerations of legal certainty', the decision about the direct effective of Treaty rights should apply prospectively only. A number of cases followed where the Court occasionally followed the line it took in *Defrenne* but, more often, took the position that a Court of Justice ruling was retrospective as well as prospective. Furthermore, in Cases C-6 and 9/90 *Francovich v Italy* (1991), where the Court imposed financial liability for signatory States for non-implementation of directives, there was no question of deploying the *Defrenne* tactic of 'prospective overruling', despite the serious financial consequences this would have for State enterprises. To make matters worse for the losing party, in Case C-271/91 *Marshall v South West Hampshire Area Health Authority (No 2)* (1993), the Court of Justice's preliminary ruling had the effect of invalidating a statutory limitation on awards in sex discrimination cases, preventing governments from imposing a ceiling on the amounts of compensation available in certain types of action. This means that anyone who has been dismissed by a State organ in violation of a right protected by EC law has a limitless claim, a fact which did not escape the attention of women who had been dismissed from the army on grounds of pregnancy (a clear breach of EC law: see below, 26.2.2). Carol Harlow observes that:

> ... by 1994, 3,918 claims had been disposed of and £6 million paid out in compensation; rising to £55 million by 1996 – no mean sum even in the perspective of a Welfare State budget! It is not wholly irrelevant that the affair attracted a great deal of unfavourable publicity; war veterans' organisations reminded the public that young women who had chosen to rear a family, and many of whom had found new employment, were receiving much greater sums in damages than the pensions awarded to seriously incapacitated war victims or their widows [Harlow, C, 'Francovich and the problem of the disobedient State' (1996) 2 ELJ 199, p 216].

22.3 Retrospective criminal measures

The power of Parliament to pass retrospective criminal measures may be assessed in the light of the judgment in the *Case of Proclamations*, which decided, as early as 1611, that the monarch no longer had the authority to make new offences (see above, 3.6.1). Although there is nothing to stop the Government introducing Bills into Parliament which create new offences, it encounters particular difficulties when such offences create retrospective liability. In 1991, a Bill making it possible to prosecute individuals for crimes committed during the Second World War was rejected twice by the Lords with Lord Shawcross maintaining that 'even if there was the slightest evidence that the electorate as a whole were in favour of this Bill, it would still be our duty to vote against it if we believe that it is wrong' (HL Deb Vol 528 col 643). The view of the House was that such a retrospective measure offended against the principle of the rule of law. The Government, however, was determined to get it through and they did this by invoking the Parliament Acts 1911 and 1949 (see above, 6.5.1). In fact, there has only been one trial for offences under the War Crimes Act 1991, resulting in Anthony Sawoniuk being given two life sentences for the murder of three Jewish people in Belarus during the 1940s (see Ganz, G, 'The War Crimes Act 1991 – why no constitutional crisis?' (1992) 55 MLR 91).

Article 7 of the ECHR

The ECHR contains a specific prohibition on retrospective criminal measures. Article 7(1) of the ECHR provides that:

No one shall be held guilty of any criminal offence on account of any act or omission which did not constitute a criminal offence under national or international law at the time when it was committed. Nor shall a heavier penalty be imposed than the one that was applicable at the time the criminal offence was committed.

Article 7(2) provides an exception for 'the trial and punishment of any person for any act or omission which, at the time when it was committed, was criminal according to the general principles of law recognised by civilised nations'. The War Crimes Act comes within the exception in Art 7(2). However, there are some measures in national law which have been challenged in the European Court of Human Rights before Art 7 was incorporated by the Human Rights Act 1998. In 1991, the criminal offence of rape did not cover forced sexual intercourse within marriage. In that year, the House of Lords responded to overwhelming pressure to remove this outdated exemption in *R v R* (1991). As a result, a number of convictions were founded on the new offence of rape in marriage. Some of those convicted applied to the European Court of Human Rights on the basis that they had been made criminally liable for acts which were innocent at the time they had been committed. In *SW v UK*; *C v UK* (1995), the Court rejected this argument, saying that the applicants must have anticipated the necessary evolution of the law on marital rape and that it was reasonably foreseeable that they would be prosecuted. The Commission has also stated that Art 7 does not require a restrictive reading of the criminal law:

> It is not objectionable that existing elements of the offence are clarified and adapted to new circumstances which can reasonably be brought under the original concept of the offence [*Application No 8710/79* (1982)].

The rule against retrospectivity is not limited to common or statute law: it applies to 'soft law' as well. A recent judicial review case decided that 'soft law', such as ministerial announcements of policy in Parliament, should comply with principles of legal certainty. In *R v Secretary of State for the Home Department ex p Pierson* (1997), the applicant, a prisoner serving a life sentence, complained that the penal element of his life sentence had been retrospectively increased. The Home Secretary relied on a policy statement made in Parliament in 1993 that he would reserve to himself the power to increase the penal element of life sentences. The House of Lords, however, held that the Home Secretary was, in effect, acting as a sentencing judge and, therefore, should be bound by the principle of law that a lawful sentence pronounced by a judge may not retrospectively be increased:

> The critical factor is that a general power to increase tariffs duly fixed is in disharmony with the deep rooted principle of not retrospectively increasing lawfully pronounced sentences. What Parliament did not know in 1991 was that in 1993 a new Home Secretary would assert a general power to increase the punishment of prisoners convicted of murder whenever he considered it

right to do so. It would be wrong to assume that Parliament would have been prepared to give the Home Secretary such an unprecedented power, alien to the principles of our law.

Article 7 of the ECHR also prohibits the imposition of greater criminal penalties than would have been imposed at the time the offence was committed. On the strength of this, a convicted drugs dealer won compensation from the European Court of Human Rights when he complained that a confiscation order made under the Drug Trafficking Offences Act 1986 had been applied retrospectively in his case (*Welch v UK* (1995)). The Act had been passed since W's conviction and permitted the Government to assume that all property passing through an offender's hands during the previous six years was the fruit of drug trafficking, unless proved otherwise. Under the Act, the courts had considerable leeway in exercising their discretion to make a confiscation order. In finding that there had been a violation of Art 7 in imposing the order, the European Court of Human Rights said:

> ... whatever the characterisation of the measure of confiscation, the fact remains that the applicant faced a more far reaching detriment as a result of the order than that to which he was exposed at the time of the commission of the offence for which he was convicted.

The outcry which followed national press coverage of this case did some damage – albeit temporarily – to the perceived legitimacy of the European Court of Human Rights, although the punitive nature of the Act was clearly within the scope of Art 7. The Act's sweeping assumption that all money in the possession of a convicted trafficker was to be considered the proceeds of crime and the possibility of imprisonment in default of compliance with the confiscation order constituted serious penalties which should not have been retrospectively imposed.

European Community law

The principle of non-retrospectivity of criminal liability also forms one of the general principles of Community law: Case C-63/83 *R v Kirk* (1984). National provisions prohibiting fishing within a 12 mile zone off the English coast had come into force to fill a gap between Community rules in this area. The effect of this was that Captain Kirk was prosecuted under a national law which was retrospectively authorised by a Council Regulation. He claimed that his right to be protected against retrospective penal laws under Art 7 of the ECHR had been violated, and that this, like other provisions of the ECHR, was one of the general principles of law observed by the European Court of Justice in assessing the legality of Community and national measures. The Court of Justice upheld this argument.

In Case C-80/86 *Officier van Jusititie v Kolpinghuis Nijmegen* (1987), a retailer of mineral water was charged with selling mineral waters which did not accord with the requirements of a 1980 Council Directive on Marketing of Mineral Waters. The directive had not yet been implemented, but the Dutch authorities were seeking to rely on it for the prosecution. The Court of Justice held that the general obligation on courts of Member States to interpret national law in accordance with EC law, even where the directive was not yet implemented, could not extend to the imposition or aggravation of criminal liability on the part of individual citizens:

> ... a directive cannot, of itself and independently of a law adopted for its implementation, have the effect of determining or aggravating the liability in criminal law of persons who act in contravention of the provisions of that directive.

22.4 Assessment

In general, successive UK governments have respected the rule of law requirement that laws, particularly in the area of criminal law, should be prospective. Although the War Crimes Act of 1991 has been criticised as departing from that principle, it is covered by the exception under Art 7(2) of the ECHR.

The issue of retrospectivity of Community law is, as it has been pointed out, a controversial one. The fact remains, however, that the imposition of liability by the Court of Justice is for obligations under Community law that have existed since the passing into force of the particular EC Treaty provision or Directive. True retrospectivity involves the imposition of legal liability after the action in question has been performed; so, in a sense, the retrospectivity problems created by Francovich and ensuing case law are procedural only. Criticisms such as those voiced by Harlow (see above, 22.2) could be met, not by the disapplication of *Francovich* liability (see above, 7.9.4), but by recognition by the Court of Justice of national limitation provisions which prevent dated claims for compensation being made.

RETROSPECTIVITY

The prohibition on retrospectivity is an important requirement of the rule of law, closely linked with another requirement, that laws be certain and accessible. You cannot know your liability under the law until that law has been properly formulated. Equally, individuals should not be subject to liability under the law for acts which gave rise to no liability at the time they were performed.

Retrospective civil measures

Judges may reach decisions which impose retrospective liability without offending the rule of law because they are fulfilling their function of settling disputes, rather than passing laws which govern conduct. The rulings generally do not extend beyond the private parties in court.

Civil claims are regarded as property under the ECHR and, therefore, Art 1 of the First Protocol, which requires States not to interfere with individuals' peaceful enjoyment of their possessions, prevents the retrospective extinguishing of civil claims – except in the field of taxation, where a wide margin of discretion is accorded to the legislature to cover tax loopholes retrospectively.

Community law creates retrospective rights and obligations which appear to infringe the rule against non-retroactivity although, in truth, the doctrine of supremacy of Community law means that Community obligations exist since the passing into force of the relevant EC Treaty provision or Directive, even if these have not been implemented into domestic law. State liability in Community law for damages may, therefore, be imposed retrospectively.

Retrospective criminal measures

Article 7 of the ECHR prohibits the imposition of retrospective criminal liability and the retrospective increasing of penalties.

The War Crimes Act, which imposes retrospective liability for war crimes, comes within the exception to Art 7 for actions which were criminal under international law principles at the time they were committed.

Article 7 does not prohibit the development of the criminal law to adapt to the morals of the times: people convicted of intra-marital rape could not complain that they had been subject to retrospective criminal liability, since they should have known at the time that the law would evolve to criminalise their acts.

Community law prohibits the imposition of criminal liability or the aggravation of penalties even if these measures are passed in order to ensure compliance with Community Directives.

CHAPTER 23

PRIVACY

23.1 Introduction

Respect for privacy operates on two levels: political and personal. In Chapter 19, it was argued that one of the functions of constitutional rights in a democracy is to keep open the channels of dissent, so that governments may be made aware of public criticism and the strength of opposition views. A right to privacy prevents those in power from keeping too watchful an eye on their political opponents by taking advantage of the considerable power of the State to monitor dissent. State intrusions into people's privacy may take a number of forms; either in the course of criminal investigations, or by keeping a check on suspected terrorist communications in the interests of national security, or the use of personal information held by public authorities, such as the Inland Revenue, housing authorities, the police or family welfare authorities.

But privacy should not only protect us from these more obvious forms of intrusion. To comprehend how privacy interests may be injured in other ways, it is necessary to mark out the boundaries of the scope of privacy. In his book, *Principles of Political Economy* (1848), Mill defined privacy as:

> ... a circle around every individual human being which no government ought to be permitted to overstep [and] some space in human existence thus entrenched around and secured from authoritative intrusion.

This broad notion of privacy has come to be known as the 'right to be left alone'. A more modern definition sets it out as follows:

> ... a clearly defined realm [that] is set aside for that part of existence for which every language has a word equivalent to 'private', a zone of immunity to which we may fall back or retreat, a place where we may set aside arms and armour needed in the public place, relax, take our ease, and lie about unshielded by the ostentatious carapace worn for protection from the outside world. This is the place where the family thrives, the realm of domesticity; it is also a realm of secrecy [Duby, G, 'Foreword to a history of private life', quoted in Feldman, D, 'The developing scope of Art 8' (1997) 3 EHRLR 264].

'The right to be left alone' entails not only a negative obligation on the State – not to interfere with the private zone of its citizens – but a positive duty to prevent private parties from interfering with each other's privacy. This includes regulation of the press and also the activities of other private organisations which routinely carry out infringements of privacy rights, such as credit rating agencies, banks, employers and the medical profession.

Technological developments and global communications have made it easier than ever before to gather details of peoples' private affairs in the interests of commerce. In order to retrieve a right to privacy intact from the state of atrophy into which it has fallen for the past few decades, it may be necessary for the State to take positive steps to control the activities of private parties in this respect. For a forceful argument in support of the positive obligations on the State to protect privacy, see Markesinis, B, 'The right to be let alone versus freedom of speech' [1986] PL 67.

At a personal level, privacy can be defined as the guarantee of the freedom to make moral choices. Without a sphere of autonomy in which a person is free of interference or scrutiny by others, he or she cannot be said to be exercising true freedom of choice. The difficulty lies in determining where this sphere begins and ends; whilst it no doubt covers the home, does it protect the workplace? Does privacy depend on status – so that a celebrity's sexual activities belong in the public sphere in the way that those of a private individual do not? Does respect for this sphere of private autonomy present dangers for vulnerable members of society, like battered wives and children? And, if so, how is the State to balance the conflicting interests of these groups with the right to privacy within the family circle? For these reasons, privacy has not been accepted in all circles as an unqualified good. It has been pointed out, for example, that too much respect by the State accorded to the family circle leaves women open to domestic violence and children open to abuse (Lacey, N, 'Pornography and the public/private dichotomy' [1993] JLS 93).

There are other criticisms of the manner in which the notion of privacy has developed in law. Raymond Wacks believes that the ambit of privacy invading conduct should be confined to the transfer or communication of private information, so that privacy is a function of information or knowledge about the individual (see *Personal Information: Privacy and the Law*, 1993, OUP). The essence of his argument is that at the heart of the concern about privacy is the use and misuse of personal information. This excludes other areas which Wacks does not think are privacy questions, such as noise, odours, prohibition of abortion, contraception and 'unnatural sexual intercourse', inter alia. The key function of the law, in his view, is to define what amounts to 'personal information'. Whether information is personal relates both to the quality of the information (details about one's sexual history, for example) and the reasonable expectations of the individual concerning its use (you would not expect your doctor to reveal your medical records to a third party).

However, the following argument will demonstrate that the right to privacy has been held to cover a far wider range of issues than information. Article 8 of the ECHR, for example, is one of the most flexible of the rights in the Convention, applying to a range of issues from transsexualism to the relationship of parents to their children. It provides:

1   Everyone has the right to respect for his private and family life, his home and correspondence.

2   There shall be no interference by a public authority with the exercise of this right except such as is in accordance with the law and is necessary in a democratic society in the interests of national security, public safety or the economic well being of the country, for the prevention of disorder or crime, for the protection of health or morals, or for the protection of the rights and freedoms of others.

This chapter will explore the extent to which the law achieves a satisfactory balance between these various interests.

23.2   Rights to privacy against the State

Clearly, most litigation concerning privacy interests involves the right of the individual not to be subject to unjustifiable surveillance by the State.

23.2.1   Secret surveillance by the police and security services

Covert surveillance techniques are invaluable in the process of investigating crime and potential threats to national security, terrorist or otherwise. However, the public order arguments in support of the use of this technology should always be weighed against the rights of the individual whose privacy is being infringed. This balancing exercise is relatively new to English law. In *Malone v Metropolitan Police Commissioner (No 2)* (1979), Malone, who had been acquitted of fraudulent trading, brought civil proceedings against the police, claiming a declaration that their interception of his telephone conversations had been unlawful on the grounds of trespass, breach of confidence and invasion of privacy. The High Court found that there had been no trespass, since the surveillance took place away from Malone's premises; there had been no breach of confidence, since there was no duty of confidence on those who took part in the conversation; and, finally, that there was no right to privacy in English common law. Therefore, nothing in law prohibited what the police had done; their actions could not be described as unlawful. This case would arguably have been decided differently had the Human Rights Act 1998 been in force; and, indeed, when Malone applied to European Court of Human Right, it upheld his claim that there had been a violation of his privacy rights. Article 8 allows for measures to be taken by the signatory States that may infringe privacy and family life in the interests of the detection of crime or the protection of national security, but the onus is on the respondent State to satisfy the Court that such measures are prescribed by law, that they are necessary in a democratic society and that they are proportional to the aim in question.

The requirement that a measure is 'prescribed by law' does not oblige all such measures to be written law. However, such unwritten law – in this case, the existence of the prerogative powers of the Crown to intercept communications in order to prevent crime – should be adequately accessible. According to the European Court of Human Rights, 'a norm cannot be regarded as "law" unless it is formulated with sufficient precision to enable the citizen to regulate his conduct'. The decision of the Home Secretary to issue a warrant for the police surveillance was not held by the European Court of Human Rights to meet the standards of accessibility and precision and, therefore, the interference with Malone's property could not be justified under Art 8(2) (*Malone v UK* (1984)).

In response to this ruling, the UK brought in the Interception of Communications Act 1985, which makes it illegal to intercept any communication over the public telephone system without a warrant from the Secretary of State. A warrant may only be obtained for certain purposes, limited to the grounds upon which States can legitimately derogate from the obligation to respect privacy under Art 8 of the ECHR.

The problem of telephone tapping, however, has not been solved by the Act, since the Tribunal set up to enforce its provisions has no powers to deal with unauthorised interceptions, which, in most cases, cannot be traced anyway. Therefore, there is no remedy under national law for bugging by individuals. On the face of it, incorporation of the Art 8 privacy right will not assist in cases where there is no public authority involved. However, since the obligations under the Human Rights Act 1998 extend to courts, which are themselves 'public authorities' (see above, 19.10.4), there may be pressure on the judiciary to develop existing torts, such as breach of confidence, to cover certain invasions of privacy, such as unauthorised intercepts by private individuals – provided that the interceptor can be traced and summonsed.

Before the Convention was incorporated, it was generally impossible to mount an action for breach of confidence where telephone conversations have been intercepted, because there is no relationship of confidence between the speaker and the interceptor. Indeed courts have taken the position in the past that committing one's communications to the public telephone network itself amounts to a waiver of confidence. Even in circumstances where privacy should be a reasonable expectation, for example in the workplace, there is very little regulation to protect such interests in English law. This lack of protection for employees has been criticised by the European Court of Human Rights. In *Halford v UK* (1997), Halford, an assistant chief constable who had brought discrimination proceedings against her employers, alleged that, as a result of these proceedings, the police authority had started a campaign against her which involved intercepting her private telephone conversations at work. The Home Office informed her that tapping by the police of their internal lines fell outside the Interception of Communications Act 1985 and, therefore, there was no requirement for a warrant. The European Court of Human Rights upheld her claim that the tapping of her calls was an invasion of her right to privacy under Art 8 and rejected the UK's justification under

Art 8(2). Since there was no legal basis for such interception, they said, it could not be said to be 'prescribed by law'. A similar complaint, this time involving the lack of regulation of closed circuit television surveillance, has been submitted to the Strasbourg authorities for scrutiny under Art 8 (*R v Brentwood Borough Council ex p Peck* (1997)).

The Interception of Communications Act 1985 has other limitations. It does not cover the use of bugging devices deployed by the police or anyone else. Although it is necessary for the police to obtain a warrant in order to place a surveillance device in private premises, the Act provides very wide grounds for the issue of such a warrant. The Chief Officer of the Police may authorise the issue of a warrant himself, on establishing that a serious offence is about to be committed. Since the definition of 'serious crime' under the Act is extremely broad, warrants could, theoretically, be issued for the bugging of anything from a Catholic confessional to a solicitor's office.

Members of MI5 are able to apply to the Secretary of State for a warrant to place surveillance devices on the premises of private individuals in the interests of national security (Security Services Act 1989, as amended by the Security Services Act 1996). The Intelligence Services Act 1994 permits the issue of warrants to MI6 for similar purposes. Tribunals have been set up under both Acts to investigate complaints; however, these provide limited protection since they may not inquire into whether the surveillance was objectively justified, only as to whether there were 'reasonable grounds' for the security services' actions – a lower threshold test. In addition to these statutory powers, the Special Branches of police forces are required by Home Office Guidelines to carry out intelligence gathering operations. Any complaints about their behaviour must be submitted to the Police Complaints Authority, although proceedings will only be taken by that authority if there has been some criminal or disciplinary offence. Since invasion of privacy is not a crime under English law, it is unlikely that redress can be sought via this avenue. It is possible, however, that breach of their statutory duty to observe individuals' right to privacy under the Human Rights Act may provide sufficient grounds for a disciplinary investigation.

23.2.2 The police and entry and search powers

Under English law, the police are permitted to invade the privacy of the person and home under certain circumstances; consent must be given, or they must hold a valid search warrant, or they must have reasonable grounds for suspecting that a person who is to be arrested is on the premises. Failure to satisfy any of these preconditions would provide valid grounds for a claim in trespass against the police, although it is particularly difficult to prove lack of consent, since it can be easily implied from most spontaneous actions of the property owner, such as stepping aside to let the police officer in. Most of the powers of entry and search are set out in the Police and Criminal Evidence Act

1984 (PACE) and its Code of Practice B, so the details will not be repeated here. The circumstances in which the police may exercise their search powers generally are discussed above, 21.2.

Entry without warrant

Police may enter premises in order to arrest someone for an arrestable offence or to recapture someone unlawfully at large or to prevent injury or damage to property. Police officers of a certain rank also have powers of entry without warrant under the prevention of terrorism legislation.

Search warrants

Search warrants are governed by PACE. Under PACE, magistrates may grant warrants to search premises if there are reasonable grounds for believing that a serious arrestable offence has been committed and where there are materials connected to the offence. The requirement of 'reasonable grounds' is discussed in more detail above, 21.2. The warrant itself must contain certain specifications, such as the number of people permitted to enter and the material which is sought.

Forcible entry

Forcible entry is permitted by PACE to make an arrest where the police have reasonable grounds for believing that the person they are seeking is on the premises. Powers of entry and search are conditional on compliance with certain procedures, such as an explanation to the property owner of his or her rights and the use of reasonable force only for entry

Seizure of goods

Under PACE, when the police are searching premises following arrest, they can seize evidence of certain offences besides that for which the arrest is made. When they are searching premises under a search warrant (that is, where no arrest has yet been made), they are entitled to seize anything connected with the offence which they are there to investigate and any other offence.

Breach of the peace

Under both common law precedents and PACE, if a police officer reasonably believes that a breach of the peace is about to occur in a private dwelling place, he has the power to enter that place to prevent it (the concept of 'breach of the peace' is given detailed attention in Chapter 25 since it usually arises in relation to public meetings). This power's compatibility with Art 8 has been considered on several occasions by the European Court of Human Rights, notably, in *McLeod v UK* (1999). Here, a claim was made under this Article by a woman whose estranged husband had arrived with the police to collect his property from the former matrimonial home. The applicant was not present at the property when the police decided to enter to prevent a breach of the peace. When the applicant took an action against the police in trespass, the English court stated that it was satisfied that PACE preserved the common law power of the police to enter premises to prevent a breach of the peace as a form of preventive justice. The European Court of Human Rights agreed that that the statutory authorisation under PACE as well as the common law precedents provided adequate legal basis for the infringement of her privacy rights in the interests of preventing disorder. Therefore, it found that the power of the police to enter private premises without a warrant to prevent a breach of the peace was defined with sufficient precision for the interference to 'be in accordance with the law'. However, the failure of the police to verify whether the husband was in fact entitled to enter the home (which he was not), and their decision to enter the home even though they had been informed that the applicant was not present, suggested that their action was disproportionate to the legitimate aim of preventing a breach of the peace. Thus, closer judicial scrutiny will be applied to the use of this power in future cases, although the existence of the power to enter to prevent breach of the peace has been declared compatible with the Convention.

23.2.3 The European Commission

Because Art 8 is justiciable before the European Court of Justice, it has often been raised in the context of the European Commission's extensive powers of search and seizure in the implementation of EC competition rules. On the whole, challenges to these powers do not meet with success. In Case C-136/79 *National Panasonic v Commission* (1980), the applicant company complained that the unannounced arrival of Commission officials at its offices to investigate the company books as part of competition proceedings violated its right to privacy under Art 8. The Court of Justice held that the Commission's action was justified under the exception in Art 8(2), which permits action in the interests of the economic well being of the country. The power of the Commission to carry out investigations without prior notification was considered to be justified by the need to avoid a distortion in competition. Indeed, nine years after the decision in *Panasonic*, the Court further restricted the scope of Art 8 in the area of competition proceedings by ruling that the protective scope of Art 8 did not extend to business premises at all (Case C-46/87 *Hoechst v Commission* (1989)). This ruling should now be reconsidered in the light of the European Court of Human Rights' judgment in *Halford v UK* (see above, 23.2.1).

23.2.4 Search orders

Orders may be granted by the court in the course of civil proceedings, giving the claimant and his or her solicitors a limited right to enter and search the defendant's premises in order to take possession of documents and other evidence which are crucial to the claimant's case. Search orders (previously known as known as Anton Piller orders, but see, now, Part 25 of the Civil Procedure Rules 1999) are typically obtained in business secrets cases or claims against the bootleg record industry, to prevent the defendant concealing or destroying important evidence. Although the purpose of the order is to protect the claimant's rights, its execution, which usually involves the claimant's solicitors and a team of assistants arriving without warning at the defendant's premises demanding entry, has raised serious concerns about breach of privacy rights, particularly in view of the fact that none of the safeguards available in criminal proceedings apply here. The order may be obtained from a judge in the absence of a defendant, and the defendant will be in contempt of court if he or she does not comply within a reasonable time with the request to allow the claimant onto his premises. In practice, many of these search orders have been exercised in conjunction with the police executing a search warrant for some related criminal offence (*Chappel v UK* (1990)) with the result that the property owner has no idea who is exercising what powers and what remedies he has against any of them. In *Chappel*, the applicant argued that, in those particular circumstances, his Art 8 rights had been breached. The European Court of Human Rights considered that the availability of Anton Piller orders *in general* were compatible with the ECHR and, although it criticised the manner in which the order had been obtained and executed in this particular case, it did not agree with the applicant that the exercise of the power was disproportionate to the aim of protecting the rights and interests of others. The power to enter, search and seize under search orders has now been put on a statutory footing in s 7 of the Civil Procedure Act 1997.

23.2.5 Private information held by public authorities

The right to respect for personal information is relevant to the right to respect for privacy generally, and this is closely related to access to private information, since, in some cases, it is only by virtue of knowing what data is held by the State about oneself as an individual that one can operate true freedom of choice. One feature of the modern State is the requirement that information be disclosed to a range of institutions such as the Inland Revenue, the Benefits Agency, the Home Office, hospitals and banks, to name but a few.

Access to information

The Access to Personal Files Act 1987 gives a right of access in respect of files containing personal information, if held by a local authority (see above, 2.9.1) in relation to its housing or social services functions. This enables those in the care of local authorities social services departments to find out certain details about their treatment, subject to the decision of the authority not to release the information on grounds of confidentiality. The relevance of this to privacy was made out in a case decided by the European Court of Human Rights in *Gaskin v UK* (1989). Gaskin had been denied access to some of his files which he wanted to rely on in order to support his case that he had been ill treated whilst in the care of the local authority. Access was denied on the basis of confidentiality. The European Court of Human Rights held that his claim did raise a privacy issue under Art 8 and ruled that the lack of any independent authority to determine the justifiability of the confidentiality claim amounted to an infringement of that right.

In response to this judgment, the Government passed the Access to Personal Files (Social Services) Regulations in 1989, under which social services departments are obliged to provide information to individuals unless the contributor of that information does not consent to the access. In addition to these provisions, the Access to Medical Reports Act 1988 and the Access to Health Records Act 1990 allow access to medical information held on an individual by that individual if he or she is identifiable from the information provided that the information would not harm the physical or mental health of the patient or anyone else.

The position taken by the European Court of Human Rights in *Gaskin* does not mean that Art 8 will provide grounds for access to information in all circumstances. The court's scrutiny of the justification depends upon the nature of the information which is secretly compiled. In *Leander v Sweden* (1987), the use of information kept in a secret police register when assessing a person's suitability for employment on a post of importance for national security was not considered by the court to carry with it a positive obligation to give the applicant an opportunity to see the content of the files held about him:

> When the implementation of the law consists of secret measures, not open to scrutiny by the individuals concerned or by the public at large, the *law itself* rather than the accompanying administrative practice, must indicate the scope of any discretion conferred on the competent authority with sufficient clarity to give the individual adequate protection against arbitrary interference.

In this case, the court found that Swedish law gave citizens an adequate indication as to the scope and manner of the exercise of discretion conferred on the responsible authorities to record information under the personnel control system.

Privacy includes the right not only to have access to personal information but the right to demand that this information is not disclosed to others. Like other aspects of privacy, there are justifications for infringing this right. In *MS v Sweden* (1998), the applicant made a claim for compensation for work related back injury. In the course of the investigation, the Social Insurance Office ascertained that this back problem was not connected with her occupation at all and refused her claim. She then applied under the Convention, contending that the submission of her medical records to the Office constituted an unjustified interference with her right to respect for her private life under Art

8. The European Court of Human Rights held that the disclosure had involved an interference with that right because of the highly personal and sensitive data contained in the medical records in question. However, the interference served the legitimate aim of the protection of the economic well being of the country, as it was potentially decisive for the allocation of public funds.

Disclosure to third parties

Like all rights, the right to privacy of personal information is not limited to law abiding citizens. It extends to the least popular members of society, such as sex offenders. Under the Sex Offenders Act 1997, individuals who have been convicted of certain types of sexual offence are to be placed on a Sex Offenders Register. This includes those offenders who have completed their sentences. The Act requires offenders convicted or cautioned for a range of sex offences after this date to tell the police where they live and when they move. The case of *R v Chief Constable of the North Wales Police ex p Thorpe* (1998) is illustrative of the factors which a court will take into consideration when balancing the duty of confidence against the public interest. Two convicted paedophiles challenged the decision by the police to disclose details of their convictions to the site owner of a caravan park where they were living. The ordinary duty of confidence entails a balancing act between the confidence in the material itself and the duty of the recipient – in this case, the police – to disclose it in the public interest. The applicants claimed, first, that the police had breached confidentiality. The Divisional Court had decided in favour of the police on public interest grounds. However, the Court of Appeal reconsidered the merits of the police's action against the background of the Home Office policy guidance (Home Office Circular 39/1997), published in consequence of the coming into force of the Sex Offenders Act 1997, with its notification requirements for sex offenders. While this policy does not apply retrospectively to those in the position of the applicants in this case, the court had to take it into account in deciding the appeal. The Court of Appeal also referred to Art 8 of the ECHR (although it had not yet been incorporated). Rejecting the applicants' contention that the police had acted unfairly, the court observed:

> ... in order to accord with the Convention, a policy [the Home Office Circular] does not have to be incapable of improvement ... There can be a margin of appreciation as to the proper application of the Convention in different jurisdictions.

But, to 'accord with the law' under the ECHR, the policy which authorised a breach of the applicant's Art 8 rights in these circumstances should have been made available to the public, so that it could be predicted that the police would manage certain types of information in a certain way. Having said that, the Court of Appeal concluded that, as a matter of domestic law and under the ECHR, the police were entitled to use information about the applicants if they reasonably concluded, having taken into account the interests of the applicants, that that was necessary in order to protect the public.

AIDS cases

The question of protecting private information arises frequently in relation to disclosure of evidence relating to HIV status. In *Z v Finland* (1998), the applicant complained that her rights under Art 8 had been breached when, in the trial of her husband for rape and attempted manslaughter, her doctors were compelled to testify as to her HIV status. The European Court of Human Rights held that the procedure had been adopted in pursuit of two legitimate aims under Art 8: the prevention of disorder or crime and protection of health and morals. But the court did uphold the applicant's claim in respect of the publication of the full judgment, which included references to this confidential medical data; the national court had had the discretion, which it should have used in favour of the claimant, not to publish its full reasoning but to put out an abridged version of the judgment which would have protected witnesses in the position of the applicant.

The European Court of Justice considered a similar claim in respect of the act of one of the Community institutions. When a staff member of the Commission complained that he had been submitted, against his will, to an AIDS test, his allegation that his privacy had been invaded was upheld (Case C-404/92P *X v Commission* (1994)).

23.2.6 Data Protection Act 1998

The Data Protection Act 1984 regulates, to a certain extent, the storage of information on computers and seeks to prevent certain types of disclosure or unauthorised access to it. No person or body can collect information on another individual unless they are registered with the Data Protection Registrar under the Act, which imposes strict compliance conditions to prevent abuse. Data held for the purpose of enforcing tax or criminal law is, however, exempted from this Act. The 1998 Data Protection Act, which is to implement the EC Directive on the matter, regulates the use not only of manually held information but also restricts the use which may be made of files held in private hands, such as private detectives (whose information gathered in breach of the data protection rules have hitherto been relied upon in litigation, for example, matrimonial finance disputes). The Act imposes a direct requirement to comply with its 'data protection principles' and is, therefore, not dependent on the data holder having registered first. This legislation may have the effect of restricting the ability of the press to collate information about the private lives of individuals since, under this legislation, the Data Protection Registrar has powers to demand access to files which have been 'unfairly' collected by the media. Under this Act, the Data Protection Registrar will have much wider enforcement powers than he held under the 1984 Act.

23.2.7 Immigration decisions

In refusing entry to a non-national who happens to be related to someone lawfully resident in this country, or by subjecting an applicant for residence to close interrogation to establish the veracity of their claims to family connections, Immigration Officers regularly infringe the privacy of individuals at ports of entry. Most immigration decisions, in fact, have succeeded before the European Court of Human Rights on the basis of the right to a 'family life', under Art 8. Until the Human Rights Act 1998, Art 8 did not have any formal role to play in national law in appeals against immigration decisions, although it was often raised by applicants whose spouses faced refusal of entry or deportation (*R v Secretary of State for the Home Department ex p Phansopkar* (1976)). However, for a time, Art 8 was included in Home Office Guidance Notes to immigration officers as a consideration to be taken into account when deciding applications for entry. As with other forms of 'soft law', these guidance notes were not binding and, therefore, even while the Human Rights Bill was completing its progress through Parliament, the alleged disregard by the Home Secretary of the right to a family life under Art 8 was not considered to be a basis for a ruling that his action was unlawful (*R v Secretary of State for the Home Department ex p Khan* (1998)). To what extent incorporation of Art 8 into national law will change this practice depends on how widely the courts will interpret the permissible infringement of the right in Art 8(2). Indeed, the case law of the European Court of Human Rights does not hold out much promise for would-be immigrants here. Challenges to immigration decisions have had mixed success, reflecting the Court's cautious approach to matters involving entry into signatory States. In *Berrehab v Netherlands* (1988), it was held that a parent could not be deported after marriage which gave right of abode ended, since the child-parent relationship is entitled to respect. In *Abdulaziz v UK* (1985), on the other hand, the court concluded that Art 8 did not impose an obligation on the State to accept non-national spouses for settlement. It is worth noting that, in the latter case, the applicants were successful on Art 14 sex discrimination grounds, since British immigration rules would have allowed wives of residents to have the right of abode, but not husbands. The UK reacted to the judgment by removing the right of all spouses and fiancées, male or female, to join their partners. Thus, a judgment which is favourable to the applicants in one case may backfire on future individuals in the same position.

The relationship between privacy rights and immigration issues has also arisen in a Community law context. In Case C-249/86 *Commission v Germany* (1989), the Court of Justice upheld a challenge to German housing policy under Art 8, ruling that the State could not impose a minimum standard of accommodation as a precondition for the exercise of the right to residence by an EC national as a worker under the EC Treaty. Such administrative action violated the applicant's right to privacy and family life under Art 8 of the ECHR and was, thus, unlawful under Community law.

In its White Paper on immigration and asylum (*Fairer, Faster and Firmer – a Modern Approach to Immigration and Asylum*, Cm 4018, 1998), the Government has proposed tougher pre-entry controls on immigration to cut down on trafficking in illegal immigrants. Some of these measures have important implications for the right to privacy. For example, it is proposed to extend the use of closed circuit television in airports to develop the Home Office's intelligence system (see para 5.16). Joint operations between the Immigration Service and other agencies targeting benefit and housing fraud by illegal entrants have already been set in place; the Government is now proposing (see para 11.9) the extension of the enforcement powers of immigration officers to enter private property, search and seize items. A Europe-wide database for fingerprints of asylum seekers is also proposed (see para 11.31). The adoption of these measures appear to fall within the public interest exceptions to privacy; we have seen in the *MS v Sweden* case that the disclosure of personal information may be justified, for example, by the interests of the economic well being of the country. However, the approach by the European Court of Human Rights in *McLeod* suggests that the actual use of some of these proposed powers, such as search and entry, will be subject to strict scrutiny on proportionality grounds.

23.2.8 Family relationships

As we have seen, Art 8 of the ECHR requires States to respect individuals' right to a family life as well as their rights to privacy. This means, amongst other things, that any rule of national law that interferes with the relationship between parent and child will violate Art 8. The leading example of this is the European Court of Human Rights decision in a case concerning a Belgian law regulating the relationship between an unmarried mother and her child; such legislation, said the court, would only survive attack under Art 8 if it allowed those concerned to lead a normal family life. If domestic law discriminated against illegitimate children, then the State was obliged to adjust it to take into account the requirements of Art 8 (*Marckx v Belgium* (1979)). This ruling was followed in an Irish case in which the European Court of Human Rights took a cautious position with regard to Irish laws prohibiting divorce – these did not, in its view, interfere with private family life under Art 8(1), since nothing in Irish law prevented estranged couples from forming unions with other people. But the Irish law on illegitimacy, which subjected the child of those subsequent (extra-marital) unions to legal disadvantages compared with the children born in wedlock were held to be in breach of Art 8 (*Johnston and Others v Ireland* (1987)). On the other hand, where the matter involves an area where there is little consensus between individual signatory Sates, the Court, although prepared to concede that Art 8 rights may have been infringed, is willing to give a wide margin of discretion to the State concerned. In *X, Y and Z v UK*, the Court ruled that X, a female to male transsexual, could not rely on

Art 8 in order to require the Government to register him as the father of a child (Z), conceived by artificial insemination during his relationship with Y.

Many Art 8 claims in this context are made together with claims under Art 12. Article 12 grants individuals the right to marry and found a family. This right may provide a platform for challenges to a range of regulations, particularly those enforced by the Human Fertilisation and Embryology Authority, restricting the circumstances in which fertility treatment may be provided by clinics. Diane Blood, for example, may have been able to avail herself of Art 12 of the ECHR if the Human Rights Act had been in force when she challenged the Authority's decision to prevent her from having her dead husband's child because she could not obtain access to his frozen sperm without his consent (*R v Human Fertilisation and Embryology Authority ex p Blood* (1997)).

23.2.9 Sexual activity

The European Court of Human Rights has recognised that sexual relations are at the core of the sphere of autonomy protected by privacy. Most challenges under this heading have been made in respect of national laws criminalising certain types of sexual activity. An application made to challenge laws in Northern Ireland which criminalised homosexual acts between consenting adults was successful, even though the applicant himself had never been prosecuted (*Dudgeon v UK* (1982)). However, in the same case, the court ruled that the UK government could set a minimum age at which men could lawfully consent to homosexual activity. A minimum age of 21 (as opposed to 16, the legal age of consent for heterosexual acts) was within the State's margin of appreciation (see above, 19.5). The age was then lowered to 18, although the European Commission of Human Rights Commission subsequently admitted a claim that this breached the right to privacy (*Sutherland v UK* (1998)). A recent attempt to lower the age of consent for male homosexuals in the Crime and Disorder Bill was defeated twice by the House of Lords, in July 1998 and April 1999. The Government has announced its intention to use the Parliament Act 1911 in order to bypass the Lords to get this provision onto the statute book (see above, 6.5.1).

In a series of claims by transsexuals, alleging breaches of Art 8 the European Court of Human Rights has tended to accept signatory States' arguments that Art 8 does not require them to recognise, for legal purposes, the new sexual identity of individuals who have undergone sex change operations (see, in particular, *Rees v UK* (1986)). Again, the lack of common ground between signatory States on this issue gives each State a wide margin of appreciation under Art 8. The European Court of Human Rights has recently rejected an Art 8 challenge in respect of birth registration laws in this country which are based on the principle that sex is fixed immutably by conventional biological considerations as existing at the time of birth. In

Horsham v UK (1998), the court ruled that the applicant's privacy rights were not breached when, for legal purposes such as court appearances or obtaining insurance and contractual documents, transsexuals were forced to show certificates revealing their previous names and gender. Equally, the relationships of gays and lesbians do not, in the view of the Court, fall within the scope of the right to family life under Art 8, an approach which maintains the emphasis on the traditional heterosexual couple as the core of the notion of family life (see *Kerkhoven v the Netherlands* (1992), where the Commission held that Art 8 did not import a positive obligation on a State to grant parental rights to a woman who was living with the mother of a child).

When a group of homosexual men were prosecuted under the Offences Against the Person Act 1861 for engaging in sado-masochistic activities they claimed that their Art 8 rights had been infringed (*Laskey, Jaggard and Brown v UK* (1997)), the European Court of Human Rights agreed that the criminal law did indeed interfere with their privacy, but held that it was in pursuit of a legitimate aim under Art 8(2), namely, the protection of health and morals.

23.2.10 Children

The laws of signatory States for protecting children may infringe the rights of parents to a private family life, particularly by not allowing the parents sufficient involvement in decisions taken by public authorities in fostering arrangements, decisions to take children into care or decisions denying parents access to their offspring once in care. In *W, B v UK* (1987) and *R v UK* (1988), the European Court of Human Rights found a breach of Art 8 because parents were denied proper access to their children held in care and insufficient involvement in the local authority's decision making process. As a consequence of these adverse judgments, the UK enacted the Children Act 1989 which fortifies the role of parents in care proceedings. When the State intervenes by removing children into care, Art 8 requires that the natural parents be properly involved in the decision making process and that full account is taken of their views and wishes: *Johansen v Norway* (1996).

Sometimes, the parents' right to a family life under Art 8 can conflict directly with a child's right to privacy under the same provision. When a 14 year old girl ran away to live with her boyfriend, the authorities returned her to her parents. She petitioned the European Court of Human Rights under Art 8 but the Commission rejected her claim, finding that the action of the authorities came within the 'health and morals' exception to Art 8:

> As a general proposition ..., the obligation of children to reside with their parents and to be otherwise subjected to particular control is necessary for the protection of children's health and morals, although it might constitute, from a particular child's point of view, an interference with his or her private life [*Application No 6753/74*].

The issue of privacy has also arisen in relation to the matter of physical chastisement of children. In *Costello-Roberts v UK* (1995), a schoolboy attending a private school complained that the practice of 'slippering' – being struck three times with a soft-soled shoe – violated several provisions of the ECHR, in particular, his right to privacy under Art 8. The Court held that the punishment being complained of 'did not entail adverse effects for his physical or moral integrity sufficient to bring it within he scope of the prohibition contained in Art 8'.

More recently, in *A and B v UK* (1998), the European Court of Human Rights considered a challenge under Arts 3 and 8 to English criminal law, which provides a defence for the charge of assault on a child if the court is satisfied that the action qualified as 'reasonable chastisement'. The child in question had been beaten regularly by his stepfather with a garden cane. He was prosecuted but he relied successfully on this defence in the magistrate's court and was acquitted. The court held that Art 3 imposed a positive obligation on signatory States to take measures to ensure that private individuals did not subject others to torture or inhuman or degrading treatment. By allowing the stepfather in this case the defence of reasonable chastisement, English criminal law had not provided the child with adequate protection and, thus, Art 3 had been breached. Since the court was satisfied that the treatment had reached the higher threshold for Art 3, it did not consider the complaint under Art 8; however, it is probable that a less severe form of physical ill treatment would be successfully challenged under Art 8 and the same considerations about the State's obligations to protect private individuals from one another would apply.

Article 8 has also been invoked in a claim *protecting* a family's right to chastise their child. In *Application No 8811/79*, DR 29, Swedish parents claimed (unsuccessfully) that a statute prohibiting corporal punishment violated their right to family life under Art 8.

23.3   The right to privacy against private bodies: the news media

Although companies publishing newspapers and making radio and television programmes are not organs of the State and not liable under the Convention, Art 8 requires the State to 'respect' the right to privacy; it should, therefore, pass laws that prevent private bodies such as news media businesses interfering with the privacy rights of individuals (see above, 19.9, on the horizontal effect of the ECHR). In *X and Y v Netherlands* (1985), the European Court of Human Rights said:

> [Article 8] does not merely compel the State to abstain from ... interference: in addition to this primarily negative undertaking, there may be positive obligations inherent in an effective respect for private and family life ... These

obligations may involve the adoption of measures designed to secure respect for private life *even in the sphere of relations between individuals themselves* [emphasis added].

In the UK, any attempt, legislative or judicial, to restrain the coverage by the news media of intimate details of people's lives is usually trumped by claims to the public interest in a free press. Clearly, the role of investigative journalism is of great significance in a free democracy, since it is one of the first bastions against the development of tyrannical power. But it is debatable whether all forms of press coverage can lay claim to the respect accorded to serious political reporting. There is a long running debate over whether people in the public eye should be allowed some protection against media intrusion, both in respect of their methods of collecting the information and the eventual coverage of intimate details in the press or the broadcast media. Over a hundred years ago, two American jurists wrote a seminal article about the scope of privacy. Their observations have an uncanny prescience:

> The intensity and complexity of life, attending upon advancing civilisation, have rendered necessary some retreat from the world, and man, under the reigning influence of culture, has become more sensitive to publicity, so that solitude and privacy have become more essential to the individual; but modern enterprise and invention have, through invasions upon his privacy, subjected him to mental pain and distress, far greater than could be inflicted by mere bodily injury [Warren, SD and Brandies, LD, 'The right to privacy' (1890) 4 Harv L Rev 193].

Where the courts are satisfied that there has been some reprehensible behaviour in collecting the information, they are sometimes prepared to prohibit disclosure. In *Francome v Daily Mirror Group Newspapers Ltd* (1984), the claimants sought an interlocutory injunction to restrain a newspaper from publishing information obtained through the tapping of the claimant's telephone in breach of the Wireless Telegraphy Act 1949, the predecessor to the Interception of Communications Act 1985. The newspaper argued that, since the tapes revealed breaches of the rules of racing by the first defendant, a well known jockey, publication of the contents of the tapes was 'justifiable in the public interest'. Lord Denning MR rejected this argument in the strongest possible terms:

> I regard Mr Molly's [the defendant newspaper editor's] assertion as arrogant and wholly unacceptable. Parliamentary democracy as we know it is based upon the rule of law. That requires all citizens to obey the law, unless and until it can be changed by due process. There are no privileged classes to whom it does not apply. If Mr Molly and the Daily Mirror can assert this right to act on the basis that the public interest, as he sees it, justifies breaches of the criminal law, so can any other citizen. This has only to be stated for it to be obvious that the result would be anarchy.

In general, however, national courts have not been prepared to restrain the publication of details about the lives of people in the public eye. It was an important factor in the *Francome* case that the information had been collected unlawfully. Until the Human Rights Act 1998, there were very limited protections in English law against the intrusions by the press on the privacy of individuals. Under the Sexual Offences (Amendment) Act 1976, it is an offence to publish or broadcast the name of a rape victim, although victims of lesser types of sexual offence are not covered by this provision. The Rehabilitation of Offenders Act 1974 prohibits the disclosure of criminal records of a convicted criminal once a certain number of years have passed and his or her conviction is 'spent'. The wardship jurisdiction of the High Court has on occasion been relied upon to protect the anonymity of the children and family members involved in the proceedings, and a range of other cases involving sensitive family problems are conducted in private. But, in between these rather isolated instances, freedom of expression in the press has been allowed to prevail over the privacy rights of individuals.

The common law provides equally unsatisfactory and patchy protection for individual privacy. A notorious example of this is *Kaye v Robertson* (1991). Here, the claimant tried to obtain an injunction to prevent the *Sunday Sport* from publishing photographs of him taken without his permission when he was seriously ill in hospital. It was necessary for his lawyers to sew together a complicated patchwork of ill fitting rules and precedents from the fabric of the common law, most of which proved inadequate in the end. They tried defamation, on the basis that the pictures would imply, damagingly, that Kaye had consented to be interviewed by the newspaper; but this failed because the courts are reluctant to impose prior restraint on the press should the allegation later turn out at trial to be substantiated; a claim in trespass to the person also failed because it was not held that photographing amounted to the common law tort of trespass. However, a claim in malicious falsehood did succeed, since the journalists must have known that the claimant had not given informed consent to the publication of the story, and the story had been published with the headline 'exclusive', falsely implying that such consent had been forthcoming. But this is a very narrow tort and it will only be established if the claimant shows that he or she stands to suffer financially from it; here, Kaye was said to have risked losing the exclusive right to sell his pictures elsewhere. The narrowness of the tort is matched by its remedy; *Kaye* was only a limited injunction to prevent the newspapers contriving to publish the offending pictures and comments, rather than a permanent injunction and damages he might have received under a fully fledged privacy right. The artificiality of the reasoning in this case demonstrates the difficulty of using the available common law to obtain a remedy for breach of privacy, even when the courts are sympathetic, as they were in this case.

It is questionable whether the incorporation of Art 8 into domestic law will greatly enhance the protection of privacy in English law, despite the pressure it will bring to bear on the courts to develop existing torts to cover forms of privacy invasion in accordance with the Convention. The case law of the European Court of Human Rights, which will influence national courts in this area, generally gives considerable weight to press freedom under the exception listed in Art 8(2) for measures taken in the interests of the 'rights and freedoms of others'. There has been manifest reluctance by the European Commission and the Court of Human Rights to accept that Art 8 rights should provide a platform for press regulation. In *Earl Spencer and Countess Spencer v UK* (1998), the applicants claimed, inter alia, that the absence in English law of a legal remedy for intrusions by the popular press into their private lives amounted to a breach of the State's positive obligations under Art 8. The Commission declared the application inadmissible, since the Spencers had not exhausted their remedies under domestic law and, therefore, did not fulfil the 'victim' requirement under Art 26 (now 34) of the Convention (see above, 19.7). It took the view that an action for breach of confidentiality might have availed the applicants in this case, rejecting their argument that they could not have relied on this cause of action since the information was already in the public domain when they became aware of it. Because this application was stopped in its tracks, there has been no recent definitive ruling from the Court on the adequacy of the common law of confidence to protect privacy rights. However, the European Court of Human Rights has recently expressed its disapproval of the disclosure of private information by the press, even where, in the end, the judgment came down in favour of freedom of expression. In *De Haes and Gijsels v Belgium* (1998), the applicants were journalists who had published articles accusing four Belgian judges of bias in their handling of a controversial custody case. The articles contained strong personal attacks on the judges and journalists were convicted of defamation. The court observed that the penalty had been justified in respect of one of the aspects of the published articles, exposing the subject to opprobrium because of matters concerning a member of his family. As far as the other comments by the journalists were concerned, the court ruled that the convictions were disproportionate since it had not been established that these allegations had no basis in fact.

Despite the somewhat cautious approach by the European Court of Human Rights to privacy interests when freedom of the press is at stake, the press lobby fought a strong rearguard action in the passage of the Human Rights Bill through Parliament when they apprehended a possible threat to their freedom. They were quick to point out that the Act would catch the Press Complaints Commission (PCC), the newspapers' self-regulatory body which was set up to monitor compliance with its Code of Practice, since this qualifies as a 'public authority' for the purposes of s 6 of the Human Rights Act (see above, 19.10.4). Anyone challenging a decision by the PCC not to take action against some alleged breach of privacy by a particular newspaper, it was argued, could apply to an English court for judicial review of the PCC's decision – arguing a violation of Art 8 – and, thus, privacy laws would be introduced 'by the back door'. In response to these anxieties, the government included a provision (s 12 of the Human Rights Act) which restricts parties' ability to obtain injunctions against newspapers on without notice applications. Section 12 also requires the courts to have particular regard to freedom of expression in any challenge to the press under Art 8. Since this is a countervailing interest listed in Art 8 anyway, it is hard to see what these provisos add to the Act, apart from the implication that there is some hierarchy of rights which was never intended by the draftsmen of the ECHR.

23.4 Assessment

Despite recent changes in the law in response to adverse rulings from Strasbourg, there are still considerable shortcomings in the available protections for individual privacy in the UK.

23.4.1 Rights of privacy against the State

As we have seen, the power of the Home Secretary to issue warrants for covert surveillance to the security services and the police, though limited by statute, may be triggered by the very broad aims of the prevention or the detection of 'serious crime'; complaints by citizens to the Tribunals set up under the Security Services Act 1989 and the Intelligence Services Act 1994 do not elicit any information as to why the surveillance was conducted and there is no obligation on the tribunal to direct the cessation of surveillance. The fact that the tribunals cannot even inquire into whether the surveillance was justified in the first place reduces the protection they offer to a mere formality. The introduction of a general right to privacy in the Human Rights Act may resolve this problem, although there is still a risk that judges, in the spirit of the *GCHQ* case (*Council of Civil Service Unions v Minister for the Civil Service* (1985)), will give a broad interpretation to the exceptions to this right, such as the interests of prevention of crime and national security.

23.4.2 Rights of privacy against private parties

Before the Human Rights Act 1998 was passed, there was no recognised right in English law to privacy, either in statute or in common law. Where the invasion of privacy violated other interests recognised by the law, such as private property or confidential information, the victim had a limited range of remedies, but, as the *Kaye* case demonstrated, these fell far short of the UK's obligation under Art 8 of the Convention. The common law on private nuisance was extended to cover the infringement of a woman's privacy in the form of constant phone calls to her parent's house (*Khorasandjian v Bush* (1993)), but that case has now been effectively overruled by a House of Lords decision that private nuisance is a cause of action only available to property owners (*Hunter v Canary Wharf* (1997)). The insistence in the common law on some prior interest – particularly property interests – has stifled the growth of any useful tort of privacy,such as has developed in the US. The introduction of Art 8 will inevitably have an impact on the common law here, extending the scope of the available torts and removing some of the current obstacles to pursuing privacy actions in the courts.

Less is to be expected from legislation. Although some types of press intrusion will be restricted by the Data Protection Act 1998, it is worth noting that the press managed to negotiate an important amendment in the parliamentary stages of the legislation, with the result that s 31 of the Act prevents them from having to disclose data if those data are being processed for a journalistic, literary or artistic purpose and if, 'having regard to the special importance of freedom of expression, publication would be in the public interest'. It is debatable whether the first three justifications would survive scrutiny under the ECHR, unless they fell within the rubric of the Art 8(2) aims of securing 'journalistic, literary or artistic' material which would require proper forensic justification on the part of the rights infringer.

The inadequacies of the law in this area are not limited to the lack of protection against press intrusions. Although private usage of surveillance devices is regulated to a certain extent under the Interception of Communications Act 1985, it can be argued that regulating such surveillance is virtually impossible, since, in most cases, it is impossible to trace the perpetrator. In addition, there is no regulation governing private use of cameras; private nuisance provides the only protection and that action is dependent on the 'victim' having a legal interest in the property where the intrusion takes place. Again, Art 8 and the relevant European Court of Human Rights case law on these issues will allow the courts to develop new torts to cover these forms of invasion.

PRIVACY

Privacy has a political function – it prevents authorities from stifling dissent by keeping too watchful an eye on their opponents' activities; and it has a non-political value in preserving, from the interference of the State, a sphere in which the individual can exercise his or her freedom. The difficulty is in striking the balance between privacy and legitimate invasions of it for the purposes of protecting others. Article 8 of the ECHR, which protects privacy and family life, contains a number of exceptions which operate to limit this protection in the interests of national security, the prevention of crime, etc (see Art 8(2)).

Secret surveillance by the police and security service

The Interception of Communications Act 1985 makes it illegal to intercept any communication without a warrant under the Act. The Police Act 1997, however, provides wide justifications for the issue of a warrant for bugging private property, and MI5 have equally wide powers under the Social Security Act 1987. Bugging is permissible 'in the interests of national security' or for 'the prevention of disorder or crime'. But such measures, in order to be upheld under Art 8(2), must be 'prescribed by law'. The law must not be so broad and permissive that the individual is at risk of having private communications intercepted for no legally recognisable reason.

Police: entry and search

The Police and Criminal Evidence Act 1984 grants wide powers to the police to enter and search private property for evidence or persons suspected of committing a criminal offence. The powers of police to enter private premises to prevent a breach of the peace have been held to be justified within Art 8.

Search orders

These are court orders issued to the legal advisers of a claimant in civil proceedings where there is a risk that the defendant will dispose of evidence essential to the trial. It permits the legal advisers to enter the defendant's private premises and remove property. Such orders may be obtained *ex parte* (in the absence of the defendant) – now called 'without notice'. Search orders have been held by the European Court of Human Rights to come within the permitted exceptions to Art 8: the prevention of crime and the protection of the rights of others.

Private information held by public authorities

A number of statutes require disclosure of details held in files and on computer on application by the individual concerned; these Acts also regulate disclosure, so that unauthorised access is not permitted. There is, however, much information held by public bodies which, for various technical reasons, is not covered by any of this legislation,so it is still impossible in some circumstances for an individual to know what information is being held about him or her. The Sex Offenders Act 1997 requires those who have been convicted of certain types of sexual offence to tell the police where they live and when they move. Information on the Sex Offenders Register is available to local authorities. Legislation restricting the use that can be made of personal information held in computers or certain categories of manual records is also in place. The restrictions imposed extend to private data holders.

Immigration decisions

Immigration procedures often involve invasions of privacy when immigration officers seek to establish the genuineness of claims to entry. Until incorporation of the ECHR, the courts have not been sympathetic to Art 8 arguments in immigration decisions concerning the refusal of entry or deportation of family members of non-nationals lawfully resident in this country. The European Court of Human Rights has ruled moreover that Art 8 does not impose an obligation on signatory States to allow entry to non-nationals except where family ties with individuals lawfully resident in that State may be established. Recent proposals on immigration and asylum raise privacy concerns, for example, extensions of immigration officers' powers of search and seizure.

Family life

Any rule of national law that interferes with the relationship between parent and child will violate the right to family life under Art 8 of the ECHR. However, in the past, the European Court of Human Rights has taken a cautious approach to laws in signatory States relating to divorce or single sex relationships. So, whilst it may not be a violation of the Convention not to allow a separated couple to divorce each other and marry other people, the disadvantages faced by the children who emerge from the consequent extra-marital union do breach Art 8.

Sexual activity

Laws which criminalise homosexual activity have been found to be in breach of Art 8, but failure to recognise the new sexual identity of individuals who have undergone gender re-assignment operations is not. Article 8 has not been extended to protect the right to participate in sado-masochistic sexual activities. In these cases, the exceptions to Art 8, particularly measures taken in the interests of the 'health and morals of others', are broadly construed.

Children

The enthusiasm of the authorities to protect the rights of children at the cost of their parents' rights to family life has been tempered in a number of Strasbourg rulings that the right to due process under Art 6 requires that parents must be allowed proper participation in care proceedings. The right to privacy has been relied upon in a challenge to the law on corporal punishment; in this sense, privacy constitutes the right to physical integrity.

The press

Although the press is a non-State body and, therefore, in principle, not liable under the ECHR, Art 8 requires that States 'respect' the right to privacy. The State should, therefore, pass laws that prevent private bodies such as media organisations interfering with the privacy rights of individuals. There are a number of common law protections against press invasions of freedom; the press may be in breach of confidentiality by publishing information held in confidence, they may be liable in trespass in their attempts to get hold of information; their publication may be attacked as malicious falsehood or libel. Freedom of the press generally prevails over the right to privacy in common law and under the ECHR.

Privacy in Community law

Article 8 is one of the general principles of Community law. Although successful claims have been made in respect of Member States' breaches of privacy, the Court has been reluctant to rule against Community institutions, particularly in the area of competition where the Commission has taken allegedly intrusive investigation proceedings.

CHAPTER 24

FREEDOM OF EXPRESSION

24.1 Introduction

Freedom of speech and of the press have presented such special constitutional concerns that they were accorded recognition by English courts long before incorporation of the European Convention on Human Rights (ECHR) by the Human Rights Act 1998. Clearly, the freedom to publish critical views of the government is essential to democracy; otherwise, government could grow corrupt and opposition views would not gather the necessary support to defeat the party in power at election time. Protection of political speech is easily justified, on the basis that the right contributes to the free flow of information. An argument may also be made out for the value of broader free speech rights in a democracy since they cultivate free choice of a range of ideas which find expression in society and thereby ensure the independence of electors and legislators in the political sphere.

Free speech is worth valuing in itself, not simply as an instrumental good. As adult members of a community, we have an important moral interest in deciding for ourselves what is good or bad, moral or immoral, within or beyond the pale. If government decides, for example, that because of someone's racist convictions, they are an unworthy participant in the democratic process, it is denying that moral interest to the people over whom it exercises power and, therefore, loses the necessary legitimacy for the exercise of that power:

> It is the central, defining premise of freedom of speech that the offensiveness of ideas, or the challenge they offer to traditional ideas, cannot be a valid reason for censorship; once that premise is abandoned, it is difficult to see what free speech means [Dworkin, R, *Freedom's Law*, 1997, Oxford: OUP, p 206].

Higher priority tends to be accorded to political speech than to other types of speech, particularly in Strasbourg. However, 'speech' or 'expression' is not limited to the disclosure of political information. If we perceive of expression as extending beyond the function of informing the public about the activities of their rulers and informing the rulers about the views of their subjects, we have to find ways of justifying why it covers a range of other forms of expression, such as avant garde films or sculpture, flag burning or advertisements. Joseph Raz described the protection of these forms of expression as the 'validating' role of freedom of expression, which is important since it allows ways of life and experience to be reflected in public culture and thus be accorded public recognition (Raz, J, 'Free expression and personal identification' (1991) 11 OJLS 303). The importance, in a democracy, of according equal status to the views of citizens is considered in Chapter 26. Guaranteeing freedom of expression in our laws is one way of ensuring that this happens.

Clearly, this wide definition of expression creates problems for itself, illustrated most starkly by the claims to protection, under the free speech banner, of pornography, exhortations to criminal activity, racism and so on. Should this freedom be guaranteed to the authors of race hate speech, tobacco advertising and pornography? How can their rights be described as 'constitutional'?

One answer to this is the utilitarian argument that the publication of opinions and facts, good or bad, true or untrue, should not be restricted, because society benefits in the long term from the process of scrutinising their worth or veracity. In his essay, *On Liberty* (1859), Mill argues that freedom of expression unleashes a certain creativity in society (see above, 1.6.1):

> If all mankind, minus one, were of one opinion and only one person were of the contrary opinion, mankind would be no more justified in silencing that one person than he, if he had the power, would be justified in silencing mankind.

Mill believed that, to lose that one dissenting opinion, would be to lose something of value. If the opinion were right, posterity would be the loser, but, in his view, there was also value in a mistaken opinion, or an assertion of untrue facts, if it forced those who were not mistaken to examine their own case more carefully and understand it better.

As Feldman notes, the modern version of this utilitarian approach to freedom of expression is manifest in the concept of the 'free market of ideas' in the US (see Feldman, D, *Civil Liberties and Human Rights in England and Wales*, 1993, Oxford: OUP, pp 547–58). The idea is that market forces will determine that good, true and valuable expressions of ideas will simply 'crowd out' unmeritorious forms of expression. Unfortunately, this model is not reflected in reality, where the marketplace did not inhibit the development of views such as those expressed by the Ku Klux Klan in 1969 that 'the nigger should be returned to Africa, the Jew returned to Israel' (quoted in Dworkin, *Freedom's Law*, 1997, Oxford: OUP). Distasteful though they were, the Supreme Court extended the protection of free speech rights under the American constitution to these declarations *(Brandenburg v Ohio)*, since a line could not be easily drawn between expressions which should attract First Amendment protection and those which should not.

It is clear, then, that freedom of speech demands that any censorship on grounds of content be prohibited; on the other hand, ways of dealing with forms of speech and expression that cause harm need to be discovered. One solution, proposed by Marshall, is that free speech protection should vary according to whether the idea expresses a 'core' value in a democracy, or is merely 'peripheral' to those values, 'so as to permit suppression of those [forms of speech] that fall outside the topmost level or privileged core of the area protected by the principle of [free speech]' (Marshall, G, 'Press freedom and free speech theory' [1992] PL 40, p 60). Attractive though this solution may be, it does not do away with the problem altogether. It still requires a measure of content based censorship in order to determine where, on the hierarchy, any particular form of expression belongs. Race hate speech or pornography must not be banned because society disapproves of the message; some instrumental justification must be found for suppressing it within the notion of freedom of speech. Such speech leads to harm; words are being used as an instrument against their audience. Therefore, it has been argued that pornography, for example, interferes with women's freedom of speech, because it changes its audience's perception about the status and intelligence of women:

> ... expression is not just talk. Pornography not only teaches the reality of male dominance. It is one way its reality is imposed as well as experienced. It is a way of seeing and using women ... so that when a man looks at a pornographic picture – pornographic meaning that the woman is defined as to be acted upon, a sexual object, a sexual thing – the viewing is an act, an act of male supremacy [MacKinnon, C, *Feminism Unmodified: Discourses on Life and Law*, 1987, Harvard: Harvard UP, p 128].

Whether one agrees with this argument or not, it is certainly more attractive than the justification for banning forms of expression on the basis of protecting people's feelings. It will be seen below that an argument was made out in the English courts that Salman Rushdie should have been prosecuted for the offence caused to Muslims by his novel, *The Satanic Verses*. If the court had upheld this claim, very many forms of expression, literary or otherwise, would have been put in jeopardy.

Having concluded that the protection and regulation of expression should depend on its effects rather than its subject matter, let us return to the issue of free speech rights against public authorities. Our consent to being subject to the coercive power of government is contingent to a certain extent on being aware of what our rulers are up to. This gives the news media an important claim to freedom of expression rights when challenged under any countervailing rights, such as individual's rights to reputation and the interests of national security. But, for this right to information to have any value, we have to be certain that the purveyors of information are giving us the whole picture. This engages the liability of private actors – the press, the independent broadcasting media, publishing corporations – under constitutional free speech rights. As Sir Stephen Sedley commented on this issue:

> For a transnational corporation on which hundreds of millions of people depend for their information about the world, [freedom of speech means another thing]: the power to suppress information, of which we would firmly deny the State control, is a power possessed by the media corporations. Are human rights there for corporations or for people? Are they a form of property

or a constraint on power [Sedley, S, 'Human rights: a twenty-first century agenda' [1995] PL 395]?

Unfortunately, for recipients of news broadcasts, at any rate, there is no mechanism in national or international provisions on the freedom of speech for the right to information (itself part of freedom of expression) to be enforced against private actors such as media corporations. There is, however, an obligation on States to ensure that the media is so regulated as to prevent concentrations of power. The 1966 International Covenant for the Protection of Civil and Political Rights has a similar provision to Art 10 of the ECHR, which includes the rights of individuals to 'receive and impart information and ideas of all kinds' (Art 19) (see above, 19.3). The UK, which is a party to the Covenant, is obliged to submit reports to the Human Rights Committee on its compliance with the provisions of the Covenant. The failure of the State to prevent media concentration is a matter which the Committee would consider as potentially giving rise to issues under Art 19. As part of its general guidelines for reporting obligations, the UN Committee has said that States should provide complete information on the legal regime that regulates the ownership and licensing of the press and broadcast media. The European Commission of Human Rights has also suggested that Art 10 may impose a positive duty on the State to guard against 'excessive press concentrations' (*De Geillustreede Pers v Netherlands* (1976)). Because freedom of expression depends to a certain extent on the prevention of media empires, the EHCR specifically permits the regulation and licensing of the media (see below, 24.7).

24.2   Protection of freedom of expression

In *British Steel Corporation v Granada Television Ltd* (1982), Lord Wilberforce said that: 'Freedom of the press imports, generally, freedom to publish subject always to the laws relating to libel, official secrets, sedition and other recognised inhibitions.' This is a very English approach, which left the residual liberty to speak one's mind vulnerable to incursions by the law. Outside the ECHR, as incorporated by the Human Rights Act 1998, there are fragments of English law which provide a positive right to freedom of expression. Under the Bill of Rights 1689, Members of Parliament have the freedom to say what they like within the precincts of Parliament without running the risk of being sued for libel or questioned in any other way in a court of law (see above, 6.6). If they wish to sue for libel, however, a defendant is entitled to adduce evidence of what they said in Parliament by way of justification. In the same way, judges, advocates, jurors and witnesses can speak freely in court without risk of a defamation action. In addition, the Education (No 2) Act 1986 provides that higher education institutions should ensure free speech on their premises, a provision designed to protect lecturers and visiting speakers with controversial views against the 'no platform' policies of student unions.

These are patchy and extremely limited legal protections for freedom of expression. However, even before Art 10 became part of national law, freedom of expression as a residual right was accorded more respect than other rights in the common law. As the cases discussed below demonstrate, the judicial approach pre-incorporation was to acknowledge in positive terms the public interest in freedom of expression, which was then weighed against the countervailing public interests, such as the administration of justice or the protection of confidentiality and privacy.

This approach is consistent with the judicial balancing exercised required by Art 10 of the ECHR:

1   Everyone has the right to freedom of expression. This right shall include freedom to hold opinions and to receive and impart information and ideas without interference by public authority and regardless of frontiers. This Article shall not prevent States from requiring the licensing of broadcasting, television or cinema enterprises.

2   The exercise of these freedoms, since it carries with it duties and responsibilities, may be subject to such formalities, conditions, restrictions or penalties as are prescribed by law and are necessary in a democratic society, in the interests of national security, territorial integrity or public safety, for the prevention of disorder or crime, for the protection of health or morals, for the protection of the reputation or rights of others, for preventing the disclosure of information received in confidence, or for maintaining the authority and impartiality of the judiciary.

There are a number of permissible exceptions set out in this Article. The scope of freedom of expression will be be evaluated below, as against the breadth of some of these exceptions.

24.3   National security and the impartiality of the judiciary

In order to ensure but justice is done in the hearing of individual cases, civil or criminal, it is clearly necessary to ensure that the tribunal, whether it consists of judge or jury, is not biased by prejudicial publicity. States also impose rules to maintain the secrecy of sensitive information. Both categories of rules involve limitations on freedom of expression.

24.3.1   Confidentiality and national security

The Official Secrets Act 1989 (discussed in more detail below) criminalises the release of certain types of classified information. However, a prosecution under this Act and its far wider ranging predecessor (the Official Secrets Act 1911) is less useful to the government than a court order preventing the information from coming into the private domain in the first place. So the English common law of confidentiality was brought into the public arena to protect sensitive information. In 1975 the plaintiff government claimed that publication of an ex-Cabinet minister's memoirs would breach the duty of confidentiality owed by the Minister to the Crown: *Attorney General v Jonathan Cape Ltd* (1976). The court upheld this novel use of the hitherto private law of confidentiality but insisted that the Government should establish that the public interest in confidentiality prevail against the countervailing public interest in disseminating the information.

When Peter Wright published his memoirs in Australia about his career in the secret services (*Spycatcher*), the Government applied for a permanent injunction to prevent publication in this country, on the basis of confidence in national security matters. Before the main trial of the action, the Attorney General also sought interlocutory injunctions to prevent newspapers serialising extracts from the foreign publication. The House of Lords granted these on the basis that they were necessary to preserve the Attorney General's case at trial (*Attorney General v Guardian Newspapers Ltd* (1987)). Since the ECHR was not then part of national law, the newspapers challenged this decision in the European Court of Human Rights (*Observer and Guardian v UK* (1991)). The Government argued that the injunction was a legitimate measure in the interests both of national security and of maintaining confidence in the judiciary. The Court agreed that the need to maintain the confidence in the judiciary and safeguard the operation of the security services were both legitimate aims under Art 10(2). However, it considered that the imposition of injunctions from the date that the extracts entered the public domain (that is, when they were published in the US) represented a disproportionate interference with press freedom.

At the hearing of the application for the permanent injunction in the national court, the Government failed to obtain its injunction against the newspapers on similar grounds, since confidentiality cannot inhere in information once it is in the public domain. During the course of the litigation, various newspapers were fined for contempt of court when they published extracts from the book, even though they themselves were not party to the interim injunctions (*Attorney General v Newspaper Publishing plc* (1990)). It was held that a newspaper which knew that proceedings were in progress against another newspaper owed a duty to preserve the rights of confidentiality in respect of the material, since this would otherwise prejudice the administration of justice. Thus, the law on confidentiality combined with common law contempt of court imposes considerable restrictions on the publication of certain types of information.

24.3.2 Contempt of court

We can see from the *Spycatcher* litigation that the law on contempt of court may, therefore, be a legitimate way of preserving the impartiality of the judiciary under Art 10(2). Again, the law on contempt of court developed in this country before freedom of expression was accorded formal protection in national law. Before the Contempt of Court Act 1981 was passed, all contempts, whether intentional or unintentional, were caught by the common law offence of contempt of court. In the *Thalidomide* case (*Attorney General v Times Newspapers Ltd* (1974)), the House of Lords upheld a finding of contempt against a newspaper for publishing an article laying out the evidence in a pending negligence action against manufacturers of a pregnancy drug which had led to deformities in thousands of children. The Lords said that the article, by pre-judging the negligence issue, was designed to put pressure on the company to come up with a generous settlement before a court of law had ruled in the main proceedings. The line between informed comment and pre-judgment, however, is hard to draw. The 'pressure' and 'pre-judgment' criteria established by the House of Lords were so extensive that it might have been a contempt to publish anything from a fair and balanced assessment of the issues in a broadsheet newspaper to a discussion of the legal issues in an academic journal.

In the Court of Human Rights, the newspaper alleged a breach of Art 10. The Court was given its first opportunity to weigh the interests of justice (impartiality of the judiciary) against freedom of expression and determine what measures to achieve this end could be said to be necessary in a free and democratic society. In *Sunday Times Ltd v UK* (1979), the Court accepted the Government's argument that contempt proceedings were a permissible restriction on Art 10 rights, but that the particular interpretation of contempt by the House of Lords went further than was necessary in a democratic society for maintaining the authority of the judiciary. The Court of Human Rights upheld the applicant's claim that the common law on contempt was an over-broad and disproportionate interference with its freedom under Art 10 of the ECHR.

The Contempt of Court Act 1981 was passed in response to this ruling, restricting the circumstances in which the publication of material concerning the issues in proceedings can amount to an offence. There must be a 'substantial risk' of serious prejudice (s 2(2)), although this has been broadly defined (*Attorney General v English* (1983)) and s 5 of the Act provides a defence of public interest; if the prejudice element is merely incidental to the publication, and the discussion is in good faith and concerns matters of public affairs, the publication will not come within the Act.

The common law offence of contempt survives the passing of the 1981 Act (s 6(c)), but it can only be made out where the contempt is intentional. The offence has proved useful where the 'contempt' has taken place in a context where proceedings are not 'pending' under the act. In 1989, successful common law contempt proceedings were brought against News Group Newspapers, on the basis that proceedings were 'imminent'. In *Attorney General v News Group Newspapers* (1989), a newspaper had decided to press for the private prosecution of a doctor who was suspected of having raped a girl aged eight. Public prosecution proceedings were not taken as there was insufficient evidence. The newspaper published the doctor's name along with incriminating statements from potential witnesses. Seven weeks later, private prosecution proceedings were initiated; the doctor was eventually acquitted. When the Attorney General took this action for contempt it was argued that proceedings, although not active or even pending, had been 'imminent' because a private prosecution had been intended by the newspaper. The Divisional Court upheld this conclusion and they also accepted the Attorney General's argument that there was no authority precluding liability for contempt even before proceedings were imminent. The administration of justice, therefore, was the paramount concern. Although the judgments indicate that the newspaper or publisher must be aware of the likelihood of proceedings to follow, nevertheless, this case suggests that any controversial subject which may lead to proceedings is fair game for a contempt order, even though no litigation is under way.

24.3.3 Protection of sources

The Contempt of Court Act 1981 provides additional protection for free speech rights by specifying that no one may be subject to contempt proceedings for failing to disclose the source of their information, provided that refusal to disclose does not interfere with 'the interests of justice or national security or for the prevention of disorder or crime' (s 10).

Promising though that provision seemed for the free flow of information when the Contempt of Court Act was passed, s 10 has not fared well at the hands of the judiciary. In the Sarah Tisdall case (*Secretary of State for Defence v Guardian Newspapers Ltd* (1985)), the national security exception was upheld on the basis that a civil servant who leaked a sensitive Ministry of Defence document to the press might attempt to do so again and, therefore, presented an ongoing threat. In *X v Morgan Grampian* (1991), the House of Lords ruled that the protection of journalists' sources under s 10 could be outweighed by the 'interests of justice' to the employer of the source of the leaked document. Factors which will weigh in the balance include the interest the claimant is seeking to protect in wishing to have the source disclosed and whether the source had (as in this case) stolen the information or breached a strong duty of confidence. The journalist in *X v Morgan Grampian* took his case to the Court of Human rights where he succeeded in his argument that this breached his rights under Art 10 and the Government had to pay him compensation and costs of £37,595 (*Goodwin v UK* (1996)). With this precedent in mind, one might have thought that national courts would be hesitant to remove the protection for sources offered by the Contempt of Court Act. But, in *Camelot Group plc v Centaur Communications Ltd* (1998), the permitted exceptions under that provision were given even wider scope. Here, an unknown person sent the draft accounts of C to a journalist, who published them in an article. When C sought the return of the documents to identify the source, the paper relied on s 10. The Court of Appeal ruled, however, that the interests of C in ensuring the continuing loyalty of its employees and ex-employees should outweigh the public importance attached to the protection of sources. Lest this judgment was seen to be in defiance of the ruling in Goodwin, the court observed that it was applying the same test as the Court of Human Rights and any apparent difference between *X v Morgan Grampian* and *Goodwin v UK* was attributable to the different view taken of the facts. This illustrates that the broad principles to be interpreted and judicial balancing exercises undertaken under the ECHR will not always lead national courts and the Court of Human Rights along the same path.

24.3.4 Whistleblowers

Whistleblowers – people who speak out in the public interest against wrongdoing or malpractice in the workplace – such as Goodwin's source in *X v Morgan Grampian* need to be protected from victimisation by their employers. The Public Interest Disclosure Act 1998, a Private Member's Bill, has recently added a number of rights to employment legislation by preventing employees from being dismissed or made subject to other sanctions for drawing attention to malpractice. The disclosure, however, must be 'reasonable' in the view of the Employment Tribunal (the adjudicative body which deals with employment disputes); and, if the disclosure was in breach of an obligation of confidentiality owed to a third party, the whistleblower is unlikely to be protected under the Act.

In these kinds of cases, it is sometimes difficult to distinguish whether the 'expression' for which protection is sought under Art 10 of the ECHR is the information which is originally leaked or the subsequent publication by the newspaper. As far as European Court of Human Rights case law is concerned, it seems that it is the publication which attracts the protection of Art 10. In *Fressoz and Roire v France* (1999), the applicants were journalist and editor of a newspaper who were convicted of the offence of handling the fruits of a breach of professional confidence. They had published a tax assessment which had been leaked to them by an anonymous source. The details of the assessment were available to the public, although the document itself was not. In ruling that the conviction for handling was a breach of Art 10, the Court observed that 'the purely technical offence of handling photocopies disguised what was really a desire to penalise [the applicant journalists] for publishing the information, although publication in itself was quite lawful'. Therefore, there was no overriding requirement for the information to be protected as confidential and, thus, the convictions could not be justified.

24.3.5 Official Secrets Acts

Another way of protecting sensitive information is by criminalising its disclosure. The main offence of leaking official secrets is contained in the

Official Secrets Act 1989. Whereas its predecessor, the Official Secrets Act 1911, made it an offence to be the recipient of unsolicited information, the 1989 Act only covers the publication by present or former servants of the Crown of information which has come into their possession by virtue of their position, and it is a defence that the informer was under the impression that he or she had lawful authority to pass on that information. Disclosure of material by intelligence officials will be an offence if the disclosure causes 'damage' or is likely to cause damage to the security services – a very broad test. The disclosing civil servant will escape liability if he or she did not know that the material came into any of the forbidden categories, honestly and reasonably believed either that disclosure would not be damaging or that disclosure had been authorised. Any third party who receives and then discloses material covered by the 1989 Act will only be liable if he or she is conscious of the damaging effects of publication, both actual and potential. This 'damage' test does not apply to the disclosure of information relating to the investigation of crime; so the leak by an M15 officer of the contents of a telephone conversation obtained as a result of tapping, to a journalist, will result in criminal liability for them both under the Act even if no harm was intended. The most important shortcoming of the Act is that it provides no public interest defence; any civil servant whistleblowing about what he or she believes to be corruption in high places will not be protected from prosecution.

The Official Secrets Act 1989 is only one of a raft of laws which criminalise the disclosure of information: the White Paper, *Open Government* (Cmd 2290, 1998), noted that some 200 other pieces of legislation restrict the publication of certain types of information. The Official Secrets Act may be combined with other legislation, such as the Security Services Act 1989 or the Interception of Communications Act 1985, to create a zone of secrecy over large tracts of information by making any disclosure a statutory offence.

Although it was noted above that the prosecution of 'leaked' information may be of little use to a government anxious to prevent the information getting out in the first place, an effective measure for stifling information has been found in the combination of criminal liability of members of the security services under s 1 of the 1989 Act and the civil law duty of confidence, explored in another ex-Security Service case, *Attorney General v Blake (Jonathan Cape Ltd)* (1998). The Attorney General applied for an injunction to prevent the defendant, a former spy, from profiting from his memoirs concerning his activities as a double agent. The publication of information obtained in the course of his duties as an SIS officer was a crime under the Official Secrets Act, but, of course, no prosecution could be brought against Blake who was in Moscow when the book was published. The House of Lords upheld the grant of the injunction, even though there had been no continuing duty of confidentiality (the information being already in the public domain). Lord Woolf was at pains to point out that this was not a matter of private law, since no compensatory or restitutionary remedy would be available to the Crown. This was a matter of legislative policy, that 'a criminal should not be allowed to retain the benefits derived from his crime'. Since the motivation behind many publications is profit related, this decision may cast a chilling an effect on many similar publications.

24.3.6 Broadcasting controls

If a proposed programme is likely to prejudice national security, the Defence and Broadcasting Committee, a joint board of the Ministry of Defence and broadcasters, may issue a 'Defence Advisory Notice' (the so called 'D' notice), requesting the voluntary compliance of the broadcaster to refrain from publishing certain matters which may threaten certain elements of national defence. Ultimate authority rests with the Home Secretary, who has the power under the Broadcasting Act 1990 to issue a notice ordering the holder of a broadcasting licence to broadcast a specific announcement or to refrain from broadcasting something if he considers it is expedient to do so in connection with his offices as Secretary of State. The House of Lords considered the scope of this power and its relationship to Art 10 of the European Convention in *R v Home Secretary ex p Brind* (1991), and rejected the applicants' claim that the Home Secretary had acted unlawfully (see above, 15.5). Although the arguments based on the protection of free expression afforded by the Convention were rejected by the majority, it is unlikely that the applicants would have succeeded even if the Convention had then been part of national law. It must be remembered that the ban did not prevent the broadcasting of the message from members of proscribed organisations; it only prohibited the broadcasting of their voices. The fact that these speeches could be voiced by BBC actors considerably reduced the impact of the ban on freedom of expression. In 1994, the Commission rejected the journalists' complaint that their Art 10 rights had been violated, holding the ban to be proportionate to the aim of combating terrorism (*Brind v UK* (1994)).

24.4 The reputation of others

Article 10 permits restrictions on freedom of expression 'for the protection of the reputation or the rights of others'. This category, therefore, legitimises, to a certain extent, the law of defamation, which, in this country, is designed to protect the reputations of individuals and companies from unjustified allegations which tend to 'lower them in the estimation of right thinking members of society'.

Civil libel

In English law, the defamatory statement in question may be one of fact or opinion. Once this is established, the burden then shifts to the defendant, who may seek to justify the statement he has made, in other words, prove the truth of the allegation. If the report was a fair and accurate coverage of court or parliamentary proceedings, it would be covered by absolute privilege. If the statement was of an opinion only, the defence of 'fair comment' may be available, provided the defendant is able to establish that the views could honestly have been held by a fair minded person on facts known at the time. It is not always easy to distinguish between fact and opinion: the test is one for ordinary readers. The question is whether they, on reading or hearing the words complained of, say to themselves, 'this is an opinion' or 'so that is the fact of the matter'? Such a conclusion may be inferred from a piece of writing which contains words like 'it seems to me' or 'in my judgment'. The difficulty of distinguishing between assertions of fact and opinion and the consequences, in terms of the available defences, makes the law of libel particularly hazardous to those wishing to air information that cannot readily be justified.

Another defence is available under statute (Defamation Act 1952), which allows the defendant to plead that the statement was 'fair comment' in the public interest. The defendant may also argue that the statement is covered by 'qualified privilege', which only applies where the publisher has a specific duty in communicating the words to another party who has a specific interest in receiving them, such as the communication of a public grievance to the proper authorities. There is a long established rule of the English common law that 'qualified privilege' does not extend to press reports of matters in the public interest (*Adam v Ward* (1917)), although it has been argued that the public's legitimate interest in the functions and powers vested in public representatives should bring the communication of this kind of information under the protection of qualified privilege (see Loveland, I, 'Political libels and qualified privilege – a British solution to a British problem' [1997] PL 428). It has been contended recently, in the Court of Appeal, that New Zealand and Australian precedents in this area should be persuasive authority for the adoption by the courts in this country of a defence of qualified privilege for all reports concerning the activities of an elected politician, when the words complained about related to his conduct in his public role (*Reynolds v Times Newspapers and Others* (1998)). The court, however, refused to follow the New Zealand and Australian precedents, observing that the conduct of those engaged in public life should not be the subject of factually untrue defamatory statements 'unless the circumstances of the publication were such as to make it proper, in the public interest, to afford the publisher immunity from liability in the absence of malice'.

The reasonableness of the defendant's conduct will thus be scrutinised before the defence of qualified privilege will be allowed and, therefore, no newspaper editor can be sure that his publication will be protected. It is debatable whether the continued 'chilling effect' caused by the uncertainty in the law of qualified privilege breaches Art 10. We have seen that the European

Court of Human Rights affords considerable protection to those who criticise politicians and other public figures, and it is increasingly the case that justifications, such as preserving the impartiality of the judiciary, that used to prevail (*Barfod v Denmark* (1991)) no longer legitimise the imposition of sanctions for criticisms of public figures, no matter how gratuitous or personal (*De Haes and Gijsels v Belgium* (1998)). However, the *Reynolds* case involves a conflict between freedom of expression and an important countervailing right – the right of the claimant to a fair trial in defamation proceedings. If qualified privilege were to apply to all political speech, this would impose an effective bar to defamation actions taken by all political claimants. This would present an impermissible restriction on those individuals' rights of access to court guaranteed by Art 6 of the ECHR. It is unlikely, therefore, that the incorporation of Art 10 in national law and the influence of European Court of Human Rights case law in this area will make any significant changes to the current limitations on qualified privilege.

In any event, not all criticism of figures in public life attracts the overriding protection of Art 10. In *Janowski v Poland* (1999), the court considered a challenge under Art 10 to a provision of national law which made it an offence to insult civil servants whilst acting in the execution of their duty. In considering whether the penalty offended the requirement of proportionality, the court held that the applicant's remarks to the civil servants in question, calling them 'oafs' and 'dumb', did not constitute criticism that should be protected by Art 10, since they did not form part of an open discussion of matters of public concern. The court also rejected the Commission's finding that civil servants acting in an official capacity should be subject to wider limits of acceptable criticism.

Whatever the outcome of the current litigation on qualified privilege, it remains the case that the low threshold for liability for libel and the limited nature of the defences available has given the UK a certain notoriety for its draconian libel laws. In most actions for damages in tort, the claimant has the burden not only of proving that he suffered the injury but that it was caused by the fault of the defendant; in other words, that his action was unreasonable. Libel claimants – if they can afford it, since there is no legal aid for defamation – can launch a court case against a defendant on the simple allegation that what the defendant said was damaging to them. There has been one important decision limiting the threat that libel actions pose to political speech: in *Derbyshire County Council v Times Newspapers Ltd* (1993), the House of Lords held that local authorities and government departments could not sue for defamation, although individual ministers can and do frequently. Despite the fact that the *Derbyshire* principle is being extended by judges to non-statutory entities – in *Goldsmith v Bhoyrul* (1998), a political party was prevented from bringing a libel action - there has not yet been an attempt to apply the principle to individual politicians. This contrasts with the position in the US, where politicians may only sue for libel if they can prove that the defendant has acted maliciously or recklessly (*New York Times v Sullivan* (1964)) (for further comment on this issue, see Loveland, I, 'Defamation of government: taking lessons from America?' (1994) LS 206).

Remedies for libel also pose a threat to freedom of expression. Interim remedies are not a problem. The courts, in this country, do not generally grant interim injunctions to prevent allegedly libellous articles from being published if the defendant intends to justify the content of the article at trial. Such remedies would impose too chilling an effect on the defendant's right of free speech to be justified by the interests of the administration of justice. The real issue arises out of the damages awards made at the end of successful actions. These are designed not only to compensate the claimant for the injury to his or her reputation but also to deter others from publishing similarly unjustified allegations. The jury decides the amount of the award, but, fortunately for libel defendants and free speech in general, the figure reached by the jury is now subject to assessment by the Court of Appeal. The power of the Court of Appeal to set aside jury awards on the grounds that they are excessive (or inadequate) was introduced by legislation passed in response to an appeal against a jury award of £250,000 in *Rantzen v Mirror Group Newspapers* (1993). The magnitude of jury awards in this country was held to be a violation of Art 10 by the Court of Human Rights in *Tolstoy Miloslavsky v UK* (1995).

The restrictive effect of libel laws in this country has been demonstrated recently by the epic '*McLibel*' trial, in which two indigent defendants spent three years defending a defamation action taken against them by a fast food multinational in respect of a series of allegations they had made – ranging from environmental degradation to cruelty to animals (*McDonald's Corporation v Steel and Morris* (1997)). The corporation had nothing to gain financially from the action since no damages would have been forthcoming, but they were determined that the two could not take advantage of the court case as an inquiry into allegedly iniquitous practices by multinationals. The claimants persuaded the judge that the issues involved in the justification defence would be too complex for a jury to comprehend and, therefore, the defendants were deprived of their chance of convincing a jury of the truth of their allegations. It was noted, during the course of the case, that juries in the Old Bailey were hearing cases of infinitely greater complexity in fraud trials. The claimant corporation ultimately won its action against the defendants, the judge finding, on balance, that the truth of the allegations had not been established. In general, the case demonstrated that the trap of litigation lies open for the unwary campaigner. Whilst it is commendable that libel laws force one to check one's facts before opening one's mouth, it does also mean that most small publishers will simply not consider it worth pursuing speculative claims of wrongdoing and will drop the controversial issue in order to publish some safe story instead. Aspects of the *McLibel* case are currently under consideration by the Strasbourg authorities – a challenge which brings the most important features of civil libel law under scrutiny.

Whatever the outcome, this litigation has, in David Pannick QC's words 'achieved what many lawyers thought impossible: to lower further the reputation of our law of defamation in the minds of all right thinking people' ((1999) *The Times*, 20 April).

Criminal libel

Although the offence of criminal libel is very rarely invoked in England and Wales, it still forms an important part of the national laws of other States which are parties to the ECHR. The Court of Human Rights has, on a number of occasions, considered the conformity of criminal libel with Art 10. In *Lingens v Austria* (1986), the applicant was prosecuted under a section of the Austrian Code which made it a criminal offence, punishable by imprisonment, to defame someone. The applicant had allegedly committed this offence by accusing the Austrian Chancellor of minimising Nazi atrocities in the Second World War. The only way the applicant could escape criminal liability was by justifying his statement. The Court of Human Rights ruled that the relevant Article in the Austrian Criminal Code, which was no doubt legitimate within Art 10(2), since it sought to protect the reputation of others, was not a necessary measure in a democratic society for achieving that purpose. The Court was of the view that is unacceptable to impose criminal proceedings for value judgments, the truth of which cannot be proved without a great deal of difficulty.

24.5   The rights of others

This exception to free speech rights in Art 10 has been relied upon to support measures criminalising certain forms of expression that cause offence to others. The common law offence of blasphemy is an example of this. In England and Wales, the common law prohibits forms of expression that cause offence to practising Christians. In *Chief Metropolitan Stipendiary Magistrate ex p Choudhury* (1991), Muslim critics of Salman Rushdie's novel, *The Satanic Verses*, applied for judicial review of the magistrates' decision not to prosecute the author. The court ruled that the law on blasphemy did not extend to the protection of other religions. It has been argued that this is anomalous in a multicultural society and that the law on blasphemy should either be extended to all religions or abolished altogether. The applicants in *Choudhury* complained that the English common law on blasphemy breached the rights of Muslims to freedom of religious thought under Art 9, but the Commission rejected their claim because the publication posed no threat to the applicants' religious freedom (*Choudhury v UK* (1990)). The Court of Human Rights has taken the approach that a wide margin of discretion operates in the area of blasphemy law and it therefore tends not to interfere with signatory Sates' laws protecting religious sensibilities (see *Otto Preminger Institut v Austria* (1995), where forfeiture of a film containing material offensive to Roman

Catholics was held to be justified on the basis of the high proportion of Roman Catholics living in the area of its distribution). In *Wingrove v UK* (1995), the applicant, the director of an 18 minute video depicting a 16th century nun engaged in erotic activity with the crucified figure of Christ, complained that the refusal by the British authorities to classify his work on the ground that the video infringed the criminal law of blasphemy was a breach of her Art 10 rights. However, the court held that the interference was 'prescribed by law' under Art 10(2) and that it pursued the legitimate aim of protecting the 'rights of others'. Some commentators have expressed disappointment that the court was prepared to find that the notoriously vague and ill defined common law offence of blasphemy has been considered to meet the standards set by the 'prescribed by law' requirement in the ECHR.

There is considerable uncertainty over whether the protection of the rights of others may also protect provisions outlawing race hate speech from attack under Art 10. In the UK, there are certain restrictions on this category of expression, although their compatability with Art 10 has not yet been tested. Under the Public Order Act 1986 (ss 17–19), speech which is likely to incite racial hatred is prohibited, not merely when it is likely to lead to violence, but where the defendant is aware that the words are abusive, threatening or insulting. The offence of inciting racial hatred may also be committed by the transmission of television or radio programmes (s 164 of the Broadcasting Act 1990).The rationale for this legislative curtailment of free speech is that ethnic minority groups should be protected from racial insults. It is not necessary to prove, in establishing the offence under any of these acts, the intent to stir up racial hatred, merely the 'likelihood' of such a thing happening. Although, in theory, the law represents a serious threat to freedom of speech, in practice, very few prosecutions for this offence are followed through.

The laws on race hate speech may be contrasted, on the one hand, with those in the US, which permits no restrictions of freedom of expression unless there is some compelling necessity, not just official or majority disapproval, for imposing those restrictions; and Germany and France, on the other, where laws have been passed criminalising Holocaust denial. The United Nations Human Rights Committee has considered and rejected a complaint that such a law interfered with the right to freedom of expression protected by Art 19 of the International Covenant on Civil and Political Rights (*Faurisson v France* (1997)). Whilst there are ample policy reasons for prohibiting race hate speech, such a prohibition is much more difficult to justify in principle. Once a government legislates to prevent expression on the basis of its content, however offensive, there is no reason in logic or law why all types of expression should not be censored.

This is a notoriously difficult area of free speech jurisprudence and, until recently, there has been very little case law from the European Court of Human Rights to provide guidance for the national courts. Two recent developments, however, illustrate the approach of the Court to this issue. In

Lehideux and Isorni v France (1998), the applicants were prosecuted for writing and publishing an article in a national newspaper in support of the memory of Marshal Petain, convicted and executed for collaboration in 1945. They were convicted of making a public defence of the crimes of collaboration. The applicants claimed that they had been denied their rights of freedom of expression under Art 10. In response to this, the French Government argued that the publication in issue infringed the very spirit of the Convention and the essential values of democracy enshrined in it and, therefore, that the applicants were debarred from relying on the ECHR. They relied, further, on Art 17 of the ECHR which provides that the ECHR could not called in aid to support any activity 'aimed at the destruction of any of the rights and freedoms' that it sets forth. The Court rejected the State's argument, since it found nothing in the applicants' advertisement that was specifically directed against the Convention's underlying values; they were praising a man, not a policy. The convictions were, therefore, held to be a disproportionate interference with Art 10.

In *Jersild v Denmark* (1995), the Court distinguished between the making of racist statements and reports and debates about them. In this case, a journalist had made a documentary for broadcast which included racist remarks by youths. He was convicted by the Danish authorities for assisting in the dissemination of race hate. The Court held that the conviction infringed Art 10 because it was disproportionate to the aim of protecting the rights and freedoms of others. It was significant that the Court stressed the news value of the information in the contested programme; bare racist statements do not, by themselves, attract the protection of Art 10 (*X v FRG* (1982)) in which a complaint that suppression of Nazi pamphlets infringed the freedom of speech provision was declared manifestly ill founded by the Commission).

Finally, the 'rights of others' have been given a generous interpretation by the Court of Human Rights in the area of commercial speech. While the highest degree of protection under Art 10 is generally accorded to political speech, the court has, on several occasions, considered the right to freedom of commercial expression and has held that it comes within Art 10 (*Marktintern v Germany* (1990)). Here, the injunctions issued under unfair competition regulations in Germany prevented a small traders' magazine from publishing articles making critical comments about a competing company. These were held by the court to pursue the legitimate aim of protecting the 'rights of others' under Art 10(2). It can be seen from this ruling that the court takes a very different approach to the 'rights of others' when the expression in issue is commercial speech rather than political discussion; respondent States' reliance on the 'rights of others' by way of justifying their defamation laws is very rarely successful in the Court of Human Rights (*Lingens v Austria* (1986)). This difference in approach may be justified by the central democratic role of political speech; nevertheless, in respect to the *Marktintern* decision, it is debatable whether the permissible restriction on the freedom under Art 10 for measures aimed at protecting the 'rights and reputation of others' was really designed to protect business interests.

The European Court of Human Rights does not always defer to the complexities of unfair competition, as was demonstrated in the case of *Hertel v Switzerland* (1998). The applicant, who had written and published articles suggesting that the use of microwave ovens was hazardous to human health, submitted that a ban subsequently imposed upon him by the Swiss courts under the unfair competition rules, at the behest of an association of oven manufacturers, infringed Art 10. The provisions of the Unfair Competition Act covered the activities, not only of economic agents, but of non-market players such as the applicant, whose activities affected relations between competitors. While acknowledging that there was a considerable margin of appreciation involved in determining the compatibility of competition rules with the ECHR, given the fluctuating nature of the market, the Court of Human Rights took special note of the importance of the contribution by the applicant to the continuing public debate on the safety of microwave ovens. In the light of this, his articles attracted a higher level of protection than the purely commercial expression at issue in *Marktintern*. The injunction was, therefore, considered a disproportionate interference with his rights under Art 10.

24.6 Protection of health or morals

This is another area in which the Court of Human Rights allows signatory States a wide margin of discretion. This exception has usually been considered in relation to signatory States' laws on obscenity. The main provisions in this area in the UK are to be found in the Obscene Publications Act 1959, which makes it a criminal offence to publish, sell or keep materials which may 'deprave or corrupt'. This test extends beyond sexual activity to other conduct generally disapproved of in society, such as drug taking. The applicability of the test depends upon the likely audience for the publication; habitual customers of pornography are less likely to be depraved and corrupted than young children. The Act provides a defence of 'artistic merit' or 'public good', evidence of which can be balanced against the depraving effect of the material. This test has been criticised as putting the jury in the impossible position of weighing up these incompatible and disparate concepts (Robertson, G, *Obscenity*, 1979, London: Weidenfeld & Nicolson, p 164).

A number of statutes criminalise the use of 'indecent' language or material, ranging from the prohibition on indecent photographs of children under the Children Act 1978, to the power of customs officials to seize indecent literature in luggage under the Customs and Excise Management Act. It is also possible for prosecutions to be brought for indecency under the common law and conspiracy to corrupt morals also provides a wide ground for punishing immoral conduct. There is no defence of public good or artistic merit to these common law offences, so the artist who displayed a human head wearing freeze dried embryos as earrings was convicted (*R v Gibson* (1990)). These offences, like many features of the common law, have ancient and rather enlightening origins:

> The crime of corrupting public morals had been created by the King's judges in 1663 to punish the drunken poet Sir Charles Sedley for urinating from a Covent Garden balcony over a crowd below. The law reports, the last to be written in Norman French, are not unanimous on the nature of Sir Charles's momentous act. One contemporary translation has him 'inflamed by strong liquors, throwing down bottles, piss'd in', whilst another avers that 'pulling down his breeches, he excrementaliz'd into the street' [Robertson, G, *The Justice Game*, 1998, London: Chatto & Windus, p 14].

Sedley did not claim any artistic merit in his performance and was heavily fined for his conduct.

Approach of the European Court of Human Rights

Although national obscenity laws have been challenged under Art 10, the Court of Human Rights has been prepared to accept the legitimacy of signatory States' measures in this area since it accords a wide margin of appreciation to signatory States to determine the best measures for protecting morality (*Handyside v UK* (1979)). This cautious approach by the court has been explained in the case of *Muller and Others v Switzerland* (1991). The applicants claimed that the forfeiture of several sexually explicit paintings and the fines that had been imposed on them for exhibiting obscene material violated their rights under Art 10. The Court upheld the State's argument that the measures were justified in the interests of protecting morals, observing that:

> By reason of their direct and continuous contact with the vital forces of these countries, State authorities are in principle in a better position than the international judge to give an opinion on the exact content of these requirements as well as the 'necessity' of a restriction or 'penalty' intended to meet them.

This decision appears to impose a heavy burden on artists to observe the 'duties' and 'responsibilities' (which condition the enjoyment of freedom of expression) by avoiding gratuitous offence to the public. Since this is a highly subjective matter, it is debatable whether the national authorities' view is always going to be justifiable; indeed, in the *Otto Preminger* blasphemy case, which also addressed the issue of gratuitous offence, the Commission and the Court of Human Rights reached directly opposing views (see above, 24.5).

In any event, signatory States must ensure that any restrictions on Art 10 rights are clear and accessible. In the *Open Door Counselling* case (see 20.7), concerning a complaint by the applicants that their prosecution under the Irish Constitutional provision on the sanctity of life, for providing 'non-directional abortion counselling', breached their Art 10 rights, the Court of

Human Rights did not consider this to be a justifiable interference under Art 10(2). Whilst the interference was, on the *Handyside* principle, in pursuit of a legitimate aim – the protection of morals – it failed the certainty test. Given that travel abroad was not illegal in Ireland, the counsellors could not have foreseen that they were committing a constitutional tort and, therefore, the interference with their freedom of expression did not properly fulfil the requirements of Art 10(2) that it should be 'prescribed by law'.

Approach of the European Court of Justice

The European Court of Human Rights decided this case after the European Court of Justice had rejected a similar claim in Case C-159/90 *SPUC v Grogan* (1991). This decision provides an illustration of the unreliability of Community law as a vehicle for the protection of fundamental human rights (rather than economic rights) (see above, 19.4). Here, the applicants were student groups against whom an injunction had been issued to stop them disseminating information about abortion clinics in England. They brought a claim in respect of their Community rights to provide services which, they claimed, had been breached by the Irish authorities. In his opinion preceding the court's decision, the Advocate General concluded that the prohibition on the provision of information in Ireland about abortion facilities in other Member States could be tested for compliance with the ECHR right to freedom of information and expression. However, the Court of Justice held that the provision of information and the abortion clinics themselves were not sufficiently connected to come within the freedom of services provisions of the EC Treaty and, therefore, they failed on the merits. By deciding against the applicants on the facts, the Court avoided what could have been a very controversial judgment upholding a fundamental Treaty provision over an Irish constitutional provision of fundamental importance. Had British abortion clinics sought to advertise in Ireland in contravention of Irish law, it would have been less easy for the Court of Justice to avoid this difficult decision on the basis of 'insufficient link'.

In considering the approach of the Court of Justice to Art 10 issues, it has to be remembered that EC law is aimed primarily at protecting commercial interests, not the incidental rights that arise from commercial freedoms. As long as the principle of freedom of expression is part of one of the 'four freedoms' protected by the EC Treaty (see above, 7.2.1), it is likely to win the day, as illustrated by the ruling on the ability of Member States to derogate from the free movement provisions in Case C-121/85 *Conegate Ltd v Customs and Excise Comrs* (1987). In 1986, English customs officials had the power to seize items which they deemed to be 'indecent or obscene' under the Obscene Publications Act. This prejudiced the right of producers of pornographic material abroad, where there were fewer restrictions, to sell their goods across boundaries. When the actions of the customs officials were challenged under Art 30 (now 28) of the EC Treaty, the Court of Justice found the UK to be in breach of the EC Treaty, and required that customs officials only had the power to seize 'obscene' items.

24.7 Media regulation

This is an interference with freedom of expression permitted by the first part of Art 10(1) . States may licence broadcasting, television or cinema enterprises without falling foul of the main right protected by the Article. Such measures have been scrutinised by the European Court of Human Rights in the same way as it approaches the permitted interferences in Art 10(2). In *Informationsverein Lentia v Austria* (1994), a network of local broadcasters and advertisers who had been refused a licence challenged the State's monopoly over broadcasting licences. Austria argued that this was a justifiable limitation under Art 10, since it enabled it to control the quality and balance of programming. But the Court ruled that total State monopoly over broadcasting could not be justified, given the co-existence in many signatory States of private and public broadcasters.

The licensing of media outlets has also come up for consideration by the European Court of Justice in relation to Art 10 of the ECHR; indeed, one of the most important statements by the Court of Justice on the role of Convention rights in the interpretation of Community law was made in the context of a freedom of expression case, Case C-260/89 *ERT v DEP*, which concerned the establishment by the Greek Government of a monopoly broadcaster. The Court of Justice held that this was contrary to Art 59 (now 49: freedom to provide services) and the Greek Government's reliance on the derogation provisions in the EC Treaty had to be interpreted in the light of the freedom of expression protected by Art 10 of the ECHR. In this case, the right under Art 10 was said to outweigh the Greek Government's interests in regulating broadcasting.

At a national level in the UK, regulation of film and the broadcast media is much stricter than that governing the printed press, which is self-regulating. The Press Complaints Commission adjudicates on the compliance by newspapers with their own Code of Practice laying down standards of taste and decency. It has no powers of enforcement or sanction and cannot require a newspaper to publish a reply by an individual aggrieved by an article it has published. Although, in principle, an individual may apply for judicial review of the Commission's decision not to take action in respect of a particular publication, the courts have signalled their reluctance to interfere in the exercise of the Commission's discretion in this area (*R v Press Complaints Commission ex p Stewart-Brady* (1997)).

The broadcast media is governed by the standards laid down in the BBC Charter and ss 6 and 152 of the Broadcasting Act 1990 (which applies to the independent sector). The Broadcasting Complaints Council, set up under the

Broadcasting Act, hears complaints on programmes and publishes its adjudications, and the Broadcasting Standards Council considers complaints relating to taste and decency, level of violence or sexual activity in the programmes broadcast. The Independent Television Commission and the Broadcasting Complaints Commission consider complaints by people and parties who allege unfair treatment or invasions of privacy by radio or television broadcasters.

The system of licensing exercised by the Government over the BBC and the Independent Television Commission over broadcasters other than the BBC has been set up to ensure that no broadcast will be permitted that will 'offend against good taste and decency' (s 6(1)(a) of the Broadcasting Act 1990). Codes on decency have been drawn up which are monitored by the Broadcasting Complaints Commission and the ITC. Difficult problems arise in relation to the regulation of non-terrestrial broadcasting, such as satellite television, particularly from other European Union Member States, since Community law requires that television services should be freely received across borders. Similar concerns have been expressed in relation to pornography published on the Internet, because, although it is covered by the Obscene Publications Act, it is, in practice, impossible to impose sanctions on remote service providers

Films and videos are regulated by the powers of the British Board of Film Classification (BBFC), which grants certificates to films and videos. The BBFC is a non-statutory organisation and, even if it does decide to issue a certificate, a local authority has the power under the Cinemas Act 1985 to refuse to issue a licence. This happened in the case of the controversial film *Crash* by David Cronenberg, which was refused a licence in 1997 by Westminster City Council despite having been certified by the BBFC.

24.8   Access to information

The right of individuals to receive information is a corollary to their right to impart it. However, the dissemination of information, statistics and ideas requires positive steps to be taken by States, a requirement which international law does not readily impose.

24.8.1 Access to information under the ECHR

The right to freedom of expression under Art 10 includes the freedom to 'receive ... information without interference by public authority'. Whether this right extends to an obligation on governments to provide information has not been settled in Strasbourg. In *Guerra v Italy* (1998), the European Court of Human Rights indicated that Art 10(2) may prevent a government from restricting the dissemination of otherwise open information, but does not extend so far as to require the State to make positive steps to collate and disseminate information.

Apart from the rather limited provisions of Art 10, there is, as yet, no general right to information in English law. There is, instead, a haphazard collection of statutory provisions dealing with limited categories of information and providing a right of access or a duty to publicise. The Citizen's Charter grants individuals a limited right of access to records and imposes an obligation on public service providers to publish full and accurate information on how they are run. The 1997 Code of Practice on Access to Government Information places a non-binding obligation on government departments to release certain types of information relating to their policies. There is also a limited right to environmental information in certain regulations implementing European Directives on environmental matters.

In 1999, the Labour Government published a draft Freedom of Information Bill, giving individuals a legally enforceable right to information held by most public authorities in England and Wales. An independent Information Commissioner, answerable to the courts, will be appointed to monitor compliance with the Act and handle appeals against refusals to disclose information. The Act will cover some private organisations carrying out duties on behalf of the Government and privatised utilities. However, the proposed Act limits access to certain types of information, such as sensitive security or intelligence matters, or information which would undermine crime prevention or prosecution. In addition, information can be withheld if disclosure would cause substantial harm to a range of protected interests, such as national security, safety of individuals and the environment, trade secrets and law enforcement. This broad range of exceptions raises the question of whether the public's access to information will, in fact, be enhanced in any real fashion if the Bill becomes law. After all, most of the major cases over information have been fought and lost on the battlegrounds of national security and trade secrets already. At least, however, there will be a presumption in favour of information, rather than the present patchwork of limited legislation and non-binding codes.

24.8.2 Access to information in the European Community

Because of the increasing impact of Community law on domestic legislation, freedom of information about the deliberations of Community institutions that lead to the formulation of Community laws is, or should be, a central condition of Brussels legitimacy. The Council has issued a declaration on access to information which states that 'The Conference considers that the openness of the decision making process strengthens the democratic nature of the institutions and the public's confidence in the administration' and, in Case C-58/94 *Netherlands v Council* (1996). Advocate General Teaser said in his Opinion that 'the right of access to information is increasingly clearly a fundamental civil right'. There has been much criticism of the 'closed door' nature of Council deliberations and the lack of transparency in the comitology system (see above, 8.2.6) has also come under attack. It has been observed by critics that even the European Parliament does not know how many Management Committees there are, and the recent report by the Committee of Experts on the mismanagement of Commission business revealed practices that have diverted some of the Commission's £65 million a year budget into the pockets of corrupt officials (see above, 7.5.1). The new Commission will, no doubt, be under heavier obligations of transparency and accountability. As far as the Community as a whole is concerned, the EC Treaty, after the Amsterdam revisions, now contains a right of access to European Parliament, Council and Commission documents (Art 255). Freedom of information at a Community level is, however, not going to be solved by the promulgation of more rules; it is primarily a political, rather than a legal matter.

24.9 Assessment

The area of law most in need of amendment – and one least likely to be affected by the incorporation of the ECHR protection of free speech into national law – is defamation. As Geoffrey Robertson observes:

> Today, London is the libel capital of the world. Foreign claimants prefer to sue in this country, because the law favours them more than anywhere else. Tax-free damages awarded in cases which actually come to court are just the tip of a legal iceberg which deep freezes large chunks of interesting news and comment, especially about wealthy people and companies which have a reputation for issuing writs [Robertson, G, *Freedom, the Individual and the Law*, 7th edn, 1993, London: Penguin, p 317].

A number of committees have recommended, over the years, that libel laws in this country be reformed by incorporating the defence of innocent publication and providing a level of reporting and broadcasting privilege to the media (see, for example, the Faulkes Report, Cmnd 5909, 1975). However, these recommendations have never been taken up by the legislature. There is another solution to this problem – a judicial one. The ECHR, although primarily enforceable only against public authorities, may have a horizontal effect that would influence the common law on defamation (see above, 19.9). Under s 3 of the Human Rights Act 1998, judges are required to read primary legislation 'in a way which is compatible with the Convention rights'. Section 6 makes it 'unlawful' for a public authority to act in a way which is incompatible with Convention rights, and 'public authority' includes a court. It is suggested that the combination of these two provisions may oblige a court to interpret the common law liability for defamation more restrictively to comply with Art 10. We have seen above, 24.4, that the *Derbyshire* case provides a precedent for this approach: public bodies, such as local authorities, should not be able to bring defamation proceedings, since such a power would impose too great a restriction on press debates on matters of legitimate public interest. The same approach should be possible even in proceedings where the parties themselves are private and the only 'public authority' involved is the court itself. This would open the way to the judicial application of Court of Human Rights case law under s 2(1)(a) of the Human Rights Act to the law of defamation, in particular, the pronouncement by the European Court of Human Rights in *Thorgierson v Iceland* (1992) that publishers are protected by Art 10 so long as their claims are based on public opinion, do not disparage specific named individuals and are primarily intended to promote a positive aim, such as institutional reform.

Another area of the law which still presents a threat to freedom of expression is the common law offence of contempt of court. As described above (see above, 24.3.2), this has been interpreted to cover contempts where no litigation is pending or even imminent. The time is ripe for a definitive ruling that liability in these cases should only arise when proceedings are about to take place, in circumstances where protection is truly necessary.

FREEDOM OF EXPRESSION

Freedom of expression is a fundamental right in a democracy; it keeps clear the channels of dissent and allows individuals freedom of choice to decide for themselves what is offensive and inoffensive. Freedom of speech was accorded special status in English law even before incorporation of the ECHR, with some judges referring to it as a 'constitutional right'.

Article 10 of the ECHR protects the right to freedom of expression, which includes the right to receive and impart information, subject to a number of restrictions.

At a Community level, any interference with the free movement of goods will be a breach of the EC Treaty; the protection afforded to this freedom sometimes has the incidental effect of protecting certain types of expression. In addition, freedom of expression, like all the other rights in the ECHR, is included in the Court of Justice's general principles of law which are to be applied in assessing the legality of Member States' actions.

National security and the impartiality of the judiciary

The common law of confidence has been combined with the criminal laws on official secrets to prevent the disclosure of certain types of information relating to national security. It is also possible to restrain publication of information in the course of litigation in order to preserve the impartiality of the judiciary. The law of contempt of court covers any publication that is likely to prejudice proceedings, subject to the defence of public interest. The Contempt of Court Act only covers active proceedings, but the common law offence of contempt of court may be made out where the contempt is intentional and proceedings are not actually active or even pending, provided they are imminent. The Contempt of Court Act prevents contempt proceedings being taken against anyone who refuses to disclose the source of their information, subject to certain exceptions, such as the prevention of crime and national security.

The broadcasting of information relating to national security is subject to voluntary compliance by the media with 'D' notices issued by the Defence and Broadcasting Committee. In addition, The Home Secretary has the power under the Broadcasting Act to prohibit the broadcasting of 'any matter'. The use of this power to prevent the direct broadcast of the voices of members of prohibited organisations in Northern Ireland was upheld in a judicial review challenge in 1991 (*R v Home Secretary ex p Brind* (1991)); such a decision might not survive attack today under the incorporated Art 10 of the ECHR.

The reputation of others

Defamation laws which restrict freedom of expression are permitted by Art 10. However, England has some of the most oppressive libel laws in the world. Defendants have the burden of proving that they are not at fault, instead of the claimant proving fault or unreasonableness (as with all other tort actions). Cases are heard by juries who, until recently, have had unlimited power to award astronomical damages. Although local authorities and government departments may not sue in defamation, a range of other public officers, such as the police and government ministers, may stifle criticism through the libel courts. On the other side of the equation, a number of defences are available to defendants and the Court of Appeal now has the power to limit the jury award to reasonable levels.

Although Art 10 permits defamation laws in order to protect the rights and reputations of others, these measures must not be disproportionate; in other words, Art 10(2) does not extend to criminal sanctions for the expression of defamatory opinions.

The rights of others

Certain statutes prohibit the use of speech inciting race hatred and likely to lead to violence, although very few prosecutions are brought under these provisions. European Court of Human Rights case law indicates that such laws will survive challenge under Art 10. The law on blasphemy criminalises any forms of expression which cause offence to practising Christians; this has also been justified successfully under Art 10.

Protection of health or morals

Censorship of printed material is governed by the Obscene Publications Act 1959, for which there is a defence of artistic merit and public good. A number of common law offences of indecency and conspiracy to commit indecency also restrict certain types of expression and, here, no such defences are available. Films, broadcasting and videos are subject to stricter censorship, in the form of licensing which allows for prior restraint. The Court of Human Rights has accorded Member States a wide margin of discretion in the area of morality, since there is relatively little consensus on these issues amongst Member States.

There are a number of statutory agencies which regulate the content and balance of the programmes put out by the broadcast media. The press is governed by a less powerful self-regulating body, the Press Complaints Commission.

Access to information

This is a negative right under Art 10; in other words, governments are required not to put obstacles in the way of access to information already available. However, in the UK, there are proposals to bring in a Freedom of Information Act, which will create a presumption in favour of information from most public authorities, subject to a number of limited exceptions.

CHAPTER 25

FREEDOM OF ASSEMBLY AND ASSOCIATION

25.1 Introduction

Like freedom of speech, the right of individuals to gather together to express their views is an important democratic safeguard, since criticism of those in power (whether justified or not) can be made much more forcibly by 20 people than by one lone voice. As with freedom of speech, the protection extends to non-political debate and protests against the actions of private parties, such as an anti-vivisection vigil held outside a private laboratory. As a vehicle for political discussion, public assemblies provide generally the only opportunity to people who are not members of the media to make a point, either about law reform or about government policy generally, when they feel that other avenues (such as the electoral process) have been closed off to them. The law on public order should, arguably, recognise that peaceful demonstrations sometimes prove ineffective and it should, thus, be open to citizens to make their point forcibly, even disruptively. If lying in front of a bulldozer is the only way to prevent a motorway being built through a green belt area, it may (in some circumstances) be inappropriate to prosecute the protester. However, because this kind of 'direct action' threatens the rights and freedoms of others, the law tends to accord more protection to public order than to public protest.

Freedom of association entails the right to belong to organised groups, political or otherwise. Writing about the importance of associations in a civil society in the early 19th century, the French political theorist Alexis de Tocqueville observed that:

> ... no countries need association more – to prevent either despotism of parties or the arbitrary role of the prince – than those with a democratic social State ... In countries where such associations do not exist, if private people did not artificially and temporarily create something like them, I see no other dike to hold back tyranny of whatever sort, and a great nation might with impunity be oppressed by some tiny fraction or by a single man [*Democracy in America*, 1994, New York: Fontana, p 192].

The two rights of assembly and association are said to be mutually dependent, since effective protest in groups (assembly) sometimes depends upon those groups having legal status and some sort of a structure (association). The two are closely related to freedom of speech, at least in their instrumental value to a democracy, of keeping open the channels of dissent (see Barendt, E, *Freedom of Speech*, 1985, Oxford: Clarendon, pp 280–98). The right to freedom of association also extends to the right to form and join trades unions. However, a discussion on trades union rights (which have been much legislated and litigated) is outside the scope of this book and the following sections will focus on two main issues: the right to assemble and the right to join organised groups, including political parties and pressure groups.

As with all the rights and freedoms discussed in Part D of this book, assembly was only a residual freedom (until the Human Rights Act 1998 came into force). Dicey's perception of this level of protection was that it was more than adequate:

> ... the right of assembling is nothing more than a result of the view taken by the courts as to individual liberty of person and individual liberty of speech [*An Introduction to the Study of the Law of the Constitution*, 10th edn, 1959, London: Macmillan, p 271].

As the following sections will illustrate, however, the inroads made by the common law and legislation have considerably reduced the residual protection of the right to assemble. This is because we cannot dissociate the notion of public protest from the concept of public order. Conor Gearty describes this as the 'schizophrenia that afflicts the treatment of the subject by both politicians and members of the public. The law manifests the same confusion, being rooted simultaneously in two opposites' (Gearty, C, 'Freedom of assembly and public order', in McCrudden, C and Chambers, G (eds), *Individual Rights and the Law in Britain*, 1993, Oxford: Clarendon, p 39). This schizophrenia is, however, the inevitable consequence of the particular nature of the right to protest, involving as it does the occasional interference with the rights of movement and even the privacy and speech of others. Feldman has pointed out that whereas most rights, such as the freedom from arbitrary arrest or interference with privacy, require mere restraint on the part of others, the right to assemble and protest:

> ... require (if they are to be effectively used) some form of communication with others, and so presuppose that the freedom of other people from annoyance is to be restricted at least so far as necessary to allow the protester to impart the nature of the protest and invite people to join in protest or discussion. It therefore goes beyond pure liberalism, which would permit people and groups to buy or hire a private hall to ventilate their grievances or policies ... but would not allow them to force their opinions on non-consenting adults [Feldman, D, *Civil Liberties and Human Rights in England and Wales*, 1993, Oxford: Clarendon, p 784].

Another threat to the freedom of assembly is posed by Community law, since the expression of public opposition to certain areas of trade interferes with the freedom of movement of goods, fundamental to the EC Treaty. The cases discussed below, in 25.7, ask whether we should accept that there is an EC right to free transport of property which should always override the right to demonstrate.

The following sections will look at the various common law, legislative and Community law inroads into the right of assembly and association and assess them for their conformity with Art 11 of the ECHR, which provides as follows:

1   Everyone has the right to freedom of peaceful assembly and to freedom of association with others, including the right to form and to join trade unions for the protection of his interests.

2   No restrictions shall be placed on the exercise of these rights other than such as are prescribed by law and are necessary in a democratic society in the interests of national security or public safety, for the prevention of disorder or crime, for the protection of health or morals or for the protection of the rights and freedoms of others. This Article shall not prevent the imposition of lawful restrictions on the exercise of these rights by members of the armed forces, or the police, or of the administration of the State.

25.2   Breach of the peace

'Breach of the peace' is an ill defined and ancient concept which triggers the exercise of police powers in many areas, particularly in the context of public order (see the discussion of *McLeod v UK* (1999), above, 23.2.2). The police can take preventative measures against an *apprehended* breach of the peace. It does not take much imagination, therefore, to conjure up a range of controversial issues which, when aired in public, will create a risk that the peace will be breached in some way or another. The present law is that the requirement of reasonable apprehension of breach of the peace will be satisfied 'whenever harm is actually done or is likely to be done to a person ... or where a person is in fear of being so harmed ...' (*R v Howell* (1982)).

Difficult questions of responsibility arise where such meetings are likely to breach the peace because of the intervention of rowdy opposition. The common law position on this used to be quite liberal: the authorities could not prevent a meeting on these grounds, otherwise, private groups would have powers of censorship over the lawful expression of opinion of others (*Beatty v Gilbanks* (1882)). The principle in *Beatty v Gilbanks* was undermined in a number of later cases where the likelihood of a violent response provided grounds for preventative action on breach of peace grounds. In 1963, a speaker in Trafalgar Square expressed extreme right wing views to an assembled crowd, including a number of Communists and Jewish people. When violence broke out in response to his more provocative statements, the defendant was arrested and prosecuted for public order offences, even though he himself had not engaged in the acts of violence himself. The court considered that, in such situations, a speaker 'must take his audience as he finds them' (*Jordan v Burgoyne* (1963)). This case can be distinguished from *Beatty v Gillbanks*, in that the plaintiffs in the first case were conducting a peaceful procession to disseminate the message of the Salvation Army; the disorder was caused by their opponents, the 'Skeleton Army'. In *Jordan*, on the other hand, the plaintiff himself had insulted the audience, thereby provoking a response. The principle in *Beatty* has been revived by the House of Lords in *Brutus v Cozens* (see below, 25.7.4); the current state of the law is that, provided the behaviour of the speaker or protester himself is not 'insulting', the adverse reaction of the audience should not provide grounds for a public order action against him. In *Nicol and Selvanayagam v DPP* (1996), the Court of Appeal said that breach of the peace would not be found where the violence provoked was wholly unreasonable; so, if all the defendant is doing is exercising his or her basic rights, 'whether of assembly, demonstration or free speech', any violent response would be considered unreasonable and the breach of the peace would not be laid at the speaker's door.

This ruling is consistent with Strasbourg jurisprudence on the right to assemble under Art 11, which may be limited 'in the interests of disorder or crime'. The problem of violent opposition to an otherwise peaceful protest was addressed by the Court in *Platform Ärzte für das Leben v Austria* (1991). An association of doctors campaigning against abortion in order to secure changes in Austrian legislation complained that the failure by the police to control violent counter-demonstrations violated their free assembly rights under Art 11. On the facts, the Court decided that the Austrian authorities had taken sufficient measures to protect the exercise of this right; but the Court did stipulate that:

> Genuine, effective freedom of peaceful assembly cannot ... be reduced to a mere duty on the part of the State not to interfere: a purely negative conception would not be compatible with the object and purpose of Art 11 ... Article 11 sometimes requires positive measures to be taken, even in the sphere of relations between individuals, if need be.

Such positive measures are limited in English law. Fragmentary protection is given to lawful meetings under statute law: s 1 of the Public Meeting Act 1908 makes it is a criminal offence to act in a disorderly fashion at an otherwise lawful public meeting with the intention of breaking up that meeting and, if a meeting is organised on private premises, it is lawful to employ stewards to preserve order (s 2(6) of the Public Order Act 1936). There is, in addition, the offence of 'aggravated trespass' which criminalises the obstruction of lawful activities that are taking place on 'land in the open air' (s 68 of the Criminal Justice and Public Order Act 1994). Since this provision was aimed specifically at hunt saboteurs, it is rarely relied upon to shift the burden of responsibility for breach of the peace from the holder of a lawful assembly to the rowdy opposition.

25.3   Binding over orders

Magistrates have the power to bind over any person appearing before them under the Magistrates' Courts Act 1980, under common law and under the Justices of the Peace Act 1361. This means that magistrates may order someone to undertake to 'keep the peace or be of good behaviour' on pain of forfeiting a certain sum of money if it is found that they have been acting in an anti-social fashion. If the person thus bound over refuses to enter into this undertaking, or 'recognisance', the court may impose a sentence of imprisonment for up to six months. A binding over order can be imposed even if the breach of peace has not yet occurred – in other words, criminal sanctions may be applied to non-criminal behaviour. For this reason, these common law and statutory powers have been challenged under the ECHR. In *Steel v UK* (1999), various environmental protestors who had been imprisoned for their refusal to be bound over claimed violation of their rights to liberty, fair trial, freedom of expression and freedom to protest under the ECHR (Arts 5, 6, 10 and 11). In particular, they argued that the custodial sentence for refusing to be bound over fell short of the requirements of Art 5. The Court rejected the Art 5 claim, observing that breach of the peace was an offence in English law and that the applicants could have foreseen that their refusal to keep the peace would be followed by a custodial sentence. As far as the claim under Art 10 was concerned, the Court agreed with the State's arguments that the arrests and detention were permissible infringements of some of the applicants' freedom of expression in preventing disorder and in protecting the rights of others under Art 10(2), and the detention following the applicants' refusal to be bound over was an infringement of this freedom justified by the need to maintain the authority of the judiciary. Other applicants whose mode of protest had been, in the Court's view, less disruptive, succeeded in their Art 10 argument; handing out leaflets outside a nuclear power plant was a form of expression that was unjustifiably suppressed by the short prison sentence that followed. Since it had reached this decision under Art 10(2), it did not consider the equivalent exception in Art 11(2). This decision indicates that challenges under the ECHR to the binding over jurisdiction of magistrates are unlikely to succeed before national courts.

25.4   Obstruction of the highway

This offence has been codified in s 137 of the Highways Act 1980 and is arrestable without warrant, which means that, if the police suspect that this offence is being or is about to be committed, they can order the meeting to move off and, if those in charge of the assembly fail to comply with police instructions, they can be prosecuted for obstructing a constable in the execution of his duty under the Police and Criminal Evidence Act 1984 (*Arrowsmith v Jenkins* (1963)). The activity must be conducted in such a manner that there is no 'lawful excuse' for it; the test for this is whether the activity is reasonable or not. The handing out of leaflets by animal rights protesters in a shopping centre outside a furrier's store was not considered unreasonable and convictions for s 137 offences were overturned: *Hirst and Agu v Chief Constable of West Yorkshire* (1985). Protest about matters of public concern can, therefore, sometimes constitute a 'lawful excuse', although this very much depends upon the magistrate's perception of what constitutes a matter of public concern.

25.5 Nuisance actions

People using the highway for assemblies or processions run the risk of being prosecuted for the offence of public nuisance or being sued in private nuisance. The offence of public nuisance is committed when the 'public' suffer a disturbance or interference with the rights they enjoy in common with others as a result of the unlawful activities of others. Private nuisance, unlike public nuisance, is a civil wrong and is actionable only when a private individual has suffered particular damage beyond the general inconvenience suffered by the public. However, the activities giving rise to the nuisance need not be unlawful; they simply have to be unreasonable. Private nuisance actions are based on property rights and the concept that you should be allowed peaceful enjoyment of your property free from interference by others. The activities of a small group of protesters handing out leaflets outside an estate agent on Islington High Street were stopped by the successful application for an injunction by the estate agent owners in a nuisance action (*Hubbard v Pitt* (1976)), because the applicants satisfied the court that 'unreasonableness' was established by showing that passage outside their office was obstructed. This decision has been much criticised and the dissenting opinion of Lord Denning MR was cited with approval in a recent case on trespassory assemblies, *DPP v Jones* (1999) (see below, 25.7.3). Lord Denning observed that the plaintiffs had not made out a *prima facie* case of private nuisance against the protestors; their real grievance was not the alleged obstruction (which only went on for three hours on Saturday mornings), but the words on the placards and the leaflets which they claimed were defamatory of them.

25.6 Trespass and private property

Despite its name, the 'public highway' is not the property of the public at all; most roads belong to local authorities and the use of them is limited to passing and re-passing and activities incidental thereto. Other popular sites open to the public have different owners; London parks, for instance, belong to the Crown and activities that take place within them are subject to bylaws. The use of the streets leading to Parliament is subject to the powers of the Metropolitan Police Commissioner, under the Metropolitan Police Act 1839, to make directions regarding the passage of traffic during parliamentary sessions.

Since there is now a specific statutory power under the Public Order Act 1986 available to the police to prohibit 'trespassory assemblies' on land to which the public has 'limited access' (see below, 25.7) it is important to know what constitutes 'activities incidental to the use of the highway'. The matter came up for consideration in the House of Lords in *DPP v Jones*, where the majority found that there was no hardcore meaning to this test and that 'very little activity could accurately be described as "ancillary to passing along the highway"' and that peaceful, non-obstructive assembly could not be regarded as unlawful for simply being non-incidental to passing and repassing. On the general point, Lord Hutton observed that:

> ... if ... the common law recognises the right of public assembly, I consider that the common law should also recognise that in some circumstances this right can be exercised on the highway, provided that it does not obstruct the passage of other citizens, because otherwise the value of the right of public assembly is greatly diminished.

Private obligations to recognise assembly

There are some statutory and common law restrictions on the right of property owners to prevent the exercise of freedom of expression or assembly on their land. We have seen an example of one of these restrictions in the *Hirst* decision, where the court's finding that the activities of animal rights protesters were not unreasonable was fatal to the obstruction offence charged. Contractual obligations may override property considerations in this context; if a local council has entered into a binding agreement with an association to allow a meeting on their land, a newly constituted council of a different political persuasion cannot renege on that agreement on the basis of the unpopularity of the hiring organisation. In *Verral v Great Yarmouth Borough Council* (1981), the Court of Appeal held that the Council had to go ahead with a conference booking by the National Front. Universities are bound by statute to allow free speech within their precincts (Education (No 2) Act 1986). The way this obligation has been interpreted and applied over the years has been somewhat relaxed; in general, universities are permitted to impose substantial conditions on a meeting which is likely to be controversial. In *R v University of Liverpool ex p Caesar-Gordon* (1991), a case concerning the proposed address by a member of the South African Embassy in an area with a largely ethnic population, the Divisional Court upheld the conditions imposed on the meeting, including the ban on publicity, the requirement of proof of identity and the reservation of the right to charge the Conservative Association, who organised the meeting, the cost of security. In practice, then, the ability to impose these kinds of conditions, particularly the last one, makes it difficult for less well endowed organisations to provide a university platform for controversial speakers.

25.7   The Public Order Act 1986

This Act was introduced to provide a legal basis for the State's regulation of assemblies and processions. Before this legislation was passed, many of the police powers in this context relied on the common law for their legitimacy.

25.7.1 Processions

Processions are governed by s 11 of the Act. The police can require previous notice of processions to be given six days before a procession is due to take place, if it is likely to cause public disorder or damage to property or disruption to the community. Once notice is given, conditions may be imposed under s 12 which effectively undermine the purpose of the demonstration. If the authorities are satisfied that such conditions will not prevent serious disorder under s 13, they can arrange for *all* processions in any given area to be prohibited for 30 days. Such a blanket ban would seem to be a disproportionate measure under Art 11(2). However, since the European Court of Human Rights ruled in *Ärzte für das Leben* that States are under a positive obligation to legislate in order to protect those exercising their right to peaceful assembly from violent opposition, it is easier for governments to satisfy the Court that restrictive measures, such as prior authorisation, geographical conditions and limitations in numbers, are justifiable as part of this duty. Indeed, in *Christians Against Racism and Fascism v UK* (1980), the Commission rejected as 'manifestly ill-founded' a claim that a blanket ban on processions that were likely to provoke violent disorder from opponents was a breach of Art 11. The general ban, issued because of possible violent counter-demonstrations, was deemed to fall within the exceptions to the general freedom, laid down in para 2, particularly since there seemed no less restrictive alternative to avoid the trouble. The applicants themselves did not present any threat to public order, although the Court accepted the respondent State's argument that conflicts between the National Front and their opponents had taken place before, and the applicants, being one of the opponents, might well trigger another disruption. In *Friedl v Austria* (1995), the dispersal of a sit-in, following the evidence of disruption to passers by, was also accepted as being for the 'prevention of disorder'. These precedents render it less likely that the powers of the police to ban processions that threaten 'public disorder' under the Public Order Act 1986 might be challenged for incompatibility with Art 11 of the ECHR.

Special problems arise in respect to processions and sectarian marches in Northern Ireland. The government has attempted to address this by passing the Public Processions (Northern Ireland) Act 1998 which created a Parades Commission to monitor public processions and 'other expressions of cultural identity', giving the Commission broad powers to impose conditions on any proposed procession. The Secretary of State may ban the procession altogether if it threatens public disorder or disruption to the life of the community. These two conditions are similar to the powers under the Public Order Act 1986. But additional criteria are included in the Northern Ireland Act, reflecting the extreme sensitivity of processions in that part of the UK. A ban may be imposed by the Secretary of State, if, in addition, he takes into account the 'impact of the procession on relationships in the community', or 'demands on the police or military forces', and comes to the conclusion that these cannot be satisfied by anything less than a total prohibition on the march. In July 1998, a ban was imposed on a Protestant march which was planned through a Catholic enclave of the Northern Irish town of Portadown. Marches staged by members of the Protestant Orange Order commemorate historic British victories over the Irish and, given the sensitivity of the area, the authorities feared that such a demonstration would spark off enough violence to bring down the fragile peace process in Northern Ireland. The response to this ban was a wave of unrest and a series of protest marches staged by the Orange Order through Belfast and other towns and villages. Troops were called in to control the rioting and outbreaks of violence while the stand-off between the authorities and the organisers of the march continued over weeks. This incident demonstrates that legislative controls do not always provide a solution to the public order problems posed by political demonstrations. On 5 July 1999, fears of a similar outbreak of violence were abated when the Orangemen of Portadown prepared their annual march at Drumcree Hill. The security services prepared to stop the marchers from passing through the town's nationalist areas by constructing a formidable line of fortifications. In the event, these measures were not needed; the march was peaceful. These events underline the importance of the approach taken to policing itself, as opposed to the use of formal powers in seeking to prevent disorder.

25.7.2 Assemblies

The police have the same powers to impose conditions on the holding of assemblies to be held in the open air as they have in respect of processions. They can also ban a particular assembly altogether under s 14A, provided they apprehend 'serious damage to property' or 'serious disruption to the life of the community' (s 14 of the Public Order Act). Their powers in relation to assemblies can only be applied to meetings of 20 or more people in public places. Once the police have imposed conditions, either in writing before the procession or assembly or by oral instructions at the scene, failure to follow them will amount to an offence punishable by three months in prison.

25.7.3 Trespassory assemblies

Section 14A of the Public Order Act 1986 allows the police to apply for consent from the Secretary of State to impose a ban on trespassory assemblies, the definition of which has been considered in *DPP v Jones* (1999). A group of New

Age travellers had gathered on a part of the highway next to Stonehenge where there was a s 14A order in force. The police then arrested two travellers for obstruction when they failed to disperse and they were convicted for breaching the order. The Divisional Court ruled that the holding of a meeting, however peaceable, on the highway, has nothing to do with the right of passage and, therefore, could constitute a trespassory assembly contrary to s 14B(2) of the Act. On appeal to the House of Lords, this ruling was overturned. The limitation of the lawful use of the highway to activities incidental to passing and re-passing would render unlawful 'such ordinary and useful activities as making a sketch, taking a photograph, handing out leaflets, collecting money for charity, singing carols, playing in a Salvation Army band, children playing a game on the pavement, having a picnic or reading a book' (*per* Lord Irvine), and this would place an 'unrealistic and unwarranted restriction on commonplace day to day activities'. It will be remembered (see above, 25.4) that 'reasonable use' of the highway exonerates the user from criminal liability for wilful obstruction. In *DPP v Jones*, the Lords noted that it was undesirable in theory and practice for activities on the highway not to count as breaches of the criminal law, yet to count as trespasses. This judgment was handed down before the passing into force of the Human Rights Act 1998, but it is influenced by ECHR principles. As Lord Irvine pointed out, if an assembly on the public highway was always trespassory, 'then there is not even a *prima facie* right to assembly on the public highway in our law. Unless the common law recognises that assembly on the public highway may be lawful, the right contained in Art 11(1) of the Convention is denied'.

25.7.4 Disorderly behaviour

The line between peaceful protest and disorderly behaviour has been drawn by the offences of riot, affray and threatening, insulting and abusive conduct codified in ss 1–5 of the Public Order Act 1986. The offences which concern us are those where lawful assembly risks becoming unlawful by virtue of random types of behaviour which are very widely drawn in the Act.

Section 4 makes the use of 'threatening, abusive or insulting' words or behaviour, or the use of visible representations of that nature, an offence if it is intended to cause or is causing an apprehension of immediate unlawful violence. There is no special meaning to be attached to the words 'insulting' or 'abusive' and they do not cover 'innocuous conduct which happens to draw a violent response' (*Brutus v Cozens* (1973)). An unexpected spin was put on this provision when a group of Muslim fundamentalists relied on it in an attempt to obtain a summons against the publishers of Salman Rushdie's controversial novel *The Satanic Verses* (*R v Horseferry Road Magistrates ex p Siadatan* (1991)). They said the book was deeply offensive to many Muslims and the violence it had already provoked indicated that the publishers were continuing to commit a s 4 offence by not withdrawing the edition from sale. The application was unsuccessful; the court ruled that the violence that was to be provoked had to be immediate, although this was to include a relatively short period of time within which violence would be likely to erupt.

Section 5 is a much wider offence than s 4. It covers insulting or threatening and abusive conduct which is likely to cause alarm, harassment or distress to anyone in hearing range. Unlike s 4, intention is not necessary. The force of many protest messages depends on the use of distressing images; the use of images of aborted foetuses, in a pro-life protest, was, therefore, not said to amount to a s 5 offence, if the protesters genuinely did not intend them to be so (*DPP v Clark* (1991)). Police constables are included in the group of people who are likely to be caused 'alarm, harassment or distress' (*DPP v Orum* (1988)) and the alarm need not be confined to the prospect of danger to oneself; it could extend to fear of danger to a third party (*Lodge v DPP* (1988), where the apprehension of danger was to the offender himself, who was gesticulating in the traffic).

25.7.5 Harassment

The Prevention of Harassment Act 1997 creates a new hazard for unwitting protesters. Under this Act, it is an offence to pursue a course of conduct amounting to 'harassment' (undefined by the Act) which may cause alarm or distress. Although this Act was designed to cover the activities of 'stalkers', it has recently been used in an application for an injunction against the British Union for the Abolition of Vivisection, restraining it from harassing a company which uses animals for research purposes. However, the High Court rejected the application, saying that Parliament had clearly not intended the Act to be used to prevent individuals from exercising their right to protest and demonstrate about issues of public interest (*Huntingdon Life Sciences Ltd v Curtin* (1997)). Whilst the offence of harassment may certainly be committed once peaceful protest has deteriorated in such a way as to interfere with the freedoms of others, it is to be hoped that future courts will take a restrictive approach to the application of the offence in the public order context.

25.7 Freedom of assembly versus free movement of goods

There have been two Community law decisions which dealt peripherally with the issue of freedom of assembly, both involving claims under the freedom of movement provisions in the EC Treaty. In *R v Chief Constable of Sussex ex p International Trader's Ferry Ltd* (1998), a cross channel livestock transporter challenged a decision by the police to reduce the level of cover provided to ferry services against animal rights demonstrators. The Chief Constable had been concerned that the financial and manpower resources committed to policing the port area were interfering with the efficient policing of the county generally. By reducing the level of policing, the applicants claimed, the police had effectively created an obstacle to the movement of goods across borders in breach of Art 30 (now 29) of the EC Treaty. The House of Lords ruled that, even if the Chief Constable had been in breach of this Article, his decision could be justified on the ground of public policy, permitted by the Treaty, since he was trying to make the best use of limited resources available. The Lords distinguished this case from an earlier judgment by the Court of Justice which involved similar facts. In Case C-265/95 *Commission v France* (1997), the Commission sought a declaration that France had failed in its free movement obligations by failing to control the actions of French farmers who, over the years, had committed acts of vandalism against the imports of agricultural goods from other signatory States. It was alleged that the French authorities had been reluctant to intervene when incidents arose and failed to prosecute the perpetrators. The Court of Justice granted the declaration, holding that France, by not taking adequate steps to prevent farmers from committing or repeating offences, had failed to adopt all appropriate and necessary measures to ensure the free movement on its territory of goods originating from other signatory States as required by the EC Treaty.

Although the implications of the Court of Justice's decision in *Commission v France* have yet to be felt, one major concern that arises out of the case is that Member States will be concerned to avoid an enforcement action by the Commission and an adverse ruling by the Court of Justice in any situation where demonstrations threaten to interfere with the free movement of goods on their territory. In a sense, this judgment will legitimise draconian State action against such demonstrations. Whilst Art 11 does not, and should not, entail an unrestricted right to impede the free flow of trade and goods across borders, the distance that many EU citizens perceive to exist between their wishes and the EU legislative process makes it particularly significant that the democratic importance of freedom of assembly should be given its due weight when it comes into conflict with Community freedoms.

25.8   Restrictions on the freedom of association

Until recently, the European Court of Justice's case law on the Art 11 right to freedom of association outside the sphere of trades union legislation has been rather sparse. In fact, most of the case law on freedom of association concerns individuals' rights *not* to be compelled to join certain associations (*Young, James and Webster v UK* (1982), confirmed by the ruling that Art 11 confers negative freedom of association in *Sigurjonsson v Iceland* (1993)). There have been some judgments in relation to employment law. In *Vogt v Germany* (1996), the European Court of Human Rights held that a teacher who had been dismissed from her post because she belonged to an extreme left wing group had suffered a violation of her free speech rights under Art 10, as well as her association rights under Art 11.

The Convention guarantees the freedom to join pressure groups and other voluntary organisations and, in a recent judgment (*Socialist Party and Others v Turkey* (1998)), the European Court of Human Rights ruled that the dissolution of the United Communist Party of Turkey was a violation of Art 11. This judgment, in effect, brings political parties within the scope of Art 11, on the basis that such organisations are forms of association essential to the proper functioning of democracy. It did not accept that the message put out by the party leader (that a federal system should be established in which Kurds would have an equal footing to Turks) amounted to a call for the use of violence. Since no connection could be found between the terrorist situation in Turkey and the statements made by the party leader, the Court found that the dissolution of the party was disproportionate to the aim of national security and could not, as such, be said to be a measure which was 'necessary in a democratic society'. A few weeks later, the Court considered a similar issue in a case concerning a political association in the Greek administrative region of Macedonia. The question here was whether the applicants' Art 11 rights had been breached by the refusal of the authorities to register an association called 'The Home of Macedonian Civilisation', because it was felt that the real aim of the association was to promote the idea that there was a Macedonian minority in Greece, undermining Greece's national integrity, contrary to Greek law. The Court held that this amounted to an interference with the applicants' exercise of their right to freedom of association, since one of the most important aspects of that freedom was that citizens should be able to form a legal entity in order to act collectively in a field of mutual interest. Whilst the authority's aims – the protection of national security and the prevention of disorder – were legitimate, the refusal of registration, based on unproven suspicions about the association's motives, was held to be disproportionate to these aims (*Sidiropoulos and Others v Greece* (1998)).

The right to join political associations is often decided under Art 10 rather than Art 11, the rationale for this being that expression is one of the objectives of freedom of association. In *Ahmed v UK* (1998), the applicants, local government officers who took active roles in local politics, challenged regulations which restricted the political activities of certain categories of local government officers. Under the regulations, which had been passed to maintain local government political impartiality, the applicants had been obliged to resign from their respective political parties and cease canvassing for election. The European Court of Human Rights rejected their claim that this was a disproportionate interference with their rights under Arts 10 and 11, holding that the regulations were justified by the pressing social need to strengthen the tradition of political neutrality.

There is, in addition to the 'clawback' provisions of para 2 of Arts 10 and 11, a more general restriction in the ECHR on political associations. Article 17 allows States to impose restrictions on programmes pursued by those groups, to prevent them interfering with the rights protected elsewhere in the ECHR.

Strasbourg case law on the scope of Art 17 indicates that it may be relied upon by respondent governments to justify restrictions on a number of ECHR rights, particularly Art 11, although it should be a last resort (*Purcell v Ireland* (1991)) and the Court is generally reluctant to allow respondent States to rely on it: see the discussion of *Lehideux v France* (see above, 24.5). The specific question has not yet arisen, but it is possible that most anti-terrorist legislation in this country would come under the protective umbrella of Art 17 as well as being justified by the Art 11(2) exceptions. The Prevention of Terrorism (Temporary Provisions) Act 1989 prohibits membership of a number of proscribed organisations in Northern Ireland, irrespective of whether those organisations have indulged in terrorist activities or not (the organisations currently proscribed under the PTA are the IRA and INLA). The other main restriction on political associations is to be found in the Public Order Act 1936, which makes it an offence to form an organisation which is 'organised or equipped entirely for the purpose of enabling them to be employed for the use or display of physical force in promoting any political object or in such a manner as to arouse reasonable apprehension that they are organised or equipped for that purpose' (s 2(1)(b)).

The Public Order Act 1986 criminalises the wearing of uniforms by participants in public gatherings. The offence is only committed if the uniform is so worn as to signify the wearer's association with any political organisation. Section 1 was introduced in response to the use of uniforms by Fascist groups between the two World Wars; now, it is of relevance largely in the context of political activities by the IRA and Unionist groups (*O'Moran v DPP; Whelan v DPP* (1975)). The Act also prohibits the gathering of vigilantes in quasi-military groups (s 2). The prevention of terrorism legislation extends these prohibitions to proscribed organisations in Northern Ireland: it is an offence to wear any item which arouses a reasonable apprehension that a person is a member or supporter of any of those organisations.

25.9 Assessment

Sections 11, 13, 14 and 14A of the Public Order Act 1986 are in most urgent need of reform. The problem rests not so much in the specific restrictions laid down by the legislative wording but the broad margin of discretion left to the police in determining whether any particular public act is likely to lead to certain consequences which, in turn, give them authority to prevent that act from taking place or impose sanctions when it does (see the criticisms of this legislation by Bonne, D and Stone, R, 'The Public Order Act 1986: steps in the wrong direction?' [1987] PL 202; and Smith, ATH, 'The Public Order Act 1986: Part I' [1987] Crim LR 156). It has been seen, from the foregoing pages, that bans may be imposed on assemblies if there is a risk of serious disruption to the life of the community. What constitutes 'serious' disruption or, indeed, who precisely makes up 'the community' and what kind of 'life' it is that risks disruption are all questions that are very much left to the discretion of the authorities. Such bans may amount to infringements on the right to assemble that extend beyond those permitted under Art 11(2), such as the prevention of disorder and crime (see Fitzpatrick, B and Naylor, M, 'Trespassers might be prosecuted' (1998) 3 EHRLR 292). Authorities should only be permitted to impose blanket bans on processions and trespassory assemblies if there are no alternative methods of preventing apprehended disorder. Although it is possible, in principle, to challenge the imposition of a blanket ban by way of judicial review, precedents show that this is unlikely to be successful in practice, In *Kent v Metropolitan Police Commissioner* (1981), the CND attempted to challenge a blanket ban which had caused it to cancel a number of planned marches. But it conceded that any demonstration, whatever the purpose, would have led to disorder and, therefore, the Divisional Court refused an order to quash the ban, since the applicant had not been able to establish that there had been no reasons for imposing it in the first place. If the burden of justifying the ban were on the authorities, rather than the burden of arguing for its removal remaining on those wishing to proceed with a peaceful protest, the temptation to impose automatic blanket bans would be much reduced.

Since very little land in the UK is truly 'public' and thus available as a platform for public protest, the widening of permissible uses of quasi-public spaces such as the highway in *DPP v Jones* is a welcome and timely development, at least as far as the public law on trespassory assembly is concerned. There are still shortcomings, however, in the private law of nuisance, which is still firmly associated with property interests (*Hunter v Canary Wharf* (1996)) and the tendency of the courts to favour the rights of landowners suggest that they are likely to give significant weight to the countervailing interest in protecting the 'rights and freedoms of others' under Art 11(2) (an assessment of the restrictions on public protest in non-public places can be found in Robertson, G, *Freedom, the Individual and the Law*, 7th edn, 1993, London: Penguin, pp 66–68). One of the most significant restrictions to freedom of expression in modern Britain is traffic control: anything which interrupts the flow of traffic is fair game for a banning order (see the discussion in Klug, F, Starmer, K and Weir, S, *The Three Pillars of Liberty*, 1996, London: Routledge, p 198, on the failure of the Campaign Against Arms Trade to find anywhere to release their slogan bearing balloons). As roads are built, extended and widened, we can see that the residual protection of certain liberties which may have been regarded adequate in Victorian England cannot be relied upon to protect public protest against practical obstacles like this.

The common law on breach of the peace is also ripe for reform, even though the European Court of Human Rights has considered that this wide concept – which does not, in itself, amount to an offence – is sufficiently certain and ascertainable to rank as a restriction 'prescribed by law'. Nevertheless, national case law demonstrates that a finding of potential breach of the peace can have a significant chilling effect on lawful public protest. Given the current precedents on breach of the peace, it may be that only the House of Lords has sufficient authority and flexibility to change the law in this area.

FREEDOM OF ASSEMBLY AND ASSOCIATION

Freedom of assembly is an important democratic freedom because, like freedom of expression, it provides a platform for open criticism of those in power. Sometimes, protest interferes with the rights of others and, in order to make freedom of assembly an effective right, it is necessary to take measures to legitimise this interference. Freedom to associate entails the right to belong to organised groups, political or otherwise. Article 11 protects the right to freedom of assembly and association, subject to a number of exceptions, notably the rights and freedoms of others and the prevention of disorder. In addition, there are various other statutory and common law restrictions on these rights.

Breach of the peace

The police may take steps to prevent an apprehended breach of the peace. Those exercising their rights to lawful protest will not be liable for breach of the peace where the violence they may have provoked is entirely unreasonable. The standard of reasonable apprehension of breach of the peace will be satisfied whenever harm is actually done or is likely to be done or where a person is in fear of being harmed.

Binding over orders

Magistrates have common law and statutory power to bind people over to keep the peace. Such measures have been found to be compatible with Art 11(2).

Obstruction of the highway

People exercising their rights of assembly on the highway may be charged with the offence of obstruction if their use of the highway is considered to be unreasonable.

Nuisance

Participators in assemblies and processions may be liable for the offence of public nuisance if the public are disturbed by their unlawful activities; they may also be sued in private nuisance if their activities interfere with the lawful enjoyment of land adjoining their protest site.

Trespass

Trespass actions may be taken in respect of many 'public' places which are not in fact public at all. Even the 'public highway' does not belong to the public and the use of the highway is limited to passing and re-passing and activities incidental to that. Private landowners may prevent meetings taking place on their land. But universities are under a statutory obligation to permit free speech within their premises.

The Public Order Act

There are a number of limitations on processions and assemblies under this Act. The police may impose conditions if the proposed procession is likely to lead to certain disruptive consequences and a blanket ban on all processions may be imposed if a serious breach of the peace is predicted. A ban may also be imposed on trespassory assemblies, and the present position is that an assembly will not be 'trespassory' if the use of the highway by its participants is considered 'reasonable'. The Public Order Act also creates a number of offences for random types of disorderly behaviour which may turn a lawful assembly or protest into an unlawful one. Such behaviour is an offence if it is 'insulting, threatening or abusive'.

Freedom of assembly versus free movement of goods

The European Court of Justice has recently ruled that the failure by a Member State to take positive measures to prevent protests that interfered with the free movement of goods was a breach of EC law. This judgment may be relied upon by State governments to justify draconian measures against protesters in areas involving Community law.

Restrictions on freedom of association

The European Court of Human Rights has recently ruled that the dissolution of a political party was an unlawful infringement of this right and could not be justified on the basis of the party leader's message advocating constitutional change – this did not amount to a call to violence. A number of statutory provisions, such as the anti-terrorist legislation and the Public Order Act 1936, prohibit or restrict association with certain types of proscribed organisations.

CHAPTER 26

EQUALITY

26.1 Introduction

Liberal democracies do not consist of identical individuals. It is a random collection of men and women ranging from convicts, millionaires, evangelical Christians, fundamentalist Muslims, to hereditary peers or refugees. Each one of these is recognised by others as belonging to a group or groups in society and this recognition determines their status. Hence the importance of the principle that all men and women, whatever group they belong to, should enjoy equal application of the law. This is easy enough to state, but far harder to implement. It is not enough to ensure that the law places no obstacles in the way of different groups of people on their way to the ballot box. This is the purely 'formal' notion of equality, espoused by libertarians like John Stuart Mill, who suggested that equality for women could be secured by ensuring their access to education, the franchise and employment. According to the libertarian view, after that was achieved, nothing more needed to be done; women should achieve their goals by talent alone. This model of equality imposes no obligation on society to adopt positive measures to ensure that sectors of the population whose status is irredeemably different are afforded true equality of opportunity. Nor does it impinge on the freedoms of others to live as they desire.

Clearly, this purely *formal* model of equality is insufficient to ensure effective equality in society. Women, for example, may still suffer the legacy of discrimination from centuries past. In order to eradicate such long established practices, *substantive* equality requires that the marketplace should adapt to women employees, not vice versa. (For an outline of this view, see Gardner, J, 'Liberals and unlawful discrimination' (1989) OJLS 1.) For the same reason, ensuring that everybody has equal access to the ballot box does not achieve true equality unless each individual feels there is some point in exercising his or her right to vote. Therefore, the State must guarantee to individuals or groups of individuals that their views and conduct will not be ranked at a lower level than those of other members of society. Without this guarantee, people will not see any link between their vote and the decisions and actions of the party in power. People have to be treated in such a way that they can and want to exercise that right to vote. A minority group routinely discriminated against by the majority and relegated to the lowest echelons of society in terms of employment, services, housing and so on will care little about the objectives of the democratic process since the views of its members are disregarded at a day to day level. So measures to ensure equality have to start somewhere further down the scale that leads to the ballot box. This is to ensure that we can achieve what Ronald Dworkin calls a 'communal' democracy:

> This means not only that everyone must be allowed to participate in politics as an equal, through the vote and through freedom of speech and protest, but that political decisions must treat everyone with equal concern and respect [*Freedom's Law*, 1997, Oxford: OUP, p 365].

Meaningful equality thus requires certain measures to be taken by the State to coerce private bodies not to act in such a way as to reduce the status of groups of individuals in society by discriminating against them. How to reconcile this with the principle of a free society in which private individuals should be allowed to get on with their lawful activities without interference from the State is one of the most pressing problems of a modern liberal democracy. The freedom of private parties to contract with others – mainly in the field of employment, but also in the provision of goods and services – must be curtailed in order to secure the equality rights of others. But how is the balance to be struck? The trouble is that, once our rulers start justifying the imposition of laws on people in the name of justice, or equality, or some higher value, they are necessarily subordinating what we think is right to what they deem to be right and good for us. As Isaiah Berlin observes,

> This is the argument used by every dictator, inquisitor, and bully who seeks some moral, or even aesthetic, justification for his conduct ['Two concepts of liberty', in *Four Essays on Liberty*, 1975, Oxford: OUP, p 151].

If real equality is incompatible with individual liberty, how much rein should we give our rulers to decide what is best for us? The legislature that decides one day, quite sensibly, that employers should not recruit a man if an equally well qualified female applicant has put in for the post, may, the next day, declare that practising Christian Scientists are under-represented in the education system and pass a law to scrutinise the employment procedures of all schools for discrimination against Christian Scientists. This may seem far fetched, but it could be justified on the same principle that authorises interference by the State with the contracting powers of private bodies in the areas of sex, race and disability discrimination. The only way to reconcile coercive anti-discrimination laws with the principle of liberty is by acknowledging, again in the words of Isaiah Berlin, that:

> ... respect for the principles of justice, or shame at gross inequality of treatment, is as basic in men as the desire for liberty. That we cannot have anything is a necessary, not a contingent, truth [p 151].

Even if we accept that liberty must be curtailed to a certain extent to secure equality, the question remains as to who should decide when and what equality interests will prevail. It has been argued in Chapters 19–25 that most rights and freedoms, if threatened, may be relied upon in the courts to challenge State action. But to what extent can we claim that a general democratic principle of equality entitles us to equality of laws and executive actions and that this is enforceable through the courts? This question arose recently in a Privy Council case concerning the scope of the right to equality in the constitution of Mauritius. The applicants claimed that the changes made to school examination regulations discriminated against pupils who did not speak oriental languages. Although the constitution prohibits discrimination in the enjoyment of rights on a number of limited grounds, there is no positive right to education or access to a particular school to be found in the constitution. The applicants nevertheless argued that there was a general substantive right to equality that went beyond the rights specified. The Privy Council did not doubt the principle that equality before the law requires that persons should be uniformly treated, unless there is some valid reason to treat them differently. But Lord Hoffmann observed that:

> ... the very banality of the principle must suggest a doubt as to whether to state it can provide an answer to the kind of problem which arises in this case. Of course persons should be uniformly treated, unless there is some valid reason for treating them differently. But what counts as a valid reason for treating them differently? And, perhaps more important, who is to decide whether the reason is valid or not? The reasons for not treating people uniformly often involve, as they do in this case, questions of social policy on which views may differ. These are questions which the elected representatives have some claim to decide for themselves. The fact that equality of treatment is a general principle of rational behaviour does not entail that it should necessarily be a justiciable principle – that it should always be the judges who have the last word on whether the principle has been observed. In this, as in other areas of constitutional law, sonorous judicial statements of uncontroversial principle often conceal the real problem, which is to mark out the boundary between the powers of the judiciary, the legislature and the executive in deciding how the principle is to be applied [*Matadeen v Pointu* (1998)].

These judicial observations are borne out by the fact that the political instinct since the 1960s has been to legislate on these issues first and then to leave the interpretation to the judges, rather than relying on the common law to determine in what circumstances unequally placed persons should be treated unequally in order to achieve equality of opportunity. Nevertheless, as the cases discussed below demonstrate, judges are generally prepared to disagree openly with the lines drawn by the legislature, even in the sensitive areas of equality and discrimination.

So, inequality of treatment is sometimes necessary because the most insidious forms of discrimination appear in the guise of neutral requirements for all comers, which can only be fulfilled by a select few. Educational and linguistic requirements may disclose a form of indirect discrimination if not objectively necessary for the task in hand; see below, 26.3.2. To combat this, it is necessary for the State to ensure that people in similar circumstances should be treated similarly and that any differences in treatment should be objectively justified.

Before tackling the scope of anti-discrimination rights, it is perhaps worth asking why we think it important to achieve the substantive equality which they are designed to secure. True democracy, it has been said, rests on this equality, but are there any other values that can be identified on the way? McCrudden has pinpointed a few objectives about which there is some consensus in this area (McCrudden, C, 'Introduction', in *Anti-Discrimination Law*, 1991, Dartmouth: International Library of Essays in Law and Legal Theory). It is said, probably correctly, that routine discrimination against certain groups in society sometimes erupts in protest and other public order problems that are best avoided by preventative legislation. Disruptive protests – such as those carried out by the suffragettes at the turn of the century – may be averted by appropriate measures prohibiting discrimination. The utilitarian argument is that permitting discrimination is economically inefficient since it gives an unfair competitive advantage to those players on the market who are prepared to be unfair. Allowing prejudicial and discriminatory practices to pass unchecked may have the consequence that less qualified candidates are given an uncompetitive advantage, thereby distorting the field. Anti-discrimination laws also open the market to more people and therefore allows for more efficient use of the talents and skills available in society. In addition, the recognition of plurality in society contributes to its richness and diversity. Instead of learning only about the Bible, for example, children should be educated about Buddha, Mohammed and Ganesh; in this way, they will not only be better equipped to make their own choices but the tapestry of education will acquire a few more strands (see Poulter, S, 'Minority rights' in McCrudden, C and Chambers, G (ed), *Individual Rights and the Law in Britain*, 1994, Oxford: Clarendon, pp 457–62; and Poulter, S (1987) 36 ICLQ 589, pp 614–15).

Finally, it has been argued that 'equality' should be regarded as a constitutional principle, like 'access to justice' and 'freedom of expression'. These constitutional rights recognised by the common law were used by judges to determine judicial review applications before the ECHR became part of national law. The substantive ground of challenge in judicial review proceedings, 'unreasonableness', is sufficiently open textured to yield a right to equality as one of its protected norms (see Jowell, J, 'Is equality a constitutional principle?' (1994) 47 CLP 1). However, not many cases have succeeded on this basis, because of the difficulties of establishing that the respondent's justification for differential treatment crosses the high threshold of irrationality required in judicial review proceedings. When four service personnel were discharged from service under the Ministry of Defence's policy of excluding homosexuals from the army, they argued that the interference with their rights to equality was unreasonable (see above, 15.5.1). While the court acknowledged that, where their rights to equality were at stake, any measure infringing on those rights should be subject to the strictest scrutiny, it accepted, in the end, the Ministry's justification for the policy of differential treatment (*R v Ministry of Defence ex p Smith* (1996)).

26.2 The scope of anti-discrimination laws

The common law provides a limited protection against discrimination. For example, there is an ancient rule of the common law that public inns and taverns (and by analogy, all providers of public services) are under an obligation to serve all comers without discrimination: *Constantine v Imperial Hotels* (1944). More recently, in *Nagle v Fielden* (1966), the applicant complained that she had been denied a trainer's licence by the Jockey Club because she was a woman. Lord Denning MR granted the declaration sought, that the refusal of the licence was an unreasonable restraint of trade and the Club had interfered with her 'right to work'. In effect, this judgment deployed a common law interest (albeit of somewhat dubious origin) to protect a fundamental right to equality (see, further, Oliver, D, 'Common values in public and private law' [1997] PL 630).

The main protections against discrimination, however, are to be found in the statutes that prohibit discrimination on the grounds of race, sex and disability. Since the Human Rights Act 1998, Art 14 of the ECHR has brought a much wider range of prohibited grounds into discrimination law. Article 14 provides:

> The enjoyment of the rights and freedoms set forth in this Convention shall be secured without discrimination on any ground such as sex, race, colour, language, religion, political or any other opinion, national or social origin, association with a national minority, property, birth or other status.

This right differs significantly from other anti-discrimination laws in that it is parasitic – it is of no use to someone wishing to complain of discrimination who cannot point to a breach of another freestanding Convention right. And Art 14 is, of course, only actionable against the State and public authorities as defined by the Human Rights Act 1998 (s 6 and see above, 19.9 and 19.10.4). The interpretative obligation on the courts under this Act (s 3) may provide a route for Art 14 application in private cases, but the complainant would have to have a case under a substantive Article as well.

26.2.1 The scope of Art 14

As we have seen, there are many grounds of discrimination set out in Art 14 of the ECHR and the list is open ended ('other status'). But the case law of the European Commission and Court has established that some grounds are more prohibited than others. The 'suspect' grounds are limited to sex, race and legitimacy of children. In these cases, the European Court of Human Rights will scrutinise very strictly any justifications advanced on the part of the signatory State. In other words, in these cases the State's margin of appreciation, or its ability to stray from the requirements of the ECHR, is narrower here than in other areas of discrimination. The European Court of Human Rights has been particularly robust in its approach to sex discrimination, holding that

> ... the advancement of the equality of the sexes is today a major goal in the Member States of the Council of Europe and very weighty reasons would have to be put forward before such a difference of treatment could be regarded as compatible with the Convention [*Schuler-Zgraggen v Switzerland* (1993)].

Article 14 must be pleaded in relation to some other substantive right in the ECHR. It is not necessary to establish a violation of another Article; if the claim comes within the ambit of another protected right, then it is possible for the applicant to succeed on discrimination alone, even if the primary violation has not been established, or the signatory State's action has been found to come within one of the permissible exceptions to that right (*Belgian Linguistic* case (1979)). A good example of this is *Abdulaziz and Others v UK* (1985). The UK's policy of not letting in husbands of lawfully settled immigrants was considered to come within the permitted exceptions to the right to privacy under Art 8, so they failed on that point. Article 8 does not require signatory States to grant the right of family members to enter and reside. But the fact that the applicants could allege a difference in treatment without a legitimate justification under Art 14 carried their claim through.

Equally, even if the right does not itself arise directly out of one of the ECHR provisions, once a State has introduced additional rights, it cannot implement them in a discriminatory manner. The right to have a system of appeal courts, for example, is not implicit in the fair trial provisions of Art 6 – once a Member State has put such an appellate system into place, it cannot operate it in a discriminatory fashion, since Art 14 prohibits discrimination in allowing access to courts throughout the whole judicial system.

Even if the European Court of Human Rights finds a violation of a substantive right, it is still theoretically possible to obtain a ruling that Art 14 has been infringed as well. In *Marckx v Belgium* (1985), the court concluded that the unfavourable treatment of illegitimate children under Belgian inheritance laws violated their right to a family life under Art 8 and breached the requirement under Art 14 that Convention rights should be secured without discrimination. But, in most cases, the court will content itself with a finding that a substantive right has been breached. In another case involving Art 8, the applicant challenged laws criminalising homosexual behaviour in Northern Ireland (*Dudgeon v UK* (1982)). The court, having found a violation of Art 8, left it at that, without going on to consider the applicant's claim that the imposition of these laws in Northern Ireland and not in the rest of the UK was a breach of Art 14.

The court has been reluctant to be drawn into disputes about discriminatory allocation of State resources where direct inequality is not in point. In *Botta v Italy* (1998), it rejected a claim that the lack of disabled facilities at a seaside resort violated the applicant's right to equal enjoyment of his right to a private life under Art 8, together with Art 14. The court held that such 'social' rights as the participation by disabled people in recreational and leisure facilities could not come within the scope of Convention rights such as Art 8 and, therefore, Art 14 did not apply.

26.2.2 Anti-discrimination legislation

Before incorporating Art 14, the UK legislature took action to prohibit discrimination in three main areas: race, sex and disability. The Race Relations Act 1976, the Sex Discrimination Act 1975 and the Disability Discrimination Act 1995 each define direct discrimination as unfavourable treatment of a person on grounds of race, sex and physical capacity. Indirect discrimination is the application to that person of a requirement that cannot be justified other than by reference to the person's race, sex and physical capacity, and is to the detriment of that person because they cannot comply with it. These Acts protect anyone, not just a victim of discrimination, who claims that they have been penalised for complaining about discriminatory practices. Discrimination on grounds of someone else's race is prohibited. Employers for example who prevent their staff from serving black customers will be committing an offence under the Act (*Zarcynska v Levy* (1979)). Despite these broad prohibitions, it will be seen below that it is possible for discrimination on all these grounds to be justified in certain circumstances (see below, 26.3).

Legislation has also been passed to prohibit discrimination on grounds of religion or political belief in Northern Ireland, since it is in this region that this form of discrimination causes the most violent civil strife. Here, it is a statutory tort to discriminate against someone because of their or their family's religious affiliations and compensation is available for anyone who can establish that such discrimination has taken place (s 76 of the Northern Ireland Act 1998). The Fair Employment (Northern Ireland) Acts 1976 and 1989 prohibit such discrimination in the workplace.

Race

The main statutory prohibition on racial discrimination is to be found in the Race Relations Act 1976 (RRA). 'Race' as defined by this act means colour, nationality or ethnic or national origins. Discrimination on these grounds is unlawful in employment, education and in the provision of goods, services, and facilities to the public. The Act also applies to advertising which has the effect of excluding members of particular racial groups. However, the Act does not cover the activities of those bodies whose function is not to provide a service but to control people – so, for example, the conduct of immigration authorities or the police cannot be challenged under the Act. Special provision is made in the Act for discriminatory practices by private institutions, such as clubs, since it would be possible for a club to escape legislative control of its discriminatory practices by arguing that it is not providing a service to the 'public'. All clubs are, therefore, covered by the Act, provided they have 25 or more members. Unlike the Sex Discrimination Act 1975, race discrimination law in this country has only been indirectly influenced by Community law in this field. For this reason, public authorities carrying out official duties are still immune from the provisions of the RRA, unlike practices by public bodies that discriminate on grounds of sex. On the other hand, the strict scrutiny of the justifiability of discriminatory measures, applied by the European Court of Justice in C-170/84 *Bilka-Kaufhaus v Weber* (1986), is applied under the RRA as much as the SDA.

The provisions of the RRA are enforced by the Commission for Racial Equality which conducts formal investigations into an activity which it believes to be discriminatory. At the conclusion of this process, a non-discrimination notice requiring the party concerned to cease their discriminatory practices may be issued. The Commission may also assist individuals who wish to apply for compensation for breach of their rights under the RRA before an industrial tribunal, if their complaint concerns employment, or through the ordinary courts if they have been discriminated against in other areas covered by the Act. Damages may be awarded for injury to feelings, and there is no limit on the amount of compensation which may be awarded.

Sex

The Sex Discrimination Act 1975 (SDA) covers discrimination on grounds of sex and marital status in the fields of employment, education, the provision of goods and services to the public, the disposal and management of premises and advertising. The SDA also protects employees who bring complaints or evidence under the Act from being victimised. The Act only covers non-contractual discriminatory practices; matters relating to pay are governed by the Equal Pay Act 1970. The scope of this legislation was, therefore, somewhat limited and it was only when the European Community's laws in this area became part of national law that discrimination on grounds of sex took centre ground in national courts. So, for example, the immunity enjoyed by public officials under the SDA was greatly restricted when the Court of Justice ruled that the issue of a certificate that prevented the bringing of a discrimination claim in respect of employment by the Royal Ulster Constabulary, on the basis of national security, amounted to a failure to provide an effective remedy for breach of Community law (see above, 18.2) (*Johnston v Chief Constable of the RUC* (1986)). As a result of this judgment, the Sex Discrimination (Amendment) Order was adopted in 1988 to remove the exclusion on grounds of national security for discriminatory practices in employment and education. It is important to remember, however, that in challenges to other forms of discrimination, this Order is not applicable, so important evidence may be withheld on grounds of national security. This legislative gap led to the decision by the European Court of Human Rights in *Tinnelly and McElduff v UK* (1998). Here, a firm, most of whose members were Catholics, had been unable to proceed in its claim that it had been discriminated against on religious grounds by a major contractor because crucial evidence was excluded on national security grounds. The Court ruled that it had been denied its right to a fair trial under Art 6 of the ECHR.

The development of European Community law on sex discrimination is discussed in detail later (see below, 26.4). As far as the SDA is concerned, the Equal Opportunities Commission is responsible for monitoring compliance with its provisions, although, unlike the Commission for Racial Equality, it relies on litigation rather than investigation to get its message across. This takes the form of assistance to individuals in taking discrimination claims before the courts as well as judicial review. The Equal Opportunities Commission scored a notable success in the role of public interest litigator in 1994, when it successfully challenged provisions in domestic law which discriminated against part time workers (who are usually women) in respect of qualification for redundancy payments. The House of Lords granted their application for a declaration that this was in breach of European Community law (*R v Secretary of State for Employment ex p Equal Opportunities Commission* (1995)). The most important advance made in this case was the recognition by the courts of the Equal Opportunities Commission's standing to bring judicial proceedings in their own right.

Disability

The only form of statutory prohibition is set out in the Disability Discrimination Act 1995 (DDA). Like the RRA and the SDA, the DDA prohibits discrimination against disabled people in the context of employment, education, provision of goods and services and in the provision of property. The Act applies to all UK employers who have 20 or more employees. It does not apply to a number of occupations, including the armed forces, the police, fire fighters, prison officers and people working on boats or aircraft. There are complex definitions within the Act as to who should come within the scope of its protection. After all, 'disability', in its literal sense, can extend from paraplegia to a very minor disability such as short-sightedness. The DDA sets a minimum standard for disability – the person concerned must have a physical or mental impairment which has a substantial and long term adverse effect on their ability to carry out normal day to day activities, but includes within its scope conditions which may not be very significant at the time but may be progressive, such as HIV, multiple sclerosis or muscular dystrophy. The DDA also covers people who have had a disability in the past, even if they have since recovered.

As with the RRA and the SDA, a criterion of 'less favourable treatment' applies for direct discrimination. This means that a person will be able to establish direct discrimination under the Act if he or she can prove that more favourable treatment would have been meted out but for the fact that the victim of discrimination had been disabled. The Act will also be infringed if an employer or a provider of services, etc, fails to comply with a duty of 'reasonable adjustment' (s 6), for example, by installing ramps, Braille keyboards, or making the necessary alterations to working hours and procedures. In relation to service provision, a shop owner may be in breach of the DDA if he fails to allow access to a blind person's guide dog, even though a general prohibition on animals on his premises is lawful. Like the RRA and the SDA, the DDA makes it unlawful to victimise anyone, whether disabled or not, who complains that the provisions of the DDA are being breached. The Act also imposes restrictions on recruitment for vacancies, so that employers may not include requirements in job advertisements or interview questioning which would unjustifiably exclude people with disabilities. A requirement for a driving licence which would discourage a candidate with cerebral palsy or epilepsy for applying, for example, will breach the Act if driving is not essential to the job.

Like the other anti-discrimination laws, there is to be a regulatory body, the Disability Discrimination Commission, established by the Disability Discrimination Act 1999. It will have powers to conduct formal investigations, issue non-discrimination notices and assist individuals in litigation concerning disability matters.

26.2.3 Justified discrimination

Because of the particularly intrusive nature of anti-discrimination legislation, which affects the behaviour of public and private actors alike, the courts are ready to accept circumstances where technically discriminatory behaviour should be permitted.

Objective grounds

Discriminatory measures may be justified on objective grounds and if there are no alternative ways of avoiding discrimination. In the work place, it is open to employers to seek to justify recruitment qualifications as long as they are required by the reasonable needs of the employer. A requirement of English fluency, for example, may indirectly discriminate against certain ethnic groups; it will be justifiable if the employer is an English language teaching school, but not, perhaps, if the employer is a motor repair business. In the *Equal Opportunities Commission* case (discussed above, 26.2.1), the Secretary of State's arguments that discriminatory provisions in employment law could be justified on the basis of preserving part time employment did not hold in the absence of objective evidence to that effect. In the context of disability discrimination, as with the RRA and the SDA, an employer may only permit himself less favourable treatment towards a disabled person if there is a relevant and substantial reason and this objection cannot be overcome by making adjustments, for example, by supplying additional training or by the allocation of some duties to another employee. Service providers may be justified in refusing to make 'reasonable adjustments' if they are prevented from so doing for health and safety reasons, or where providing a service to a disabled person would ruin or jeopardise the service for others.

Positive discrimination

The assumption that individuals have a right not to be treated as members of a particular group cuts both ways. It applies to favourable treatment as well as negative treatment. The RRA and the SDA are symmetrical in operation, in other words, practices which favour disadvantaged groups over others will be as unlawful as ordinary or negative discrimination. Substantive equality requires, in some circumstances, formal measures to be put in place to afford certain sectors of the population true equality of opportunity (see the introductory section to this chapter). For this reason, the 'symmetrical' operation of anti-discrimination legislation in this country is subject to some limited exceptions. In offering vocational training to a particular group in areas of employment where that group has been under-represented in the past, the institute may specify race or sex. The DDA requires that measures be adopted to open up opportunities for disabled people, so this, to a certain extent, is an Act authorising positive discrimination as a whole.

The effect of Art 14 on positive discrimination is more debatable. It is a classic 'negative' obligation, in other words, it imposes no positive duties on States to run affirmative action programmes, for example, or to provide resources for the improvement of opportunity for traditionally disadvantaged groups. Conversely, a State may take measures for positive discrimination without violating Art 14, provided there is an objective justification for increasing disproportionately low representation of a particular group in some area.

However, this Article does require signatory States to 'secure' the enjoyment of rights and freedoms without discrimination. The precise meaning of that obligation has not been settled by the European Court of Human Rights and the import remains obscure, particularly since the ECHR does not require incorporation of any of its substantive provisions into the national law of signatory States. Under the Human Rights Act 1998, this obligation may be interpreted in the UK courts so as to impose an obligation on the government to prevent private discrimination on the grounds set out in the ECHR. While the discriminating organisation (club, private school, private medical clinic) may escape a claim under Art 14 because it is not a public authority (see above, 19.10.4), it may be possible for the government itself to be challenged for not having 'secured' the equal enjoyment of Convention rights, in other words, for not legislating to prohibit such discriminatory practices by private actors. In disputes between private parties, it will also be possible to argue that the court, as 'public authority' under the Human Rights Act, is itself obliged to develop the interpretation of statute or common law in accordance with the principle of equality enshrined in the Convention.

26.3 Equality in European Community law

Much European Community law is concerned with the creation of a single market through the elimination of barriers to trade between Member States. This entails the prohibition of measures that discriminate on the basis of nationality. From the outset, the EC Treaty also required equal pay for equal work by men and women and, subsequently, Community law has sought to prohibit other forms of sex discrimination. In recent judgements and opinions, the Court of Justice and Advocates General have appeared sympathetic to the broader aims of equality, extending the scope of the equality provisions in the EC Treaty and subordinate law to areas beyond the specific grounds of sex and nationality. The cases considered below were decided before the Amsterdam revisions to the EC Treaty and Treaty on the European Union (see above, 7.2), which considerably widened the scope for anti-discrimination measures. Article 13 of the EC Treaty gives the Council express power to 'take appropriate action to combat discrimination based on sex, racial and ethnic origin, religion or belief, disability, age or sexual orientation'. This provision is, however, unlikely to be held to create any directly effective rights enforceable in national courts (see above, 7.9.2) nor does it actually prohibit discrimination in these listed fields. It simply enlarges the Community's legislative competence in these areas. On the other hand, it is potentially a very useful basis for the enlargement of equality rights in the Community sphere. Since Community legislation is aimed at the harmonisation of the laws of Member States to achieve the aims of the single market, a number of different areas can now be brought within the sphere of Community competence, providing a legal basis for measures promoting equality. Under the new Art 13, for example, Community institutions could pass laws prohibiting discrimination on the listed grounds in the areas of environmental standards, construction, transportation, communication and a number of other very important fields of economic activity.

26.3.1 Sex discrimination in European Community law

Prohibitions against sex discrimination in Community law apply in the context of employment and provision of social security. Article 141 of the EC Treaty states that 'Each Member State shall ensure that the principle of equal pay for male and female workers for equal work or work of equal value is applied'. This Treaty provision is directly effective (see above, 7.9.2) and may be relied on in national courts against both public authorities and private firms (Case C-43/75 *Defrenne v Sabena (No 2)* (1976)). Article 141 is supported by a raft of directives (in particular, the Equal Treatment Directive 76/207 and the Equal Pay Directive 75/117) and judgments of the Court of Justice on the liability of Member States for breach of these provisions. Other directives have been passed which require equal treatment in matters of social security (Directive 79/7), pension schemes (Directive 86/378), equal treatment for self-employed persons (Directive 86/613) and conditions of work relating to pregnancy and maternity leave (Directive 92/85). Directives are required to be transposed into national law by Member States (see above, 7.6.2); if a Member State has failed to do this, a person may be able to rely on a directly effective provision in a directive to bring proceedings in a national court or tribunal – but only against public authorities, not against private firms or other individuals (Case C-152/84 *Marshall v Southampton and South West Hampshire Area Health Authority (Teaching)* (1986)).

This has been of huge significance to women employees; in the UK, Community law has been invoked more frequently than in any other Member State, in particular, testing the legality of retirement provisions, which, in this country, are linked to the statutory pensionable age (60 for women, 65 for men). In *Marshall*, M, a public health sector employee, challenged the compulsory retirement policy which obliged her to retire five years before her male colleagues. The Court of Justice found that her case was not within the exceptions laid out by the Social Security Directive, which excluded from the equal treatment principle the determination of pensionable age for the purposes of granting retirement pensions, but ruled instead that her pensionable age was being determined for 'other purposes' and, therefore, fell foul of Community law. The Sex Discrimination Act 1986 has now rendered discriminatory retirement ages illegal, and men and women both have to reach the age of 65 before they qualify for pensions.

26.3.2 Justified discrimination: objective grounds in European Community law

The European Court of Justice has distinguished between direct discrimination (when men and women are treated differently by virtue of their sex) and indirect discrimination (sexually neutral rules adversely affect a significant proportion of one sex more than another). Indirect discrimination may, as in domestic law, be objectively justified (Case C-170/84 *Bilka-Kaufhaus GmbH v Weber von Harz* (1986)). Discrimination on grounds of sex is also permissible under the Equal Treatment Directive, but only on the very narrowly construed grounds that the sex of the worker is a determining factor, in other words, that a person of one sex could not in any possible sense carry out the work designed for someone of the other sex; differential treatment may also be justified if it concerns the protection of pregnant women, which excludes, for example, special provision for maternity leave for women from the scope of the Directive. Dismissal on grounds of pregnancy constitutes direct discrimination under the Directive (Case C-177/88 *Dekker v VJV Centrum* (1990)) and it cannot be justified by comparing the state of pregnancy with an illness or disability (Case C-32/93 *Webb v EMO Air Cargo (UK) Ltd* (1995)). Dismissal on grounds of absence due to pregnancy related illness does not offend the provisions of the Directive, however, since a man could also be dismissed for overlong absence due to illness (Case C-179/88 *Handels-og Kontorfunktionaerernes Forbund i Danmark v Dansk Arbejdsgiverforening for Danfoss* (1990)).

26.3.3 Positive discrimination in European Community law

The Equal Treatment Directive does not prohibit measures designed to remove existing inequalities which affect women's opportunities, even though they might amount to discrimination in favour of women. These measures, however, must not overstep the mark – in Case C-450/93 *Kalanke v Freie Hansestadt Bremen* (1996), the Court of Justice held that national rules requiring the appointment of female candidates over equally qualified male candidates were in breach of the directive. On the other hand, if the Member State is careful to include in its positive discrimination programmes provisions which allow men to get the post if particular characteristics tilt the balance back in their favour, then they will not fall foul of the directive (Case C-409/95 *Marschall v Nordrhein-Westfalen* (1997)). However, these cases were decided before the Amsterdam revisions to the EC Treaty took effect. Article 141 was amended to include the following provision:

> With a view to ensuring full equality in practice between men and women in working life, the principle of equal treatment shall not prevent any Member State from maintaining or adopting measures providing for specific advantages in order to make it easier for the under-represented sex to pursue a vocational activity or to prevent or compensate for disadvantages in professional careers.

26.3.4 Discrimination on grounds of nationality in European Community law

Article 12 (formerly Art 6) of the EC Treaty provides that:

> Within the scope of application of this Treaty, and without prejudice to any special provisions contained therein, any discrimination on grounds of nationality shall be prohibited.

This is a central element in Community law which is based on the rationale that the internal market will not function correctly until all borders, financial, physical and psychological, between Member States are removed. Discrimination on grounds of nationality can only form the basis of a complaint under the EC Treaty and directives if the complainant is an EC national; no protection is afforded to third country members within the European Union. The protection against this form of discrimination is carried forward by the EC Treaty's provisions on free movement of workers, establishment and services (Art 39, 43 and 49). These Treaty provisions and relevant directives all have direct effect (see above, 7.9.2) and, therefore, provide an important protection at a domestic level against discrimination. However, it is important to remember that, originally, these rights could only apply in the context of workers. Discrimination on grounds of nationality was outside the scope of Community law if it had nothing to do with economic activity. The claimant, in order to attract the protection of the Court of Justice against discriminatory practices, had either be a worker or a member of a worker's family. However, the Court of Justice has extended the principle of non-discrimination to cover a broader category of EC nationals, such as the recipients of services (see below, Chapter 27).

26.3.5 Equality as a general principle of European Community law

The EC Treaty expressly prohibits discrimination between producers and consumers in achieving its objectives under the Common Agricultural Policy (Art 34). Equality is also a *general principle* behind the Court of Justice's review of the legality of Community measures and there have been a number of successful appeals to this principle in disputes between producers. Aids or subsidies may be granted to one group of producers at the expense of another, or levies imposed on an agricultural sector which those affected may feel has a disproportionate impact on them. In Cases C-103 and 145/77 *Royal Scholten-Honig Holdings Ltd v Intervention Board for Agricultural Produce* (1978), glucose producers challenged the imposition of levies on their production that were used to finance subsidies for sugar producers. This, they argued, was in breach of the general principle of equality between producers in competition with one another. The court upheld their complaint and annulled the regulations imposing the levy.

As stated above, the general principle of equality as developed and applied by the Court of Justice is only relevant in cases involving areas of Community competence. In the wake of the BSE scare and the consequent European Union ban on beef products being exported from the UK, the Ministry of Agriculture, Fisheries and Farming (MAFF) set up a 'beef stocks transfer scheme' to provide financial aid to beef exporters with their own slaughtering activities. Those exporters who did not run their own facilities challenged MAFF's scheme in judicial review proceedings, saying that they were being discriminated against in breach of the equality principle in Community law. In *R v Ministry of Agriculture, Fisheries and Food ex p First City Trading* (1997), the High Court ruled that, since this case concerned matters internal to the UK only, general principles of Community law could not apply.

26.4 Discrimination on the basis of sexual orientation

There are, as yet, no clear precedents for prohibiting discrimination on grounds of sexual orientation. Of all the systems of law, the case law of the European Court of Human Rights has gone furthest in this respect. As early as 1982, that court ruled, in *Dudgeon v UK* (1982), that sexual orientation should be immune from interference by the State, and the European Commission of Human Rights has declared admissible a complaint that the higher age of consent for male homosexuals in England than that applicable to heterosexuals constitutes a violation of Art 14 of the ECHR in conjunction with Art 8. In the Commission's view, this amounted to discrimination on the basis of sex, because only homosexual *males* under the age of 18 were prohibited from engaging in sexual conduct according to their orientation (*Sutherland v UK* (1996)). There are also cases pending before the Commission questioning the basis for dismissing gays and lesbians from the armed forces (*Lustig Prean v UK* (1996)).

The Human Rights Act 1998 requires courts in the UK to interpret legislation so far as possible to comply with the ECHR and relevant case law from the European Court of Human Rights (see above, 19.10.1). Before the ECHR became part of national law, the Court of Appeal considered whether a homosexual partner of a deceased tenant could take over the tenancy under the Rent Act 1977 which limited such succession to persons who had lived with the original tenant 'as wife or husband' or that they were a member of his 'family' (*Fitzpatrick v Sterling Housing Association Ltd* (1998)). The majority of the court dismissed the application, holding that the term 'family' was to be construed in its popular contemporary sense, taking into account prevailing social attitudes. Family, in this light, meant an entity which bound together 'persons of the opposite sex cohabiting as man and wife'. In a strongly worded dissent, Ward LJ held that the exclusion of same sex couples from the protection of the Rent Act proclaimed the message that society judges their relationship to be 'less worthy of respect, concern and consideration than the relationship between members of the opposite sex'. He noted that a number of European countries had started permitting same sex couples to enter into agreements regulating their property and inheritance rights just as unmarried heterosexual couples can do, and that the US Supreme Court had recently held that the view of a family should include 'two adult lifetime partners whose relationship is long term and characterised by an emotional and financial commitment and interdependence' . In the context of the UK Rent Act, which is designed to protect tenants and their families from sudden eviction, the concept of the family should move with the times:

> The trend is to shift the focus, or the emphasis, from structure and components to function and appearance – what a family is rather than what it does, or, putting it another way, a family is what a family does [*per* Ward LJ].

While this was a minority judgment, the emphasis given to the applicant's 'constitutional right to equal treatment under the law' suggests that the claims of minorities will not be discounted so readily in future cases marking out the scope of concepts such as the 'family'. More recently, in an employment case, the Court of Appeal upheld an argument that discrimination against a male homosexual could provide grounds for a claim under the Sex Discrimination Act 1976 (*Smith v Gardner Merchant Ltd* (1998)). However, such a claim could only be made out if the complainant could show that a gay woman would have been treated differently. In this sense, no new ground was broken by this judgment, since discrimination on the basis of homosexuality alone would not be illegal under the Act if a homosexual woman in a similar position would be equally prejudiced.

26.4.1 Homosexuals

In Case C-249/96 *Grant v South-West Trains Ltd* (1998), the applicant claimed that the refusal by her employer to grant travel concessions to her female partner, on the basis that the concessions were not available to partners of the same sex , constituted discrimination based on sex, contrary to the provisions of Community law on equal pay for men and women. The Court of Justice held however that this claim of sex discrimination had not been made out since South-West Trains also refused travel concessions to partners of gay men. Given the lack of consensus amongst Member States in this area, the Court did not feel in a position to extend the protection of Community law to this type of discrimination. It therefore remains for the Community to pass legislation under Art 13 of the amended EC Treaty (see above, 26.4) to give the court sufficient legal basis for outlawing discrimination on the grounds of sexual orientation.

26.4.2 Transsexuals

Individuals who wish to obtain recognition for their change of gender raise difficult issues in EC law since such recognition often involves positive obligations on Member States in an area where there is little international consensus. Nevertheless, in Case C-13/94 *P v S and Cornwall County Council* (1996), the Court of Justice ruled that the protection offered by the Equal Treatment Directive 76/207 covered discrimination against an individual wishing to undergo gender re-assignment. Rejecting the argument of the UK that the employer would have dismissed P if P had been a woman and had undergone an operation to become a man, the Court indicated that the principle of equal treatment would no longer be based on the comparison between a female and a male employee:

> ... where a person is dismissed on the ground that he or she intends to undergo or has undergone gender re-assignment, he or she is treated unfavourably by comparison with persons of the sex to which he or she was deemed to belong before undergoing gender re-assignment.

In response to this judgment, UK law was changed by the Sex Discrimination (Gender Re-assignment) Regulations 1999 (SI 1999/1102) which make direct discrimination against transsexuals contrary to the SDA 1975 in some circumstances.

26.5   Assessment

The scope of anti-discrimination is a fast developing area of human rights law. However, there remain some inadequacies. Individual citizens may still be discriminated against on grounds of age or health (if that does not amount to disability). The scope of Art 14 is limited to the rights set out in the ECHR and

Community laws on discrimination are restricted to matters within Community competence. The provision for extended grounds for anti-discrimination measures in the Community field in the EC Treaty raises the possibility that issues not presently covered by Community law – such as disability – might in future be encompassed by the Court of Justice within its general principles of equality and non-discrimination. However, no amount of directives and regulations under the amended EC Treaty on a number of grounds of discrimination will prove of much assistance to people whose cases raise no Community law element. The protection of EC Treaty rights, such as the right to free movement, only applies to people operating within the open labour market. Therefore, as things stand at present, disabled people, for example, who are employed within specially targeted training or vocational schemes, are denied the status of 'worker' under Community law and cannot enforce the rights associated with that status because national schemes adopted to help disabled people back into work do not constitute an 'effective and genuine economic activity' (Case C-344/87 *Bettray v Staatsecretaris van Justitie* (1989)). This approach has been confirmed recently by the Court in Case C-199/95 *Kremzow v Austria* (1997), where it said that, 'where national legislation is concerned with a situation which ... does not fall within the field of application of Community law, the Court cannot, in a reference for a preliminary ruling, give the interpretative guidance necessary for the national court to determine whether the national legislation is in conformity with the fundamental rights whose observance the Court ensures, such as those deriving in particular from the ECHR'.

EQUALITY

Equality is a cornerstone of democracy. To establish real equality it is necessary, not only to ensure equal participation at election time, but to guarantee to each individual that his or her views or conduct will be given equal status to those of other members of society.

Equality of treatment means that people in similar circumstances should be treated similarly and any differences should be objectively justified. Equality also demands that different cases should be treated differently.

Prohibition of discrimination

Statutes have been passed to restrict discriminatory practices in the context of race, sex and, lately, disability. Discrimination on grounds of religion is prohibited in Northern Ireland.

Race relations

The Race Relations Act 1976 prohibits discrimination on grounds of colour, nationality or ethnic or national origins. It applies to employment, provision of goods and services to the public, and certain types of private clubs. The Commission for Racial Equality is the statutory watchdog.

Sex equality

The Sex Discrimination Act 1975 prohibits unequal treatment between men and women in the context of employment and provision of goods and services to the public. The Equal Opportunities Commission is the statutory watchdog.

Physical capacity

The Disability Discrimination Act 1995 prohibits discrimination on grounds of disability in the context of employment, provision of goods and services and in the provision of property.

Equality under the ECHR

Article 14 requires that the rights and freedoms in the ECHR must be available without discrimination on a number of grounds. The Strasbourg Court will scrutinise most closely those laws and practices of signatory States that discriminate on grounds of sex, race and legitimacy of children. Article 14 is a procedural right only and must be pleaded in tandem with another substantive ECHR right.

Justified discrimination

An employer or service provider may get away with a discriminatory practice if he or she is able to prove objective grounds for it.

Positive discrimination, or affirmative action programmes, are discriminatory on their face and may fall foul of any of the above statutes unless the practice comes within one of the limited grounds authorised by the legislation.

Remedies

Individuals may sue under these Acts in industrial tribunals for employment cases and in the ordinary courts for all other forms of discrimination; damages are at large, which means they can claim compensation for injury to feelings as well as financial loss.

Equality in European Community law

Community law prohibits discrimination on grounds of sex and nationality. Originally, these prohibitions related to 'economic actors' only, to ensure a level playing field for goods and services in the internal market, but the Luxembourg Court has extended the equality requirements to other areas, where, for example, people who are benefiting from tourism services in other Member States are discriminated against. The Amsterdam Treaty now provides a basis for legislation against discrimination in any area of Community competence on a wide range of grounds, including disability and sexual orientation

Sex discrimination

Community law in this area only applies in the context of employment. Women are entitled to equal treatment and equal pay to men; this includes benefits as well as remuneration. Transsexuals may not be discriminated against on the basis of a gender re-assignment operation; on the other hand, employees in same sex partnership relationships may not rely on Community law for equal provision of benefits.

Justified discrimination

It is possible to justify discriminatory practices, but only on the very narrowly defined grounds set out in Community law and only if sex of the worker is a determining factor. The Luxembourg Court will scrutinise very closely any affirmative action measure; if it is unnecessarily unfavourable towards male workers, it may be in breach of Community discrimination law.

Equality as a general principle of law

EC law prohibits discrimination between producers and consumers; in addition, the Court of Justice, as part of its 'general principles of law', will rule out any legislative measure that favours one group of producers against another.

Nationality

Community law prohibits discrimination on grounds of nationality. Only EC nationals crossing over inter-State boundaries may rely this prohibition; it does not extend to cover the rights of nationals within Member States, nor can it be relied upon by non-EC nationals.

Sexual orientation

This ground has not yet become a firm basis for action under any national or international prohibition of discrimination. Strasbourg jurisprudence prohibits the criminalisation of homosexual activities, but Community law and the Sex Discrimination Act 1975 may only be invoked by homosexuals if a gay person of the opposite sex would not have been similarly treated. Discrimination on grounds of homosexuality *per se* is, therefore, not yet illegal.

CHAPTER 27

FREEDOM OF MOVEMENT

27.1 Introduction

Freedom of movement within the territory of a Nation State is a fundamental right in a democracy; without such a freedom, we cannot be said to be truly free to make independent choices. Restrictions on individuals' movement across international boundaries are more generally accepted, partly due to historical circumstance, partly due to the need for controls to deal with advances in global travel. This chapter deals with the ability of people to move within and across State frontiers.

The law on freedom of movement has developed in three main areas: immigration; the rights of asylum seekers; and the rights of citizens of the European Union to move across inter-State boundaries.

There is no right to be free of border controls when moving into and out of the UK. This level of restriction on the freedom of movement of non-nationals and, to a certain extent, of nationals as well is due in part to the geography of the UK. In March 1992, the then Home Secretary suggested that this could have the effect of liberating residents of the UK from other controls common in landlocked countries:

> Our island geography enables us to place the main weight of our immigration control at ports of entry. For us, that is by far the most effective way of doing it. It also means that we can avoid the need for intrusive in-country controls such as sanctions on employers who employ illegal immigrants or identity cards or random police checks, which other countries without effective means of controlling their borders find necessary [(1992) HC Deb Vol 73 col 31].

The Secretary of State's speech does not give the whole picture; in fact, employers who disregard the visa status of their employees may be subject to sanctions if it comes to light that the employee in question has overstayed or did not have right of entry in the first place.

Immigration control is one of the most controversial areas of government policy. Feldman suggests that if we take as the litmus test of a democracy the mood of the general public, it may be that, in the field of immigration control, 'rights' (of free movement) tend in one direction, 'democracy' in another (Feldman, D, *Civil Liberties and Human Rights in England and Wales*, 1993, Oxford: OUP, p 349). On the other hand, a generous spirited approach towards the admission of foreigners has allowed into the country people such as Marx, Engels, Garibaldi and Lenin. As Robertson has observed, some of their modern counterparts would today be deported as undesirable aliens

(Robertson, G, *Freedom, the Individual and the Law*, 7th edn, 1993, London: Penguin, p 387).

As far as asylum seekers are concerned, the UK is bound in international law by the provisions of the United Nations Convention relating to the Status of Refugees 1951. It has been said that they enjoy a right 'to humanity', 'anterior to all law'. So basic are the human rights here at issue that it cannot be necessary to resort to the European Convention on Human Rights (ECHR) to take note of their violation (*R v Secretary of State for Social Security ex p Joint Council for the Welfare of Immigrants* (1997)). International law on the rights of asylum seekers falls outside the scope of this book, though the recognition of these basic rights in the procedures governing asylum decisions are discussed in this chapter (see below, 27.5).

Freedom of movement has been given a much more significant role to play in the hierarchy of rights in the UK by accession to the EU. Free movement of persons is one of the fundamental freedoms protected by EC law (see above, Chapter 7). The UK's obligation under these provisions of Community law has not yet had a significant impact on rights of entry to non-EC nationals to the UK. In fact, it has been argued that British immigration law and practice have signally failed to reflect Community law since joining the Community (see Vincenzi, C, 'European citizenship and free movement rights in the UK' [1995] PL 259). The European Court of Justice has found the UK to be in breach of its obligations on several occasions, particularly where the Home Office purports to deport someone on grounds of public policy. Advocate General Jacobs said in an opinion in 1992 that a Community national who goes to another State is entitled:

> ... to assume that, wherever he goes to earn his living in the European Community, he will be treated in accordance with a common code of fundamental values, in particular, those laid down in the ECHR. In other words, he is entitled to say *civis europus sum*, and to invoke that status in order to oppose any violation of his fundamental rights [Case C-168/91 *Konstantinidis v Stadt Altensteig* (1993)].

It is, therefore, to Community law that we will have to turn to find a developed jurisprudence regarding the right to free movement and it may be that Community law in the future will prove the source of that right in respect of the movement of people who do not qualify for EU citizenship now. As Vincenzi says:

> In a State without a written constitution, and without a constitutional court, the burden of giving effect to the rights of an estimated eight million EU citizens who annually visit this country falls entirely on those individuals in the ordinary courts and tribunals, usually without the assistance of legal aid. The fact that other Member States have a similarly undistinguished record in this field cannot justify this country's failure [p 274].

27.1.1 The scope of freedom of movement

Although there is no absolute right of non-nationals to enter the country, the laws on immigration and citizenship do not draw a clear line between nationals and aliens. At any given time, there are large numbers of people in this country with limited rights of entry and abode who fall between these two categories. It is the manner in which these limited rights are granted which gives rise to most litigation in this area, challenging the Home Office's standards of fairness and observation of procedural rights. Several other rights are often taken into consideration in this litigation, such as the right to life or privacy. Although the ECHR does not impose obligations on signatory States to allow entry to non-nationals (*Abdulaziz, Cabalas and Balkandali v UK* (1985)), the rights set out in the ECHR may be enjoyed by nationals and non-nationals alike. This provides certain important safeguards to aliens who face deportation or whose asylum applications are turned down. There is a Protocol to the ECHR – not yet ratified by the UK – which guarantees freedom of movement of lawful residents and the rights of entry of nationals into their own country (Protocol 4 to the ECHR). This Protocol also prohibits expulsion of nationals and the collective expulsion of aliens.

The government also has a limited power to curb the movement of its own nationals by restricting them to one part or other of the UK. The following sections will explore the extent to which the power to make exclusion orders under prevention of terrorism legislation infringes basic rights of movement. In addition, the movement of nationals and lawful residents alike are restricted by a range of restrictions imposed by the civil and criminal law, in particular, trespass.

27.2 Movement out of the UK

British people think of their freedom of movement in and out of the UK as dependent on having a valid passport. In fact, the grant of a passport is an exercise of prerogative power (see above, 2.4.3) which was based originally on the need to protect British subjects abroad; far from being a condition of travel out of the country, it was a document issued to those who wished to leave the country (freely) to ensure their safety. In fact, the right to leave the country is one of the rare breed of rights that were protected in statutory form in English law long before the Human Rights Act 1998; the Magna Carta guaranteed the right of individuals to travel abroad as early as 1215. The only measure that prevented movement out of the country was the writ of *ne exeat regno*, under which the Crown could prevent someone from leaving the realm when the interests of the State demanded it. Although the writ (a formal order of the court) still exists, its significance has been reduced by modern practicalities of travel. Since all countries require possession of a valid passport before allowing entry to a traveller, it is not in the carriers' interests to allow a passenger to embark without a passport. Indeed, one commentator has observed that the most effective method of limiting asylum applications is through imposing heavy fines (£2,000 per passenger) on the airlines and shipping companies which carry fugitives whose entry documents are not correct:

> The government has in effect 'contracted out' immigration control of refugees to the airlines, which have avoided financial penalties by refusing to fly refugees and in several cases by removing them from passenger planes by tricks or force [Robertson, G, *Freedom, the Individual and the Law*, 7th edn, 1993, London: Penguin, p 412].

Although carriers are legally obliged to ensure that they bring into the UK only passengers with valid identity and entry clearance documents, there is still no legal requirement for a passenger to possess a passport before leaving the country. In the light of this it ironic that national law obliges people to be in possession of a British passport in order to prove British citizenship *within* the UK. There is no statutory appeal against a decision by the Home Office to refuse or revoke a passport but, in judicial review proceedings, an applicant may challenge a decision on the basis that no reasons have been given (*R v Foreign Secretary ex p Everett* (1989)). There is, on the other hand, no legal entitlement to a passport (see Finlay CJ in *Attorney General v X* (1992)).

27.3   Movement into the UK

As was noted above, the majority of cases in this area are taken by non-nationals who wish to challenge immigration officers' decisions to refuse entry, or the Home Office's decision to deport. Before considering the case law, it is first necessary to set out in a very basic form the complex distinctions laid down by UK law between different types of nationals and non-nationals, or aliens.

27.3.1 Nationals

Under the British Nationality Act 1981, the right of abode in the UK is primarily enjoyed by British citizens and their offspring, grandchildren or parents. Entry and residence are also allowed to some Commonwealth citizens. There are other complex categories of British citizenship in the Act which do not entail an automatic right of abode, including the following:

- British protected persons;
- citizens of the Republic of Ireland;
- British dependent territories citizens: these are people who were citizens of the UK and colonies before the British Nationality Act came into force but only had a connection with a British dependent territory, such as Gibraltar;

- British overseas citizens;

- residents of Hong Kong who became British nationals (overseas) citizens at the end of British rule in 1997;

- those born in an independent Commonwealth country before 1949: these are British subjects without citizenship.

The rules and procedures governing the entry of citizens of EC Member States are dealt with below, 27.4.

27.3.2 Non-nationals

The category of the British Nationality Act 1981 which most clearly excludes citizenship and with it the right of entry and abode is the residual provision referring to 'aliens'. Even without any prospect of achieving British citizenship by naturalisation or other means, some non-nationals may qualify for limited entry under the Immigration Rules 1994 which allow in students, patients seeking private medical treatment, people with work permits and people wishing to establish themselves as investors (the present minimum is £1 m).

However they seek entry into this country, non-nationals have to comply with procedures and qualifications laid down by the immigration legislation, not all of which is subject to judicial control. Short term visitors and students, for example, may find that they have no redress from a refusal of an immigration officer to grant entry on the basis of misinformation. Some decisions made by immigration authorities to refuse entry, impose conditions or curtail leave to enter have to be accepted without further hearing. Those decisions that are appealable fall broadly into the following four categories:

(a) refusal of entry;

(b) decisions on deportation and removal (see below, 27.5);

(c) refusals to extend leave, the imposition of conditions and admission and the curtailment of leave;

(d) asylum decisions (these are appealable to a Special Adjudicator (see below, 27.9)).

Appeals against these are heard in the first instance by a board of Home Office 'Adjudicators'. It is possible to appeal with leave from the Adjudicator to the Immigration Appeal Tribunal and, from there, on a point of law, to the High Court. In most instances, applicants can only pursue their appeals from abroad, and even asylum seekers may be removed from the country to pursue their claims if they can be sent to a safe third country (see below, 27.8). Judicial review is available of the Home Secretary's decisions in these cases but permission will be refused if the applicant has not exhausted all their avenues of appeal (*R v Secretary of State for the Home Office ex p Swati* (1986)). As with all judicial review challenges, applicants complaining about deportation or removal decisions have to base their challenge on the three grounds for judicial review: legality; rationality; and procedural fairness (see above, Chapter 11). The courts have, however, reserved their power to apply a stricter level of scrutiny to judicial review applications in asylum decisions where the applicant's life is at stake (*R v Secretary of State for the Home Department ex p Bugdaycay* (1987), see above, 15.5.1).

Clearly, there is a range of decisions on residence permits and citizenship that remains outside these categories. This does not mean to say that the court's supervisory jurisdiction is excluded altogether. Under the British Nationality Act 1981, the Home Secretary used to refuse the issue of a naturalisation certificate without giving reasons. The Act also states that his decision should not be reviewable in any court of law. However, in *R v Secretary of State for the Home Department ex p Fayed* (1997), the Court of Appeal held that the Home Secretary had a duty to act fairly by affording applicants who have been refused citizenship an opportunity to make representations on any matters of concern relating to their application. The Government has indicated in its White Paper (*Fairer, Faster and Firmer: A Modern Approach to Immigration and Asylum*, Cm 4018, 1998) that applicants for British citizenship will now always be told why their application was rejected. The existence of statutory rights of access to some forms of personal data (see above, 23.2.7), coupled with increased computerisation of immigration and nationality casework will also increase the availability of information to applicants.

27.4   Involuntary removal from the UK

The government has wide discretion under the Immigration Act 1971 to deport individuals with no or limited rights of residence. Grounds for deportation are:

(a) breach of residence conditions;

(b) entry obtained by deception;

(c) family member subject to a deportation order;

(d) commission of a criminal offence;

(e) if the Home Secretary deems that a deportation order would be conducive to the public good.

Such decisions have been made in relation to persons threatening national security, or where the individuals concerned are members of cults or religious groups which are generally disapproved of in this country (there is a long line of decisions either refusing entry to or deporting members of the Church of Scientology on 'public good' grounds, see, for example, *Van Duyn v Home Office* (1974)). It was mentioned above that appeals against deportation orders on national security grounds are now heard by a special Immigration Appeals

Commission and there is a right of appeal on a point of law to the Court of Appeal.

On occasion, deportation has been challenged on the basis that the authorities have used it as a form of disguised extradition. If, for example, the person in question has committed an offence which could be described as 'political', he or she may not be extradited. In *R v Brixton Prison Governor ex p Soblen* (1963), the decision of the Home Secretary to deport S for public good reasons was challenged on the basis that the deportation order was issued for another purpose – to comply with the US's request for the applicant's return. The Court of Appeal rejected this argument on the basis that this purpose did not undermine the validity of the Home Secretary's order. The Court held that the Home Secretary could act for a plurality of purposes.

There is no specific provision in the main body of the ECHR dealing with the right to freedom of movement. However, the right not to be subject to inhuman or degrading treatment under Art 3 has often been relied upon either to prevent deportation or to seek compensation for the deportation, without a proper hearing, of refugees to their State of origin where they face persecution. As early as 1978, the European Commission of Human Rights ruled that the refusal of entry to Asians fleeing persecution in Uganda amounted to inhuman and degrading treatment. In the Commission's view, the immigration rules in operation at that time were racially motivated, since they targeted, in particular, people in the applicants' position, despite the fact that they held British passports:

> ... differential treatment of a group of persons on the basis of race might be capable of constituting degrading treatment in circumstances where differential treatment on some other ground, such as language, would raise no such question [*East African Asians* case (1973)].

The *Chahal* judgment (discussed further below, 27.8) limits the ability of States to rely on national security considerations when deporting an asylum applicant who faces a well founded risk of persecution in the State of destination. Chahal was a prominent Indian Sikh who had been arrested for suspected involvement in Sikh terrorism in the UK. The Home Secretary decided that there were sufficient grounds to justify a deportation order. Chahal argued that there was a strong probability that he would be exposed to persecution in India due to his high profile position in the Sikh separatist movement; nevertheless, his application for asylum was turned down since the Secretary of State held that that the question whether he qualified for refugee status became irrelevant once the decision to deport him had been made. The European Court of Human Rights ruled that, in view of the potential risk he faced in the destination State, any deportation order issued against him would breach his rights under Art 3 not to be subject to torture or inhuman treatment.

Deportation of someone suffering from a terminal illness to a country where there is insufficient medical care may also amount to inhuman and degrading treatment in breach of Art 3 (*D v UK* (1997)). The applicant, a convicted drugs smuggler who was in the final stages of AIDS, was to be deported to St Kitts where there was no adequate medical treatment, shelter or family support. The court held that the duty to secure to the applicant the guarantees contained in Art 3 engaged the liability of the State in this case. Application of Art 3 is, therefore, no longer confined to situations where the individual to be expelled faces a real risk of being exposed to forms of treatment which are intentionally inflicted by the receiving State (see, also, the Commission's admissibility decision in *BB v France* (1998)).

The threshold for inhuman and degrading treatment is high. Breaking up a family will not breach Art 3, but it may amount to an infringement of the right to family life under Art 8. In order to rely on Art 8, non-nationals must satisfy the court that they have established family connections over a long period of time in the deporting State (*Beldjoudi v France* (1992)). Even before incorporation of the ECHR the rights of entry in this country were altered to include unmarried partners in a relationship akin to marriage.

27.5   Movement within the UK

The most important restriction on this freedom of movement is the ability of the Home Secretary to issue exclusion orders under the Prevention of Terrorism (Temporary Provisions) Act 1989 against anyone suspected of being involved in terrorist activities. This means that a person may be prevented from entering Great Britain (see above, 2.4) and vice versa if it appears expedient to the Home Secretary for the prevention of acts of terrorism connected with Northern Ireland. These orders are not subject to any form of independent review by a judicial body and the very situation which gave rise to this legislation is fraught with sensitive security issues. This allows the Home Secretary to impose exclusion orders without giving reasons (for fear that important sources of information might be betrayed). It is possible to seek judicial review of a decision to impose an order, but national courts tend to accept the government's defence that it is necessary on grounds of national security. In *R v Secretary of State for the Home Department ex p McQuillan* (1995), the applicant challenged an exclusion order against him because the Home Secretary had failed to provide reasons justifying the order. The application for judicial review was based on breach of the principle of procedural fairness. The court, although sympathetic to this argument, had to accept as conclusive the Home Secretary's statement that national security prevented the disclosure of reasons. The exclusion order could not, therefore, be ruled to be unlawful on that basis.

27.6 Freedom of movement in the European Union

One of the original purposes of the EC Treaty was to ensure that all obstacles to the free movement of economic actors, such as employees and service providers and their goods and capital, were removed. The purposes have now broadened beyond these economic aims and citizenship of the European Union has been created:

Article 17 [formerly Art 8]

1 Citizenship of the Union is hereby established. Every person holding the nationality of a Member State shall be a citizen of the Union. Citizenship of the Union shall complement and not replace national citizenship.

2 Citizens of the Union shall enjoy the rights conferred by this Treaty and shall be subject to the duties imposed thereby.

Article 18 [formerly Art 8a]

1 Every citizen of the Union shall have the right to move and reside freely within the territory of the Member States, subject to the limitations and conditions laid down in this Treaty and by the measures adopted to give it effect.

2 The Council may adopt provisions with a view to facilitating the exercise of the rights referred to in paragraph 1; save as otherwise provided in this Treaty, the Council shall act in accordance with the procedure referred to in Art 251. The Council shall act unanimously throughout this procedure.

As we have noted before, rights and freedoms under Community law only apply to EC nationals and those third country nationals with recognised links to citizens of EU Member States, such as spouses. Even these applicants have to satisfy certain conditions before they can claim the protection of Community law; individuals who are not engaged in some economic activity and who do not qualify under one of the limited directives on residence discussed below are not able to bring claims under Community law. In addition, it is necessary for applicants to establish a 'jurisdictional link' between their case and Community law. The Court of Justice will not make preliminary rulings on questions which are internal to Member States (Case C-175/78 *R v Saunders* (1979)). For this reason, claims have been made to the recently adopted right to citizenship in the EC Treaty in matters relating to restrictions on movement within the borders of a Member State (see below, 27.7).

EC nationals and their spouses are not the only ones to be affected by developments at a Community level. One of the consequences of the Schengen Agreement, signed in 1985, was that, once a non-EC national is lawfully resident within one Member State, he or she may travel unobstructed by border controls within the EU (with the exception of the UK and Ireland, which have reserved the right to operate their own border checks). However, a side effect of this arrangement is that asylum seekers are passed from one country to the other with no evenhanded determination of their claims. The hardships caused by what has come to be known as 'fortress Europe' were illustrated vividly in the case of Kenyan asylum seekers who arrived in the UK in early 1998 having been given 'notices to quit' by the Belgian authorities, where they had arrived ((1998) *The Times*, 26 March). They were the latest apparent victims of 'dumping' which the Home Office claimed had happened to more than 900 asylum seekers from Kenya and the former Yugoslavia since the beginning of 1998. The proposals for harmonisation of Member States' rules on asylum under the Amsterdam Treaty will be discussed below.

27.6.1 Economic actors

Community law protects free movement in a number of ways. Article 12 of the EC Treaty (formerly 6) prohibits discrimination on the basis of nationality. Articles 39 (formerly 48) protects the freedom of movement of workers. This includes the right to travel to find work. Article 43 (formerly 52) protects the right of EC nationals to establish their business in other Member States. This right applies to self-employed persons and to companies, and Art 49 (formerly 59) applies to services; individuals and companies are free to provide services across EC borders and EC nationals have the right under this Article to travel to receive services.

Articles 43 and 49 have been followed by various forms of secondary legislation (Directives 89/48 and 92/51) requiring Member States to recognise the qualifications of other EC nationals and restricting the imposition of re-qualification rules.

EC nationals claiming lawful entry and abode under Arts 39, 43 and 49 may avail themselves of the provisions of Directive 68/1612 which entitles them to 'family reunion'; in other words, they may be joined by their spouse, dependent children, parents, grandparents and, in certain circumstances, anyone who was living under the same roof as them in their State of origin. This is an important accessory to the right to freedom of movement because there must be no major disincentives that would prevent, say, a German national from taking a job in France because members of his family would lose out on valuable benefits in their new place of residence.

27.6.2 Other European Community nationals

Family members of EC workers may avail themselves of the same benefits and educational facilities available to nationals of the host State (Regulation 68/1612, Art 12: rights of workers' dependants to education on the same terms of children of host State nationals).

Article 18 (formerly 8a) of the EC Treaty enshrines the concept of European citizenship (see above). Since this Article refers to 'citizens', rather than workers, the freedom of movement it bestows is no longer restricted to economic actors. The implications of this provision are considered below, 17.7.

In addition to the Treaty provisions and Regulation 68/1612, the Council has passed three directives which guarantee the freedom of movement (that is, granting of residence permits) of non-workers and their families. Directive 90/366 grants rights to students undergoing vocational training; Directive 90/365 entitles self-employed people who have ceased to work certain rights of residence; and Directive 90/364, a catch-all piece of legislation governing all those persons who do not already enjoy a right in EC law, guarantees a right of residence for EC nationals who are of independent means and have private medical insurance. This Directive is designed to ensure free movement of individuals within the Community who will not present a financial burden to the host State.

The freedom of EC nationals under Art 50 to move in order to provide services also covers the freedom to receive services. This has the consequence of extending the application of Community law to many areas which would not appear to be within the commercial framework of the original Treaty objectives. In Case C-286/82 *Luisi and Carbone v Ministerio del Tesoro* (1984), L and C were fined for exporting excessive amounts of capital out of Italy. They invoked Art 60 (now 50), claiming that they would have been protected by EC law if they had wanted this money to pay for services. The Court of Justice held that that the freedom to go to the State where the service provider is established is a corollary of the express freedom in Art 60 (now 50) of the service provider to move to the recipient's State. This freedom to receive services, therefore, applies to a wide range of people, such as tourists, persons receiving medical treatment and persons travelling for the purposes of education or business, although even these wide categories have been further extended by the recent ruling on this issue in *Bickel v Italy* (1998). Here, the court ruled that the scope of the provisions on freedom of services could cover situations where the applicants 'intend or are likely to receive services', a definition which arguably applies to such a wide variety of situations that the original link with the Treaty freedoms has been eroded away.

The broad principle of non-discrimination has also been responsible for the extension of Community law into areas unrelated to employment or services. France used to have compensation laws which limited payments for criminal injury to victims who were resident in France or who held French nationality. In Case C-186/87 *Cowan v French Treasury* (1989), C, a visitor to France, was denied State compensation for injuries incurred in a criminal assault. The Court of Justice, referring to Art 6 (now 12), observed:

> When EC law guarantees a natural person the freedom to go to another
> Member State, the protection of that person from harm in the Member State in
> question, on the same basis as that of nationals and persons residing there, is a
> corollary of that freedom of movement.

Thus, it is not only lawful residence as a citizen of a Member State, but lawful
presence as a visitor which furnishes the basis for a claim under the non-
discrimination provisions of Community law. In *Bickel*, the court allowed a
claim under Art 6 of the EC Treaty by two EC nationals who faced criminal
proceedings in northern Italy. There was a local regulation which permitted
German speaking residents to be tried in German, but they did not qualify
since they were not lawfully resident in the area. They complained that this
violated the principle of non-discrimination on the basis of nationality. The
Court upheld their claim. It considered that their presence in the host State
indicated that they were intending or likely to receive services; this then
brought them within the personal scope of the EC Treaty and entitled them to
rely on Art 6 to challenge the discriminatory measure in question. A similar
position was taken by the Court in Case C-85/96 *Martinez Sala v Germany*
(1998).

27.6.3 Derogations from rights of free movement

The rights outlined above are, as always, not absolute. They are subject to the
ability of Member States to refuse entry or restrict the issue of residence
permits on the basis of public policy and health grounds. States may also
refuse permits to those wishing to seek work in sensitive areas of the public
sector which it is permissible to reserve to nationals. However, these
limitations are very strictly policed by the Court of Justice. There is also a
Council Directive (64/221) which specifies the grounds upon which entry and
residence for workers may be restricted. These grounds are similar to those
referred to in the EC Treaty, but they are much more detailed and, therefore, it
is difficult for a Member State to rely on them if the case in question does not
fit into the provision.

In Case 36/95 *Rutili v Minister for the Interior* (1975), R, an Italian married to
a French national, had his temporary residence permit in France endorsed so
that he was only able to travel to certain parts of the country. He suspected
that this was because of his role as a trades union activist and he applied to
the Court of Justice, claiming this was a violation of his right under Art 48
(now 43) of the EC Treaty to travel freely in the Community as a worker. The
Court upheld the claim. They refused to accept the defendant State's
argument that the order was justified on the basis of public policy. Such a
derogation from a fundamental EC Treaty right, they said, would only be
permissible if it was necessary in a democratic society, applying the same
reasoning to State derogations under the EC Treaty as the Court of Human
Rights applies to the permitted derogations under Arts 8–11 of the ECHR.

Since the Court of Human Rights has taken the position that the provisions of the ECHR are relevant considerations in assessing the legitimacy of a Member State's derogation from a particular right in Community law, this means that the Member State's courts must consider whether a restriction on an individual's movement, such as the imposition of a deportation order, would be in breach of any of the rights listed in the ECHR, such as the right of free association under Art 11, or the right to privacy under Art 8, or the right not to be subject to degrading treatment under Art 3. If there is a risk of such a breach, the derogation may not be permissible, even if it is based on one of the grounds for derogation listed in the EC Treaty or in a directive.

In addition to this strict scrutiny of derogations from the right of freedom of movement, Community law requires that the power to restrict movement of EC nationals may only be justified on the basis of personal unacceptability; past membership to a proscribed organisation or a spent offence will not justify any derogation on public policy grounds (Case C-41/74 *Van Duyn v Home Office* (1974)). It was established in Case C-30/77 *R v Pierre Bouchereau* (1977) that a national authority may only rely on the public policy exception if the applicant presents a genuine and sufficiently serious threat affecting one of the fundamental interests of society.

This reasoning applies, of course, only if the case involves a point of Community law; the individual concerned must be an EC national, or the spouse of an EC national, who is a member of one of the protected classes outlined above. Neither the Treaty nor the Convention would be relevant if the case concerns a non-EC citizen (an illegal entrant of Indian nationality could not rely on Art 8, via Community law, to prevent the Home Office from refusing him leave to stay in the UK (*R v Secretary of State for the Home Department ex p Tejinder Singh* (1993)).

27.7 'An ever closer union': rights of movement for European Union citizens

The extent and scope of the rights under Art 18 (formerly 8a) of the EC Treaty – set out above – have been considered by national courts and the Court of Justice. The question is whether this EC Treaty provision confers any new rights in addition to those available under pre-existing EC Treaty provisions and directives. The issue is central to any discussion on free movement because, if Art 18 is a freestanding right, the applicant who wishes to claim the protection of EC law need no longer qualify as an economic actor or bring himself within the scope of one of the limited directives on residence rights discussed above, 27.6. Nor would it be necessary to establish a jurisdictional link with Community law; in other words, the claim to citizenship under Art 18 could exist irrespective of any inter-State element in the State action complained of.

The question first arose in the national courts in relation to exclusion orders, since they involve restrictions on the movement of EC citizens within the borders of a Member State, the UK. When EU citizenship was first created after the Maastricht treaty revisions, the leader of Sinn Fein, a political party in Northern Ireland with an association with the IRA, challenged an exclusion order preventing him from coming to Great Britain to attend a political meeting at the House of Commons (*Secretary of State for the Home Department ex p Adams* (1995)). However, the reference to the Court of Justice for a preliminary ruling was withdrawn after the Home Secretary revoked the exclusion order, so the court did not consider the applicability of Art 18 to wholly internal situations. In *R v Secretary of State for the Home Department ex p Vitale* (1996), the national court took the position that this Article does not create any new rights of free movement, but simply takes the existing rights created by the EC Treaty in its original form, together with all the implementing legislation and related qualifications, as the basis for the new citizenship. This has been borne out to an extent by comments of the Court of Justice to the effect that citizenship of the Union, established by Art 18, was not intended to extend the scope of the EC Treaty to internal situations which have no link with Community law (Case C-64/96 *Ücker v Germany* (1997); and see Vincenzi, C, 'European citizenship and free movement rights' [1995] PL 261).

Another application has been made under Art 7a of the EC Treaty (now Art 14), to the effect that the expressed aim of the Treaty, the abolition of internal frontiers, had been disregarded by the UK who had maintained border controls. The provision states:

Article 14 [formerly Art 7a]

1   The Community shall adopt measures with the aim of progressively establishing the internal market over a period expiring on 31 December 1992, in accordance with the provisions of this Article and of Arts 15, 26, 47(2), 49, 80, 93 and 95 and without prejudice to the other provisions of this Treaty.

2   The internal market shall comprise an area without internal frontiers in which the free movement of goods, persons, services and capital is ensured in accordance with the provisions of this Treaty.

3   The Council, acting by a qualified majority on a proposal from the Commission, shall determine the guidelines and conditions necessary to ensure balanced progress in all the sectors concerned.

The national court ruled that the Article was insufficiently clear and unconditional to produce direct effects between Member States and their subjects (*R v Secretary of State for the Home Department ex p Flynn* (1995)).

Earlier in this chapter, the byzantine provisions of domestic law for the determination of British citizenship were considered. Because of the implications of Community law for immigration, the UK, on entry into the Community in 1972, took the precaution of limiting the definition of a UK national for the purpose of Community law to two categories within the British Nationality Act 1981: British citizens (who have the right of abode in the UK) and Gibraltarians (who come within the category of British dependent territories citizens, who do not necessarily have the right of abode in the UK).

However, if the right of EU citizenship is set to expand, such unilateral action by Member States may soon become a thing of the past. Exclusive competence of Member States in this area is bound to come under pressure, since Member State citizenship is determinative of EU citizenship. The Court of Justice has observed recently that this determination must be carried out with respect for and in accordance with Community law (*Ücker v Germany*), and the question of the competence of Member States to determine citizenship is presently under consideration by the Court after a referral was made in relation to the status of British overseas citizens in *R v Secretary of State for the Home Department ex p Kaur* (1998).

27.8 Asylum

The final part of our inquiry into the right to freedom of movement concerns the assertion of that right by those *in extremis*. The 1999 NATO bombing raids on Yugoslavia following Serbia's attempt to 'clear' the province of Kosovo of ethnic Albanians was only the most recent crisis precipitating the mass movement of people from their homes, seeking safety and protection elsewhere. Not all such disasters are so cataclysmic; asylum seekers may constitute only small groups or individuals, fleeing persecution from countries which have not made it to the front pages of the Western press. The urgent nature of the refugee problem after the end of the Second World War brought about the ratification of the International Convention Relating to the Status of Refugees 1951 (the Refugee Convention). This Convention defines a refugee as one who, 'owing to a well-founded fear of being persecuted for reasons of race, religion, nationality, membership of a particular social group or political opinion', is outside his or her country of nationality and because of such fear is unwilling to return to it.

The Refugee Convention has been adopted into national law by the Asylum and Immigration Appeals Act 1993 and the Asylum and Immigration Act 1996. There is no right to asylum, even by genuine refugees; however, the Refugee Convention obliges signatory States not to subject genuine refugees to refoulement, in other words exposing them to the danger of persecution by returning them to their State of embarkation. In order to qualify for refugee status under the Refugee Convention, an applicant for asylum must satisfy the immigration authorities that there is objective justification for their fear of persecution in their country of nationality.

Even if they are able to cross this threshold by supplying objective evidence to satisfy the authorities that their fear of prosecution is well-founded, applications for asylum often fail to meet the legal criterion for 'membership of a particular social group'. The unifying characteristics of gender, for example, do not, on the whole, go to constitute a 'particular social group' and, therefore, persecution on grounds of sex does not qualify applicants for refugee status, although, if there is some specific consequence of being of a particular gender – women, for example, threatened with flogging on suspicion of adultery – it might be possible to qualify as belonging to a 'particular social group' (*R v Immigration Appeal Tribunal ex p Shah* (1999)).

The Home Office decides upon the merits of asylum applications and the decision of the Home Secretary is appealable to Special Adjudicators whose decision in turn may be reviewed by the Immigration Appeal Tribunal on a point of law. The lawfulness of the detention of immigrants depends, to an extent, on the opportunity of the detainee to have the legality of his detention assessed by an independent tribunal (see above, 21.4.1). The Special Adjudicator, who usually sits in a panel of three ('three wise men') has been said by the European Court of Human Rights to be insufficiently independent of the executive to afford asylum applicants properly independent scrutiny of their claims as required by Art 5(4) of the ECHR (*Chahal v UK* (1997)). The European Court of Human Rights decided in this case that Chahal, a deportee claiming asylum, had not been afforded this opportunity, even though he could have challenged the decision of the Special Adjudicator by way of judicial review. Such a challenge did not, in the view of the Court, provide proper consideration of the merits of the decision. In response to this ruling, the UK has passed legislation under which an independent Commission, including a judge and at least one lawyer, has been appointed to hear appeals in cases of deportation on the grounds of national security (Special Immigration Appeals Commission Act 1997).

Obstacles for asylum seekers

The applicant for asylum faces severe practical as well as legal difficulties. In 1996, a pressure group acting on behalf of asylum seekers challenged social security regulations which deprived such applicants of income support while waiting for their claims and appeals to be decided (*R v Secretary of State for Social Security ex p Joint Council for the Welfare of Immigrants* (1996)). This, said the court, was a breach of their (common law) right to a fair hearing, since it made it impossible for them to stay in the country until their claims were determined and so it was, in practice, unrealistic that they would be able to appeal at all. In response to this judgment, the Government introduced the Asylum and Immigration Act 1996, which effectively deprives asylum seekers of the right to receive various social benefits if they claim asylum after entering the country and not at the port of entry. The courts' reaction to this manoeuvre was to move the burden onto local authorities and ratepayers when, in October 1996, they ruled that s 21 of the National Assistance Act 1948 meant that local authorities had a duty to provide the resources for care and accommodation to asylum seekers who were without other means of support (*R v Hammersmith and Fulham LBC ex p M* (1997)). In its White Paper, *Asylum and Immigration* (Cm 4018, 1998), the Government signalled its intention to resolve this problem by removing cash benefits for asylum seekers and replacing them with benefits in kind – such as food and accommodation – the idea being to remove the main incentives for economic refugees.

The 'third country' rule

The 1996 Act also expedites asylum claims by introducing a procedure whereby an asylum seeker may be returned to a safe third country without the authorities in this country having to investigate the merits of his claim. In *R v Secretary of State for the Home Department ex p Canbolat* (1997), C, an asylum seeker from Turkey, applied for judicial review of the immigration officer's refusal to grant her entry and the decision of the Home Secretary to remove her to France, arguing that the Home Secretary did not properly evaluate the material that suggested there might be a risk that this third country would send her back to Turkey. This material was the finding of Special Adjudicators in a number of other cases that France was not a third country from which asylum applicants could continue their appeal. The Court of Appeal rejected the challenge, holding that the Secretary of State could grant a removal certificate if he was satisfied that the third country's system for dealing with asylum applications would, in general, provide the required standard of protection. This case demonstrates the difference between the function of the judicial review court and that of the Special Adjudicators. The former was unable to interfere with an administrative decision that was not Wednesbury unreasonable; whereas the Special Adjudicators, who could have examined her argument on its merits, may have come to a different conclusion (as, indeed, they had done in other cases).

The 'safe third country' rule in the Refugee Convention has particular significance for the handling of refugee claims across the EU. The Dublin Convention, which came into force in 1997, governs arrangements for safe third country cases in Europe. The basic rule is that asylum claims should be examined just once in the EU and that the Member State 'responsible' for the presence of the asylum seeker in the EU should be responsible for examining their claim. Whilst the aim of this Convention was to prevent asylum seekers from being passed between Member States without anybody taking responsibility for examining their claim, the effect has been rather the opposite, with a certain amount of buck-passing on who had responsibility in the first place. Where an asylum seeker has no documentation and is unwilling or unable to provide information as to where he or she has just been, it is practically impossible to establish which Member State was 'responsible' for their arrival.

Future proposals for asylum law

At the intergovernmental conference leading up to the Amsterdam revisions to the EC Treaty and Treaty of EU (see above, Chapter 7), Member States expressed concern that differing asylum rules across the EU afforded an opportunity for terrorist suspects to escape extradition by taking advantage of asylum procedures in other Member States. So a Protocol to the Amsterdam Treaty was drawn up which provides that Member States should regard each other as safe countries of origin for all legal and practical purposes relating to asylum applications from EC nationals. It will be remembered that the 'third country rule' is a relevant consideration in the Refugee Convention. This Protocol, in effect, provides an opportunity for Member States to reject asylum applications on the basis of a presumption that other Member States are safe, which suggests that Member States will not apply the level of scrutiny required by the 1951 Refugee Convention.

Decisions on asylum and immigration have now been brought within the 'European Community pillar' (see above, 7.2.1). Thus, they are subject for the first time to interpretation and review by the Court of Justice. Article 63 of the EC Treaty now provides for measures to be taken by the Council harmonising asylum policy, laying down minimum standards on the reception of asylum seekers and uniform procedures in Member States for granting or withdrawing refugee status. The aim of this is less to promote the rights of asylum as to ensure that the burden of dealing with refugees is equally shared between Member States ('balance of effort'); however, it is to be hoped that, once consistent asylum procedures are adopted under the EC Treaty, the tendency of Member States to 'pass the buck' in this area will come to an end.

27.9   Assessment

The main shortcoming in the UK's system of immigration controls is in relation to the guarantee of due process. The fact that most immigration controls are carried out via non-justiciable rules, internal regulations, guidance notes to immigration officers and circulars gives rise to a number of variable criteria that are difficult to anticipate, comply with or challenge in appeal proceedings. The operation of this system also depends on very wide discretionary powers which, again, have proved in the past very difficult to challenge in judicial review proceedings.

Asylum seekers fare slightly better, because of the strict scrutiny approach adopted by UK courts to cases involving a possible threat to the applicant's safety. The decision by the House of Lords holding the Home Secretary in contempt for deporting a Zairean citizen in breach of a court order in *M v Home Office* (1994) illustrates this approach. As Robertson has observed:

> ... although the court exonerated Baker of personal liability, the prospect of a
> criminal conviction will henceforth concentrate the minds of ministers who

may be tempted to ignore inconvenient court orders made to protect asylum seekers [*Freedom, the Individual and the Law*, 7th edn, 1993, London: Penguin].

This spirited approach by the courts to what they perceive to be genuine asylum seekers (see *ex p Shah*, above) will be bolstered by the provisions available to them under Arts 3, 6 and 8 of the ECHR, incorporated into national law by the Human Rights Act 1998, without the necessity to observe the margin of appreciation doctrine that has hampered the development of freedom of movement case law under these Articles in the Court of Human Rights. However, the tough approach to illegal immigration and bogus asylum seeking signalled in the Government's 1998 White Paper will bring with it a range of measures that may interfere with these rights. It remains to be seen how robust the judiciary is prepared to be in the face of primary legislation designed to combat immigration crime that overrides the rights of some genuine refugees and applicants for entry and residence.

EU citizenship, which got off to a slow start, is developing into a promising basis for claims to free movement, not only across EC boundaries, but within Member States. This will, no doubt, improve the situation for EC nationals and their families, but there may be a price to be paid by third country nationals as Member States draw in their entry requirements and clamp down on immigration criteria to compensate for the greater pressure imposed on their social welfare systems, by Community citizens within their borders.

FREEDOM OF MOVEMENT

The law on freedom of movement has developed in three main areas: immigration; the rights of asylum seekers; and the rights of EC nationals to move across inter-State boundaries. Community law has the most sophisticated case law regarding the right to free movement, although rights under Community law are only enjoyed by EC nationals and their spouses. The ECHR does not guarantee a right to non-nationals to enter and reside in the territory of signatory States, although there are Protocols annexed to the Convention (as yet unratified by the UK) which guarantee free movement for anyone lawfully within a Member State, prohibiting signatory States from refusing entry to or expelling their own nationals and prohibiting the mass expulsion of aliens.

Since there is no specific right to free movement in the ECHR, deportation and immigration decisions are considered in relation to three related rights: the prohibition on torture, degrading or inhumane treatment (Art 3); the right to family life under Art 8 and the right to an effective remedy before the national judicial authorities under Art 13.

Movement out of the UK

There are no restrictions on nationals wanting to leave the country; possession of a valid passport is not a precondition for travel abroad, although, in practice, travellers are not accepted on the main carriers without a passport.

Movement into the UK

Immigration laws and regulations determine who has the right of abode and who has only limited rights of entry. There are nine categories of nationality under the British Nationality Act 1981; out of these categories, only one, that of British citizenship, guarantees right of abode.

Persons claiming asylum can only be granted entry if they are considered to be political refugees for the purposes of the Refugee Convention. The Refugee Convention prohibits deportation of an asylum seeker to any country where his or her life is endangered ('refoulement') and the State's liability for breach of Art 3 of the ECHR is engaged in these circumstances even if the risk to which the deportee is exposed is not the direct responsibility of the State.

Article 8 may be invoked to invalidate a refusal to allow entry where family ties within the Member State territory are well established, although there is no obligation on States to allow non-nationals in to marry people lawfully within the territory.

Determination of claims

The immigration officer's initial refusal of entry, decision on deportation and removal, refusal to extend leave, imposition of conditions on right to remain and refusal of asylum are appealable to an Adjudicator and then to the Immigration Appeal Tribunal. The Immigration Appeal Tribunal's decision may be appealed to the High Court on a point of law, otherwise, judicial review is the only available scrutiny.

A non-national may be deported on a number of grounds, most broadly, on the basis that their expulsion is conducive to the public good. Appeals against deportation on national security grounds are heard by a panel of judges selected to sit on the Special Immigration Appeals Commission.

Article 13 of the ECHR imposes an obligation on signatory States to put the substance of his or her ECHR rights to the judicial authorities of the Member State before being deported. The availability of judicial review of decisions relating to deportation and extradition in the UK has been held to fulfil this requirement. Article 13 has not been incorporated by the Human Rights Act and, therefore, may not be relied upon as an argument in national courts.

Restrictions on freedom of movement within the country

Under the Prevention of Terrorism Act 1989, a person may be excluded from the mainland or Northern Ireland if he or she is suspected of being involved with terrorist offences.

Freedom of movement in community law

Treaty provisions

The EC Treaty guarantees free movement of workers, establishment and services. The Treaty provision prohibiting discrimination on grounds of nationality also provides a general protection for the freedom of movement of EC nationals. Although the Treaty of EU grants a right of citizenship of the EU, this has not yet been successfully relied upon by individuals challenging restrictions on their freedom of movement within Member States.

The Treaty of Amsterdam revisions to the EC Treaty and Treaty of EU has improved the position of third country nationals by moving asylum and immigration policy into the Community 'pillar' of the EU, which means that the Court of Justice may scrutinise national measures with a view to harmonising Member States' laws in this area.

Secondary legislation

In addition, secondary Community legislation in the form of directives oblige host States to guarantee to family members of migrant workers, students and persons of independent means various benefits that would be available to their own nationals.

Member States may refuse entry or restrict the issue of residence permits on the basis of public policy and health. Derogations on these grounds will be assessed for their legality in the light of the provisions of the ECHR, in particular, the right to a family life and freedom of association and assembly. If the measure is deemed to have a disproportionate effect on these rights, it will be in breach of Community law. Migrant workers may also be refused permits to work in sensitive areas of the public sector.

'Third country' nationals

Non-EC citizens are not entitled to the rights to free movement guaranteed in the EC Treaty and secondary legislation. The difficulties of these 'third country' nationals arise partly out of the Schengen Agreement 1985 which, in the view of critics, has created a 'fortress Europe' in which asylum seekers are passed from one country to the other with no evenhanded determination of their claims. Article 73k of the EC Treaty provides for measures to be taken by the Council harmonising asylum policy, laying down minimum standards on the reception of asylum seekers and uniform procedures in Member States for granting or withdrawing refugee status. The aim of this is less to promote the rights of asylum than to ensure that the burden of dealing with refugees is equally shared between Member States ('balance of effort').

BIBLIOGRAPHY

Chapter 1, Principles in Public Law

Berlin, I, 'Two concepts of liberty' (1958) published in various collections of his works, including *Four Essays on Liberty*, 1969, Oxford: OUP

Dahl, RA, *On Democracy*, 1998, New Haven: Yale UP

Dworkin, R, *Freedom's Law*, 1997, Oxford, OUP, especially Chapter 1, 'The moral reading and the majoritarian premise'

Chapter 2, The New Constitutional Settlement

Hazell, R (ed), *Constitutional Futures: A History of the Next Ten Years*, 1999, Oxford: OUP

Chapter 3, Principles from History

van Caenegem, RC, *An Historical Introduction to Western Constitutional Law*, 1995, Cambridge: CUP

Chapter 4, Politicians and Their Principles

Conservatism

Hague, W, 'Change and tradition: thinking creatively about the constitution', lecture delivered to the Centre for Policy Studies on 25 February 1998 (see <www.cps.org.uk>)

Lansley, A and Wilson, R, *Conservatives and the Constitution*, 1997, London: Conservative 2000 Foundation

Scrutton, R, *The Meaning of Conservatism*, 2nd edn, 1984, London: Macmillan

The Third Way

Giddens, A, *The Third Way: The Renewal of Social Democracy*, 1998, London: Polity

Giddens, A, 'After the Left's paralysis' (1998) *New Statesman*, 1 May, pp 18–21

Marquand, D, 'The Blair paradox' (1998) *Prospect*, May, pp 19–24

Perryman, M (ed), *The Blair Agenda*, 1996, London: Lawrence and Wishart

Chapter 5, Textbook Writers and their Principles

Craig, PP, 'Dicey: unitary, self-correcting democracy and public law' (1990) 106 LQR 105

Harlow, C and Rawlings, R, *Law and Administration*, 2nd edn, 1997, London: Butterworths, Chapters 1–5

Jowell, J, 'The rule of law today', in Jowell, J and Oliver, D (eds), *The Changing Constitution*, 3rd edn, 1994, Oxford: OUP

Loughlin, M, *Public Law and Political Theory*, 1992, Oxford: Clarendon

Mount, F, *The British Constitution Now*, 1993, London: Mandarin

Chapter 6, The UK Parliament

Drewry, G (ed), *The New Select Committees*, 2nd edn, 1989, Oxford: Clarendon

Hansard Society Commission on the Legislative Process, *Making the Law*, 1992, London: Hansard Society

Riddell, P, *Parliament under Pressure*, 1998, London: Gollancz

Silk, P, *How Parliament Works*, 2nd edn, 1989, London: Longman

Chapter 7, The European Union

Gowan, P and Anderson, P (eds), *The Question of Europe*, 1997, London: Verso

Weiler, J, *The Constitution of Europe*, 1999, Cambridge: CUP

Chapter 8, Government and Administration

Baldwin, R, *Rules and Governmental Process*, 1995, Oxford: Clarendon

Ganz, G, *Quasi-legislation: Recent Developments in Secondary Legislation*, 1987, London: Sweet & Maxwell

Harlow, C and Rawlings, R, *Law and Administration*, 2nd edn, 1998, London: Butterworths

Greer, P, 'The Next Steps initiative: an examination of the agency framework document' (1998) 68 Public Administration 89

Freedland, MR, 'Government by contract and public law' [1994] PL 86

Austin, R, 'Administrative law's reaction to the changing concepts of public service', in Leyland, P and Woods, T (eds), *Administrative Law Facing the Future*, 1997, London: Blackstone, p 28

Galligan, DJ (ed), *A Reader in Administrative Law*, 1996, Oxford: OUP

Freedland, M, 'Public law and private finance – placing the private finance initiative in a public law frame' [1998] PL 288

Wellens, KC and Borchardt, GM, 'Soft law in European Community law' (1989) 14 ELR 267

Klabbers, J, 'Informal instruments before the European Court of Justice' (1994) 31 CML Rev 997

Jowell, J, 'The rule of law today', in Jowell, J and Oliver, D (eds), *The Changing Constitution*, 3rd edn, 1994, Oxford: Clarendon, pp 62–26

Chapter 9, Introduction to Dispute Resolution

Birkinshaw, P, *Grievances, Remedies and the State*, 2nd edn, 1994, London: Sweet & Maxwell

Chapter 10, Commissioners for Administration ('Ombudsmen')

JUSTICE/All Souls, *Administrative Justice: Some Necessary Reforms*, 1988, Oxford:OUP, Chapter 5

Lewis, ND and Birkinshaw, P, *When Citizens Complain: Reforming Justice and Administration*, 1993, Buckingham: Open UP

Drewry, G and Harlow, C, 'A "cutting edge"? The Parliamentary Commissioner and MPs' (1990) 53 MLR 745

Gregory, R and Drewry, G, 'Barlow Clowes and the Ombudsman' [1991] PL 192 and 408

Select Committee Report on the PCA, *First Report for Session 1994–95 on Maladministration and Redress*, HC 112

Chapter 11, Introduction to Judicial Review

Jowell, J, 'Of *vires* and vacuums: the constitutional context of judicial review' [1999] PL 448

Craig, P, 'Competing models of judicial review' [1999] PL 428

Le Sueur, AP and Sunkin, M, *Public Law*, 1997: London: Longman, Chapter 20

Wade, HWR and Forsyth, CF, *Administrative Law*, 7th edn, 1994, Oxford: Clarendon, pp 24–49

Chapter 15, Grounds of Judicial Review IV: Irrationality

Jowell, J and Lester, A, 'Beyond *Wednesbury*: substantive principles of administrative law' [1987] PL 368

Peiris, GL, '*Wednesbury* unreasonableness: the expanding canvas' [1987] CLJ 53

Irvine (Lord), 'Judges and decision makers' [1996] PL 59

Jowell, J and Lester, A, 'Proportionality: neither novel nor dangerous', in Jowell, J and Oliver, D (eds), *New Directions in Judicial Review*, 1988, London: Sweet & Maxwell

Chapter 17, Judicial Review Procedures and Remedies

Bridges, L, Mészáros, G and Sunkin, M, *Judicial Review in Perspective*, 2nd edn, 1995, London: Cavendish Publishing, especially Chapter 7

Cane, P, 'Standing up for the public' [1995] PL 276

Le Sueur, AP and Sunkin, M, 'Applications for judicial review: the requirement of leave' [1992] PL 102

Schiemann J, '*Locus standi*' [1990] PL 342

Chapter 18, European Community Litigation

Maher, I, 'National courts as European Community court' (1994) 14 LS 226

Craig, P and de Búrca, G (eds), *The Evolution of EU Law*, 1998, Oxford: OUP

Chapter 19, Civil Liberties and Human Rights

Dworkin, R, *Freedom's Law*, 1997, Oxford: OUP

Griffith, JAG, 'The political constitution' (1979) 42 MLR 1

Higgins, R, *Problems and Processes: International Law and How We Use It*, 1994, Oxford: OUP

Home Office, *Rights Brought Home: The Human Rights Bill*, Cm 3782, 1997, London: HMSO

Chapter 20, Right to Life

Dworkin, R, 'Life, death and race', in *Freedom's Law*, 1997, Oxford: OUP, pp 39–146

Klug, F, Starmer, K and Weir, S, *The Three Pillars of Liberty*, 1996, London: Routledge, pp 238 *et seq*

Chapter 21, Liberty of the Person

Ashworth, A, 'Should the police be allowed to use deceptive practices?'(1998) 114 LQR 109

Reiner, R and Leigh, L, 'Police power', in McCrudden, C and Chambers, G (eds), *Individual Rights and the Law in Britain*, 1994, Oxford: Clarendon

Richardson, G, 'Discretionary life sentences and the ECHR' [1991] PL 34

Sanders, A and Bridges, L, 'Access to legal advice and police malpractice' [1990] Crim LR 494

Chapter 22, Retrospectivity

Craig, P, 'Formal and substantive conceptions of the rule of law: an analytical framework' [1997] PL 467

Fuller, L, *The Morality of Law*, 1969, Yale: Yale UP

Ganz, G, 'The War Crimes Act 1991 – why no Constitutional Crisis?' (1992) 55 MLR 91

Shklar, JN, *Legalism, Law, Morals and Political Trials*, 1974, Harvard: Harvard UP

Chapter 23, Privacy

Eady, D, 'Statutory right to privacy' (1996) 3 EHRLR 243

Feldman, D, 'Secrecy, dignity or autonomy? Privacy as a civil liberty' (1990) 43 CLP 41

Feldman, D, 'The developing scope of Art 8' (1997) 3 EHRLR 264

Leander, S, 'The right to privacy, the enforcement of morals and the judicial function' (1990) CLP 115

Markesinis, B, 'The right to be left alone versus freedom of speech' [1986] PL 67

Wacks, R, *Personal Information: Privacy and the Law*, 1993, Oxford: OUP

Warren, SD and Brandeis, LD, 'The right to privacy' (1890) 4 Harv L Rev 193

Chapter 24, Freedom of expression

Gardner, J, 'Freedom of expression', in McCrudden, C and Chambers, G (eds), *Individual Rights and the Law in Britain*, 1994, Oxford: Clarendon

Loveland, I, 'Political libels and qualified privilege – a British solution to a British problem' [1997] PL 428

MacKinnon, C, *Feminism Unmodified: Discourses on Life and Law*, 1987, Harvard: Harvard UP

Marshall, G, 'Press freedom and free speech theory' [1992] PL 40

Raz, J, 'Free expression and personal identification' (1991) 11 OJLS 303

Robertson, G, *Obscenity*, 1979, Oxford: Clarendon

Robertson, G, *Freedom, the Individual and the Law*, 7th edn, 1993, London: Penguin

Chapter 26, Equality

Dworkin, R, *Taking Rights Seriously*, 1994, London: Duckworth, pp 272–78

Gardner, J, 'Liberals and unlawful discrimination' (1989) 9 OJLS 1

Jowell, J, 'Is equality a constitutional principle?' (1994) 42(2) CLP 1

MacKinnon, C, 'Reflections on sex equality under law' (1991) 100 Yale LJ 1281

McCrudden, C, 'Introduction', in *Anti-Discrimination Law*, 1991, Aldershot: Dartmouth

Oliver, D, 'Common values in pubic and private law' [1997] PL 646

Raz, J, *The Morality of Freedom*, 1986, Oxford: Clarendon

Wintermute, R, 'Sexual orientation discrimination', in McCrudden, C and Chambers, G (eds), *Individual Rights and the Law in Britain*, 1994, Oxford: Clarendon

Chapter 27, Freedom of Movement

Feldman, D, *Civil Liberties and Human Rights in England and Wales*, 1993, Oxford: Clarendon

Robertson, G, *Freedom, the Individual and the Law*, 7th edn, 1993, London: Penguin, Chapter 9

Vincenzi, C, 'European citizenship and free movement rights in the UK' [1995] PL 259

INDEX